Nina. Bramhall

Quest of a Hemisphere

By the same author

American History Was My Undoing

QUEST OF A HEMISPHERE

by

Donzella Cross Boyle

Pro Patria Series

Published by WESTERN ISLANDS ★ BOSTON ★ LOS ANGELES

This book is dedicated to the girls and boys in my classes, whose interest in their country's history guided the research for writing QUEST OF A HEMISPHERE.

Preface

QUEST OF A HEMISPHERE is a factual American history written from documents, manuscripts, journals, diaries, letters, newspapers, and rare books in the Library of Congress, National Archives, Henry E. Huntington Library and Art Gallery, Pan American Union, and private collections of Americana.

Although QUEST OF A HEMISPHERE is basically a history of the United States, the title indicates that events in neighboring countries, vitally affecting the way of life in this nation, are interwoven chronologically into the text. By recording the varied political, social, and economic history of both Americas, the point of view becomes hemispherical.

Illustrations feature the art of historical periods — reproductions of sketches and paintings, portraits of famous men by artists of their time, and copies of documents in the original style of printing. Legends are vital history, serving to supplement the text.

In narrative style, each chapter renders a factual account of the struggle, achievement, and vision of the peoples who forged new nations in the Western Hemisphere. Who were they? Why did they come? Where did they go? What did they do? What destiny were they seeking? That is the story in this book.

Acknowledgements

To the Henry E. Huntington Library and Art Gallery of San Marino, California, grateful thanks are extended for research privileges, and permission to print excerpts from the following manuscripts: *Orderly Book of Francis Marion; Diary of Charles Willson Peale;* Letter of Nathanael Greene to George Washington (Greene Papers); *Orderly Book of Henry Dearborn; Diary of Elkanah Walker.*

Grateful acknowledgement is extended to the Henry E. Huntington Library and Art Gallery for the following reproductions from the Library's collections: Boston Massacre, Paul Revere; Benjamin Franklin's account of New Invented Fireplace; *Histoire Generale des Antilles,* Du Tetra; *Cristobal Colon,* Roselly de Largues Conde; *Genesis of the United States,* Brown; *New Discourse of Trade,* Child; *Diary of the American Revolution,* Moore; *History of the Navy,* Boynton; *Memorial History of the City of New York,* Wilson; *Pioneer History of Ohio Valley,* Hildreth; *Ferdinand Magellan,* Guillemand; *Essex Gazette* (1768); *Pennsylvania Journal and Advertiser* (1765); *Dunlap's Pennsylvania Packet* (1775); *Harper's Weekly* (1862); Currier and Ives: Bombardment of Fort Sumter, Marion's Brigade Crossing the Peedee River, S.C. 1778, Canadian Voyageurs, Mink Trapping; *Pictorial Field Book of the Revolution* by Benson J. Lossing (1850): Jacques Cartier, Continental Bills, American Troops at Valley Forge, Washington's Mission to the Ohio, Washington, Henry and Pendleton, Braddock's Field, St. John's Church, Skirmish at Lexington, Declaration of Independence Approved; Inauguration; *Pictorial Field Book of the War of 1812*: Fight on Deck of Serapis; Facsimile of Perry's Dispatch; Harbor of Lisbon; Fort Amsterdam; Peter Stuyvesant; Colonial Kitchen; Reading of the Declaration of Independence; Marietta, Ohio.

Thanks for additional illustrations are extended to the Library of Congress for: Indenture, Patrick Henry, Independence Hall, Liberty Bell, Benjamin Franklin, Jonathan Dayton, Edmund Randolph, James Madison, John Langdon, Daniel Carroll, Charles Cotesworth Pinckney, Gouverneur Morris, Roger Sherman, Alexander Hamilton, James Wilson, George Mason, The Capitol; Pan American Union: Francisco de miranda, Miguel Hildalgo y Costilla, Jose Maria Morelos, San Martin Monument, Pan American Union Building; National Film Board of Canada: Houses of Parliament; American Museum of Natural History, New Mexico Department of Development, Kansas State Historical Society, New Mexico State Tourist Bureau, Chamber of Commerce of New Orleans, Jamestown Foundation, Province of Quebec – Archives, Meeting House in Gloucester, Massachusetts from collection of Rev. Peter Knost, Mount Vernon Ladies Association, Helena Chamber of Commerce, Montana Power Co.,

Thomas Jefferson Memorial Foundation, Bank of Venezuela, Bureau of Indian Affairs, Oklahoma Historical Society, Eastern National Park and Monument Assoc., Valentine Museum, Tuskegee Institute.

Grateful acknowledgement is made to the following publishers and authors for permission to reprint excerpts from copyrighted material: The Hispanic Society of America for *The Diary of Francisco de Miranda, 1783-1784,* edited by W.S. Robertson; Jose Porrus E. Hijos for *La Vida Economica y Social de Nueva España* by Gonzalo Gomez de Cervantes; Bank of Venezuela for *Selected Writings of Bolivar,* Lecuna and Bierck; Historical Society of Pennsylvania for *Indian Treaties, Printed by Benjamin Franklin* and *The Pennsylvania Magazine of History and Biography,* XXXVII (1913); The Filson Club Publications for the *Journal of Doctor Walker* and the *Journal of William Calk.*

Generous thanks are extended to teachers, librarians, and citizens from many walks of life for their helpful cooperation and kindly interest in the preparation of this book.

Author

Table of Contents

List of Illustrations

Note to the Reader

The attention of the reader is called to the map references at the end of various chapters in this text. These maps can be found in the *Atlas of American History* or in the larger *Our United States*, both by Edgar B. Wesley and published by Denoyer-Geppert Company, 5235 Ravenswood Avenue, Chicago, Illinois.

PART ONE

The Old World
Finds the Western Hemisphere

COLUMBUS SEES A LIGHT, INDICATING THAT LAND WAS NEAR.

Copied from "The Journal of the First Voyage of Columbus." October 11, 1492:

. . . the Admiral at ten o'clock at night being in the stern forecastle saw a light, but it was so concealed that he would not declare it to be land. But he called Pedro Gutierrez, the Groom of the Chamber of the King, and said to him that it appeared to be a light, and asked him to look at it, and he did so and saw it. He also told Rodrigo Sanchez de Segovia, whom the King and Queen sent with the fleet as Inspector . . . . After the Admiral told it, it was seen once or twice, and it was like a small wax candle which rose and fell, which hardly appeared to be an indication of land. But the Admiral was certain they were near land.

Although a sailor on the Pinta first saw land two hours after midnight, Columbus received the award of 10,000 maravedis (small gold coins) offered by the King and Queen of Spain to the man who first saw land. Columbus had seen the light two hours before midnight, and received the award each year of his lifetime.

Chapter 1

Spanish Civilization Invades the Americas

A SAILOR RETURNS

ON A BALMY April day in 1493, Columbus made his triumphal entry into Barcelona to report his famous voyage to the King and Queen of Spain. A special messenger had summoned Columbus to the Court as soon as Their Majesties had learned of his return to the city. In August, 1492, he had ventured into unknown seas to prove that the earth was round, that he could find the east by sailing to the west.

On this day, the port city on the Mediterranean welcomed a seaman who came with a strange caravan. As the train of horses and mules approached the city, runners dashed along the streets and shouted, "The Admiral! The Admiral!"

The news created an uproar. Merchants left their shop doors open and swarmed into the lanes. Women unlocked their ironbarred windows and stood on the balconies. Church bells clanged throughout Barcelona.

Armed sailors on horseback led the procession. They cleared a path through the excited mob that choked the narrow street leading to the royal palace. Next in line were the dark-eyed, copper-colored men from the newly-discovered islands which Columbus thought were off the coast of India. These natives were in feathered hats made from the brilliant plumage of tropical birds. In little cages, carried on the shoulders of these men, were bright green parrots with yellow heads and red-tipped wings. Columbus was fond of parrots. The screeching chatter of the birds mingled strangely with the cheers and laughter of the noisy crowd. It was circus day in Barcelona, the city by the sea.

The nuggets of gold in the noses and ears of the native Indians caught the eye of many a Spaniard. Columbus had his natives wear gold in their dress so that Spain would be impressed with the importance of his discovery. Servants walking in the procession carried baskets of tropical fruits and flowering plants. One basket was filled with chunks of quartz that glittered in the bright sunlight of the warm, spring day.

Columbus showed cunning in displaying his wares first, instead of leading the procession. He rode in the middle of the train with his two young sons. At his side was the King's chamberlain, dispatched by Ferdinand to escort him into the royal presence. A wild clamor broke loose whenever the crowd caught sight of Columbus in the slowly-moving line. The fiery Spaniards waved their arms and shouted his name. They sang the ballads of Spanish heroes and clicked their heels in Spanish dances. Their joy knew no bounds.

A train of pack mules, guarded by soldiers, brought up the rear of the parade. The packs bulged with boxes containing the secret treasure of the Indies. What was this loot that Columbus hoarded to show to the King and Queen? The curious throng could only wonder. Was it gold?

ADMIRAL OF THE OCEAN SEA

AS COLUMBUS APPROACHED the throne, Ferdinand and Isabella rose to greet him as "Admiral of the Ocean Sea and Viceroy of the Indies." The audience gasped at the honor accorded a common seaman as Columbus knelt before the King and Queen and kissed their hands. A still greater honor awaited him. Columbus was invited to sit beside Their Majesties and the young prince, Don Juan.

Looking out over that well-dressed audience, perhaps the sailor's mind wandered back to that day in May, seven years earlier, when he had first met the beautiful, auburn-haired queen at Cordova. Isabella, though inclined to believe his story that the world was round, and that he could sail *west* to reach the east had felt obligated to consult the learned men of her kingdom. "All in one voice said that it was complete folly and vanity."

The weary years had dragged on, but Columbus had not given up. He had a real friend at court, Luis de Santangel, who said to Isabella:

I have wondered much that your Highness did not accept an empire such as this Columbus has offered. This business is of such a quality that, if what your Highness thinks difficult or impossible should be proposed to another King and prove successful, the result would be an injury to your kingdom.

Since Spain was impoverished by war, the Queen had suggested waiting, but Luis de Santangel had shaken his head. He knew that Columbus was then on his way toward the border of France to seek aid from the French king.

Santangel, a rich man, offered to lend the money to Isabella for fitting out an expedition for Columbus. He assured her that it would be a small favor to lend her over a million *maravedis* from his own family. He wanted Isabella to send a messenger in haste to overtake Columbus and ask him to return for an audience with Her Majesty.

Well did Columbus remember the day that an officer had overtaken him on the road to France, with a royal summons to return to the Court of Spain. Now, having made his great voyage, he would not disappoint the woman who had believed in him. This was his great moment, and the Queen's.

Like an actor in a play, Columbus leaned forward to tell his story to a breathless audience. For five weeks his three ships had sailed through uncharted seas. They had met wind and rain, and hours of calm without a breeze. The fretful sailors had threatened to turn back toward home and loved ones, but hopes had been revived with signs of land. A sailor on the *Pinta* killed a land bird with a stone; a pelican rested on the deck of the *Santa Maria;* the crew of the *Nina* saw a berry bush floating in the sea. After dark one night, Columbus had seen a light moving up and down. Who was carrying the torch? Four hours later, at two o'clock in the morning, a sailor on the

Pinta sighted land. That was the twelfth day of October in the year 1492.

Columbus praised the kindness of the natives. Knowing Isabella's zeal for her faith, he assured her that the gentle natives could easily become good Christians. At a signal, the Indians walked out with jingling steps. The rulers of Spain fastened curious eyes upon them and their gold. Columbus displayed ears of corn, sweet potatoes, bananas, rhubarb, coconuts, palm oil, and medicinal herbs found in the Indies. In the animal exhibit were lizards, fish, and tropical birds. The parrots chattered glibly, to the delight of the listeners.

The royal audience waited anxiously to learn what loot was stored in the boxes. Columbus lifted a lid and picked up samples of gold ore, grains of gold dust, and little nuggets of the yellow metal for which his sailors had traded thongs of leather and cheap trinkets. He handed the specimens to the King and Queen, who examined them like delighted children with a new toy.

Brass trumpets and shrill woodwinds joined the Queen's chapel choir in a loud Te Deum (Hymn of Praise). The reception ended in a blaze of glory for Columbus, Their Majesties, and Spain.

The reception was the last real glory Columbus experienced. He thought he had discovered islands off the Asiatic coast. Instead, he had landed in the West Indies. Four times he set sail in search of the Asiatic mainland and oriental treasure. If Columbus had explored the mainland, he might have realized it was not Asia but a New World. It was not until Magellan, another explorer, and his crew sailed westward around the world in 1522 that the people of Europe knew that the New World was not Asia.

Columbus died before his countrymen fully appreciated the importance of his discovery. As Spaniards migrated to the West Indies, however, the bold adventurers among them explored the shores of Central America. New World lands might mean more gold! The hunt for treasure continued.

CORTES LEADS
A GOLD-SEEKING EXPEDITION

A YOUNG BOY who was to find the treasure came to the Indies in the same year that Columbus returned from his last voyage. The bold adventurer who found the gold was the ruthless soldier and leader of men, Hernando Cortes.

Cortes was only nineteen when he left Spain on a sailing ship bound for the Indies with colonists and supplies. In Cuba he was given a land grant with a small gold mine on it and Indian slaves to till the soil and dig the ore. The easy-going life of a plantation owner, however, failed to satisfy his craving for excitement.

The governor of Cuba had previously sent two expeditions to the mainland to seek gold. Although the natives greeted the strangers with showers of lances and arrows, the Spaniards succeeded in trading green glass beads, which the Indians prized, for little idols, animals, and trinkets made of gold. Always, the natives pointed toward the rising sun. They wanted to know if the palefaced men had come from the east. From captured natives, the Spaniards learned that the tribes on the coast were ruled by a powerful emperor called Montezuma, who lived inland in a great city surrounded by water.

In battle with these natives along the

shores of Yucatan, a large number of Spaniards were killed, a few were captured, and most of those who returned had been wounded with poisoned arrows. This did not stop the Cuban governor, who was after the gold in the new land. Ten ships idled at anchor in the harbor of Santiago, within sight of the governor's palace, awaiting a commander to take the fleet on a third expedition.

The chosen man was Hernando Cortes. At once, he began to collect matchlocks, armor, cross-bows, powder, cannon, cassava bread, salted bacon, and other supplies. He spent his own money and all that he could borrow from his friends. Cortes hired men to walk through the streets of Santiago to advertise his voyage. Tooting trumpets and beating drums, they spread the news that Cortes would share gold, silver, and jewels with every man who joined the expedition. Also, he would give a large piece of land and Indian slaves to any man who wished to settle in the lands he conquered. Such lavish promises led many colonists to seek their fortunes with Cortes. They sold their plantations and slaves to buy food, clothing, ammunition, and horses.

With three hundred soldiers on board, the ten vessels sailed out of the harbor of Santiago. A few days later, the fleet dropped anchor in the harbor of Trinidad, another port on the southern coast of Cuba. Cortes made a speech in the public square of the town. He invited men to join him and promised them great wealth in gold, land, and slaves. One of the richest men in Cuba joined the party in Trinidad. He brought his own ship, food, Negro servants, and, most important of all, his spirited chestnut mare. At the time, horses were scarce and costly in the Indies. At Havana, where the fleet delayed, more supplies were loaded and more men joined the expedition.

In a holiday mood, as if on a pleasure cruise, the fleet of eleven vessels put out to sea early in the year 1519. On board were poor men seeking a fortune, rich men hunting more gold, landowners wanting more land, noblemen searching for thrills, and young men seeking adventure. The chief pilot was Alaminos, navigator for Columbus on his fourth and last voyage to the Indies.

Alaminos had piloted the two former expeditions from Cuba to the mainland and was familiar with the coast line of Yucatan. There was plenty of battle equipment, including four small falcons and sixteen horses. This was real adventure and hopes were high. Little did those on board dream of the hardships that awaited them. They had yet to learn that the persuasive gentleman, Cortes, was a stern commander who would never turn back once he had set a goal. From this day on, his mission was to lead, and theirs, to follow. Cortes had come to the New World for adventure and gold.

GODS OR MEN?

AMONG THE MANY GODS worshipped by the Mexican Indians was one named Quetzalcoatl, a prophet with a white skin and a black beard. According to the legend, this god had once lived among the tribes. He taught them to be kind to each other and not to cut out the hearts of their brethren in sacrifice to their idols. The natives loved this kind man and obeyed him while he lived among them. When he went away, he promised to return someday from the east, bringing men like himself to conquer and rule the land. In his honor, great temples were built. In time, however, the people forgot his teaching and returned to their old custom of human sacrifice.

When Montezuma heard that palefaced men with dark beards had landed on the coast, he trembled with fear. He was the rich and powerful emperor of the warlike Aztecs, who had conquered neighboring tribes and demanded from them a tribute of young men and women to be sacrificed to the war-god. Montezuma had disobeyed the laws of Quetzalcoatl. Now the god must be returning, as he had promised, from the east. Montezuma walked the floor and wrung his hands, wondering what move to make.

The Emperor sent his trusted lieutenant, Tendile, a clever, bright fellow, to head a group of messengers with gifts for the strangers. The messengers brought corn-bread, pheasants, plums, and choice dishes to feed the strangers. War captives were included in the party in case the bearded men were cannibals and might wish to feast on human flesh. Among the presents were ceremonial hats and capes made of brilliant feathers, and a tiger skin coat of the Aztec priests which was like the one Quetzalcoatl used to wear. When Cortes failed to recognize these sacred emblems, the shrewd Tendile began to doubt. Later, when a bell rang calling men to prayer and Cortes knelt with his men before a wooden cross stuck into the sand, Tendile concluded this bearded stranger was not a god.

During the interview, the church service, and the meal, the artists in Tendile's party were busy painting what they saw on long sheets of white cotton cloth. Cortes suddenly realized that these painters must be impressed with his power, although he did not know they were sketching him so that Montezuma could determine whether he was a god. He ordered his officers to mount their horses. The Indians had never seen horses. With the spirited chestnut mare in the lead, all sixteen horses galloped down the beach at breakneck speed. The Aztecs stood in awe, thinking the horses, and not the men, were the gods. Next, Cortes had a cannon fired. The sketches of the round ball tearing through the air greatly amused the Spaniards.

In exchange for the Indian gifts, Cortes gave cheap glass beads, a string of imitation pearls, and a decorated armchair for Montezuma to sit in when Cortes called at the palace of the mighty Aztec emperor. He sent to Montezuma a bright red cap trimmed with a medal engraving of St. George slaying the dragon. One of the messengers asked for a gilded helmet worn by one of the Spanish soldiers. Cortes handed it over and requested that it be returned filled with gold dust.

Montezuma was so frightened when these messengers returned that he ordered more war captives to be sacrificed to the gods before he dared to look at the paintings. The horses and cannon ball puzzled him, but the helmet alarmed him. In shape, the headpiece resembled the helmets worn by his forefathers in battle. How could he keep his bearded stranger out of his kingdom? For hours at a time, Montezuma locked himself in his own room in the palace and refused to eat the meals which servants brought to him. He called in fortunetellers to advise him what to do. Finally, he decided to send such costly gifts that the strangers would be satisfied and sail away as others had done who came to Yucatan. If the palefaced leader was not Quetzalcoatl, he would accept the bribes and leave, Montezuma concluded.

THE GOLDEN BRIBE

CORTES HAD THE good fortune to find excellent interpreters at the start. At his first stop after leaving Cuba, he rescued a Spaniard named Aguilar, who had been shipwrecked on the coast of Yucatan eight years before. Aguilar had been a slave of Indian masters for all of that time. The Indians of Tabasco gave Cortes an orphan girl called Malinche. Bright and attractive, Malinche had learned to speak several languages. Without her the conquest of Mexico by Cortes might have failed. Since she could speak both Tabascoan and Aztec, and Aguilar could speak Tabascoan and Spanish, Cortes was able to carry on a conversation with Tendile. He sent word directly to Montezuma that he desired to visit him in his palace. The Emperor did not want him and sent a golden bribe.

In the short space of seven days Tendile returned to the coast with a hundred Aztec porters, their backs bent over with the weight they carried. Tendile uncovered the treasure, each article having been wrapped in white cotton cloth. First, he presented Cortes with a solid gold plate, round like the sun and as large as a wagon wheel, with the Aztec calendar engraved upon it. From another porter's back, he lifted a heavy silver plate, still larger, representing the moon. The third gift was the helmet filled with grains of gold. The Spaniards were speechless with wonder. A treasure, given without asking, was spread before them.

It took a long time to display all the gifts strapped to the backs of the hundred porters. Among the presents were thirty golden ducks, solid gold figures of lions, tigers, dogs, monkeys, deer, and some wild animals which the Spaniards had never seen. A golden bow, with a string attached, gave Cortes an idea of the Aztec weapons. The carriers unloaded rolls and rolls of white cotton cloth with designs woven in bright feathers, fans made of the gay plumage of tropical birds, sandals of deerskin embroidered in gold thread, feather ornaments in gold and silver cases, necklaces of pearls, emeralds, and rubies, and ten gold chains with lockets. With this loot Montezuma hoped to bribe Cortes to leave the country.

The Spaniards could scarcely believe their eyes. They knew now, beyond any doubt, that Montezuma ruled over an empire of fabulous wealth. An Aztec stepped forward to deliver a message from his Emperor. Indeed, this message was the real purpose of the gifts. In polite terms, he stated that Montezuma would be pleased to give Cortes and his men all the food they needed as long as they remained on the coast, but that the Emperor would not see him. In equally polite language, the messenger hinted that the strangers might regret the blunder of trying to enter Mexico uninvited. Cortes thanked the messenger for the gifts and the speech, but insisted that his king, Charles V, had sent him across a wide ocean to pay the respects of His Majesty to the great ruler of Mexico. (Charles V had never heard of Montezuma.) These speeches were translated by Aguilar and Malinche.

When this message was brought back to Montezuma, he grew more worried. In his fright, he ordered young children to be sacrificed. He begged the war-god for power to outwit this stubborn paleface with a beard. Day and night the question haunted him, "Was he Quetzalcoatl?" The Emperor made his last attempt to prove that the stranger was or was not the god. As a final bribe, he sent four green stones, sacred to the Mexicans, because Quetzalcoatl had taught them how to polish these jewels. To the Spaniards, who wanted gold, the stones were worthless.

While the stones were being delivered to Cortes, the church bell rang, calling the Spaniards to prayer. One of the Aztecs inquired why Cortes humbled himself to kneel before a wooden cross. The answer was a sermon preached by a friar and translated by Aguilar and Malinche. The friar explained that the white strangers had come from the east to stop human sacrifice, kidnapping, the eating of human flesh, and other crimes.

When the third mission returned, Montezuma was even more confused. The bearded man had ignored the precious green stones. He was not Quetzalcoatl. The strangers said they had come from the east to stop human sacrifice. Cortes was Quetzalcoatl. At last, Montezuma stopped brooding over his fate and called a meeting of his war council to dispatch runners to all the conquered tribes with orders to fight the strangers.

In a few days the Indians who had been bringing food disappeared as if by magic. Cortes and his men went up the coast to a better location to start a settlement which they called Vera Cruz. The friends of the Cuban governor wanted to return home with the golden treasure, which they would divide among themselves and the governor who had sent out the expedition. The majority, however, voted to stay and perhaps gain more gold.

It was agreed to send most of Montezuma's bribe to Spain as the fifth which the King claimed of all the gold found in the New World. The best vessel in the fleet was outfitted for the voyage. The charge of the golden loot was given to Alaminos, the best navigator who had ever come to the Indies. In 1513 he had piloted Ponce de Leon to Florida in his vain search for the "Fountain of Youth." On that expedition, Ponce de Leon crossed the Gulf Stream four times. Consequently, Alaminos learned much about this warm river sweeping out of the Gulf of Mexico into the Atlantic Ocean.

Near the end of July Alaminos left for Spain. He cruised up the coast of Florida to gain speed and time in the swift current of the Gulf Stream, and to avoid the danger of capture by pirates lurking in the sea lanes to the Indies. He delivered the golden bribe to His Majesty, who melted the treasure to pay for his wars in Europe. Thus ended the golden sun and the silver moon, pride of the Aztecs whose works of art were wasted in a futile effort to bribe Cortes.

ON TO MEXICO

TO PROHIBIT THE FRIENDS of the Cuban governor from deserting, Cortes suggested that the ten remaining ships be run onto the sands. The majority agreed. After the vessels were beached, the sailors and pilots joined the expedition. The older men, unable to march, stayed in the new Spanish town of Vera Cruz. Now, there was no retreat!

Going inland from the coast, the invaders cut their way through dense jungle. Parrots screeched in the tree tops and butterflies swarmed in the air. A steady climb brought them out of the steaming lowland into the cooler air of the plateau region, where hills were patched with little plots of corn. At first, the tribes along the way fought the invaders, either through fear of Montezuma or loyalty to him. In these encounters, the Spaniards lost both men and horses, and many were wounded. It was a bloody road to the inland province on a high plateau. After these battles, however, Cortes gained allies for his conquest by promising to free them from paying tribute to the mighty Emperor of the Aztecs. The chiefs complained that Montezuma's taxgatherers stole their gold, robbed their fields, and kidnapped their daughters. Montezuma grew more fearful when some of his vassals joined the invaders. He sent more gifts hoping Cortes would turn back before he reached the high range of mountains encircling his kingdom.

As if standing on guard, two lofty peaks towered above the mountain barrier to the Aztec kingdom, and one was afire. This was the first active volcano the Spaniards had ever seen and it aroused their curiosity. The natives told them why the mountain smoked. A long time ago, a handsome prince loved a beautiful princess of an enemy tribe. Forbidden to marry, they eloped and perished. According to the Mexican legend, their spirits were united in the two volcanoes. In his wrath, the prince, Popocatepetl belched hot rock and ashes to hide the sun and destroy the crops. The Aztecs named the highest volcano after him. Popocatepetl became the word in their language for "smoking mountain." At his side, the princess sleeps on the summit of the other volcano. The snow which never melts moulds her figure in a long white gown. The "sleeping woman" is Ixtaccihuatl. With a rumbling sound like distant thunder, the earth trembled beneath the feet of the invading army crossing the divide near the spouting volcano. The native warriors were very frightened at this ill omen. Popocatepetl was muttering angry words at them, they said.

As the army descended from the cold

IXTACCIHUATL (Sleeping Woman)

According to legend, the lovely princess slumbers on top of the mountain by the side of Popocatepetl. The "Sleeping Woman," wrapped in her shroud of eternal snow, is Ixtaccihuatl.

Pan American Union

POPOCATEPETL (Smoking Mountain)

Popocatepetl is no longer a "smoking mountain," as in the time of Cortes. Years ago, as the crater cooled, snowflakes healed the ugly scar. Today, the glistening white cone of this volcano can be seen for many miles in the clear dry air of the high plateau of Mexico.

heights, the climate grew warmer. Pine forests gave way to groves of oak and sycamore. After days on twisting trails, a sudden turn in the road gave the Spaniards their first view of the beautiful basin of Mexico, a high plateau hemmed in by mountains. In the bright sunlight of the autumn day, the lakes were as blue as the sky. On an island in the center rose the temples and palaces of the Aztec capital. This was their goal.

Fearing a rebellion among his conquered tribes, Montezuma decided to receive Cortes as the visiting ambassador of a foreign monarch. He sent his nephew to invite Cortes and his army into the city. The Spaniards entered the capital over a long dike wide enough for eight horsemen to ride abreast. The foreigners "did not amount to four hundred and fifty, but

there were about a thousand natives for the baggage and artillery," and others joined along the way. The lakes swarmed with sight-seers in canoes. From roofs and terraces, the curious crowds eyed the strangers and their horses. They viewed with some alarm the entrance of their old tribal enemies. As Cortes passed through the main gate of the city, Montezuma came forth to meet him. Seated in his throne chair, the Emperor was carried on the shoulders of favorite nobles. A canopy of royal green feathers shielded him from the sunlight. On his head he wore an ornament with green feathers which floated down his back. The soles of his shoes were made of gold and the uppers were studded with jewels. As he stepped from the royal sedan, attendants unrolled yards of cotton cloth for him to walk upon.

9

CORTES VISITS MONTEZUMA

Tenochtitlan.

Pan American Union

In this old sketch, Cortes and Montezuma are carrying on a conversation with Aguilar translating Spanish into Tabascoan, and Malinche — her Christian name was Donna Marina — translating Tobascoan into Aztec.

Bernal Diaz, who went with Cortes into Mexico, wrote an account of this meeting in his journal:

The next day (November 9, 1519) was fixed on by Cortes for his visit to Montezuma. (He took four officers and five soldiers for his bodyguard.) He went to his palace, which as soon as Montezuma was informed of, he came as far as the middle of the hall to meet us, attended by his relations, no other persons being allowed to enter where he was, except on most important business. With great ceremony on each side, the king took Cortes by the hand and leading him to the elevated part of the room, placed him upon his right, and with affability, desired the rest of us to be seated.

The artist included samples of the food Montezuma furnished for his pale-faced guests from overseas.

Parrots in cages were provided for entertainment during their meal.

Cortes got off his horse and walked forward with his interpreters to greet the Emperor of Mexico. Montezuma received him cordially, as thousands of Aztecs looked on and wondered. Were these white men with beards the gods whom the prophet foretold would come from the east to conquer and rule them? A brother of the Emperor escorted the Spaniards to their quarters, while Montezuma returned by a shorter route to arrive ahead of his guests. In his father's palace, large enough to accommodate the four hundred Spaniards, Montezuma welcomed Cortes and his soldiers.

"You are in your house," he said. "Eat, rest, and enjoy yourself. I shall return presently."

He did, with gifts in gold for every man.

THE PRICE OF GOLD AND GLORY

AFTER FOUR DAYS Cortes asked Montezuma for permission to go on a sight-seeing tour of the city. The Emperor assured him safety to go wherever he pleased. With a bodyguard of his own officers, Cortes visited the huge market place. Here, as many as forty thousand people came on special days to buy and to sell their many products, ranging from honey cakes to gold dust. From the market place, the Spaniards went to the great temple of the war-god, the place which they wanted most to see. A steep climb up the 114 steps of the temple rewarded them with a bird's-eye view of the city with its aqueduct, bridges, lakes, market, and two volcanoes in the distance. The sight of prisoners stretched and tied to slabs of stone, waiting to be sacrificed, made the Spaniards shudder.

Montezuma stepped forth from an inner

10

chamber, where he had been worshipping and watching in fear that the strangers would offer any kind of an insult to his idols. Through Malinche, Cortes asked to go inside. Montezuma entered with him. Three bleeding hearts, freshly cut from victims, dripped on the stone altar before the statue of the war-god. The floors were black with dried blood and the stench was terrible. The Spaniards did not ask to stay long.

With uneasy minds, they returned to their quarters where they learned from their Indian allies that the war-god had advised Montezuma to welcome the strangers into the city. There they were, on an island, surrounded by thousands of natives who could make them prisoners at any time. Like other prisoners, they might be sacrificed on the foul-smelling altars of that hideous idol, the Aztec god of war. It was not a comforting thought. How could they escape? Again, as at Vera Cruz, gold made the fatal decision.

It was a custom of the Spaniards to look for gold wherever they went. In searching the palace, two soldiers discovered traces of an old doorway in one of the apartments which they occupied. Secretly, they tore down the sealed doorway and found the treasure which Montezuma had inherited from his father. Sheets of solid gold, pounded thin, were stacked in piles upon the floor. Mounds of gold and jeweled trinkets were strewn around the room. The news spread rapidly among the soldiers. Plans were made to escape and take with them the riches of the Aztec kings.

They agreed upon a bold scheme to kidnap Montezuma and hold him in their quarters as a hostage to guarantee their safety. Cortes and several of his officers called upon the Emperor and forced him to accompany them under threat of death. Although Montezuma was treated with every courtesy and held court for his chiefs as usual, Spaniards were always present. The Aztecs grew suspicious that their ruler was held against his wishes and made plans to rescue him. The nephews of Montezuma gathered an army of warriors pledged to fight until not one Spaniard was left alive. When battles broke out around the palace, Cortes pleaded with Montezuma to tell the Aztecs that the Spaniards would leave the city if the warriors would return to their homes.

A hush fell over the packed square when Montezuma spoke, but it was soon broken by the angry mob, shouting, "Coward! Woman! Traitor!" The air grew

THE CALENDAR STONE

The Calendar Stone, completed in 1479, is thirteen feet in diameter and weighs twenty tons. The carving represents the history of the world with the face of the sun god in the center. This stone shows the extent of Aztec civilization in art and science. It is now exhibited in the National Museum in Mexico City.

Pan American Union

thick with arrows and stones hurled at the speaker. The great Emperor was knocked senseless with a rock and was struck with several arrows. Although the Spaniards waited upon him with every care, he refused to eat. Montezuma wept bitter tears, declaring he wanted to die because he had betrayed his people and his gods. As Montezuma breathed his last, he asked his conqueror to take good care of his most precious jewels, his daughters. Cortes, deeply touched by this request, promised he would guard and provide for them. He kept his word.

After the death of Montezuma, Cortes decided to sneak out of the capital with his army and the golden treasure of the Aztec rulers. The backs of wounded horses were loaded with sheets of gold, and the backs of eighty Indian porters were weighted down with loot. Each soldier helped himself to all the gold and jewels he could stuff into his pockets and strap onto his shoulders. Cautiously, in a drizzling rain, the army crept across the bridges which connected the island city to the mainland.

The Aztecs were waiting in the darkness. Suddenly, the lakes became alive with canoes. Thousands of fierce warriors pounced upon the Spaniards and their Indian allies. There was not much room to fight on the bridges and horses and men tumbled off into the water. Most of the stolen gold was lost. During the night, the long-haired priests were busy sacrificing Spanish captives to the greedy god of war. Their weird chants mingled with the blast of trumpets, and the boom of drums drowned the cries of their victims.

Although Montezuma's warriors avenged

CENTRAL SQUARE OF MONTEZUMA'S CAPITAL IN 1519

The temple of the War God towers above all the buildings. To the left of this tall monument is the palace of Axayacatl, Montezuma's father, where Cortes and his soldiers were housed. At the right of the great temple is the palace of Montezuma. The square is crowded with temples to lesser gods, the round sacrificial stone in the center, and the skull rack to the far right.

Courtesy of the American Museum of Natural History.
Great Temple of Tenochtitlan by Ignacio Marquina

his death on this terrible "night of sorrows," their victory was short-lived. Cortes and part of his army escaped. The Spanish forces grew as more and more pale-faced men from the land of the rising sun came to conquer and rule the native tribes. The ancient prophecy was fulfilled.

After the conquest, Cortes settled in Cuernavaca, the center of a fertile and beautiful valley where he ruled over a vast estate. For leading the conquest, the King gave him a title, "Marquis of the Valley." His wealth and fame brought him neither peace of mind nor peace of conscience. Jealous Spaniards plotted against him and Indian tribes rebelled. Another man was sent to govern the country which Cortes had discovered and conquered for Spain without costing the Crown and government a single penny. Cortes returned to Spain seeking justice at the Court and remained to die, like Columbus, a "forgotten man."

The winner was Spain. This bold and ruthless conquest gave that nation the first colonies in the New World and a foothold in America. The results were far-reaching. More adventurers came, hunting Montezumas and golden treasures. They stayed to build a Spanish empire in the Western Hemisphere.

Pan-American Union

PLAZA de la CONSTITUCION — MEXICO

The great central square in the heart of Mexico City is named "Plaza of the Constitution," but commonly called Zocalo. It marks the heart of the ancient city destroyed by Cortes. The Cathedral of Mexico, with altars covered in gold leaf, stands on the site of the ancient temple to the god of war. Today, in Montezuma's capital, busy streets cover the old canals; an open paved park hides the spots of temples; a new civilization builds a new way of life.

THREE SPANIARDS AND A MOOR

EIGHT YEARS AFTER Cortes sailed from Havana, Narvaez landed at Tampa Bay in Florida on another gold-hunting expedition. With him were about four hundred men and forty horses. Travel was slow in the swampy wilderness. The land was strewn with fallen trees blown down by hurricanes. As they stumbled over logs and waded through streams, both the men and their horses were targets for hostile Indians. The explorers found gold maize, needed for food, but no signs of a golden treasure. Discouraged, the conquistadores begged to return to New Spain (Mexico), although their fleet had sailed away, leaving them stranded in a foreign land.

Out of their stirrups, spurs, and crossbows, the Spaniards made axes, saws, and nails. The one carpenter in the group supervised the building of boats for their escape. Every third day, a horse was killed for food, and the skin on the legs was dried to make water bottles. In about three weeks, five boats were completed. Their ropes and rigging were made from horses' tails and the sails were fashioned from the shirts of the men. This strange and rickety fleet, carrying the 242 survivors, sailed from Apalachee Bay late in September, 1528.

The frail vessels followed the coast line of the Gulf of Mexico westward, toward the mouth of the Rio Grande. They kept a safe distance from the shore until hunger and thirst drove the men into some inlet for fresh water and shellfish. Once, when suffering terribly from thirst, the men discovered a river of fresh water running through the salty sea. They dipped into the muddy current and drank their fill, not knowing this water came from the Mississippi River that drained the central part of a continent.

In a storm, the boat of Narvaez drifted away into the Gulf and was never seen again. The vessel commanded by Cabeza de Vaca was washed ashore with such violence that men lying unconscious on the bottom were jolted to their senses. Here, they were found by Indians who brought them fish, roots, and water. Other shipwrecked Spaniards were enslaved by Indians wherever they were found along the coast. A wealthy gentleman and his slave were both forced to dig for roots under water until the flesh was torn from their fingers. They had to carry loads of firewood until their bare shoulders were streaked with blood. Summer and winter, they went without clothing.

The captives managed to meet several times a year when the tribes gathered. Finally, after eight years of slavery, only a few of the forty captives were left when the tribes met to feast. The survivors were the son of a physician; the

rich Spaniard and his slave, a black Moor from Africa; and Cabeza de Vaca, the only living officer of the ill-fated expedition. While the Indians were busy feasting, dancing, and singing, the captives made their escape.

The fleeing men had the good fortune to come upon the Indians of the plains of Texas. These Indians were more friendly than those along the Gulf coast. These tribes wandered from place to place as they tracked the "hunchback cows." De Vaca was the first white man to write about the wild bison which roamed the plains of North America. The natives were kind to the strangers. They sent guides to lead them through a pass in the mountains near the present site of El Paso, where they crossed the Rio Grande. The four that were left of the four hundred conquistadores finally reached the town of Culiacan on the western coast of Mexico, to tell a story stranger than fiction. The three Spaniards were the first white men, and the Moor, the first black man, to cross the continent of North America from the Atlantic to the Pacific.

The journey of Cabeza de Vaca and his companions changed the maps of the day, which had pictured Mexico as an island with a waterway north of it. Now the world knew that Mexico was a peninsula attached to a large land mass on the north. Having lived with a number of the tribes, these men learned their languages and their ways. They returned with first-hand information of the natives and their customs, of trees and plants, of birds and beasts, of rivers and mountains, of deserts and forests, of climate and rainfall.

Although de Vaca's report to the King of Spain told of suffering hardships and not of finding gold, more adventurers came on treasure-hunting expeditions. Among these were Hernando de Soto and Francisco Vasquez de Coronado, who started from opposite borders of the continent. De Soto landed in Florida and traveled north and west until he crossed the Mississippi River into Arkansas. At one time, unknowingly, the two expeditions were not far apart. After de Soto's march had begun, Coronado started from western Mexico and traveled north and east as far as the Arkansas River in Kansas. Not long after this near meeting, de Soto died from fever. He was buried at night in the Mississippi River near the present town of Natchez. His watery grave was intended to hide his body from the Indians, who believed he was an immortal god from the land of the rising sun.

Coronado's expedition was prompted by tales from the ex-captive, black Moor. At Culiacan, the Moor told the story of the golden cities of Cibola, where the people lived in three-and four-story houses whose doorways were studded with jewels. He related what Indians had told him of these cities to the north. Because the Moor could talk with the natives wherever he went, the viceroy of Mexico sent him with Friar Marcos and Indian guides to locate Cibola.

When nearing one of the Seven Cities, the Moor and some of his Indian guides raced ahead to be the first to arrive in the Zuni village. When he told the people that white men were coming from the east, they did not believe him because he was black. Offended by his arrogant manner, the Zunis killed the Moor. His frightened guides hurried back to tell the friar, warning him to go no farther. Marcos did go on to get a distant view of the village from a hilltop. He returned to report what he had seen and heard to Coronado, the new governor of New Galicia, in the western part of Mexico. Together, they rode to the capital to tell the exciting news to the viceroy, Mendoza, who was Coronado's intimate friend. Then and there, plans were made to conquer the rich and powerful "Seven Cities of Cibola."

GENTLEMEN ON HORSEBACK

THE SONS OF Spanish noblemen continued to pour into Mexico seeking adventure and gold. Since they usually carried letters of introduction from the King, the viceroy was obliged to entertain them with barbecue dinners at his ranches and with gay parties at his palace in Mexico City. The favorite sport of these noblemen was to ride about the city on sleek horses from the viceroy's farms. Since these "gentlemen on horseback" wanted adventure and not work, Mendoza turned a willing ear to Coronado's story of the riches of Cibola. A gold-hunting expedition might prove entertaining and attract a number of these "gentlemen."

The equipment for this expedition was costly and today would be calculated in hundreds of thousands of dollars. The captain-general was Coronado. The starting point was Compostela, an inland town near the western coast of the Mexican peninsula. Mendoza traveled on horseback from Mexico City to this distant village to review the troops for this expedition. A blast of trumpets and a roll of drums announced the parade in his honor. Coronado was dressed in gold-plated armor and a shining helmet, tipped with red and white plumes. His horse wore a long, fringed blanket which almost touched the ground. Next in line were his officers, riding prize mounts from Mendoza's stock farms. Their armor glistened in the sunlight, their lances were held erect, and their swords dangled at their sides. Hundreds of Indians armed with bows and arrows walked in the great procession. It was Sunday, the twenty-second day of February in 1540.

The next morning, about three hundred mounted men, holding silk banners to the breeze, started north from Compostela on the great adventure. It took nearly a thousand Indian and Negro servants to carry the baggage, to lead the pack horses, and to drive the herds of cattle and sheep that were provided to give the men fresh meat on the journey. The friars, except Marcos who remained as a guide, had left weeks before on foot, refusing to ride in luxury. With Indian interpreters, they aimed to make Christians of the inhabitants of the Seven Cities.

In the rough mountain country to the north, the expeditions made slow progress. Along the way, the "gentlemen" gave away their fine clothes to make room on the pack horses for food and water. Many a proud nobleman carried his own belongings

INDIAN VILLAGE OF TAOS, NEW MEXICO

Coronado found Indians living in large apartment houses much like the homes of some Indians in New Mexico today. The old Indian village of Taos was a center of revolt against the Spaniards in the 16th century.

New Mexico Department of Development

on his back. Grass was thin and scattered in the desert region. The plump saddle horses looked like bony nags after five long months of travel.

There was great rejoicing among the Spaniards when they sighted the first of the Seven Cities, a Zuni pueblo in the western part of the present state of New Mexico. The natives saw the strangers approaching. Coronado found the warriors drawn up in battle line to defend their homes. When the chief refused Coronado's terms for peace, the Spaniards attacked and captured the town. Great was their disappointment to find the palaces of their dreams to be mud-brick houses, two and three stories high. Colored rocks and turquoise stones, pressed into the bricks while wet, made the "jewelled doorways." However, they found corn, beans, fowl, and dried meat, which the hungry men needed more than gold and jewels.

In some villages, the frightened natives rushed out to bring gifts of buffalo hides, tanned deerskins, dried melons, wild turkeys, corn meal, turquoise stones, and everything they had with which to buy peace. In other towns, the warriors fought, killing and wounding the Spanish soldiers and stealing their horses. The Spaniards were forced to depend upon the natives for food and clothing. The tramp through cacti and sagebrush had torn their fine clothes into shreds and worn out their shoes. The natives were not prepared to feed and clothe this large, invading army. The demands of the Spaniards took the shirts off their backs and the corn from their bins. In some villages, the natives fled at night into the hills. From their hiding places, the Indians raided the Spanish camps and captured the horses and mules, which they prized. In this way, the Indians acquired a herd of these fleet-footed animals, unknown to them until the white men came.

The hard-pressed tribes schemed to get rid of their unwelcome guests. Among these tribes was a man from the plains whom they had captured in war and made a slave. A chief promised to free him if he would lead the palefaced strangers into his own country. Here they would die on the prairie without food and water. The slave made up a fairy tale about a wonderland, Quivira, where little gold bells, tied to branches of the trees, tinkled in the breeze to lull the chief to sleep on summer afternoons.

Coronado left the sick and weak men in his base camp near the site of Albuquerque while he took his best soldiers on the journey to Quivira. The slave led them into Kansas, probably as far as the Arkansas River where, he had told them, the fish were as big as horses. On the prairie the Spaniards found wandering tribes of Indians who lived in tents made of buffalo skins and hunted wild cattle for food. The palefaced men did not perish on the plains. They saved themselves by living as the Indians lived. They hunted buffalo and dried the meat in the sun. With wild cherries, grapes, and herbs, they made stews of the dried meat in native fashion. Finally, when the slave, whom they called the "Turk," confessed that he had led the Spaniards out to the plains to die, they killed him. Coronado and his men returned from the "wild-goose chase" hale and hearty.

After searching two years for gold and finding none, Coronado was convinced that the metal did not exist in that country. He was homesick and wanted to return to his wife and children. Rather than endure the

CORONADO HEIGHTS

According to legend, Coronado and some of his men stood on this knoll and gazed across the level plain. They were seeking a mythical land of gold, Quivira. If they could return to the same spot today, they would see golden grain in a patchwork design laid down on the prairie. The place would be Kansas, the wheat-growing state.

walk home through desert land, some of his soldiers remained with the Indians. The friars stayed to preach Christianity and established the first missions in this country.

Shamefaced and weary, Coronado entered Mexico City with a small band of soldiers, the remnant of his army. He reported his journey to his best friend, Mendoza, who received him coldly. For weeks afterwards, the "gentlemen on horseback" straggled into the capital on foot. Dirty, unshaven, thin and worn, the survivors were a sorry sight. They went away in silk and velvet and came back in skins and rags. Coronado returned to his rancho, grateful to join the list of forgotten men and live out his days in the peace and quiet of the countryside.

History rates him a great explorer who contributed to the world's knowledge of geography in his day. Coronado had sent

FRIJOLES CANYON — NEW MEXICO

Natives were living in this canyon when Coronado came in 1540. Cliffdwellers had chiseled caves in the rocky walls with tools made of stone and bone. Surprised to find beans growing along the banks of a little stream flowing through the gorge, the Spaniards named the place Frijoles Canyon, and the creek, "El Rito de los Frijoles" — the Little River of the Beans.

small groups of his men in all directions to explore the country. A band of soldiers under Cardenas were the first white men to view that great wonder of the world, the Grand Canyon of the Colorado River.

Coronado's thorough job of exploration, following the journeys of de Vaca and de Soto, convinced the Spaniards that the country north of the Rio Grande was not a land of gold. They turned their attention to colonizing South America, where riches were flowing from the fabulous mines of Peru. They built a Spanish empire on the southern continent.

THE CONQUEST OF PERU

IN 1510, as a stowaway in a barrel, Balboa sneaked aboard a vessel leaving a port in the West Indies for the unexplored mainland. The mainland turned out to be the Isthmus of Panama. There, a story told by the young son of an Indian chief started Balboa on an expedition which wrote his name on the pages of history. The story was of a rich country where the people drank from goblets of shining gold.

With a few Spaniards and native allies, Balboa started on his search, cutting his way through a tropical jungle. On a Sunday morning in late September in the year 1513, Balboa climbed alone to the top of a high hill, eager to claim the honor of being the first white man to look upon the Pacific Ocean. When he gave his soldiers permission to follow him, they scaled the peak, shouting, "The sea! The sea!" Balboa named the large body of water, the South Sea, because it lay directly south of the spot where he stood.

One of the sixty-seven men with Balboa on this eventful day was Francisco Pizarro, who could neither read nor write, but who became the conqueror of Peru.

In this conquest, Pizarro followed the pattern set by Cortes in Mexico, although his methods were more cruel than those of Cortes. The conquest of Peru was a bloody, violent affair for both the natives and the Spaniards, who quarreled among themselves. After Pizarro had arrived in Peru, he invited the Inca Emperor, Atahualpa, to a banquet where he was seized and held for ransom.

The Inca ruler, like Montezuma, tried to bribe his captors, trading gold and jewels for life and freedom. The ransom, amounting to millions of dollars, was a room full of gold and silver plates torn from temples and a bench of gold on which they said the sun was wont to sit down. The ransom was given to the Spaniards but it did not save Atahualpa, who was killed because the Spaniards were afraid to let him go. Almagro, the partner of Pizarro, was not pleased with his share of lands, slaves, and loot. In the civil war that followed, both men were murdered. They died as violently as they had lived.

Spanish goldseekers continued to pour into the new countries. New Spain was colonized. Under the encomienda system which the Spaniards established, the natives became the slaves of their Spanish masters. The society developed by the conquistadores still affects the pattern of living in Latin American countries. How did it grow?

ENCOMIENDA

SOLDIERS WHO CONQUERED new territory for the King of Spain, as well as favorites at his Court, received land grants in the New World. Since the soil was worthless without servants to till it, these grants included the people living on the land. Thus the natives became the serfs of the new landlords, whose titles to the property were recorded in Madrid. There was much rivalry among aristocrats near the King over who would get land with the most servants to dig the gold and plow the fields.

The men who had borne the hardship of conquering and subjugating the country, the conquistadores, felt they had prior right to these awards of lands and serfs, called "encomiendas." Today, thousands of acres of land in Latin America still belong to the descendants of these first colonists, by right of original titles from the Court of the Indies in the sixteenth century. Some of the natives were already serfs, having been conquered by the warlike Incas before the white men came. Although the Indians no longer owned the land, they still lived on it. Under the encomienda system, they were not driven from their homelands.

Since there was not enough land to go around, an encomienda also came to mean smaller favors, such as the right to demand the labor of a certain number of Indians for any kind of servile work. In a short time,

ATAHUALPA, LAST INCA EMPEROR

The warlike Incas conquered their neighboring tribes in all directions. Atahualpa inherited an empire as large as the United States east of the Mississippi River, extending in places from the forests of the Amazon River on the east to the Pacific Ocean on the west.

Pan American Union

some regions were almost depopulated. Greedy masters had worked the natives to death, and it was necessary to import Negro slaves from Africa. The abuses of the encomienda system were loudly protested by both government and church officials. They pleaded that the King should protect the natives from cruel landlords. The report of Gonzalo Gomez de Cervantes, a governor in Mexico in 1598, deals largely with the abuses of the encomienda system. His description of conditions in the mines explains why so many natives perished in the frantic search for gold. Indians were hunted and captured for forced labor in the mines. Governor Cervantes wrote:

After eight days laborer gets four reales (coins), leaving his clothes torn in a manner to be of no service to him. Besides, when he draws out metal from the mines, he is covered with mud. When the miserable Indian goes to sleep, he has only these torn clothes to cover him, wet, and full of clay.

By 1598 laws had been passed that limited the laborer's time underground to eight days. Before these laws were made, the laborer often remained in the depths of the mines until he died. The new laws required the mine owners to pay wages to the laborers, although the wages were too small to provide even a bare existence. The abuses continued. Natives would be apportioned for gardening, cleaning, and housework by the judge, and then, be driven to break stones for granaries erected "by the sweat and labor of the miserable Indians." It was mining, however, that caused the most deaths. Cervantes said:

MACHU PICCHU — INCA RUINS — CUZCO, PERU
Inca architects used heavy stones of irregular size, cut and fitted so closely together that a thin knife blade could not be wedged between them. Without cement, walls are still standing where the stones have not been removed for later building.

Pan American Union

All this can be remedied by letting each owner of each mine have only a certain number apportioned to him. And, when their work is done, send them to the judge to be paid and given liberty. Anything that can be carried by pack mules, it is right that it should not be done by the poor Indians. Even if it is more work for the judge who apportions, it is better to preserve the Indian than to have the abuse.

All governors, however, were not as considerate of the natives as was de Cervantes. A chart written in a book published about 1575 lists the number of Spaniards and slaves then working in some mining sections of Mexico.

Place	Spaniards	Negroes	Indians	
Zultepec	200	500	200	
Temascaltepec	60	150	300	(paying tribute)
Taxco	100	700	900	
Pachuca	90		2700	(paying tribute)
Zacatecas	300	500		

Some idea of the amount of gold shipped to Spain from the colonies in America can be gained from a fraction of the report submitted by de Cervantes, who carefully recorded the amounts for each viceroy of Mexico from 1522 to 1594.

Viceroy	Date	Pesos
Don Antonio de Mendoza	1535 - 1548	1,794,224
Don Luis de Velasco	1549 - 1564	4,295,073
Don Martin Enriquez	1570 - 1580	8,769,093
Marques de Villa Manrique	1586 - 1589	3,850,463
Don Luis de Velasco, II	1590 - 1594	4,966,166

Since all Indians paid tribute, a law was passed demanding that each Indian bring in a hen as part of this tribute to get chicken raising started in the colonies. In his report de Cervantes complains that mulattoes who were free went into the country and bought chickens from the natives, carried them to the towns, and sold them at too big a profit. He declared that it is only right that all business be carried on by the descendants of the conquistadores, and asked the King to pass laws to that effect. To this day, in much of Latin America, business and governments are carried on by the descendants of the first families who settled in the Spanish colonies. However, as time goes on, more and more citizens in these countries are sharing in the responsibility of government. More and more of the big land grants given to the early settlers are being divided among the descendants of the native peoples who were living on this land when the Spaniards came.

Thus did a Spanish civilization invade the Americas. It was a duty of conquistadores to spread Christianity. Church towers marked the centers of villages where natives gathered to pray, to play, and to sell their wares. In time, Spain lost her empire in the Western Hemisphere, but her culture remains and flourishes in the republics of Latin America from the Rio Grande to the Strait of Magellan.

MAPS:

WA6r
Atlas of American History by Edgar B. Wesley

WA7r
Our United States by Edgar B. Wesley

Chapter 2

Portuguese Navigators Explore the Seas

VASCO DA GAMA

IT WAS THE HOPE of reaching Asia that had brought Columbus across the Atlantic. He was seeking the gold and spices that Europe wanted from the Orient. Other explorers also were lured across uncharted seas in search of a water route to the Far East. If the precious oriental cargo could be loaded on ships rather than land caravans, Europeans would get more goods at less cost. The land route over deserts and mountains brought a mere trickle of trade to Mediterranean ports.

Portugal was an established rival of Spain in this race for trade. Bordering the Atlantic Ocean, Portugal had early turned to the sea for a livelihood. A school for navigators was founded by Prince Henry, a member of the royal family. The sailors from Prince Henry's school gained the reputation of being the most daring navigators in Europe. Before Columbus had sailed for Spain, these Portuguese mariners had been venturing out into the Atlantic Ocean to the Azores and beyond. They had been sailing down the western shore of Africa and trading trinkets for gold on the Guinea Coast. In May of 1493, less than a year after the first voyage of Columbus,

action was taken to remove a possible cause of war between these two rivals. Pope Alexander VI issued his famous decree that separated the hunting grounds of Spain and Portugal. These two countries sealed the papal edict with the Treaty of Tordesillas in 1494. They agreed to a line of demarcation:

From the Arctic Pole to the Antarctic Pole, which is from North to South, which mark or line — must be drawn straight, as is said, at 370 leagues from the islands of Cape Verde to the West, — . And all that which up to the present shall be found and discovered by the said King of Portugal, or by his vessels, — going by the Eastern side within the said line to the East, — may belong to the said Lord, the King of Portugal and to his successors for ever after.

— From this day, henceforward, the King and Queen of Castile and of Leon, etc. (Spain) will not send any ships, by this part of the line on the Eastern side which belongs to the said Lord the King of Portugal. In like manner the representatives of the King of Portugal agreed not to send ships for trade and territory west of this line, which belongs to the said Lords, the King and Queen of (Spain) to discover and search for any lands or islands, or make treaties, or barter, or conquer in any manner.

In the first part of July, 1497, Vasco da Gama's little fleet of three vessels sailed from Lisbon, Portugal, to gain for that city

The harbor of Lisbon, Portugal as it looked when Diaz, da Gama, and Cabral were making their famous voyages that brought land, trade, and wealth to that country.

the envied title, center of the spice trade. Vasco da Gama did not creep cautiously down the coast of Africa as former explorers had done. Instead, he steered southwest, in a huge curve, to take advantage of the trade winds and to escape the dreaded region of equatorial calms. He was the first mariner to explore the South Atlantic Ocean. Not until the fourth of November did he sight the African mainland. On this day the unidentified keeper of the journal on this voyage wrote the following entry, which reported the joy of the crews:

At nine o'clock, we sighted land. We then drew near to each other, and having put on our gala clothes, we saluted the captain-major (da Gama) by firing our bombards, and dressed the ships with flags and standards.

Four days later the fleet anchored in a bay that:

extended east and west, and we named it Santa Helena. We remained there eight days, cleaning the ships, mending the sails, and taking in wood.

Then da Gama headed for the Cape of Good Hope, discovered ten years before by Bartholomew Diaz, another Portuguese navigator. The wind blew so hard at the Cape that it took four days to round the stormy point.

On the way up the eastern coast of Africa, Vasco da Gama stopped at ports where Arab traders eyed the Europeans with unfriendly suspicion. Why had they come? Did they have goods to sell? Would they be competitors in the future? The

23

keeper of the journal described the people seen at Mozambique:

They are Mohammedans, and their language is the same as that of the Moors (Arabs). Their dresses are of fine linen or cotton stuffs, with variously colored stripes, and of rich and elaborate workmanship. They are merchants and have transactions with white Moors, four of whose vessels were at the time in port, laden with gold, silver, cloves, pepper, ginger, and silver rings, as also with quantities of pearls, jewels, and rubies, all of which articles are used by the people of this country.

Continuing the voyage the three vessels arrived at Calicut, a town on the southwestern coast of India. The name Calicut means cock's crow. The town was called Calicut because the territory of the first king there extended only as far as the crow of a rooster could be heard. Taking thirteen men with him, Vasco da Gama called upon the King, whom he found reclining on a couch covered with green velvet. His Majesty was chewing a betel nut and spitting out the husks into a large golden cup held in his left hand. The two men talked about merchandise and the articles each country had to offer. The King of Calicut then wrote a letter with an iron pen on a palm leaf. Vasco da Gama was to take the letter to the King of Portugal. It read:

Vasco da Gama, a gentleman of your household, came to my country, whereat I was pleased. My country is rich in cinnamon, cloves, ginger, pepper, and precious stones. That which I ask of you in exchange is gold, silver, corals, and scarlet cloth.

Although the King was friendly, the Arab merchants who controlled the trade, resented the coming of any rivals. They made trouble for the Portuguese when the latter tried to display their merchandise. When agents of the King came to inspect the display, they did not buy because the Arab merchants made fun of the Portuguese goods. Since the Portuguese could not speak the native languages, and the Arabs could, the Europeans were at a disadvantage. The journal entry for Wednesday, August 29, 1498 reads:

The captain-major and the other captains agreed that, inasmuch that we had discovered the country we had come in search of, as also spices and precious stones, and it appeared impossible to establish cordial relations with the people, it would be as well to take our departure. — We therefore set sail and left for Portugal.

Sometime about the middle of September in 1499, after an absence of over two years, Vasco da Gama reached Lisbon. He was honored with a title, Count of Vidigueira, in recognition of his feat in discovering a water route to India. Less than half of his men survived this epoch-making voyage that put the little kingdom of Portugal in the front rank of commercial nations for years to come.

CABRAL SEEKS TRADE IN THE NEW WORLD

WHEN VASCO DA GAMA told about the riches he had found in the East, the King of Portugal wanted him to return there with shiploads of merchandise to trade for spices, herbs, and jewels. Da Gama was tired and suggested that his friend Cabral go in his place. Cabral could take along some members of da Gama's crew to act as guides and captains.

It was a gala day when fourteen ships assembled in the Tagus River a few miles below Lisbon. This was the first commercial fleet sailing from Portugal with goods to trade for spices in the fabulous East. The cargo consisted of copper, vermilion, mercury, amber, coral, and rolls of woolen, velvet, and satin cloth. Dom Manuel, the King, was there to bid Cabral farewell and present him with a banner carrying the royal arms. The music of fifes, drums, horns, and bagpipes mingled with the cheers of the crowds that lined the riverbanks. It was the ninth of March, 1500 and a great day for Portugal, for whom Cabral was to win both trade and empire.

To avoid the calms off the Gulf of Guinea, Cabral followed the mid-Atlantic route of da Gama. The trade winds and ocean currents, however, carried the vessels far off the course. After almost two months in the South Atlantic, the Portuguese set foot on the mainland of South America at a spot which they named Porto Seguro. Cabral named the newly found land, "land of the true cross." He took possession of it for the King of Portugal. Since Porto Seguro is east of the line of demarcation, Cabral's landing gave Portugal a claim to the country. The territory was soon renamed Brazil, because a valuable dyewood by that name became the leading product exported to Europe.

The unknown keeper of the journal wrote:

During these days which we stayed there, the captain determined to inform our Most Serene King of the finding of this land, and to leave in it two men, exiles condemned to death, who were in the same armada for this purpose. (It was the custom to offer condemned prisoners freedom if they agreed to take the chance of living among natives in new lands to learn the languages.) And the said captain promptly dispatched a small supply ship which they had with them. This small ship carried the letters to the King. In these were contained what we had seen and discovered. After the said

small ship was dispatched, the captain went on shore and ordered a very large cross to be made of wood, and he ordered it to be set up on the shore, and also, as has been said, left two convicts in the said place. They began to weep and the men of the land comforted them and showed that they pitied them. The following day, which was the second day of May of the said year (1500), the armada made sail on its way to go round the Cape of Good Hope.

Approaching the windy region of the Cape, the fleet ran into a storm that wrecked four vessels and all on board were lost. The captain of one of these ill-fated vessels was Bartholomew Diaz, who perished off the "Cape of Storms" which he himself had discovered. The surviving ships rounded the Cape without further damage and continued the voyage to Calicut, India.

Arabs controlled the spice trade. They resented the efforts of the Portuguese to take some of this business from them. In riots started by Arab merchants, Cabral lost fifty men who were killed or captured. He left Calicut to seek cargo in other ports. However, he did not find cloves, the most profitable spice. The Moors had purchased the entire supply on the market.

On the long return voyage around Africa the expedition took a short rest in a harbor near Cape Verde. During this stop-over three vessels under the leadership of Amerigo Vespucci dropped anchor in the same harbor. The King of Portugal had sent Vespucci, an Italian, to explore the new land that Cabral had described in the letters from Brazil. Amerigo Vespucci later wrote such interesting letters about his travels in the New World that he became better known than the men who had discovered the countries he later visited. In 1507 Martin Waldseemuller wrote a geography in which he suggested that the newly-discovered lands to the west be called "America" after Amerigo Vespucci. At first the title was applied only to the southern continent, and later, to North America.

In July, 1501 seven ships of Cabral's fleet returned to Lisbon. Two of the ships were empty. Five held a cargo of spices, drugs, and jewels. The cargo was enough to pay, in part, for the seven vessels that did not come back. The loss of life cast a pall of gloom over the little kingdom. This voyage, however, netted Portugal both commerce and an empire. The opening of a sea lane to the Orient brought about a decline of the power of Venice, Florence, and other commerical cities of the Mediterranean that had prospered on the overland spice trade by the old caravan routes.

At the beginning of the sixteenth century the Portuguese did not realize the value of Cabral's detour to land in the New World. Little did they dream that the time would come when a Portuguese monarch would flee from a conqueror and set up a throne for the royal family in far away Brazil. Portugal's ambition was to win the spice trade of the East, which seemed more important than empire in those days.

MAGELLAN STARTS
AROUND THE WORLD

ONE OF THE GREATEST Portuguese explorers was Magellan, leader of the expedition that was the first to sail around the world. However, this accomplishment brought glory and land to Spain, rather than Portugal. Spain financed this voyage.

In August of 1519, the year that Cortes began the conquest of Mexico, Magellan sailed from Seville. The fleet of five vessels gathered supplies as they went down the Guadalquivir River to the Atlantic Ocean. There were men from many lands on this expedition. Magellan, the captain-general, was Portuguese. With him went between 235 and 268 men; the exact number is not known. They were Spaniards, Portuguese, Sicilians, Genoese and other Italians, Germans, French, Dutch, English, Malays, Moors, Negroes, and natives of the Madeira, Azores, and Canary Islands. The pilots were Portuguese, and the chief gunners were German, French, and English. On board the vessels were sailors, common seamen, carpenters, calkers, coopers, stewards, interpreters, notaries, accountants, barbers, shepherds, blacksmiths, servants, and cabin boys. In addition there were the officers and five priests, one for each ship. There were other men, "extras," going along for adventure. They took the part of soldiers, defending the crews if the expedition was attacked by enemies. Among these "soldiers of fortune" was a well-to-do Venetian named Pigafetta, who kept the journal of the voyage.

By the time Magellan entered the service of the King of Spain, it was known that two continents connected by a narrow isthmus blocked the western water route to India. Spanish explorers had searched in vain to find a strait across this narrow strip of land linking the Atlantic Ocean and the "South Sea," discovered by Balboa. Magellan determined to find this waterway in another direction. Touching the eastern shore of South America near Bahia (old name for Salvador) he turned south, following the coast line and exploring inlets like All Saints Bay and the Rio de la Plata in search of the mythical strait.

At Port St. Julian mutiny broke out

when the crews learned the captain-general intended to spend the winter of 1520 in this cold and barren region. All had been put on rations to save food. The men declared Magellan "was taking them all to destruction." When requested to turn back, Magellan replied that he would either die or accomplish what he had promised. He said that he had to sail until he found the end of the land or some strait which must surely exist. He scolded the men for complaining "since the bay had an abundance of fish, good water, many game birds, and quantities of wood, and that bread and wine would not fail them if they would abide by the rule regarding rations." To quell the mutiny, however, some of the leaders were executed by Magellan.

The fleet remained at Port St. Julian from the last day of March to the twenty-fourth of August. These are winter months south of the equator. On the twenty-first of October Magellan discovered by chance the strait that bears his name. Although this body of water is approximately 300 miles long, Magellan traveled over 400 miles while investigating arms of the strait to find one with an outlet. Some men scaled the snow-covered mountains flanking the waterway to find the way out. It was the twenty-eighth of November before Magellan emerged from the puzzling network of gulfs and bays that link the two oceans. He had only three ships. The *Santiago* was wrecked before entering the strait, and Gomez, pilot of the *San Antonio*, had slipped away with his vessel while under orders to explore an inlet of the waterway. Gomez skirted the coast of both continents in the Western Hemisphere looking for a passage through either one of them. Failing in the attempt he turned home and arrived safely.

For three months and twenty days Magellan sailed the vast Pacific Ocean. When food ran low, the crews ate wormy biscuits, ox hides taken from the main yard, and sawdust. Many died of scurvy. The survivors were overjoyed when they at last came upon some islands. Magellan named these islands "Ladrones" (robbers) because natives swarmed over the ships and stole everything they could, even rowboats. Not far away, however, on another island the Europeans found friendly natives with whom they traded red caps, mirrors, combs, bells, and ivory for fish, figs, bananas, rice, and coconuts.

Magellan discovered the Philippine Islands. This rich archipelago was held by Spain until 1898 — over 375 years. The territory, however, cost Magellan his life. He and sixty of his men joined forces with an island prince who had become a Christian, to force another chief at Matan to accept the Christian ruler, to obey the King of Spain, and to pay tribute. In the battle that followed, a warrior hurled a poisoned bamboo lance into Magellan's face after he had been wounded in the leg with an arrow. Magellan died on the battlefield. The day was April 27, 1521. A week later two new captains who had been elected to replace Magellan were dead. They were among those killed at a banquet given by the Christian king whom they had defended. Choosing new captains again, the survivors continued the voyage in two vessels. They had burned the third ship before they left the Philippines because there were not enough men left to sail it.

The crews fired guns for joy when they arrived in the Moluccas, the Spice Islands. On these islands were a few Portuguese traders who had arrived after the voyages of da Gama and Cabral. Here, the men in

Magellan's ships traded cloth, hatchets, linen, quicksilver, knives, scissors, and broken mirrors for cloves, a spice that sold at a high price in Portugal. At other islands they gathered nutmeg, mace, and cinnamon.

The little ship *Victoria* was the only ship in the expedition that finally returned to Spain. The other ship, the *Trinidad,* was captured by the Portuguese, who claimed the exclusive right to trade in the East Indies. When the *Victoria* reached Spain, Pigafetta wrote in his journal:

On Saturday, September six, 1522, we entered the Bay of San Lucar with only eighteen men and the majority of them sick, all that were left of the sixty men who left Malucho (the Molucca Islands). Some died of hunger; some deserted at the island of Timor; and some were put to death for crimes. From the time we left that bay (San Lucar) until the present day of our return, we had sailed fourteen thousand four hundred and sixty leagues, and furthermore had completed the circumnavigation of the world from east to west.

Magellan, a Portuguese navigator in the service of a Spanish King, was the first European to sail across the Pacific Ocean. He discovered another water route to India, proved beyond any doubt that the earth was round and that the lands Columbus discovered were not Asia. The voyage was a success commercially. The cargo on the *Victoria* consisting of cloves, cinnamon, nutmeg, mace, and sandalwood, was sold for a sum profitably exceeding the original cost of the four lost vessels and equipment.

The visit of Magellan's men to the Moluccas gave Spain a claim to these rich spice islands, where mountains were covered with clove trees. Therefore Portugal and Spain again reached a trade agreement by extending the line of demarcation to the Eastern Hemisphere. Portugal took

the Moluccas, but paid an indemnity to Spain. For nearly a century after Vasco da Gama's first voyage on the Indian Ocean, that body of water was practically a Portuguese sea. Portugal prospered on spices until Dutch traders swooped down upon the rich East Indies and gradually took that business to the Netherlands.

THE PORTUGUESE SETTLE IN AMERICA

PORTUGAL PLANTED COLONIES in Brazil to hold the country against invaders, especially the French, who threatened to settle there. The colonial plan resembled the encomienda system established by Spaniards in the Americas. The King of Portugal gave huge land grants to nobles of his realm. In turn these nobles accepted the responsibility of conquering and pacifying territory allotted them, of inducing settlers to go there, and of governing the territory as vassals of the King. These original land grants were called captaincies, and their owners, captains. Brazil began with eight captaincies, south of the equator, from which developed the coastal provinces of present-day Brazil. These grants extended along the Atlantic Ocean and inland as far as the line of demarcation separating Spanish and Portuguese territory in South America.

About seventy years after Cabral touched the coast of Brazil, a Portuguese named Pero de Magalhaes wrote the first history of that country. His aim was to encourage poor people in Portugal to migrate to the nation's colony in America. The title of his book was *History of the Province of Santa Cruz* because the name had not been officially changed to Brazil. Magalhaes tells of life on the estates:

The first thing which the inhabitants seek to obtain is slaves to work the land and to till their plantations and ranches, because without them, they cannot maintain themselves in the country. One of the reasons why Brazil does not flourish much more is that the slaves revolt and flee to their own land and run away every day. The crops from which they obtain the greatest profit are sugar, cotton, and brazil wood, and, because there is little money in the country, they pay with these the merchants who bring them goods from the Kingdom. All the inhabitants of the country have plantations of food stuffs. There are also many Guinea slaves (Negroes). These are more certain than the Indians of the country, because they never flee as they have nowhere to go.

Since Brazil was an agricultural country, landowners imported Negro slaves from Africa to work on their ranches and plantations. The landowners also held the natives in bondage. In order to develop the resources of the country, the Portuguese established a social order based upon master and slave from which evolved a society much like that in Spanish colonies. Although the aristocratic landowners became the ruling group in rural sections, towns in Brazil had a form of self-government similar to the plan commonly used in New England towns during colonial times. The Portuguese captains defended their provinces against invaders, mainly French and Dutch, and held the country. Today, the land of Brazil is Portuguese America, where the people celebrate Cabral's Day with national rejoicing on the third day of May each year.

MAP:

WA6r
Atlas of American History by Edgar B. Wesley

Chapter 3

New Netherland and New Sweden Are Started

THE DUTCH SEEK TRADE
IN THE EAST AND THE WEST

THE NETHERLANDS (HOLLAND), ruled by Spain in the early part of the sixteenth century, was a little nation hemmed in by neighboring countries. Like Portugal, with an open door to world waterways, she also turned to the sea for a livelihood. Dutch traders challenged the trade of Portugal in the Indian Ocean by organizing the Dutch East India Company in 1602. For almost a century before the formation of this company, bold Dutch sailors had been attacking and robbing Portuguese vessels laden with spices. These pirates, known as "beggars of the sea," broke the power of Portugal in the Far East. They opened the ports of the East Indies to Dutch traders who followed them. During the time Spain ruled Portugal (1581-1640), these daring marauders of the sea lanes had a patriotic excuse for their piracy, since the people of the Netherlands were trying to break away from Spain.

Merchants of the Dutch East India Company were anxious to find a shorter route to the East Indies than the long voyage around the Cape of Good Hope. They hired the English navigator, Henry Hudson, to explore the Arctic in search of a northeast passage to the Orient. Early in April, 1609, Henry Hudson sailed from Amsterdam on the *Half Moon* with "a crew of eighteen or twenty men, partly English, and partly Dutch." A month later, he rounded the North Cape and headed for Novaya Zemlya, an island in the Arctic Ocean north of Russia. Some of his men who had been sailors in the East Indies grumbled about the bitter cold. Finding the sea blocked with ice, Hudson held a conference with his crew. He proposed that they abandon the search for a northeast passage and seek one in the northwest. Maps which a certain Captain John Smith had sent him from Virginia indicated that a strait might pass through the continent of North America.

Early in September of 1609, the *Half Moon* anchored in New York Harbor. Exploring the region, Hudson soon discovered a wide river (later named for him), which he hoped was the Northwest Passage to Cathay. He sailed up the stream as far as the present site of Albany and sent scouts to test the depth of the river beyond. On the twenty-second of September, Robert Juet recorded in the ship's journal:

In the morning our Masters Mate and foure more of the companie went up with our Boat to sound the River higher up. At three of the clocke in the afternoone they (Indians) came aboard, and brought Tabacco, and more Beades, and gave them to our Master (Hudson), and made an Oration, and shewed him all the Countrey round about. They sent one of their companie on land, who presently returned, and brought a great Platter full of Venison, dressed by themselves. This night at ten of the clocke, our Boat returned in a showre of raine from sounding of the River; and found it to bee at an end for shipping to goe in.

The stream did not lead into the fabled Northwest Passage. Early in November of 1609, the *Half Moon* reached England where Hudson and the Englishmen in the crew were held. It was months before the East India Company in Amsterdam received the written report of the voyage, a total loss as far as that trading company was concerned. Hudson had returned with furs from North America instead of cloves from the Spice Islands.

In the following year Hudson made another voyage, this time in the *Discoverer*, in search of the Northwest Passage. The venture was financed largely by three English merchants, one of whom was Sir Thomas Smith, treasurer of The London Company that founded Jamestown in Virginia. During the winter months the *Discoverer* was ice-bound in a polar bay. The men were placed on rations of meal and biscuits, although fowl was plentiful. Mutiny began to brew on board. When the ice broke up in the late spring, the crew were afraid that Hudson would continue the search for the waterway. Under the leadership of Juet, keeper of the journal on the voyage up the Hudson River, the men rebelled. The master of the *Discoverer,* John Hudson, who probably was Henry's son, and the sick and lame were bound,

lowered into a boat, and abandoned. The ship's carpenter, refusing to join the mutineers, asked to share Hudson's fate. He begged permission to take along his kit of tools. The nine doomed men had a gun, powder and shot, an iron pot, some meal, and the carpenter's chest in the boat when cast adrift upon the icy waters of the Hudson Bay. No trace of the party was ever found. Juet did not get home. When the *Discoverer* was almost in sight of the Irish coast, Juet died of starvation and was buried at sea. The remnant of the crew that survived were thrown in prison when they finally reached England.

THE DUTCH WEST INDIA COMPANY HELPS SETTLE THE NEW WORLD

THE FURS BROUGHT BACK by Hudson in 1609 created a stir among Dutch traders. They were excited, also, by the report describing lands "as pleasant with Grasse and Flowers, and goodly Trees, as ever they had seene," and fish caught in the harbor, "ten great Mullets of a foot and halfe long a peece." The little country of the Netherlands, proud of independence finally won from Spain, looked forward to trading with the world.

The year after Hudson's voyage, a group of Amsterdam merchants outfitted a ship and loaded a cargo of trinkets and baubles to be traded for valuable furs in the country Hudson had explored. This first venture was so successful that two vessels, the *Little Fox* and the *Little Crane,* were officially licensed the next year to look again for a northerly passage to the Orient. Their real mission was to trade with the Indians. Soon, the New Netherland Company was formed and trading posts

This view of Fort Amsterdam on the Manhattan is copied from an ancient Engraving executed in Holland. The Fort was erected in 1623 but finished upon the above model by Governor Van Twiller in 1635.

FORT AMSTERDAM ON MANHATTAN ISLAND

In the "New World" published by Johan De Laet in 1625, this fort and the surroundings are described as follows:

The fort was built here in the year 1614, upon an island on the west side of the river, where a nation of savages dwell called the Mohawks, the enemies of the Mohicans. On this river there is a great traffic in the skins of beavers, otters, foxes, bears, minks, wild cats and the like. The land is excellent and agreeable, full of noble forest trees and grape vines, and nothing is wanting but the labor and industry of man to render it one of the finest and most fruitful lands in that part of the world.

were erected on the island of Manhattan, claimed by the right of discovery.

After the New Netherland's charter expired, plans were made for another trading company, the Dutch West India Company. The organization of the Dutch West India Company followed the pattern used by most of the trading companies of those days. The first step was the meeting of a group of merchants who agreed to form a company, invest their own money, and sell stock to other "adventurers." Any adventurer who bought stock in the company would be entitled to a share in the profits. The money he paid for his stock would be used by the company to run its ships and carry on trade.

The next step, usually assured in advance, was to get permission to form the company from the king or government in power. When the patent, or charter, was granted, the company had the legal right to sell stock and to seek colonists. The members of the company could make all the rules for operating the company itself and for the conduct of the colonists.

Since the charters made these trading companies into sub-nations, enjoying special privileges, each company set up its own form of government. Usually, the government was modeled upon that of the mother country. The highest governing board was composed of leading stockholders. This board was commonly called the council. The council managed the company's affairs in much the same way that the directors of modern corporations conduct a business. This council, the home council, carried on its work from the mother country, and it appointed a governor to work in the colony. The governor ruled the colonists with the help of another council, or governing body, that operated in the trading settlement. Sometimes the governor chose the members of this advisory group from the colonists themselves. Sometimes the home council selected these men. The governor and his advisory body represented the home council in the colony. These representatives were charged with the responsibility of operating the colony for the benefit of the company.

The regulations of the French and English trading companies were much like those of the Dutch West India Company in that the company held a monopoly on trade for profit. Naturally, the settlers wanted to trade on their own account and keep the profits for themselves. The governors had difficulties enforcing the rules of their companies. In the friction that developed, the trading companies eventually lost their control of trade to the colonists.

THE PATROON SYSTEM DEVELOPS

TO GET SETTLERS, the Dutch West India Company used the land-grant plan of Spain and Portugal, but adapted it to the needs of trade. Free land was the lure held out to emigrants from crowded European countries. Any man in whom the company had confidence could become a patroon by agreeing to plant a colony of fifty persons over fifteen years of age within four years in New Netherland. Each patroon was entitled to a grant of land extending for sixteen miles along the bank of any navigable river, or for eight miles on each side of the stream, and as far inland as he could go successfully. He also received the plants, minerals, rivers, springs, and rights to fishing, hunting and grinding on this property. The patroon system of the Dutch differed from the Spanish encomienda and the Portuguese captaincy in that the land grant did not include the natives living on it. The Dutch did not enslave the Indians. Since the West India Company had trading rights in Africa, Negro slaves were shipped from that continent and sold throughout the Americas. Patroons were promised that "the company will endeavor to supply the colonists with as many blacks as they possibly can." However, white laborers were preferred by the patroons. These landowners paid for the passage of white laborers across the ocean and maintained them while they worked out this expense in terms of servitude. When their contracts expired, the servants were free.

The lordly patroons had the privilege of trading in fish, slaves, and merchandise, except furs, provided they returned to Manhattan with their cargoes and paid duty of five percent to the West India Company. The company also claimed one third of the booty taken from ships at sea by vessels belonging to patroons. Dutch privateers continued to capture the Spanish treasure ships and the slavers bringing Negroes from Africa to the Spanish colonies.

Realizing that some persons might want to settle in New Netherland without the rank of patroon, the Company welcomed colonists who brought over fewer than fifty settlers. These people were allowed to hold as much land as they could cultivate properly. In an effort to create a perfect state, the Dutch West India Company purchased land from the Indians; granted it to patroons in exchange for a share of their profits; and provided for the support of the Dutch Reformed Church, along with aid for individual colonists.

The most famous purchase was the site of present downtown New York. In the spring of 1626 Peter Minuit, first governor of the Dutch West India Company in New Netherland, opened negotiations with Indian chiefs to buy Manhattan Island. The Dutch intended to build their capital on this island. Minuit made a treaty with the natives to transfer ownership of the island to the West India Company for goods that would be worth about twenty-four dollars three centuries later.

The early settlers had no idea of the future value of land on Manhattan Island. In 1682 a lot in the old sheep-walk was recorded as follows:

Lot on Wall Street, south side, 23 feet front, 60 feet deep, sold by Mrs. Drissius to John Pound, a laborer, for about $30.

The patroon system crumbled within and without. In an open country, rich in natural resources, both patroons and colonists wanted freedom to make the most of their opportunities. The patroons objected to the company's exclusive right to the fur trade and to paying a duty to the company. The colonists wanted to go into business for themselves instead of working for the patroons. Also, the English Government was making claim to New Netherland under charters granted to the Plymouth and London Companies, rivals of the Dutch West India Company for general business as well as fur trade. In addition, a blow was struck by Peter Minuit, whom the company had discharged. He returned to plant a Swedish colony in their territory and to take some of the fur trade from them.

SWEDES AND FINNS SETTLE ALONG THE DELAWARE RIVER

THE FOUNDING OF NEW SWEDEN grew out of the need to sell Swedish copper to finance the Thirty Years War in Europe. The Swedish commissioner to the Netherlands was told by Blommaert, a director of the Dutch West India Company, that a market for Swedish copper might be found in North America. Shortly afterwards, Minuit, the discharged governor of New Netherland, called upon Blommaert, who was displeased with the way the Dutch West India Company was managed. The two men made a proposition to the Swedish chancellor that a Dutch Swedish company be formed to trade on the Delaware under the protection of the Swedish flag.

After a charter was obtained from the Swedish Government, it took considerable time to sell enough stock to finance the first voyage to North America. Dutch merchants waited for the Swedish merchants to pay for half the shares before they invested enough money to pay for their part. Finally, supplies were purchased, ships were secured, sailors were hired, and the expedition sailed from Sweden to the Netherlands, and across the Atlantic, with Minuit in charge.

About the middle of March, 1638, the *Kalmar Nyckel* and the *Fogel Grip* sailed into Delaware Bay with colonists from Sweden. The cargo consisted of several thousand yards of cloth, several hundred hatchets, axes, knives, tobacco pipes, and dozens of mirrors, combs, earrings, and necklaces to trade for furs with the Indians. Minuit brought over farming tools — spades, hoes, and rakes, since the colonists would need to raise a supply of food during the summer months; and also, two barrels of wheat and two barrels of barley for seed.

Since Minuit had been governor of New Amsterdam, he had some knowledge of the region. Sailing up the Delaware River, he entered a tributary leading into the country occupied by the Minquas, a tribe of expert hunters, with whom he wanted to trade. Two miles up this branch of the Delaware, Minuit found a natural rock wharf, a good landing place, away from the beaten path of Dutch traders who claimed the "South" River trade under a charter issued to the Dutch West India Company. Guns on the *Kalmar Nyckel,* a man-o'-war, fired a Swedish salute denoting possession. It also notified the natives that white men had arrived to trade with them. The cannon brought the desired results. In a few days five Indian chiefs came on board. Minuit entertained them in his cabin and gave them presents. From them, he purchased territory along the Delaware extending sixty-seven miles along the western bank of the river, south to Duck Creek and north to the Schuylkill. When the chiefs had traced their totem marks on the treaty, all went ashore. They erected a pole with the Swedish coat of arms nailed to it, and a cannon fired a salute. The territory was christened New Sweden. On the rocky shore, Minuit built Fort Christina, named for the girl queen of Sweden. The stream, Minquas Kill, today is Christina River. It winds its lazy way through Wilmington, which was built on the site of the old fort, and is now the largest city in Delaware.

Early in the summer of 1638, the *Fogel Grip* sailed for home. Three weeks later, Minuit left New Sweden on the *Kalmar Nyckel* to exchange a cargo of wine brought from Europe for tobacco in the West Indies. While anchored in the harbor of St. Christopher Island, the captain of *The Flying Deer,* a vessel from Rotterdam, invited Minuit and his skipper to be his guests. While aboard, a storm rose suddenly and swept the ship out to sea. It was never seen nor heard of again. After waiting three days for Minuit, his crew returned to the Netherlands. The tobacco was sent to Sweden, and the furs were turned over to Blommaert, director of the Dutch Swedish trading company. The two vessels brought back 1769 beaver skins, 314 otter, 132 bear hides, and some other skins of lesser value. Blommaert sold these pelts to pay part of the expense of the first voyage, which had been disappointing. He had hoped Minuit, with a man-o'-war, would be able to capture one or more of Spain's silver ships and return with a big prize. Unfortunately, the leader himself did not get home.

A few years later the Dutch members of the trading company sold out to the Swedish members. Among the colonists brought over by the New Sweden Company were many Finns who had been reduced to poverty by the wars they were forced to share under the rule of Sweden. The hardy Finnish peasants cut down trees, built log houses, planted crops, and traded with the Indians. Both Swedes and Finns had begun to prosper on farms along the Delaware River when a Dutch squadron of seven vessels appeared, in 1655, and demanded the surrender of the colony. The Dutch West India Company had been complaining to the Government in the Netherlands about the Swedish settlement in territory belonging to the company.

Peter Stuyvesant, governor of New Netherland, came in person to demand the surrender. He was backed by a force of over 300 men. New Sweden was added to New Netherland under an agreement respecting private property, granting religious freedom, and permitting anyone to return to Sweden. All who remained in the Swedish colony were required to swear allegiance to the Dutch authorities in New Amsterdam. Thus ended Swedish rule on the Delaware River. However, Swedes and Finns continued to come in greater numbers to seek new homes among their countrymen who had settled in the colony. The change of ownership did not stop the migration.

Nine years later, four British frigates with soldiers on board anchored in Gravesend Bay. The commanding officer, Sir Richard Nicolls, demanded the surrender of New Amsterdam. Lacking ammunition, soldiers, and supplies, Stuyvesant was forced to obey this order. The name was changed to New York in honor of the Duke of York, brother of the King of England. Thus ended both Dutch and Swedish rule in North America, but Dutch and Swedish colonists stayed in their homes along the Hudson and the Delaware. New York joined the British colonies in 1664.

MAPS:

WA9r, WA12r
Atlas of American History by Edgar B. Wesley

Chapter 4

France Plants Her Banner in North America

VERRAZANO —
PIRATE AND EXPLORER

GIOVANNI DA VERRAZANO was born in Florence, Italy, probably about ten years before Columbus made his famous voyage in 1492. In those days Florentine lads with a longing for the sea spent days and days on the docks. They watched the ships unload their cargoes of spices brought to the Mediterranean ports by slow-moving caravans, over long and dangerous land routes. Verrazano learned the art of navigation on this inland sea that was the mariner's cradle. Indeed, he must have crossed the Mediterranean many times because he lived in both Egypt and Syria before he embarked upon the voyages which made him famous. As a French corsair, or pirate, the Spaniards called him Juan (John) Florin or Florinus. He lived in a time when piracy was a respectable business if a captain had a commission from the king of a country to prey upon the merchant fleets of an enemy nation. With papers issued by the King of France, Verrazano became the terror of the seas.

As an explorer for Francis I, King of France, the Florentine navigator was Verrazano, searching for a northwest passage to the Spice Islands and not Florin, the corsair, waylaying the treasure ships of Spain. In January of 1524, he sailed from the Madeira Islands in the *Dauphine,* steering directly west to avoid the Spanish sea lanes to the West Indies. In less than two months, the light of fires burning on a beach directed him to land. It was the coast of New Jersey. There, Indians gathered in the early spring to feast on shellfish and to manufacture wampum, which were strings of shells they used for money. Skirting the shore line in search of a strait, Verrazano entered New York harbor and anchored off Sandy Hook. In his explorations he found many natives huddled around fires on Rockaway Beach. Although Verrazano entered New York harbor eighty-five years before Henry Hudson, he failed to find the great river. Having only one vessel, he did not risk it in passing through the Narrows. Continuing the northern voyage, he touched the east coast of Newfoundland and then turned homeward.

After his arrival in France in July, Verrazano wrote a letter to Francis I, the King of France, telling what he had seen on his voyage — the natives, the forests, and the fertile lands. Verrazano had brought back no gold and had failed to locate the

Northwest Passage to the spice-laden Orient. Francis I was too deeply involved in war to profit by Verrazano's discoveries, although the pilot recommended the country he had seen for colonization. Ten years passed before the King of France was able to turn his attention again to America.

CARTIER — THE BOLD BUCCANEER

SPAIN'S SUDDEN WEALTH from the New World tempted the hardy seamen of the French coast and many a captain turned pirate to raid the Atlantic sea lanes. From the sheltered harbor of St. Malo on the coast of Brittany, these daring buccaneers sallied forth to pounce upon the treasure ships of Spain. Among them were the Italian Verrazano and the Frenchman Cartier.

Jacques Cartier was born in St. Malo about the time that Columbus was making his first voyage to America. When the lad was old enough to play on the wharves, he eyed with childish wonder the booty from the Indies, brought in by the buccaneers. It was not long until Cartier was one of them, sharing danger and adventure to capture the Spanish vessels with gold and silver from Mexico and Peru.

When the King of France had a breathing spell from war, his thoughts turned to the spice trade. Was there a Northwest Passage to Cathay? If not, was there land beyond the line of demarcation that might be added to the domain of France? Searching for a strait through a continent claimed by Spain was entirely within the bounds of the Treaty of Tordesillas. Neither Spain nor Portugal could reasonably object to such a venture, especially, if the leader of the expedition was respected and feared. While

looking around for the right man, the Vice Admiral of France took Cartier to the court and personally introduced him to Francis I. No one knows now what the King, the naval officer, and the bold buccaneer said at this meeting. One can only guess.

Cartier, to whom the broad Atlantic was as familiar as the Breton shore, came away from the meeting with a commission from the King placing him in command of an expedition to search for a western waterway to India.

On an April day in 1534, with two small ships and sixty-one hardened sailors, Cartier sailed from the harbor of St. Malo to cross the North Atlantic. He followed the route of the French fishermen who had been coming to the rich fisheries of Newfoundland since 1500. It was a pleasant voyage for Cartier and his men. A strong wind filled the sails, wafting the vessels to the shores of Newfoundland in only twenty days. The sea was so full of icebergs that the ships took shelter in a harbor for ten days. Here, the men feasted on waterfowl. They salted four or five casks of great auk to eat when no fresh fowl could be obtained. Continuing their voyage toward the mainland, the sailors caught their first glimpse of a polar bear "as big as a calf and as white as a swan." Boats were lowered for his capture, and bear steaks were served on board that evening.

The two vessels poked in and out of bays, slipped through narrow straits, and drifted along the coast of Labrador. They explored gulfs and bays, large and small, for a water opening leading westward. For days at a time, dense fog blotted out the shore line. When a strong wind blew, the fog parted to reveal a barren land, bleak, cold, and gloomy. Returning from one of his many trips ashore to explore the country, Cartier was heard to remark: "In all the Northland, I have not seen a cartload of good earth."

Undaunted, the explorer turned westward, still hoping to win for France the glory of discovering the passage to the East. On the first day of July, Cartier and his men went ashore on Prince Edward Island. They feasted on wild strawberries, blackberries, and gooseberries while they listened to birds chattering in the cedars, pines, white elms, ash, and willow trees. After the fog-bound coast of Newfoundland this island seemed a paradise. With renewed courage Cartier sailed up the coast until he found a widemouthed bay which he hoped would lead into a strait to the Orient. He named it Chaleur Bay (Bay of Heat) because the weather was warm. Chaleur Bay proved to be landlocked.

Leaving the ships anchored, Cartier and a small party of sailors rowed up a river in small boats to explore the country. They had not gone far upstream when about fifty canoes, crowded with Indians, cut across their path and paddled for the shore. With shouts that rang through the woods, the natives leaped ashore and waved pelts of fox, marten, and beaver stretched on paddles. With signs and yells they made it plain that they wanted to trade with the strangers. Cartier feared to run the risk of going ashore — a few white men among so many Indians. The next day a few daring sailors rowed up the same stream to barter with the natives. For furs the Frenchmen traded knives, needed to skin animals, and iron tools, glass beads, combs, and trinkets.

Cartier explored the St. Lawrence River as far as the site of the present city of Montreal.

Delighted with their bargains, the Indians danced and sang, clasping their hands and looking heavenward as though they were thanking the sun for their good luck. Thus began the fur-trading business which came to be the treasure France gained in the New World.

Before leaving for home, Cartier planted a wooden cross thirty feet high at the entrance to the harbor of Gaspé. At the center of the cross, he placed a shield with the French emblem, and above that, a board upon which was carved, LONG LIVE THE KING OF FRANCE. While the natives looked on in wonder, the French explorers knelt in prayer, bidding farewell to this new land destined to become New France. Without the loss of a man, Cartier and his crew sailed into the harbor of St. Malo early in September of that same year, 1534.

Eight months later, at the command of Francis I, Cartier sailed from St. Malo on his second voyage to search for a strait leading to Cathay, and to explore new lands he found. On this voyage, he discovered the St. Lawrence River. He explored the river as far as Montreal and beyond, searching for a rich country where the Indians said gold and jewels could be found. The mythical land was probably the Lake Superior region, and copper, not gold, would be the metal the Indians told him about. On Cartier's first voyage, he had kidnapped two Indians, to whom he taught the French language. He could now talk with the natives through these interpreters.

During the long cold winter a number of Frenchmen died of scurvy before an Indian chief told Cartier how to cure the disease by drinking water from boiled bark of a certain tree. It was the middle of July in 1536, before Cartier reached St. Malo again to report to the King on the country he had explored.

In 1541, Cartier left St. Malo on his third voyage. John Francis de la Roche, Knight, Lord of Roberval, was to go with him as lieutenant and governor to start a French colony. Since Roberval was not ready, Cartier went ahead of him, taking along cattle, hogs and goats to stock farms in the new land. Roberval arrived later with two hundred colonists, including soldiers and mariners, who took possession of Cartier's old fort on the St. Lawrence River. Many of these newcomers were prisoners released from jail as recruits. The majority did not live through the first, harsh winter. The survivors, Roberval among them, abandoned the colony and returned to France.

FURS SET THE PATTERN OF FRENCH COLONIZATION

AFTER THE FAILURE of Roberval's colony, it was fifty years before the French King renewed efforts to establish a settlement in the New World. Meanwhile French fishermen were coming to the banks of Newfoundland as they had been doing for years. Some ventured to the mainland where they traded for a few packs of furs to take back with their fish. When beaver skins brought more money than codfish, fishermen turned traders, following the rivers to barter trinkets for pelts. Instead of sending over prisoners, forcing them to be colonists, as was done with Roberval, the King granted permits to trading companies. These trading companies were given exclusive rights to the fur business in certain territories. Then the trading companies found their own colonists, provided for them, and established centers where trappers and hunters, both French and Indians, brought their furs to market.

In the year 1608, on the third of July, Samuel de Champlain marked out the site for the first building in Quebec, the Indian name for the spot where the St. Lawrence River becomes narrower in its course. The structure was both a dwelling for traders and a storehouse for skins. From this trading post grew the largest fur market in the New World and the city of Quebec. Champlain represented merchants in France, bought and sold furs, organized a trading company of his own, served as lieutenant and governor of New France, and still found time and energy to explore the region of eastern Canada as well as the Atlantic Coast. He traveled among the Indian tribes, seeking to win and to hold their friendship. Upon the Indians' good will depended the fur business that supported the colonies in New France. Champlain established missions among tribes to convert them to Christianity and he took an interest in their welfare.

Champlain had a hard time persuading men to stay in one place and till the soil. The French gold that grew on the backs of wild animals lured the colonist deep into the wilderness. Hunters and trappers migrated to the lakes and streams of the Canadian woods. These voyageurs learned to like the carefree life of the wilderness. Men without licenses for fur trading were known as "coureurs de bois" (runners of the woods). In frail canoes made from birch bark or hollowed from tree trunks, the fur hunters paddled up the St. Lawrence River, skirted along the shores of the Great Lakes, and ventured into the back country where no white man had ever

been before. Often a trader went alone in search of furs, with no one to talk to for weeks at a time. His only friend was his trusty canoe. The northern woods rang with the paddling songs which the jolly voyageurs sang to their little boats upon which their lives and · their profits depended.

A TRADER AND A PRIEST
EXPLORE THE MISSISSIPPI RIVER

AS THE FUR BUSINESS became more profitable, trading companies established posts along lakes and rivers farther inland. To these posts, voyageurs in the region brought their packs of skins and gained supplies for their wilderness trips. Priests followed the trails of the voyageurs. They built missions in the trading centers where they preached the gospel of Christianity to the Indians. In accompanying traders on fur hunting expeditions, these priests, most of whom were Jesuits, explored the wild country and wrote what they had learned.

For protection against Indian attacks, forts were erected in these frontier settlements. Around the log store, church, and fort were clustered the huts of the voyageurs and their Indian wives and children. Thus did furs set the pattern of French colonization in North America.

From tribes in the Great Lakes region the missionaries learned of a wide river, the "Great Water" called by the Indians, "Messipi," or "Missi-Sipi." It flowed into a sea, the natives said. Could this body of water be the South Sea? Maybe the "Great Water" was the long-sought waterway to the East. The two men who finally set out to find this river were a trader, Joliet, and a priest, Marquette. These close friends were once students together at the Jesuit seminary in Quebec.

In the middle of May, 1673, Joliet and Marquette left the Jesuit mission of St. Ignace, near the Strait of Mackinac, with five companions and two canoes. The only food they took along consisted of bags of cornmeal and some smoked meat. The seven men carried the two canoes and supplies over the portage of 2700 paces that brought them to the Wisconsin River, and then to the Mississippi, in one month of travel time. Late in June the French explorers reached the prairie country of the Illinois Indians. Here fields of green corn lined the riverbank. These natives seldom suffered from hunger because their fertile soil produced abundant crops of maize, beans, squashes, and melons. The friendly Illinois gave the strangers cornmeal mush seasoned with buffalo fat, and invited them to remain with the tribe. Although they declined the invitation, Marquette promised to return and preach the gospel to them. Later, he kept his word.

When the Frenchmen insisted on traveling farther down the stream, the Indians warned them that the heat would make them ill. They said that sea monsters infested the lower region of the "Great Water." Some time later Marquette was tempted to believe the tale when a huge catfish almost upset his canoe. About seven hundred Illinois men, women, and children crowded the riverbank to watch their chief present a calumet (peace pipe) to his white visitors to protect them in their journey. The long-stemmed pipe with streamers of bright feathers saved the lives of the daring explorers on more than one occasion. When hostile Indians shot arrows from the shore or swam out to tip over the light canoes, Marquette held up the peace pipe. It worked like magic, turning enemies into friends.

Not far from the mouth of the Arkansas River and near the spot where de Soto had been buried, the Frenchmen met a tribe whose advice changed their plans. The natives gathered on the riverbank to welcome the palefaced strangers. The Frenchmen were greeted by the chief, who performed the calumet dance and presented the peace pipe as a token of friendship. At the banquet in their honor, the explorers were feasted with boiled cornmeal and roast dog. They did not relish this course as much as they did the dessert of sweet, ripe melons. The Indians apologized for the meager fare. They explained that they did not dare go out to the prairie on buffalo hunts. Their tribal enemies were friends of white men (Spaniards). These tribes killed the buffalo hunters with guns that barked like dogs.

Joliet and Marquette held a council and decided it would be foolhardy to continue their journey down the Mississippi River and risk capture by Spaniards or their Indian allies. They had gone far enough to prove that the "Great Water" ran directly south into the Gulf of Mexico and not west to the Pacific Ocean. It was not the waterway to the Orient. They turned back, paddling against the current, until they reached the mouth of the Illinois River. Steering from this stream into the Des Plaines River they crossed a portage to the Chicago River and finally reached Lake Michigan. It was the end of September when the party arrived at the mission in Green Bay. Marquette was ill.

After spending the winter at the mission, Joliet started to Quebec in the late spring when the ice broke up in the lakes and streams. In the outskirts of Montreal, the rowers became so overjoyed at the sight of farmhouses that they carelessly turned into a strong current that capsized the canoe in the rapids. All were drowned except Joliet. He was dashed upon a rock where he was found unconscious by fishermen and rescued. Joliet mourned the loss of his companions, and most of all, the death of an Indian boy given to him by one of the chiefs he had met in the Mississippi country. Frontenac, governor of New France, deplored the loss of Joliet's journal of his expedition, written during the winter at Green Bay. He asked Joliet to write another one, as best as he could remember, and draw another map to replace the one lost when his canoe turned over. With this information Frontenac determined to continue the exploration of the Mississippi Valley.

LA SALLE DREAMS OF A
FRENCH EMPIRE IN NORTH AMERICA

IN 1666 LA SALLE, member of a wealthy French family, migrated to Canada. He received a large land grant near Montreal at the rapids afterwards named La Chine. The name suggested adventure, the search for the waterway to China. Like most colonists La Salle entered the fur business. From the Indians he learned enough of their languages to barter with them. The Senecas told him about a great river to the west that flowed to the sea. Being an explorer at heart, La Salle traded the comforts of his estate for the hardships of the wilderness. While hunting for the headwaters of the great river in the region of Lake Ontario, he met Joliet returning from Lake Superior. Joliet had gone to locate copper deposits which Indians told him

were numerous. Although there are no records to prove absolutely that La Salle discovered the Ohio River in his wanderings, it is quite possible that he found the upper course of that stream in 1670.

In the year (1673) that Joliet and Marquette started on their journey to the Mississippi River, La Salle, as an assistant to Frontenac, the governor of New France, was assigned the task of erecting a fort on Lake Ontario. The purpose of this fort was to shut out the Iroquois who were taking furs to Dutch and English traders on the Atlantic Coast. Since a number of forts were necessary to control the western fur trade, La Salle went to France to present his plan for a chain of forts and missions along the inland waterways of North America. He received the right to own the land he might discover. He also received rights to the fur business with tribes that were not then sending furs into Montreal. He was to pay the expenses of his explorations and he was not to ask financial help from the King.

The French were careful not to antagonize the Indian tribes upon whom their business depended. The French trader found a welcome because he brought knives, kettles, cloth, and other articles the Indians needed to exchange for furs. Then he went away. He did not take their land from them. With few exceptions, the tribes were friendly toward the French. With the natives on their side, La Salle figured that soldiers stationed in the scattered forts could prevent the English colonists from crossing the Allegheny Mountains. Likewise they could keep the Spaniards from moving north of the Gulf of Mexico.

Before he built his forts, La Salle realized that he had to know more about the geography of this vast central region of

CITY OF NEW ORLEANS

La Salle's dream of a city like Paris at the bend of the Mississippi River came true in New Orleans. Here, the language and customs of France still cling to the city.

the continent. He had to prove beyond any doubt that the "Great Water" emptied into the Gulf of Mexico. In the middle of the winter of 1681-82 La Salle started for the Mississippi River. In his party of fifty-four persons were French woodsmen, Indian guides, ten Indian women to do the cooking, and three of their children. The loaded canoes were dragged on sleds over the frozen Chicago and Illinois rivers, enroute to the Mississippi. Travel was slow down the stream, with time out to hunt wild turkey, quail, and deer to feed the party. The only food carried was cornmeal.

Like Marquette, La Salle took along a calumet, the Indian symbol of peace. The pipe of peace warded off Indian attack, assuring tribes that the strangers were friends. In the lower part of the Mississippi

the weather was warm and pleasant. La Salle was delighted to find mulberry trees and dreamed of raising silk worms in the mild climate. At a bend in the river where the ground was dry, he envisioned a city with spires and towers, like Paris.

In April the party reached the broad flat delta where the Mississippi River divides into three channels. La Salle sent a group down each of the branches. A week later all three parties met to celebrate the first successful journey to the mouth of the Mississippi River. They set up a pole and nailed the arms of France to it. La Salle stood beside the column and said in a loud voice:

In the name of the most high, mighty, invincible, and victorious Prince, Louis the Great, by the

44

Grace of God King of France and of Navarre, Fourteenth of that name, this ninth day of April, one thousand six hundred and eighty-two, I, in virtue of the commission of his Majesty which I hold in my hand, and which may be seen by all whom it may concern, have taken, and do now take, in the name of his Majesty and of his successors to the crown, possession of this country of Louisiana, — Mississippi and rivers which discharge themselves therein, from its source, — as far as its mouth at the sea or Gulf of Mexico, —

When he had finished speaking, claiming the entire heart of North America for France, the explorers shouted, "LONG LIVE THE KING!" They fired a salute with guns. Beside the pole, a wooden cross was raised. La Salle pledged the King of France to establish missions for the natives in this vast territory. All sang a hymn. One by one before a notary, Frenchmen signed the paper that La Salle had read, amid hearty shouts of LONG LIVE THE KING!

Five years later, on another exploring expedition in Louisiana, La Salle was murdered by one of his own men. Although he did not live to carry out his plan, the chain of forts and missions was built. At the bend in the river, the city of New Orleans was founded. In this city, today, many people still speak the French language and follow French customs. LaSalle's dream came true, but his empire did not survive. It takes people living on the land to hold a new country, and the French were traders rather than farmers. French colonization consisted of relatively few men scattered over a large territory. Their English rivals, who had settled along the Atlantic seaboard, cultivated the land first and then indulged in trade. They were colonizers.

MAPS:

WA6r, WA9r, WA11r
Atlas of American History by Edgar B. Wesley

PART TWO

England Bids for the New World

TYPICAL PURITAN MEETING HOUSE
Gloucester, Massachusetts 1780

THE MAYFLOWER COMPACT

In ye name of God Amen. We whose names are underwriten, the loyall subjects of our dread soveraigne Lord King James by ye grace of God, of Great Britain, France and Ireland king, defender of ye faith, and having undertaken, for ye glorie of God, and advancement of ye Christian faith and honour of our king and countrie, a voyage to plant ye first colonie in ye Northerne parts of Virginia, doe by these presents solemnly and mutualy in ye presence of God, and of one another, covenant, and combine our selves togeather into a civill body politick; for our better ordering, and preservation and furtherance of ye ends aforesaid; and by vertue hearof to enacte, constitute, and frame such just and equall lawes, ordinances, acts, constitutions, and offices, from time to time, as shall be thought most meete and convenient for ye generall good of ye Colonie, unto which we promise all due submission and obedience. In Witnes wherof we have hereunder subscribed our names at Cap-Codd ye 11 of November, in ye year of ye raigne of our soveraigne lord King James of England, France, and Ireland ye eighteenth, and of Scotland ye fiftie-fourth, Ano. Dom. 1620.

Chapter 5

"We Hope to Plant a Nation"

ENGLAND WINS
FREEDOM OF THE SEAS

THE STORY THAT COLUMBUS told at the Court of Spain stirred London as it had the capitals on the continent of Europe. The news of red-skinned natives decked with gold set tongues wagging in England. During the excitement John Cabot, like Columbus a navigator from Genoa, was presented to the King of England. With maps and charts, he convinced the tightfisted Tudor, Henry VII, that he could do for England all that Columbus had done for Spain, and more. He would find a northwest passage to India and bring the rich spice trade to England.

Early in May of the year 1497 John Cabot and his son, Sebastian, sailed from Bristol in an English ship manned by British sailors. On June 24 land was sighted. The captain and his crew went ashore, probably on Cape Breton Island, where they planted a cross and raised the flag of England. After searching along the coast and not finding the imaginary strait, Cabot turned homeward because supplies were running low. Like Columbus, he did not know he had touched the shores of an unknown continent. The King's stingy

reward for the voyage upon which England later based a claim to North America was recorded as follows:

10th Aug. 1497. To hym that founde the new isle, 10 pounds. (Less that $50.)

Queen Elizabeth I, crowned in 1558, encouraged merchants to form trading companies and to seek markets in distant lands. The Baltic Company provided timber, pitch, and tar from Russia, Poland, and other countries on the inland sea. These materials helped build the ships for England's growing commerce. Grocers joined the Turkey Company, trading along the Mediterranean as far away as Persia and the Bible lands, to get spices and herbs brought to eastern ports by camel caravans.

Other men, not merchants, also bought stock in these trading companies and shared in the profits according to their investments. Although the seas were infested with pirates, the risk and the danger lured men to "adventure" their money, their goods, and their lives. When voyages were successful, the profits were large and the adventurers were suddenly rich. "When my ship comes in" is still a familiar saying in the English language.

Trade was to become the nation's might, and England's future was on the seas. Freedom of the seas, however, was yet to be won.

When English merchants ventured into the Atlantic, their ships were often captured and sacked by rival Spaniards. On one of these looted vessels was a young man named Francis Drake. He had invested his small fortune in merchandise and gone forth to try his luck in foreign trade. Returning penniless, he vowed to fight the power of Spain to the end of his days. With the help of Queen Elizabeth, Drake became the terror of the seas. He captured, plundered, and sank the treasure ships of Spain. Others joined him in this patriotic privateering. They amassed big fortunes in Spanish booty — the gold and silver from the mines of Mexico and Peru.

Angered by Elizabeth's privateers, King Philip of Spain sent a fleet (armada) of about 130 ships and nearly 30,000 men to destroy the British Navy and to invade England. In the channel, the British fleet and its "sea dogs," Hawkins, Frobisher, and Drake, awaited the arrival of the grand Spanish Armada. After days of unsettled fighting, the remains of the Armada skulked away into the misty North Sea. In the flight around Scotland and Ireland, wind, weather, and starvation completed the destruction of the mighty fleet. Only a few vessels, with crews more dead than alive, returned to the ports of their homeland.

The defeat of the Spanish Armada in 1588 opened the sea lanes of the Atlantic to British commerce. In the English Channel the "sea dogs" started the island kingdom on the march toward world empire.

To carry on world trade England had to build more ships. The eyes of merchant adventurers turned toward the New World for shipbuilding products. Although a Spanish empire was rising in Mexico and South America, Spain no longer controlled the sea lanes to North America. Lumber for shipbottoms and poles for masts would find a ready sale on the London market. Could North America supply this timber?

The merchant adventurers were cautious and sent trustworthy men to explore the country and report on the trees before they risked too much money. It was well known throughout England that Sir Walter Raleigh had lost about $200,000 in his attempts to plant a colony in the New World. This made traders wonder if America were a good investment.

WAS AMERICA A GOOD INVESTMENT?

THREE YEARS BEFORE the defeat of the Spanish Armada, Sir Walter Raleigh sent his first colonists to Roanoke Island, off the coast of North Carolina. He named the country Virginia in honor of Elizabeth I, known as the Virgin Queen. A year later, in 1586, Sir Francis Drake anchored his fleet of twenty-three raiders off the Carolina coast and the homesick colonists returned with him to England.

Undismayed by failure, Raleigh sent more colonists under Governor White the following year. After a fort had been erected on Roanoke Island, White returned to England for supplies and was held there by the threat of the Spanish Armada. When he did return in 1591, not a trace of the colony could be found. Among the missing was White's little granddaughter, Virginia Dare, the first child born of English parents on the soil of the United States. On a voyage up the James River in 1607, one of the early colonists saw an Indian boy with light hair and blue eyes. Did Raleigh's colonists join an Indian tribe to survive? Or were they captured and carried away into slavery? To this day their fate is unknown.

Sir Walter Raleigh's experience made businessmen in England hesitate to invest their money in any attempt to plant an English colony in North America. Raleigh, however, did not give up. He published a report by Thomas Hariot, a man he had employed to explore the resources of the new country. As Raleigh had hoped, the little book encouraged his fellowmen to believe in the future of America.

A group of merchant adventurers hired the highly respected navigator, Bartholomew Gosnold, to explore the coast of North America. Raleigh, still believing that America was a good investment, contributed to the fund that chartered the ship *Concord* for this voyage. On the fourteenth day of May in 1602, Gosnold landed on the coast of Massachusetts. After a fishing trip which netted a big catch of cod, the explorer named the "mighty headland" with a "very bolde coast," Cape Cod.

Some friendly Indians on the nearby islands gave the strangers boiled fish to eat and tobacco to smoke. The natives brought deer skins, wolf hides, and costly furs of beaver, otter, and martin to trade for gaudy trinkets. They helped to cut down trees and to load the boat with timber. Like Columbus, Gosnold took back evidence to England in case anyone doubted his word.

Brereton, one of the explorers, kept a diary telling what he saw and learned about the country. This report, also published with Raleigh's help, captured the interest of merchant adventurers in the lumber trade. America was a land of forests with a store of timber. Brereton praised the climate, declaring the members of the crew had better health on the voyage than at home in England. This pleasant land was only thirty-five days away on the shorter northern route across the Atlantic Ocean.

The people who read books like Hariot's story of Roanoke Island and Brereton's report on Massachusetts told their neighbors about the new country. The stories traveled quickly. All classes in England began to take notice of North America.

After Elizabeth's death, Sir Walter Raleigh was thrown into prison, and finally beheaded by her successor, James I. Although Raleigh lost his fortune, his freedom, and his head, his life was not a failure. He was a great patriot with a vision beyond the day in which he lived. Raleigh did more than any other one man to convince the British public that America was a good investment. He SOLD a continent.

A GREAT GAMBLE

THROUGHOUT THE NATION the feeling grew that it was a patriotic duty to plant English colonies on the coast of North America, between the French along the St. Lawrence River and the Spaniards on the Gulf of Mexico. Without colonies how could England hope to build up trade in the New World?

Officials of the government favored colonization as a scheme to rid the country of returned soldiers who were getting into mischief. The defeat of the Spanish Armada had ended the wars with Spain. Thousands of recruits from the Netherlands and Ireland were mustered out of service. Many of these men were not anxious to return to their former homes and settle down. A quiet country life did not appeal to many lads from the farming districts, after they had tasted adventure in foreign lands. Unable or unwilling to toil with spade and hoe, these idle soldiers became the terror of city streets and country lanes. Their officers, too, were unemployed and chafing to unsheathe their swords again. Fighting men could be kept busy in the New World.

From their pulpits, clergymen also urged the people to invest money in North America. It was their Christian duty, said the preachers, to convert the natives in the pagan land across the sea.

Who would pay the bill? It took money to charter ships, to hire sailors, and to provide food, clothing, and ammunition to begin life anew in a wilderness. Bartholomew Gosnold, the navigator, and Richard Hakluyt, a geographer who wrote about explorations, held meetings with merchants in Bristol. They told of vast forests of oak, cedar, beech, elm, walnut, sassafras, hazelnut, and cherry trees found by explorers in North America. The shipbuilding industry was growing rapidly and traders were seeking timber. These learned men assured the adventurers that profits would be large on any investment in America.

It took Gosnold a year to gather enough investors to form a trading company. It was known as the Virginia Company of London and it was commonly called the London Company. Only four percent of the investors belonged to the high-ranking nobility of England. Most of the men who backed the company were the merchant adventurers seeking business in the New World. "Bills of Adventure" were purchased by the bakers, grocers, cloth-workers, drapers, goldsmiths, ironmongers, tailors, skinners, salters, leathersellers, dyers, embroiderers, stationers, and fishmongers. Sometimes whole towns bought shares of stock.

A "Bill of Adventure" stated that the buyer would share in new lands according to the sum he had "ventured." This first stock certificate in United States history assured the owner his just share "of such mines and minerals of gold, silver, and other metals or treasure, pearls, precious stones, or any kind of wares or merchandise, commodities or profits whatsoever, which shall be obtained or gotten in the said voyage, according to the portion of money by him employed to that use, in as ample manner as any other adventurer therein shall receive for the like sum."

It took about a hundred dollars to equip each settler for the colony. After the money had been raised, it took Gosnold and others another year to find enough colonists to start the venture. Finally, on the sixth of April, 1606, King James granted permission to Gosnold, Sir Thomas Gates, and others to found a colony in "that part of America called Virginia," between 34° and 41° of north latitude. (In unexplored country the charters of colonies sometimes overlapped. See Charter of New England, Page 58.) Excitement ran high as talk in the streets turned to Virginia. With a patent from the King, an English settlement in North America was no longer an idle dream. With great enthusiasm the London Company prepared for the voyage.

A few days before Christmas in 1606, three ships sailed down the Thames. Captain Newport was in command with seventy-one passengers on the *Sarah Constant*. On a small craft, the *Discovery*, were twenty men. At the helm of the *Goodspeed*, with fifty-two colonists on board, was the promoter of the venture, Captain Bartholomew Gosnold. One of the ships carried a sealed box in which were written the names of the men who were to govern the colony. It was not to be opened until the coast of Virginia had been found. Delayed by storms, the colonists did not reach the West Indies until the twenty-third of March. While cruising among the islands, the three vessels dropped anchor in a number of good harbors and the men caught fish, hunted wild boars, and filled the casks on board with fresh water. On the twenty-sixth of April, at four o'clock in the morning, the coast of Virginia was sighted. Thirty of the men went ashore and named this first landing spot Cape Henry. While wandering along the coast, the party was attacked by five natives, and two colonists were wounded.

On board was Captain John Smith, a trained soldier, who had fought with foreign armies in wars against the Turks. However, he arrived in chains. Suspected of mutiny, he had been held a prisoner during most of the voyage. Later, in England, he wrote a history of the founding of the colony, published in 1624. The following quotation was copied from a first edition of Smith's *Generall Historie of Virginia:*

That night (April 16, 1607) was the box opened and the orders read, in which Bartholomew Gosnold, John Smith, Edward Wingfield, Christopher Newport, John Ratliffe, John Martin, and George Kendall, were named to be the Councell, and to choose a President amongst them for a yeare, who with the Councell should governe . . . . Until the 13 of May they sought a place to plant in, then the Councell was sworne, Mr. Wingfield was chosen President, and an oration made why Captaine Smith was not admitted of the Councell as the rest.

When the colonists landed in Virginia, the struggle to survive severely tested the governing ability of these chosen leaders.

THEY MET IN PHILPOT LANE

CANDLES BURNED far into the night in a house in Philpot Lane. It was the home of Sir Thomas Smith, treasurer of the London Company. Here the officers met to discuss ways of supporting their settlement in America. All was not well in Virginia.

After exploring the country on Chesapeake Bay, the first colonists had selected a site on the James River, named for the King. The stream was lined with trees that would give them timber for building ships. Unfortunately, Jamestown was in a swampy region, which was not a healthy place to live. Nearly every day during the hot and humid summer of 1607, a new grave was dug. On the twenty-second of August the colony lost the ardent promoter of the settlement. Captain Gosnold died of the swamp fever and was honorably buried, "having all the guns of the fort shot off with many vollies."

Food for the colonists was kept in a general storehouse, and each man received the same daily rations. The toiler had no more to eat than did the loafer. As a result, many men spent their time in hunting and fishing instead of plowing and planting. They showed little concern for the interests of the company that had paid for these supplies and the expenses of the voyage.

Since the colonists needed a military man both for defense from Indian attacks and for discipline within their own ranks, Captain John Smith was elected to the council on the tenth of September. He put men to work repairing the church, cutting

Jamestown Foundation

KEEPING WATCH IN JAMES FORT

A uniformed soldier, armed with a halberd used in the fifteenth and sixteenth centuries, greets visitors at James Fort. Another guardsman looks on from the second floor of the wattle-and-daub house, reconstructed to show the houses built by the first permanent settlers in Jamestown.

down trees, building a larger store house for supplies expected from London, improving the fort, and keeping guard. Every Saturday, the able-bodied men were exercised and drilled like soldiers. His success in dealing with the Indians and maintaining discipline was rewarded. A year later Smith was elected president of the council.

Food received from home was never enough, and colonists complained of being left in a wilderness to starve. Smith wrote:

In searching our casked corne, we found it halfe rotten, and the rest so consumed with so many thousands of rats that increased so fast, . . . as we knew not how to keepe the little we had. This did drive us all to our wits ends, for there was nothing in the countrie but what nature afforded.

Smith held two Indians as prisoners to show the colonists how to plant corn and live off the country. When food became so scarce, he was forced to free them:

for want of victuall. But so well they liked our companies they did not desire to go from us. And to express their loves, for 16 days continuance, the Countrie people brought us 100 a day of Squirrels, Turkeyes, Deere and other Wilde beasts.

The natives saved the remnant of the colony by this act of charity.

Among the first settlers were listed thirty gentlemen, four carpenters, and only twelve laborers. It was not long until both the governing council in Virginia and the officials of the company in London realized that the success of their colony depended upon the settlers. A wilderness was not the place for ne'er-do-wells. Before Lord Delaware left England in 1610, the Virginia Council distributed handbills in London. The wording was plain. The company did not want "such an idle crew as did thrust themselves in the last voyage, that will rather starve for hunger than lay their hands to labor."

In an unsettled wilderness, there was much need for laborers with brawny backs and skilled hands. There was little room for "gentlemen" who could not plow and build.

The company had hoped to ship enough timber, ore, and other raw materials to pay dividends to the stockholders. In the spring 1608, Captain Newport sailed from Jamestown with a load of cedar logs, walnut boards, and sassafras wood. In the autumn of the same year, he brought over seventy colonists. He returned with a cargo of iron ore which was sold to the East India Company.

Lumbering and farming failed to pay dividends. The London Company then turned to manufacturing in an effort to put the colony on a paying basis. They advertised for tradesmen. In 1611, before Sir Thomas Dale sailed with new settlers and supplies, this broadside appeared in London:

It is not intended any more to burden the colony with vagrant and unnecessary persons. This is to give notice to so many honest and industrious men, as carpenters, brickmen, gardeners, smiths, coopers, fishermen, tanners, shoemakers, shipwrights, brickmen, farmers, and laboring men of all sorts, that if they repair to the house of Sir Thomas Smith in Philpot Lane in London, before the end of the present month of January, the number not full, they shall be entertained for the voyage, upon such terms as their quality and fitness shall deserve.

To the mansion of Thomas Smith came all classes of people, from laborers to rich adventurers.

The officials of the London Company were leading men in England. They would be disgraced if their trading venture failed. When would Virginia begin to pay?

VIRGINIA MUST NOT FAIL

SWAMP FEVERS, crop failures, homesick colonists, bickering leaders, and Indian troubles made progress slow in Virginia. The governing council of the colony asked for help again and again, until the members of the company grew weary of giving money without receiving profits. Investors did not readily buy stock in the London Company. England would lose the respect of France, Spain, and the Netherlands, her rivals in trade, if the

ADVERTISEMENT OF A LOTTERY FOR VIRGINIA

This drawing and a printed list of prizes advertised a lottery in 1615 to collect money for the Virginia colony. The ad bears the seals of the King and the London Company. A man dressed in the costume of the day is pulling duplicates of chances from two large drums, and calling the names of the winners.

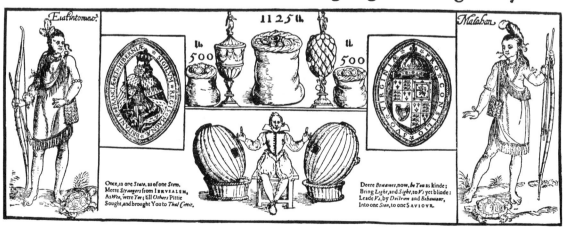

A Declaration for the certaine time of dravving the great ſtanding Lottery.

ARRIVAL OF MAIDS "TO MAKE WIFES"

In 1619, the first boatload of maids arrived in Jamestown to marry the lonely men in the settlement and make homes for them. Planters paid the cost of the voyage at the rate of 120 to 150 pounds of tobacco per wife. In early Virginia, tobacco was used for money.

Jamestown settlement failed. The success of Virginia became a matter of national honor.

The council appealed to the Lord Mayor of London, who sent copies of the letter to the merchant associations. He ordered the appeal to be read at their next meetings. He personally asked each one "to make some adventure in so good an action." The merchants could not well ignore such a request from the Lord Mayor, himself. The fishmongers were generous, perhaps with an eye on the cod and mackerel so plentiful in American waters. The clothmakers, on the other hand, were so stingy that their officers had to levy an extra assessment to raise the "petty sum" to one hundred pounds. The grocers published the names of the loyal men who invested in Virginia and a list of the unpatriotic members who did not contribute.

A poem appeared, "Newes From Virginia," praising the citizens who invested money:

And to the adventurers thus he writes,
　Be not dismayed at all,
For scandal cannot doe us wrong,
　God will not let us fall.
Let England knowe our willingnesse
　For that our work is good.
WEE HOPE TO PLANT A NATION,
WHERE NONE BEFORE HATH STOOD.

A new day dawned when Sir Edwin Sandys was elected treasurer of the London Company to replace Sir Thomas Smith. In April of 1619, Sir George Yeardley, appointed governor by the new treasurer, arrived in Jamestown with another charter. The common storehouse was closed, and martial law, needed to enforce the communal plan, was abolished. Under the revised charter, each man worked for himself and was entitled to the benefits gained from his own labor. Land was assigned to settlers for farming. Four corporations were created to market their products and carry on trade. This was not enough.

Sandys and the board in London agreed that their colonists would take more interest in the settlement if they had a share in governing it. The most important reform was an invitation to each plantation and village, asking that delegates be sent to a general assembly to cooperate with the governor and council of the company in framing the laws of the colony. This meeting of the first representative assembly in Virginia laid the foundation for government by the people on this continent. From that day on, "something new" began to grow in the New World.

THE FIRST COLONIAL REPRESENTATIVE ASSEMBLY

IT WAS A HOT and humid day near the end of July in the year 1619. The governor, himself, had gathered flowers to decorate the little church in Jamestown for this historic event. The new governor was born a commoner, plain George Yeardley, the son of a merchant tailor in London. The King had knighted him, with the idea that men in high places needed titles to command respect.

Sir George Yeardley sat in the green velvet chair in the choir loft of Jamestown church and presided at the first meeting of the first representative assembly. With him were the members of his council, also appointed by the London Company. Who

were they? One was John Rolfe, who had returned to his tobacco plantation in Virginia after burying his young Indian wife, Pocahontas, in England. Captain West, the president of the council, was a direct descendant of William, the Conqueror. Two were graduates of Cambridge University, one of whom was John Pory who had served in Parliament and knew about law making. He wrote down the proceedings and sent the papers on a Dutch ship, for safe keeping, to a member of the London Company living in the Netherlands.

For the future of America, however, the most important men were the twenty-two representatives called burgesses. These men were elected by eleven communities to work with the council of the company in framing laws for the colony. Who were these representatives? The first settlement, Jamestown, preferred military men, and elected the gunner and flag-bearer as burgesses. From a seacoast plantation came a tough Indian fighter, who farmed the land now occupied by the United States Naval Base at Norfolk. Walter Shelley, related to the famous English poet, Percy Bysshe Shelley, did not return to his neighbors who had elected him. He died on the third day of the meeting, probably from the heat. The plantation, Flowerdieu, sent a young man by the name of John Jefferson.

This meeting opened with a prayer by the minister, "that it shall please God to guide and sanctify all our proceedings to His own glory and to the good of this plantation." This custom is still followed by Congress. In fact, the Virginia House of Burgesses set the pattern of our present legislative body. Our Senate is comparable to the company council. Our House of Representatives is comparable to the House of Burgesses.

The seeds of the American war for independence were sown at this first meeting in 1619. The burgesses sent a petition to London demanding the right to veto any of the company's laws to which they objected. This was bold indeed, considering that the London Company owned Virginia under a patent from the King, and had invested large sums of money in the colony. Edwin Sandys did not object to the plan, which forecast the "something new" destined to grow up in the New World. It was to be a *constitutional* republic based upon the idea *that the human rights of man are above the rights of government.*

Immediately, James I plotted to get rid of the new treasurer, Sandys. A man who would permit His Majesty's subjects in a distant land to have a share in governing themselves was not a friend of monarchy. The idea might grow and threaten the authority of a king who ruled by *divine right.* According to this doctrine, the right to a throne was conferred by God. The king ruled by divine right, and his subjects were granted only the rights which he chose to give them. Sandys had served only a year and two months when he was forced out of office by James I. Then the London Company elected another man who was sympathetic toward the rights of the colonists.

The King kept a watchful eye on the colonists. In a few years, an Indian attack provided James with an excuse for annulling the charter of the trading company. This act meant that Virginia became a royal colony. The trading company was no longer in control. The governor and his advisers now were appointed by the King rather than by merchant adventurers. The House of Burgesses, however, continued to represent the colonists themselves.

The London Company had spent 200,000 pounds and transported 9000 persons across the sea to establish the first permanent English settlement in America. Yet, as a business venture, the London Company failed. Some of the larger stockholders traded their "bills of adventure" for plantations that were from two to five thousand acres in some cases. From this land-owning class would come the great statesmen of our country — George Washington, general of the war for independence; Thomas Jefferson, author of the Declaration of Independence; and James Madison, "father of the Constitution." Thus did a band of merchant adventurers sow seeds of freedom in a wilderness. They fulfilled the prophecy of the poet and founded a nation WHERE NONE BEFORE HATH STOOD.

THE STRUGGLE FOR RELIGIOUS LIBERTY

IN ONLY A FEW COUNTRIES in the entire world did freedom of worship exist when the first little band of religious refugees landed on American shores. One of these nations was the Netherlands. A group of people called Separatists fled to the Netherlands to escape persecution in their native England. These people had refused to worship in the Anglican Church, which was the Church of England. The English Government persecuted any group who separated themselves from the Anglican church.

After a dozen years in the Netherlands, where these Separatists were kindly treated, they decided to migrate to

America. They wanted a colony of their own. They wanted to rear their children in the faith of their fathers, and at the same time, to teach them English ways and language rather than Dutch.

The Pilgrims were too poor to pay for their passage across the ocean, so they appealed to the London Company owning settlements in Virginia. Sir Edwin Sandys, then treasurer of the company, listened sympathetically to their plea for help. He encouraged his friends to invest money in a trading company to finance their voyage to the New World. At a meeting in Sandys' house in February of 1620, a patent was granted to a company of merchant adventurers to settle these refugees in the northern part of Virginia. The charter of New England, 1620, stated that the second colony should extend from "forty degrees of northerly latitude . . . to forty-eight degrees of the said northerly latitude."

These Pilgrims wanted a guarantee that they could worship as they pleased and not be bound by the laws of the English Church. Although Virginia did not have religious freedom, the London Company petitioned the King to grant this privilege to the refugees. Sandys assured James I that these thrifty colonists would send timber, fish, and furs to the London market. Trade was England's power. The King slyly consented to ignore the fact that these colonists did not attend his church, but declared that he would not openly grant freedom of worship to any of his subjects, anywhere.

Seventy merchant adventurers, forming the Plymouth Company, paid for the voyage of the first religious refugees to our shores. In November of 1620, the *Mayflower*, with 102 passengers, dropped anchor in Cape Cod Harbor. This was beyond the limits of Virginia. As they were too far north to be governed by the laws of the southern colony, the Pilgrims found themselves without a government. Since nearly all the Pilgrim fathers had lived in the Netherlands, then a republic, they were familiar with local self-government, town meetings, and voting by ballot. The men met in the cabin of the *Mayflower* and drew up an agreement.

This document was the Mayflower Compact. It established self-government in the second English settlement in the Americas. Among the forty-one men who signed the compact were the first three governors of Plymouth — John Carver, William Bradford, and Edward Winslow; Myles Standish, the soldier; and John Alden, the youngest signer, who had boarded the *Mayflower* at Southampton where the ship took on supplies. Alden was a cooper, engaged to mend leaks in the wooden vessel and keep it seaworthy. Although he was not one of the religious refugees, he chose not to return on the *Mayflower*. He married Priscilla Mullins and stayed in Massachusetts, where they reared a family of eleven children.

In a letter to a friend in England, Edward Winslow described the first Thanksgiving after the first harvest in Plymouth:

Our harvest being gotten in, our Governour sent foure men on fowling, that so we might after a more special manner rejoyce together, after we had gathered the fruits of our labour.

They foure in one day killed as much fowle, as with a little help beside, served the company almost a weeke, at which time amongst other recreations we exercised our Armes; many of the Indians coming amongst us, and among the rest their greatest King Massasoyt, with some ninetie men, whom for three days we entertained and feasted, and they went out and killed five deere, which they brought to the Plantation and bestowed on our Governour, and upon the Captaine and others.

The Pilgrims had come to America to worship in their own way, in a colony of their own, and they wanted no one of another religion to live among them. Others, not of their faith, were sent over by the merchant adventurers who had financed the colony. This displeased the Pilgrims. To them, the Plymouth Plantation was a refuge; to the traders, it was an investment. Under a communal plan, established by the trading company, the colonists were fed and clothed from the common storehouse, and the products of their labors went into the common storehouse. As in Jamestown, the industrious men toiled and the lazy ones loafed. Plymouth, like Jamestown, suffered a starving time.

At the end of seven years the Pilgrims demanded and obtained the right for each man to keep what he had earned. The adventurers agreed that the settlers could have complete ownership of their houses and lands, and the profits from their trade in fish, timber, and furs. In return the colonists would pay the adventurers 1800 pounds sterling in yearly payments of 200 pounds each for nine years. Although this was a large sum in those days, seven of the leading citizens, including Governor Bradford and Elder Brewster, personally signed the agreement in behalf of the colonists and guaranteed the payments to win the privilege of managing their own affairs and working for themselves.

Under the system where each man worked for himself in his own way, the colony began to prosper. With fish, timber, and furs, the hard-working colonists paid off the adventurers, who were glad to sell out to these independent people who wanted to be left alone. Then the Pilgrims ruled themselves under a charter from the King.

On a winter day in 1620, a shivering band of religious refugees set foot on American shores. They pursued a fleeting vision of religious liberty. It was something they could not see nor understand because they had never known it, except in a foreign land. Yet, unknowingly, they laid the foundation for freedom of worship in the New World.

PURITANS ESTABLISH UNION OF CHURCH AND STATE

SEVEN YEARS AFTER the landing of the Pilgrims, "some friends being together in Lincolnshire fell into discourse about New England and the planting of the Gospel there." From this friendly conversation in the house of Lincolnshire stemmed plans for the Puritan migration to Massachusetts. The Puritans wished to reform the Church of England and remain in it, while the Pilgrims were Separatists who had quit the English church and broken all ties. The Puritans especially disliked the ceremony of the established church. They were often arrested and thrown into jail for preaching against it. To gain freedom of worship, this small group of merchants, ministers, and landowners agreed to organize a trading company to plant a Puritan colony in New England. The colonists would be Puritans intent upon promoting their reformed faith, and not concerned only with making money for themselves. In 1628 they bought land from the Council of New England, the former Plymouth Com-

59

pany, that had sent over the Pilgrims. A few months later, the *Abigail,* with forty men on board, sailed from Weymouth, England to plant the first Puritan colony at Salem.

The next spring the company was granted a charter from the King to "The Governor and Company of Massachusetts Bay in New England." This charter

granted, bargained, sold, – and confirmed to Sir Henry Rosewell, Sir John Young, Knights, Thomas Southcott, John Humphrey, John Endecott, and Simon Whetcombe, their heirs and assigns, and their associates forever, all that part of New England in America, which lies and extends between a great river there, commonly called Monomack, alias Merrimack, and a certain other river there, called Charles River, being in the bottom of a certain bay there, commonly called Massachusetts, –

The new corporation was to be ruled by a governor, a deputy governor, and eighteen assistants who were elected by the "freemen." They were to meet four times a year and make the laws. The charter warned the company that practicing the Christian faith and converting the Indians to Christianity were the "principall ende of this Plantacion."

Each shareholder, according to his investment, would receive land. For 50 pounds invested in the company, he would get 200 acres. If he came himself as a settler, he was entitled to 50 acres more and fifty for each member of his family. Each emigrant not owning any shares in the company was allotted 50 acres for himself and the same amount of land for each servant whose way he paid.

However, it was the government set up by the Massachusetts Bay Company that attracted the settlers. A measure of self-government and freedom to worship in the Puritan way appealed to Englishmen persecuted for their religion. In 1629, year of the charter, Francis Higginson brought over five boatloads of emigrants, and one of the vessels was the *Mayflower* that had carried the Pilgrims to Plymouth.

In that same year, a few leading members of the Massachusetts Bay Company met in Cambridge, England, agreeing to move to their colony and take their families with them, if the company would permit. The company consented. The big Puritan migration was in 1630 when John Winthrop, chosen governor, brought over a thousand colonists in seventeen ships and landed at Boston. He also brought the company's charter to escape the fate of the London Company whose charter had been seized six years before. Thus, the charter of a trading company founded in England, and transferred to America, grew into a constitution of an almost independent government in Massachusetts.

The governor and company of Massachusetts Bay provided settlers with warm clothing, seeds for planting, fishing nets, guns, powder and shot, horses and cattle. More important than these supplies was the number of colonists skilled in making pitch and salt, in working with iron and other metals, and in surveying land and building fortifications.

Since the Massachusetts Bay Company had been formed primarily for religious purposes, the ministers held a conference soon after the arrival of colonists in 1629. They met to decide upon the kind of church they wanted to establish. The Puritans had left England and settled in America so that they could worship as they pleased. Unfortunately, they brought over with them the system that had caused their persecution in their homeland. This system was called union of church and state. Under this system the same people who made the laws of the land also made the laws of the church. In England, the King had ruled that all people worship in the Church of England. In the Massachusetts Bay Colony the Puritan ministers established a church which all their colonists had to attend. In the Puritan colony, as in England, any man or woman who disobeyed a law of the church was guilty of a crime against the state. In other words, if someone refused to follow the specific practices of the Puritan church, he would be subject to fines, imprisonment, banishment, or sometimes, death.

The Puritan ministers passed laws that said only Puritans in good standing could be freemen and citizens, enjoying the rights to vote and hold office. They made laws that interfered with freedom of worship, such as:

— no master or commander of any ship, barque, pinnace, ketch, or other vessel, shall henceforth bring into any harbor, creek or cove within this jurisdiction, any known quaker or quakers, — upon the penalty of the forfeiture of one hundred pounds, to be forthwith paid to the treasurer of the country — . And for default of payment of the said fine of one hundred pounds, or good security for the same, such master shall be committed to prison by warrant from any magistrate, there to continue till the said fine be satisfied to the treasurer.

This court doth order and enact, that every person or persons of the cursed sect of the quakers, — shall be apprehended by any constable, commissioner or selectman (official), and conveyed from constable to constable until they come before the next magistrate, who shall commit the said person or persons to close prison, there to remain without bail until the next court of assistants, where they shall have a legal trial by a special jury, and being convicted to be of the sect of the quakers, shall be sentenced to banishment upon pain of death.

Thus, the rules of the Puritan church were also the laws of the Puritan colonies, just as the rules of the Anglican Church were the laws of England. There was one great difference between New England and old England, however. As more and more Puritans came to Massachusetts, the ministers fought among themselves about the kind of reforms they wanted in their new church. When several newcomers felt the same way about a particular reform, they were free to leave the original Massachusetts Bay Colony and make a new colony with a church to their liking.

ROGER WILLIAMS —
THE DISSENTING MINISTER

ELEVEN YEARS AFTER the Pilgrims landed in Massachusetts, John Winthrop, governor of the Massachusetts Bay Company, wrote in his diary:

The ship *Lyon,* Mr. William Pierce, master, arrived at Nantasket. She brought Mr. Williams a godly man, with his wife, Mr. Throgmorton, Perkins, Augre and others with their wives and children, about twenty passengers, and about 200 tons of goods. She had a very tempestuous voyage. All their people came safe except Waye, his son, who fell from the spritsail in a tempest, and could not be recovered tho he kept in sight near a quarter of an hour. Her goods came also in good condition.

Roger Williams, a young man from a well-to-do family, was welcomed to Boston. He was invited to take the place of the church teacher who was returning to England on the same ship, *Lyon.* Williams was a well-educated and farseeing man. It was a great disappointment to him to find no more religious liberty on this side of the ocean than on the other side. He quickly

61

found the cause of the religious squabbles in Massachusetts. It was the union of church and state.

In Boston, Plymouth, and Salem, he began to preach against the rules of the Puritan Church and the laws of the colony. He declared that every one had the right to worship as he pleased, and that no man should be asked to attend or support any church against his wishes. These were radical doctrines in those days, and even Roger Williams did not fully succeed in practicing them. The new preacher was a forceful speaker. Families moved to Salem to hear his sermons, and his followers grew in number. It was embarrassing to have a minister of the gospel preaching against the Puritan laws. Williams was brought to trial. The colonial record reads:

Whereas Mr. Roger Williams of the church at Salem hath divulged new and dangerous opinions, — it is therefore ordered that the said Mr. Williams shall depart within six weeks, not to return anymore without written license from the court.

In his own home, the fiery minister began to preach on week days as well as on Sundays. Crowds flocked to hear him. Boldly, he declared that no government had the right to establish a *state* religion, and that every man had the right to worship in his own way. This doctrine, complete *separation of church and state,* was contrary to the laws of Massachusetts and to the legal code of England. It was treason.

Could such a man be permitted to remain six weeks? Officers were sent to kidnap Williams and carry him secretly to a ship lying in the harbor of Nantasket. As soon as he would be safely on board, the captain was to sail for England. When the officers arrived at Williams' house, the minister was not at home. He had learned of the plot and left three days before.

Roger Williams had long wanted to be a missionary to the Indians. In trading, he had lived among them enough to learn their language. He had often preached to them. Now, in a way quite unexpected, his wish came true. The Narragansetts wintered in the woods, cutting logs for fuel and killing game for food. Although in poor health, Williams plodded for days through deep snow to seek shelter among his Indian friends. Of his flight into the wilderness in 1635, Roger Williams wrote:

I was unmercifully driven from my house to a winter's flight, for fourteen weeks, in a bitter winter season, I knew not what bread or bed did mean.

The Indians welcomed him into their smoke-filled huts and shared their corn and venison. In the spring he left the hospitable Narragansetts and searched for a pleasant spot where he could build a cabin for his wife and children, whom he had left at home. He selected a site near a spring of good water and named it Providence. He invited all who were persecuted in other colonies to join him in the new settlement, where he would share with them the land he had purchased from the Indians. To all he promised religious liberty without taxation to support an established church, although he carried on heated debates with ministers of other faiths who did not agree with him. Although some men believed in complete religious liberty, the idea was too new for men to live up to.

The little settlement, dedicated to religious freedom, grew into the colony of Rhode Island. As long as Williams lived, all went well. After his death Rhode Island lost that freedom of worship for which the colony had been founded. People could not grasp the new idea. The "godly minister" lived ahead of his time. However, the doctrine he preached, separation of church and state, was written into the constitution of a republic yet unborn — the United States of America.

FOR LIBERTY OF CONSCIENCE

IN SEPTEMBER OF 1633, two ministers, Thomas Hooker and John Cotton, arrived in Massachusetts with a company of Puritan emigrants from England. Hooker went to Newtown, now Cambridge, where about a hundred families lived, and Cotton remained in Boston. Hooker's parsonage stood on land that is now part of Harvard University.

When Thomas Hooker became the pastor of the Newtown congregation, three thousand Englishmen were settled in the region. They were occupied in planting, fishing, herding sheep and cattle, building houses and barns, and trading with the Indians for furs. Already, there were about fourteen ministers, all well-educated, dwelling among them. Many of the settlers were not accepted as freemen and were denied the right to vote under the strict laws of the colony.

Although Hooker was disturbed over this injustice, he was not outspoken against the union of church and state as was Roger Williams. However, he was not long in the Massachusetts colony until he applied for permission to move his congregation to the valley of the Connecticut River. Since boatloads of emigrants were arriving from England and taking up the land, the members of Hooker's congregation needed more pasture for their sheep and cattle. Although

this reason was sufficient, Hooker's plea was refused the first time. Some persons had an idea that Hooker was not altogether pleased with the strict laws of the Massachusetts Bay Colony, and that the need for more land was not the only cause of removal. His second request was granted.

On the last day of May in 1636, Thomas Hooker and his congregation set out for the valley of the Connecticut River (claimed also by the Dutch). Driving 160 head of cattle, they tracked their way over Indian trails in the wilderness. "They fed of their milk by the way." Mrs. Hooker, being too ill to walk, was carried in a litter. The emigrants carried packs, guns, and cooking utensils strapped on their backs. Furniture, farm tools, and other supplies were sent round by water. With only the aid of a compass, they made their way to a site on the Connecticut River, a hundred miles away, in two weeks' time. The settlement was named Hartford, after the home town in England of Samuel Stone, Thomas Hooker's assistant and teacher. Ground was purchased from the Indians and two acres were parcelled out to each family.

Thomas Hooker was both minister and statesman. His ideas were woven into the laws of the new colony, which was called Connecticut. In sermons, he declared that the people had the right to choose their own officials and to limit the power of these men. Unlike Massachusetts Bay, the right to vote in Connecticut was not limited to church members selected by church authorities. Thus, more colonists were able to have a share in their government.

Although the settlers suffered from Indian wars, the colony grew rapidly after the destruction of the Pequots, a hostile Indian tribe. Towns along the river formed a union for their own protection, and this idea of federation probably originated with Hooker. He was usually consulted about all matters pertaining to the welfare of the people. Thomas Hooker stood for the liberty of the individual person and the liberty of the individual church.

In 1637 he was summoned to Boston for the meeting of the church council that tried Anne Hutchinson, a dissenter from the accepted Puritan views on doctrine. After deliberating for twenty-two days, the synod, at which Thomas Hooker was a moderator, condemned many of Mrs. Hutchinson's opinions on doctrine. In March of 1638, she was called to trial in the court of Boston and banished from the colony. About six years later Anne Hutchinson and all her children, except one, were killed on the frontier by the Indians.

Like Anne Hutchinson, the Quakers suffered for defending their rights to think as conscience dictated. Public opinion and an order from Charles II brought an end to capital punishment for religious belief in Massachusetts. Thereafter, although the Quakers were not welcome in the Puritan colonies, they were endured, more or less. Since Massachusetts had an established church, only Puritans were allowed to vote and hold office, and real religious liberty did not exist for a long time.

Even the tolerant Dutch had only a vague idea of religious liberty. Governor Stuyvesant attempted to force Quakers in New York to follow rules of the Dutch Reformed Church. He found it necessary to arrest one of their leaders and send him to Amsterdam for trial. In a year, the sturdy Quaker returned with a letter from the Dutch Government to Peter Stuyvesant.

The document, dated Amsterdam, April 16, 1663, contained the following rebuke to the Governor:

In the youth of your existence, you ought rather to encourage than check the population of the colony. The consciences of men ought to be FREE and UNSHACKLED, so long as they continue moderate, peaceable, inoffensive, and not hostile to the government.

It took men a long time to grasp the meaning of liberty of conscience.

LORD BALTIMORE'S DREAM

THE NEW WORLD BECAME the place to experiment with new ideas for the benefit of mankind. George Calvert, elevated to the peerage as Lord Baltimore, had long cherished a plan to help his fellowmen. Where could he try it out?

Lord Baltimore and Edwin Sandys were neighbors and friends, although they did not always agree in the councils of the London Company to which they both belonged. They had a common bond. Both men believed in religious liberty. They worked together to plant freedom of worship in the New World. Lord Baltimore was a secretary of state and adviser to the King when Sandys had invited the Pilgrims to settle in northern Virginia. These men had wangled the faint promise from James I that the Pilgrims would not be forced to attend the Anglican Church.

Baltimore resigned from public office to carry out his secret ambition of founding a colony with complete religious freedom. He believed that men of all Christian faiths could live and work together in peace and contentment if church and state were entirely separate and the people, themselves, had law-making rights to preserve religious liberty. Although many made fun of his ideas, ridicule did not stop Lord Baltimore. In 1632 he received from Charles I a grant of land north of the Potomac River. He named this land Maryland in honor of the queen, Henrietta Maria. The charter that Baltimore received made him the proprietor of the colony he would establish. As a proprietor, he had the right to set up the kind of government he wanted.

Baltimore invited many Catholic families to his colony. Through fines, forfeits, and imprisonment, these Catholics had lost their land, their homes, and their belongings in England, and were a burden to the nation. Lord Baltimore also invited Protestants to his colony. He promised them freedom of worship and no taxation to support a state church.

George Calvert did not live to see his dream come true. His son, Cecil, the second Lord Baltimore, carried out his father's wishes. Thirteen years after the landing of the Pilgrims, the *Ark* and the *Dove*, owned by the Baltimore family, sailed for America with another band of religious refugees. The founder asked his colonists not to talk about religion during the voyage. Although a Catholic himself, Baltimore requested that his church ceremonies be held as privately as possible in order that the services not offend the Protestants, who were in the majority. "And this is to be observed on land as well as at sea," he wrote.

Boldly, Baltimore added some political liberty to religious freedom. Every freeman had the right to sit in the assembly and take part in making the laws of the colony. The settlements grew so rapidly that it soon became necessary to elect representatives to the General Assembly at St. Mary's. Religion was not a consideration for holding office. Each governor of Maryland under the Baltimores was requested to take this oath:

Nor will I make any difference of persons in conferring offices, rewards or favours proceeding from the authority which his said Lordship hath conferred upon me, as his Lieutenant here, FOR OR IN RESPECT OF THEIR SAID RELIGION respectively, but merely as I shall find them faithful and well deserving of his said Lordship, and to the best of my understanding, endowed with moral virtues and abilities, fitting for such rewards, offices, or favours, wherein my prime aim and end from time to time, shall sincerely be the advancement of his said Lordship's service here, and the public unity and good of the province, without partiality to any — .

With liberty of conscience guaranteed by the Baltimores, Maryland became the home of Puritans, Quakers, other Protestant sects, and Roman Catholics. This ideal of many sects living together worked out well until the Baltimores lost control of their colony. Then Maryland was the scene of bitter religious strife. Catholics, Quakers, Anabaptists, and others lost their right to share in their government when Puritan refugees from England gained control of Maryland. Every one had to obey the laws of the Puritan Church. For a long time Puritans clung to the old-world idea that church and state should not be separated.

The Calverts were practical business men. Their motto was to practice freedom of worship, not preach it. Each man should be allowed to go his own way and to mind his own business. Maryland was to be a way of life. To liberty of conscience the Calverts added *security of person and property*. The founder had unusual foresight for his day. He realized that religious freedom and political liberty go hand in hand, and that neither one can long exist without the other. This idea was his great contribution to the "something new" growing up in the New World. Lord Baltimore was a dreamer. Like Roger Williams in New England, he lived ahead of his time.

"PENN'S HOLY EXPERIMENT"

WILLIAM PENN, well-built and athletic, was a handsome young man with charming manners and a friendly way. Being the son of an admiral in the British Navy, he was educated to take his place in the world as a wealthy English gentleman. Instead, he became a Quaker, trading dinner parties, fox hunts, and tea dances of society for sermons, reforms, and prisons. Penn traveled over western Europe preaching that slavery was wrong; that prisons should be places of reform, not punishment; and, most disturbing of all, the doctrine that every man had the right to worship in his own way. Penn's ideas and Quaker ways proved embarrassing to his father, who once drove his son from his house with angry words.

"You may 'thee and thou' the other folk as much as you like, but you cannot 'thee and thou' the King or me," his father declared.

William did 'thee and thou' the King, who had a sense of humor, and enjoyed the queer ways of the likeable son of his friend, the admiral. One of the Quaker customs was that men did not remove their hats in the presence of others. One day, Charles II snatched off his hat quickly when he met young William.

"Why dost thou remove thy hat, Friend Charles?" Penn asked.

"Because only one can be covered in the presence of the King," he replied. The "Merry Monarch" chuckled heartily, thinking this was a good joke on the Quaker.

Although Penn's friendship with Charles II did not save him from being thrown into prison with other Quakers, it did help him gain a refuge for the Quakers in the New World. The King owed the admiral 16,000 pounds. The younger Penn fell heir to the debt when his father died. William traded the sum for a grant of land, north of Maryland, named Pennsylvania in honor of his father. Here Quakers could live in peace and worship as they pleased. Penn was another dreamer with ideas for the benefit of his fellowman. This grant gave him a colony of his own. Because he was made a proprietor of the colony, he could try out his scheme of government. His idea as stated in his own words was:

Any government is free to the people, whatever be the frame, where the laws rule and the people are parties to those laws.

Penn guaranteed religious freedom to all sects who "live peaceably and justly in civil society," and assured his colonists a share in the government.

"You shall be governed by laws of your own making," he wrote, "and live a free, and if you will, a sober and industrious people. I shall not usurp the right of any or oppress his person . . . ."

Like Baltimore, Penn had the wisdom and the foresight to know that political liberty and religious freedom cannot long exist apart. His whole charter was so generous that many people made fun of it. They dubbed his colony "Penn's Holy Experiment."

The Quaker leader was a shrewd business man. He advertised for settlers in countries where hard-working, honest people had suffered from religious persecution, feuds, and wars. Penn welcomed the thrifty farmers and skilled craftsmen from the German states, where many people had been reduced to poverty by thirty years of war. So many came that, before the Revolutionary War, nearly one third of Pennsylvania's population was German. From Switzerland and nearby states came Mennonites, who were dairymen and cheesemakers. Among the Scotch and Irish refugees were skilled weavers of linens and woolens. Quakers from England and Wales, Catholics, Jews, Anabaptists, and other persecuted sects migrated to "Penn's Woodland." The people worked together and made use of their abilities.

These newcomers soon made Pennsylvania a busy colony. Mill wheels in little streams ground corn into meal and wheat into flour. In 1690, eight years after the first refugees came, an immigrant from the Netherlands built the first paper mill in the colonies on a creek in Germantown. In Pennsylvania farming and manufacturing grew at the same time, adding material prosperity to political liberty and religious freedom. Also, there was freedom from the fear of Indian massacre. From the Indian owners, Penn had purchased the land "given" to him by the King. With the chiefs of the tribes, he made a treaty that never was broken. The colony with the most freedoms grew the fastest and became the richest of the English settlements in America. "Penn's Holy Experiment" was no longer a joke, either in America or in England. Men liked to live where they could be free.

Of all the thirteen colonies Pennsylvania was the only one that practiced religious freedom from the date of its founding in 1682. This was possible because the heirs of William Penn never lost ownership of their colony.

It took our forefathers a long time to learn that freedoms increase when shared with others, and that the safest guarantee of religious liberty for one sect is to extend the privilege to all. It is fitting that the law which guarantees our freedom of worship should have been written in Penn's City of Brotherly Love, Philadelphia.

The first amendment to our Constitution reads: CONGRESS SHALL MAKE NO LAW RESPECTING AN ESTABLISHMENT OF RELIGION, OR PROHIBITING THE FREE EXERCISE THEREOF.

Only sixteen words. Yet, for this victory, Roger Williams was banished; Lord Baltimore was ridiculed; William Penn was imprisoned; and Mary Dyer, a Quaker, was hanged on Boston Common. With a vision that foretold the future, they were prophets in their day. They lived ahead of their time and their dreams came true in the law of our land.

A charter from the King of England gave one man or a group of men permission to start a colony in new lands claimed by Great Britain. However, all charters were not alike.

Colonies in New England whose charters granted the most local control came to be known as "the charter colonies."

When a charter granted land and many privileges of government to one man, the settlement was called a proprietary colony. Although the proprietors appointed governors, judges, and other important officials in their colonies, as a rule, the people had a share in making the laws through assemblies of freemen who were elected.

In royal colonies, the governors were appointed by the King, but the people shared in governing themselves through their elected assemblies. In some colonies, these assemblies had the right to pay the royal governor his salary, and the governor found it convenient to please the people.

Although most of the British colonies eventually became royal in name, the people insisted in sharing more and more in governing themselves. As a result, the British colonists acquired the experience in self-government that led to their independence.

MAPS:

WA6r, WA9r, WA11r
Atlas of American History by Edgar B. Wesley

Colony	Date	Founded by	Reason	Government
Virginia	1607	London Company	Trade	Charter 1606 Royal 1624
Massachusetts	1620	Plymouth Co. Pilgrims (Separatists)	Trade Religion	Self-governing – 1620 Charter – 1629
	1628 - 1630	Massachusetts Bay Co. (Puritans)		Charter – 1629 Charter – 1691 with governor appointed by the King
New Hampshire	1623	John Mason	Religion	Charter – 1629 Royal – 1679
(Maine	1623	Fernando Gorges)	Trade	(Maine was proprietary in 1629 – Mass. bought rights in 1677.)
Maryland	1634	George Calvert (Lord Baltimore)	Religion	Proprietary – 1632 Royal – 1692 Proprietary 1720
Rhode Island	1636	Roger Williams	Religion	Self-governing 1636 Charter – 1663
Connecticut	1636 1638	Emigrants from Massachusetts	Land Religion	Self-governing Charter – 1662
Delaware	1638	Swedish South Co.	Trade	Swedish rule – 1638 Dutch rule – 1655 English rule – 1664 (proprietary) Merged with Pennsylvania – 1682 Separate governor – 1691
North Carolina South Carolina	1663	Earl of Clarendon Duke of Albemarle William, Earl of Craven John, Lord Berkeley	Trade	Proprietary 1663 N. Royal 1729 S. Royal 1729 Separated in 1729

Colony	Date	Founded by	Reason	Government
		Lord Ashley		
		Sir George Carteret		
		Sir John Colleton		
		Sir William Berkeley		
New York (New Amsterdam)				
	1614	United Netherlands Company	Trade	Dutch rule
	1622	Dutch West India Co.	Trade	Dutch rule
	1664	Captured by England	To destroy Dutch power in America	
	1664	Named for Duke of York, proprietor	Trade	Proprietary, 1664 Royal – 1685
New Jersey	1623	Dutch West India Co.	Trade	Dutch rule – 1623
		Swedish South Co.	Trade	Swedish rule – 1638
		Dutch West India Co.	Trade	Dutch rule – 1655
	1664	Lord Berkeley – George Carteret, proprietors	Trade	Proprietary – 1664 Royal – 1702
Pennsylvania	1682	Quakers-William Penn	Religion	Proprietary
Georgia	1732	James Oglethorpe	Debtors	Proprietary 1732 Royal 1752

Chapter 6

For Freedom of Opportunity

FREEDOM FROM WANT

THE PATTERN OF LIFE was set for a tenant farmer living in a wee thatched cottage on the huge estate of an English nobleman. Year after year he and his children plowed the duke's fields, stored feed in his barns, milked his cows, tended his sheep, and toiled in his garden. The pay was small, providing the barest necessities of life, and leaving little or nothing with which to seek a better way. Few schools were provided for the poor in England and there was little hope for change. One evening a neighbor of one of these tenant farmers dropped in to bring the news from London. He carried a little pamphlet, thin as a pancake, which he had purchased for a penny at a London book stall. He was a welcome guest — this neighbor who had learned to read and write in the big city, where he went on frequent trips to sell his master's cattle. The farmer seated him on a wooden stool, lighted a candle, and the family gathered around the table to hear the news.

First, the neighbor read the front-page notice from the publisher, assuring the reader that every word was the truth, because the letter (not intended for the press) was written by a minister living in New England.

In America land was free for the taking. A man standing on a hilltop could see thousands of acres of the finest corn land cleared by the Indians. Along the Charles River the soil was rich and black. Cattle grew fat on the long thick grass, and milk was cheap, a penny a quart. The great crop was Indian corn, which grew wherever the seed was planted. One man paid about $1.60 for seed, traded his corn crop to the Indians for beaver pelts, and sold the furs for $1600. Turnips, parsnips, carrots, peas, cucumbers, and pumpkins grew larger in America than in England. Greens, onions, herbs, berries, grapes, fruits, and nuts grew wild in the woods. There were many turkeys, partridges, wild ducks, and geese. Pigeons were so numerous that their flights sometimes darkened the earth like a cloud. Deer and bear roamed in the forests. The minister wrote enthusiastically about the abundance of fish — cod, herring, mullets, mackerel, haddock, crabs, and oysters. He declared that he had seen lobsters weighing as much as sixteen pounds and had heard of others weighing twenty-five pounds. Lobsters were so plentiful that even small boys could catch all they could eat. Such a variety of food was unknown to the poor in Europe, who always seemed hungry. It was free in New England for those who hunted, fished, and farmed.

In a country where land was easy to obtain and the woods were thick with trees, any man could own his home, be he ever so poor. Stone, too, was plentiful. Not far from Salem was a place with "marble-stone" which the settlers called Marble Harbor. The minister praised the climate of Massachusetts.

"A sup of New England Aire," he said, "is better than a whole draft of Old England's Ale."

The winters were cold but wood was plentiful. A poor servant with fifty acres of land could afford to use more logs for heating than many a nobleman in England. "Here is good living for those who love good fires."

It was a long letter, nearly 5000 words, praising New England. In closing, the minister wrote:

We that are settled in Salem make what hast (haste) we can to build Houses, so that within a short time we shall haue a faire Towne . . . . We have plentie of Preaching . . . . And thus we doubt not but God will be with us, and IF GOD BE WITH US, WHO CAN BE AGAINST US?

The New World was a land of plenty. Without money to pay for the voyage, how could they get there? Alas! America was only a dream. Then, months later, the neighbor returned from another selling trip to London. He brought good news.

INDENTURED SERVANTS PROVIDE WORKMEN FOR THE COLONIES

THE PLANTERS IN AMERICA needed men in their fields and shops. They advertised for help in London and seacoast towns. They offered to pay the passage across the ocean for men, women, and families willing to bind themselves to a term of service until they had repaid their master for the cost of the voyage. To guarantee their freedom after a specified number of years, both master and servant signed duplicate papers, indented or notched in the same places to prove the agreement was mutual and legal. When a servant's time expired, he and his master took their papers to an officer of the law. One paper was placed on top of the other to prove that the notches were identical and were made at the same time. Sometimes, both parts were written on one sheet which was torn with jagged edges. Then the master and servant fitted them together to prove that the two pieces were part of one sheet of paper. These papers protected the rights of the servants to become freemen when their time expired. The papers were known as "indentures." Thus, men and women possessing these papers came to be called "indented" or "indentured" servants. They were not treated as slaves. They had rights in the courts to protect them from unjust and cruel masters.

Although the abuses of the system were many, tens of thousands from England, Ireland, Scotland, Germany, and other countries were willing to sell themselves into bondage to escape poverty and want in their homelands. For them, America was a land of hope as well as a land of plenty. When their debt was paid, they could build their own homes, plow their own fields, raise their own cattle, and market their own products.

In fact, this trade in servants became so

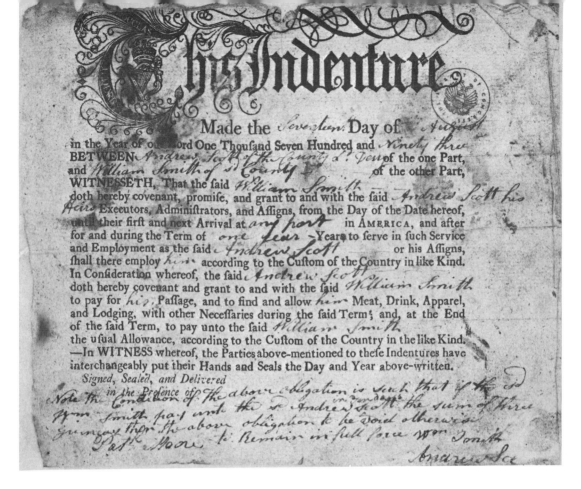

Photograph of original indenture between William Smith and Andrew Scott, witnessed by Patrick Moore. Both Smith and Scott received identical copies with edges torn in the same way to prove the indenture was legal. When presented in court, a judge declared that the servant had completed the time required to pay for his passage and was free to go his own way.

THIS INDENTURE made the seventeenth day of August in the year of our Lord, one thousand seven hundred and ninety three, between Andrew Scott of the County L. Derry of the one part, and William Smith of said County . . . of the other part, WITNESSETH, that the said William Smith doth hereby covenant, promise, and grant to and with the said Andrew Scott, his heirs, admininstrators, and assigns, from the day of the date hereof, until their first and next arrival at any port in America, and after for and during the term of one year to serve in such service and employment as the said Andrew Scott or his assigns, shall there employ him according to the custom of the country in like kind. In consideration whereof, the said Andrew Scott doth hereby covenant and grant to and with the said William Smith to pay for his passage, and to find and allow him meat, drink, apparel, and lodging, with other necessaries during the said term; and, at the end of the said term, to pay unto the said William Smith the usual allowance, according to the custom of the country in like kind. - In WITNESS whereof, the parties above-mentioned to these indentures have interchangeably put their hands and seals the day and year above-written.

SIGNED, SEALED, AND DELIVERED IN THE PRESENCE OF
PATRICK MOORE

William Smith
Andrew Scott

(The added note in Moore's handwriting states that Smith can be free before his term is completed by paying Scott three guineas.)

72

profitable that thousands of persons, including young children, were kidnapped and sold into servitude in the colonies. The King used the system to get rid of criminals and undesirables. Many of these "undesirables," however, had been thrown into prison for political and religious reasons, and were not guilty of crime. They made good citizens in the New World. Two of the signers of the Declaration of Independence came to this country as indentured servants. Twenty Negroes sold in Virginia by a Dutch captain in 1619 were more like indentured servants than slaves. Actual slavery came later.

Of course, there were indentured servants who did not live up to their bargains. The following excerpt from a colonial paper is one of many advertisements for runaway servants:

Six Pounds Reward

RAN AWAY from the subscribers, two servant lads, one named JAMES HAMBLETON, seventeen years of age, about five feet three and four inches high, wears his own red hair, a little knock-kneed; had on a new felt hat, a check shirt, striped outside jacket, a silk vest, new leather breeches, and old shoes.

The other named WILLIAM HALL, about the same age and height, full face and eyes, down look, and had light colored hair; had on a blue and white striped vest, a kersey jacket, a coarse linen shirt with a patch on the left shoulder, striped trousers, and a pair of double-soled calfskin shoes with square brass buckles in them. Whoever takes up said servants and secures them, so that their masters may have them again, shall have the above reward, or THREE POUNDS for either of them, and reasonable charges, paid by

JOHN HILLIAS
JONAH WOOLMAN

Skilled tradesmen and professional men, as well as laborers, came to this country as indentured servants seeking freedom from

A PLACE in the Country is wanted for a likely, active NEGRO GIRL, who is about nine years old, and has had the small pox; she is to be bound until twenty-four years old.— For further particulars enquire of the Printer.

Sometimes owners freed the children of their slaves when they were old enough to take care of themselves. These Negroes were given legal papers assuring their freedom at a given time, and these papers were recognized by the courts.

TO BE SOLD, THE TIME of an English servant Man, by trade a blacksmith, and understands forging gun barrels. Enquire of the Printer.

Only the time of an indentured servant could be sold. This advertisement offers the time an English immigrant has yet to serve to pay back the expenses of his voyage to America.

want. The desire to possess land is strong in the Anglo Saxon and Celtic peoples of northern Europe. Many humbled themselves in servitude to win a title to fifty acres of land when they became freemen in America. Without these servants to build up the colonies, it would have taken England a longer time to gain a foothold in the New World. To the poor in Europe, America was a land of promise. Even debtors, thrown into prison, found a haven in the New World.

GEORGIA IS FOUNDED FOR DEBTORS

IN ENGLAND at this time whole families were thrown into prison for debt.

In jail they could not earn money to pay their debts. They lived on in the filthy, wretched prisons until they died. Many kind-hearted Englishmen were moved to pity by the plight of these unfortunate people. The support of these prisoners, poor as it was, made the taxpayers complain of the burden.

A rich and kindly man, James Oglethorpe, asked his friends and Parliament to help him provide the funds to start a colony where these debtors could work to support themselves. The men who invested money in the colony expected some profits and believed that Oglethorpe could make the venture pay. George II favored the founding of the colony because it would place Englishmen farther south to push the Spaniards back and hold them in Florida. The new settlement would protect Carolina, founded in 1663 as a grant to proprietors who were favorites of the King. Oglethorpe's colony was named Georgia in honor of King George and was the last of the thirteen colonies. It was a proprietary colony, in a way, under Oglethorpe's direction. Oglethorpe was granted a charter in 1732, the year George Washington was born. In January of the following year, Oglethorpe arrived at Charleston, South Carolina, with his first colonists, where he was received cordially by the governor and given a pilot to guide his ships to the Savannah River.

Since the debtors had nothing at all, Oglethorpe's company furnished passage, food, and clothing for a year until they could harvest their first crop. The father of each family was given fifty acres of land and a start in cattle, hogs, and sheep. Many families who could afford to pay their way migrated to Georgia from England, Scot-land, Ireland, and Germany. The men who invested their money in this colony had visions of gaining riches in the silk and wine industries. These adventurers asked the colonists to plant mulberry trees, which they did. In spite of the mild climate, silkworms did not thrive in Georgia. In a new country, where land was plentiful, the farmers planted rice and sugar cane and worked in the fields. Raising silkworms was a tedious, stay-at-home chore which did not appeal to men in a country rich with game. They planted the grape vines but failed to make much wine.

Although Oglethorpe did much to make his colonists happy and successful, the colony did not prosper so much as those farther north.

Some of the debtors were not thrifty. They failed to take care of themselves in the New World as they had failed in the Old World. Like all of the proprietary colonies, except Pennsylvania, Georgia eventually became the property of the Crown.

LITTLE TRADE BEGINNINGS OF OUR GREAT INDUSTRIAL NATION

INTO THE HARBORS along the Atlantic Coast sailed boatloads of Europeans. They were seeking freedom from want, food to eat, clothes to wear, and fires to warm them. As soon as these simple needs were filled, they grew "trade-minded." They were no longer content merely with freedom from want. Many desired to own a farm, a shop, a store, a mill, a factory, a fishing boat, a merchant vessel, and to go into business for themselves.

Land was cheap, sometimes free for the taking. Most families built their own homes and raised their own food. To provide other needs and some of the luxuries, most farmers made something to sell or trade from the natural resources of the country. In the northern colonies during the winter, farmers cut down trees. From pine and spruce they made poles for masts on sailing ships. White and red oak were used for ship timber and they had a ready market in the shipbuilding industry in England and the colonies. From the refuse of pine forests they made pitch, tar, turpentine, rosin, and potash. In farm homes, barrels, shingles, and clapboards were made by hand. These products were traded for merchandise made in neighboring colonies and in England. Women and girls made linen from flax grown in the fields and woolen cloth from the fleece of barnyard sheep. In early colonial days it was hard to tell who was a farmer and who was a manufacturer, because nearly every man had some little business of his own.

One product led to another from the natural resources of the country. The forests supplied the timber that built the boats for the fishing industry. These vessels were constructed in sheltered coves on the seaboard, on the banks of larger rivers, and sometimes in the deep woods where the timber was cut, miles from water. Then, in the winter, the boats were drawn on sledges to the nearest stream.

When Captain John Smith was in Jamestown, he learned from the Indians that gold and copper deposits could be found along the Atlantic Coast north of the Virginia settlement. Several years after he had returned to England, he had been employed by some merchants to explore the North Atlantic Coast, which he named New England. Not finding either gold or copper, John Smith wrote in his *Description of New England* in 1614:

Fish and furs were now our guard. By our late arrival and long lingering about the whale, the prime of both those seasons were past ere we perceived it, we thinking that their seasons served at all times. But we found it otherwise, for, by the middle of June, the fishing failed. Yet in July and August some was taken, but not sufficient to defray so great a charge as our stay required. Of dry fish we made about 40,000; of salted fish, about 7000. While the sailors fished, myself with eight or nine others that might best be spared, ranging the coast in a small boat, we got for trifles near 1100 beaver skins, 100 martins, and near as many otters, and most of them within the distance of twenty leagues.

John Smith and his men probably boiled ocean water to get the salt to "cure" their fish. The early colonists followed this tedious process, using 250 gallons of water to obtain a single bushel of salt. In 1629 Cape Cod fishermen walking along the rocky shore noticed that salt was sticking to their shoes. They discovered that the salt covering the rocks had evaporated from the tide water. They tried it on their fish and liked the flavor. Soon, salt was made by filling shallow vats with ocean water and leaving the water to be evaporated by the sun and the wind. Thus, because the fishing business created a demand for salt, another industry was started. Lumbering, shipbuilding, and fishing grew together. Then the demand arose for merchants who would sell these products in markets at home and abroad.

Less than fifteen years after the Pilgrims landed in Massachusetts, a sawmill was built at Salmon River Falls on the Piscataqua in New Hampshire. This was years before England had a sawmill. These mills, built near streams and operated by water power, sawed the lumber that made the ships that carried the fish, lumber, and fur of the colonies to the West Indies and ports of Europe. Salem, Boston, Plymouth, Dorchester, Salisbury, and New Bedford were shipbuilding centers in early days. In 1692 one man had twenty-one vessels trading with the West Indies, the isle of Jersey, and the ports of France. Sometimes a skipper sold both his vessel and his cargo in a foreign port, returning home as a passenger on another ship.

In New England where the winters were long and the growing seasons were short, more and more people turned from farming to trading as a means of earning a living. This created a demand for more things to sell and home manufacturing increased. On long winter evenings boys in farm families hammered out homemade nails in tiny forges in chimney corners. Yankee traders brought bales of raw cotton from islands in the West Indies and sold them to farmers in the colonies. The farmers' wives and children carded and spun the cotton. The fathers, many of whom had learned to weave in the old country, plied their looms during spare time from labor in their fields. When woven and dyed, the cloth was taken to the nearest town and offered for sale or trade. In fact, every family was expected to make some article of commerce. In Massachusetts in 1656, a law was passed demanding that each family spin three pounds of linen, cotton, or wool each week for thirty weeks of each year. This law excused them from spinning during the twenty-two weeks of the growing season in spring and summer.

In the beginning, commerce thrived on these homemade articles and farm products. Gradually, the demand grew for more goods than home manufacturing could produce. This situation created a demand for mills and factories to produce more goods. Manufacturing outside the home made slow progress because of the lack of capital and scarcity of labor and equipment.

CAPITAL, LABOR, AND MONOPOLY IN COLONIAL DAYS

MONEY FOR INVESTMENT is commonly called "venture capital." Although the colonists had food, clothing, and shelter, and were not in want, they had little money or venture capital. Business was carried on by barter. Taxes were paid and trades made in furs, cattle, corn, leaden bullets, and beaded belts called wampum. In Virginia tobacco was used for money to pay taxes and fines. At a meeting of the House of Burgesses in 1629, a law was passed that every master of a family and every freeman must pay a tax of five pounds of tobacco to support three Indians who lived in the colony and who were public charges. Another law stated that everyone absent from church on Sunday was to be fined one pound of tobacco.

The London Company furnished the money to build the first factory in the colonies. Captain Newport, on his second voyage to Jamestown in 1608, brought over eight skilled workmen from Poland and Germany to make glass, pitch, tar and soapashes. The following year, in the woods about a mile from Jamestown, the company built a "glass house" to make beads and trinkets to trade for furs brought in by Indian trappers. During the first year this plant also produced fifty barrels of tar, pitch, and soapashes. The workmen dug a well in the fort, made nets for fishing, and

A TOBACCO PLANTATION IN THE WEST INDIES

According to tradition, a sailor who came with Columbus in 1492 took tobacco home and smoked a pipe of it to show his friends how the Indians used the plant. At first, Europeans raised tobacco in their gardens as a curiosity, and did not use it. As the smoking habit increased, tobacco became the leading export from some colonies in the New World. Sometimes, colonists to Virginia stopped over in the West Indies to learn how to raise and market tobacco. In 1619, the first Negro servants were sold in Jamestown to work in the tobacco fields as in the West Indies.

erected a block house for the Indian trade. They built twenty houses for themselves, and cleared, plowed, and planted forty acres of land. Then, during leisure time, they made clapboards and wainscot by hand to be shipped to the London Company for sale in England. A "master of all trades" was the factory toiler in colonial days. The "glass house" near Jamestown was the first manufacturing plant to operate in what is now the United States. Ten years later the company erected an iron works in the same forest. In a few years both little factories were destroyed in an Indian attack on the Jamestown settlement. The officials of the London Company made further efforts to establish manufacturing in Virginia, but the colonists

preferred to be planters and raise tobacco.

To get manufacturing started in New England, where money was scarce, the people turned to barter. In town meetings the people voted to give land and special privileges to anyone or any group willing to invest money in a mill or a factory. In 1665 Groton, Connecticut, gave 20 acres of land within the limits of the town to a group of men to erect a mill for grinding corn. At the same time the townsmen voted that the property would be free of taxes for twenty years. They also prohibited the erection of another mill for the same length of time.

In 1646 a man in Lynn, Massachusetts, was granted a monopoly for fourteen years on his invention for using water power in mills, including a sawmill, "so his study and cost may not be in vayne or lost." The town of Lynn became famous for shoes instead of lumber. The first shoemaker settled there only fifteen years after the Pilgrims arrived. As cattle became more plentiful in New England, leather was tanned for shoes and clothing. The first tannery was in Lynn. The town became a great center of the shoemaking industry. The fisheries furnished oil for tanning and the woods were full of oak and sumac.

In 1641 the townsmen of Salem, Massachusetts, voted to give two acres of public land to each of three men if they would start a glass factory. Since the men lacked enough capital to complete the factory, the citizens in town meeting voted to lend them tax money which they were to repay, "if the work succeeded, when they were able."

The colonial manufacturer had a more difficult time in getting helpers than he did in getting money. Although hundreds of skilled mechanics came to America as industrial servants, there was always more to be done than people to do it. Some men made a business out of supplying workmen for the manufacturers. This was true especially in the middle colonies of Pennsylvania, New York, and New Jersey. Advertisements like the following appeared in colonial papers:

Just Arrived
On Board The Brigantine, Friendship,
John Bean, Master, from Dublin
A NUMBER of healthy indented SERVANTS, Men and Women, among whom are several valuable Tradesmen, whose times are to be disposed of, on reasonable terms, by JOHN LYNCH, at the corner of Third and Lombard Streets, or the master on board vessel, now lying off the Drawbridge.
(Dunlap's Pennsylvania Packet.)

Many a factory owner failed in business because the "indentured servants" left his employ when their terms of servitude were ended. These workmen had come from countries where the land was largely owned by noblemen and aristocrats. When free, both skilled mechanics and common laborers in the colonies preferred to struggle on a farm and work for themselves, rather than live easily in a town and work for wages. It was land that lured workmen from the mills and hindered the growth of manufacturing. The old-world idea that a gentleman lived on the land greatly influenced the way of life in the British colonies, where even a poor servant could become a land-owning aristocrat. Agriculture was considered more respectable than commerce. Today, the average citizen of this nation desires to own his own home, be it large or small.

Since labor was always scarce and costly, all kinds of labor-saving machinery were welcomed and America became a land of inventions. The English colonists from the beginning took a decided stand against monopoly. They passed laws to prevent a few men from controlling the goods and services that contributed to the welfare of all the people. As early as 1641, the legislators of Massachusetts decreed "there shall be no monopolies granted or allowed among us but of such new inventions as are profitable to the country, and that for a short time." Men were given monopolies to invest their money in mills and factories to help a community, but these all had time limits placed upon them. The colonists who had come to this country for freedom of opportunity made an effort to maintain this privilege for all. They resented attempts to deprive them of the freedom of buying and selling at their own free will.

When the London Company tried to get back Virginia after James I had taken the settlement from them, the House of Burgesses, established by the trading company, voted to belong to the Crown. The planters declared that a return to ownership by the London Company would give that group of men a monopoly of their trade. Freedom of opportunity, sometimes called free enterprise, lured men across three thousand miles of ocean to venture their lives and fortunes in the New World.

NORTH AMERICA WAS COLONIZED BY TRADERS.

IN THE RACE for territory in the Americas, France, England, and the Netherlands depended largely upon trading companies to populate their colonies. Usually, these corporations operated under government charters which gave them a monopoly on trade for a specified number of years.

The Cent Associés, a French trading company headed by Champlain, received a monopoly on the fur trade forever and on all other commerce for fifteen years. In spite of this monopoly, farmers and tradesmen slyly set traps in the woods. They sold pelts to independent buyers instead of to the company that had brought them to Canada. However, the monopolies of trading companies hindered the growth of population in Canada and discouraged manufacturing. Although the shipbuilding industry made a feeble start and some grain was milled for export, the fur business absorbed the energy of New France.

The Netherlands gained a foothold in the New World by granting a charter to the Dutch West India Company. In the instructions issued to colonists in January of 1625 is the following paragraph:

The Director of New Netherland shall give the colonists and other free persons full permission to trade in the interior and to catch the animals with the skins, but they must deliver up the said skins and goods to the Company at the price for which we obtain them at the trading place from the Indians, and he shall not permit them, by selling the skins to others, to make the Company pay a higher price.

The King of England did not grant such sweeping privileges of monopoly to the Plymouth Company and the Virginia Company, although both were purely commercial enterprises for profit. In order to get timber, furs, and minerals, it was necessary for these companies to maintain settlements for families who would produce these articles for sale. Not finding gold and silver and sudden riches, the English colonists settled down to the hard task of cutting timber and planting crops, through which prosperity came the slow way.

When tobacco became an important export in Virginia, the Crown saw a chance to gain revenue by taxing the article. By the time the adventurers of the Virginia Company were hopeful of profits on their investments, the charter was revoked in 1624. Virginia became a Crown colony. The trading companies did not last in the British colonies because the settlers wanted free enterprise for themselves. The settlers did not want to be limited to trade through the company. Therefore, more emigrants came to the English settlements. Here they could eventually have more freedom of opportunity than in the French and Dutch colonies which were largely controlled by trading companies.

The Dutch West India Company lost its

New Netherland colony to the English, who greatly outnumbered the Dutch. England claimed this region under the Plymouth and Virginia charters. Late in August of 1664, a fleet of four men-of-war cast anchor in the harbor of New Amsterdam. On the four English vessels were trained soldiers. Stuyvesant, governor of New Netherland, had less than a hundred men to defend his town. He called a meeting of the leading citizens who advised surrender after securing the best terms possible. Colonel Richard Nicolls, the English commander and new governor, promised to follow the terms suggested by Stuyvesant if the fort would surrender. Stuyvesant asked that the people be permitted: to keep their houses and lands; to have the privilege of remaining there or returning to the Netherlands; to have liberty of conscience; and the right to choose their local officers by vote. Nicolls agreed.

It was the eighth of September and a sad day for the governor who had ruled New Netherland for seventeen years. Peter Stuyvesant, hobbling on a wooden leg, led his Dutch troops down Beaver Street with drums beating and flags flying to board the *Gideon* for the Netherlands. Three years later, he returned to his farm, the "bouwery" on the east side of Manhattan Island to end his days in peace among his Dutch and English neighbors. His New Amsterdam had another name, New York, and he had another friend, Colonel Nicolls.

Many of the Dutch citizens welcomed the change to English rule which gave them more freedom of opportunity. Nicolls proved to be a wise and popular governor. New York began to grow into a flourishing colony. The city began to spread over the island of Manhattan under a form of government which encouraged individual enterprise. The Dutch gradually became as jealous of their rights as any Englishman. They took an active part in their government. Through town meetings and colonial assemblies the early settlers of this country gained the political liberty that insured their freedom of opportunity. New England colonies led the way. In the British possessions of North America, government by the people evolved but freedoms were hard won.

POLITICAL LIBERTY GROWS IN THE TOWN MEETING

The freeholders and other Inhabitants of the Town of Topsfield Quallified according to Law for voting are to Take notice to meet at our meeting house in Topsfield on the first

PETER STUYVESANT

Peter Stuyvesant, Dutch governor of New Netherland was enraged when he received the summons to surrender New Amsterdam to the commander of the British fleet.

Tuesday in march next at eight of ye clock in ye forenoon.

Dated in Topsfield:
14th of February: 1718
Elisha Putnam
Constabel of Topsfield (Mass.)

It was the custom to list the reasons for calling a town meeting. This gave neighbors time to talk over the business at hand before they gathered in the meeting house. The purpose of this meeting in Topsfield, Massachusetts on March 8, 1718 was to choose officers; to consider the petition of Isaac Peabody who wanted some land near the mill pond; to agree upon some way to preserve the timber on the common land owned by the town; to choose jurymen for Ipswich Court; and to do any other thing for the benefit of the town.

The town meetings were New England's way of carrying on local government. At each meeting the townsmen chose one man to conduct the gathering. He was called the moderator. Any townsman had the right to ask for a vote on any matter affecting the public welfare.

School and church were common subjects for discussion at these meetings because each was necessary to the other. All good Puritans had to be able to read the Bible. Since both men and women needed to learn to read in order to practice their religion, schools were important in Puritan colonies. However, most of these schools were not free. Although some public funds were voted to support education, the parents paid tuition if they were able to afford it.

The school teacher and the minister were selected by vote at these town meetings and their salaries were set. Before school-houses were built, committees were appointed to find homes in which the schoolmaster could live and teach for a few weeks in each neighborhood. In the early days of the Puritan colonies in New England, the church was supported by public funds voted by the citizens in town meetings. From old records these items were copied:

Ye towne have agreed to build ye new meeting house two and forty foot wide and four and forty foot long.

The town agreed that ye committee shall have power to Draw Money out of ye Treasury to pay Mr. Eliot for his service in ye ministry as Long as he shall Preach to & amongst us.

Disputes over boundaries, permits for mills and shops, construction of roads, building of fences, payment of bills, help for the poor, protection from Indian attack, and other neighborhood problems were discussed in open meetings. Decisions were made by vote. This was self-government at work under charters obtained from the King of England. Although the Puritans in New England had the privilege of self-government, obligations went with it. It was the duty of every freeman to attend these meetings. Absence carried a penalty. When a member was late as much as thirty minutes, he was fined. When he was tardy an hour, the sum was doubled. No man was permitted to leave until all the matters under discussion had been settled by voting. The meeting was announced by drums beating a thunderous summons thirty minutes before the time set for roll call.

The stern Puritans believed in discipline. A notice of a town meeting, posted by the village constable, was not passed by unheeded. The paper amounted to a summons and citizens obeyed the call. "Ye Olde Towne Meeting" was a training school in political liberty. It laid the foundations for our present local governments. When James II tried to destroy this system of self-government, the independent New Englanders staged their own rebellion.

IN DEFENSE
OF POLITICAL LIBERTY

IN 1686 JAMES II sent Sir Edmund Andros to Massachusetts to be:

Our CAPTAIN-GENERAL and GOVERNOR IN CHIEF in and over all our territory and dominion of New England in America commonly called and known by the name of Our Colony of the Massachusetts Bay, Our Colony of New Plymouth, and Our Province of New Hampshire and Maine, the Narragansett country otherwise called the King's Province with all the islands . . .

Andros was given almost unlimited authority by King James, and he used it. He demanded the surrender of the early charters upon which depended the colonial rights of property and self-government. All obeyed the order, except Connecticut, where, according to tradition, the precious piece of parchment was hidden in the hollow of an oak tree. New York, taken from the Dutch in 1664, and the neighboring province of New Jersey also came under the control of Andros. A one-man rule was established from Delaware to the St. Croix River. Then Andros set himself up as a dictator with an advisory council.

Three years later, when a revolution in England swept James II from the throne, the long-suffering New Englanders captured Sir Edmund Andros and held him a prisoner, along with men on his council. Boston was filled with armed colonial soldiers and 1500 more awaited a call at

Charlestown. Andros tried to escape from the fort by wearing women's clothes. In this disguise he passed two guards, but the third one noticed his shoes, which he had neglected to change. He was recaptured and held a prisoner until he was deported to England. The colonists defended their action in a long paper sent to the new rulers of England, William and Mary. The colonists declared:

It was absolutely necessary for the people of New England to seize Sir Edmund Andros and his associates. They made what laws they pleased, WITHOUT ANY CONSENT OF THE PEOPLE OR THEIR REPRESENTATIVES. In New England, by constant usage under their charter governments, the inhabitants of each town did assemble to consider the welfare of their respective towns, the relief of the poor, and the like. Sir Edmund Andros, with a few of his council, made a law prohibiting any town meeting except once a year, the third Monday in May. The inhabitants of the country were startled at the law, fearful the design of it was to prevent the people from meeting to make complaints of their grievances.

It took about 20,000 words to list the crimes of Sir Edmund Andros against liberty, in the opinion of the colonists. What did he do? One paragraph lists a number of grievances with complete frankness:

In the time of his government, without form or legal authority, he made laws destructive of the liberty of the people, imposed and levied taxes without the consent of the people either by themselves or by an assembly, threatened and imprisoned them that would not be assisting to the illegal levies, denied that they had any property in their lands without patents from him, and during the time of actual war with the Indians, he did supply them with ammunition. Several Indians declared that they were encouraged by him to make war upon the English.

At the trial of a minister in Ipswich, Massachusetts, who had organized a movement to fight taxation without representation, a member of the council of Andros said to the defendant:

You have no more privileges left you than not to be sold for slaves.

In the report, the colonists asked this question:

What people that had the spirit of Englishmen could endure this?

Andros denied the colonists freedom of the press, the right to assemble, their own general courts, and many other liberties to which they had become accustomed. A hundred years later, the basic human freedoms defended in this lengthy document were briefly stated in Article One of the Bill of Rights, the First Amendment to the Constitution of the United States:

Congress shall make no law respecting an establishment of religion, or prohibiting the free exercise thereof; or abridging the freedom of speech or of the press; or the right of the people peaceably to assemble, and to petition the government for a redress of grievances.

FREEDOM OF THE PRESS

THE RIGHT TO PRINT the truth is a necessary part of political liberty. Freedom of the press was won in colonial days by a poor printer, John Peter Zenger. Zenger had come to America in 1710 at the age of thirteen, a religious refugee born in Germany. His father died on shipboard, and the lad became a printer's apprentice in New York to obtain a living. He served for eight years to learn his trade. In 1726

Zenger set up his own print shop on Smith Street.

In 1726 New York was an English royal colony. It was ruled by a governor appointed by the King. Although the people had an assembly to which they sent representatives, the governor had the power to dismiss this legislative body at will. English officials collected revenues and spent the tax money as they pleased. They paid little attention to the needs of the colonists. A storm broke when William Cosby became governor in 1732. His acts fomented discontent. The people felt the need of an independent newspaper in which they could expose the acts of the governor and get him recalled. They selected the German printer, Zenger. A paper called *New York Weekly Journal* was started. The first issue appeared November 5, 1733.

In 1697 censorship of the press had been established in New York by law, "that no person keep any press for printing, nor that any book, pamphlet, or other matter whatsoever be printed without your (Governor's) especial leave and consent first obtained." When articles appeared in the *New York Weekly Journal* criticizing the governor, Cosby ordered the arrest of Peter Zenger, who had printed the sheet. When Zenger was lodged in jail, his wife put out the paper. Through a hole in the door of his cell, she would discuss the content with her husband. The anger of the people increased. They determined to free the German printer.

The trial began on the fourth of August, 1735, in the City Hall on the corner of Nassau and Wall Streets. The courtroom was jammed long before the opening. The crowd overflowed into the street. The twelve jurymen took their seats. Seven of them were Dutch. A principle was at stake, a cornerstone of political liberty. It was the trial of a basic freedom as much as it was the trial of a man. Zenger had a famous lawyer, Andrew Hamilton from Philadelphia, who took advantage of the occasion to defend the human rights of man, such as trial by jury, freedom of speech, press, and religion. He said, among many statements:

The loss of liberty to a generous mind is worse than death . . . . The man who loves his country, prefers its liberty to all other considerations, well knowing that without liberty, life is a misery.

·When both sides had presented their cases, the jury retired to reach a decision. The men were not out long. The foreman of the jury stood and spoke clearly and firmly — NOT GUILTY. Three deafening cheers filled the courtroom. In the evening forty citizens entertained Zenger's attorney at a dinner in the Black Horse Tavern. When he left New York the next day, after the printer had been released from jail, guns fired a salute in his honor, "as a public testimony of the glorious defense he made in the cause of liberty in this province."

Thus, in colonial days, did the people of the colonies stand firmly against any form of dictatorship. Thousands of immigrants came to the settlements along the Atlantic seaboard, with only a vague idea of the freedoms they were seeking, because they had not known many of them. They were pursuing a vision. Freedoms sprouted in a wilderness like flowers on a vacant lot, because each person who came had broken the pattern of life in his old country and he was starting all over again. "Something new" began to grow in the New World — a mere idea. People began to question the right of government to interfere with their freedom to come and go, to buy and sell, to own or lease, to talk or listen, to vote and elect. In other words, people began to think they had the right to govern themselves. Yet, a new nation had to rise in the Western Hemisphere before this idea gained the force of law.

PART THREE

A New Nation Rises

**MEMBERS OF THE CONTINENTAL CONGRESS WHO
APPROVED THE DECLARATION OF INDEPENDENCE**

Chapter 7

France and Great Britain Clash

WESTERN TREK
LEADS TO WAR

VIRGINIA, through her charter, claimed a large share of the land lying between the Appalachian Mountains and the Mississippi River. This area was also included in the French claim to all the territory drained by the Mississippi. Since the practical Virginians realized that the way to hold a disputed territory was to occupy it, they gave away land freely in this region.

A company of men who had received a grant of 800,000 acres from the governor of Virginia wanted to learn about their new land in the "West." To explore their grant they hired a man called Dr. Walker, who liked to wander in an unknown wilderness. He kept a diary of this journey which lasted from early in March to the middle of July in 1750. Every day Walker wrote down what happened to his party. His diary is a story of life in the wilderness. For twenty days the party of five men traveled among frontier settlers from whom they bought hominy, bacon, corn meal, and other supplies. On the twenty-sixth of March they ventured into unknown country. The next day it snowed and the Appalachians were white in the distance.

The trials of this journey for both man and beast can best be told in Walker's own words. The following entries were taken from his diary:

April 7: We rode eight miles over broken land. It snowed most of the day. In the evening our dogs caught a large bear, which, before we could come up to shoot him, had wounded a dog of mine so that he could not travel. We carried him on horseback till he recovered.

April 19: This afternoon Ambrose Powell was bit by a bear in the knee. (Powell River was named for this man.)

April 27: Another horse was bit in the nose by a snake. I rubbed the wounds with bears oil, and gave him a dose of same and another of rattlesnake root some time after. This day Colby Chew and his horse fell down a bank. I bled and gave him drops, and he recovered.

May 6: The Sabbath. I saw goslings, which shows that wild geese stay here all year. Ambrose Powell had the misfortune to sprain his well knee.

July 13: I got home about noone. We killed in the journey 13 buffaloes, 8 elk, 53 bears, 20 deer, 4 wild geese, about 150 turkeys, besides small game. We might have killed three times as much meat, if we had wanted it.

Walker was probably the first white man to go through Cumberland Gap. He named the pass in honor of the Duke of Cumberland, a son of George II, King of England at the time. Beyond the gap Walker found coal. Today this region is mining country in the state of Kentucky.

These explorers were typical early Americans, men of action to whom adventure and danger were everyday living. To them, the great continent of North America was a challenge. In meeting it they scorned fear and hardships and developed self-reliance and courage. Like all explorers Dr. Walker mapped the rivers, mountains, gaps, valleys, and named many of them. He located mineral deposits, lumber regions, and farming lands. He took notice of the trees, shrubs, and flowers, and listed the wild geese to be found in the region.

Although the land owners who had hired Walker were pleased with his report, the company was not able to hold the grant. Families began to move in and help themselves to land. They were called "squatters."

The legislature of Virginia passed the "cabin law," giving any man a title to four hundred acres of land when he had built a log house and planted one acre of corn. To land-hungry English people four hundred acres of ground was an estate for a nobleman. As the news spread over Europe, boatloads of immigrants arrived in Atlantic ports. The more daring newcomers among them filtered inland where even the poorest could own a farm. While the French were busy nailing plates to trees, declaring the Ohio Valley belonged to their King, hundreds of families from the English colonies were quietly moving into the territory. Trouble then began with both the French and the Indians.

Most of the Indian tribes were friends of the French and enemies of the British. The reason was plain. The French trader visited, bought furs, and departed. He brought the Indians guns and powder to hunt their food, blue and red cloth to make their clothes, knives to skin their game, copper kettles to boil their meat, tobacco to fill their pipes, vermilion to paint their faces, and brandy to quench their thirst. The British colonists cut down the trees and destroyed the breeding grounds of the fur-bearing animals which the Indians trapped to trade to the French. He plowed the land, planted a crop, built a house, moved in his family, and stayed.

Both the British and the French, however, realized the value of Indian allies when "King George's War," an extension of a war in Europe, broke out in North America in 1744. Both sides sought Indian support in the struggle which was eventually to determine who was to control North America. The British had few Indian friends outside the powerful Iroquois Confederacy.

THE VALUE OF INDIAN ALLIES

WILLIAM PENN, in starting his colony, met with a group of Indian chiefs under an elm tree. He paid them for the land granted to him by the King. When the Indians danced to celebrate that first treaty with the Quaker, Penn who was quite an athlete asked to join in the fun as their brother. In a short time he mastered the difficult dance steps and jumped as high as an Indian. Then and there he won their hearts with his physical strength and ready wit. Through the years he gained their lasting respect because this treaty, neither signed nor sworn to, was never broken.

Because the Quakers did not believe in waging war and shooting their enemies, tribal chiefs frequently chose some town in

88

Pennsylvania for treaty conferences with any of the British colonies. Thus a meeting called by Virginia and Maryland to gain more land from the Iroquois Indians was held in Penn's town of Lancaster, Pennsylvania.

The Iroquois were organized in a strong and well-run confederacy consisting of six nations – Mohawk, Oneida, Onondaga, Cayuga, Seneca, and the newly admitted Tuscarora. They lived in a large area extending from the Appalachians to the Mississippi River and north to the Great Lakes. This land also was claimed by the British Colonies. It was some of this "western" land that Virginia and Maryland wanted. In the opening meetings at Lancaster, which lasted for ten days, both Virginia and Maryland had gained the lands they wanted in exchange for gold.

Now, on the fourth of July, 1744, the final meeting was to be held. The little courthouse at Lancaster was crowded to the doors. For many years the British had been on good terms with the Iroquois and were anxious to remain so, especially in view of the conflict with France. Great Britain and France were already engaged in King George's War. Would the Iroquois support the British or the French? The people in the courthouse waited to hear. Canassatego, chief of the Onondagas, was the spokesman for the Six Nations of the Iroquois Confederacy. He stepped to the platform to answer the question that, in no small way, decided the fate of a nation. At a table beside him sat the trusted Iroquois interpreter, Conrad Weiser. Weiser's father had brought him to this country with his seven brothers and sisters from Germany after their mother's death. When he was a young lad, Conrad ran away from his father's house in New York to live among the Mohawk Indians. The German boy learned to speak the languages of the Iroquois tribes. Years later, with his family of fifteen children, he lived on a thousand-acre farm near the bank of the Schuylkill River in Pennsylvania. Always the red man's friend, Weiser became a powerful backwoods diplomat and worked earnestly with the Iroquois chiefs to keep peace.

Politely, the dignified chief bowed to his host, the governor of Pennsylvania, whom he called Onas in his Indian language. Then he bowed to the representatives from Virginia and Maryland.

"Brother Onas," the chief began, "we assure you we have great pleasure in this meeting with our brethren of Virginia and Maryland, and thank you for bringing us together in order to create a good understanding."

The Indians shouted, "Yo-hah! Yo-hah!" the red man's way of saying, "We all agree."

"Brother Onas," he continued, "the friendship chain between us and Pennsylvania is of old standing and has never gathered any rust. In token of our wishes we present this belt of wampum."

Conrad Weiser read the English translation. The governor of Pennsylvania accepted the wampum presented by the chief to show his gratitude, and the colonists applauded in the white man's way. The Iroquois would protect Pennsylvania, but what about Massachusetts, Connecticut, and New York, if they were attacked by the French and their Indian allies? The anxious listeners fanned themselves and waited while Canassatego rested and took his own time. These treaties were always made according to Indian ritual and the white man had to accept the red man's way. With each promise or transaction there was time out for presenting wampum, the seal of authority.

When the chief rose to answer the one question which most concerned all those gathered together, his face was serious. The men leaned forward in a tense silence.

"Brother Onas," he said, addressing the Pennsylvania governor, "we shall never forget that you and we have but one heart, one head, one eye, one ear, one hand. Before we came here, we sent word to the governor of Canada that neither he nor any of his people could come through our country to hurt our brethren, the English, or any of the settlements belonging to them. In token of our sincerity we present you with this belt of wampum."

The yo-hahs of the Indians could scarcely be heard above the noisy hand-clapping and loud huzzas which rang through the halls of the little courthouse at Lancaster. It was a great fourth of July for the British colonists. Seeing their joy at his words, Canassatego arose to sound a warning. He continued, "We have one thing further to say, and that is, we heartily recommend union between you and our brethren. Never disagree, but keep a strict friendship for one another, and you, as well as we, will become the stronger. Our wise forefathers established a union of nations. This gave us weight with our neighboring peoples. We are a powerful confederacy. If you will use the same methods of our wise forefathers, you will acquire fresh strength and power. Therefore, whatever befalls you, never quarrel one with another."

This was good advice from a wise, farseeing man. At this time the British colonies were not united and did not work together in harmony.

With the British in their front yard and the French at their backs, the Iroquois played one against the other in a clever diplomatic game. Through treaties with their neighbors, both red men and white men, the Six Nations managed to keep peace for themselves. However, they had to pay for it. They gave up more and more of their hunting grounds to the fast-growing British colonies. Sandwiched between two strong warring nations, the Iroquois realized their best weapon was compromise and they used it. The British colonists, too, knew the value of compromise, and put forth much effort to keep the Iroquois on their side in all the wars between France and Great Britain. Well they knew that defeat and massacre might overtake them if the Six Nations suddenly joined with the French and their Indian allies. The friendship of the Iroquois did not prevent, entirely, a border warfare that raged at intervals among the frontier settlements.

BORDER WARFARE

IN THE MIDDLE of winter a party of French coureurs-de-bois (runners of the woods) and their Indian allies made a raid on Schenectady, New York. The raid occurred on a cold night in February. After a village party, the sentinels at the palisade had jokingly built two snowmen to guard the gate. The sentinels went home to sleep in their warm beds. Although they were warned by the military commander to keep watch, the two young men had ridiculed the thought of an attack on such a bitter night.

When all the villagers were asleep, the raiding party crept cautiously on snowshoes up to the gate. The Indian warriors and the French woodsmen stared dumbly at the ghostly sentinels of snow. The party divided into two bands, one going to the left of the silent snowmen and the other to the right. Then they walked quietly between the palisade fence and the houses until the leaders met at the opposite end. At a signal, a mighty war whoop broke the stillness. The raiders began chopping down doors with their hatchets. The settlers jumped from their beds, but only a few had time to get to their guns. Sixty men, women, and children were killed that night. Thirty-eight men and boys, ten women, and twelve children were carried off as captives. By noon the next day, the settlement of Schenectady was in ashes.

By 1750 this border warfare had terrorized the frontier settlements of the English colonies. The colonists fought back with raids on French towns and Indian villages. They contributed large sums of money to send their own armies on military expeditions into enemy territory.

By the Lancaster Treaty Virginia had gained land in the upper Ohio Valley, both north and south of the river. For this territory, Canassatego was paid one hundred pounds of gold. Governor Dinwiddie sent a young man only twenty-one years of age to explore this wilderness and to report what could be done to protect settlers seeking homes in the new country. The young man was George Washington, major and adjutant-general of the Virginia Militia, who delivered a message to the commandant of the French fort near the present site of Erie, Pennsylvania. Dinwiddie's letter politely asked the French to vacate and leave the land claimed by Virginia under the treaty with the Iroquois in 1744.

Returning from this mission to the headwaters of the Ohio River, Washington narrowly escaped drowning when his log

WASHINGTON ON HIS FIRST JOURNEY TO THE OHIO

On the last day of October, 1753, George Washington left Williamsburg, capital of Virginia, to deliver a message from Governor Dinwiddie to de St. Pierre, the French commandant at La Boeuf, now the town of Waterford, Pennsylvania. The distance was 500 miles. At Fredericksburg, Washington hired a Dutchman as a French interpreter and an Englishman as an Indian interpreter. At Cumberland, Maryland, Christopher Gist, who had gone into the Ohio country before, joined the party as guide along with four more men, two of whom were traders.

raft tipped over, dousing him into the icy current of the Allegheny River. Upon arrival at the junction of this stream with the Monongahela on the twenty-fourth of November in 1753, he wrote in his journal:

As I got down before the canoe, I spent some time in viewing the rivers, and the land in the fork, which I think extremely well situated for a fort, as it has absolute command of both rivers.

In January of 1754, Washington reported to Governor Dinwiddie in Williamsburg, the capital of Virginia. He told him that the French commandant at Fort La

Boeuf insisted that territory drained by the Ohio River and its tributaries belonged to France by right of La Salle's discoveries. Therefore, British traders and settlers entering this country would run the risk of being taken prisoners by the French. The governor acted upon Washington's suggestion that a fort be erected upon the strategic triangle where the Allegheny and Monongahela Rivers join to form the Ohio. Forty men were busy cutting down trees and sawing logs for a fort where Pittsburgh now stands, when several hundred French and Indians arrived in canoes on the Allegheny River. They demanded the woodsmen's surrender. Outnumbered, the British troops made no resistance. Afterwards the British officer was invited to dine with the French commander who treated him kindly. Little did either man realize that on this day, the seventeenth of April in 1754, they had launched the struggle between France and Great Britain for the possession of a continent. The French completed the stockade started by the British and named it Fort Duquesne.

Later in that same year, Washington returned to this western country with Virginia militiamen to defend the right of British colonists to trade for furs with the natives. At the time of his death, Washington still owned the Great Meadows and surrounding territory where he had been forced to surrender the hastily erected Fort Necessity because his soldiers had been eight days without bread. They lacked the strength to carry their baggage in a hurried retreat.

After the second failure to hold the country purchased from the Iroquois, the British Government became alarmed and decided to send troops to defend the American possessions. The colonists were expected to aid in supplies and men. Early in 1755 General Braddock arrived in Virginia with a small British force to train a colonial army for the capture of Fort Duquesne. This maneuver was the beginning of the French and Indian War, so named, perhaps, because the native tribes played a decisive part in the long and bitter conflict. The Iroquois kept their promise made in the Lancaster Treaty, but the majority of the Indian tribes fought with the French.

BRADDOCK'S ROAD TURNS DEFEAT INTO VICTORY

DAY AFTER DAY at Fort Cumberland, Braddock drilled the raw frontiersmen. In their deerskin shirts and moccasins, the backwoodsmen looked strange as they marched beside the British soldiers in their smart red coats and His Majesty's sailors in their trim, blue uniforms. Among the backwoodsmen who enlisted in the army was a young man remembered today as an outstanding explorer. His name was Daniel Boone.

When the June day arrived for the start to Fort Duquesne, Boone was ordered to the rear of the train to shoe horses, to mend wagons, and to serve the needs of the roadbuilders. This was not a frontiersman's idea of going to war, building a road through a wilderness to get the army and supplies to the place to fight. The free lad who had roamed the Carolina hills in his favorite sport, hunting, was having his first taste of military discipline under a strict and stubborn commander.

With Boone was another blacksmith and wagon-mender, a Scotch-Irish trader, who had bartered with the Indians living along the Ohio River. Always a hunter at heart, Boone inquired about the game. Around the evening fire, the lad from Carolina listened wide-eyed to the exciting tales of the Scotch-Irish trader who had crossed the mountains. The two became close friends while serving under Braddock. They planned to go together, when the war ended, to that wonderful hunting ground which the Indians called "Kentucky."

In the evenings, the men could talk of pleasure, but their days were filled with work, the hard labor of roadbuilding. The road they were building to Fort Duquesne was no more than a track. When rain fell, the artillery and wagons dug ruts into the soft and mushy earth, and sometimes they stuck in the mud. Surveyors went ahead to stake the route. The army followed to chop down trees, to hack the underbrush, and to fill the swampy spots with logs.

Gordon, the engineer in charge of the road building, was in the front line staking the roadbed when he sighted the enemy lurking behind trees. The battle began only eight miles from Fort Duquesne. George Washington, leading the Virginia troops, advised his commander to fight in Indian fashion from behind logs, rocks, and trees. Instead, Braddock ordered his men to march in a column, the battle formation used in Europe. Their bright red coats made perfect targets against the green of the forest. Of Braddock's thirteen hundred men, more than eight hundred were killed or wounded. After having five horses shot under him, the General, with a bullet in his chest, was carried to the rear in a wagon. Before he died, three days later, he gave his favorite

BRADDOCK'S FIELD

This wooded area along the Monongahela River has been the scene of important events in American history. Here, in 1755, General Braddock was defeated and mortally wounded. Although Washington had two horses shot under him and four bullet holes in his clothing, he escaped unhurt. Years later along the Kanawha River in territory that was then in western Virginia, Washington was surveying farms to be used to pay his soldiers. An old Indian came to his camp. He had traveled for days through the forest to greet his former enemy, a man with a charmed life, he said. The Indian told Washington that he was the marksman ordered to shoot him during the battle, but that he stopped firing when four bullets failed. He predicted that Washington would not die in war.

horse to Washington, the young officer from Virginia, whose advice he had scorned.

The brave general was buried in the middle of the road, near the cluster of apple trees where he had died. The remnant of Braddock's army retreated over his grave to pat down the fresh mound with their marching feet. Wagon wheels leveled the spot to hide his burial place from the Indians. In later years immigrants by the thousands trudged over his lost grave to seek new homes beyond the mountain ranges. About seventy years after his burial, workmen repairing the road dug up human bones wrapped in the faded uniform of the British general. They buried them on a slope above the road he had pushed through a wilderness.

Braddock lost the battle, but his road turned defeat into victory. No longer were the mountains a barrier to keep the colonists huddled along the Atlantic seaboard. In the years to come they followed this road to board the flatboats which carried them down the great inland waterway to rout the French from the Ohio Valley forever. This humiliating loss at Fort Duquesne was the first defeat, but not the last the British were to suffer in eight years of war with the French and their Indian allies. The victorious engagements were about equally divided between the French and British in America, where geography played an important part in winning the war.

THE BRITISH AIM FOR
THE GREAT RIVER VALLEYS

THE FRENCH BUILT and fortified a network of water routes to carry on their trade with the Indian tribes. La Salle's dream came true. Sixty forts protected the inland waterways in the heart of North America from Canada to the Gulf of Mexico. With land travel over a few portage trails, it was possible to paddle a canoe from Montreal to New Orleans. The practical British mapped their military campaigns on the same geographical pattern the French had used in building their empire in the New World. They both aimed for control of the rivers, highways of transportation in wilderness country.

To guard the entrance to the St. Lawrence River, the French raised Louisburg on Cape Breton Island. It was the strongest fort in America and cost six million dollars. Although it took twenty years to build it, a British fleet, with the aid of land troops, battered the thick stone walls into ruins in less than two months. By this victory, Great Britain closed the St. Lawrence River to French ships bringing troops and supplies to Quebec, and gained control of the fishing industry in Canadian waters.

Soldiers from the colonies crossed Lake Ontario in open boats to capture Fort Frontenac. The fall of this key position cut the water route to the Mississippi River and interfered with the Indians who sold their furs in Quebec.

Three years after Braddock's defeat, Washington went west again, this time with General Forbes who was so ill that he had to be carried on a litter. The capture of Fort Duquesne was an easy victory. When the troops arrived, the stockade was smoldering in ashes. The French garrison set fire to it when Indian scouts informed them that the approaching British soldiers were greater in number than the trees in the forest. The French retreated down the Ohio River, leaving the strategic triangle to the enemy. Washington had the satisfaction of helping to erect a log shelter on the spot, later known as Fort Pitt. General Forbes, a Scotsman, had named the place Pitt's Borough in honor of the British prime minister, a friend of the colonists. From this humble beginning grew the city of Pittsburgh, at the junction of the Allegheny and Monongahela Rivers. The control of the Ohio Valley passed into the hands of the British with the fall of Fort Duquesne.

In June of 1759, an English fleet of twenty-eight ships of war with transports carrying ten thousand land troops under Major-General Wolfe, sailed up the St.

MONUMENT ERECTED TO MONTCALM AND WOLFE, FRENCH AND BRITISH GENERALS WHO LOST THEIR LIVES IN THE BATTLE OF THE PLAINS OF ABRAHAM, September 13, 1759.

The inscription is in Latin: MORTEM VIRTUS COMMUNEM — FAMAM HISTORIA — MONUMENTUM POSTERITAS DEDIT (Courage gave them the same death; history, the same fame; posterity, the same monument.)

Province of Quebec Film Bureau

Lawrence River to Quebec. Located on a steep bluff overlooking the river, the city was well fortified.

After losing over five hundred men while attempting to unload soldiers and supplies on the opposite shore, the British ships moved up and down the river under fire from French guns, searching for a spot to land. At daybreak on the thirteenth of September, British troops in small boats discovered a steep trail poorly guarded. Although a French sentinel fired a gun, the soldiers climbed up the rocky path, hauled cannon, and sent word for others to follow them.

Due to heavy fog, it was the middle of the morning before Montcalm, the French commander of Quebec, saw the enemy lined up to fight on the Plains of Abraham behind the city. In the battle that followed, Wolfe died on the field. Montcalm, dashing forward on horseback to rally his troops, was wounded and died a few hours later. Quebec surrendered to the victorious British. Today Canada is a part of the British Commonwealth, but Quebec retains its old French atmosphere.

By the Treaty of Paris, signed in 1763 after eight years of war, Great Britain gained all of the French lands east of the Mississippi River except New Orleans and a few fishing islands off the coast of Newfoundland. France lost her empire in North America to Great Britain, her ancient rival with colonizing ways.

WHY DID THE BRITISH WIN?

GREAT BRITAIN had sea power and France did not. Many French ships carrying soldiers and supplies to New France were

95

captured or sunk in crossing the Atlantic. The British had the advantage in numbers because their colonies had twenty times as many persons as the French had in a territory twenty times as large. The French colonists made little or no attempt to rule themselves since most of their settlements were administered by trading companies with privileges granted by the King. In the British colonies, with more or less self-government, the people elected their own officials. In a way each British colony was a small republic, independent of the mother country, and often, too independent of one another. They were self-reliant and strong, taking action in peace and war without orders from their homeland.

In the conflict with the French the colonists learned a valuable lesson. They learned the necessity of working together for the common good of all. When this war appeared to be near at hand, Benjamin Franklin had proposed a plan of union at the Albany Congress, but it was not adopted. The King of England rejected the plan because it was too lenient. The colonies did likewise because it gave some authority to the King. The Albany meeting took place ten years after the Onondaga chief had advised the colonies to unite as the tribes of Iroquois had done. Although the war was unpopular in some of the colonies where it interfered with trade, the people were forced to help in fighting a common enemy and to share the cost of the conflict. After the peace had been signed, Benjamin Franklin declared in the House of Commons in England:

The colonies raised, paid and clothed near 25,000 men during the last war, a number equal to those sent from Britain, and far beyond their proportion. They went deeply into debt in doing this, and all their taxes and estates are mortgaged, for many years to come, for discharging this debt.

In sharing this burden, the colonists found new strength and gained more confidence in themselves. Soon after the Treaty of Paris was signed, settlers from the Atlantic seaboard crossed the mountains to find new homes in the territory France had ceded to Great Britain. They were there to claim this land when war broke out twelve years later between the colonies and the mother country. The French and Indian War turned out to be a dress rehearsal for a still greater conflict, the American War for Independence, that spread to this new frontier.

THROUGH CUMBERLAND GAP AND OVER THE WILDERNESS ROAD

TWO WAGON MENDERS in Braddock's army agreed to seek adventure beyond the mountains when the war with France had come to an end. The Scotch-Irish trader kept his word and included his young friend, Daniel Boone, in the hunting party that was going into Kentucky. Boone wrote, years later, in his autobiography:

It was on the first of May, in the year 1769, that I left my family in North Carolina, to wander through the wilderness of America in quest of the country of Kentucky . . . . On the seventh of June, we found ourselves on Red River . . . . From the top of the hill, we saw with pleasure, the beautiful level of Kentucky. . . . At this place we encamped and made a shelter, . . . and began to hunt.

The hunting party followed the Scotch-Irish trader and Boone into the wilderness country to find the rich furs that were there. They passed through a natural opening between the mountains, the Cumberland Gap.

Late one afternoon, near the Kentucky River, Boone and a companion were captured by the Indians hunting in the same country. On the seventh night, while the Indians slept, the captives escaped and made their way back to camp. The Scotch-Irish trader and two hunters with him had vanished. To this day it is not known what happened to them. Of the five men who went on this hunting trip, Daniel Boone was the only one who returned home, after an absence of two years. He had with him a pack of valuable skins. Boone, a natural woodsman, survived in the wilderness where others, not trained to live off nature, perished.

In January of 1775, Judge Henderson of North Carolina and nine associates formed a company and purchased the present state of Kentucky and part of Tennessee from the Cherokee Indians. The company then offered land for sale to homeseekers. Daniel Boone was hired to mark a trail for the settlers to follow enroute to their new lands beyond the mountains. Boone's party of sturdy woodsmen cut down trees, removed fallen timber, filled sinkholes, chopped underbrush, and burned thickets to blaze this narrow trail through two hundred miles of wilderness.

Boone's wilderness trail followed through Cumberland Gap, the natural gateway to the vast acres of unsettled lands that were called Kentucky. Many landseekers going to the West traveled through this gateway.

Before the roadbuilders had completed their work, pack trains of settlers were on the track behind them. In one party was Abraham Hanks, the uncle of Nancy Hanks, who came over the Wilderness Road fourteen years later, when she was only five years old. It is believed that this Nancy Hanks grew up to become the mother of Abraham Lincoln. William Calk kept a diary of this early journey over the Wilderness Road. He recorded in his diary that Abraham Hanks and his friend, Drake, had more than their share of bad luck and turned back.

There were few schools on the frontier, Many bright boys and girls had no opportunity to learn to read, write, and spell. William Calk had a little schooling, but not enough to spell correctly. Nor did he know the rules for capital letters, commas, and periods. Try reading from his diary exactly as he wrote it:

MARCH

1775, Mon. 13th – I set out from prince wm. to travel to caintuck on tuesday Night our company all got together at Mr. Priges on rapadon which was Abraham hanks philip Drake Eaneck Inoith Robert Whitledge and my Selfthear Abrams Dogs leg got broke by Drake's Dog.

thursed 30th – We set out again and went down to Elk gardin and there suplid our Selves With Seed Corn and irish tators then we went on a littel way I turned my hors to drive before me and he got scared ran away threw Down the Saddel Bags and broke three of our powder goards and Abrams beast Burst open a walet of corn and lost a good Deal and made a turrabel flustration amongst the Reast of the Horses Drakes mair run against a sapling and noct it down we cacht them all agin and went on . . . .

APRIL

Saturday 8th – We all pack up and started crost Cumberland Gap about one oclock this Day Met a good maney peopel turned Back for fear of the indians but our Company goes on Still with good courage . . .

tuesday 11th – this a very loury morning and like for Rain but we all agree to start Early and we cross Cumberland River and travel Down it about 10 miles through some turrabel cainbrakes as we went down abrams mair Ran into the River with her load and swam over he followed her and got on her and made her swim back agin – Mr. Drake

Baked Bread without washing his hands we Keep Sentry this Night for fear of the indians.

thursday 13th — Abram and Drake turn Back we go on and git to loral River . . .

thursday 20th — this morning is clear and cool. We start early and git Down to caintuck to Boons foart about 12 o'clock where we stop they come out to meet us and welcome us in with a voley of guns.

(Filson Club Publications)

Boone and the roadbuilders arrived first and started a settlement at Boonesborough. Their horses feasted upon the rich blue grass growing thick and long in the limestone soil on the banks of the Kentucky River. Today, this region is known as the blue grass country, a breeding center for race horses. The settlers lost no time. How did a settlement begin in a wilderness? Calk's diary told how:

tuesday 25th — in the eavening we git us a plaise at the mouth of the creek and begin clearing.

Wednesday 26th — We Begin Building us a house and a plaise of Defense to Keep the indians off this day we begin to live without bread.

Satterday 29th — We git our house kivered with Bark and move our things into it at Night and Begin housekeeping.

May, tuesday 2nd — I went out in the morning and killed a turkey and come in and got some on for my breakfast and then went and sot in to clearing for Corn.

The settlers would have little to eat except meat and wild greens until the first corn crop was harvested. By the middle of June, 1775 the fort of Boonesborough was ready. Log cabins, connected by high fences, formed a rectangle, with block houses at the four corners from which the settlers could fire upon Indians if attacked. Then Boone departed for the stockade on the Clinch River where he had left his large family. They had been forced back by an Indian attack in which his eldest son was killed.

Mrs. Boone and her daughters were the first white women on the banks of the Kentucky River. Daniel's tales of the beautiful Kentucky country with tall blue grass and rich soil lured others to follow him. During the summer more families arrived at Boonesborough. Women were the homemakers. For them, the men made tables, chairs, tubs, and washboards. With patchwork quilts and turkey-tail fans, the bare log cabins of Boonesborough began to look like homes. Other settlers went on to found Harrodsburg. Kentucky pioneers named another settlement Lexington when the news reached them about the Battle of Lexington, the first engagement in a war that would overtake the settlers on this western frontier.

MAP:

WA12r
Atlas of American History by Edgar B. Wesley

Chapter 8

A Family Quarrel Leads to War

BRITISH COLONIAL POLICY

SINCE KINGS HAD granted charters to the American colonies, the Government of England expected the settlers to work for the prosperity of the mother country. The colonists, however, were more interested in securing trade for themselves than for their homeland across the sea. Rivalry in trade provoked the long quarrel which led to the American Revolution.

In 1694 Sir Josiah Child, chairman of the East India Company, published a book defining British colonial policy. His words expressed the views of British merchants who had been gaining power in Parliament since the days of Queen Elizabeth I, when the big trading companies were started. He stated "that all colonies or plantations do endanger their mother-kingdoms, if the trades of such plantations are not confined by severe laws," because "the greatness of this kingdom depends upon foreign trade." He then explained why "New England is the most prejudicial [harmful] plantation to this kingdom."

I am now to write of a people whose frugality, industry, temperance, and the happiness of whose laws and institutions, do promise to themselves long life, with a wonderful increase of people, riches, and power. No man ought to envy that wisdom and virtue in others, — but rather to commend and admire it. Yet, I think it is the duty of every good man primarily to respect the welfare of his native country. Therefore, though I may offend some, — I cannot omit in the progress of this discourse to take notice of some particulars wherein Old England SUFFERS BY THE GROWTH OF THOSE COLONIES SETTLED IN NEW ENGLAND.

The southern colonies, being farming communities, sold their tobacco, rice, and timber in England. They bought their manufactured products from British merchants. This was what the British Government wanted. New England, with a rocky soil and long cold winters, was not a farming country. There, many people earned a living through fishing, trade, and shipbuilding. During the icy winter weather in New England, when fishing was not so profitable, both fishermen and boat owners turned to trading. The fishing sloops were loaded with salt, rum, molasses, bundles of cloth, hats, caps, stockings, iron kettles, wooden bowls, hooked rugs, and other items made in the homes and little shops of New England. The fishermen traded these wares for pork, corn, pitch, tar, leather, and other products

A New
DISCOURSE
OF
TRADE,

Wherein is Recommended feveral
weighty Points relating to Companies of Merchants.

The Act of NAVIGATION.
NATURALIZATION of Strangers.
And our Woollen Manufactures.
The
BALLANCE of TRADE.

And the Nature of Plantations, and their Confequen-
ces in Relation to the Kingdom, are ferioufly
Difcuffed.

And fome Propofals for erecting a Court of Merchants for determining Controverfies, relating to
Maritine Affairs, and for a Law for Transfer-
rance of Bills of Debts, are humbly Offered.

By Sir Joliah Child.

The fecond Edition.

London Printed, and fold by Sam. Crouch,
Tho. Horn, & Jof. Hindmarfh in Cornhill. 1694.

A NEW DISCOURSE OF TRADE

**This book written by Sir Josiah Child, Chair-
man of the East India Company, expressed the
views of British merchants of that time in England.
Their ideas on trade with the colonies became laws
in Parliament as Navigation Acts to regulate trade
with the colonists for the benefit of merchants in
England. The colonists objected to these laws,
claiming they gave the mother country an unfair
monopoly of their trade.**

in the Carolinas. In 1726, a fisherman-
trader chartered a fishing boat for his cargo
of sixty sheep, sixteen bales of coarse
homespun, furniture, and billiard tables
from New England, which he sold at a
profit in Charleston, South Carolina. Massachusetts made saddles and shoes for the
southern colonies. Connecticut exported

cheese and made woolens and linens, caps
and mittens.

British merchants complained that the
colonists were trading with one another instead of with the mother country. The enterprising Yankees went out for business
and found it. They formed their own trading companies, built their own ships, and
sold their wares in foreign lands. As early as
1694, Sir Josiah Child wrote in his book on
trade:

Many of our American commodities, especially
tobacco and sugar, are transported directly in
NEW ENGLISH shipping to Spain and other
foreign countries without being landed in England,
or paying any duty to His Majesty. This is a loss to
the King, to the navigation of OLD ENGLAND,
and to the English merchant in those ports where
NEW ENGLISH vessels trade. Since no custom
dues are paid in NEW ENGLAND, and great custom paid in OLD ENGLAND, the NEW ENGLISH
merchant will be able to sell cheaper than the OLD
ENGLISH merchant. And those who sell cheaper
will get the whole trade sooner or later.

This paragraph tells the whole story in a
few words. Instead of working for the
prosperity of the mother country, the
merchants of New England went into business for themselves. They became the competitors of merchants in the homeland. The
mother country felt that laws had to be
passed to enforce the British colonial
policy.

NAVIGATION ACTS FORCE
COLONISTS INTO MANUFACTURING

MOST OF THE TRADE laws dealt with
shipping and were known as Navigation
Acts. These laws were passed over a period
of nearly a hundred and fifty years. Their
purpose was to make the British merchants

rich at the expense of the colonies. No foreign vessels could bring goods directly to the colonies; colonists could not trade with foreign countries except under certain conditions; tobacco, cotton, indigo, and dye woods could be shipped only to England; European goods had to be shipped first to England, where a duty was paid, before going to the colonies; goods could be shipped only in British vessels manned by British subjects. Other restrictions of trade forbade the manufacture of goods in the colonies, that England made for export. These regulations, however, were not strictly enforced until the middle of the eighteenth century.

In 1731 a petition to the Board of Trade asked that the manufacture of woolens, hats, and shoes be stopped in the colonies. The importation of sheep was forbidden, but sheep were smuggled from Spain. Poor, indeed, was the farmer without his own fleece; and poor, indeed, was the farmer's wife without some yardage of hand-loomed woolen cloth. Furs were plentiful in America, and colonial hatters continued to do business. Colonial shoemakers were kept busy making footwear for their neighbors. As early as 1661 Virginia passed a law that any man found guilty of exporting a hide would be fined a thousand pounds of tobacco. Nearly all the colonies passed similar laws.

With timber near and plentiful, New Englanders went into the shipbuilding business. In the year of 1741 Massachusetts had about 400 vessels engaged in the fishing business. Nearly all these had been built in ports of New England. Cod fish was salted and dried for shipment to distant countries. Since there was no refrigeration, tons of fish spoiled in the process. The refuse was carried to the West Indies to be used for fertilizer. It was exchanged for molasses, a waste product on the sugar plantations. In New England the molasses was distilled into rum. This molasses and rum traffic became part of a triangular trade route which included the Guinea Coast of Africa, the West Indies, and New England. The rum distilled in New England was shipped to Africa, and there it was exchanged for Negro slaves. The slaves were then taken to the Americas and sold.

To stop this profitable trade, Parliament passed the Molasses Act in 1733. Any vessel caught in this trade was confiscated. This law did not stop the daring young skippers of Salem, Boston, and other ports. For thirty years ships from the colonies carried on the molasses trade with the Dutch and French West Indies. It was exciting and adventurous to outrun a British patrol and escape capture. Now and then, however, notices like this one appeared in the papers in Salem:

On Friday night last were brought in here as prizes, a large snow and a brig, lately taken by His Majesty's ship, Glasgow, Captain Allen, for being concerned in a contraband trade.

The New Englanders openly disobeyed the Navigation Acts and traded where they pleased, because the British Government could not keep enough vessels on the high seas to catch many of them. As a joke the General Court of Massachusetts laid a duty on English goods and a tax on English-built ships. Such impudence, though amusing, caused the dignified Lord Justices of England "to express their great displeasure."

The Navigation Acts and other trade laws were supposed to hinder the growth of manufacturing as well as foreign trade. The colonists were expected to sell raw

A COLUMN FROM THE ESSEX GAZETTE
Published in Salem, Massachusetts
August, 1768

By Capt. Samuel Grant, who arrived here laft Lord's Day, from Martinico, in 28 Days, are come to Hand, Copies of an Arret of the French King's Council of State of April 1, 1768; and an Ordinance of the King, dated the 9th of July laft, permitting foreign Veffels to import Timber of all Kinds, Dying Woods, Live Stock of all Kinds, green or tanned Hides, Furs, Pitch and Tar, Rice, Indian Corn, Beans, Peafe, Coffee, Sugar, Cotton and Cocoa, into any Harbour or Road of the Ifland of *St. Lucia.* The particular Articles and Regulations will pe publifhed in our next.

CUSTOM-HOUSE, Port of SALEM & MARBLEHEAD, Auguft 8.

INWARD ENTRIES ———— From

Saunders, Stanford,	Martinico.
Nabby, Dodge,	Guadaloupe.
Betfey, Boden,	Falmouth.
Union, Grant,	Martinico.
Alexander, Ellery,	Lifbon.

CLEARED OUT ———— For

Live Oak, Kidveal,	Weft-Indies.
Molly, Knight,	Newfoundland.
Endeavour, Harris,	St. John's.
Hitty, Burnham,	Barbados.
Nancy, Bartlet,	Weft-Indies.
Friendfhip, Pearfon,	Ditto.

OUTWARD BOUND ———— For

Patty, Archer,	Weft-Indies.
Polly, Bartlett,	Philadelphia.
Jofeph, Elkins,	Weft-Indies.

Salem, Auguft 23, 1768.
The Merchants and Traders of

this Town are defired (efpecially thofe concerned in importing Goods from *Great-Britain*) to meet at the *King's-Arm* Tavern this Evening, at feven o'Clock, to confider the prefent State of our Trade, &c.

WANTED, a half-decked Schooner, 2 or 3 Years old, between 60 and 80 Tons burthen. Any Perfon who has one to difpofe of, may hear of a Purchafer by enquiring of the Printer hereof.

Cuftom-Houfe, Bofton, Auguft 20.
Entered-In. *Meferut and Littlefield from Rhode-Ifland; Wetmore, Griffing and Lutler from New-London; Raymond from New-Haven; Smith from New-York; Joyne from Virginia; Cuffing and Taylor from No.Carolina; Emerfon from So. Carolina; Ford from Halifax; Ball, Turne and Axworth from Newfoundland; Lavner from Quebec; Saunders from Grenadoes; Crocker from Guadaloupe; Allen from St. Chriftophers; Hunter from St. Ubes; St. Barbe from Lifbon and Falmouth.*

Colonial papers prove that the Navigation Acts were not strictly enforced.

The first news item in the column notifies ship owners that timber, livestock, rice, and many other products can be sold in St. Lucia, a French possession in the West Indies. Such trade was forbidden by the Navigation Acts except under certain conditions.

In the list of ships coming and going in the harbor of Salem on August 8, 1768, some are bound for ports in the West Indies, and the others are returning from the same islands.

Any effort to enforce the Navigation Acts caused merchants and traders to meet and discuss new ways to evade them. In this column is a notice calling such a meeting at the King's Tavern.

A merchant adventurer advertises to buy a schooner.

The custom house at Boston lists the vessels arriving on August 20, 1768. Out of 21 ships, 16 were from ports in the British colonies of North America. This coastal traffic aided home industries and helped to unite the thirteen colonies.

materials to the mother country and to buy their manufactured products from the mother country. They were to make for themselves only those articles that they could not buy from Great Britain. This plan was generally accepted by nations as their colonial policy.

The main purpose of the trade laws was to keep the colonies dependent on the mother country. Since most of the colonists could not afford to buy many of the imported articles, they were forced to weave their own woolens and linens, make their own hats and shoes, and build their own furniture. Every house was a little factory, in so far as it produced these articles. In the end, these trade laws defeated their purpose and made the colonies more independent of the mother country.

HOME INDUSTRY PAVES
THE WAY TO INDEPENDENCE

IN THE SOUTH, where people lived in the country and towns were far apart, clothing and tools for the laborers were made on the big plantations. *A Perfect Description of Virginia,* published in 1649, mentioned a planter, Captain Mathews, one of the governing council of the colony:

He hath a fine house. He sowes yeerly store of hempe and flax and causes it to be spun. He keeps weavers, and hath a tan-house; causes leather to be dressed; hath eight shoemakers employed in this trade; hath forty Negro servants, and brings them up to trades in his house. He yeerly sowes abundance of wheat, barley, etc. The wheat he selleth at four shillings the bushell; kills stores of beeves, and sells them to victual the ships when they come thither; hath abundance of kine, a brave dairy, swine, and poltery. He married the daughter of Sir Thomas Hinton, lives bravely, and is a true lover of Virginia. He is worthy of much honour.

Each plantation had its own small factory that supplied daily needs. The produce that was left over was used to trade for china, silver, furniture, silks, and other luxuries imported from England. The southern planters were good customers of the British merchants.

Sixteen hundred and fifty yards of woolen, linen, and cotton cloth were made in Washington's weaving house at Mt. Vernon in the year 1767. Of this amount, about 450 yards were woven for neighbors who brought their own yarns to the weaving house. There were 1200 yards for use in Washington's household and for sale. To pay Washington for weaving fourteen yards of woolen cloth, one farmer gave him two turkeys and seven chickens. This system of trading farm products for manufactured articles was in common use in the South long after the Revolutionary War. In a Kentucky paper with a date line of September 12, 1829, a factory owner advertised that he would accept wool, wood, pork, lard, feathers, bacon, and any farm products in trade for carding, spinning, coloring, and weaving wool fleece brought to his factory. Not until the War Between the States destroyed the plantation system of home manufacturing did factory towns in the South begin to grow to any size.

Meanwhile, New England became a manufacturing country. During the winter months women and girls on New England farms carded, spun, wove, knitted, and sewed, making articles for use of the family and for sale to stores. The men and boys tanned leather, made shoes, built furniture,

A COLONIAL KITCHEN

In the early days, each member of the family worked to maintain the home for all. While the able-bodied men in the family were doing the heavy chores, women were toiling in the kitchen, the living room of the house. In this sketch, mother is cooking, grandmother is spinning, daughter is churning, grandfather is paring apples, and the "hired girl" is rolling the pie dough. Only the children have time to play.

tinkered with metals, and fashioned their own tools for field and workshop. Since the people could not make a living by farming, they needed to have industries to provide jobs. Towns had societies for raising funds to start factories. This notice was printed in a Boston paper on August 8, 1754:

THE COMMITTEE OF THE SOCIETY for encouraging industry and employing the poor, give public notice, that the annual meeting will be on Wednesday, August 14, when a sermon will be preached at the OLD SOUTH MEETING HOUSE by the Reverend Mr. John Barnard of Marblehead, at eleven o'clock in the forenoon. After the sermon, there will be a collection when such persons as do not belong to the society may have the opportunity of contributing what they think proper toward its encouragement. – All those who would be truly charitable are hereby invited to become members of the Society.

The bounty system encouraged business and industry. According to this system merchants offered prizes for the best weaving of linen, cotton, and woolen cloth, and for the largest number of yards woven in a given time. The public was asked to donate prizes for crews who caught the most fish in a single season in order to get more men to go into the fishing business. A notice in a Boston paper in 1754 instructed the owners of fishing schooners to meet at

FRANKLIN STOVE INVENTED IN 1742

In 1744, Benjamin Franklin printed and sold a pamphlet describing his fireplace, and extolling its merits. Franklin, the diplomat, was also a shrewd business man. The smiling face of the sun and the motto, "Alter Idem," suggests to the buyer that Franklin's fireplace will warm a room as the sun warms the earth, and even better, according to the poem.

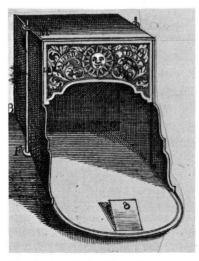

On the DEVICE of the NEW FIRE-PLACE,
A SUN; *with this Motto,* ALTER IDEM.
i.e. A fecond Self; or, *Another, the fame.*
By a Friend.

ANOTHER Sun! — 'tis true ; — but not THE SAME.
   Alike, I own, in Warmth and genial Flame :
But, more obliging than his elder Brother,
This will not fcorch in Summer, like *the other* ;
Nor, when fharp *Boreas* chills our fhiv'ringLimbs,
Will *this Sun* leave us for more Southern Climes ;
Or, in long Winter Nights, forfake us here,
To chear new Friends in t'other Hemifphere :
But, faithful ftill to us, this *new Sun's* Fire,
Warms when we pleafe, and juft as we defire.

Faneuil Hall, with proof of the quantity of fish caught by the crew of each vessel. It was an honor to win these prizes.

A town meeting in Salem issued this order to the two newly elected representatives, one of whom was the richest man in town, Richard Derby, merchant and ship owner:

We earnestly recommend you to promote the fishery, so material a branch of the business of this county, by every encouragement in your power.

On May 29, 1769 the town meeting of Marblehead, Massachusetts instructed the representatives, who had been elected on that day:

That you promote all you can every rational scheme for employing the poor in manufactures, in every part of this province.

The advertisements in Boston papers, a year before the French and Indian War broke out, listed many items for sale, some large and some small. Among these were the following: three copper kettles for soap-making; rice, sole leather, and deer-skins from South Carolina; 20,000 bricks; garden and flower seeds, fruit trees, herbs and garlic; looking glasses, pictures, spectacles, chinaware, tea, violins, flutes, toys, and silver; Connecticut pork by the barrel; choice Newcastle coal; window glass sold for cash or wheat; bar-iron and rod-iron; and a mill for twisting linens and woolens. One store advertised books sold cheaply for cash or traded for rum, pork, and grain. The list of books included the *Bible, Pilgrim's Progress, Arabian Nights, Aesop's Fables, Goody Two Shoes, World Turned Upside Down*, grammars, arithmetics, and spelling books. To a lesser extent the middle colonies had to develop industry in order to support their population. Pennsylvania had more indentured servants than any other colony. William Penn encouraged poor, hard-working people to settle in his "woodlands." His advertisements were cleverly written. This one appeared in an English paper:

The richness of the air, the navigable rivers, the increase of corn, the flourishing conditions of the city of Philadelphia make Pennsylvania the most glorious place . . . . Poor people, both men and women, can get three times the wages for their labor they can in England and Wales.

Many people who were skilled tradesmen came as indentured servants. It was necessary to provide shops and mills to give them employment, so that they could serve their time in labor to repay their passage to the New World. From its founding in 1682 Pennsylvania made rapid gains in manufacturing. In December of 1719, the first newspaper in the middle colonies began printing on paper made in the first mill of its kind, located on a creek near Germantown. It was the Rittenhouse mill, founded by a Dutch immigrant. Soon, paper from Pennsylvania mills was shipped to other colonies.

The waters of Wissahickon Creek, now in the city of Philadelphia, turned wheels for grinding corn into meal and wheat into flour. Bakers in nearby towns made ship's bread, called hardtack by the sailors, to supply the fishing fleets of New England and the vessels in the overseas trade. The industries of the colonies produced both goods and good will. This coastal trade helped to tie the colonies together.

The Navigation Acts had failed to yield the expected revenue because they were not generally enforced. Smuggling was almost universal. Even some of the King's governors ignored the offenders because the prosperity of their colonies depended upon smuggling. The Navigation Acts made lawbreakers out of many good citizens. Aware of the growing prosperity of the colonies, the British Government attempted a stronger enforcement of the Navigation Acts. They also levied more taxes. This strict policy took effect in the years following the French and Indian War.

Parliament maintained the right to tax the colonies for purposes of revenue because, in the opinion of the time, colonies existed for the benefit of the mother country. The colonists in America did not all agree with this point of view. Many insisted upon the right to work independently for their own personal welfare at home and abroad. These opposing ideas led to conflict. No nation dares to defend itself, at the risk of war, unless it has natural resources and is able to use them. Through home industry, many colonists were ready to defend their point of view. Thus they used their economic independence to gain political liberty.

TAXATION WITHOUT REPRESENTATION

THE COLONISTS fought the threat of oppression as much as oppression itself. In fact they enjoyed more freedom than any other people of the civilized world of 1775. With grim determination, they opposed every attempt to rob them of any liberty they had gained. The privilege of the colonial assemblies to levy taxes for support of colonial governments was zealously guarded. This privilege meant that the colonial assemblies voted the tax levy that paid the governor's salary in most of the colonies. If the King's executive opposed the will of the people, it was a simple matter to "forget" to vote the governor's pay. Thus, in some cases, the governor was little more than a figurehead.

Until the middle of the eighteenth century, the colonies had been taxed mainly by their chosen representatives in town meetings and colonial assemblies. They maintained that the British Parliament in London did not have the *right* to tax them because their own elected delegates were not seated in Parliament. The British Government's idea of representation was different. Both the King and Parliament declared the colonists were as much represented in the government as were the people of England. Among the members of Parliament were farmers, doctors, lawyers, merchants, and tradesmen. Therefore the British Government claimed that all farmers, all doctors, all lawyers, all merchants, and all tradesmen were represented whether they lived in England or the colonies.

The colonists refused to accept this class representation and demanded to be taxed *only* by men for whom they had personally voted and sent to their own assemblies. Since the taxes levied by Parliament were less for the colonists than for the Englishmen at home, the Government was amazed at the protest raised in the colonies. However, it was not so much the amount as the *principle* of taxation that the colonists opposed. They realized that the money obtained in taxes levied by the British Parliament could be used to support the governors and other royal officers in the colonies. These officers would then be free to enforce the will of the King.

The American War for Independence was not caused by the tyranny of England, but by a lack of understanding on the part of George III, Parliament, and the British people in general of the American point of view. Across an ocean three thousand miles away "something new" was growing. The colonists did not want these new freedoms to be taken away from them.

To enforce the Navigation Acts, Parliament made legal WRITS OF ASSISTANCE, which gave the King's officers authority to search a store or a home for smuggled goods. Those found with merchandise forbidden by any of the Navigation Acts were arrested and tried in an "admiralty court" by judges sent over from England. The defendants were denied a trial by jury. In a Boston court, on February 24, 1761 James Otis argued against these writs. Boldly, he stated that a law was void if it violated the human rights of man. Otis declared that the writs denied "the privilege of the house." He said:

A man who is quiet, is as secure in his house as a prince in his castle . . . . For flagrant crimes and in cases of great public necessity, the privilege may be infringed on.

The Stamp Act of 1765 fanned the flame of rebellion throughout the colonies. This law forced the colonists to buy stamps to put on legal papers, magazines, and newspapers. For example, a stamp costing about ten dollars was demanded for each college diploma. The colonists did not buy many of these stamps. In Boston, the boxes of stamps were seized and burned. In New York, an angry mob captured the governor's carriage and dragged it through the streets. In the carriage there was a dummy of the governor sitting with the devil. Then they burned the carriage in the open square

The TIMES are
Dreadful
Doleful
Dismal
Dolorous, and
DOLLAR-LESS.

THE

PENNSYLVANIA JOURNAL;
AND
WEEKLY ADVERTISER.

EXPIRING: In Hopes of a Refurrection to LIFE again.

Adieu Adieu to the LIBERTY of the PRESS

I am forry to be obliged to acquaint my readers that as the Stamp Act is feared to be obligatory upon us after the *firft of November* ensuing (The Fatal To-morrow), The publifher of this paper, unable to bear the Burthen, has thought it expedient to ftop awhile, in order to deliberate, whether any methods can be found to elude the chains forged for us, and efcape the infupportable flavery, which it is hoped, from the laft reprefentation now made againft that act, may be effected. Mean while I muft earneftly Requeft every individual of my Subfcribers, many of whom have been long behind Hand, that they would immediately difcharge their refpective Arrears, that I may be able, not only to fupport myfelf during the Interval, but be better prepared to proceed again with this Paper whenever an opening for that purpofe appears, which I hope will be foon. WILLIAM BRADFORD.

REACTION TO THE STAMP ACT

Copy from front page of a Philadelphia newspaper, October 31, 1765, the day before the Stamp Act was put into force.

Skull and crossbones mark the death of the paper printed by William Bradford, who refused to buy stamps. In mourning for the last edition, he wrote in one corner:

"The times are dreadful, doleful, dismal, dolorous, and dollarless."

in front of the governor's house. In the House of Burgesses in Virginia, Patrick Henry made a speech against the Stamp Act. He finished with:

"Caesar had his Brutus, Charles the First his Cromwell, and George the Third — "

"Treason!" interrupted the speaker of the house, seated on a high platform. "Treason! Treason!" echoed voices from the floor of the assembly.

" — may profit by their example." After completing the sentence, he waited until the hall was quiet, and added, defiantly:

"If THIS be treason, make the most of it."

These fiery outbursts aroused the people. They organized to defeat the law by refusing to buy British goods. Many colonists wore homespun garments with patriotic pride, scorning others who dressed in linens and woolens imported from England. The boycott caused unemployment and injured British trade. The merchants opposed the tax for another reason. They had to buy the revenue stamps to place on clearances of their ships from colonial ports. With so many complaints, Parliament repealed the Stamp Act after four and a half months. However, it was closely followed by the Declaratory Act, stating Parliament had the right to tax the colonies.

In 1767, the Townshend Acts levied a tax on glass, paper, paints and tea. Again the colonists resorted to boycott, refusing to buy, and signed non-importation agreements. Merchants who stocked British goods and raised their prices found their names printed in the papers. They were in disgrace and lost their customers. Public opinion had the force of actual law.

Nearly every edition of a colonial newspaper told of a gathering of spinners, usually at the home of a minister. The following news item is from *The Essex Gazette* of June 22, 1769. It is flattering praise:

It gives a noble prospect to see what a spirit of industry prevails at this day in the American young ladies, working willingly with their hands.

Yesterday morning, very early, the young ladies in the parish of the town called Chebacco to the number of 77, assembled at the house of the Reverend Mr. John Cleaveland with their spinning wheels. Though the weather that day was extremely hot, and many of the young ladies were about thirteen years of age, yet by six o'clock in the evening, they carded and spun 177 ten-knot skeins of yarn.

After the music of the wheels was over, Mr. Cleaveland entertained them with a sermon. He concluded by observing how the women might recover to the country the full and free enjoyment of all our rights, properties, and privileges, —

Unhappy Boston! see thy Sons deplore,
Thy hallow'd Walks besmear'd with guiltless Gore:
While faithless P—n and his savage Bands,
With murd'rous Rancour stretch their bloody Hands;
Like fierce Barbarians grinning o'er their Prey,
Approve the Carnage, and enjoy the Day.

If scalding drops from Rage from Anguish Wrung,
If speechless Sorrows lab'ring for a Tongue,
Or if a weeping World can ought appease
The plaintive Ghosts of Victims such as these;
The Patriot's copious Tears for each are shed,
A glorious Tribute which embalms the Dead.

But know, FATE summons to that awful Goal,
Where JUSTICE strips the Murd'rer of his Soul:
Should venalC—ts the scandal of the Land,
Snatch the relentless Villain from her Hand,
Keen Execrations on this Plate inscrib'd,
Shall reach a JUDGE who never can be brib'd.

Engrav'd Printed & Sold by PAUL REVERE BOSTON

The unhappy Sufferers were Mess.ᵈˢ SAM.ˡ GRAY SAM.ˡ MAVERICK, JAM.ˢ CALDWELL, CRISPUS ATTUCKS & PAT.ᵏ CARR
Killed. Six wounded two of them (CHRIST.ʳ MONK & JOHN CLARK) Mortally

Henry E. Huntington Library

THE BOSTON MASSACRE

On the night of March 5, 1770 a fire bell sounded, and about fifty or sixty youths rushed into the streets of Boston. It was a false alarm. The youths then began throwing snowballs at a British sentry on duty at the Custom House. Captain James Preston sent a squad of soldiers to his aid, and they were greeted with snowballs and jeers. The soldiers fired into the crowd to scatter the youths.

In this drawing, "engraved, printed and sold by Paul Revere" are listed the names of five killed and two who died later of wounds. As news of the "massacre" spread, drums beat, bells rang, and angry Bostonians poured into the streets. The British soldiers were arrested and jailed to be held for trial.

108

which is more than the men have been able to do, namely: BY LIVING, AS FAR AS POSSIBLE, UPON THE PRODUCE OF THIS COUNTRY; AND TO BE SURE TO LAY ASIDE THE USE OF ALL FOREIGN TEAS; BY WEARING ONLY CLOTHING OF THIS COUNTRY'S MANU-FACTURE.

Notices like this one from *The Essex Gazette* in Salem, Massachusetts appeared in the papers:

May 1, 1770
The selectmen have issued a warrant for calling a town meeting at 2 o'clock this afternoon, in order to determine upon proper measures to be pursued in the common cause, by preventing British goods being imported into this town, till the detested revenue acts are TOTALLY repealed. It is expected that every freeholder who regards the right of disposing of his own property as a blessing worth fighting for, will attend this meeting.

In November of 1772, Samuel Adams of Boston organized the Committees of Correspondence to send circular letters from town to town and colony to colony, keeping the people informed on happenings. The idea spread throughout the colonies. Groups of young men banded together as the Sons of Liberty. Riding their horses over country roads and wood-land trails, they carried these messages from Boston to Williamsburg.

On December 16, 1773, three British tea ships were moored in Boston harbor with cargoes that could not be unloaded until the tax on tea was paid. Although the tea had been so priced, that, after paying the tax, it would cost less than the tea smuggled in Dutch ships, the merchants dared not accept it with the tax. Crowds gathered in the streets. After dark, with a war-whoop, about fifty young men dressed as "wild Indians" – John Hancock was one

of them – boarded the vessels and threw three hundred and forty-two chests of Bohea into the water.

In haste, Samuel Adams sent messen-gers dashing in all directions with news of the Boston Tea Party. After notifying the Committee of Correspondence in New York City, Paul Revere arrived in Phila-delphia a few days before Christmas with the circular letter. A popular ditty celebrating the event ended with these lines:

We made a plaguey mess of tea
In one of the biggest dishes,
I mean we steeped it in the sea
And treated all the fishes.
Tol-le-lol-de-riddle, Tol-le-lol-de-ray,
And treated all the fishes.

On the tenth of May, 1774, news of the Port Bill reached Boston. The harbor of the city would be closed to all shipping on June first if the citizens did not pay for the tea destroyed by the "wild Indians." On that same day, the Committee of Corre-spondence sent letters to the neighboring towns of Boston inviting their Committees of Correspondence on the twelfth. Follow-ing their arrival, it was agreed to notify all the colonies and not to pay for the tea, which would be admitting that Parliament had the right to tax them. Samuel Adams wrote the circular letter and sent the riders in all directions. Again, Paul Revere carried the message as far as Philadelphia in six days.

Five days later, General Thomas Gage, the new military governor of Massachusetts arrived from London with orders to arrest the ringleaders of the "tea party." On the raw, rainy day, John Hancock, who was one of the leaders, boldly marched his cadets to the wharf to greet General Gage and escort him to welcoming ceremonies in Faneuil Hall. Sensing the temper of the people, Gage made no arrests. Wisely, he waited for more British troops to arrive.

Soon, help and sympathy arrived from other colonies as far away as Georgia. That colony sent rice, money and supplies of various kinds. All rallied to the needs of Boston, realizing that if Massachusetts lost its freedom, others would suffer the same fate. In order to show sympathy, church bells tolled throughout the colonies, and flags flew at half-mast.

The Journal of the House of Burgesses records what happened in Williamsburg, Virginia, when a messenger delivered the circular letter written by Samuel Adams.

HOUSE OF BURGESSES May 24, 1774
This House, being deeply impressed with apprehension of the great dangers to be derived to British America from the hostile invasion of the City of Boston in our sister colony of Massachusetts Bay, whose commerce and harbor are, on the first day of June next, to be stopped by an armed force, deem it highly necessary that the said first day of June be set apart, by the members of this House as a day of fasting, humiliation, and prayer, devoutly to implore the divine interposition for averting the heavy calamity which threatens destruction to our civil rights, and the evils of civil war; to give us one heart and one mind firmly to oppose, by all just and proper means, every injury to American rights . . . .

Ordered, therefore, that the members of this House do attend in their places at the hour of ten in the forenoon, on the said first day of June next, in order to proceed with the Speaker, and the Mace, to the church in this city, for the purposes aforesaid; and that the Reverend Mr. Price be appointed to read prayers, and the Reverend Mr. Gwatkin to preach a sermon suitable to the occasion.

Members of this House of Burgesses included five future signers of the Declaration of Independence: Thomas Jefferson, Benjamin Harrison, Thomas Nelson, Francis Lightfoot Lee and Richard Henry Lee. Four future delegates chosen to attend the Constitutional Convention were members, also, including George Washington.

George Mason, who was in Williamsburg on this day, sent word by a friend to his home, Gunston Hall: "please to tell my dear little family that I charge them to pay a strict attention to it (day of prayer and fasting) and that I desire my three eldest sons and my two oldest daughters may attend church in mourning, if they have it, as I believe they have." (They were wearing mourning for their mother, whose death occurred the year before.)

Closing the Port of Boston was only one of the "Intolerable Acts." In Massachusetts, judges were to be appointed by the crown; British soldiers accused of crime were to be tried in England; and town meetings could be called only by the Governor. Added to these was the Quebec Act which extended Canada into territory claimed by Massachusetts and other colonies.

A COMMON CAUSE UNITES THE COLONIES

JOHN DICKINSON — farmer, lawyer, statesman — wrote a series of newspaper articles for the Pennsylvania Chronicle in 1767 and 1768, under the title LETTERS FROM A FARMER. These letters, later printed in book form, were widely read in the colonies and in England where many people sympathized with the colonists. In France they were also popular in translation. What did the farmer say?

Let these truths be indelibly impressed on your minds — that we cannot be happy without being

WASHINGTON, HENRY, AND PENDLETON ENROUTE TO THE FIRST CONTINENTAL CONGRESS

On the last day of August in 1774, Patrick Henry and Edmund Pendleton arrived at Mount Vernon in time for breakfast with Washington. All day long, the three men discussed the problems facing the colonists. Early the next morning, they left on horseback for Philadelphia. These delegates from Virginia to the First Continental Congress arrived the evening before the meeting opened, and were present when the first session began at ten o'clock on Monday morning, September 5, 1774.

free — that we cannot be free without being secure in our property — that we cannot be secure in our property, if, without our consent, others may as by right take it away.

In common with most colonial writers, the farmer agreed that "TAXATION WITHOUT REPRESENTATION IS TYRANNY," which became a slogan of the Revolutionary War. Dickinson wrote:

Here then, let my countrymen ROUSE themselves, and behold the ruin hanging over their heads. If they ONCE admit, that Great Britain may lay duties upon her exportations to us, FOR THE PURPOSE OF LEVYING MONEY ON US ONLY, she then will have nothing to do, but

to lay those duties on the articles which she prohibits us to manufacture — and the tragedy of American liberty is finished.

The unity gained through a common problem led to calling the First Continental Congress, to meet in Philadelphia in September, 1774. Delegates were present from every colony except Georgia. The first to arrive were the South Carolinians, who came by boat. The men from New England traveled by stagecoach and on horseback. Their journey was a march of triumph. In towns along the way, church bells were rung, salutes were fired, and feasts were spread in their honor. Massachusetts chose Samuel Adams and his

111

cousin, John Adams, as two of the five delegates from the colony. One of the Pennsylvanians was John Dickinson, author of the well-known Farmer's Letters. George Washington, Edmund Pendleton, and Patrick Henry left Mt. Vernon and rode together on horseback to Philadelphia to join other delegates sent to the meeting from Virginia.

The fifty-five delegates to this congress sent resolutions to King George and Parliament, stating their rights as British subjects. One of the demands was the right to be taxed by their own elected assemblies. No mention was made of separation from the mother country, but the last few

An old print of St. John's Church in Richmond, Virginia in which Patrick Henry urged the colonists to fight for their rights in his famous speech, closing with these words:

"Give me liberty or give me death."

St. John's Church.[1]

lines carried a veiled threat, a resolve not to buy or use goods made in England until the unjust laws were repealed. Probably the most important act of this First Continental Congress was a vote to meet again in May of the next year, 1775. By that time war had begun.

In St. John's Church of Richmond, Virginia, the second revolutionary convention of Virginia met to consider military plans for defense. At this meeting on March 23, 1775 a burgess made his famous "We-Must-Fight" speech.

The delegates filled the auditorium of the little church, leaving the end gallery for the anxious spectators. The day was warm and the windows were open. A tall thin man with shoulders slightly stooped arose from his seat in the third pew on the north side and walked awkwardly down the aisle. In the pulpit of St. John's Church, the sun-tanned face of this man of the woods seemed strangely out of place. He was Patrick Henry, fiddler, hunter, fisherman, farmer, lawyer, elected from a frontier county in Virginia. Among the delegates he faced were two Virginia planters, George Washington and Thomas Jefferson. They knew his fighting spirit from other speeches he had made. What would he say?

Henry recited the wrongs suffered by the colonists under "taxation without representation," and declared there was no hope for peace. The closing lines of his speech are well known in American history:

Is life so dear, or peace so sweet, as to be purchased at the price of chains and slavery? — I know not what course others may take; but as for me, give me liberty or give me death.

The words of the fiery orator stunned his listeners. Patrick Henry walked to his

PATRICK HENRY 1736-1799

seat in the third pew in tomb-like silence. Then from scattered spots in the church, men arose to agree with him. Most of the delegates were silent and solemn, but they voted for his resolutions to arm for defense.

Later, when Henry asked for volunteers to gather for drill on the grounds of the Culpepper Court House, three hundred and fifty minutemen came, armed with knives, tomahawks, and rifles. They carried a yellow flag with a coiled rattle-snake and the words, "Don't tread on me!" Throughout the war soldiers from Culpepper and several other counties in Virginia wore the motto, LIBERTY or DEATH, embroidered in white on their green homespun shirts.

British troops were quartered in the city of Boston, the trouble center, and British warships were anchored in the bay. Samuel Adams and John Hancock, who had been elected to the Second Continental Congress, were hiding in Lexington until they were ready to leave for the meeting. The British commander, General Gage, learned of their hiding place and sent troops to capture the trouble makers who were to be sent to England for trial. The same scouting party had orders to capture the guns and powder which the colonists had stored at Concord. A watchman in the tower of North Church saw the troops crossing the Charles River in boats. With a lantern, he gave the signal which sent William Dawes and Paul Revere dashing through the countryside on horseback to awaken the people. Adams and Hancock were aroused by Paul Revere who was shouting, "The regulars are coming!" Before daylight the two delegates from Massachusetts were on their way to Philadelphia to serve in the Second Continental Congress. This Congress held together the thirteen separate colonies in the War for Independence.

The British colonies were largely settled by people who had revolted against their living conditions in other lands. They were rebels, in a sense, who had the courage to flee from want and persecution, and face the perils of a wilderness to seek a better form of life. When they found a better way, they fought to keep it. Their children, grandchildren, and great-grandchildren did not want any monarch to change their way of life. They had plowed their own land, built their own homes, and made their own clothes. They had hunted in the forests, fished in the streams, and slept under the stars. Who was their master?

Chapter 9

The Revolutionary War

THE WAR BEGINS
IN THE NORTHERN COLONIES

ON TUESDAY NIGHT, April 18, 1775, about midnight, General Gage dispatched troops on a supposedly secret mission to capture the cannon and military supplies at Concord. As the infantry approached Lexington, the ringing of bells and the roll of drums warned the British regulars that their march was known. By five o'clock in the morning of April 19, about a hundred colonists with loaded muskets were gathered on the Lexington green near the meeting house. Scarlet uniforms appeared in the gray morning light. The soldiers halted to load their guns. The colonial militia did not budge, as they were under orders not to fire the first shot.

"Disperse, you villains! Lay down your arms!" called out Major Pitcairn, the British officer in charge.

The colonists did not obey immediately. Pitcairn gave the order to surround the militia. In the confusion, shots were fired. Three British soldiers were wounded and eight militiamen were killed. The British continued the march to Concord where they destroyed a few cannon, burned sixteen new carriage wheels, and chopped

down a liberty pole. Most of the supplies had been hidden in the woods. When British soldiers began to tear off the planks of the bridge crossing the river, militiamen gathered to stop the destruction, and shots were fired on both sides. As such action had not been anticipated, British officers ordered a retreat to Boston for further orders. Along the way, the regulars were fired upon from behind walls and trees, houses and barns, by marksmen who seemed "to drop from the clouds." During the eventful day, the British lost 65 killed, 183 wounded, and 28 who were made prisoners. The colonists or provincials had 49 killed, 39 wounded, and 5 who were missing. Thus began a long and bitter struggle, the American War for Independence.

BREED'S HILL IS ATTACKED

COLONEL WILLIAM PRESCOTT, with orders to fortify Bunker Hill, decided to include Breed's Hill and began there. All night soldiers were busy building defenses of earth and, as protection from heavy shells, walls made of rail fences stuffed with newly cut grass. Before they could get

114

to Bunker Hill, the battle began on Breed's Hill. One of the officers, Israel Putnam, who had hurried to Boston from his farm in Connecticut, took command under Prescott. Smoking a pipe, "Old Put," who had served in the French and Indian War, walked back and forth among his men shouting the order, "Don't one of you shoot till you see the white of their eyes!" Ammunition was scarce. The British charged the hill three times before the patriots ran out of powder. Although troops were arriving and some were at work building defenses on Bunker Hill, the actual battle of that name was fought on Breed's Hill.

In this battle, the British lost one-third of their men, killed or wounded. Gage was replaced in Boston by General Howe who had led the British troops on three charges up Breed's Hill. The Americans suffered a great loss in the death of Dr. Joseph Warren, a political leader as well as a physician. Boston was occupied by British troops and war had begun, not only for Massachusetts but for all the thirteen colonies. The colonies were not united in their determination to prosecute the war. The burden of the conflict fell upon the Second Continental Congress meeting in Philadelphia, with John Hancock presiding.

Two days before the Battle of Bunker Hill, Congress had resolved to appoint a commander for the American armies which were being recruited from volunteers. A delegate from Maryland nominated Colonel George Washington of Virginia, who was unanimously elected commander-in-chief of the colonial forces. In accepting the appointment, Washington said:

Mr. President, Though I am truly sensible of the high honor done me in this appointment, yet I feel

SKIRMISH AT LEXINGTON

Among the Minutemen was an artist who made this sketch of the battle from eye-witness accounts. The largest building was the meeting house; the one with two chimneys, the tavern. Major Pitcairn, on horseback, is ordering his British regulars to fire upon the Minutemen who had gathered on the village green during the night. However, historians have not been able to prove who fired the first shot.

great distress, from a consciousness that my abilities and military experience may not be equal to the extensive and important trust. However, as the Congress desire it, I will enter upon the momentous duty, and exert every power I possess in their service, and for the support of the glorious cause. —As to pay, sir, I beg leave to assure the Congress that, as no pecuniary consideration could have tempted me to accept the arduous employment at the expense of my domestic ease and happiness, I do not wish to make any profit from it. I will keep an exact amount of my expenses. Those, I doubt not, they will discharge, and that is all I desire.

On the twenty-first of June, Washington left Philadelphia, arriving in New York four days later. It was there that he first heard of the battle on Breed's Hill in Boston, on June seventeenth. At nine o'clock on the morning of July 3, 1775, on Cambridge Common, Washington took command of the Continental Army, an untrained group of men from all walks of life. Several days later, Washington called a council of his officers, who voted to maintain the siege of Boston. During the remainder of the summer, neither army felt strong enough to make an attack. Both followed a purely defensive policy. Washington was busy establishing discipline and training raw recruits to fill his regiments, and he also gave much attention to outfitting privateers to harass the enemy. The year ended without a major battle.

However, when Washington took command in Cambridge, Massachusetts, the "Green Mountain Boys" who had captured Crown Point and Ticonderoga were back on their New England farms after a brief fling at war. Benedict Arnold, one of the officers at Ticonderoga, was anxious to proceed with the invasion of Canada before the forces of Sir Guy Carleton, governor of that British province, were increased with regiments from overseas.

About the middle of August in 1775, a committee from the Continental Congress visited Washington at his headquarters. There a plan was made to invade Canada with armies approaching from two directions. Major General Philip Schuyler, belonging to a Dutch patroon family with a large estate near Albany, was given command of one army. He was to advance north through the Hudson Valley to capture Montreal. Benedict Arnold took charge of 1100 hardy men detached from Washington's army. He left Cambridge in the middle of September to follow the route of the Kennebec River in Maine. He planned to join forces with Schuyler for the attack upon Quebec.

Arnold's men started up the Kennebec in flat-bottomed boats which they paddled up stream, carried around seventeen waterfalls, and pushed through swamps. Hastily built from green lumber, the boats leaked and supplies were ruined. Sometimes, the men waded in slushy swamps up to their armpits during storms of rain, snow, and sleet. The troops depended upon salmon trout for food, although sometimes they chewed on their moccasins to ease the pangs of hunger. One company roasted the captain's dog. Arnold and a party went ahead to buy food from French Canadians, who were friendly but not much interested in joining the colonial armies. However, they took sick and wounded men into their homes and cared for them.

By the time Arnold's army reached the St. Lawrence River, one fourth of the troops had been lost from exposure or desertion. With bare feet on frozen ground, this small force appeared before the fort in Quebec where Arnold attempted an assault. The British, snug and warm inside, made no reply, leaving Arnold and his invaders out in the cold Canadian winter. Then the Americans retreated to await the army from the south.

Meanwhile, Schuyler had been forced by illness to turn over his command to his Brigadier, Richard Montgomery, a more aggressive officer. Early in December, Montgomery joined Arnold with only about half the number of troops expected, but he brought the uniforms of captured British soldiers to clothe Arnold's tattered army. On a dark night when heavy snow was falling, about a thousand Americans stormed the citadel of Quebec. When light dawned on the following morning, the last day of December in 1775, Montgomery's body was found lying half buried in the deep snow. Arnold suffered a leg wound and was carried to the rear. Daniel Morgan, commander of Virginia riflemen, took his place. Continuing the attack, Morgan and about 400 of his soldiers, fought until they were surrounded, captured, and held as prisoners. Later Morgan was exchanged and returned to Washington's army. Carleton,

116

governor of Canada, treated his prisoners with extraordinary kindness, and ordered Montgomery to be buried with military honors. Storms, swamps, freezes, sickness, and desertions made the invasion of Canada a dismal failure.

BRITISH EVACUATE BOSTON

HOWEVER, THE Canadian campaign aided Washington in the siege of Boston. Following is an excerpt from a letter written by Ethan Allen to the Massachusetts Congress (Council of War):

Ticonderoga, May 11, 1775
GENTLEMEN: I have to inform you with pleasure unfelt before, that on break of day of the tenth of May, 1775, by the order of the General Assembly of the Colony of Connecticut, took the fortress of Ticonderoga by storm. The soldiery was composed of about one hundred GREEN MOUNTAIN BOYS, and near fifty veteran soldiers from the Province of the Massachusetts Bay .... As to the cannon and warlike stores, I hope they may serve the cause of liberty instead of tyranny .... From, gentlemen, your most obedient humble servant,
— ETHAN ALLEN

In November of that year, Washington sent General Knox north to bring back the sorely needed armaments that Ethan Allen mentioned. He returned with 42 sleds, loaded with 14 mortars, 39 cannons, one barrel of flints, and more than a ton of lead. With this added equipment, Washington decided to bombard Boston although British warships in the harbor had over 150 guns. Months before, the Continental Congress had given Washington the authority to destroy the city, if necessary, to dislodge Howe's army. John Hancock personally urged the bombard-

ment although he would probably suffer the heaviest loss, being one of the largest landowners in Boston.

Early in February of 1776, the arrival of ten militia regiments boosted Washington's army to 17,000 men. Many of the recruits had received little or no training and were not dependable in battle. However, the attack could not be delayed. Howe was expecting reinforcements from Ireland and Halifax. During the first week in March, on a moonlit night, Dorchester Heights was fortified with cannon pointing toward the city.

A few days later General Howe agreed to evacuate Boston to save the city and its inhabitants from gunfire. A smallpox epidemic sweeping through the city hastened Howe's withdrawal. The disease was spreading among his troops. Word was sent to Washington that the retreating army would not fire the city if the troops were not harassed while embarking upon vessels in the harbor. The patriots calmly watched the departure. About a thousand loyalists fled with the soldiers. On the seventeenth of March, a fleet of more than a hundred ships sailed from Boston Harbor for Halifax. The Tory refugees so crowded the vessels that Howe left behind 250 cannon, more than 3000 tons of coal, over 5000 bushels of grain, 100 barrels of oil, and 150 horses, a boon to the poorly supplied patriots.

Since Washington did not know the destination of Howe's fleet, he dispatched the major portion of his army to defend New York, thinking that port would be invaded by the fleeing British army. He left Boston on the fourth of April, leaving a few regiments to defend the city. The war moved into the middle colonies, where more supplies could be obtained.

THE DECLARATION OF INDEPENDENCE

IN JANUARY OF 1776, the Massachusetts General Court passed this resolution:

As the happiness of the People is the sole end of Government, so the consent of the People is the only foundation of it, — . Therefore, every act of Government — against or without the consent of the People is injustice, usurpation, and tyranny.

This statement was read in court, in town meetings, and in churches. The New Englanders and the Virginians were ready to declare independence before a majority of the people in the middle colonies would accept the idea. The loyalists were strong in New York and Pennsylvania. Many staunch patriots believed it was wise to remain colonists of Great Britain if King and Parliament would meet their demands for justice and liberty. Among these was John Dickinson, author of the widely-read Farmer's Letters. John and Samuel Adams of Massachusetts, George Washington and Thomas Jefferson of Virginia, and Benjamin Franklin of Pennsylvania did not agree with him.

In their homes, at the crossroads, and in town meetings, the colonists argued for and against independence. On April 12, 1776, North Carolina took the lead by instructing her delegates in Congress to vote for a complete separation from England. Rhode Island was second. On May 15, Virginia declared her own independence of England. Virginia instructed her representatives in Congress to ask all thirteen colonies to do likewise. Only five days later, the neighboring colonies of Maryland and Delaware voted against independence. It was June before the Second Continental Congress felt that public opinion would support a declaration of independence. The following is copied from the Journals of the Second Continental Congress:

TUESDAY, June 11, 1776
RESOLVED, That the committee to prepare the declaration, consist of five members:
The members chosen, Mr. Thomas Jefferson, Mr. John Adams, Mr. Benjamin Franklin, Mr. Roger Sherman, and Mr. Robert Livingston.
RESOLVED, that a committee be appointed to prepare and digest the form of a federation to be entered into between these colonies.
RESOLVED, That a committee be appointed to prepare a plan of treaties to be proposed to foreign powers.

Independence made necessary a central government with treaty-making powers. Six months before, Franklin had presented a plan to unite the colonies but it was voted down. Many people felt that a strong central government might rob them of the liberty they enjoyed in their own colonies.

When the committee of five met to draft a declaration of independence, John Adams and Thomas Jefferson were nominated for the task. Each one politely suggested that the other one do it. Finally, John Adams insisted that Jefferson pen the document, remarking "you can write ten times better than I." John Adams was the better speaker, but Thomas Jefferson could put strong words on paper. Seventeen days later, Jefferson's draft was read and debated in Congress, and suggestions were made for changes. On July 4, 1776, the final version was read to Congress and approved unanimously, except by New York whose delegates had not been instructed to vote for independence.

THE DECLARATION OF INDEPENDENCE

In Congress July 4, 1776

The Unanimous Declaration of the Thirteen United States of America

When in the Course of human events, it becomes necessary for one people to dissolve the political bands which have connected them with another, and to assume among the powers of the earth, the separate and equal station to which the Laws of Nature and of Nature's God entitle them, a decent respect to the opinions of mankind requires that they should declare the causes which impel them to the separation.

We hold these truths to be self-evident, that all men are created equal, that they are endowed by their Creator with certain unalienable Rights, that among these are Life, Liberty and the pursuit of Happiness. That to secure these rights, Governments are instituted among Men, deriving their just powers from the consent of the governed. That whenever any Form of Government becomes destructive of these ends, it is the Right of the People to alter or to abolish it, and to institute new Government, laying its foundation on such principles and organizing its powers in such form, as to them shall seem most likely to effect their Safety and Happiness. Prudence, indeed, will dictate that Governments long established should not be changed for light and transient causes; and accordingly all experience hath shewn, that mankind are more disposed to suffer, while evils are sufferable, than to right themselves by abolishing the forms to which they are accustomed. But when a long train of abuses and usurpations, pursuing invariably the same Object, evinces a design to reduce them under absolute Despotism, it is their right, it is their duty, to throw off such Government, and to provide new Guards for their future security. Such has been the patient sufferance of these Colonies; and such is now the necessity which constrains them to alter their former Systems of Government. The history of the present King of Great Britain is a history of repeated injuries and usurpations, all having in direct object the establishment of an absolute Tyranny over these States. To prove this, let Facts be submitted to a candid world.

He has refused his Assent to Laws, the most wholesome and necessary for the public good.

He has forbidden his Governors to pass Laws of immediate and pressing importance, unless suspended in their operation till his Assent should be obtained; and when so suspended, he has utterly neglected to attend to them.

He has refused to pass other laws for the accommodation of large districts of people, unless those people would relinquish the right of Representation in the Legislature, a right inestimable to them and formidable to tyrants only.

He has called together legislative bodies at places unusual, uncomfortable, and distant from the depository of their public Records, for the sole purpose of fatiguing them into compliance with his measures.

He has dissolved Representative Houses repeatedly, for opposing with manly firmness his invasions on the rights of the people.

He has refused for a long time, after such dissolutions, to cause others to be elected; whereby the Legislative powers, incapable of Annihilation, have returned to the People at large for their exercise; the State remaining in the meantime exposed to all the dangers of invasion from without, and convulsions within.

He has endeavored to prevent the population of these States; for that purpose obstructing the Laws for Naturalization of Foreigners; refusing to pass others to encourage their migrations hither, and raising the conditions of new Appropriations of Lands.

He has obstructed the Administration of Justice, by refusing his Assent to Laws for establishing Judiciary powers.

He has made Judges dependent on his Will alone, for the tenure of their offices, and the amount and payment of their salaries.

He has erected a multitude of New Offices, and sent hither swarms of Officers to harass our people, and eat out their substance.

He has kept among us, in times of peace,

Standing Armies without the Consent of our legislatures.

He has affected to render the Military independent of and superior to the Civil power.

He has combined with others to subject us to a jurisdiction foreign to our constitution, and unacknowledged by our laws; giving his Assent to their Acts of pretended Legislation:

For quartering large bodies of armed troops among us:

For protecting them, by a mock Trial, from punishment for any Murders which they should commit on the Inhabitants of these States:

For cutting off our Trade with all parts of the world:

For imposing Taxes on us without our Consent:

For depriving us in many cases of the benefits of Trial by Jury:

For transporting us beyond Seas to be tried for pretended offenses:

For abolishing the free System of English Laws in a neighbouring Province, establishing therein an Arbitrary government, and enlarging its Boundaries so as to render it at once an example and fit instrument for introducing the same absolute rule into these Colonies:

For taking away our Charters, abolishing our most valuable laws, and altering fundamentally the Forms of our Governments:

For suspending our own Legislatures, and declaring themselves invested with power to legislate for us in all cases whatsoever.

He has abdicated Government here, by declaring us out of his Protection and waging War against us.

He has plundered our seas, ravaged our Coasts, burnt our towns, and destroyed the lives of our people.

He is at this time transporting large Armies of foreign Mercenaries to complete the works of death, desolation and tyranny, already begun with circumstances of Cruelty and perfidy scarcely paralleled in the most barbarous ages, and totally unworthy the Head of a civilized nation.

He has constrained our fellow Citizens taken Captive on the high Seas to bear Arms against their Country, to become the executioners of their friends and Brethren, or to fall themselves by their Hands.

He has excited domestic insurrections amongst us, and has endeavored to bring on the inhabitants of our frontiers, the merciless Indian Savages, whose known rule of warfare is an undistinguished destruction of all ages, sexes and conditions.

In every stage of these Oppressions We have Petitioned for Redress in the most humble terms: Our repeated Petitions have been answered only by repeated injury. A Prince, whose character is thus marked by every act which may define a Tyrant, is unfit to be the ruler of a free people.

Nor have We been wanting in attentions to our British brethren. We have warned them from time to time of attempts by their legislature to extend an unwarrantable jurisdiction over us. We have reminded them of the circumstances of our emigration and settlement here. We have appealed to their native justice and magnanimity, and we have conjured them by the ties of our common kindred to disavow these usurpations, which would inevitably interrupt our connections and correspondence. They too have been deaf to the voice of justice and of consanguinity. We must therefore, acquiesce in the necessity which denounces our Separation, and hold them, as we hold the rest of mankind, Enemies in War, in Peace Friends.

WE, THEREFORE, the REPRESENTATIVES of the UNITED STATES OF AMERICA, IN GENERAL CONGRESS, Assembled, appealing to the Supreme Judge of the world for the rectitude of our intentions, do, in the Name, and by the authority of the good People of these Colonies, solemnly PUBLISH and DECLARE, That these United Colonies are, and of Right ought to be FREE AND INDEPENDENT STATES; that they are Absolved from all Allegiance to the British Crown, and that all political connection between them and the State of Great Britain, is and ought to be totally dissolved; and that as FREE AND INDEPENDENT STATES, they have full Power to levy War, conclude Peace, contract Alliances, establish Commerce, and to do all other Acts and Things which INDEPENDENT STATES, may of right do. And for the support of this Declaration, with a firm reliance on the protection of Divine Providence, We mutually pledge to each other our Lives, our Fortunes, and our sacred Honor.

When the document had been engrossed on parchment, each member of Congress signed his name with the delegates of the state he represented. (Their ages and occupations or professions were added by the author. The average age was forty-four.)

Massachusetts

John Hancock, President	39	Business
Samuel Adams	54	Politics
John Adams	41	Law
Robert Treat Paine	45	Law
Elbridge Gerry	32	Business

New Hampshire

Josiah Bartlett	47	Medicine
William Whipple	46	Business
Matthew Thornton	62	Medicine

Rhode Island

Stephen Hopkins	69	Business
William Ellery	49	Law

Connecticut

Roger Sherman	55	Law
Samuel Huntington	44	Law
William Williams	45	Government
Oliver Wolcott	50	Government

New York

William Floyd	42	Agriculture
Philip Livingston	60	Business
Francis Lewis	63	Business
Lewis Morris	50	Agriculture

New Jersey

Richard Stockton	46	Law
John Witherspoon	54	Ministry
Francis Hopkinson	39	Law
John Hart	68	Agriculture
Abraham Clark	50	Government

Pennsylvania

Robert Morris	42	Business
Benjamin Rush	31	Medicine
Benjamin Franklin	70	Diplomacy
John Morton	52	Government
George Clymer	37	Business
James Smith	57	Law
George Taylor	60	Manufacturing
James Wilson	34	Law
George Ross	46	Law

Delaware

Caesar Rodney	48	Government
George Read	43	Law
Thomas McKean	42	Law

Maryland

Samuel Chase	35	Law
William Paca	36	Law
Thomas Stone	33	Law
Charles Carroll of Carrollton	39	Agriculture

Virginia

George Wythe	50	Law
Richard Henry Lee	44	Agriculture
Thomas Jefferson	33	Law
Benjamin Harrison	36	Agriculture
Thomas Nelson, Jr.	38	Government
Francis Lightfoot Lee	42	Agriculture
Carter Braxton	40	Agriculture

North Carolina

William Hooper	34	Law
Joseph Hewes	46	Business
John Penn	35	Law

South Carolina

Edward Rutledge	27	Law
Thomas Heyward, Jr.	30	Law
Thomas Lynch, Jr.	27	Law
Arthur Middleton	33	Agriculture

Georgia

Button Gwinnett	41	Agriculture
Lyman Hall	52	Medicine
George Walton	36	Law

INDEPENDENCE HALL, PHILADELPHIA, PENNSYLVANIA IN 1876

In that year, the Centennial Exposition was held in Philadelphia to celebrate the one-hundredth anniversary of The Declaration of Independence.

A number of these men who pledged their lives and fortunes lost either or both in the war. On their way to Charleston in 1780, British soldiers ransacked the beautiful home of Arthur Middleton, destroyed his collection of paintings, and damaged the house while he was serving in the army defending Charleston. When that city fell, Middleton was captured and held on a British prison ship in the harbor. When the British invaded Georgia, Lyman Hall moved his family north. His property was destroyed. Richard Stockton was also captured by the British and confined in a military prison in New York, where ill treatment wrecked his health and hastened his death. British soldiers burned his fine library, drove off his horses and cattle, and laid waste his farm near Princeton, New Jersey.

The Declaration of Independence stated the principles of government based on the

THE LIBERTY BELL
INDEPENDENCE HALL – PHILADELPHIA
"Proclaim Liberty throughout all the land unto all the inhabitants thereof."

God-given human rights of man; cited examples proving that the British government had interfered with these rights; and justified the colonies, in defense of these human rights, to declare their independence.

John Hancock, President of the Second Continental Congress, and Charles Thomson, the Secretary, signed their names. That was all. Business went on as if nothing extraordinary had happened. Congress ordered copies to be printed and sent to the assemblies of the thirteen states, to councils of safety, and to commanding officers of the continental troops. With an order to sell twenty-five pounds of powder to a man in North Carolina, the day's business came to an end. The meeting "adjourned to 9 o'clock tomorrow."

A few days later, Philadelphia celebrated. A crowd gathered in the statehouse yard to hear the Declaration of Independence read to them. The bell in the tower rang the news and church bells joined the celebration. Soldiers paraded on the common and fired salutes. It was a gala day.

Although the United States of America had declared its independence, the new nation had yet to win its freedom by force of arms. The grim duty of providing for this necessity fell largely upon the Second Continental Congress. The delegates could only ask for men and supplies, as they did not have enough authority to compel obedience to any demands.

MEN AND SUPPLIES
FOR A CONTINENTAL ARMY

WHEN THE Second Continental Congress met on May 10, 1775, fighting had already begun between British and colonial troops. The members had been sent to this meeting in Philadelphia to demand certain rights from the King of England. Upon arrival, they found a war on their hands. Since there was no national government, as each colony was separate, this body of men fell heir to the difficult task of raising and supplying an armed force to wage war with Great Britain. It took arms to equip a soldier, ammunition to fire the guns, and saltpetre to make the gunpowder. Since there were no large mills for manufacturing saltpetre when war broke out, the people in every community searched for the earth containing the necessary minerals, and refined it with crude home-made apparatus. Bounties were offered for the product, and men were encouraged to become munitions-makers. Advertisements like the following appeared in colonial papers:

THE READING OF
THE DECLARATION OF INDEPENDENCE
The Declaration of Independence was received with loud cheers when read to Washington's troops in New York.

BOUNTY ON SALTPETRE
Connecticut, July 17, 1775
THE GENERAL ASSEMBLY OF THE COLONY OF CONNECTICUT, in May last, voted Ten pounds reward for every fifty pounds weight of SALTPETRE that should be made in the Colony within the year ensuing. Any person, master of the process, and willing to undertake, if able to carry on the works, may (if his character is good), by inquiring of the printer, be informed of the best places in that colony to set up the business, and assisted with every necessary direction.

From Dunlap's Pennsylvania Packet
PHILIP and HENRY SHEETS
GUN-SMITHS
In Shepherd's Town, Berkley, Virginia
INTEND carrying on their business extensively; and as they are in want of hands that understand said business, they will give great wages either by the week, month, year, or otherwise as they may desire it, to any such that would choose to be employed, by applying speedily at their place of residence as above mentioned.

From Dunlap's Pennsylvania Packet
COMMITTEE OF SAFETY
Philadelphia, January 17, 1776
Such persons as are willing to erect POWDER MILLS in this province, within fifty miles distant of this city, are desired to apply to the Committee of Safety, who will lend them money on security, if required, for that purpose, and give them also other encouragement.
Extract from the Minutes
William Govett, Secretary

The non-importation agreements had shut out woolens from England and there was no supply on hand when war broke out. Upon women and girls fell the duty of providing part of the clothing for the soldiers. They knitted socks, caps, and mittens for the fighting men in their own families. In their homes, they carded, spun,

123

and wove linens and wool, but home manufacture could not supply the demand. In 1776 Congress promised every enlisted man a new suit of clothes each year, but this pledge could not be kept. Congress could only ask for needed supplies, since this body did not have the power to tax the separate states. Each one maintained its own militia for its own defense. Enlistments were slow in the Continental Army. Promised necessities were not always delivered on time, if at all.

Any costume was a uniform for a Continental soldier. About 11,000 Americans took part in the Battle of Brandywine. The best dressed of these fighting men wore long, loose hunting shirts over long pants, and wide-brimmed hats, turned up at three places and decorated with a bright feather or a green sprig. Many of the soldiers were almost naked. In the winter of 1777-78 at Valley Forge, nearly half the soldiers lacked good shoes and warm stockings. Some cut up their blankets to wrap around their feet, and then were forced to sit up all night huddled around the fire to keep warm. In December of 1777, 3000 men were unfit for military duty because they lacked warm clothing. Six weeks later, the number was 4000. Even officers were without uniforms and wore blankets and bed-coverings on parade. Some of the manufacturing states were able to supply clothing for their own recruits. Every man from Connecticut at Valley Forge was ready for duty at a moment's notice, if in good health.

A soldier's ration called for bread and meat each day, but this allowance was cut in half for weeks at a time during the winter at Valley Forge. The Second Continental Congress issued paper money to purchase provisions for the army, and patriotic citizens accepted it in payment for goods. However, as the war lagged, this paper went down in value. Farmers as well as manufacturers wanted coins, "hard money," for their produce and wares, and less could be purchased. During January of 1778, the soldiers encamped with Washington lived for days on pancakes made of flour and water, baked on flat stones heated in the fireplace. When food could not be purchased, forage parties were sent out to take supplies, a certain amount being assessed to each farmer. Some soldiers took more than the allotment, according to the item found in Dearborn's Orderly Book, dated January 14, 1778, at Valley Forge:

As several farmers have complained, notwithstanding the certificates granted by the Commanding General of Forage of their having furnished their quotas of Forage assigned them, further demands have been made upon them of what was reserved for the use of their own families. The General strictly prohibits such unjust proceedings, and desires that more respect may be paid the Forage Master General's certificates for the future.

The health of the troops presented a problem. In May of 1777, General Greene wrote a letter to Washington saying scurvy was found among some of the troops because they lived mainly on animal food and did not have enough vegetables to eat. Greene recommended that each man be allotted about a half a pint of vinegar per day to prevent this ailment.

"I think it, my dear General, an object of great importance to preserve the health of the troops," he wrote. "What can a sickly army do? They are a bother to themselves and the state that employs them."

The Committees of Safety in Pennsylvania and other states sent men from door to door collecting window weights, clock weights, and anything made of lead, needed for bullets. In New York City, during the celebration of the Declaration of Independence, the gilded leaden statue of King George III was dragged from its stone base in the Bowling Green to be melted for bullets. Washington mildly rebuked his soldiers for their part in this rowdyism, ordering that in the future, "these things shall be avoided by the soldiery." Lead was so scarce that even weights on fishing nets were confiscated. Window leads were removed from the houses of more than 500 citizens in New York City. The total was 100 tons. According to the records of the Auditor-General of New York, some of the bills were not paid until years after the war ended.

Some families donated or sold their pewter dishes as material for bullets. Munitions could be obtained overseas when money could be raised to provide ships and engage crews.

The problem of pay for fighting men plagued Congress throughout the war years.

A free farm was tempting bait to a Celt or an Anglo-Saxon. However, an offer more exciting and more adventurous lured men onto the high seas.

AMERICAN SEAMEN FIGHT FOR INDEPENDENCE

WHEN WAR BROKE out in 1775, a few armed merchantmen were hastily added to Washington's army to capture the British supply ships headed for Boston. The officers and crews were taken from Washington's forces. To encourage enlist-ments, Washington offered prize money to the crews: "one-third part of the cargo of every vessel by you taken and sent into port." Special detachments of soldiers on these vessels were forerunners of marines, and all on board were part of the Continental Army. This fleet led to the formation of a Continental Navy and Washington's fleet was disbanded.

On a chilly morning in January of 1776, Commodore Esek Hopkins left the Walnut Street wharf of Philadelphia to take command of eight armed vessels with these names: *Alfred, Columbus, Andrew Doria, Cabot, Providence, Hornet, Fly,* and *Wasp;* all were made-over merchant ships. Although Esek Hopkins was a soldier when he was chosen to command the first American fleet, he belonged to a seafaring family in Rhode Island. He had been a seaman for over thirty years and in command of a number of ships. As the commodore reached the deck of the *Alfred,* his flagship, the captain gave a signal to First Lieutenant John Paul Jones to hoist the flag. Historians are still undecided about this flag. Some claim that the first pennant to wave over an American man-of-war was a yellow silk flag with the image of a coiled rattlesnake, ready to fight, and the motto "Don't tread on me." A British spy who saw the fleet sail described the flag as "English colors but more striped."

Although the officers received their commissions from the Continental Congress during December of 1775, the exact date on which they boarded the vessels in the Delaware River is not known. November tenth is the birthday of the Marines, because on that date in 1775, the Second Continental Congress ordered a Marine Corps to be organized. However, marines had been serving in local navies.

There were eleven naval units belonging to the separate states, besides Washington's fleet and the Continental Navy, that served in the War for Independence.

The first orders received by the first commander of a United States fleet were instructions to defend the coast of Virginia from attacks by a British squadron under Lord Dunmore. However, one paragraph of these orders issued by the Continental Congress provided a loophole. It stated:

Notwithstanding these particular Orders, which 'tis hoped you will be able to execute, if bad winds or stormy weather, or any other unforseen accident or disaster disable you so to do, you are then to follow such courses as your best judgment shall suggest to you as most useful to the American cause and to distress the enemy by all means in your power.

Since the weather was stormy and many of the men were sick, and Hopkins had little chance to succeed if he attacked warships with his made-over merchant vessels and inexperienced crews, he took advantage of the permission to use his own judgment, and sailed for the Bahamas.

The first cruise of this Continental Navy was to these islands in the West Indies to capture guns and ammunition stored there.

On the third of March, 1776, marines landed on the beach near the town, Fort Nassau, under cover of guns from the ships. Since an attack was unexpected and the garrison was small, the fort was soon taken. The booty, loaded on the vessels, included cannon, 15 mortars, shells, and shot, but only 24 barrels of gunpowder were captured. The British governor had managed to ship out 150 casks of powder during the night. Hopkins took over a vessel lying in the harbor, and loaded it also, as his own fleet could not hold all the stores obtained.

Some members of the crew contracted fever in the islands. It was a heavily laden and poorly manned fleet that sailed away.

The voyage home was made in bad weather, but only one ship, the *Wasp,* was lost from sight. That vessel made the port of Philadelphia on the thirteenth of April, eleven days after the main fleet reached the eastern end of Long Island. Sailing into the sound, Hopkins captured a British schooner with six guns, and on the next day, a brig of eight guns. Two merchant ships bound from New York to London fell as prizes of war to this navy.

Off the coast of Rhode Island, near the end of the voyage, the little fleet met up with the *Glasgow,* a British sloop of war carrying twenty-four guns. Hopkins' flagship, the *Alfred,* bore the brunt of the battle which began shortly after midnight on the sixth of April and lasted for nearly three hours. The *Glasgow,* badly damaged, headed for Newport with one man killed and three wounded. The American loss was ten killed and fourteen wounded. Among the wounded men was the commodore's son. In this first sea fight of the United States Navy, no ships were sunk, and the much needed guns and ammunition were delivered to army units. The states quarreled over the booty. Hopkins was accused of favoring New England in distributing cannon, especially his home state of Rhode Island which received twenty-six of the captured guns. The crews were paid in Continental money, which, according to Lieutenant Trevett, one of the navy officers, "would pay for one pair of shoes."

The venture to the Bahamas was the only cruise of the entire fleet during the war. The engagements on the sea were between individual vessels for the most part. John Paul Jones, aboard the *Alfred* in the first sea battle, was soon promoted and given his first command, the *Providence.* Later, as captain of the *Ranger,* the *Bon Homme Richard*, and other vessels, he captured tons of supplies for the Continental Army and harassed the British Navy. He is honored today as the outstanding naval hero of the Revolutionary War.

The official navy had a powerful competitor — the privateer. Owners of ships idled by the war applied to Congress for "letters of marque," legal permission to mount guns on their vessels and turn them into privateers. Captains of these armed ships roamed the seas, capturing British merchantmen and their cargoes, towing them into an American port, and collecting their share of the prize money. Part of the loot was given to Congress for support of the war. In letters to Congress, Hopkins bitterly complained that seamen refused to enlist in the official Navy and ships were idle for lack of men. Yet, the owners of privateers had no difficulty in securing crews because they offered larger prize

THE CAPTURE OF THE SERAPIS

In the middle of August, 1779, John Paul Jones sailed from a French port with a fleet of five vessels to raid British shipping. His flagship was the *Bon Homme Richard, (Good Man Richard)* named for Benjamin Franklin's paper, *Poor Richard's Almanac.*

Cruising along the coast of Scotland, Jones sighted the Baltic fleet of forty merchantmen convoyed by the British warship, *Serapis.* He ordered a chase, and all of his captains obeyed except Landais of the *Alliance.* Early in the evening of September 23, 1779, the desperate sea battle began off Flamborough Head near Scarsborough. Richard Dale, First Lieutenant of the *Bon Homme Richard,* who was in the fight, wrote an account of this bloody engagement:

At about eight, being within hail, the *Serapis* demanded, "What ship is that?"

He was answered, "I can't hear what you say."

Again the *Serapis* hailed, "What ship is that? Answer immediately, or I shall be under the necessity of firing into you."

At this moment, I received orders from Captain Jones to commence the action with a broadside which, indeed, appeared to be simultaneous on board both ships.

(Later in the battle, Dale wrote:) We were again hailed by the *Serapis,* "has your ship struck?"

Captain Jones answered, "I have not yet begun to fight."

By 9:30 when the moon rose, both ships were on fire. After three hours of hand-to-hand combat, Pearson, the Captain of the *Serapis* who had nailed the flag to the mast, handed it down and surrendered. With the *Bon Homme Richard* sinking, the able-bodied men boarded the *Serapis,* now commanded by Jones, who took it to a Dutch port. Most of the wounded on the *Bon Homme Richard* went down with their ship.

For this victory, Congress presented John Paul Jones with a gold medal, and the King of France gave him a gold sword.

money, usually one half, while the Navy offered only a third. There was less delay and bickering in settling the prizes of privateers than with the Continental vessels. When a privateer brought a prize into port, the goods were sold quickly, and the booty divided among the men, while seamen in the Navy suffered delay in receiving their shares because agents were forced to await orders from Congress before they could dispose of the captured cargoes. Privateering became so profitable that men did not enlist readily in the regular Navy, where the pay ranged from $6 to $8 per month. Some states even offered a bonus. The risk and danger of this licensed piracy appealed to many adventurous young men, and the privateers were numerous and well-manned. In time of dire need, these patriotic pirates supplied Continental soldiers with food, clothing, and ammunition, from the beginning of the war to the end.

Early in 1777, the American privateer, the *Montgomery,* captured the *Hannah,* and brought the prize into Baltimore where the cargo of cheese, ale, port wines, handkerchiefs, stockings, spices, linen, beef, pork, and peas was sold for nearly £7000. After the Government's share was taken to supply troops, and all expenses were paid, the sum remaining was divided among the officers and members of the crew according to agreement. Esek Hopkins, commander of the Continental Navy, complained about the competition of the privateers when his vessels were marooned in port for lack of sailors. He tried to get the General Assembly of his home state to pass a law that the privateers could not enlist seamen until the quotas of navy vessels in Rhode Island ports were filled. Since most of the men in the General

Assembly were merchants possessing letters of marque, the law was not passed although Hopkins knew many of them personally and had sailed ships for them before they had turned to privateering.

The deeds of the unsung heroes of the privateers are seldom recorded on the pages of history. Privateering was real adventure on the high seas — and it PAID.

THE WAR CENTERS IN LOYALIST STRONGHOLDS

FOLLOWING THE evacuation of Boston by Howe, Washington and the major portion of the Continental Army moved to New York where the armed rebellion was not so popular as it was in Massachusetts. Since the state of New York bordered on Canada, its citizens were inclined to remain loyal to the King. They preferred to plead for justice rather than fight for it. In New York City, a trade center, the wealthy landowners and merchants whose prosperity depended upon commerce did not want a war that would endanger their property and ruin business.

Shortly after his arrival in New York, Washington recommended to the Committee of Safety that the inhabitants of the city not be permitted to go back and forth freely to the British vessels anchored in the harbor. Information and supplies were reaching the enemy. This order marked merely the beginning of the hardships which the Tories, as the loyalists were called, would be forced to endure while the city was occupied by the American Army.

Loyalists who wished to remain neutral, or who preferred to join the King's armies, hid in swamps and out-of-the-way places when the troops of Washington took over the city. Since many of these men belonged to the militia of the state and had been called into service, they were considered to be deserters. Orders were issued by army officers to apprehend them. In the army records are many such commands, like the following:

Queens County, June 19, 1776
To Mr. Thomas Mitchell, Lt. —
You are hereby required to march your company into Capt. Peter Nostrand's district, and divide them into as many parts as you may think proper, for the purpose of aiding and assisting him to bring forth — with 283 defaulting persons belonging to that company, or such of them as you can find, and forthwith send or bring them to Samuel Nicolls', and there safely secure them until further orders. Given under my hand and seal.
John Sands, Col.

Strangers were stopped and questioned by American soldiers, and messengers carried identification. Warrants were given to search the homes of Tories and seize all arms found.

Tories often did not attend conventions called to elect delegates to the state congress or the Continental Congress in Philadelphia. With less than a majority, the patriots went ahead, and boldly chose their representatives to operate the government. At first, Tories were only disarmed. Soon, however, they were arrested, thrown into jail, and sometimes banished. Then, gradually, their property was confiscated, and families of soldiers who had joined the British forces suffered from want. Two weeks after independence was declared, Congress ordered that livestock on Long Island be driven inland to prevent their capture by the enemy, who was expected to land at any time. Some Tories were able to escape on British vessels and return to England,

leaving their belongings and property behind. Some fled from New York to Connecticut.

Washington managed to erect a few forts around New York before General Howe reached Sandy Hook on June 28, 1776, with ships carrying 10,000 men. A few days later, his brother, Lord Richard Howe, arrived with a British regiment and Hessian soldiers. Soon Clinton and Cornwallis came up from the South, bringing the combined British force to over 31,000 men. The Americans had less than 20,000 fit for duty, and these were poorly equipped. Howe tried to bring about a reconciliation and have the Americans lay down their arms. After Washington's refusal, Howe landed troops on Long Island.

The evening before the resulting battle, Washington made this speech to his soldiers.

The time is near at hand which must probably determine whether Americans are to be freemen or slaves; whether they are to have any property they can call their own; whether their houses and farms are to be pillaged and destroyed, and themselves consigned to a state of wretchedness from which no human efforts will deliver them. The fate of unborn millions will now depend, under God, on the courage and conduct of this army . . . . We have, therefore, to resolve to conquer or to die.

The next day, August 27, in the Battle of Long Island, Washington's troops were routed. The Americans lost the battle with five hundred men killed or wounded and eleven hundred officers and men taken prisoner. In rain and fog, Washington escaped with his army and supplies across the river to Manhattan without discovery. General Howe lost an opportunity "to end the war with a single stroke," his critics said in England.

After defeat in the Battle of Long Island,

Washington desperately needed information on the plans of the enemy. Where would Howe attack next? He asked Lieutenant-Colonel Knowlton to find a young officer to serve as a spy. Only one volunteered, Captain Nathan Hale, twenty-one and a graduate of Yale.

He entered the British camp disguised as a school teacher and loyalist, looking for a job, and gathered the news Washington wanted. With his notes written in Latin on thin paper stuffed between the soles of his shoes, he escaped to the appointed spot where he was to be met on the beach by patriots who would row him back to his regiment. The boat arrived on schedule, but the six men aboard were British marines. Hale was

STATUE OF NATHAN HALE
CITY PARK, NEW YORK

Encircled by a wreath are these words:
"A captain in the regular army of the United States who gave his life for his country."

Circling the column above the base are his last words:
"I only regret that I have but one life to lose for my country."

Courtesy of The New York Historical Society, New York City

captured and hung. When asked for his last words, he said:

"I only regret that I have but one life to lose for my country."

Lord Howe, the British naval commander, now tried to end the war peacefully. He sent General Sullivan, captured in the Battle of Long Island, to ask the Continental Congress to send delegates to discuss peace. John Adams, Franklin, and Rutledge met Howe on Staten Island where they were courteously received and entertained. Lord Howe was friendly to the Americans and earnestly desired to come to some terms on which the so-called rebellion could end without further bloodshed. On September 19, 1776, he announced that the British Government was willing to reconsider the acts and laws which had caused the rebellion, if the Declaration of Independence were repealed. The three delegates from Congress held out for independence. Four days later, with little difficulty, his brother, General Howe, took New York City.

It was soon plain to Washington that the British planned to separate New England from the other states by occupying the Hudson Valley. After the Battle of White Plains, in which the British lost more men than the Americans, Washington crossed to New Jersey, escaping a trap by a masterly retreat across that state. He ordered General Charles Lee to follow but the officer disobeyed and was captured. The war shifted to New Jersey and Pennsylvania, also strong loyalist centers.

The Tory governor of New Jersey, a son of Benjamin Franklin, had been arrested in June of 1776 and removed to Connecticut for safe keeping while delegates were chosen to vote for independence. In Pennsylvania, Quakers refused to fight because of their religious beliefs. Some of the large German population preferred to solve the problems as colonials rather than as independents. However, many Germans aided the American cause and joined the state militia. Neighbors, friends, and families disagreed on the war.

Washington's retreat from New York was a dark hour in the fight for independence. General Howe remained in the city, assigning Lord Cornwallis to pursue the fleeing enemy. Washington outran him and crossed the Delaware River with his troops, establishing headquarters at Newtown, Pennsylvania. Congress, meeting in Philadelphia, adjourned to Baltimore.

Upon leaving New York, Washington advised Greene to evacuate Fort Washington on Manhattan Island and Fort Lee on the opposite bank of the Hudson River. Instead, Greene reinforced Fort Washington, which was taken by the British along with about 2600 of the best American troops. Flushed with success, the King's commissioners issued a proclamation granting pardons to all persons who, within sixty days, agreed to remain peaceable, not to take up arms against the King, nor encourage anyone else to do it. In those dark hours, an American victory was desperately needed. It came as a surprise.

The diary of Charles Willson Peale who painted portraits of Washington, reveals how well the commander-in-chief kept a secret of his plans. Peale's entry for Christmas Day, 1776, begins as follows:

We were ordered to join brigade. Many of the men were unwilling to turn out, as it was a Day that they would wish to enjoy themselves. However, with small battalions we went through several maneuvers.

Late in the day, there was no warning of the eventful night to come because Peale left camp at Bristol, where his division was stationed. He wrote in his diary:

In the afternoon, one of our men informed me that he had heard of a person about three miles out of town had butter and cheese that he would only sell for hard money. I set out on foot with some men and got there just before it was dark. But on asking to buy with hard money, I found that the man had been slandered. I tempted as much as I thought was justifiable, finding the man never expected to get any other than Continental Money, and that he constantly sold his butter of it.

By the time Peale arrived at camp with two quarts of fresh butter, he found that orders had come to cross the Delaware, and his troops were waiting for their officer. Peale marched his men about six miles to a ferry and they tried to cross the stream, rowing against the wind in a storm of icy rain. Some succeeded in reaching the Jersey side, but the ice gathered so rapidly at a distance from the shore that the artillery could not be landed. Therefore, the entire force was ordered to march back to Bristol "at which place I arrived just before day of 26, — very much fatigued having walked 18 miles at least, 11 of them with very heavy baggage. The storm continues with hail and rain," wrote Peale.

General Putnam was expected to cross the Delaware River from Philadelphia with a thousand men. He did not attempt it, since his troops were needed to discourage a loyalist rebellion, simmering under cover in the city. Washington was the only one who succeeded in crossing the river on that stormy night. With a force of about 2400 men, he marched from Newtown to Taylorsville, nine miles above Trenton, where guns, ammunition, and troops were prepared for action. The crossing was made at McConkey's Ferry after dark. Fishermen from Marblehead, Massachusetts, were the first to row across the Delaware, which was full of floating ice. Washington was among the first to land on the Jersey side of the river. In the sleet storm it was difficult to handle the artillery. It was three o'clock in the morning before the last gun was unloaded. An hour later, with a strong wind blowing snow and ice into their faces, the troops were marching toward Trenton where Hessian soldiers were encamped.

Snow deadened the rumble of the artillery as the Americans approached the village about eight o'clock in the morning. In such bad weather, an attack was not expected. Everyone was indoors asleep after the revels of Christmas Day. At the entrance to the village, Washington saw only one man, and he was chopping wood. The surprise was complete. The Hessians did not have time to get out their artillery and any cannon that appeared was quickly captured. Rahl, the Hessian commander, tried to rally his men. He was mortally wounded and died that evening. In half an hour, nearly 1000 Hessian soldiers surrendered. Washington sent his prisoners to Philadelphia and scattered them in Pennsylvania and Virginia. Washington had notices posted explaining to citizens that these soldiers, for the most part, were serving in the British army against their will, and some had even been kidnapped in their German kingdoms and sold into military service by their rulers. Some of the hired soldiers had their wives and children with them and were burdened in the march with pots and pans, bundles and blankets. In crossing New Jersey, these Hessian soldiers had plundered farmhouses for supplies. Some of the Hessian women stripped American children to put warm clothing on their own little ones. When Americans learned the truth of their plight, a Hessian corporal wrote that "many came out of the towns and brought us provisions, and treated us with kindness and humanity."

Since the enlistments of most of the soldiers Washington had at Trenton would end on the last day of December, he sent an appeal to Robert Morris in Philadelphia for money to offer them to reenlist. Early on New Year's Day, 1777, Morris went from house to house and managed to borrow, partly by signing the notes personally, about $50,000 and sent it to Washington.

On the next day, Cornwallis reached Trenton, and the two armies were facing each other. Washington left his camp fires burning brightly and slipped away in the dark to surprise the British from the rear, at Princeton. These two victories electrified the Americans struggling for independence, and startled the British who had considered the rebellion almost ended. Volunteers enlisted in the Continental Army, giving Washington enough troops to recover control of New Jersey. Then the war shifted back to the state of New York, which bore the brunt of the conflict. Out of 308 engagements of the war, 92 were fought on the soil of New York, the most important one being the decisive battle of Saratoga.

BRITISH PLAN
TO ISOLATE NEW ENGLAND

ON THE SIXTH of May, 1777, General Burgoyne, who had witnessed the Battle of Bunker Hill, arrived at Quebec from London to take command of the British

132

army from General Carleton. He commanded a force of about 8000 men, of whom 3000 were hired German soldiers, 150 were Canadians, and 500 were Indians. His orders were to follow the Hudson River route south to prevent another invasion of Canada, and to split the rebellion in two, separating the leaders, Massachusetts and Virginia. In the middle of June he dispatched Colonel St. Leger from Montreal with a small force, instructing him to go up the St. Lawrence to Lake Ontario, thence to Fort Oswego and down the Mohawk Valley. General William Howe, in possession of New York, was to go up the Hudson with an army and a fleet, capture forts along the way, and join Burgoyne and St. Leger at Albany. It was a well-laid plan on paper — divide and conquer.

Burgoyne moved up Lake Champlain where his Indians paddled their way in canoes. His overland journey was hampered by poor weather and roads. It rained and both troops and guns wallowed in mud and water. The trails were blocked with fallen trees laced together in a web, the work of General Schuyler's men. When Burgoyne reached Fort Edward at the end of July, his provisions were low. On a tip from a loyalist, he sent Colonel Baum with 500 men to capture flour and other supplies stored at Bennington. Colonel Stark, with state militia, interfered with this scheme, winning the Battle of Bennington and taking over 500 prisoners, most of them loyalists. Burgoyne was forced to proceed without the needed food, horses, and wagons. Vermonters cut off other supplies to Burgoyne's army as he advanced toward Albany.

St. Leger reached Oswego the middle of July where loyalists under Johnson and Butler and Indians under Brant joined his force, making a total of 1700 men. Early in August, St. Leger appeared before Fort Stanwix (sometimes called Fort Schuyler) on the Mohawk River, and demanded surrender. Although he threatened the garrison with an Indian massacre, the Americans held the frontier post. In a ravine near Oriskany, Indians fired from behind trees upon county militia under General Herkimer, marching to the relief of Fort Stanwix. When rain fell in torrents, the Indians fled and the loyalists retreated, leaving their equipment on the battleground. As soon as the storm subsided, the garrison marched out of the fort and invaded St. Leger's camp, capturing over twenty wagon loads of food, blankets, guns, clothes, and ammunition. Hearing from scouts that Arnold was approaching with as many men as there were leaves on the trees, St. Leger continued his retreat to Montreal.

The order for Howe to join Burgoyne was left on a desk when the messenger hurried away on a hunting trip. When he returned the ship had sailed.

Since General Howe had not received definite orders to go himself to meet Burgoyne, he evacuated New York, leaving the city under Sir Henry Clinton. General Howe started for Philadelphia. He seems not to have worried about the fate of Burgoyne. The Americans were as much surprised as were the British at Howe's move. Both agreed it was a colossal blunder. The voyage from New York to Philadelphia was more like a pleasure cruise than a military expedition. Although Howe embarked his troops at New York on the fifth of July, he did not sail up the Chesapeake Bay to land until late in August.

The Continental Congress fled to Lancaster, Pennsylvania, but moved on shortly to

Benson J. Lossing

WASHINGTON'S ARMY WINTERING AT VALLEY FORGE
1777-1778

It was a bitter winter at Valley Forge near Philadelphia, where Washington's troops suffered from lack of food, clothing, shelter, and medical care.

York to hold meetings in the courthouse there.

The British did not march into Philadelphia unopposed. When Admiral Howe's fleet sailed from New York harbor with the army of his brother on board, Washington left his encampment in New Jersey and headed south to defend Philadelphia. He passed by the city, taking a position at Newport to challenge the march of British troops advancing from Elk River where they landed early in September. Although the Americans were forced to retreat after the Battle of Brandywine, the action delayed Howe's march. He did not enter the city until the twenty-sixth of September. Eight days later, Washington attacked Howe's headquarters at Germantown. Fighting in a dense fog, friends were mistaken for enemies, prisoners were captured and recaptured, and army units became confused. The Americans finally deserted the field of combat, leaving Howe in full possession of Philadelphia, guarded by his brother's fleet anchored in the Delaware River. Nearby at Valley Forge, Washington established his winter quarters.

Meanwhile, a decisive action was developing in central New York. Following the plan for the three generals to meet at Albany, Burgoyne had steadily advanced although his pace was only a mile a day as

Schuyler's troops had blocked trails, flooded roads, and wrecked bridges. Howe's failure to proceed according to schedule to march north from New York, and St. Leger's defeat in the Mohawk Valley, maneuvered Burgoyne into a trap. The possible capture of Burgoyne's army encouraged enlistments. These were especially heavy from New England after Horatio Gates replaced Schuyler, who was a descendant of a Dutch patroon and was therefore not popular in Puritan communities. In the fighting that took place on his estate, Schuyler lost his residence. Afterwards, Burgoyne apologized for ordering Schuyler's mansion to be burned.

As the two armies lined up for a contest, Burgoyne's Indians deserted in large numbers and went home. The regiments under Gates were adding recruits day after day. Clinton waited for fresh troops to arrive from England before starting up the Hudson with 3000 men. He had not gone far when a decisive battle developed around Saratoga. The British were hemmed in and shut off from sources of supply. Defeated in combat, Burgoyne asked for terms of surrender. These were quite generous. The Canadians were sent home. Free passage was granted to Burgoyne's army for their march to Boston where they would await the arrival of British transports to take them home.

In the afternoon of October 17, 1777, British soldiers piled their guns in scattered heaps near the riverbank. There were less than 6000 able-bodied British, Canadian, and German soldiers left to lay down their arms on that day when the American army numbered about 24,000 men. Gates had ordered the American forces to remain within their own lines to spare the prisoners undue humiliation. Burgoyne and his officers rode to the American camp to give themselves up. Burgoyne handed his sword to Gates who promptly returned it. According to a page added to Burgoyne's orderly book, probably by Governor Clinton of New York, the British and American officers celebrated the surrender in a congenial manner in Albany.

"They all dined at General Schuyler's," the note read. "At table, General Gates drank the King of Britain's health. General Burgoyne in return thanked him, and in the next glass drank the Continental Congress."

Thus ended the engagement at Saratoga, listed by historians as one of the decisive battles of the world. It was the turning point of the War for Independence. This victory encouraged enlistments at home and brought help from abroad. Convinced that the Americans could win with aid, the King of France agreed to send supplies, men, and ships to the former colonists of Great Britain.

THE WAR
ON THE WESTERN FRONTIER

THREE YEARS before the Revolutionary War broke out, a surveyor from Virginia traveled over Braddock's Road to Fort Pitt, and made the trip down the Ohio River in a canoe. He was only nineteen years old and his name was George Rogers Clark. Like many young men of his day, he was looking for land where it was cheap and plentiful. He found acres that pleased him, where a creek furnished water for his needs. Here he built a log cabin and planted corn. Clark was more a soldier than a farmer. In the spring of 1774, following Indian raids on the frontier settlements, troops from Virginia passed near his cabin on their way to punish the tribes north of the Ohio River. Clark left his farm and joined the ranks of the soldiers. He proved to be such a good Indian fighter that he was offered a commission in the British Army. He refused the offer. The colonists were then quarreling with the mother country over the right to tax themselves. Clark wanted to fight with the colonies if the quarrel led to war.

When the war broke out the following year, George Rogers Clark was living on the Kentucky frontier, where Indian raids were destroying houses and crops. The British, in forts north of the Ohio, were furnishing guns and powder to the Indians and inciting them to war upon the settlers in their old hunting ground, Kentucky. For protection, the people turned to George Rogers Clark, the able soldier with experience in Indian warfare.

With a few companions, Clark made the dangerous journey from the wilderness to Williamsburg, then the capital of Virginia, to lay his plans for defense before the governor, Patrick Henry. Patrick Henry listened eagerly to the daring scheme of the tall, athletic young officer. Clark asked for money and men to threaten the British strongholds north of the Ohio. Since this was a bold venture, Patrick Henry sought the advice of Thomas Jefferson and other Virginians. After several weeks of debate, Clark left Williamsburg with orders signed by the governor allowing him to enlist seven companies of fifty men each, to purchase flatboats for the journey down the Ohio, and to buy guns, powder, and supplies. To encourage men to enlist in this expedition, Jefferson made this promise in a letter to Clark:

We think it just and reasonable that each volunteer entering as a common soldier in this expedition, should be allowed 300 acres of land and the officers in proportion, out of the lands which may be conquered.

On a little island in the Ohio, opposite the present site of Louisville, Clark established a base of supplies. He then started north into British territory.

THE CAPTURE
OF KASKASKIA AND VINCENNES

IT WAS JULY 4, 1778. Clark's small army was sighted at Kaskaskia, a fort the British had taken in the French and Indian War. This army had marched from old Fort Massac on the Ohio, without wagons or pack horses, and had carried their munitions and supplies on their backs. For the last two of the six days, they had marched on empty stomachs.

After dark, the Americans quietly surrounded the town while Clark and a few men captured the British governor. Then, pretending their force was much larger, the soldiers burst noisily into the town. Those who could speak French ran up and down the streets, shouting at the tops of their voices, "Stay inside your houses, or be shot." During the night, the Americans searched the French homes and took all the guns. The surprise was complete. Without the loss of a man on either side, the fortified town of Kaskaskia fell to a handful of bold frontiersmen.

The next morning, Father Gibault and several aged men called at Clark's headquarters to learn their fate. They were shocked at the sight of these officers. In the march of a hundred and twenty miles through a swampy wilderness, their clothes were torn by briers, their leggings were crusted with mud, and their bare toes stuck out of holes in their homemade moccasins. These were the frontiersmen whom the Indians called "Long Knives" because a hunting blade hung from each man's belt. The village priest offered the surrender of his people, expecting the Americans to take their homes and cattle as prizes of war. He pleaded that enough food and clothing be left for the women and children.

"Do you mistake us for savages?" Clark asked. "My countrymen disdain to make war upon helpless innocence. It was to prevent the horrors of war upon our own wives and children that we took up arms and came to this remote stronghold."

The French villagers gathered in the church to receive Clark's orders, which they thought would be exile. When they learned that they could remain in their homes, unmolested, and could worship as they pleased, they rang the church bell and sang hymns of thanks. Father Gibault supported the American cause and aided Clark in many ways. He sent word to the Indian tribes, who always had been friendly to the French, asking them to make peace with the "Long Knives." He went ahead of Clark to Vincennes to get French aid for the Americans.

The fifth of February in 1779 was an exciting day in the frontier village of Kaskaskia. Clark's army of 170 men marched down the lane of log houses with fifes shrieking and drums beating. The soldiers cheered and waved their wide-brimmed hats while the women dabbed their tear-stained faces with their long white aprons. Children clung to their mothers' long full skirts and waved

ARMY OF GEORGE ROGERS CLARK MARCHING TO FORT VINCENNES

When George Rogers Clark and his small army arrived at the Little Wabash, they found the river had overflowed its banks and flooded the plain between two forks of the stream. The troops were forced to wade through miles of icy water to surprise the British garrison in Fort Vincennes.

Benson J. Lossing

goodbye to their fathers going along with Clark to capture the strong British fort at Vincennes.

It rained nearly all the time. The little army slushed through mud and water during the day, and slept without tents in the cold drizzly night. Between them and the fort, the Wabash River had overflowed its banks and turned the plain into a shallow lake. When Clark saw his men hesitate at the brink of a five mile stretch of water, he gave a war whoop and marched into the flood. He ordered those nearest him to start singing a favorite tune. Down the line, the men began to sing, and fell in behind their leader.

At night, the army camped on little islands of hilltops in the vast swamp. The flood seemed endless to the tired and hungry men. Each morning ushered in another day of wading. Sometimes, the water reached their armpits, forcing them to carry their rifles above their heads. The short troopers clung to floating logs and branches of trees. When soldiers dropped exhausted, their comrades pulled them into canoes to save them from drowning.

A little drummer boy, only fourteen years old, kept up the spirits of the men with his funny antics. When the water was too deep for wading, he floated on his drum, bobbing up and down like a cork, and paddled with his feet and hands. One morning when the water was coated with a film of ice, Clark hoisted the little drummer to the shoulders of a tall, comical sergeant. With his drum perched on the sergeant's head, the lad beat the charge, while Clark followed close behind them into the icy flood, waving his sword and shouting the command, "Forward! MARCH!"

Not expecting an army to wade through miles of water, the attack upon the fort at Vincennes was another complete surprise. The French inhabitants had been warned by Father Gibault that the Americans were coming. When Clark sent word ahead that the King of France was helping the Americans, the villagers refused to fight in defense of the village. The British fort soon fell to these brave frontiersmen. Clark changed the name to Fort Patrick Henry, in honor of the man who had backed the expedition. In the East and in the West, the help of France proved to be the turning point of the war.

FOREIGNERS AID THE AMERICAN CAUSE

IN AUGUST OF 1775, the Duke of Gloucester, a brother of George III of England, had stopped over in the city of Metz, France, on his way to visit Italy. The governor of Lorraine, a French province, gave a dinner in the capital to honor his royal guest from England. Among the invited guests was a young French army officer, Marquis de Lafayette, whose regiment was stationed in the town. During the meal, the conversation turned to the war between England and her colonies. The Duke of Gloucester, who did not agree with his brother, the King, talked freely and explained why the colonists had rebelled. Lafayette, a lad not quite eighteen, listened to every word and asked the duke many questions about the rights the colonists were demanding. He knew neither the country nor the people of the American colonies and he did not speak their language. Before he left that dinner table, he had made up his mind to offer his services to a strange people struggling for freedom across the Atlantic.

His family and his government opposed every attempt he made to leave for the New World. It would be embarrassing, indeed, to have a member of the French nobility helping the common people of any country to fight their king. Finally, in secret, Lafayette bought a ship which he christened *La Victoire* (The Victory), hired a crew, and loaded it with supplies for a voyage. Before he could sail, however, he received orders to report for duty with his regiment. His ship, ready to sail, lay at anchor in a Spanish port beyond the reach of French officials. Lafayette had to make his decision — and quickly.

Disguised as a postboy, he rode on horseback ahead of the coach he had hired to take him and his friend across the border into Spain. French officers sent to capture him inspected the coach, but ignored the shabby looking postboy in the lead. At an inn where the party stopped to rest, the young daughter of the innkeeper, recognized the rich nobleman disguised as a servant. The postboy shook his head and the girl kept silent. A few hours later, when French officers caught his trail and inquired for him at the inn, the girl sent them on a wild-goose chase in the opposite direction.

On a Sunday in April, 1777, *La Victoire* unfurled her sails and slipped quietly out of the harbor of Los Pasajes in Spain. On board was the owner, Marquis de Lafayette, other officers in the French army, Baron de Kalb, a German, serving in the French army, the friend who had ridden with Lafayette in the coach, and an American named Price. It took fifty-four days to cross the Atlantic in a sailing ship. To escape capture, Lafayette had been forced to leave France without saying goodbye to his young wife and year-old daughter. On shipboard, he spent much time in writing letters asking his wife's forgiveness and explaining why he had come to the New World against the wishes of his family. He wrote:

As a defender of that liberty which I adore, coming as a friend to offer my services to this most interesting republic, I bring with me nothing but my own free heart and my own good will, no ambition to fulfill and no selfish interests to serve. — The happiness of America is intimately connected with the happiness of all mankind. She is destined to become the safe and venerable asylum of virtue, of honesty, of tolerance, of equality, and of peaceful liberty.

La Victoire was bound for Charleston, South Carolina. At the time, British warships were cruising off that part of the Carolina coast. Fortunately, a strong southerly wind blew Lafayette's ship off its course, and the captain dropped anchor farther north at the mouth of an inlet near Georgetown. Not knowing where they were, Lafayette, de Kalb, and several officers, with eight sailors, started for the shore in the ship's yawl. It was early in the afternoon on a warm June day. They rowed up North Inlet until ten o'clock that night, when they found some Negroes fishing for oysters. These men said they belonged to an officer in the American Army, and offered to guide the strangers to their master's house. With the tide out, the water was not deep enough for the yawl. Lafayette took de Kalb and one more, leaving the others on the yawl, and climbed into the little oyster boat. It was midnight when the Negroes put them off at their master's landing. The three men stumbled through the darkness toward a light burning in a window. As they approached the house, the dogs began to bark. The noise awakened the family who thought the prowlers were sailors from an enemy ship out to raid their chicken roost.

From the darkness, a voice called out, "Who's there?"

"We are French officers," answered de Kalb, who could speak English.

"What do you want?"

"We've just come ashore to serve in the Continental Army," de Kalb replied. "We want a pilot to bring our ship into the harbor."

"Come in!" the voice spoke.

The three men entered a room where they were cordially welcomed and were invited to spend the night. Thus, to Major Benjamin Huger of South Carolina, fell the unexpected honor of welcoming Lafayette to America. Later the French nobleman went to Charleston. From this place, he wrote to his wife about the country and the people. Lafayette wrote:

What gives me most pleasure is to see how completely the citizens are all brethren of one family. In America there are none poor and none that can be called peasants. Each citizen has some property, and all citizens have the same rights as the richest individual, or landed proprietor, in the country.

It was a long journey overland from Charleston to Philadelphia, seat of the Continental Congress. Lafayette bought carriages and horses for the trip, but the coaches soon broke down on the rough roads, and the party completed the journey on horseback. Lafayette was given an army commission by the Continental Congress. Some of his fellow officers received none and returned to France, disgruntled.

Another foreigner, a Pole named Kosciuszko, helped the American cause.

He left Poland after his country, defeated in war, was partitioned by its powerful neighbors. When his own country could not be free, he sought consolation in fighting for the freedom of a new nation across the seas. He arrived a year ahead of Lafayette. As an engineer, his services were in demand for building roads, defenses, and fortifications. In the Journal of the Continental Congress for Oct. 18, this item appears:

RESOLVED, that Thaddeus Kosciuszko be appointed an engineer in the service of the United States, with the pay of sixty dollars a month, and the rank of colonel.

A Polish patriot, Count Pulaski, also preferred fighting for freedom in a strange land to living in his own country under foreign rule. He was killed in an attack on Savannah. De Kalb also lost his life. In the battle of Camden, South Carolina, he was badly wounded, and died a few days later. During his last hours, he dictated a letter to Colonel Smallwood who took over his command. In this note, he expressed his satisfaction in dying for a cause as dear to the friends of liberty in Europe as it was to those in the United States. Baron Steuben, another German, survived the war. He had been educated for a military career and had been a general in the Prussian Army under Frederick the Great. He was a hard drill-master who trained raw recruits for the Continental Army, rendering a great service to Washington during the trying winter of 1777-78 at Valley Forge. Of all the foreigners who fought in the war for independence, Lafayette was the most popular man with the people, perhaps, in part, because his country helped the United States.

During a visit in Baltimore, Lafayette was invited to a ball. He attended but did

FAC-SIMILE OF THE CONTINENTAL BILLS.[1]

Benson J. Lossing

CONTINENTAL MONEY

The plates for this paper money were engraved on copper by Paul Revere of Boston. One bill shows a beaver patiently gnawing at the trunk of a tree. The motto — PERSEVERANDO (by perseverance) suggests that the colonists will win if they are as determined as the beaver. On another bill a circular chain is engraved with each link named for one of the thirteen states. In the center is the slogan, WE ARE ONE.

This paper money so depreciated in value that one pair of boots cost $600 in January of 1781. The Continental Congress could ask the states for taxes to support the war, but could not force the states to pay.

not join in the fun. When he was introduced as the honored guest, he said to the ladies who had planned the party for him, "You dance very prettily; your ball is fine; but my soldiers need *shirts.*"

Quite embarrassed, the ladies soon went home. In a few weeks, bundles of shirts were on the way to clothe Lafayette's troops.

THE FRENCH ALLIANCE ENCOURAGES AMERICANS

HISTORY RECORDS that wars breed strange alliances like the "Treaty of Amity and Commerce" between France and the United States in 1778. Why did a French king help the Americans, whom he

regarded as rebels, to wage war against another king? The answer is long and involved because the reasons were many and varied. Was revenge a motive? France was still smarting under defeat by Great Britain in the Seven Years War. The loss of Canada and the territory lying between the Allegheny Mountains and the Mississippi River was a blow to French pride, and also closed the door to French colonization in a large part of North America. Great Britain's victory over France was attained in a large measure with the resources of men and supplies from her American colonies. Therefore, the loss of these possessions would injure British commerce and the British navy, lessening the power of Great Britain in world affairs.

Although the King, Louis XVI, listened to this argument from his ministers, he was not easily persuaded to risk another war with Great Britain, until Burgoyne was captured at Saratoga. This victory convinced him that the Americans had a chance to win the war if given some help and encouragement. Or, at least, so his ministers convinced him. At the time, following Burgoyne's surrender, there was considerable opposition in the British Parliament to continuing the war. Early in 1778, a member of Parliament testified that American privateers had captured or destroyed 559 British vessels according to the register at Lloyd's Coffee House, where a record was kept "with the most minute correctness" of every vessel sailing out from or entering into ports of Great Britain and Ireland. Lloyd's insurance rates on ships sailing for the United States had doubled, even with convoy, because about 175 American privateers with 2000 guns and 13,000 seamen were raiding British shipping.

141

On the thirteenth of March, the French Ambassador in London announced that his Government had signed a "Treaty of Amity and Commerce with the United States of North America." A week later, Benjamin Franklin and other envoys were presented to Louis XVI, who appointed a Minister to the United States. In only another week, a letter was on the way to the Continental Congress that the King was sending a fleet under the Count D'Estaing "to endeavor to destroy the English forces upon the shores of North America." With France at war with Great Britain, American privateers were free to use French ports, taking their raids into waters washing the shores of England.

When news of the French treaty reached Washington encamped at Valley Forge, he ordered a day set aside "to offer up a Thanksgiving" and to celebrate the important event.

With money loaned by investors, after the treaty of France increased the chances for victory, Washington's army gained uniforms, guns, and much needed equipment. The French Minister, Gerard, visited the General's headquarters in northern New Jersey a year later. A troop review was arranged in his honor. Dr. Thacher remarked in his journal, with pride, that the "ragged Continentals" of Valley Forge had been drilled into a first class army by Baron Steuben. The doctor's entry for May 28, 1779, began with a description of Steuben's inspection of the brigade to which he was assigned:

The Baron Steuben reviewed and inspected our brigade. The troops were paraded in a single line with shouldered arms, every officer in his particular station. The baron first reviewed the line in this position, passing in front with a scrutinizing eye; after which, he took into his hand the muskets and accoutrements of every soldier, examining them with particular accuracy and precision, applauding or condemning, according to the condition in which he found them. He required that the musket and bayonet should exhibit the brightest polish; not a spot of rust or defect in any part could elude his vigilance. He inquired also into the conduct of the officers toward their men, censuring every fault and applauding every meritorious action. Next, he inquired of me, as surgeon, a list of the sick, with a particular statement of their accommodations and mode of treatment, and even visited some of the sick in their cabins. — The continental army has improved with great rapidity under his inspection and review.

THE WAR ENDS IN THE SOUTH

TEN DAYS AFTER celebrating the French alliance, Washington's troops were rejoicing over the departure of General Howe, who turned over his command in Philadelphia to General Clinton on the eighteenth of May, 1778. Howe was called home to answer for his failure to end the rebellion. A month later, Clinton evacuated Philadelphia and marched toward New York. Lafayette in command of the advance column was pursuing him. Washington overtook the British forces at Monmouth, New Jersey. Joining forces with Lafayette, an indecisive battle was fought on the twenty-eighth of June, a day of oppressive heat which increased the number of casualties.

During the battle, Molly Pitcher, wife of one of the officers in charge of a cannon, carried water from a spring for her husband's gun crew. When he fell, overcome by the heat, the officer in charge ordered the gun taken off the field. Molly rushed forward, however, and continued to fire the gun until a retreat was ordered. The engagement ended without a decision in favor of either side. Washington and Lafayette lay down under a tree on the moonlit night, to be ready at daybreak to resume the battle. During the night, Clinton silently slipped away, and continued his march to New York. Washington followed, establishing his headquarters nearby at White Plains; later moving to Morristown, New Jersey, for the winter.

Meanwhile, the final campaign of the war was slowly developing in the South. After Burgoyne's surrender at Saratoga and the failure of the British plan to isolate New England, a new scheme was developed to conquer the southern states, one by one. This strategy was good, since there were many loyal Tories in these former proprietary colonies. From the beginning of the war, patriots and loyalists had been engaged in civil war, destroying each other's property and murdering one another. Taking advantage of this bitter personal feud among former neighbors and friends, the British outlined their southern campaign.

The arrival of a French fleet carrying French troops during the summer of 1779 helped the development of action in the South. In the autumn of that year, ships commanded by Count D'Estaing appeared off the coast of Georgia. They landed troops to aid the Americans and laid siege to Savannah. However, the British held the city and the French squadron sailed away to defend the West Indies from attack. With the loyalists in control of the government, the patriots were forced to retreat into forests and swamps to carry on warfare.

Encouraged by the British success at Savannah, Clinton sailed from New York during the Christmas holidays with an army to invade the South. He took Lord Cornwallis as second in command and left Knyphausen to hold New York and to keep Washington anchored at his headquarters in Morristown, New Jersey. With the departure of the French fleet, it was safe to transport his army by sea for an attack on Charleston, South Carolina.

The expedition ran into stormy weather which caused the loss of one vessel carrying guns for the siege. Nearly all the horses belonging to the cavalry perished at sea. It was the end of January before the transports reached Savannah, from which place Clinton sailed to a spot about thirty miles south of Charleston. He landed his troops on John's Island. His plan was to attack Charleston by land while his fleet bombarded the city from the harbor.

About the middle of May, after resisting a siege, the Americans surrendered Charleston. When news came a few weeks later, that a French fleet was enroute across the Atlantic, Clinton sailed for New York. He left Cornwallis in command of 8000 troops. Lacking numbers and equipment, roving bands of militiamen harried the march of Cornwallis with hit-and-run warfare. They hid in the woods by day and raided the British camps at night. A page from the small orderly book of Francis Marion, whom the British nicknamed the Swamp Fox, reveals the alert method by which he earned this title:

Before George Town May 28, 1781

All the guards and pickets to keep their arms so near as to be able to take them at an instant and without confusion, night and day. No officer to leave his guard on any pretense. Should an alarm take place, all guards and pickets must be ready to make the utmost opposition and not to quit their posts but on the greatest necessity or by orders

MARION'S BRIGADE CROSSING THE PEEDEE RIVER

During the Revolutionary War, Marion and his followers roamed through the swampy region between the Peedee River and the Santee River in South Carolina. From their hidden camps, day and night, the Swamp Fox and his fighting men raided the British quarters.

from the commandant or field officer of the day. — Every officer to remain with his men during the night. — All horses must be picketed in the rear of the encampment at night.

Nathaniel Greene, who early in the war had taken over the difficult job of furnishing supplies for the army, asked to be relieved of the quartermaster's duties. He wanted to return to the field of combat in the southern campaign. Generals Greene, de Kalb, Gates, and Lafayette were among the officers dispatched to meet Cornwallis on his march northward from Charleston. Although the Americans lost more battles than they won, they managed to drive Cornwallis inland, drawing him farther and farther away from his supply bases on the coast.

The main battles in the Carolinas were Camden, King's Mountain, Cowpens, Guilford Court House, Hobkirk's Hill, and Eutaw Springs. At Petersburg, Virginia, on the twentieth of May, 1781, Cornwallis joined forces with Benedict Arnold, the able general who had deserted the Continental Army and joined the British Army.

Lafayette with a small force was encamped at Richmond, not far from Petersburg. A French fleet, commanded by Count de Grasse, was on the way to block a British retreat by sea. For good measure, de Grasse brought about 4000 troops from Haiti to enlarge the forces under Lafayette. Late in August, Washington left part of his army along the Hudson. He slipped away with his main force and headed south toward Chesapeake Bay. Clinton thought Washington intended to attack him in New York, and the troops had passed Philadelphia before the British General realized that Washington was enroute to Virginia.

While his army was embarking for a short voyage at the head of Chesapeake Bay, Washington paid a brief visit to his home at Mount Vernon. It was the first time in six years that he had been home.

Protected by a French fleet, Washington landed at Williamsburg. He assembled about 16,000 soldiers to close in on Cornwallis who was trapped on Yorktown peninsula. The siege of Yorktown began late in September, with a combined force including about 8000 French troops. On October 17, 1781, four years to the day after Burgoyne's defeat at Saratoga, Cornwallis was ready to surrender. Two days later, his soldiers marched out and stacked their guns while their army band played the old British tune, "The World Turned Upside Down."

Eight years after the Battle of Lexington, merely a skirmish on the village green, Great Britain acknowledged the independence of her former thirteen colonies in North America. By the Treaty of Paris, negotiated by John Adams, John Jay, and Benjamin Franklin in 1783, the United States extended from Canada in the north to Florida in the south, and west to the Mississippi River. The eyes of the world were turned toward the first new nation to rise in the Western Hemisphere. People everywhere wondered how long it would last. What kind of government would it have? Would the country grow and prosper? In war, could the nation defend itself?

MAP:

WA13r
Atlas of American History by Edgar B. Wesley

145

PART FOUR

New Government for New Nation

GEORGE WASHINGTON

This statue of Washington was made by the great French sculptor, Houdon, five years after the end of the Revolutionary War. The inscription on the pedestal was written by James Madison:

The General Assembly of the Commonwealth of Virginia have caused this statue to be erected, as a monument of affection and gratitude to GEORGE WASHINGTON, who, uniting to the endowments of a HERO the virtues of the PATRIOT, and exerting both in establishing the liberties of his country, has rendered his name dear to his fellow-citizens, and given the world an immortal example of true glory. Done in the year of CHRIST, one thousand seven hundred and eighty-eight, and in the year of the Commonwealth, the twelfth.

Chapter 10

People Choose Republican Form of Government

EXPERIMENTS PAVE
THE WAY TO UNION

AS EARLY AS 1754 at a meeting in Albany, Benjamin Franklin had submitted a plan for uniting the colonies. It had not been favorably received. When war had started with the mother country in the spring of 1775 and the Second Continental Congress had sent aid to Massachusetts, Franklin again urged the colonies to unite under a federal government. He had presented a plan for a confederacy to Congress on July 21, 1775, three months after the War for Independence began at Lexington. Article II of Franklin's draft stated:

The said United Colonies hereby severally enter into a firm league of friendship with each other, binding on themselves and their posterity for their common defense against their enemies, for the security of their liberties and property, the safety of their persons and families, and their mutual and general welfare.

Nearly a full year later, seven days after independence had been declared, John Dickinson, well-known author of the "Farmer's Letters," introduced different Articles of Confederation for Congress to consider. Although the states felt the need for closer cooperation in carrying on the war, all were wary of surrendering their newly acquired independence in managing their own affairs. Not until November 17, 1777, after Burgoyne's defeat at Saratoga, had members of Congress finally agreed upon the Articles of Confederation which were submitted to the states for approval. In July of the following year, the official text of the document was elegantly engrossed on a roll of parchment about ten feet long, ready for signatures of the men representing the thirteen states.

It was the First of March, 1781 when Maryland, the thirteenth state, agreed to sign the document. This made the Articles of Confederation the law of THE UNITED STATES OF AMERICA. Maryland's signature had been withheld until other states, especially Virginia, surrendered all claims to western territory to the Confederation. In October of the same year, Cornwallis surrendered at Yorktown, and the Revolutionary War came to an end. In meeting the problems that followed the war, it was soon plain to many citizens that Article II of the final draft was a stumbling block:

Each state retains its sovereignty, freedom and independence, and every power, jurisdiction and

BENJAMIN FRANKLIN 1706-1790

right, which is not by this confederation expressly delegated to the United States, in Congress assembled.

With thirteen states levying import duties, making treaties, printing money, regulating commerce, and calling militia, the result was confusion and bickering. Under the Articles of Confederation, Congress could ask the states for money to meet expenses, to pay the soldiers, to apply on the national debt, but had no power to enforce payment. The fundamental weakness of the Articles of Confederation was the inability of Congress to collect taxes. No government can function properly without money to meet expenses. Another fatal weakness was that Congress lacked the power to regulate commerce.

During the war, machinery operated by steam engines increased the number of mills in England. When the war was over, British manufacturers, anxious to recover their markets in the former colonies, sent boatloads of cloth and merchandise to the United States. The Americans, so long without goods from abroad, were as eager to buy as the British were to sell, since cloth made by machinery sold cheaper than yardage woven on hand looms. The money that Americans paid for these imports left the country and went to England. Soon the people did not have the money to buy the goods merchants carried on their shelves. Respectable businessmen who had always paid their bills before were bankrupt and closed their doors.

News items from *Columbian Magazine* describe what was happening to commerce and what people thought about it:

A sloop laden with cheese, potatoes, and produce from Newport, Rhode Island, sailed for Charleston, South Carolina. After disposing of her cargo, the charges amounted to more than the net proceeds of her whole cargo. If dear-bought experience has not already convinced the northern states of the necessity of an energetic federal government to control and regulate trade, that foreigners may not supply our markets, we shall soon be convinced of it to our greater injury.

Factories are needed to encourage emigrants to come to our shores. It is necessary to encourage our own manufactures and employ our own people as we did during the Revolution in order to be truly independent. Now it seems we must employ manufacturers that live 3000 miles away and leave our own poor to wander in the woods and wilds of the back country to live like Indians and be useless to the nation.

In October of 1785 James Bowdoin, Governor of Massachusetts, in a speech to the legislature urged an appropriation to pay the national debt. He said:

Punctuality in the payment of taxes is so essential to public credit that the existence of the latter depends upon it.

147

Governor Bowdoin suggested that Congress acquire the authority to apportion the national debt among the states according to population to restore the nation's credit, as "every day's delay is embarrassing to the Union." Since the National Government lacked credit, it could not borrow money. The same was true of individuals. Business was hampered everywhere, but less in the southern states where people depended more upon agriculture and less upon manufacturing. Although clothing and many necessities were made on the plantations, southerners imported goods from Europe.

Some farmers in New England who could not pay their debts lost their land. In Massachusetts citizens took to armed rebellion in seeking redress for their grievances against the commonwealth. In the fall of 1786 Daniel Shays, formerly a captain in the Continental Army, led a band of about 600 men to Springfield and closed the court in session there. The General Court issued a public letter asking the legislature to investigate the causes of the insurrections and to remedy them, since much of the discontent was due to lack of funds. The report stated:

It is even said by some that a new Constitution is necessary. Soldier certificates must be redeemed, taxes cut, and duties levied upon imports.

Following an agreement between Virginia and Maryland for regulating trade and navigation on the Potomac River, another meeting was called by the legislature of Virginia for September, 1786, in Annapolis, Maryland to view the trade of the Union. When delegates from only five states — New York, New Jersey, Pennsylvania, Delaware, and Virginia — attended the meeting, only one thing was done, and that was important. Alexander Hamilton of New York wrote the report to the legislatures of these five states and to Congress, suggesting another meeting to which all states would be invited to discuss trade and other matters. The Annapolis Convention paved the way for the Federal Convention that framed the Constitution.

Meanwhile, mechanics were leaving the northern states for the Ohio Valley to claim cheap land and to try their luck at farming. In wagons and on horseback the emigrants headed westward over Braddock's Road and other trails to the frontier settlement of Pittsburgh. There they chopped down trees, built their own flatboats, loaded their few belongings and drifted down the Ohio. It was a dangerous journey. Sometimes Indians fired from the shore to halt the pioneers. More often they paddled their canoes into the stream and surrounded the clumsy arks, killing or capturing all on board. The tribes north of the Ohio River fought hard to keep settlers out of their hunting grounds. They were not successful. This area was known as the Northwest Territory and was ceded to the United States by Great Britain after the War for Independence. By 1787 so many emigrants had arrived there that it was necessary to provide some kind of government for them.

The last and greatest act of Congress under the Articles of Confederation was the Ordinance of 1787 for governing the Northwest Territory. This famous document guaranteed freedom of worship, trial by jury, right to own property, personal liberty, and representative government. Since most of the settlers had come from New England, where people generally were opposed to slavery, this ordinance forbade the system. It also stated that "schools and means of education shall forever be encouraged." When sufficiently populated, the Northwest Territory was to be divided into not less than three nor more than five states. These became Ohio, Indiana, Illinois, Michigan, and Wisconsin.

By 1787, after the rebellions in Massachusetts, people began to realize the need for a centralized authority. They were more willing to give up some of their flaunted independence under state rule for increased security under a stronger national government. In May of that year a meeting was called in Philadelphia to revise the Articles of Confederation. This gathering became the Constitutional Convention.

REPRESENTATIVES OF THE PEOPLE MAKE A CONSTITUTION

FULLY AWARE OF the great importance of this meeting, every state, except Rhode Island, sent delegates. About twenty-five per cent of the men chosen did not attend for various reasons, leaving fifty-five to carry the burden of the convention. Who were they? Why were they selected? What were their qualifications?

Members of colonial or state legislatures	46
Members of Continental Congress	42
Members of State constitutional conventions	10
Lawyers	34
Officers in the Revolutionary War	18
Signers of the Declaration of Independence	8
Signers of the Articles of Confederation	6
College men	25
Attended Annapolis Convention	7
Governors (had been or were to be)	16

After the Constitution was ratified, a number of men who had drafted it were elected to high positions in the new government.

Presidents of the United States	2
Vice President of the United States	1
Members of President's Cabinet	4
Justices of the Supreme Court of the United States	5
Justices of State Supreme Courts	5
Congressmen	14
Senators	19

The average age of the delegates to the Constitutional Convention was forty-four. Jonathan Dayton, twenty-six, of New Jersey was the youngest. The oldest was Benjamin Franklin — printer, scientist, diplomat — whose wisdom and wit enlivened the meetings he was able to attend. He was eighty-one and in poor health.

JONATHAN DAYTON 1760-1824

Although Jonathan Dayton was the youngest member of the Constitutional Convention, his experience exceeded his years. In 1776, at the age of sixteen, he graduated from the College of New Jersey, and joined the army, where he received the

149

commission as paymaster in the Third Battalion of New Jersey in which his father was a colonel.

He served under General Sullivan, becoming his aide-de-camp with the rank of major. He took part in the Battles of Brandywine and Germantown, endured the trying winter at Valley Forge, and fought under Lafayette at Yorktown. After serving throughout the Revolutionary War, he remained in the army until he was discharged in 1783.

Three years later, Dayton was elected to the General Assembly of New Jersey, and in the next year, delegate to the Constitutional Convention. He took an active part in the debates and signed the Constitution. Later, he again served in the legislature of New Jersey, and was elected Speaker of the General Assembly. He was elected to Congress five times, was chosen Speaker of the House of Representatives in the Fourth Congress, and was re-elected in the Fifth Congress. In 1798, he was sent to the Senate of the United States from New Jersey.

He took a great interest in the Northwest Territory, and acquired land in Ohio where the city of Dayton was named for him.

THE CONSTITUTIONAL CONVENTION

ALTHOUGH MAY 14, 1787 was the opening date of the convention, it was the twenty-fifth of May before a majority of the delegates arrived. On this day the first business meeting took place in the same city, in the same building, and in the same room where the Declaration of Independence had been signed. Who would be president of the convention? Benjamin Franklin was granted the honor of nominating George Washington

to preside over the meeting. Franklin's health, however, kept him home on that rainy day and Robert Morris took his place to propose the General's name. The motion was seconded by John Rutledge of South Carolina. When the ballots were counted every delegate had voted for Washington.

After several days occupied with the necessary chore of deciding upon rules of procedure, one being to debate in secret, the main subject of the meeting was introduced — revision of the Articles of Confederation. On the twenty-ninth of May, Edmund Randolph, Governor of Virginia, opened the discussion of the main topic by stating that the meeting had been called because the confederation of practically independent states had provided no security against foreign invasion; no power to check quarrels among states; no authority to levy taxes for support and defense; and no way for Congress to compel states to obey laws and treaties. In revising the federal government, Randolph suggested that the delegates inquire into: the properties which such a system should possess; the defects of the Confederation; the dangers faced by the nation; and the remedy for these conditions. It soon became plain to most of the delegates that their work would be framing a new constitution rather than revising the Articles of Confederation.

Edmund Randolph

Edmund Randolph, born in Williamsburg, Virginia, studied law after graduating from William and Mary College. Since both his father and his grandfather had held the office of Attorney General under the King, his family expected him to follow in line. Instead, Edmund embraced the cause of the Revolution and joined Washington's

EDMUND RANDOLPH 1753-1813

the same year attended the Annapolis Convention.

In 1787, Randolph was chosen as a delegate to the Federal Convention in Philadelphia, where he introduced the "Virginia Plan" which was adopted as the basis of the Constitution. His training in law and his experience in government made him a leader in the debates. In 1789, Washington appointed Randolph the first Attorney-General of the United States; and, in 1794, Secretary of State.

After spending years in government, he returned to his law practice. He liked to read philosophy and great English poetry.

Randolph's "Virginia Plan" was based upon a paper written by James Madison. This plan proposed a national government of three departments: legislative, to make the laws; executive, to enforce the laws; judicial, to interpret the laws according to the Constitution. On May 29, 1787, also, Charles Pinckney of South Carolina introduced a plan for three departments, but not exactly like the one presented by Randolph. On the fifteenth of June, William Paterson, a delegate from New Jersey came forth with a plan more like the confederation than a national government, the "New Jersey Plan," favored by the smaller states. From the debates on these ideas, the final form of the Constitution emerged, based largely upon the "Virginia Plan."

staff in Boston in 1775. His father promptly disinherited him, and sailed for England with the British governor of Virginia.

Edmund was soon forced to return to Virginia upon the death of his uncle who left several plantations in his care. Not being a success as a planter, he returned to law. Randolph's office seldom lacked clients. Neighbors "beset him on his way to court with their papers in one hand and with guineas in the other."

In 1776, he was elected a delegate to the convention that framed a new constitution for Virginia, under which he became first Attorney General of the independent state of Virginia. The people of Williamsburg, the capital, elected him mayor. After one session as clerk of the House of Delegates, he served three years in the Continental Congress. In 1786, he was elected Governor of Virginia, and in

ARTICLE I
LEGISLATIVE DEPARTMENT

Power to make laws

Section I. All legislative powers herein granted shall be vested in a Congress of the United States, which shall consist of a Senate and House of Representatives.

Representation in this national legislature stirred up a long and heated debate that lasted for weeks. Some of the delegates, including James Wilson of Pennsylvania and James Madison of Virginia, argued that the lower branch, the House of Representatives, should be elected by the direct vote of the people. Others wanted this body chosen by the state legislatures. Wilson insisted that one branch of the lawmaking body should be drawn from the people, where "all government ought to rest." Madison added another reason for this plan, because allowing the people to vote directly for their representatives in Congress would "inspire confidence, and induce the Government to sympathize with the people."

How Representatives are elected

Section II. Clause 1. The House of Representatives shall be composed of members chosen every second year by the people of the several States, and the electors in each State shall have the qualifications requisite for electors of the most numerous branch of the State Legislature.

Since each State had its own voting laws, the Constitution allowed any citizen who could vote for members of the House of Representatives or Assembly in his own State, to vote for members of the House of Representatives in Congress.

Who may be a Representative

Clause 2. No person shall be a Representative who shall not have attained to the age of twenty-five years, and been seven years a citizen of the United States, and who shall not, when elected, be an inhabitant of that State in which he shall be chosen.

JAMES MADISON 1751-1836

James Madison was born on a large plantation in Orange County, Virginia. His education began in a school taught by a learned Scotsman, where he studied Latin, Greek, arithmetic, geography, algebra, geometry, and literature. He was tutored for college by the clergyman of his parish, and entered the College of New Jersey at Princeton when he was eighteen years old. His favorite subject was the history of governments in all times. In two years, he completed the three-year course, and returned to his home in Virginia.

Not being in good health, he remained at home, giving much of his time to teaching his six younger brothers and sisters. He was a diligent student of the Bible and spent much of his time in learning all he could about Christianity. This knowledge served him well when he

152

decided to study law and led him into spending most of his life in government. He lived to be eighty-five.

Madison's public life began with the Revolutionary War in 1775 when he was chosen for the Committee of Public Safety in his home County of Orange. While serving in the Convention that replaced the former colonial legislature, he voted to instruct the delegates from Virginia in the Continental Congress to cast their votes for independence.

Madison served in Congress during the last year of the Revolutionary War and for a year after the Treaty of Paris was signed. He learned, at first hand, in what ways the Articles of Confederation were weak. On April 18, 1783, he spoke in Congress on the necessity of the states providing a means for the government to pay the debts of the Revolution, if they were to enjoy the fruits of it. He said:

Let it be remembered, that it has ever been the pride and boast of America, that the rights for which she contended, were the rights of human nature. By the blessing of the Author of these rights on the means exerted for their defense, they have prevailed over all opposition, and form the basis of thirteen independent states . . . . In this view the citizens of the United States are responsible for the greatest trust ever confided to a political society.

His first term in Congress was followed by three years in the legislature of Virginia where he presented Thomas Jefferson's bill for freedom of religion, while Jefferson was out of the country as Ambassador to France. Madison, who advocated a stronger union of the states, urged delegates to attend the meeting at Annapolis. When only five states responded, he added his support to another meeting in Philadelphia in May of 1787, the Constitutional

Convention, to which he was elected as a delegate from Virginia.

Madison's influence in calling this meeting, his knowledge of law and experience in government, his skill in debates, his journal of the proceedings, and his success in winning Virginia's acceptance of the Constitution earned for him the title – FATHER OF THE CONSTITUTION.

Madison was elected to the House of Representatives in the First Congress. He introduced amendments to the Constitution that became the Bill of Rights, copied largely from those written by George Mason for the Constitution of Virginia. He was Secretary of State in Thomas Jefferson's cabinet, and succeeded him in 1809 as the fourth President of the United States.

Representation according to population

Clause 3. Representatives and direct taxes shall be apportioned among the several States which may be included within this Union according to their respective numbers, which shall be determined by adding to the whole number of free persons, including those bound to service for a term of years, and excluding Indians not taxed, three-fifths of all other persons. The actual enumeration shall be made within three years after the first meeting of the Congress of the United States, and within every subsequent term of ten years, in such manner as they shall by law direct. The number of Representatives shall not exceed one for every thirty thousand, but each State shall have at least one Representative; and until such enumeration shall be made the State of New Hampshire shall be entitled to choose 3; Massachusetts, 8; Rhode Island and Providence Plantations, 1; Connecticut, 5; New York, 6; New Jersey, 4; Pennsylvania, 8; Delaware, 1; Maryland, 6; Virginia, 10; North Carolina, 5; South Carolina, 5; and Georgia, 3.

The real argument centered on how many men each State could have in each branch of Congress. Delegates from the small state of Delaware had been instructed to vote against any proposition to change the equal vote per state under the Articles of Confederation. The large states wanted representatives apportioned according to population.

The small states, fearing rule by the larger ones, wanted each state to have the same number of representatives. When the convention was dead-locked on the issue, Hugh Williamson of North Carolina stood up.

"If we do not concede on both sides," he said, "our business must soon be at an end."

JOHN LANGDON 1741-1819

John Langdon, born in Portsmouth, New Hampshire, became a successful merchant and an ardent patriot. Before the actual fighting began in the Revolutionary War, he and John Sullivan (General Sullivan) led a raid on Fort William and Mary in Portsmouth, carried off all the cannon, and ninety-seven kegs of powder. They hid the loot under the pulpit of Durham Church. Several cartloads of this powder were used in the Battle of Bunker Hill.

Langdon sold seventy hogsheads of tobacco, borrowed money, and used his own funds to equip the New Hampshire militia, making possible General Stark's victory at Bennington in 1777.

In between terms as Speaker of the Assembly, Judge of the Court of Common Pleas, delegate to the Continental Congress, and President of the State Convention to frame a constitution for New Hampshire, he was a soldier in the field.

When he and Nicholas Gilman, a young lawyer, were chosen as delegates to represent New Hampshire in the Federal Convention, the state treasury apparently lacked funds to send them. Langdon offered to pay expenses for both of them, and they arrived in July. Although late, they took part in the debates, and signed the Constitution.

As temporary President of the First Congress under the new Constitution, Langdon had the honor of notifying Washington of his election as first President of the United States. He was twice elected Governor of New Hampshire, and both he and Gilman served in the United States Senate.

THE CONNECTICUT COMPROMISE

BEFORE THE MEETING was adjourned on July 2 to celebrate Independence Day, a committee of eleven members, one from each state, was chosen by ballot to work during the holiday recess to obtain the compromise requested by Ellsworth and

Sherman from Connecticut. (The delegates from New Hampshire had not yet arrived.)

The following delegates were selected:

Massachusetts	Elbridge Gerry
Connecticut	Oliver Ellsworth
New York	Robert Yates
New Jersey	William Paterson
Pennsylvania	Benjamin Franklin
Delaware	Gunning Bedford, Jr.
Maryland	Luther Martin
Virginia	George Mason
North Carolina	William Davis
South Carolina	John Rutledge
Georgia	Abraham Baldwin

On the fifth of July, Elbridge Gerry, chairman of the committee, reported to the convention the compromise:

That in the first branch of the legislature each of the states now in the Union shall be allowed one member for every 40,000 inhabitants;

That each state not containing that number shall be allowed one member;

That all bills for raising or appropriating money, and for fixing the salaries of the officers of the Government of the United States shall originate in the first branch of the legislature, and shall not be altered or amended by the second branch;

That no money shall be drawn from the public treasury, but in pursuance of appropriations to be originated in the first branch;

That in the second branch each state have an equal vote.

This compromise was for the most part accepted. In the Constitution, however, there was one Representative for every 30,000 people.

A new argument arose. Shall slaves be counted as population? This was settled with another compromise, counting "three-fifths of all other persons." Indians who did not pay taxes were not counted in the population.

Clause 4. When vacancies happen in the representation from any State, the Executive Authority thereof shall issue writs of election to fill such vacancies.

Clause 5. The House of Representatives shall choose their Speaker and other officers, and shall have the sole power of impeachment.

If a Representative dies or resigns, the Governor of his State holds an election to pick a new one. Members of the House of Representatives choose one member to be the Speaker and preside over the meetings. The House of Representatives, by a majority vote, has the power to accuse officials of the Government of misconduct. This is called impeachment.

The Senate

Section III. Clause 1. The Senate of the United States shall be composed of two Senators from each State, chosen by the Legislature thereof, for six years; and each Senator shall have one vote.

By the Seventeenth Amendment (1913), Senators are now elected by the direct vote of the people, the same as Representatives.

CLASSIFICATION OF SENATORS. Clause 2. Immediately after they shall be assembled in consequence of the first election, they shall be divided as equally as may be into three classes. The seats of the Senators of the first class shall be vacated at the expiration of the second year, of the second class at the expiration of the fourth year, and of the third class at the expiration of the sixth year, so that one-third may be chosen every second year; and if vacancies happen by resignation, or otherwise, during the recess of the Legislature of any State, the Executive thereof may make temporary appointments until the next meeting of the Legislature which shall then fill such vacancies.

Senators are elected to have only one-third of them new at any time; one-third will have four more years to serve; and one-third will have two more years to serve.

QUALIFICATIONS OF SENATORS. Clause 3. No person shall be a Senator who shall not have attained to the age of thirty years, and been nine years a citizen of the United States, and who shall not, when elected, be an inhabitant of that State for which he shall be chosen.

PRESIDENT OF THE SENATE. Clause 4. The Vice President of the United States shall be President of the Senate, but shall have no vote unless they be equally divided.

Clause 5. The Senate shall choose their other officers, and also a President pro tempore, in the absence of the Vice President, or when he shall exercise the office of President of the United States.

The Vice President is President of the Senate, but he votes only when there is a tie vote. Senators elect one of their own number to preside when the Vice President is absent, or he has become President of the United States after the President's death or removal for another reason. Then the President of the Senate is the President pro tempore.

SENATE A COURT FOR TRIAL OF IMPEACHMENTS. Clause 6. The Senate shall have the sole power to try all impeachments. When sitting for that purpose, they shall be on oath or affirmation. When the President of the United States is tried, the Chief Justice shall preside; and no person shall be convicted without the concurrence of two-thirds of the members present.

JUDGEMENT IN CASE OF CONVICTION. Clause 7. Judgment in cases of impeachment shall not extend further than to removal from office, and disqualification to hold and enjoy any office of honor, trust, or profit under the United States; but the party convicted shall nevertheless be liable and subject to indictment, trial, judgment, and punishment, according to law.

Only if more than half of the Senators are present, can the Senate do its work. If two-thirds of Senators present find an impeached official guilty, he loses his job

and he cannot get another job in the Government. But the Senate cannot fine him or put him in jail. If he has broken a law, he can be tried in the regular courts. If a President is impeached, the Chief Justice presides at his trial in the Senate.

Elections of Senators and Representatives

Section IV. Clause 1. The times, places, and manner of holding elections for Senators and Representatives shall be prescribed in each State by the Legislature thereof; but the Congress may at any time by law make or alter regulations, except as to places of choosing Senators.

In 1842, Congress passed a law that Representatives must be elected by districts. In 1876, Congress passed a law that Representatives would be elected on the Tuesday after the first Monday in November.

MEETING OF CONGRESS. Clause 2. The Congress shall assemble at least once in every year, and such meeting shall be on the first Monday in December, unless they shall by law appoint a different day.

The Twentieth Amendment (1933), changed the date from the first Monday in December to noon on the third of January. Terms of new Senators and Representatives start on January 3.

ORGANIZATION OF CONGRESS. *Section V.* Clause 1. Each House shall be the judge of the elections, returns, and qualifications of its own members, and a majority of each shall constitute a quorum to do business; but a smaller number may adjourn from day to day, and may be authorized to compel the attendance of absent members in such manner, and under such penalties, as each House may provide.

RULE OF PROCEEDINGS. Clause 2. Each

House may determine the rules of its proceedings, punish its members for disorderly behavior, and with the concurrence of two-thirds expel a member.

The House and Senate decide if their members have been elected properly. If over half the members of the House or the Senate are present, work can be done. If less than half are present, they may adjourn or compel absent members to attend. They may make rules and punish members who break rules; and, with a two-thirds vote throw out a member.

JOURNALS OF EACH HOUSE. Clause 3. Each House shall keep a journal of its proceedings, and from time to time publish the same, excepting such parts as may in their judgment require secrecy; and the yeas and nays of the members of either House on any question shall, at the desire of one-fifth of those present, be entered on the journal.

Every word spoken every day in both the House and the Senate is in print by the next morning. At the demand of one-fifth, the "Yes" and "No" votes of each member will be printed in this Record. Citizens may subscribe to the Congressional Record and learn whether or not the men they elected are voting as they want them to vote.

ADJOURNMENT OF CONGRESS. Clause 4. Neither House, during the session of Congress, shall, without the consent of the other, adjourn for more than three days, nor to any other place than that in which the two Houses shall be sitting.

The President may not order Congress to adjourn. Both Houses must agree to go home at the same time. If one could quit without the other, no laws could be passed.

PAY AND PRIVILEGES OF MEMBERS. *Section VI.* Clause 1. The Senators and Representatives shall receive a compensation for their services, to be ascertained by law, and paid out of the Treasury of the United States. They shall in all cases, except treason, felony, and breach of the peace, be privileged from arrest during their attendance at the session of their respective Houses, and in going to and returning from the same; and for any speech or debate in either House they shall not be questioned in any other place.

Congress has power to fix salaries of members and the amount allowed for travel expenses. Senators and Representatives may not be arrested going to and from meetings except for serious crimes. They may not be punished for what they say in Congress except by that Congress.

OTHER OFFICES PROHIBITED. Clause 2. No Senator or Representative shall, during the time for which he was elected, be appointed to any civil office under the authority of the United States which shall have been created, or the emoluments whereof shall have been increased during such time; and no person holding any office under the United States shall be a member of either House during his continuance in office.

Senators and Representatives may not hold any other job in Government during their terms; may not take a job in Government that was started during their terms; and may not take a job for which the salary was raised during their stay in Congress. This rule prevents a Congressman from taking undue advantage of his election to create a big-paying job for himself.

REVENUE BILLS. *Section VII.* Clause 1. All bills for raising revenue shall originate in the House of Representatives, but the Senate may propose or concur with amendments, as on other bills.

This one sentence was written into the Constitution after long and heated arguments in the Convention. "No taxation without representation," the

157

slogan of the American Revolution, was fresh in the minds of the delegates. The people wanted to be taxed by their own elected representatives. Since the Senate was chosen by the State Legislatures, a number of the leading men favored the House of Representatives for tax bills.

George Mason of Virginia argued that "the Senate did not represent the *people* but the *States* in their political character. It was improper therefore that it should tax the people."

Elbridge Gerry of Massachusetts made the comment that "taxation and representation are strongly associated in the minds of the people, and they will not agree that any but their immediate representatives shall meddle with their purses."

Benjamin Franklin remarked "that it was always of importance that the people should know who had disposed of their money, and how it had been disposed of. It was a maxim that those who feel, can best judge. This end would be best attained, if money affairs were to be confined to the immediate representatives of the people."

How Bills Become Laws. Clause 2. Every bill which shall have passed the House of Representatives and the Senate shall, before it becomes a law, be presented to the President of the United States; if he approve, he shall sign it, but if not, he shall return it, with his objections, to that House in which it shall have originated, who shall enter the objections at large on their journal and proceed to reconsider it. If after such reconsideration two-thirds of that House shall agree to pass the bill, it shall be sent, together with the objections, to the other House, by which it shall likewise be reconsidered; and if approved by two-thirds of that House it shall become a law. But in all such cases the votes of both Houses shall be determined by yeas and nays, and the names of the persons voting for and against the bill shall be entered on the journal of each House respectively.

If any bill shall not be returned by the President within ten days (Sundays excepted) after it shall have been presented to him, the same shall be a law, in like manner as if he had signed it, unless the Congress by their adjournment prevent its return; in which case it shall not be a law.

Although the legislative department makes the laws, the executive department may check the laws, but not change them. As a check upon Congress, the Constitution provides that every bill be sent to the President for his signature before it becomes a law. If a President does not like the bill, he can refuse to sign it, but he must return it to Congress within ten days. This is another check, lest a President let a bill lie on his desk until Congress adjourned. If two-thirds of the Senators and Representatives again vote for the bill, it becomes a law without the President's signature. Each member of Congress has his vote, "yes" or "no," printed in the Congressional Record.

Approval and Veto Powers of the President. Clause 3. Every order, resolution, or vote to which the concurrence of the Senate and House of Representatives may be necessary (except on a question of adjournment) shall be presented to the President of the United States; and before the same shall take effect shall be approved by him, or, being disapproved by him, shall be repassed by two-thirds of the Senate and the House of Representatives, according to the rules and limitations prescribed in the case of a bill.

This same rule applies to "every order, resolution, or vote" on any duty given to Congress, lest Congress try to by-pass the President.

Powers Vested in Congress

Section VIII. Clause 1. The Congress shall have power:

To lay and collect taxes, duties, imposts, and

excises, to pay the debts and provide for the common defense and general welfare of the United States; but all duties, imposts, and excises shall be uniform throughout the United States.

Clause 2. To borrow money on the credit of the United States.

The authority to levy and collect taxes is the most important power given to Congress. Lacking this power, the Articles of Confederation failed. Under the Constitution, Congress has the right to tax imports from other countries; and goods made in the United States, especially liquors, cards, cosmetics, and items of luxury. These taxes must be the same all over the country. Congress may spend this money for three things: to pay debts; to maintain armed forces to protect the United States; and to do what is necessary in the best interests of the people. Congress may borrow money and promise to pay it back with interest.

Clause 3. To regulate commerce with foreign nations, and among the several States, and with the Indian tribes.

Under the Articles of Confederation, much confusion existed in trade because each state made its own rules for commerce. Congress has the right under the Constitution to regulate trade between states and with foreign nations.

Clause 4. To establish a uniform rule of naturalization, and uniform laws on the subject of bankruptcies throughout the United States.

Congress makes the rules for persons who come from foreign countries to make their homes in the United States. Congress also makes laws for people who are unable to pay their bills and must declare themselves bankrupt.

Clause 5. To coin money, regulate the value thereof, and of foreign coin, and fix the standard of weights and measures.

Clause 6. To provide for the punishment of counterfeiting the securities and current coin of the United States.

Only Congress may make money, both coin and paper, and declare its worth. Congress makes the rules for punishing men who duplicate Government bills, coins, stamps, or bonds. These thieves are called counterfeiters.

Clause 7. To establish post offices and post roads.

Congress builds post offices and hires the employees to transport letters and packages by truck, train, plane, and other means and to print and distribute stamps.

8. To promote the progress of science and useful arts by securing for limited times to authors and inventors the exclusive rights to their respective writings and discoveries.

An inventor may get a patent on his invention to prevent another person from copying it without his permission, and using it for his own profit. An author can get a copyright of his book, play, music and anything he has written, and no one can use any of his works without his written permission. This was done to promote science and learning.

Clause 9. To constitute tribunals inferior to the Supreme Court.

Congress has the right to set up courts lower than the Supreme Court, to handle cases which may be settled in these courts. Most legal cases are decided in the lower courts, leaving only the more difficult cases to be heard by the Supreme Court.

Clause 10. To define and punish piracies and felonies committed on the high seas, and offenses against the law of nations.

Pirates roamed the seas at the time the Constitution was written. Congress makes laws to punish crimes committed on American ships wherever the ships go, and crimes against other nations.

Clause 11. To declare war, grant letters of marque and reprisal, and make rules concerning captures on land and water.

Only Congress may declare war. However, the United States has been involved in undeclared wars, labeled "police action," such as the war in Korea, and in Vietnam. During a war, Congress may give a ship owner written permission, called a letter of marque, to capture ships and property belonging to the enemy. Rules for letters of marque usually stated what part of the captured property must be given to the Government to support the war effort.

Clause 12. To raise and support armies, but no appropriation of money to that use shall be for a longer term than two years.
Clause 13. To provide and maintain a navy.
Clause 14. To make rules for the government and regulation of the land and naval forces.

If a President could raise an army, he might become a dictator and rule the people by force without their consent. Allowing Congress to appropriate money to support the army for only two years is also a check upon Congress. Since Representatives are elected every two years, and the Constitution states that "all bills for raising revenue shall originate in the House of Representatives," the people keep a check on the armed forces. Congress makes rules for the army, navy, air force, and any means for defending the country.

Clause 15. To provide for calling forth the militia to execute the laws of the Union, suppress insurrections, and repel invasions.
Clause 16. To provide for organizing, arming, and disciplining the militia, and for governing such part of them as may be employed in the service of the United States, reserving to the States respectively the appointment of the officers, and the authority of training the militia according to the discipline prescribed by Congress.

Under the Articles of Confederation, each state had its own army, the state militia. These small groups won battles in the Revolutionary War, and the people were proud of them. A number of delegates, including Elbridge Gerry and Luther Martin, opposed federal control over the state militia, even though the officers would be appointed by the States. James Madison and Edmund Randolph favored the plan, insisting the central Government needed the authority to call out the militia for general defense. The militia is now called the National Guard, and can be ordered to serve anywhere in the world with the regular army. Congress makes the rules for their training.

Clause 17. To exercise exclusive legislation in all cases whatsoever, over such district (not exceeding ten miles square) as may, by cession of particular States and the acceptance of Congress, become the seat of Government of the United States, and to exercise like authority over all places purchased by the consent of the legislature of the state in which the same shall be, for the erection of forts, magazines, arsenals, dry-yards, and other needful buildings; — And
Clause 18. To make all laws which shall be necessary and proper for carrying into execution the foregoing powers, and all other powers vested by this constitution in the government of the United States, or in any department or officer thereof.

The men who wrote the Constitution knew Congress must be given the power to make laws for the future as well as the present. Congress may make laws to put into effect all powers in the Constitution. In Section VIII, twenty of these powers are listed.

DANIEL CARROLL 1730-1796

Daniel Carroll, the oldest of six children, was born in 1730 at the Carroll Manor in Prince George's County, Maryland. As a child he was largely taught by his mother until old enough to go to school in Europe. At eighteen he returned to his home in Maryland after spending six years at St. Omer, a school in French Flanders.

Three years later, in 1751, his father died. Being the eldest son, he took over his father's importing business, plantations, and tobacco farms. His only brother, John, five years younger, went to St. Omer,

studied for the priesthood, and became the first Roman Catholic Archbishop in the United States.

Carroll's success in business brought him into public life during the Revolutionary War. In 1777, he was elected to the five-man Council advising the Governor of Maryland. This Council had the duty of supplying Maryland's quota of animals, food, clothing, ammunition, and the scarce item of salt to Washington's army. A sample of the requests from the Continental Congress is this call for three hundred and fifty horses:

> The horses should be sound and clean-limbed not less than five years old this spring nor exceeding 12 Geldings at least 14½ Hands and not less than a quarter-blooded.

In a letter to Governor Johnson of Maryland, dated December 29, 1777, Washington asked for shoes, stockings and blankets for his soldiers:

> We had in camp not less than 2,898 men unfit for duty, by reason of their being barefooted and otherwise naked.

Daniel Carroll was elected to the Senate of Maryland and the Continental Congress in the same year, dividing his time between the two offices. He arrived at the Continental Congress on February 12, 1781, with the good news that Maryland had finally agreed to the Articles of Confederation. He promptly signed the document for Maryland, the thirteenth State, making the Articles of Confederation the first legal code for the United States as a nation.

In 1787 Carroll was chosen to represent Maryland in the Federal Convention in Philadelphia that framed the new code, the Constitution. As he had served in the

Continental Congress, he was acquainted with many of the delegates. After the meeting he returned to his home to support the Constitution and to urge its adoption by Maryland. In *The Maryland Journal,* Carroll answered a criticism by Samuel Chase who opposed the Constitution. In defense he quoted the words of James Wilson, assuring people that any errors in the Constitution could be corrected with amendments. Carroll ended with this sentence affirming his faith in the new Government:

Regarding it, then, in every point of view with a candid and disinterested mind, I am bold to assert that it is the best form of government which has ever been offered to the world.

Carroll was elected to the First Congress as the Representative from the Sixth District of Maryland. He took a leading part in locating the seat of government on land belonging to his family where "one could see the Potomac from his own back door." He was present at the laying of the cornerstone of the Capitol on March 15, 1791, being one of three Commissioners.

In the later years of his life, his public service was limited by his own poor health and the care of his ailing mother who lived to the age of ninety-two years. In the *Maryland Gazette* and *Baltimore Daily Advertiser* of May 14, 1796, this notice was printed:

Last May 7, died at Rock Creek, Daniel Carroll, Esq., a gentleman of unbounded philanthropy, and possessed of all the esteem of all who had the pleasure of his acquaintance.

* * *

During Washington's administration, Maryland gave sixty square miles on the bank of the Potomac River for the capital of the United States. This area does not belong to any state, and is governed by Congress. The city was named for the first President. The Twenty-third Amendment gave the right to vote to residents of the District of Columbia. The United States Government owns and governs all lands and buildings used for its purposes. The Government is the largest single landowner in the country.

Powers Forbidden to Congress

IMMIGRANTS, HOW ADMITTED. *Section IX.* Clause 1. The migration or importation of such persons as any of the States now existing shall think proper to admit, shall not be prohibited by the Congress prior to the year one thousand eight hundred and eight, but a tax or duty may be imposed on such importation, not exceeding ten dollars for each person.

A second compromise on slavery was added, that Congress could not stop the importation of slaves before 1808, but could tax "such persons," not exceeding ten dollars for each one entering the country. Neither the word slave nor the word slavery appear in the Constitution.

Most of the delegates in the Constitutional Convention were opposed to slavery, including many who owned slaves. George Mason of Virginia and Luther Martin of Maryland bitterly denounced the system, and did not want it to be a part of the Constitution.

Charles Pinckney was of the opinion that the southern states "will probably of themselves stop importations" of slaves. However, since the plantation owners of the South were forced to depend upon slave labor, Pinckney stated that "an attempt to take away the right as proposed will produce serious objec-

CHARLES COTESWORTH PINCKNEY
1746-1825

tions to the Constitution" which he wished to see adopted.

At seven years of age, Charles Cotesworth Pinckney left his home in Charleston, South Carolina to attend schools in England. At Oxford, he took many notes on the lectures given by the famous British judge, Sir William Blackstone. He entered the Temple, a law school in London, at the age of eighteen. He later studied for nine months in a military school in France before returning to Charleston to open his law office.

In a few years, he put his military training to good use in the Revolutionary War, rising through the ranks to brigadier-general. When the British forces took Charleston, he was captured in the fighting, and remained a prisoner for two years. To taunts from English officers trying to shake his loyalty, he replied:

I entered into this cause after reflection and through principle. My heart is altogether American, and neither severity, nor favor, nor poverty, nor affluence can ever induce me to swerve from it.

After the war ended, he resumed his practice. As he was a highly successful lawyer with experience in writing the Constitution of South Carolina, he was chosen as a delegate to the Federal Convention to use his wide knowledge of law in framing the Constitution of the United States.

After the adoption of the Constitution, Pinckney declined offers of Associate Justice of the Supreme Court, Secretary of War, and Secretary of State. He did accept the difficult task of representing the United States during the "XYZ Affair" of the French government. He was generous with his time in serving his city, state and nation, including years as president of the Bible Society of Charleston. Among his associates, he was noted for his cordial hospitality, his easy manner, and his brilliant conversation.

HABEAS CORPUS. Clause 2. The privilege of the writ of habeas corpus shall not be suspended, unless when in cases of rebellion or invasion the public safety may require it.

A person thrown into jail may get a habeas corpus (have the body) paper from the court demanding to know why he was arrested. If the jailer is unable to show good reasons for holding the person in jail, the prisoner is freed. Congress may deny this writ of habeas corpus only if it is necessary to keep the prisoner in jail for the safety of the country.

ATTAINDER. Clause 3. No bill of attainder or ex post facto law shall be passed.

In England, by an act of Parliament, a man could be denied the right of trial by jury, a hearing in court, and witnesses to prove his guilt or innocence. The accused man could not inherit property, nor could his children inherit his lands and wealth. This legal injustice was called a "bill of attainder," and was used by some of the English kings to "attain" property by punishing men they did not like.

A person may not be arrested and punished for breaking a law that did not exist at the time he failed to obey the law. This injustice would be an ex post facto law, meaning, after the time the thing was done.

DIRECT TAXES. Clause 4. No capitation or other direct tax shall be laid, unless in proportion to the census or enumeration hereinbefore directed to be taken.

Congress may not tax citizens directly unless each one pays the same amount. Capitation means a tax on every "head," usually called a "poll" tax.

REGULATIONS REGARDING CUSTOMS DUTIES. Clause 5. No tax or duty shall be laid on articles exported from any State.

Clause 6. No preference shall be given by any regulation of commerce or revenue to the ports of one State over those of another, nor shall vessels bound to or from one State be obliged to enter, clear, or pay duties in another.

Under the Articles of Confederation, each state levied its own taxes. This resulted in confusion and loss of trade. The people wanted to trade freely with one another without laws favoring one state over another, and without interference from Congress.

MONEYS, HOW DRAWN. Clause 7. No money shall be drawn from the treasury but in conse-

quence of appropriations made by law; and a regular statement and account of the receipts and expenditures of all public money shall be published from time to time.

In guarding the public purse, delegates stated rules for taking money out of the Treasury. "Appropriations made by law" means that no money can be used without a bill originating in the House of Representatives, passed by both House and Senate, and signed by the President. Congress must tell the people how much money comes into the Treasury, how much is spent, and for what purpose.

TITLES OF NOBILITY PROHIBITED. Clause 8. No title of nobility shall be granted by the United States. And no person holding any office of profit or trust under them, shall, without the consent of the Congress, accept of any present, emolument, office, or title, of any kind whatever, from any king, prince, or foreign state.

At the time, many governments were monarchies where the King bestowed titles upon his friends. The Government of the United States may not give noble titles to people. No person working for the Government may accept a title from a foreign country, or gifts. This law has caused some embarrassment. (The delegates in the Convention did not expect a President to visit a foreign country, where, as a matter of courtesy, the ruler would give him a present.)

Powers of States Defined

Section X. Clause 1. No State shall enter into any treaty, alliance, or confederation; grant letters of marque and reprisal; coin money; emit bills of credit; make anything but gold and silver coin a tender in payment of debts; pass any bill of attainder, ex post facto law, or law impairing the obligation of contracts, or grant any title of nobility.

Clause 2. No State shall, without the consent of the Congress, lay any impost or duties on imports or exports, except what may be absolutely necessary for executing its inspection laws; and the net produce of all duties and imposts, laid by any State on imports or exports, shall be for the use of the Treasury of the United States; and all such laws shall be subject to the revision and control of the Congress.

Clause 3. No State shall, without the consent of Congress, lay any duty of tonnage, keep troops or ships of war in time of peace, enter into any agreement or compact with another state, or with a foreign power, or engage in war, unless actually invaded, or in such imminent danger as will not admit of delay.

Section X lists many powers which the states had under the Articles of Confederation, but which the states will not have under the Constitution, except with the consent of Congress. Only after much debate did the states agree to surrender these powers to make a strong national government.

ARTICLE II
EXECUTIVE DEPARTMENT

Power, in whom vested

Section I. Clause 1. The Executive power shall be vested in a President of the United States of America. He shall hold his office during the term of four years, and, together with the Vice President, chosen for the same term, be elected as follows.

The delegates in the Constitutional Convention had many different ideas about the President, how he was to be chosen, the length of his term, and the number of terms allowed. Among others, Mason, Pinckney and Madison favored a term of seven years, and only one term. Wilson and

Sherman suggested three years; Ellsworth and Williamson, six years; Davie, eight years; Gerry, fifteen years; King, twenty years; and Hamilton, for life.

A compromise was finally reached on a term of four years, but none on the number of times a President could be elected. The President of the Convention heard these debates. When he was the first President of the United States, he refused to serve more than eight years. Washington established a precedent that was not broken for over one hundred and fifty years. After Franklin Delano Roosevelt had been elected four times, the Twenty-Second Amendment was added to the Constitution in 1951, limiting a President to two terms, or eight years in office.

ELECTORS. Clause 2. Each State shall appoint, in such manner as the Legislature thereof may direct, a number of electors, equal to the whole number of Senators and Representatives to which the State may be entitled in the Congress; but no Senator or Representative or person holding an office of trust or profit under the United States shall be appointed an elector.

There was as much disagreement among the delegates on how the President should be elected as there was on how long he should serve. Should he be elected by Congress? by the state legislatures? By electors chosen by Congress? By electors selected by vote of the people? By direct vote of the people? James Wilson, the great lawyer from Pennsylvania, argued throughout the debates that the President should be elected by the people, and not by the states. He finally won. Although the people do not vote directly for the President, they choose the electors who do vote for him. Each state gets as many electors as it has representatives and senators; but no one working for the federal government may be an elector.

PROCEEDINGS OF ELECTORS. — PROCEEDINGS OF THE HOUSE OF REPRESENTATIVES. Clause 3. The electors shall meet in their respective States and vote by ballot for two persons, of whom one at least shall not be an inhabitant of the same State with themselves. And they shall make a list of all the persons voted for, and of the number of votes for each, which list they shall sign and certify, and transmit, sealed, to the seat of the government of the United States, directed to the President of the Senate. The President of the Senate shall, in the presence of the Senate and House of Representatives, open all the certificates, and the votes shall then be counted. The person having the greatest number of votes shall be the President, if such number be a majority of the whole number of electors appointed, and if there be more than one who have such majority, and have an equal number of votes, then the House of Representatives shall immediately choose by ballot one of them for President; and if no person have a majority, then from the five highest on the list the said House shall in like manner choose the President. But in choosing the President, the vote shall be taken by States, the representation from each State having one vote. A quorum, for this purpose, shall consist of a member or members from two-thirds of the States, and a majority of all the States shall be necessary to a choice. In every case, after the choice of the President, the person having the greatest number of votes of the electors shall be the Vice President. But if there should remain two or more who have equal votes, the Senate shall choose from them by ballot the Vice President.

This section was changed by the Twelfth Amendment, ratified in 1804. (See Twelfth Amendment.) The electors from all the states make up the Electoral College.

TIME OF CHOOSING ELECTORS. Clause 4. The Congress may determine the time of choosing the electors, and the day on which they shall give their votes, which day shall be the same throughout the United States.

In 1872, Congress decided that the Tuesday after the first Monday in November in every fourth year would be the day for the people to vote for the electors who would choose a President.

QUALIFICATIONS OF THE PRESIDENT. Clause 5. No person except a natural born citizen, or a citizen of the United States at the time of the adoption of this Constitution, shall be eligible to the office of President; neither shall any person be eligible to that office who shall not have attained to the age of thirty-five years and been fourteen years a resident within the United States.

To be President, a man must be thirty-five years old, be born a United States citizen, and have resided in this country for fourteen years, but he can be born outside the United States.

PROVISION IN CASE OF HIS DISABILITY. Clause 6. In case of the removal of the President from office, or of his death, resignation, or inability to discharge the powers and duties of the said office, the same shall devolve on the Vice President and the Congress may by law provide for the case of removal, death, resignation, or inability, both of the President and Vice President, declaring what officer shall then act as President, and such officer shall act accordingly until the disability be removed or a President shall be elected.

In 1886, Congress passed a law that next in line to the President would be the Vice President, followed by the Secretary of State, Secretary of the Treasury, Secretary of War, Attorney General, Postmaster General, Secretary of the Navy, Secretary of the Interior, Secretary of Agriculture, Secretary of Commerce, and Secretary of Labor.

With the exception of the Vice President, all of these men are in the President's cabinet, and appointed by him. Since the Constitution provides for the President to be elected by the people through the electoral college, his possible successor should be a man elected by the people. In 1947, Congress changed the law and made the Speaker of the House of Representatives next in line to the Vice President. If he cannot serve, the elected President (pro tempore) of the Senate is the President. All of these men have been chosen by vote of the people. The line of succession then goes into the President's Cabinet, officers who were appointed, not elected, in this order: Secretary of State, Secretary of the Treasury, Secretary of Defense, Attorney General, Postmaster General, Secretary of the Interior, Secretary of Agriculture, Secretary of Commerce, Secretary of Labor, Secretary of Health, Education, and Welfare, Secretary of Housing and Urban Development, and Secretary of Transportation.

SALARY OF THE PRESIDENT. Clause 7. The President shall, at stated times, receive for his services a compensation which shall neither be increased nor diminished during the period for which he shall have been elected, and he shall not receive within that period any other emolument from the United States, or any of them.

OATH OF THE PRESIDENT. Clause 8. Before he enter on the execution of his office, he shall take the following oath or affirmation:

"I do solemnly swear (or affirm) that I will faithfully execute the office of President of the United States, and will, to the best of my ability, preserve, protect, and defend the Constitution of the United States."

During the debate on salary for the President, Benjamin Franklin asked to read his comments on the subject which he had written down, not trusting his memory. James Wilson offered to read the speech for him. Franklin, the oldest delegate, was the philosopher of the Convention. All listened with respect to his words of wisdom. Franklin spoke on what he had learned about the ways of men during his long life. A few of his remarks are quoted:

Sir, there are two passions which have a powerful influence on the affairs of men. These are ambition and avarice; the love of power, and the love of money. Separately each of these has great force in prompting men to action; but when united in view of the same object, they have in many minds the most violent effects.

And there will always be a party for giving more to the rulers, that the rulers may be able in return to give more to them. — Hence as all history informs us, there has been in every State and Kingdom a constant kind of warfare between the governing and governed: the one striving to obtain more for its support, and the other to pay less.

In all cases of public service the less the profit the greater the honor. To bring the matter nearer home, have we not seen the great and most important of our officers, that of General of our armies executed for eight years together without the smallest salary, by a Patriot whom I will not now offend by any other praise; and this through fatigues and distresses in common with the other brave men, his military friends and companions, and the constant anxieties peculiar to his station?" (Franklin referred to Washington who had refused pay for his services in the Revolutionary War. Washington later refused pay as President.)

Although Franklin pleaded for the office of President to be an honor without a salary attached, the delegates voted to pay the President. The first salary was set at $25,000 a year in 1789; $50,000 in 1873; $75,000 in 1909; $100,000 in 1949; and $200,000 in 1969. The President may not receive any other pay from the Government. Before he takes his office, a President swears to preserve the Constitution and to fight for it.

Duties of the President

Section II. Clause 1. The President shall be Commander-in-Chief of the Army and Navy of the United States, and of the militia of the several states when called into the actual service of the United States; he may require the opinion, in writing, of the principal officer in each of the executive departments upon any subject relating to the duties of their respective offices, and he shall have power to grant reprieves and pardons for offences against the United States except in cases of impeachment.

The President shall be the leader of the Army and Navy of the United States, and of the National Guard. The Secretary of Defense carries out his orders. The President has never led armed forces in a war. The duties of the Executive Department are supervised by members of the President's Cabinet, and he may ask their advice at any time. The President may pardon anyone who has done something against the government, except in cases of impeachment, which are handled in Congress.

MAY MAKE TREATIES, APPOINT AMBASSADORS, JUDGES, ETC. Clause 2. He shall have power, by and with the advice and consent of the Senate to make treaties, provided two-thirds of the Senators present concur; and he shall nominate, and by and with the advice and consent of the Senate, shall appoint ambassadors, other public ministers and consuls, judges of the Supreme Court, and all other officers of the United States whose appointments are not herein otherwise provided for, and which shall be established by law. But the Congress may by law vest the appointment of such inferior officers as they think proper in the President alone, in the courts of law, or in the heads of departments.

A number of the delegates argued over this treaty clause. Mason said the Senate "could sell the whole country by means of treaties." Rutledge and Gerry expressed the opinion that no treaty should be made without the consent of two-thirds of *all* the Senators, instead of two-thirds of those present. Gerry later agreed with Wilson's idea. Since treaties were the law of the land to be obeyed by all citizens, Wilson thought treaties should be approved by both the Senate and the House of Representatives like other laws.

The President nominates the men and women to represent the United States in other countries, and sends their names to the Senate for approval. He picks the judges of the Supreme Court in the same way. The President selects men and women for jobs whose appointments are not listed in the Constitution. Congress may authorize the President or the courts, or the members of the President's cabinet, to choose people for jobs in the Government.

MAY FILL VACANCIES. Clause 3. The President shall have power to fill up all vacancies that may happen during the recess of the Senate, by granting commissions, which shall expire at the end of their next session.

When the Senate is not meeting, the President picks men for jobs without the consent of the Senate. These men hold their jobs only until the end of the next meeting of the Senate.

MAY MAKE RECOMMENDATIONS TO AND CONVENE CONGRESS. *Section III.* He shall from time to time give to the Congress information of the State of the Union, and recommend to their consideration such measures as he shall judge necessary and expedient; he may, on extraordinary occasions, convene both Houses, or either of them, and in case of disagreement between them, with respect to the time of adjournment, he may adjourn them to such time as he shall think proper; he shall receive ambassadors and other public ministers; he shall take care that the laws be faithfully executed, and shall commission all the officers of the United States.

When Congress meets in January, the President speaks to both Houses of Congress in a joint meeting. He talks about the condition of the country and recommends laws he thinks should be passed. This is called the "State of the Union" address which can be read, but it is usually delivered by the President in person. The President may call the Congress to a meeting when he considers it is necessary for the good of the country. If the Senate and the House of Representatives do not agree on the time to quit, the President can close the meeting. This has never happened.

The President accepts ambassadors and other representatives from foreign countries. If he does not like one of them, he can tell him to go home. Although the President does not actually pick all the government officers, he signs their papers. The President's job is to see that the laws of the country are obeyed.

How Officers May Be Removed. *Section IV*. The President, Vice President, and all civil officers of the United States shall be removed from office on impeachment for, and conviction of, treason, bribery, or other high crimes and misdemeanors.

The President, Vice President, Justices of the Supreme Court, and other officers of the government can be impeached, that is, be accused of helping the country's enemies (treason); accepting bribes; or being guilty of "other high crimes and misdemeanors." Only the House of Representatives, by a two-thirds vote, can impeach an official. Then only the Senate, by a two-thirds vote, can convict that official. If found guilty after a trial in the Senate, the officer is dismissed.

When Lincoln was shot, the Vice President, Andrew Johnson, took his place as President of the United States. He was un-popular in Congress. He asked Edwin M. Stanton, Lincoln's Secretary of War to resign. Stanton refused, and Johnson appointed an army officer to take his place. Johnson was impeached on the grounds that he had no right to discharge a cabinet officer and appoint a new one without the consent of the Senate, then in session. After his trial in the Senate with the Chief Justice presiding, Johnson was declared "not guilty" by only one vote, and finished his term as President. Johnson was the only President to be impeached.

ARTICLE III
JUDICIAL DEPARTMENT

Power, how vested

Section I. The judicial power of the United States shall be vested in one Supreme Court, and in such inferior courts as the Congress may from time to time ordain and establish. The judges, both of the Supreme and inferior courts, shall hold their offices during good behavior, and shall, at stated times, receive for their services a compensation which shall not be diminished during their continuance in office.

Judging power was placed in a Supreme Court. Since one court could not handle all the cases that would come before it, Congress was given authority to establish lower courts as needed. Most cases to be heard in Federal courts start in the United States District Courts which are located throughout the country so as to be easily reached by the people. These courts handle cases involving citizens of different states, and cases involving laws of the Federal Government. Since most cases are decided in these courts, the largest number of courts are District Courts. Cases taken above the District Courts are heard in the ten Circuit Courts of Appeal located in large cities around the country. Appeals from these courts go to the Supreme Court in Washington, but not many, unless a question about the Constitution has to be answered. John Jay was the first Chief Justice, appointed by Washington in 1789, with four other judges. The present Supreme Court has a Chief Justice and eight Associate Justices. The President picks all the judges for these courts and the Senate approves them. They serve for life unless impeached and convicted.

To What Cases It Extends. *Section II.* Clause 1. The judicial power shall extend to all cases, in law and equity, arising under this Constitution, the laws of the United States, and treaties made, or which shall be made, under their authority; to all cases affecting ambassadors, other public ministers, and consuls; to all cases of admiralty and maritime jurisdiction; to controversies to which the United States shall be a party; to controversies between two or more States; between a State and citizens of another State; between citizens of different States; between citizens of the same State, claiming lands under grants of different States, and between a State, or the citizens thereof, and foreign States, citizens or subjects.

Government courts decide cases about the Constitution; the laws of the country; treaties made by the Government; representatives from foreign countries; laws on the sea. If a citizen breaks a law of the government, he is tried in a United States Court. If two states argue over boundary lines, the case is decided in a United States Court. The Eleventh Amendment was necessary to change the Constitution allowing citizens living in one state to sue another state. Now, a citizen must seek justice from the state legislature or the state Court of Claims. Cases between citizens of differ-

ent states are often settled in state courts, but can be heard in United States Courts. Cases involving a state and a foreign country, or an American citizen and a foreign citizen are heard in United States Courts.

Jurisdiction of the Supreme Court. Clause 2. In all cases affecting ambassadors, other public ministers, and consuls, and those in which a State shall be party, the Supreme Court shall have original jurisdiction. In all the other cases beforementioned the Supreme Court shall have appellate jurisdiction, both as to law and fact, with such exceptions and under such regulations as the Congress shall make.

If a State is involved, the case goes directly to the Supreme Court and does not start in a lower court. The same is true if a foreign representative is in the case.

Rules Respecting Trials. Clause 3. The trial of all crimes, except in cases of impeachment, shall be by jury, and such trial shall be held in the State where the said crimes shall have been committed; but when not committed within any State, the trial shall be at such place or places as the Congress may by law have directed.

Any person accused of crime has the right of trial by jury, except in cases of impeachment. The trial is held in the state where the crime was committed. If not in any state, Congress may rule where the trial is to be held.

Treason Defined. *Section III.* Clause 1. Treason against the United States shall consist only in levying war against them, or in adhering to their enemies, giving them aid and comfort. No person shall be convicted of treason unless on the testimony of two witnesses to the same overt act, or on confession in open court.

A person who fights against the country or helps the enemies of the United States is guilty of treason. Two witnesses must appear in court and prove an accused man is guilty of treason, or he must admit to what he did in court.

HOW PUNISHED. Clause 2. The Congress shall have power to declare the punishment of treason, but no attainder of treason shall work corruption of blood, or forfeiture except during the life of the person attainted.

Congress makes the rules to punish treason. No person convicted of treason may hold a government office. Punishment for treason may not take property from a traitor's children, or punish them for what their father did.

ARTICLE IV

RIGHTS OF STATES AND RECORDS. *Section I.* Full faith and credit shall be given in each State to the public acts, records, and judicial proceedings of every other State. And the Congress may by general laws prescribe the manner in which such acts, records, and proceedings shall be proved, and the effect thereof.

Congress makes the rules by which each state accepts the laws, records, and court decisions of all other states.

PRIVILEGE OF CITIZENS. *Section II.* Clause 1. The citizens of each State shall be entitled to all privileges and immunities of citizens in the several States.

A citizen of the United States has the same rights of his native state in every other state.

EXECUTIVE REQUISITIONS. Clause 2. A person charged in any State with treason, felony, or other crime, who shall flee from justice, and be found in another State, shall, on demand of the Executive authority of the State from which he

fled, be delivered up, to be removed to the State having jurisdiction of the crime.

LAWS REGULATING SERVICE OR LABOR. Clause 3. No person held to service or labor in one State, under the laws thereof, escaping into another, shall, in consequence of any law or regulation therein, be discharged from such service or labor, but shall be delivered up on claim of the party to whom such service or labor may be due.

If a man breaks a law in one state and runs away to another state, he can be sent back if the governor of the state he left asks the other governor to return him. The governor may examine the man's record and decide not to return him. The accused man may ask for a hearing to explain why he thinks, in fairness to him, he should not be returned. No law forces a governor to return a man accused of crime to the state he left, but most governors do.

A slave who ran away to a free state was not free. He was returned to his owner. This part of the Constitution is now meaningless; but, at the time, the slave states wanted it.

NEW STATES, HOW FORMED AND ADMITTED. *Section III.* Clause 1. New States may be admitted by the Congress into this Union, but no new State shall be formed or erected within the jurisdiction of any other State, nor any State be formed by the junction of two or more States, or parts of States, without the consent of the Legislatures of the States concerned, as well as of the Congress.

When settlers moved into new country, they formed a government and became a territory. When more and more settlers arrived, enough to make a state, the people called a convention to frame a Constitution which they sent to Congress. If Congress approved the Constitution, a bill was passed to make the territory a state. No new state shall be made inside another state. If the people wish to put states or parts of states together to form a new state, both the state legislatures and Congress must agree. For example, the Dakota Territory became North Dakota and South Dakota. Three new states – Washington, Oregon, and Idaho – shared the Oregon Territory.

POWER OF CONGRESS OVER PUBLIC LANDS. Clause 2. The Congress shall have power to dispose of and make all needful rules and regulations respecting the territory or other property belonging to the United States; and nothing in this Constitution shall be so construed as to prejudice any claims of the United States, or of any particular State.

Congress makes the rules for all Government lands. At the time, some states along the Atlantic seaboard claimed western lands, and these claims were not settled until the National Government was operating under the Constitution.

REPUBLICAN GOVERNMENT GUARANTEED. *Section IV.* The United States shall guarantee to every State in this Union a Republican form of government and shall protect each of them against invasion; and, on application of the Legislature, or of the Executive (when the Legislature cannot be convened), against domestic violence.

The United States is a republic under a Constitution establishing government by the governed. The Constitution requires each state to have a government by the people. The United States Government protects each state from invasion. If trouble breaks out within a state, the governor calls out the National Guard (militia) to keep order. If the state soldiers are unable to restore order, the President may send troops if the state legislature asks for help. If the state legislature is not meeting, the governor may ask for help.

172

ARTICLE V
CONSTITUTION, HOW AMENDED

The Congress, whenever two-thirds of both Houses shall deem it necessary, shall propose amendments to this Constitution, or, on the application of the Legislatures of two-thirds of the several States, shall call a convention for proposing amendments, which, in either case, shall be valid to all intents and purposes, as part of this Constitution, when ratified by the Legislatures of three-fourths of the several States, or by conventions in three-fourths thereof, as the one or the other mode of ratification may be proposed by the Congress; provided that no amendment which may be made prior to the year one thousand eight hundred and eight shall in any manner affect the first and fourth clauses in the Ninth Section of the First Article; and that no State, without its consent, shall be deprived of its equal suffrage in the Senate.

Amendments may be added to the Constitution in two ways. If two-thirds of the Representatives and two-thirds of the Senators in Congress agree to an amendment, it is sent to the state legislatures. If the amendment is approved by the state legislatures or by conventions called for this purpose in three-fourths of the states, the amendment is added to the Constitution.

If two-thirds of the state legislatures ask for an amendment, Congress shall call a meeting to propose the amendment. If three-fourths of the states, through their legislatures or conventions, agree to the amendment, it is added to the Constitution.

Article V of the Constitution lists two exceptions for adding amendments. No amendment could prohibit the importation of slaves until 1808. No amendment shall take away from any state, without its consent, equal number of Senators in Congress.

ARTICLE VI

VALIDITY OF DEBTS RECOGNIZED. Clause 1. All debts contracted and engagements entered into before the adoption of this Constitution shall be as valid against the United States under this Constitution as under the Confederation.

Under the Constitution, the United States would pay its debt contracted under the Articles of Confederation. All bills would be paid.

SUPREME LAW OF THE LAND DEFINED. Clause 2. This Constitution and the laws of the United States which shall be made in pursuance thereof, and all treaties made, or which shall be made under the authority of the United States, shall be the supreme law of the land, and the judges in every State shall be bound thereby, anything in the Constitution or laws of any State to the contrary notwithstanding.

The highest law of our country is made up of the Constitution, the laws passed by Congress, and the treaties made by the President and Senate. Some of the delegates were strongly opposed to making treaties the supreme law of the land without the consent of the House of Representatives where the members were elected by the direct vote of the people.

OATH: OF WHOM REQUIRED AND FOR WHAT. Clause 3. The Senators and Representatives before mentioned, and the members of the several State Legislatures, and all executive and judicial officers, both of the United States, and of the several States, shall be bound by oath or affirmation to support this Constitution; but no religious test shall ever be required as a qualification to any office or public trust under the United States.

All officers of both state governments and the national government in Washington must take an oath to defend the Constitution. A state officer swears to defend the United States Constitution before he swears to defend the state constitution. An official cannot be required to be a member of any one church.

PREAMBLE

FROM THE FIRST week to the last week of the Constitutional Convention, off and on, members of the Convention discussed the Preamble. What kind of government did they want to submit to the people? What did the people want government to do for them? How could they explain these goals in a brief introduction to the Constitution they were writing?

On August sixth, the following copy was reported:

We, the people of the States of New Hampshire, Massachusetts, Rhode Island and Providence Plantation, Connecticut, New York, New Jersey, Pennsylvania, Delaware, Maryland, Virginia, North Carolina, South Carolina, and Georgia, do ordain, declare, and establish the following Constitution for the government of ourselves and our posterity.

The next day, the delegates voted to accept this version. However, it was changed by the Committee of Style composing the final draft of the document. The five members of this Committee were skilled in writing the English language. They were:

Gouverneur Morris	Pennsylvania
James Madison	Virginia
Alexander Hamilton	New York
Rufus King	Massachusetts
William Samuel Johnson	Connecticut

The final wording was approved only five days before the end of the meeting:

173

"We, the people of the States" was changed to conform to the new union, and read, "We, the people of the United States."

PREAMBLE, We, the People of the United States, in order to form a more perfect Union, establish justice, insure domestic tranquility, provide for the common defence, promote the general welfare, and secure the blessings of liberty to ourselves and our posterity, do ordain and establish this CONSTITUTION for the United States of America.

After months of debate, the Preamble, in one sentence, stated the goals of the Constitution.

GOUVERNEUR MORRIS 1752-1816

After graduation from Columbia College, New York at the age of sixteeen, Gouverneur Morris studied law. He was admitted

to the bar shortly before his twentieth birthday. He was witty, wise, and courageous. In 1776, he spoke boldly for independence:

As a connection with Great Britain cannot again exist without enslaving America, independence is absolutely necessary.

As he was able to speak and write fluently in both English and French, he soon became a leader in public affairs. He was a member of the convention that framed a constitution for the state of New York. After his election to the Continental Congress during the Revolutionary War, he served on a committee to supply Washington's army at Valley Forge; was Assistant Superintendent of Finances of the United States; and negotiated with the English for an exchange of prisoners.

In the Constitutional Convention, as a delegate from Pennsylvania, Morris spoke on nearly every subject, outdoing James Wilson and James Madison who frequently debated the issues. The clear, elegant English in the Constitution of the United States is a tribute to Gouverneur Morris who wrote much of the final draft.

President Washington appointed him to the difficult post of United States Ambassador to France during the revolution in that country. Morris was the only foreign diplomat who remained in Paris during the Reign of Terror when the King and Queen were beheaded and savage mobs roamed the streets to destroy the French nobility. At the risk of his life, he sheltered Count D'Estaing, Vice Admiral of a French fleet serving with Americans during the Revolutionary War. Morris hid him in his own house. Through his efforts, Lafayette and his family were released from prison.

On his return, he made his home in the State of New York, and was soon elected a Senator. In the Senate, he made a powerful speech, urging the purchase of Louisiana, citing the dangers of allowing this territory to continue under the rule of Napoleon. His later years were occupied with his favorite project, building a canal between the Hudson River and Lake Erie. Until a few months before his death, he was chairman of the commissioners, who called him the Father of the Erie Canal.

ARTICLE VII
RATIFICATION
OF THE CONSTITUTION

The ratification of the Conventions of nine States shall be sufficient for the establishment of this Constitution between the States so ratifying the same.

Done in Convention by the unanimous consent of the States present the seventeenth day of September, in the year of our Lord one thousand seven hundred and eighty-seven, and of the Independence of the United States of America the twelfth. In witness whereof we have hereunto subscribed our names.

Go. WASHINGTON,
Presidt. and Deputy from Virginia.

All of the thirteen States except Rhode Island sent delegates to the Constitutional Convention. When nine of the twelve States held conventions and agreed to accept the Constitution, the Constitution would be law in those nine States. North Carolina and Rhode Island were the last States to ratify the Constitution, after the Constitution was in effect in eleven states.

The day was September 17, 1787. After nearly four months of debate, the time had come to sign the document. When the final draft had been read, Benjamin Franklin asked all members present to sign their names. Addressing his remarks to Washington, the presiding officer, he said:

For when you assemble a number of men to have the advantage of their joint wisdom you inevitably assemble with those men all their prejudices, their passions, their errors of opinion, their local interests, and their selfish views. — It therefore astonishes me, sir, to find this system approaching so near to perfection as it does.

Alexander Hamilton, the only delegate present from New York, also expressed his desire for every delegate to sign his name. John Dickinson of Delaware could not be there on that day, but he asked George Read from Delaware to sign for him. The first name was George Washington, President, and Deputy from Virginia.

A glowing sun was carved on the back of Washington's chair in Independence Hall. During the tense and solemn minutes while the delegates came forward to write their names, Franklin was heard to remark:

I have often and often in the course of the session, and the vicissitudes of my hopes and fears as to its issue, looked at that sun behind the President without being able to tell whether it was rising or setting. But now at length I have the happiness to know that it is a rising and not a setting sun.

Thirty-nine of the fifty-five delegates who had attended at one time or another wrote their names.

George Washington — President, and Deputy from Virginia

New Hampshire
  John Langdon
  Nicholas Gilman

Massachusetts
  Nathaniel Gorham
  Rufus King

Connecticut
  William Samuel Johnson

Roger Sherman

New York
  Alexander Hamilton

New Jersey
  William Livingston
  David Brearley
  William Paterson
  Jonathan Dayton

Pennsylvania
Benjamin Franklin
Thomas Mifflin
Robert Morris
George Clymer
Thomas Fitzsimons
Jared Ingersoll
James Wilson
Gouverneur Morris

Delaware
George Read
Gunning Bedford
John Dickinson
Richard Bassett
Jacob Broom

Maryland
James McHenry
Daniel of St. Thomas
  Jenifer

Daniel Carroll

Virginia
John Blair
James Madison

North Carolina
William Blount
Richard Dobbs
  Spaight
Hugh Williamson

South Carolina
John Rutledge
Charles Cotesworth
  Pinckney
Charles Pinckney
Pierce Butler

Georgia
William Few
Abraham Baldwin

Edmund Randolph and George Mason of Virginia, and Elbridge Gerry of Massachusetts watched the delegates sign, but refused to add their names. Later, these three outstanding leaders explained their action.

Washington forwarded the draft of the new Constitution to the President of Congress assembled under the old Confederation with the following resolution:

RESOLVED: That the preceding Constitution be laid before the United States in Congress assembled, and that it is the opinion of this Convention, that it should afterwards be submitted to a Convention of Delegates chosen in each state by the people thereof . . . ; and that each Convention assenting to, and ratifying the same, should give notice thereof to the United States in Congress Assembled.

With the draft, Washington added a letter with these closing lines:

. . . that it (the Constitution) may promote the lasting welfare of that country so dear to us all, and secure her freedom and happiness, is our most ardent wish.

The day was Monday, September 17, 1787. At four o'clock the meeting adjourned. Meanwhile, word spread that the convention was about to close. A few anxious citizens were gathered in the yard outside the building when the weary delegates walked out of Independence Hall. Mrs. Powell of Philadelphia stepped up to greet Benjamin Franklin.

"Well, Doctor," she asked, "What have we got, a republic or a monarchy?"

"A republic!" he assured her, quickly. Then he added the solemn warning, "If you can KEEP it."

Washington and the delegates dined at City Tavern in Philadelphia and said farewells. The delegates hurried away, eager to report the convention to the people in their own states, and to win their support for the government they had framed. When nine states had ratified the Constitution, the document they had written would become the basis of Government for the United States of America.

Fifty-five men! They were soldiers, farmers, tradesmen, lawyers, ministers, physicians, planters, merchants, professors. All loved liberty. They were Baptists, Quakers, Episcopalians, Presbyterians, Congregationalists, Catholics, Methodists, Huguenots. None were atheists. They were rich and poor; old and young; humble and haughty; tall and short; handsome and homely. They were the Founding Fathers.

So many different ideas from so many different men with so many different backgrounds were welded into the Constitution of the United States. This document has weathered the test of time to become the oldest working Constitution in the world today.

THE PEOPLE APPROVE
A NEW GOVERNMENT

DURING THE FOUR anxious months when the Fathers of the Constitution had been working behind closed doors, the citizens of Philadelphia in passing their meeting place had looked up at the windows with awe and wonder. Inside that red brick building, a handful of men were deciding the fate of a nation. For the first time in the history of the world, the people of a country, through their own representatives, were selecting their own form of government. The closing of the convention did not decide the matter. The people had yet to learn what kind of government these men had designed and whether or not the states would accept it.

In state conventions, chosen by the voters, each article of the proposed Constitution was read and debated, word for word. The vote in Delaware and New Jersey was unanimous, but the contest was close in some of the states.

Edmund Randolph wrote a letter to the Speaker of the Virginia House of Delegates explaining that he had not signed the Constitution because he thought it was better to amend it now.

"A bad feature in government becomes more and more fixed every day," he said.

In his letter, he expressed the hope that Virginia and other states would agree:

1. In making the language of the Constitution so clear and precise that it could not have more than one meaning.

2. In limiting the President's terms. (This was done by the Twenty-second Amendment, 1951.)

3. In taking from the President the power to nominate the judges to the Supreme Court and inferior courts.

4. In taking from the President the power to pardon treason at least before conviction.

5. In drawing a clear line between the powers of Congress and the powers of States, "to prevent the one from being swallowed up by the other, under cover of general words, and implication."

6. In reducing the power of the Senate "to make treaties supreme laws of the land."

7. In not allowing members of Congress to set their own salaries.

8. In limiting and defining the judicial power.

In the convention called to ratify the Constitution, Randolph urged Virginia to accept the Constitution as it was and voted for it.

Two days before the Constitutional Convention closed, George Mason, also from Virginia, expressed his opinion on changes he desired. Mason's main objection was that the Constitution did not have a Bill of Rights. He also objected to the Judiciary, stating that "the Judiciary of the United States is so constructed and extended as to absorb and destroy the judiciaries of the several States." He agreed with Randolph that the President should not have the power to pardon treason. Mason thought the Senate had too much power, because that body was elected by the state legislatures and not by the people.

Mason objected to the treaty clause, saying:

By declaring all treaties supreme laws of the land, the Executive and Senate have in many cases, an exclusive power of legislation which might have been avoided by proper distinctions with respect to treaties, and requiring the assent of the House of Representatives, where it could be done with safety.

177

Elbridge Gerry wrote a letter to the President of the Senate and to the Speaker of the House of Representatives in Massachusetts.

It was painful to me on a subject of such national importance to differ from the respectable members who signed the Constitution.

Then he listed his reasons, which are quoted below in part:

1. Some of the powers of the legislature (Congress) are . . . . indefinite and dangerous.

2. The executive (President) is blended with, and will have an undue influence over the legislature.

3. The judicial department will be oppressive.

4. Treaties of the highest importance may be formed by the President with the advice of two-thirds of a quorum of the Senate.

5. The system is without the security of a bill of rights.

He closed his letter with this sentence:

Nevertheless, in many respects, I think it (the Constitution) has great merit, and, by proper amendments, may be adapted to the "exigencies of government, and preservation of liberty" . . . .

These three men pointed the way to nearly half the amendments added to the Constitution in one hundred and seventy five years. The first Ten Amendments are the Bill of Rights. The Seventeenth Amendment (1913) changed the election of Senators from the state legislatures to the people by direct vote. The Twenty-second Amendment limited the President to two terms or eight years.

ROGER SHERMAN 1721-1793

Roger Sherman, as a shoemaker, supported his mother and younger children after his father's death. Devoting his spare time to the study of mathematics, he became a county surveyor. Later in life, he studied law and rose to be a judge of the highest court in Connecticut, where he served twenty-three years. He was tall, erect and plainly dressed as well as wise and reserved.

Roger Sherman is the only man who had the privilege of adding his name to four of the greatest documents of early American history. His signature appears on the Articles of Association of the Congress of 1774, the first Continental Congress. With Jefferson, Franklin, Adams and Livingston, he prepared the Declaration of Independence in 1776. He wrote his name on the Articles of Confederation. As a delegate to

178

the Federal Convention, he signed the Constitution of the United States in 1787. Returning home, he wrote articles for *The New Haven Gazette,* in which he urged the people of Connecticut to approve the new Constitution.

The greatest security that a people can have for the enjoyment of their rights and liberties is that no laws can be made to bind them nor any taxes imposed upon them, without their consent by representatives of their own choosing. The rights of the people will be secured by a representation in proportion to their numbers in one branch of the legislature, and the rights of the particular states by their equal representation in the other branch.

THE FEDERALISTS

MOST OF THE delegates in the Constitutional Convention went home determined to win their States for the Constitution. They wrote letters urging their friends to vote for it. They served in State conventions called to ratify it. They wrote articles praising the Constitution for newspapers. The greatest of these articles explaining the Constitution were printed in New York papers, addressed "To the People of the State of New York," and they became known as *The Federalist Papers.* The authors were Alexander Hamilton and James Madison of the Constitutional Convention, and John Jay who became the first Chief Justice of the United States. Hamilton contributed the most writings to *The Federalist Papers,* and Jay, the least. They won votes for the Constitution in New York and other states, where a number of patriotic citizens feared that a strong central government would take away their personal liberty, and deny the separate states a rightful share in government.

ALEXANDER HAMILTON 1755-1804

Alexander Hamilton was born of a Scotch father and a French mother on the little island of Nevis in the West Indies. Before he was thirteen years old, after the death of his mother, he left school and went to work for a merchant, Nicholas Cruger, in Santa Cruz. Cruger's counting-house was a beginner's school in finance for the boyish clerk destined to become the first Secretary of the Treasury of the United States. Here, he bought and sold cargoes; bartered with captains and traders in two languages; kept records and wrote letters in both French and English; learned how to handle money; and dreamed of the day when he could escape from the dreary life of a clerk. Yet, at fourteen, he was so efficient that Cruger

179

left him in charge of the business while he made a trip to the mainland.

A hurricane ended Hamilton's early mercantile career when he wrote a vivid description of the devastating storm that swept over the Leeward Islands, and a local paper printed it. His minister, friends and relatives thought a boy with such talent for writing should have a good education. With their help, Hamilton arrived in Boston late in 1772, and was enrolled in a preparatory school in Elizabethtown. In winter, he often studied until midnight. In summer, he began at dawn. In a year, he was ready for college, and applied to enter the College of New Jersey at Princeton. The President, Dr. Witherspoon, refused to accept Hamilton on his terms, that he be promoted as rapidly as he was able to complete courses of study. He then applied at King's College (Columbia) in New York, and was accepted.

After weighing both sides of the controversy between the colonies and the British government, Hamilton cast his lot with the Americans, speaking and writing in favor of the colonies. He read books on gunnery, ammunition, and military tactics before joining a volunteer corps of students, named "Hearts of Oak." The young men dressed in green uniforms, and wore the motto, "Freedom or Death," on their leather caps. Hamilton came under fire for the first time when the student corps marched to the Battery to capture the cannon there. A broadside from a British ship hit the Battery, killing one and wounding two of the young men.

Later, Hamilton was commissioned captain of a company of New York artillery. After watching the young officer drill his troops with model discipline, General Greene recommended him to

Washington. His bravery and leadership in a number of battles led Washington to place him on his staff. On March 1, 1777, Hamilton was appointed aide to the Commander-in-Chief with the rank of Lieutenant Colonel. He was barely twenty years old. He served throughout the war from the Battle of Long Island in 1776 to the final victory at Yorktown in 1781.

With peace, Hamilton settled in New York to practice law, but government still claimed its share of his time. He was sent by his home state to the Annapolis Convention, and to the Federal Convention that framed the Constitution of the United States.

Hamilton's greatest efforts for the constitution were his writings in support of it and his arguments for it in the New York State Convention.

President Washington appointed Hamilton as Secretary of the Treasury in his cabinet. In this position, Hamilton rescued the nation financially and started the government on the road to prosperity. He later returned to his own law practice in New York. In 1804, he was shot in a duel with Aaron Burr.

PHILADELPHIA CELEBRATES THE RATIFICATION OF THE CONSTITUTION

THE PEOPLE OF Philadelphia planned a celebration when nine states ratified the Constitution. By June, 1788 eight states had signed and conventions were in session in New York, New Hampshire, and Virginia. Perhaps the ninth state would sign in time to have the celebration on the Fourth of July. It would be fitting to observe both events on the same day. "TRUE FREEDOM can only be preserved by GOOD GOVERNMENT." The Constitution would guarantee the freedoms sought in the Declaration of Independence.

There was little chance for New York to be the ninth state to ratify. A majority of the delegates were opposed to the Constitution although Alexander Hamilton defended it. When New Hampshire ratified the Constitution on June 21 — 57 for and 46 against — plans began for the largest parade the city of Philadelphia had ever staged. Then a messenger arrived the evening of July 2 with the good news that Virginia had accepted the Constitution by the narrow majority of ten votes.

Early in the morning on this Fourth of July, the city was awakened with the ringing of bells and the firing of guns. The parade began at nine o'clock. It was a mile and a half long and took several hours to pass. It ended at Union Green. Behind the carriages of officials of Pennsylvania and foreign nations, rode two leading citizens, one dressed in the fashion of the day, and the other in the garb of an Indian chief. They were smoking the pipe of peace. There followed many floats on which the people showed the products they could make and exhibited their skill in making them. In all, fifty-eight trades and professions drew lots for places in the line of march. They ranged from porters to professors, plowmen to preachers, painters to physicians. Ministers of Christian churches and a Jewish rabbi walked arm in arm.

The grand float was the *Federal Edifice* representing the new national government. The roof of the temple was held up with ten white pillars. Three were left only partly finished, representing New York, North Carolina, and Rhode Island that had not yet ratified the Constitution. On top of the dome was a figure of Plenty bearing her cornucopia. The carriage was drawn by ten white horses, one for each state that had signed. Behind the *Federal Edifice* walked dozens of men of the building trades: architects, carpenters, brickmakers, stonecutters, bricklayers, house painters, plasterers, and others.

The *Federal Ship Union,* another large float, had mounted twenty guns and carried a crew of twenty-five men. The ship was built upon a barge once belonging to the *Serapis,* a British vessel captured by John Paul Jones during the war. Moving in the parade, the members of the crew performed their duties as if at sea. The captain went through the ceremony of receiving a pilot on entering a port. Behind the *Federal Ship Union* walked the tradesmen who could build and fit out a vessel — ship's carpenters, sail makers, boat builders, rope makers, and dealers in products for seamen. They carried a banner with this motto: MAY COMMERCE FLOURISH AND INDUSTRY BE REWARDED. Each group of tradesmen also carried a banner. The motto of the sixty rope makers in the procession brought a titter from the crowd. It read: MAY THE PRODUCTION OF *our* TRADE BE THE NECKCLOTH OF HIM WHO ATTEMPTS TO UNTWIST THE POLITICAL ROPE OF OUR UNION.

The Manufacturing Society, formed to offer premiums and to encourage industry, had an interesting exhibit on a long carriage drawn by ten bay horses. This float was a miniature factory. Two workmen operated a carding machine and a woman worked at a spinning machine. A weaver at a large loom wove cloth with a fly shuttle. A man designed and cut prints for shawls. A girl wove lace at another loom. An apparatus for printing muslins was exhibited. The inventor was a man named Hewson, whom Franklin had persuaded to leave England for America. His wife and four daughters rode on the carriage and displayed their skill on chintz. Weavers and clothmakers followed this float carrying a banner with these words: MAY THE UNION GOVERNMENT PROTECT THE MANUFACTURES OF AMERICA.

MAY OUR COUNTRY NEVER WANT BREAD was the slogan of 130 bakers who wore white shirts and pleated aprons with wide blue sashes. Their exhibit was a large oven in front of which master bakers rolled dough into pans and tossed piping hot buns fresh from the oven into the crowd as the parade crawled along. On a wagon drawn by two horses, men worked at a potter's wheel making cups and bowls. Twenty potters marched behind the float, some holding high a banner with the words, THE POTTER HATH POWER OVER HIS CLAY. Bricklayers, carrying trowels, hoisted the picture of workmen erecting a city in a forest clearing and the printed line, BOTH BUILDINGS AND RULERS ARE THE WORKS OF OUR HANDS.

A country boy in working clothes walked behind a plow drawn by four oxen. Then came other farmers sowing seed and millers grinding wheat. Grocers had five barrels of flour hauled on a dray splashed with the slogan, WE FEED THE POOR AND HUNGRY. The butchers, dressed in white, drove two prize steers in the line. After the parade both flour and cattle were given to the poor.

In a forge kept burning on a wagon, blacksmiths made a set of plow irons from old swords, worked a sword into a sickle, and made horseshoes to throw into the crowd for good luck. Other mechanics made nails, spikes, and tacks, selling them along the way as souvenirs. The owner of a brass foundry that had made cannon during the war, displayed his skill by making a three-inch howitzer in a furnace on his float. When the parade arrived at Union Green, he fired a salute with this gun. A chandelier of thirteen branches arched with thirteen silver stars formed the standard of the candlemakers. Their motto was, THE STARS OF AMERICA, A LIGHT TO THE WORLD.

Printers, bookbinders, and stationers set up a small printing press on their carriage, pulled by four gray horses. A man dressed as Mercury, the ancient god, tossed into the crowd copies of a poem as fast as the sheets rolled off the press. This ode was written by Francis Hopkinson, chairman of the parade committee and a signer of the Declaration of Independence. The closing lines read:

Hail to this festival! all hail the day!
Columbia's standard on her roof display;
And let the people's motto ever be,
UNITED THUS, and THUS UNITED FREE.

School boys and college students marched with their teachers and professors. Their leaders held aloft a flag with the inscription, THE RISING GENERATION. A troop of cavalry marked the end of the parade. When the rear of the line arrived, James Wilson, a Pennsylvania delegate to the Constitutional Convention and also a signer of the Declaration of Independence, stood on the *Federal Edifice* and spoke to the crowd. He began:

A people, free and enlightened, ESTABLISHING and RATIFYING a system of government, which they have previously CONSIDERED,

EXAMINED and APPROVED! This is the spectacle which we are assembled to celebrate; and it is the most dignified one that has yet appeared on our globe.

After telling his listeners what a wonderful privilege it was for a people to *choose* a government instead of having one forced upon them against their wishes, he warned that the success of the new government depended upon them:

A good constitution is the greatest blessing which a society can enjoy.

Among the virtues necessary to merit and preserve the advantages of good government, I number a warm and uniform attachment to LIBERTY, and to the CONSTITUTION. The industrious village, the busy city, the crowded port — all these are the gifts of liberty; and without a good government, liberty cannot exist.

The enemies of liberty are artful and insidious. A counterfeit steals her dress, imitates her manners, forges her signature, assumes her name. — Against these enemies of liberty, who act in concert, though they appear on opposite sides, the patriot citizen will keep a watchful guard.

The speaker impressed upon his listeners their duty in elections:

If the people, at their elections, take care to choose none but representatives that are wise and good, their representatives will take care in their turn, to choose or appoint none but such as are wise and good, also. — Let no one say that he is but a single citizen, and that his ticket will be but one in the box. That one ticket may TURN the election. In battle, every soldier should consider the public safety as depending on his single arm; at an election, every citizen should consider the public happiness as depending on his SINGLE VOTE.

Wilson praised the industries and opportunities in this country, and closed with these lines:

Peace walks serene and unalarmed over all the unmolested regions, while LIBERTY, VIRTUE, and RELIGION go hand in hand harmoniously, protecting, enlivening, and exalting all! HAPPY COUNTRY! MAY THY HAPPINESS BE PERPETUAL!

JAMES WILSON 1742-1798

James Wilson was born on a farm in the lowlands of Scotland. His parents, at his birth, decided their son should be a Presbyterian minister. Though poor, his stern, religious father sent the boy to a parish school to study Latin, Greek, geometry, rhetoric, penmanship, and catechism. After grammar school, Wilson walked six miles from his home to St. Andrews to study for the ministry. After the death of his father, Wilson found employment as a tutor for the children in a "gentleman's family," and abandoned the career that his parents had chosen for him.

183

His three older sisters could help with the farm work, but his three younger brothers were dependents. The scholar of the family was forced to be a bread-winner.

Wilson harbored a secret longing for America. After his sisters were married and his younger brothers could help themselves, he finally gained his mother's consent to leave. Friends and relatives raised the money for his passage, and he arrived in New York in 1765, the year of the Stamp Act. He went immediately to Philadelphia, armed with a letter to a trustee of the College of Philadelphia, where he got a job as a tutor.

Bored with teaching Greek, Latin and rhetoric to young boys, Wilson decided to study law. With the help of a cousin and schoolmate from Scotland, then a prosperous, land-owning minister in a frontier town in Pennsylvania, he paid the fee to study with John Dickinson. Here, he was tossed into the colonial storm that swirled around his teacher, and pondered the justice of the patriot cause of which he was to become a leading spokesman.

He signed the Declaration of Independence; served on the Continental Board of War; was Advocate-General for France; signed the Constitution of the United States; taught law in the College of Philadelphia; and was appointed by Washington as an Associate Justice of the Supreme Court.

Wilson was always the scholar, reading and studying, ever speaking and writing his unswerving belief — "THAT ALL POWER IS DERIVED FROM THE PEOPLE — THAT THEIR HAPPINESS IS THE END OF GOVERNMENT"

Wilson stepped down from his platform on the grand float, *Federal Edifice*. A crowd of 17,000 persons sat down to a picnic dinner on Union Green. It was a pleasant day with a cooling breeze. During the meal, ten toasts were given, one for each State that had ratified the Constitution. At the sound of a trumpet, the crowd rose and cheered for each toast while artillery replied with ten blasts. The ship, *Rising Sun*, moored in the Delaware River, joined each toast with ten firings of its guns. These were the ten toasts:

1. The people of the United States.
2. Honor and immortality to the members of the late Federal convention.
3. General Washington.
4. The King of France.
5. The United Netherlands.
6. The foreign powers in alliance with the United States.
7. The agriculture, manufacturers, and commerce of the United States.
8. The heroes who have fallen in defence of our liberties.
9. May reason, and not the sword, hereafter decide all national disputes.
10. The whole family of mankind.

After a gay and noisy Fourth of July, the people went home rejoicing. By six in the evening the crowd had scattered. All was quiet on Union Green.

A BILL OF RIGHTS IS ADDED TO THE CONSTITUTION

SEVERAL MONTHS before the first Congress under the Constitution met in New York, the legislature of Virginia wrote a letter to that body. The letter reminded the members that Virginia had ratified the Constitution under the promise that amendments would be submitted to the states, "to secure to ourselves and our latest posterity the great and unalienable rights of mankind." Circular letters were sent to other state legislatures asking them to make the same request.

In 1789 thousands were still living who had been denied these "unalienable rights" by colonial governments. In a long and bitter war they had gained these freedoms. Many patriotic citizens in state conventions voted against the Constitution because the document did not contain a guarantee of personal liberty.

Two months after Congress opened, the letter from Virginia was read in the House of Representatives. Debates on amendments were added to the discussions on import duties, Indian treaties, and government policy. Although Congress realized it was necessary to assure the people that the new Constitution would protect their freedoms, some members thought other business should come first. On June 8, James Madison from Virginia rose in the House of Representatives. He stated:

This day, Mr. Speaker, is the day assigned for taking into consideration the subject of amendments to the Constitution. As I considered myself bound in honor and in duty to do what I have done on the subject, I shall proceed to bring the amendments before you as soon as possible, and advocate them until they shall be finally adopted or rejected by a constitutional majority of this House.

On that same day, Madison presented his first draft of these amendments based upon the Virginia Bill of Rights by George Mason. He explained why he thought each one was necessary to guard against the abuse of power, both in state and federal governments:

I think we should obtain the confidence of our fellow-citizens in proportion as we fortify the rights of the people against the encroachments of the Government.

Almost every word in each amendment was carefully weighed and often debated. It was Madison who patiently wrote and rewrote each one until twelve amendments had secured a majority vote in Congress on September 25, 1789. The President, George Washington, forwarded copies of these amendments to the governors of the eleven states that had already ratified the Constitution and to the executives of North Carolina and Rhode Island, not yet in the Union. In the state legislatures each amendment was again debated, and ultimately, two of the amendments were rejected. On the fifteenth of December, 1791, ten amendments were approved and thus became an official part of our Constitution.

Since these ten amendments assured the human rights of man, which were ever above the rights of government, they were called the Bill of Rights. These principles were guaranteed by the new government. In no other country, at this time, were such freedoms protected for its citizens.

The man who deserves much of the credit for the Bill of Rights was George Mason. Mason of Gunston Hall and Washington of Mt. Vernon were friends and neighbors in Virginia. They visited back and forth; rode to the hunt with hounds; discussed British colonial policy; attended meetings in Williamsburg, the capital; and stood together in time of trouble. Mason gathered supplies for Washington's militia serving with General Braddock in his disastrous attempt to capture Fort Duquesne. In the Virginia assembly, Washington presented the resolutions of non-importation written by Mason. One of these resolutions pledged the planters not to buy any slaves imported after November 1, 1769.

GEORGE MASON 1725-1792

When war broke out between England and her colonies, Washington became Commander-in-Chief of the Continental Army. Mason stayed in Virginia to be the "pen of the Revolution." He refused high offices after his wife's death, explaining he could not serve because of "the duty I owe a poor little helpless family of orphans to whom I now must act the part of mother and father both."

After the Declaration of Independence, Virginia formed a new "Plan of Government" that included the Declaration of Rights written by Mason. This Virginia Bill of Rights was copied by other new states, and was closely imitated in the first ten amendments added to the Constitution of the United States.

In 1787, Mason was chosen as a delegate from Virginia to the Constitutional Convention in Philadelphia. Being a skilled debater and experienced in government, he

took an active part, staunchly defending the principle he had stated at the beginning of the War of Independence:

In all our associations; in all our agreements; let us never lose sight of this fundamental maxim that all power was originally lodged in and consequently is derived from the people. We should wear it as a breastplate, and buckle it on as our armor.

AMENDMENTS TO THE CONSTITUTION

Congress submitted twelve amendments for state ratification, prefacing them with the following preamble. The two rejected amendments are not listed.

THE Conventions of a number of the States, having at the time of their adopting the Constitution, expressed a desire, in order to prevent misconstruction or abuse of its powers, that further declaratory and restrictive clauses should be added: And as extending the ground of public confidence in the Government, will best ensure the beneficent ends of its institution:

RESOLVED by the Senate and House of Representatives of the United States of America, in Congress assembled, two thirds of both Houses concurring, that the following Articles be proposed to the Legislatures of the several States, as Amendments to the Constitution of the United States, all or any of which Articles, when ratified by three fourths of the said Legislatures, to be valid to all intents and purposes, as part of the said Constitution;

ARTICLES in addition to, and Amendment of the Constitution of the United States of America, proposed by Congress, and ratified by the Legislatures of the several States, pursuant to the fifth Article of the original Constitution.

BILL OF RIGHTS

FIRST AMENDMENT
ARTICLE I

RELIGION AND FREE SPEECH. Congress shall make no law respecting an establishment of religion, or prohibiting the free exercise thereof; or abridging the freedom of speech or of the press; or the right of the people peaceably to assemble, and to petition the Government for a redress of grievances.

Most of the early colonies followed the European custom of establishing a state religion which the people supported and attended. In Virginia, the official church was Anglican, the Church of England; in Massachusetts, Puritan; in New Amsterdam, Dutch Reformed. A few laws in the colony of Virginia afford examples of religion operated by government, and show why the people wanted a guarantee forbidding a national religion.

In 1659, 1662 and 1693, the Virginia Assembly passed laws to punish parents who failed to have their children baptized in the Church of England. In 1661, a law stated "that the canons set down in the Liturgy of the Church of England for celebrating divine service, shall be duly observed and kept."

In 1705 a law was passed punishing people who did not attend church services:

Be it enacted . . . that if any person, being of the age of twenty-one years, or upwards, shall wilfully absent him or her self from divine service at his or her parish church, the space of one month . . . shall forfeit and pay fifty pounds of tobacco. . . . If any person offending shall refuse to make payment . . . , by order of Justice . . . shall receive on his or her bare back, ten lashes, well laid on.

In 1748 the General Assembly of Virginia passed a law setting a minister's salary at 16,000 pounds of tobacco. Another law in the same year granted the church leaders in every parish the right to levy taxes on "all male persons of the age of sixteen years and upward" to support the established church.

Although such severe laws of punishment had been repealed, the people of Virginia were still taxed to support a government church after separation from England. In 1786, with Madison's support, "an act for establishing religious freedom" written seven years before by Jefferson, was made a part of the new state Constitution of Virginia. The law stated:

That no man shall be compelled to frequent or support any religious worship, place, or ministry whatsoever, nor shall be enforced, restrained, molested, or burthened in his body or goods, nor shall otherwise suffer on account of his religious opinions or belief; but that all men shall be free to profess, and by argument maintain, their opinions in matters of religion, and that the same shall in no wise diminish, enlarge, or affect their civil capacities.

Jefferson, then ambassador to France, wrote to Madison that this act of religious freedom had been received with enthusiasm in Europe, and 'that it' had been translated into French and Italian. Three years later, this "act" in the Virginia Constitution, forbidding a state religion, was condensed into sixteen words in the First Amendment to the Constitution of the United States, forbidding Congress to establish a national religion.

A man has the right to say what he thinks and write what he thinks, but he can not injure another with untrue statements.

Congress can make no law to prevent people from meeting peacefully to talk about their problems and to complain to the Government. Human rights denied to millions of people all over the world today are guaranteed to citizens of the United States in the First Amendment.

SECOND AMENDMENT
ARTICLE II

RIGHT TO BEAR ARMS. A well-regulated Militia being necessary to the security of a free State, the right of the people to keep and bear Arms shall not be infringed.

People have the right to protect themselves, and the right to keep guns for that purpose.

THIRD AMENDMENT
ARTICLE III

SOLDIERS IN TIME OF PEACE. No Soldier shall, in time of peace, be quartered in any house, without the consent of the owner, nor in time of war, but in a manner to be prescribed by law.

No soldier has the right to live in any man's house unless he is invited. Quartering of British soldiers in the people's homes was one of the causes of the Revolutionary War. In case of war, soldiers can be lodged in people's houses, but only as prescribed by law.

FOURTH AMENDMENT
ARTICLE IV

RIGHT OF SEARCH. The right of the people to be secure in their persons, houses, papers, and effects, against unreasonable searches and seizures, shall not be violated, and no Warrants shall issue, but upon probable cause, supported by Oath or affirmation, and particularly describing the place to be searched, and the persons or things to be seized.

People, their houses, papers and property can not be searched except for good reason, and then only by an official of government who shows a search warrant explaining in particular what or who is being sought.

FIFTH AMENDMENT
ARTICLE V

CAPITAL CRIMES AND ARREST THEREFOR. No person shall be held to answer for a capital or other infamous crime, unless on a presentment or indictment of a Grand Jury, except in cases arising in the land or naval forces, or in the militia when in actual service in time of War or public danger; nor shall any person be subject for the same offense to be twice put in jeopardy of life or limb; nor shall be compelled in any criminal case to be a witness against himself, nor to be deprived of life, liberty, or property, without due process of law; nor shall private property be taken for public use, without just compensation.

Death is the punishment for a capital crime; death or imprisonment for an infamous crime. No one has to go into court for either crime unless accused by a Grand Jury, a group of not more than 23 citizens. They are summoned by the county sheriff or the district marshal. This jury hears the witnesses and decides whether or not the accused person should be brought to trial. In some states the prosecuting attorney takes the place of the grand jury. This does not apply to the armed forces in time of war or any danger to the nation.

If a court finds a man not guilty of a crime, he shall not be tried again in court for the same crime unless new evidence has been found that amounts to a new crime.

Nobody shall be forced to say anything against himself in court. If an accused man is asked a question in court, he must tell the truth because he took an oath to tell the truth. If he tells a lie, and it can be proved, he is guilty of perjury and can be given a term in prison. Therefore, if an accused man thinks a truthful answer will help convict him of the crime of which he is accused, he shall not be forced to answer the question.

Nobody's life, freedom, or property shall be taken except through a fair trial under the laws of the Constitution. If government needs land for a country road, or lots and houses to clear the route of a city freeway, the owner shall be paid a fair price.

SIXTH AMENDMENT
ARTICLE VI

RIGHT TO SPEEDY TRIAL. In all criminal prosecutions, the accused shall enjoy the right to a speedy and public trial, by an impartial jury of the State and district wherein the crime shall have been committed, which district shall have been previously ascertained by law, and to be informed of the nature and cause of the accusation; to be confronted with the witnesses against him; to have compulsory process for obtaining witnesses in his favor, and to have the Assistance of Counsel for his defence.

A man accused of a crime has the right to a speedy trial before a fair jury in the state and district where the crime was committed. Witnesses who have accused him must face him in court and tell what they know against him. If witnesses who he thinks can prove him innocent refuse to come into court, they can be forced to come. If the accused man is too poor to hire a lawyer to defend him, the court will provide a lawyer for him.

SEVENTH AMENDMENT
ARTICLE VII

TRIAL BY JURY. In Suits at common law, where the value in controversy shall exceed twenty dollars, the right of trial by jury, shall be preserved, and no fact tried by a jury shall be otherwise re-examined in any Court of the United States, than according to the rules of the common law.

If a man is accused of taking money, he can ask for a jury trial if the amount is over twenty dollars. A trial can be taken before another jury, after one jury has ruled on it, only if there was some mistake made in the judicial process.

EIGHTH AMENDMENT
ARTICLE VIII

EXCESSIVE BAIL. Excessive bail shall not be required, nor excessive fines imposed, nor cruel and unusual punishments inflicted.

A man accused of a crime may deposit a required sum of money, called bail, with the court as a guarantee that he will appear at the time set for his trial. If the court is willing to accept bail, the accused man does not have to wait in jail for his trial to start. This bail shall not be excessive for the type of crime. A large bail for a small crime would be unreasonable. Courts shall not ask big fines for small crimes or offenses, such as a fine of $10,000 for illegal parking. Courts may not ask for cruel punishments, such as public whippings, stocks and pillories used in colonial times.

NINTH AMENDMENT
ARTICLE IX

ENUMERATION OF RIGHTS. The enumeration in the Constitution of certain rights, shall not be construed to deny or disparage others retained by the people.

The Constitution cannot list all the rights that belong to the people. Any rights the people had at that time, still belonged to them, in addition to those listed in the Constitution.

TENTH AMENDMENT
ARTICLE X

RESERVED RIGHTS OF STATES. The powers not delegated to the United States by the Constitution, nor prohibited by it to the States, are reserved to the States respectively, or to the people.

Although the Constitution had been adopted and put to work, many people still feared that a strong central government would take away the rights of the States. Congress hoped that the Tenth Amendment would allay this fear. It originally read: "powers not delegated by the Constitution are reserved to the states respectively." A representative from South Carolina urged that it be changed to "all powers being derived from the people." Finally, the motion by Daniel Carroll of Maryland carried, and the words "or to the people" were added.

The Bill of Rights was readily accepted and was declared in force in 1791. Two amendments were ratified within the next thirteen years. Sixty-one years elapsed before the next amendment appeared.

ELEVENTH AMENDMENT – 1798
ARTICLE XI

JUDICIAL POWER. The judicial power of the United States shall not be construed to extend to any suit in law or equity, commenced or prosecuted against one of the United States, by Citizens of another State, or by Citizens or Subjects of any Foreign State.

Citizens of one state cannot sue another state in a United States court. Citizens of a foreign country cannot sue a state in a United States court. This amendment changed Article III, Section 2 of the original Constitution.

TWELFTH AMENDMENT – 1804
ARTICLE XII

ELECTORS IN PRESIDENTIAL ELECTIONS. The Electors shall meet in their respective states,

and vote by ballot for President and Vice President, one of whom, at least, shall not be an inhabitant of the same state with themselves; they shall name in their ballots the person voted for as President, and in distinct ballots the person voted for as Vice President; and they shall make distinct lists of all persons voted for as President, and of all persons voted for as Vice President, and of the number of votes for each, which lists they shall sign and certify, and transmit, sealed, to the seat of the Government of the United States, directed to the President of the Senate; the President of the Senate shall, in the presence of the Senate and House of Representatives, open all the certificates, and the votes shall then be counted; the person having the greatest number of votes for President shall be the President, if such number be a majority of the whole number of electors appointed, and if no person have such majority, then from the persons having the highest numbers, not exceeding three, on the list of those voted for as President, the House of Representatives shall choose immediately, by ballot, the President. But in choosing the President, the votes shall be taken by States, the representation from each State having one vote; a quorum for this purpose shall consist of a member or members from two-thirds of the States, and a majority of all the States shall be necessary to a choice. And if the House of Representatives shall not choose a President, whenever the right of choice shall devolve upon them, before the fourth day of March next following, then the Vice President shall act as President, as in the case of the death or other constitutional disability of the President. The person having the greatest number of votes as Vice President shall be the Vice President, if such number be a majority of the whole number of electors appointed, and if no person have a majority, then from the two highest numbers on the list, the Senate shall choose the Vice President; a quorum for the purpose shall consist of two-thirds of the whole number of Senators, and a majority of the whole number shall be necessary to a choice. But no person constitutionally ineligible to the office of President shall be eligible to that of Vice President of the United States.

The main change in this amendment is that each elector now votes for one man to be President, and one man to be Vice President. Originally, each elector voted for two men. The one receiving the most votes became President, and the next highest became Vice President. With the rise of the two-party system, the original law had to be changed, making it impossible for the President to be of one party, and the Vice President of another party.

Formerly, if the vote in the Electoral College was a tie, the House of Representatives chose a President from the five highest on the list of candidates. The Twelfth Amendment changed the number to the three highest. If a President is not elected by March 4, the Vice President acts as President (See Article XX.)

If no man has over half of all the electoral votes for Vice President, the Senate selects one from the two highest on the list. Two-thirds of all the Senators must vote to elect a man. The man who wins more than half the votes of the Senators becomes the Vice President, in case of a tie. No person who is not eligible to be President can be Vice President. This rule is necessary because a Vice President becomes President if the President dies during his term.

THIRTEENTH AMENDMENT – 1865
ARTICLE XIII

SLAVERY PROHIBITED. *Section I.* Neither slavery nor involuntary servitude, except as a punishment for crime whereof the party shall have been duly convicted, shall exist within the United States, or any place subject to their jurisdiction.

Section II. Congress shall have power to enforce this article by appropriate legislation.

Lincoln's Emancipation Proclamation, as a war measure, freed slaves in seceded States and sections of States where people had left the Union. It did not abolish slavery.

Since slavery was legal in the original Constitution, it was necessary to add this amendment to the Constitution to forbid slavery, except as punishment for crime (prison labor), in the United States and in all territory belonging to the United States.

FOURTEENTH AMENDMENT – 1868

The Reconstruction Act, passed by Congress March 2, 1867, placed Alabama, Arkansas, Florida, Georgia, Louisiana, Mississippi, North Carolina, South Carolina, Texas, and Virginia under military control. The commanding officers of the United States Army prepared rolls of voters for conventions to establish State governments that Congress would accept. No citizen in these States could vote or hold office if he had served on the Confederate side in the War Between the States. Thus, when elections were held to choose legislatures in these States, the voters and candidates were mostly freed slaves, few of whom could read or write, and "carpetbaggers" who had come down from the north to take advantage of the situation for their own profit. The ten States could not be re-admitted to the Union until their legislatures ratified the Fourteenth Amendment. On July 21, 1868, Congress declared the Fourteenth Amendment was a part of the Constitution although Ohio and New Jersey had withdrawn their former ratifications at the time, leaving the necessary three-fourths of the States in doubt. However, on July 28, 1868, Secretary of State Seward certified that the Fourteenth Amendment was a part of the Constitution.

ARTICLE XIV

PROTECTION FOR ALL CITIZENS. *Section I.* All persons born or naturalized in the United

States, and subject to the jurisdiction thereof, are citizens of the United States and of the State wherein they reside. No State shall make or enforce any law which shall abridge the privileges or immunities of citizens of the United States, nor shall any State deprive any person of life, liberty, or property without due process of law, nor deny to any person within its jurisdiction the equal protection of the laws.

The first section of the Fourteenth Amendment made the freed slaves citizens of the United States and of the States where they lived. They were entitled to all the privileges of citizens. No State can make a law to prevent any man from his rights as a citizen of his State and the United States.

APPORTIONMENT OF REPRESENTATIVES. *Section II.* Representatives shall be apportioned among the several States according to their respective numbers, counting the whole number of persons in each State, excluding Indians not taxed. But when the right to vote at any election for the choice of electors for President and Vice President of the United States, Representatives in Congress, the Executive and Judicial officers of a State, or the members of the Legislature thereof, is denied to any of the male inhabitants of such State, being twenty-one years of age, and citizens of the United States, or in any way abridged, except for participation in rebellion, or other crime, the basis of representation therein shall be reduced in the proportion which the number of such male citizens shall bear to the whole number of male citizens twenty-one years of age in such State.

If a State prevents men twenty-one years and older from voting in an election for officials of the State or United States, that State will lose its apportionment of Representatives according to the number of citizens who had been kept from voting. (This has not happened.)

REBELLION AGAINST THE UNITED STATES. *Section III.* No person shall be a Senator or Representative in Congress, or elector of President and Vice President, or hold any office, civil or military, under the United States, or under any State, who, having previously taken an oath, as a member of Congress, or as an officer of the United States, or as a member of any State Legislature, or as an executive or judicial officer of any State, to support the Constitution of the United States, shall have engaged in insurrection or rebellion against the same, or given aid and comfort to the enemies thereof. But Congress may by a vote of two-thirds of each House, remove such disability.

Every man who had been in Congress, in a State legislature, in the electoral college, or who had held any office where he had promised to support the Constitution and later, had served on the Confederate side, could not hold office of any kind. However, he could ask Congress for amnesty (forgiveness.) If two-thirds of the House of Representatives and two-thirds of the Senate voted to forgive him, his name was removed from the black list and he could again run for office in the Government. The process was slow. Not until 1877, when Rutherford B. Hayes became President, was general amnesty granted to men who had served the Confederacy in the War Between the States. (Amnesty was not given to important men in the Confederate army and government.)

THE PUBLIC DEBT. *Section IV.* The validity of the public debt of the United States, authorized by law, including debts incurred for payment of pensions and bounties for services in suppressing insurrection or rebellion shall not be questioned. But neither the United States nor any State shall assume or pay any debt or obligation incurred in aid of insurrection or rebellion against the United States, or any claim for the loss or emancipation of any slave; but all such debts, obligations, and claims shall be held illegal and void.

Section V. The Congress shall have power to enforce, by appropriate legislation, the provisions of this article.

The southern States had to pay war debts of the United States, but debts of the Confederacy were not paid. No State could pay any debts incurred in fighting the war against the Union.

FIFTEENTH AMENDMENT — 1870
ARTICLE XV

RIGHT OF SUFFRAGE. *Section I.* The right of the citizens of the United States to vote shall not be denied or abridged by the United States or by any State on account of race, color or previous condition of servitude.

Section II. The Congress shall have power to enforce the provisions of this article by appropriate legislation.

No State shall deny the right to vote to any citizen because of the color of his skin or for his race. The right to vote cannot be denied to a citizen because he was once a slave.

The Thirteenth, Fourteenth, and Fifteenth Amendments were passed to guarantee rights of citizenship to former slaves.

SIXTEENTH AMENDMENT — 1913
ARTICLE XVI

INCOME TAXES. The Congress shall have power to lay and collect taxes on incomes, from whatever source derived, without apportionment among the several States and without regard to any census or enumeration.

The sixteenth amendment defined the meaning of "direct taxes" in Section II of Article I in the Constitution, as giving the Congress power to levy taxes upon the incomes of citizens, without trying to collect any specified sum from any one State.

SEVENTEENTH AMENDMENT — 1913
ARTICLE XVII

ELECTION OF SENATORS. The Senate of the United States shall be composed of two Senators from each State, elected by the people thereof, for six years; and each Senator shall have one vote. The electors in each State shall have the qualifications requisite for electors of the most numerous branch of the State Legislatures.

When vacancies happen in the representation of any State in the Senate, the executive authority of such State shall issue writs of election to fill such vacancies: *provided* That the Legislature of any State may empower the Executive thereof to make temporary appointments until the people fill the vacancies by election as the Legislature may direct.

This amendment shall not be so construed as to affect the election or term of any Senator chosen before it becomes valid as part of the Constitution.

This amendment changes Article I, Section III of the original Constitution. It was the intention of the "Founding Fathers" to have the House of Representatives speak for the individual citizens. Each citizen voted directly for the man to represent him in making the laws. The Senate was to be the voice of the States in Congress. Senators were elected by the State Legislatures. The Seventeenth Amendment changed this pattern by having Senators elected by the direct vote of the people, the same as the House of Representatives.

If a Senator dies or resigns, the governor of his State calls an election to choose a new one. Or, the State Legislature may give the governor the right to choose a new man to serve until the people elect a new Senator.

EIGHTEENTH AMENDMENT — 1919
ARTICLE XVIII

LIQUOR PROHIBITION. *Section I.* After one year from the ratification of this article, the manufacture, sale, or transportation of intoxicating liquors within, the importation thereof into, or the exportation thereof from the United States and all territory subject to the jurisdiction thereof for beverage purposes is hereby prohibited.

Section II. The Congress and the several States shall have concurrent power to enforce this article by appropriate legislation.

Section III. This article shall be inoperative unless it shall have been ratified as an amendment to the Constitution by the Legislatures of the several States, as provided in the Constitution, within seven years from the date of the submission hereof to the States by the Congress.

The Eighteenth Amendment stopped the manufacture and sale of any liquors that would make a person drunk. No one could sell intoxicating liquors to other countries, nor import them from other countries. Ratification of this amendment when proposed in 1917 was limited to seven years, but it became part of the Constitution much sooner, in 1919.

NINETEENTH AMENDMENT – 1920
ARTICLE XIX

WOMAN SUFFRAGE. The right of citizens of the United States to vote shall not be denied or abridged by the United States or by any State on account of sex.

Congress shall have power to enforce this article by appropriate legislation.

Although some States granted women the right to vote when their Constitutions were written, women could not vote in most States. This amendment guarantees women the right to vote in all States.

TWENTIETH AMENDMENT – 1933
ARTICLE XX

TERMS OF PRESIDENT, VICE PRESIDENT, MEMBERS OF CONGRESS, TIMES OF ASSEMBLING OF CONGRESS. *Section I.* The terms of the President and Vice President shall end at noon on the 20th day of January, and the terms of Senators and Representatives at noon on the 3d day of January, of the years in which such terms would have ended if this article had not been ratified; and the terms of their successors shall then begin.

Section II. The Congress shall assemble at least once in every year, and such meeting shall begin at noon on the 3d day of January, unless they shall by law appoint a different day.

This amendment changes parts of Article I and Article II of the original Constitution, and part of the Twelfth Amendment. At noon, on the twentieth day of January, terms of a President and Vice President end, and the terms of newly elected President and Vice President begin. The former date was March fourth.

Terms of Representatives and Senators end at noon on the third day of January, and terms of newly elected Congressmen begin. By law, the date may be changed. (If January third was on Sunday, the first meeting would probably be changed to Monday, January fourth.)

Congress is required to meet once a year, at least, and the meeting starts at noon on the third day of January.

Section III. If, at the time fixed for the beginning of term of the President, the President elect shall have died, the Vice President elect shall become President. If a President shall not have been chosen before the time fixed for the beginning of his term, or if the President elect shall have failed to qualify, then the Vice President elect shall act as President until a President shall have qualified; and the Congress may by law provide for the case wherein neither a President elect nor a Vice President elect shall have qualified, declaring who shall then act as President, or the manner in which one who is to act shall be selected, and such person shall act accordingly until a President or Vice President shall have qualified.

If the man elected President dies before his term starts, the man elected Vice President is the President. In case the President had not been elected in time to start his term, the elected Vice President is the President, serving until the President is elected. If neither a President nor Vice President has qualified for their offices,

Congress may pass a law naming a President or it may state how this man will be chosen. (Such a situation is not likely to happen.)

Section IV. The Congress may by law provide for the case of the death of any of the persons from whom the House of Representatives may choose a President whenever the right of choice shall have devolved upon them, and for the case of the death of any of the persons from whom the Senate may choose a Vice President whenever the right of choice shall have devolved upon them.

When the House of Representatives has the duty of choosing a President, Congress may pass a law on what to do if the man dies. If a Vice President chosen by the Senate dies, Congress may make a law on what to do.

TWENTY-FIRST AMENDMENT – 1933
ARTICLE XXI

REPEAL OF ARTICLE XVIII. *Section I.* The Eighteenth article of amendment to the Constitution of the United States is hereby repealed.

The Eighteenth Amendment is repealed.

Section II. The transportation or importation into any State, territory, or possession of the United States for delivery or use therein of intoxicating liquors, in violation of the laws thereof, is hereby prohibited.

The repeal of this amendment did not repeal liquor laws passed by States.

Section III. This article shall be inoperative unless it shall have been ratified as an amendment to the Constitution by conventions in the several States, as provided in the Constitution within seven years from the date of the submission hereof to the States by the Congress.

This amendment had to be ratified by conventions called to meet in each State, and not by the State Legislatures. The time limit was seven years.

TWENTY-SECOND AMENDMENT – 1951
ARTICLE XXII

PRESIDENT'S TERM OF OFFICE. *Section I.* No person shall be elected to the office of the President more than twice, and no person who has held the office of President, or acted as President, for more than two years of a term to which some other person was elected President shall be elected to the office of the President more than once. But this article shall not apply to any person holding the office of President when this Article was proposed by the Congress, and shall not prevent any person who may be holding the office of President, or acting as President, during the term within which this Article becomes operative from holding the office of President or acting as President during the remainder of such term.

Section II. This article shall be inoperative unless it shall have been ratified as an amendment to the Constitution by the legislatures of three-fourths of the several states within seven years from the date of its submission to the states by the Congress.

This amendment limits the President to two terms. He can be elected twice. Any President who finished another President's term cannot be elected more than once if he served as President for more than two years. It would be possible for one man to be President for ten years, but that would be the longest time. The law did not apply to President Truman, who was then in office and who did not seek a third term.

TWENTY-THIRD AMENDMENT – 1961
ARTICLE XXIII

PRESIDENTIAL VOTE FOR DISTRICT OF COLUMBIA. *Section I.* The District constituting the seat of Government of the United States shall appoint in such manner as the Congress may direct:

A number of electors of President and Vice President equal to the whole number of Senators and Representatives in Congress to which the District would be entitled if it were a state, but in no event more than the least populous State; they shall be in addition to those appointed by the States, but they shall be considered, for the purposes of the election of President and Vice President, to be electors appointed by a State; and they shall meet in the District and perform such duties as provided by the twelfth article of amendment.

Section II. The Congress shall have power to enforce this article by appropriate legislation.

The people living in the District of Columbia were not allowed to vote for President and Vice President. As it is the seat of the Federal Government, the District is governed by a Committee of Congress. According to the Twenty-third Amendment the people living in the District of Columbia have the right to vote for electors in the Electoral College the same as people of any State. The District may have as many electors as the least populous state. This number is three.

TWENTY-FOURTH AMENDMENT – 1964
ARTICLE XXIV

POLL TAX. *Section I.* The right of citizens of the United States to vote in any primary or other election for President or Vice President, for electors for President or Vice President, or for Senator or Representative in Congress, shall not be denied or abridged by the United States or any State by reason of failure to pay any poll tax or other tax.

Section II. The Congress shall have power to enforce this article by appropriate legislation.

A poll tax is a head tax. Each citizen under law in some states paid a tax to register as a voter. This amendment forbids any state to require any citizen to pay a tax to vote for President, Vice President, Senators and Representatives.

TWENTY-FIFTH AMENDMENT – 1967
ARTICLE XXV

PRESIDENTIAL DISABILITY AND SUCCESSION. *Section I.* In case of the removal of the President from office or his death or resignation, the Vice President shall become President.

Section II. Whenever there is a vacancy in the office of Vice President, the President shall nominate a Vice President who shall take office upon confirmation by a majority vote of both Houses of Congress.

Formerly when a Vice President became President at the death of a President, the country did not have a Vice President until the next election. During thirty-eight years of the nation's history, the office of Vice President was vacant. Section II provides for the country to have a Vice President at all times.

Section III. Whenever the President transmits to the President pro tempore of the Senate and the Speaker of the House of Representatives his written declaration that he is unable to discharge the powers and duties of his office, and until he transmits to them a written declaration to the contrary, such powers and duties shall be discharged by the Vice President as Acting President.

For example, a President facing a serious operation writes to the President pro tempore of the Senate and to the Speaker of the House of Representatives telling them that he is unable to fulfill his duties. Then the Vice President becomes the Acting President. When a President has recovered his health after an operation, he writes to the same leaders in Congress, stating that he is able again to fulfill his duties.

Section IV. Whenever the Vice President and a majority of either the principal officers of the executive departments or of such other body as Congress may by law provide, transmit to the President pro tempore of the Senate and the Speaker of the House of Representatives their written declaration that the President is unable to discharge the powers and duties of his office, the Vice President shall immediately assume the powers and duties of the office as Acting President.

The first paragraph of Section IV provides a legal way for the Vice President to become Acting President if the President does not realize he is unable to fulfill his duties.

Thereafter, when the President transmits to the President pro tempore of the Senate and the Speaker of the House of Representatives his written declaration that no inability exists, he shall resume the powers and duties of his office unless the Vice President and a majority of either the principal officers of the executive department or of such other body as Congress may by law provide, transmit within four days to the President pro tempore of the Senate and the Speaker of the House of Representatives their written declaration that the President is unable to discharge the powers and duties of his office. Thereupon Congress shall decide the issue, assembling within forty-eight hours for that purpose if not in session. If the Congress, within twenty-one days after receipt of the latter written declaration, or, if Congress is not in session, within twenty-one days after Congress is required to assemble, determines by two-thirds vote of both Houses that the President is unable to discharge the powers and duties of his office, the Vice President shall continue to discharge the same as Acting President; otherwise, the President shall resume the powers and duties of his office.

The last paragraph of Section IV was the subject of considerable debate before it was approved. Congressmen finally concluded this law provided for a situation not likely to happen, but was needed if it did happen. For many years, a law to provide for Presidential disability had been discussed in Congress, and was finally accomplished by adding this amendment to the Constitution. In brief, the Twenty-fifth Amendment provides for the country to have both a President and Vice President in office at all times.

Most of the men in the Constitutional Convention had served in colonial, state, and national governments in some way as soldiers, lawmakers, and judges. Through knowledge and experience, they knew it is the nature of government to seek power over the governed. Down through the centuries to the present day, history relates how this strong human urge for power drives chiefs, emperors, kings, dictators, and heads of state to rob their people of the rights for which "governments are instituted among men."

To guard against this tyranny, the "Founding Fathers" determined to limit the power of government over the governed. The Constitution of the United States features a plan of checks and balances whereby three departments — legislative, executive, and judicial — can work together yet still restrain one another. The Constitution grants freedom of choice. Citizens of the United States have the privilege of maintaining these three departments in balance by their votes, and the same privilege of destroying this balance by their votes. The Constitution that made men free depends upon the governed to keep men free.

Chapter 11

Government Starts Under Constitution

GEORGE WASHINGTON
BECOMES THE FIRST PRESIDENT

SINCE THE CONSTITUTION did not specify how the electors should be chosen, the procedure was left to the decision of the states. Should Presidential electors be selected by the state legislatures or by the direct vote of the people? Pennsylvania was the first state to enact an electoral law in September of 1788. The people were to vote for the men who were to choose a President and Vice President. Delaware and Maryland did likewise.

In Georgia, Connecticut, and South Carolina, state legislatures chose the electors. In New Jersey the governor and his council picked the men. Although New York had ratified the Constitution, the upper and lower houses of the legislature could not agree on the method of election. That state lost its votes for the first President. Members for both the Senate and House of Representatives had also to be elected before the electoral votes could be counted. In some states Congressmen and electors were voted upon at the same time and in others at separate elections. It was not easy to establish a new government and start it functioning.

On the first Wednesday of January in 1789, the first election took place under the new Constitution. On that day seventy-three electors were chosen to vote for the first President. However, when they met on February 4 in their respective states to cast their votes, four men were missing. One from Maryland was confined to his bed with gout. Another was prevented "from attending by the ice in the river and bay." Two from Virginia failed to appear at the electoral meeting. When, according to the Constitution, the ballots were opened at a session of Congress and counted, every one of the sixty-nine electors had voted for George Washington for President. John Adams had a bare majority for Vice President. Messengers were dispatched on horseback to Virginia and Massachusetts to notify Washington and Adams of their election.

Washington hesitated to accept the Presidency because he was fifty-seven years old. After almost a lifetime of public service, he really wanted to retire to private life and spend his days quietly on his own plantation near the Potomac River. On April 16, 1789 he wrote this entry in his diary:

MOUNT VERNON, VIRGINIA — HOME OF GEORGE WASHINGTON

Although Washington answered his country's call in both war and peace, he always expressed regret at leaving his home overlooking the Potomac River.

About ten o'clock, I bade adieu to Mount Vernon, to private life, and to domestic felicity; and, with a mind oppressed with more anxious and painful sensations than I have words to express, set out for New York, with the best disposition to render service to my country in obedience to its call, but with less hope of answering its expectations.

His journey to New York was one continuous ovation. When his carriage entered towns along the way, church bells clanged a welcome and cannon fired salutes. At the frontier of Pennsylvania, Washington was met by the governor of the state, Thomas Mifflin, who had been one of his officers during the war. At Chester, where he stopped for breakfast, troops of cavalry were waiting to escort the new President into Philadelphia. A beautiful white horse was led out for

Washington to ride, and the procession moved along the road with General St. Clair in front. About 20,000 people lined the streets and cheered, "Long live the father of his people!"

On a sunny afternoon Washington stood on the banks of the Delaware, a stream he had crossed twelve years before, through floating ice, when on his way to Trenton. His decision on that stormy Christmas night had turned the fortunes of war at a dark hour. At the bridge the women of Trenton gathered to honor the President. They had an arch built, entwined with laurel and evergreen, and inscribed: "The Defender of the Mothers Will Be the Protector of the Daughters." Young girls wearing white dresses and crowns of blossoms strewed flowers in his path over the bridge. They sang an ode composed for the occasion by an officer who had served under Washington.

Early on the morning of April 23, Washington arrived at Elizabethport, New Jersey, to complete his journey by water. Here he boarded a barge manned by thirteen master pilots dressed in white uniforms. The troops of his overland escort remained behind and fired salutes from the Jersey shore. The bay was thronged with craft, large and small, and the air was filled with music from the bands on board. Every ship in the harbor was decorated for the event, except one, a Spanish man-of-war. As Washington's barge passed by this vessel, the flags of every nation were suddenly displayed and the members of the crew manned the sails and stood at attention behind their guns. Cheers rose from the crowded boats.

Thousands of people lined the New York shore to greet the new President with loud huzzas and gun salutes. In the evening the sky was a blaze of fireworks. Throngs walked the streets shouting and singing.

The inauguration took place on April 30, 1789. At nine o'clock crowds gathered in churches throughout the city, asking divine

WASHINGTON'S RECEPTION ON THE BRIDGE AT TRENTON

On the bridge over a stream Washington's army had crossed on that snowy December 26, 1776, the newly elected President was greeted by mothers and daughters who strewed flowers in his path while singing an ode composed for the occasion:

Welcome, mighty chief, once more!
Welcome to this grateful shore!

WASHINGTON ENROUTE TO HIS INAUGURATION

Decorated boats, large and small, joined Washington's triumphal crossing from New Jersey to New York for his inauguration. At a signal, a Spanish ship suddenly hoisted the flags of many nations in the rigging, the gunners fired salutes, and the sailors dressed in their best uniforms stood at attention as Washington's barge passed nearby. The waterfront was crowded with men, women and children shouting and waving their greetings to the new President.

guidance for the first President of the new nation. At noon the procession formed in front of Washington's house on Cherry Street. The parade was led by American soldiers in fancy dress uniforms. Scotch infantrymen in their plaid kilts marched to the lively tunes of their bagpipes. Opposite Federal Hall soldiers formed in two lines, between which Washington and his party were conducted into the

building. In the Senate chamber, John Adams, the Vice President, received them.

"Sir," said Adams, "the Senate and the House of Representatives are ready to attend you to take the oath required by the Constitution which will be administered by the Chancellor of the State of New York."

Washington replied, "I am ready to proceed."

He was then conducted to a balcony

overlooking the crowd waiting outside. Washington stood in the center of the balcony between two pillars. Government officials and a few old friends found places to stand in the gallery. Not far from Washington stood Baron Friedrich von Steuben who had drilled the General's ragged continentals at Valley Forge during one of the darkest periods of the war. With his hand on the Bible, Washington spoke his oath of office slowly and distinctly for all to hear. The crowd listened in tense silence:

I do solemnly swear that I will faithfully execute the office of President of the United States, and will to the best of my ability preserve, protect and defend the Constitution of the United States.

Then the Chancellor turned to the crowd and exclaimed, "Long live George Washington, President of the United States!"

Resounding cheers filled the air. The President bowed repeatedly until he was led away to the Senate Chamber to give his inaugural address. His speech was rather brief. In it he expressed the wish "that the foundation of our national policy will be laid in the pure and immutable principles of private morality, and the preeminence of free government be exemplified by all the attributes which can win the affections of its citizens and command the respect of the world."

Washington asked again the same favor that he had requested when he took command of the American armies during the War for Independence. He asked to serve his country without pay. He would accept only the money needed for "such actual expenditures as the public good may be thought to require."

DESCRIPTION OF WASHINGTON'S INAUGURATION IN THE "GAZETTE OF THE UNITED STATES," May 2, 1789

On Thursday last, agreeable to the resolution of both houses of Congress, the inauguration of THE PRESIDENT of the UNITED STATES was solemnized.

At nine o'clock, A.M. the people assembled in the several churches, with the Clergy of their respective denominations, to implore the blessing of Heaven upon the new government, its favor and protection to the PRESIDENT, and success and acceptance to his administration.

About twelve o'clock the procession moved from the house of the President in Cherry Street — through Queen, Great Dock and Broad Streets, to the Federal State House . . . When within a proper distance of the State House, the troops formed a line on both sides of the way. The PRESIDENT, passing through, was conducted into the Gallery adjoining the Senate Chamber, and fronting Broad-Street, where, in the presence of an immense concourse of citizens, the Oath, prescribed by the Constitution, was administered to him by the Hon. R.R. LIVINGSTON, Esq. Chancellor of the State of New York.

The Chancellor then proclaimed him THE PRESIDENT OF THE UNITED STATES, which was followed by the instant discharge of 13 cannon, and loud repeated shouts. THE PRESIDENT bowing to the people, the air again rang with their acclamations. He then retired with the two Houses to the Senate Chamber, where he made his inaugural address.

THE PRESIDENT, accompanied by His Excellency the Vice-President, the Speaker of the House of Representatives, and both Houses of Congress, then went to St. Paul's Chapel, where divine service was performed, by the Right Rev. DR. PROVOST, Bishop of the Episcopal Church in this State, and Chaplain to the Senate.

The religious solemnity being ended, the President was escorted to his residence.

The people celebrated far into the night with fireworks, laughter, and song. The ship of state was launched under an untried system of government. Would the sailing be rough or smooth? The world waited to see.

THE NEW GOVERNMENT BEGINS TO FUNCTION

TWO DAYS AFTER Washington was inaugurated, a leading newspaper editor wrote that "to strengthen and complete the union of the states, to extend and protect their commerce, to explore and arrange the national funds, to restore and establish public credit, . . . will require the energies of the patriots and sages of our country."

For advisors in the executive department, Washington chose four "patriots and sages" who had served their country well. The first Secretary of State was Thomas Jefferson who had begun his public career in the House of Burgesses in Virginia. He was a member of the Continental Congress when he wrote the Declaration of Independence. During the last two years of the war he had been the governor of Virginia. After the treaty of peace was signed with Great Britain, he spent five years in France as the first ambassador from the United States to that nation. He was well versed in both domestic and foreign affairs.

For Secretary of War, Washington chose Henry Knox, an artillery officer who had fought for independence from the Battle of Bunker Hill to the siege of Yorktown. The first Attorney General of Virginia, Edmund Randolph, became the first Attorney General of the United States. He, too, had been governor of Virginia and was a delegate from that state to the Constitutional Convention.

With nearly everyone in debt to someone else, and few able to pay, the most difficult job was that of Secretary of the Treasury. This post fell to Alexander Hamilton, thirty-two years old and the youngest man in the Cabinet. When Hamilton served as Washington's aide-de-camp during the war, the General had discovered his talents for organization and finance. Hamilton was the only delegate from New York who had signed the Constitution.

The first branch of the new Government to go into operation was the legislative department. The first Congress elected under the Constitution met in the new Federal Hall in New York City on the first Wednesday in March of 1789. The ringing of bells and the roaring of cannon at sunrise, at noon, and at sunset celebrated this historic event. Immediately, the members began with the most pressing need of the new Government — money. Faced with the necessity of providing revenue to support the Government, Congressmen turned to taxes on goods imported to the United States. Not only would duties bring in funds to pay the expenses of operating the Government, but such imposts would encourage manufacturers to go into business and produce articles needed by the people. The import tax would have to be high enough to make the imported goods more expensive than those produced in this country.

The happenings in Congress were reported in the papers of the day and were read with much interest by the people.

The revenue bill was still being debated in Congress when Washington was inaugurated and for weeks after he became President.

The House agreed to reduce the duty on molasses from 5 to 2½ cents per gallon; to tax cotton 3 cents per pound; and to add playing cards to the list at a duty of 10 cents a pack.

Although the executive branch was started when the first President took office, Congress was busy setting up various departments. The passage of the Judiciary Bill established a Supreme Court at the seat of the National Government and branches in districts of the states. These courts could be reached easily by the people living in the districts. John Jay, a lawyer who helped to negotiate the peace treaty with Great Britain, became the first Chief Justice of the United States. All of this business was attended to during the first session of Congress.

The site for a national capital caused much debate in Congress. The southerners objected to New York City because it was so far away from their homes. They wanted a more central location. Offers of free land from Pennsylvania, Maryland, and Virginia poured into Congress.

The editor of a Maryland newspaper printed this comment on February 4, 1791:

Where will Congress find a resting place? They have led a vagrant life ever since 1774, when they first met to oppose Great Britain. Every place they have taken to reside in has been made too hot to hold them. Either the enemy would not let them stay, or the people made a clamor because they were too far north or too far south and obliged them to remove. If three removes are as bad as one fire, then Congress may be said to have been burnt out several times.

After two years of bickering, Washington announced in a speech that a district ten miles square had been selected on the Potomac River to become the permanent seat of the Government. The city had been laid out "agreeable to a plan which will be placed before Congress." Early in 1791, the Government moved to Philadelphia, nearer the site of the new capital. The new capital was named Washington in honor of the first President.

As the three departments of Government began to function successfully, the people gained more confidence in the Constitution and in themselves. With renewed courage, they tackled the problems of providing employment, restoring commerce, and paying their bills.

THE GOVERNMENT AND THE PEOPLE COOPERATE TO REGAIN PROSPERITY

A WAVE OF PATRIOTISM swept over the country when the Constitution was ratified. Signs of better times brought hope to the people. The manufacturers, beginning in a small way, were much encouraged when both Washington and Adams wore suits of cloth woven in the United States at their inauguration. Mrs. Washington wore with pride, before leaving Mount Vernon, a dress made of calico woven and printed in New England.

Five and a half months after his inauguration, Washington left New York City for Boston on a tour of the New England states. His eye witness accounts of mills visited, as written in his daily journal, presented a picture of early manufacturing in that section of the country:

Tuesday, October 20, Hartford, Connecticut
After breakfast, accompanied by Colonel Wadsworth, Mr. Ellsworth, and Colonel Jesse Root, I viewed the Woollen Manufactory at this place, which seems to be going on with spirit. Their Broadcloths are not of the first quality, as yet, but they are good; as are their Coatings, Cassimeres, Serges and Everlastings; of the first, that is, broadcloth, I ordered a suit to be sent to me at New York — and of the latter a whole piece, to make breeches for my servants. All the parts of this business are performed at the Manufactory except

the spinning – this is done by the Country people who are paid by the cut.

Wednesday, October 28, Boston, Massachusetts

Went, after an early breakfast, to visit the duck manufacture, which appeared to be carrying on with spirit, and in a prosperous way (Duck is cloth like light-weight canvas.) They have manufactured 32 pieces of Duck of 30 or 40 yards each in a week . . . . They have 28 looms at work, and 14 Girls spinning with Both hands (the flax being fastened to their waist). Children (girls) turn the wheels for them, and with this assistance, each spinner can turn out 14lbs. of Thread per day when they stick to it, but as they are paid by the piece, or work they do, there is no other restraint upon them but to come at 8 o'clock in the morning, and return at 6 in the evening.

Friday, October 30, Lynn to Ipswich

After passing Beverly, 2 miles, we come to the Cotton Manufactory, . . . In this Manufactory they have the new Invented Carding and Spinning Machines . . . one of which spins 84 threads at a time by one person. The Cotton is prepared for these Machines by being first (lightly) drawn to a thread on the common wheel; there is also another machine for doubling and twisting the threads for particular cloths; this also does many at a time. For winding the Cotton from the Spindles, and preparing it for the warp, there is a Reel which expedites the work greatly. A number of Looms (15 or 16) were at work with spring shuttles, which do more than double work. In Short, the whole seemed perfect, and the Cotton stuffs which they turn out, excellent of their kind; warp and filling both are of Cotton.

Washington's description of these three mills traced three steps in the growth of manufacturing during his term of office. In Hartford spinning was still done in homes of farmers and weaving was done in the factory. In Boston spinning was done in a mill. In the factory near Beverly carding, spinning, and weaving were completed by machinery in one place. The President was impressed with all of the new machinery

and its possibilities in developing manufacturing in this country. He favored a duty on foreign goods to protect the infant manufacturers. The tax would be high enough to raise the price of the imported article above the price of the article produced at home.

The members of the German Society of New York agreed to appear on every New Year's Day. They would dress entirely in garments manufactured in the United States. They would buy American-made products instead of imported articles whenever possible. Each member agreed to pay an extra fee to provide a fund for prizes to encourage manufacturing in the nation.

Other societies helped to increase the products made in the United States. The Pennsylvania Society for the Encouragement of Manufactures and Useful Arts was organized in this way in 1787:

For the better employment of the industrious poor, and in order to render the society as useful as possible, a subscription, for sums not less than ten pounds from any one person or company, shall be immediately opened to all persons whatever, for the purpose of establishing factories in such places as shall be thought suitable. These subscribers shall be entitled to all the profits attending the business and shall be the sole owners of all the lots of ground, buildings, implements, raw materials, and other things, purchased or paid for out of their subscriptions which shall be called the manufacturing fund.

The Pennsylvania Society offered twenty dollars in cash or a gold plate worth that much with an appropriate inscription to:

such person as shall exhibit on or before the thirty-first day of December, 1788, a model of a most useful engine or machine to be moved by water, fire or otherwise, to save the labor of hands in manufacturing cotton, wool, flax or hemp more than any engine or machine now used in the State of Pennsylvania.

Premiums of thirty dollars in cash or gold plate with inscription were offered to the farmer who raised the most hemp, the most flax, and sheared not less than 200 pounds of wool from his own sheep. Prizes were awarded for the best dishes, the finest glassware, and the most beautiful book printed in Pennsylvania.

Our present day corporations are the outgrowth of these manufacturing societies and are modeled after them. Today, in a number of corporations, it is the custom to give a bonus to each employee who makes or sells more products than the average. This idea was also adopted from the old manufacturing societies of early days.

Manufacturing was encouraged by Alexander Hamilton, the brilliant young Secretary of the Treasury in Washington's Cabinet, and was aided by his program. Hamilton took over the finances of a nation that had little or no credit at home or abroad and a debt of more than $50,000,000. That was a large sum of money in those days. Hamilton insisted this debt must be paid for the United States to regain credit and respect, both at home and across the seas. Both individuals and nations that fail to pay their bills find it difficult to borrow money. He declared that it was the obligation of the National Government to pay back the money that the states had borrowed to support the armies of the Revolutionary War. If men who lent this money were repaid, they would have something to invest in manufacturing that would employ workmen and aid prosperity.

Hamilton submitted plans to Congress for taxation to raise the funds to pay these debts, and for a Bank of the United States. He met with considerable opposition. Although the bill which established the Bank was passed, public opinion remained divided on the issue. Some men favored the Bank because it gathered money belonging to many persons. This provided capital for loans to the Government and to individuals; kept precious gold and silver in vaults instead of being worn out in circulation, and paper money took its place; speeded up payments in business because bank notes were easy to transmit from place to place; aided collection of taxes; and prevented persons from charging exorbitant rates of interest to borrowers. Others objected to the Bank on the grounds that a federal bank would interfere with a state bank; that states had the right to prohibit as well as to permit banks; and that the Constitution did not give the Federal Government the right to enter the banking business in competition with banks owned by citizens.

The argument that the Bank of the United States was unconstitutional divided people. It helped to lay the foundation of the two party system in this country. However, investors were waiting in line before the door opened to buy stock in the Bank of the United States. All the shares were sold on the first day. This sale proved that the public had confidence in Hamilton's measures to straighten out the tangled finances of the budding nation.

HAMILTON REPORTS TO CONGRESS

IN JANUARY OF 1790, the House of Representatives had ordered the Secretary of the Treasury to prepare and report to the House "a proper plan or plans . . . for the encouragement and promotion of such manufactories as will tend to render the United States independent of other nations for essentials, especially for military supplies."

This request was put in almost the exact words President Washington had used in a speech he had made in Congress a few days before. When Washington made his tour of the country, visiting many factories, he gathered information which aided Hamilton in writing his report. This personal interest of the President encouraged an increase in manufacturing both in homes and mills.

For nearly two years the Secretary of the Treasury gathered information in his thorough, methodical manner before he was ready to report to Congress on the subject of manufacturing. In his survey, Hamilton discovered that about three-fourths of the clothing worn by the people was made entirely at home. Nearly all families in Connecticut carried on some kind of manufacturing in their own homes to supply their own needs, and to provide goods for sale. In the homes of the 4562 inhabitants of Ipswich, Massachusetts, 41,978 yards of lace were woven in the year that Washington became the first President. In the following year, in the neighborhood of Providence, Rhode Island, 3,000,000 nails were hammered with the aid of tiny forges nestling in roomy corners of kitchen chimneys. In a county of Virginia, a record was kept of the household manufactures of twenty families, some rich and some poor. In the year 1790 they turned out 1085 yards of linen, 344 yards of woolen, 1681 yards of cotton, 174 pairs of stockings, and 237 pairs of shoes. In Lancaster, Pennsylvania, the largest inland town, one-third of the families were manufacturers. There were 14 hatters, 36 shoemakers, 25 tailors, 25 weavers of woolens, linens, and cottons, 3 stocking weavers, and 4 dyers.

Hamilton told Congress that "the objections to the pursuit of manufactures in the United States are scarcity of hands, dearness of labor, and want of capital." He suggested immigration as a remedy. Now was the time to encourage immigration when the nations of Europe were threatened with civil and foreign wars. Workmen would gladly come if they knew they could find employment. Rich foreigners would invest money in mills.

Hamilton's plans to promote manufactures included duties on foreign articles that might be produced in this country; no duty on materials needed from abroad for manufacturing; encouragement of new inventions and the use of machinery; a general circulation of money from the Bank of the United States to make payments easier; the building of roads and canals to transport goods; and bounties, premiums, and prizes. He declared that agriculture would be advanced by manufacturing because the farmer could give all of his time to producing food for the artisan while he made the articles the farmer needed. To assure the people that his plan for prosperity did not interfere with their liberty to go into business and to buy and sell when and where they pleased, Hamilton made this statement in his report:

Indeed, it can hardly ever be wise in a government to attempt to give a direction to the industry of its citizens. This, under the quick-sighted guidance of private interest, will, if left to itself, find its own way to the most profitable employment; and it is by such employment that the public prosperity will be most effectually promoted.

This system of competitive enterprise had grown up in colonial times. It meant that every man was free to establish a little business of his own. The people wished to go on doing business in this way. Hamilton's program laid the foundation of our economic system and led the nation back to prosperity. When the nation began to pay its debts, public credit was restored. The Government was able to borrow money again. The British complained that the thrifty Dutch were selling out in Great Britain and investing their money in the United States.

A mint was established in Philadelphia and banks increased in number throughout the country. When New York City had three banks, the event inspired a poem that appeared in a magazine:

> The trade and business of the nation,
> Exceeds all human computations;
> One bank no longer can suffice,
> And see in clusters how they rise!

Hamilton's plea for more manufacturing encouraged the building of factories. Although the British kept their new inventions a secret as long as they could, the machinery for making cloth found a way to the United States. Samuel Slater, from memory, built a number of Arkwright machines at Pawtucket, Rhode Island and started the first successful water-spinning mill in the United States. As more and more labor-saving machinery was invented, less and less manufacturing was done at home. Since women and children had worked at home making goods to sell, they went into factories to continue their employment. Instead of selling their own products, they worked for wages.

The immigrants that Hamilton wanted came by the thousands. A letter from Amsterdam in 1791, the same year in which Hamilton made his report to Congress, stated that Germans were arriving there in divisions of three and four hundred "to take shipping for the land of liberty and peace."

When seventy families from Switzerland arrived at Wilkes-Barre, Pennsylvania, an American newspaper editor welcomed them in his newspaper:

> They come from an industrious, frugal, and moral country, enjoying a republican form of government. This colony will be highly acceptable.

A London editor wrote in his paper:

> The preparations over all the north of Ireland for emigrating to America are truly alarming. Not less than 880 passengers have engaged to sail on one vessel, now lying at Londonderry.

Sometimes, whole parishes migrated from Ireland and came with enough money to pay their passage and travel to settlements inland. Others arrived as indentured servants and worked their way, serving a term of months or years for their master who had paid for their passage over the ocean. However, immigrants who accepted the invitation to the United States soon learned that the disorders of the continent that they had left behind affected their lives in the New World.

Chapter 12

The New Nation Defends Itself

REVOLUTIONS
LEAD TO REVOLUTIONS

DISORDERS IN OTHER PARTS of the world began to trouble this nation from its beginning. The success of the British colonists in gaining self-government inspired other peoples to break away from kingly rule. Some South Americans had served with the French in aiding the people of the United States to win independence. They returned to their Spanish colonies and spread revolutionary ideas among the people. Kentuckians complained that prices had dropped on flour and tobacco in New Orleans. Trade had fallen off with the South American colonies of Spain where revolutions were hampering business.

For some time discontent had been growing among the masses in France who had kept a watchful eye on the American war. In 1789, the same year that Washington was inaugurated, the King of France, Louis XVI, was forced to grant his people a share in government. Although representatives were elected to a national assembly, the king yielded too late to halt the conspiracy against him. He and his queen, Marie Antoinette, were beheaded four years later, and the thunder of the French Revolution echoed all over Europe and across the seas in both Americas.

In Saint Domingue, a French settlement in the West Indies, the Negro slaves rebelled against their white masters and terror swept over the island. From Port-au-Prince word reached the United States that over 300 coffee and sugar plantations had been plundered and burned. Many of the white owners had been killed. Those who escaped boarded a ship for other lands, leaving the island to the Negroes.

The rebellion was led by Toussaint L'Ouverture, a Negro slave, born on a big plantation owned by a French nobleman. Toussaint's godfather, living on the same land, had learned to read and write when serving Jesuit missionaries. The old Negro, a religious man, taught the young man to read and write French, and a little Latin. His master promoted Toussaint to a position of trust, and took him out of the sugar fields. Later, when a mob threatened his kindly master, he hid the family in nearby woods and provided for their escape on an American vessel.

After Toussaint became the governor of the French part of Haiti, he conquered the Spanish part of the island, freed the slaves, and declared Haiti independent. This freedom was short-lived. Toussaint was captured by French soldiers and sent to France where he died in 1803 a prisoner, in a dark, damp dungeon.

In 1793 when war broke out between France and Great Britain, Edmond Genet came to this country as an agent from the French Republic. By many he was received as a hero. He began to fit out privateers in American ports to prey on British commerce, although the President had issued a proclamation of neutrality. Finally, Washington asked the French government to recall Genet who approved the French Revolution in which the President did not want the new United States involved.

On the high seas the British captured American merchantmen, kidnapped the crews, and forced the sailors to serve on British ships. The excuse for this outrage was that the vessels were carrying supplies to France. Washington sent John Jay to England to get what terms he could to maintain the peace. Jay negotiated a treaty but it did not deal with the question of impressment. This treaty aroused such anger that Jay was hanged in effigy and branded a traitor.

Since Washington was a military man he frequently urged Congress to appropriate money to build and man a navy and to support an army for defense. Less than a year after his inauguration, Washington said in a speech to Congress:

To be prepared for war is one of the most effectual means of preserving peace.

During his two terms Washington managed to keep the nation out of the squabbles in other countries and to bring prosperity to the people of the United States. He refused to consider a third term. On September 17, 1796 his farewell address was printed in a newspaper for all to read. His parting advice, "Observe good faith and justice toward all nations," still influences the thinking of Americans and colors the pages of American history.

Washington lived at Mount Vernon until his death in 1799. Henry Lee's tribute to him in a funeral oration is still quoted by many Americans:

"First in war — first in peace — and first in the hearts of his countrymen."

TWO-PARTY SYSTEM DEVELOPS FROM INTERPRETATION OF THE CONSTITUTION

ADAMS, HAMILTON, and many others argued that the clause in the Constitution, "to provide for the common defense and general welfare of the United States" carried "implied powers" for the Federal Government to make any laws necessary for the benefit of the people. Those who agreed with this point of view and who believed in a strong central government were called Federalists. In this party were the citizens who depended upon manufacturing and commerce for a living. They needed a strong central government to protect their trade and their jobs. The Federalist Party was strongest in the manufacturing states of New England.

Jefferson, Madison, and many others believed that the Federal Government had only the powers definitely assigned to it by the Constitution and that all other powers belonged to the states. They wanted a strict interpretation of the document. Because Jefferson and Madison sympathized so strongly with the French people fighting for a republic, they and their followers were called Republicans, and sometimes, Democratic-Republicans. In this party were the agriculturists — the southern planters, the small farmers, and the "westerners" who had settled beyond the Alleghenies. Being able to raise their own food and make most of their clothing, they were independent and did not feel the need of a strong central government to protect their interests. They stood for states' rights.

Out of the friction that developed in Washington's Cabinet between Hamilton and Jefferson, New Yorker and Virginian, northerner and southerner, Federalist and Democratic-Republican, grew the roots of the two-party system. Washington's election had been unanimous but the vote for his successor was close. In the Electoral College John Adams, the Federalist, received only three more votes than Thomas Jefferson, the Republican. According to the Constitution, Adams became President and Jefferson, Vice President. This led to bitter rivalry between the two parties and the people took sides in the controversy.

Meanwhile, foreign troubles continued to plague the nation. After the Jay Treaty American commerce suffered less attacks from British vessels and more from the French. The French considered the treaty with Great Britain an insult to them. Americans had lost about $50,000,000 through ships and cargoes captured by the French corsairs. In an effort to keep peace, President Adams sent Elbridge Gerry, Charles Cotesworth Pinckney, and John Marshall to Paris. Although France had changed from a monarchy to a republic, the revolution was still in progress. The new government, the Directory, needed money. Talleyrand, the Minister of Foreign Relations, sent three agents, Mr. X, Mr. Y, and Mr. Z to talk with the three American ministers.

Mr. X called first. Since Pinckney was the only American who spoke French, Mr. X asked to speak with him alone. The two men stepped into the next room. Mr. X whispered that for a sum of a quarter of a million dollars given secretly to Talleyrand, the Americans could have peace. Talleyrand would use his influence with the Directory to check attacks on American ships. Pinckney explained that he had no authority to grant money.

The next caller was Mr. Y who repeated the demand for money, threatening the Americans with the rising power of Napoleon whose armies were succeeding in Italy.

"Gentlemen, you do not speak to the point," said Mr. Y impatiently. "It is money. It is expected that you will offer money."

The Americans insisted they had no authority to promise money, and they had clearly explained that fact.

"No," said he, "you have not. What is your answer?"

Pinckney answered in a loud tone of voice. "It is no, no! Not a sixpence."

A few days later, Mr. Z came to see Gerry and to invite him for a talk alone with Talleyrand. Talleyrand had spent over two years in America as an exile and he could speak English. During his stay in America, he had met Gerry.

On April 3, 1798, a report on the XYZ Affair was read in Congress, quoting the bribe: "It is necessary to pay money — to pay a great deal of money."

As this news spread through the newspapers, the public turned against France. Marshall, the first one of the three ministers to leave Paris, arrived in New York City, unannounced, to find an outburst of patriotism sweeping over the nation. Everywhere, people were singing the latest popular song, with words by Hopkinson set to the lively music of "The President's March."

Hail, Columbia! happy land!
Hail, ye heroes! heaven-born band!

To Marshall's great surprise, he was one of the heroes. Twenty years after he had passed through Philadelphia to fight in the Battle of Monmouth, he returned to the city. Marshall the soldier was Marshall the hero. Church bells rang and crowds cheered. At a banquet in his honor, a toast was made that became a slogan of national pride:

MILLIONS FOR DEFENSE BUT NOT A CENT FOR TRIBUTE!

The French revolutionists quickly sought peace without a bribe when the Americans began to prepare for war. A few weeks before the end of his term, President John Adams nominated John Marshall to be Chief Justice of the United States. He held this position until his death in 1835 in his eightieth year.

When the danger of conflict passed over, the two political parties at home quarreled, bitterly criticizing each other. The Federalists, with a majority in Congress, passed a law giving the President power to send aliens out of the country if he suspected they were dangerous to the United States. Emigrants from Europe, who had fled from governments with limited freedoms, naturally joined the Republicans who wished to reduce the power of government. Some well educated aliens became newspaper editors and writers and ridiculed the Federalists. The purpose of the Alien Act was to control the efforts to stir up ill feelings toward the government in power. Another law made written attacks upon the government punishable as a crime. It carried a penalty of fine and imprisonment. Although this Sedition Act was intended to prohibit libel (the publication of charges not true), it was interpreted as a limitation on freedom of press and speech as guaranteed in the First Amendment to the Constitution. Both Virginia and Kentucky passed resolutions condemning the Alien and Sedition Acts as unconstitutional. The acts were repealed.

The Democratic-Republicans won the election of 1800. Both Thomas Jefferson and Aaron Burr received seventy-five votes each and the House of Representatives had to choose between them. Jefferson was chosen President and Burr, Vice President. Not long afterward, the Twelfth Amendment to the Constitution was added to prevent such a happening again. Thereafter electors voted separately for a President and a Vice President.

The Federalists never won another Presidential election and the party passed out of existence. The Federalist leaders had been the fighting men of the war for independence and the far-seeing statesmen of the Constitutional Convention, on whom the people had depended in time of stress. They held the reins of Government in their hands until the Federal Union was firmly established. Their work was done. Now, men younger and less experienced could take part in their Government successfully with Jefferson, as President and Madison, the "Father of the Constitution," as Secretary of State.

The year 1800 marks the beginning of more confidence on the part of the people to govern themselves under a national union. In a letter to a friend in 1787, before the Constitution was made, Jefferson had said:

I am persuaded myself that the good sense of the people will always be found to be the best army. They may be led astray for a moment, but will soon correct themselves.

Jefferson was a man of peace but, like Washington and Adams before him, he found it difficult to keep the nation out of the feuds and wars of European countries. Although he succeeded, except for a little war with pirates of the Barbary States in Africa, he was forced to use "implied powers" of the Constitution for which he had criticized the Federalists. The Constitution did not state that a President could buy land but Jefferson purchased Louisiana to avoid war.

LOUISIANA WAS A BARGAIN

DURING THE HARD TIMES following the Revolutionary War hundreds of families left the states on the Atlantic seaboard to seek new homes in a western wilderness beyond the Appalachian Mountains. Many of these emigrants had given their fortunes, as well as their services, in the cause of liberty. Penniless but still proud, they started life all over again. Some of these Revolutionary soldiers were allotted farms in the Northwest Territory because the Government had no money to pay them for their services in the War for Independence. A large grant of land in southern Indiana, opposite Louisville, Kentucky, was divided among the soldiers who had marched with George Rogers Clark through icy waters and sticky mud to win that country. In the first year after the opening of the Northwest Territory 967 boats, carrying 18,370 men, women, and children with 7986 horses, 2372 cows, 1110 sheep, and 646 wagons went down the Ohio River, the front door to the West. Still more came on horseback and on foot through Cumberland Gap and over the Wilderness Road into Kentucky and Tennessee. Before Boone's path was widened for wagon travel, Kentucky had a population of 220,000 persons. How did they earn a living?

The majority were farmers and their living depended upon markets for their produce. The farmers had flour, cornmeal, tobacco, wool, and hickory-smoked hams for sale. The farmers could not sell to their neighbors because they, too, were farmers and had the same products for sale. There were no towns of any size, only settlements in a wilderness. Along the Atlantic seaboard lived many townsmen who would relish the woodsy aroma of smoked ham frying for breakfast. However, it was a long and dangerous journey with pack horses over mountain trails to reach the eastern markets. The trip would cost more than the sale would bring. Since water transportation was cheap, the Mississippi River became the highway of commerce for the westerners. New Orleans at the mouth of the river became their market.

However, it was not safe for a few farmers to travel to market alone. They went in small fleets of twenty or more boats and carried guns.

When the farmers arrived at New Orleans, buyers were waiting on the docks to bid for their cargo. It was not all food and tobacco. Nearly every man had a pile of skins on his boat to sell to the fur buyers. In the winter the settlers had time to trap beaver, muskrat, and other fur-bearing animals. The fur buyers would load the furs on to sailing ships for markets in Philadelphia, New York, and the ports of foreign countries. In those days drifting down the Mississippi to the "Paris of America" was a voyage of excitement and romance to the young frontiersmen.

All went well until this trade became involved in the game of international politics. By the Treaty of Fontainebleau, November 3, 1762, the King of France gave Louisiana to his cousin, the King of Spain. The treaty was kept a secret. Following the French and Indian War, the Treaty of Paris, signed on the tenth of February, 1763, publicly confirmed this gift. Spain received from France "so much of Louisiana as lay west of the Mississippi River, including both sides of the river at its mouth."

In November of 1762, British forces captured Havana, Cuba, belonging to Spain. A few months later, in the Treaty of Paris, Spain traded Florida to England for Havana and Manila, Philippine Islands, also captured by the British, in these words:

"His Catholic Majesty cedes and guarantees in full right, to His Britannic Majesty, Florida, with Fort Augustine and the Bay of Pensacola, as well as all that Spain possesses on the Continent of North America, to the east, or to the southeast of the river Mississippi."

Later in the same year, by the Treaty of Versailles, England traded Florida, which had been captured by Spanish soldiers, to Spain. By the Treaty of Paris in 1783, after the Revolutionary War, free navigation of the Mississippi River was pledged in Article VIII:

"The navigation of the river Mississippi, from its source to the ocean, shall forever remain free and open to the subjects of Great Britain and the citizens of the United States."

Since the Spanish government had not been consulted on the Treaty of Paris in 1783, it did not feel obligated to accept the document. Difficulties arose with Spain soon after Washington became President. Under a date line of February 15, 1790, Washington told in his journal of reading two letters which the Secretary of War had received from the Mississippi frontier and had forwarded to him. One letter from an army officer stationed in Nashville, Tennessee reported that the Spanish governor of Louisiana was drawing citizens of the United States to settle in his territory. He promised them land and freedom of navigation on the Mississippi River to New Orleans. There they could sell their products by paying a fifteen percent duty to the King of Spain. The officer warned that the western settlers must be assured markets in New Orleans and navigation on the Mississippi River, or they would accept the invitiation to become subjects of the King of Spain. The other letter told of the threat of war from the Creek Indian nation dwelling in territory claimed by both the United States and Spain.

In 1795, during Washington's second term, Thomas Pinckney negotiated the Treaty of San Lorenzo with Spain. This treaty settled the boundary with Florida and gave citizens of the United States free navigation of the Mississippi River and the right of deposit in New Orleans for three years. Soon afterwards the United States made a treaty with Great Britain giving that nation rights of navigation on the Mississippi. Spain objected on the grounds that this country could not legally transfer the rights of navigation to another nation. The dispute was still unsettled when Jefferson was elected third President of the United States. The issue resulted in a crisis which threatened war.

When the three-year agreement expired the Spanish governor withdrew the freedom of the port in New Orleans at a time when the cotton was almost ready to be picked and freighted down the river to market. The western farmers were indignant, threatening to raise their own army to take the city and the mouth of the Mississippi River for themselves. Jefferson, friend of the belligerent westerners, pleaded with them to control their tempers. He knew he could not long hold them back if they lost their market in New Orleans. He would buy the town and give it to them.

There was another reason. Napoleon's rising power in France was threatening all of Europe. He harbored a secret ambition to recover some of the territory once held by France in North America. By a secret treaty signed in Madrid, Napoleon traded lands he had conquered in Italy for Lousiana in North America. He gave this territory to the Duke of Parma whose wife was a daughter of the King of Spain, and made the Duke the King of Tuscany. The Spanish King was pleased with the bargain. His daughter was a queen. Jefferson, President of the United States was alarmed when the news of this treaty leaked out. He did not want Napoleon for a next door neighbor.

He instructed Robert R. Livingston, American Minister to France, to arrange for the purchase of New Orleans. He sent James Monroe to assist him in the negotiations. Napoleon needed cash to support his planned conquests in Europe. Since, in the event of war with Great Britain, he could not hold Louisiana, he offered to sell the whole territory for 80,000,000 francs ($15,000,000.) There was no time for the commissioners to consult the President and then wait weeks and weeks for a reply. Giving Napoleon no time to change his mind, the American representatives snatched the bargain. Early in May, 1803 the treaty was signed. This purchase of Louisiana removed the immediate danger of war with both France and Spain.

The western farmers were overjoyed. They owned the Mississippi River from its source near the Canadian border to the Gulf of Mexico. Although Spain objected to the deal, the territory was formally ceded to the United States December 20, 1803. The Spaniards were fearful that this purchase might doom their empire in North America. In a French Louisiana, Spain had had little to fear. The freedom loving peoples of the rising republic, the land hungry Anglo Saxons, were now their neighbors. Would they cross the Mississippi to conquer their new West?

PEOPLES AND PROBLEMS WERE PART OF THE BARGAIN

JEFFERSON LOST NO TIME in sending explorers to the territory he had purchased "sight unseen." In May of the following year an expedition left St. Louis to paddle its way up the Missouri to the river's source. It continued overland beyond the boundary of Louisiana to the headwaters of the Columbia and down that stream to the Pacific Ocean. The leaders were army officers — Meriwether Lewis, a close friend of President Jefferson, and William Clark, a brother of

George Rogers Clark who had captured the British forts north of the Ohio during the Revolutionary War.

About forty-five hardy frontiersmen, carefully picked, made up this exploring party. Among them were blacksmiths, gunsmiths, hunters, boatmen, carpenters, woodchoppers, and interpreters. Two were fiddlers, one a Frenchman and the other, a backwoods American. They furnished music for the lonely men who sang and danced around the evening fires. Many of these young men were the sons of the Scotch Irish pioneers who came into Kentucky and Tennessee through Cumberland Gap and over the Wilderness Road. Clark's big Negro servant excited the curiosity of the Indians along the way. They had never seen a black man before.

Frenchmen, half-breeds, and Indians joined the party as interpreters and guides as the explorers moved forward into unknown country. One of these was Sacajawea, the Indian-girl wife of a French trader. The couple joined the party at a trading post on the Missouri River near the present site of Bismarck, North Dakota. Sacajawea was the daughter of a Shoshone chief. As a child she had been captured by an enemy tribe from the prairie but she remembered the language of her father's people. Many times she saved the white men when their lives were threatened by hostile Indians. There was great rejoicing when she found her own people again and they welcomed the white strangers who had brought her home. With her tiny papoose strapped to her back, she rode on horseback to guide Lewis and Clark over the mountains to the Columbia River and

RYAN DAM, MISSOURI RIVER, MONTANA

On the way west in 1805, Lewis and Clark discovered the Great Falls of the Missouri River blocking their way upstream. The explorers were forced to make a long and trying portage for miles around this barrier. Their soft homemade moccasins sewn from skins of animals afforded little protection to their bleeding feet as they tramped over rocky ground thorny with cactus and spiky plants. Some boats were hauled on sleds but supplies were carried in bundles tied to the backs of the men.

Today Ryan Dam owned by the Montana Power Company spans the Missouri River at the Great Falls.

Montana Power Company

on to Everywhere-Salt-Water, Indian name for the Pacific Ocean.

After an absence of nearly two and a half years, during which time they had traveled over 8000 miles in canoes, on horseback, and on foot, Lewis and Clark returned to tell what they had seen and heard in the Louisiana Purchase. From this expedition the people of the United States gained a vague idea of the great natural resources in the vast new territory beyond the Mississippi River.

Perhaps the most important result of this expedition was a strengthened claim to the rich Oregon country where the British were establishing fur trading posts. Although British seamen had sailed through the northwest waters, an American, Captain Gray from Boston, had crossed the treacherous sand bar to enter the Columbia River. Lewis and Clark had tracked the stream from the mountains to the sea. Now, both Great Britain and the United States claimed Oregon, creating another international problem.

In the year after Lewis and Clark returned from the Northwest, Zebulon Pike explored the central part of the Louisiana Purchase to the Rocky Mountains. Pikes Peak in Colorado is named for him. Like Lewis and Clark, he found the inhabitants of the territory were Indians with a sprinkling of Spanish, French, and half-breed traders.

In the southern tip of the Louisiana Purchase, Jefferson inherited a strange and interesting mixture of people. These were Acadians, banished from Nova Scotia when the British took that province from the French in 1755. Across the mountains on foot, down the Mississippi River in canoes, and through the Gulf of Mexico on sailing vessels, the Acadians found their way to

Montana Highway Commission

GATES OF THE ROCKY MOUNTAINS

"For five and three quarter miles these rocks rise perpendicularly from the water's edge to the height of nearly twelve hundred feet . . . . Nothing can be imagined more tremendous than the frowning darkness of these rocks which project over the river and menace us with destruction. The river, of one hundred and fifty yards in width, seems to have forced its channel down this solid mass, but so reluctantly has it given way that during the whole distance the water is very deep even at the edges. For the first three miles there is not a spot except one of a few yards, in which a man could stand between the water and the towering perpendicular of the mountains . . . This extraordinary range of rocks we called the GATES OF THE ROCKY MOUNTAINS."

From the Journal of Lewis and Clark.

the coast of Louisiana where the people spoke French, the only language they knew. The French in New Orleans helped their destitute countrymen to start life anew along the Bayou Teche, west of the city. Being a rural people, the Acadians turned to farming and cattle raising. Each

217

farm had a waterfront on the sluggish bayou where the boats were moored; a stretch of prairie where cane, corn, and sweet potatoes grew; and a marsh where traps were set for mink and muskrat and timber was cut for fires. It was to this new Acadia in Louisiana that the exiled blacksmith welcomed Evangeline and old neighbors in these lines from Longfellow's poem, "Evangeline":

Welcome once more, my friends, who long have
    been friendless and homeless,
Welcome once more to a home, that is better
    perchance than the old one!

Smugglers and pirates were also a part of the great bargain. Past the farms of the honest and upright Acadians, strange vessels with even stranger cargoes moved noiselessly up the bayous into the back country. The boats were filled with Negroes, chained together, bound for hidden stockades on little islands in the marshes. In one year alone more than ten thousand slaves from Africa were smuggled into New Orleans and sold. Pirates with fleet ships sailed out into the Caribbean to capture the slavers bound for ports in the Spanish colonies. It was a prosperous business because officials of the United States Government could find neither the smugglers nor the booty. Both were swallowed up by the swampy jungle with its network of waterways.

The king of smugglers was Jean Lafitte. He was tall, dark, and slender like a storybook pirate. His hideout was Grand Isle in Barataria Bay south of New Orleans on the Gulf of Mexico. His gang of a thousand pirates roamed the seas. Becoming weary of these raids, Spain sent armed vessels with convoys of merchantmen. Then the bold buccaneers turned to plundering American

ships and the Government was forced to wage war on piracy. With a price on his head, the gay and charming Lafitte moved from the bayous of Louisiana to the island of Galveston in Mexican territory.

Long after the slave trade was forbidden by law in 1808, slaves could be bought from the smugglers of the Gulf Coast. Southerners moved to the fertile lands beyond the Mississippi River where laborers could be obtained for their fields of cotton, rice, and sugar cane. Jefferson, who opposed the system of slavery, extended the system unknowingly by the purchase of Louisiana. People and problems were part of the bargain.

NAPOLEON'S SUCCESS IN EUROPE INVOLVES THE AMERICAS

THE PURCHASE OF LOUISIANA did not remove Napoleon from the American scene. As he rose to power in France, he became ambitious to conquer Europe. His major rival was Great Britain. Three years after Jefferson bought Louisiana, Napoleon issued a decree forbidding all trade with the British Isles by any country. (Any ship bound for a British port was seized if caught by the French.) On the high seas American vessels were also often taken and their crews pressed into service by the British Navy if they were carrying goods to France. Our nation was unprepared for war and Jefferson was determined to keep the peace. With his support, Congress passed the Embargo Act forbidding American vessels to sail for foreign countries.

From the beginning it was plain that it would be difficult to enforce this law. Commerce was carried on illegally in all parts of the nation. Shippers were willing to take a chance because they figured the French would not be able to capture many vessels. Since ships could sail from port to port in United States territory, some slipped away into the open seas, or reloaded their cargoes at out-of-the-way places. Many people, especially the New Englanders, depended largely upon trade for a living. They felt they had to find ways and means of selling their goods. Many farmers transported their produce to the shores of Lake Champlain. Out of the timber they made rafts upon which they piled their flour, pork, and potash; built crude shelters on these boats; and waited for a strong south wind to fill their sails. Under cover of darkness, fleets of these rafts drifted down the lake and passed the guards unheard and unseen to the northern shore in Canadian territory. In winter, farmers in Vermont hauled their products on sleds to the Canadian border. Sometimes, if officers were on guard, a sham accident was staged. The trick was to park a sled atop a hill on the line, pull out the blocking stone, and let the barrels of pork, flour, and potash roll down the slope into Canada.

Although smuggling was bold, the embargo almost put an end to trade. In the shipping towns sailmakers, shipwrights, rope walkers, draymen, and sailors were out of work. Merchants and shopkeepers closed their doors. However, sailors suffered the most. In Boston unemployed seamen marched to the governor's house and demanded work or bread. Finally the embargo hit the farmers. Unable to sell their produce, they lacked funds to pay their debts and to buy seed for the spring planting.

Opposition in New England became so

MONTICELLO — HOME OF THOMAS JEFFERSON

As a young man, Jefferson began work on his house, completing a little at a time. During his service as Ambassador to France, he visited great buildings in that country, gathering ideas for his own home. Although Jefferson was a lawyer, a writer, a farmer, a diplomat, and a President of the United States, he probably enjoyed most being an architect, designing the house and gardens of Monticello near Charlottesville, Virginia.

Thomas Jefferson Memorial Foundation

strong that the Embargo Act was repealed. On February 27, 1809 the Non-intercourse Law was passed. It closed the ports of the United States to vessels from the warring nations, France and Great Britain, but permitted trade with all other nations. Nothing could be carried to France and Great Britain and nothing could be taken away. Jefferson signed the bill three days before his term ended.

Like Washington, Jefferson refused to accept the nomination for a third term. Although Jefferson served his country during eight stormy years when war clouds hovered on the horizon, he managed to keep the peace, to reduce taxes and the national debt, and to lessen the executive patronage. He simplified government, bringing it nearer the people. The long finger of history points to the purchase of Louisiana as the outstanding achievement of his Administration. In a storm of snow and sleet, Jefferson rode out of Washington on horseback, bound for the plantation home he cherished in Monticello. He left the office of President to James Madison, his trusted Secretary of State and neighbor from Virginia. The "Father of the Constitution" inherited the conflict that Jefferson had dodged for eight years and could be dodged no longer – the War of 1812.

THE SECOND WAR FOR INDEPENDENCE

THE WAR OF 1812, so named because it began in that year, was a mixture of conflicts embroiling Europe and both Americas. British, French, and Spanish peoples, as well as Indians and pirates, were involved in this struggle over issues left unsettled in former wars. In the long standing feud between France and Great Britain, American commerce suffered. In addition to capturing vessels and cargo, the British kidnapped American sailors and pressed them into the service of Great Britain to fight against Napoleon. However, this impressment of American sailors began during Washington's term of office. Over a period of nine months in the years 1796 and 1797, the United States Minister in London applied for the release of nearly 300 seamen, most of whom were citizens of this country. At first, the British claimed to be seeking only deserters from the British navy but the search was extended to include all British subjects. Any sailor unable to prove on the spot that he was a citizen of the United States was forced to serve on a British vessel.

Meanwhile revolutions were brewing in the Spanish colonies in North and South America. Pirates were preying on Spanish commerce. Tecumseh, the brilliant Shawnee chief, organized a confederacy of Indian tribes to halt the westward march of settlers occupying their lands. Thus, the War of 1812 spread on land from Canada to Mexico and on water from the English Channel to Chesapeake Bay.

The land struggle began on the frontier where the farmers suspected that the British were furnishing the Indians with guns and ammunition for raids upon the settlements. In Congress the frontier faction, called the "War Hawks," was led by Henry Clay from Kentucky and John C. Calhoun from South Carolina. Both the western and southern Indians were on the warpath. Although the New Englanders suffered most from French and British attacks on shipping and the impressment of seamen, they did not want war. Their prosperity depended upon commerce and an all-out war would practically destroy their trade with foreign countries. The westerners wanted to fight. On June 18, 1812 Congress declared war upon Great Britain by a vote of 79 to 49 in the House of Representatives, and 19 to 13 in the Senate. From the beginning of this conflict the nation was divided.

War began in the West on the lake border between territories of Great Britain and the United States. As in the War for Independence, the invasion of Canada was high on the docket of military strategy. The western command was entrusted to General Hull, governor of Michigan, an officer who had marched with Washington. Hull moved too slowly. A letter telling him that war had been declared was captured, along with his baggage and hospital stores, by the British commander in the territory. Meanwhile before Hull learned that Great Britain and the United States were at war, the British commander had time to prepare. Hull made only a timid defense, losing not only ground in Canada, but forts on the Great Lakes including Detroit.

Hull was bitterly criticized for his surrender of Detroit and his army without firing a shot. He was tried by court-martial and sentenced to be shot but was pardoned by President Madison. To save the northwestern frontier from invasion, an army of about 10,000 men was recruited by the westerners and placed under General William Henry Harrison, who had defeated Indian followers of Tecumseh the summer before at Tippe-canoe in Indiana. American armies stationed at Niagara and farther east were also too cautious. The initial invasion of Canada was a failure. It gave the British time to enlarge their forces and defend the country, not only with garrisons but also with a fleet on Lake Erie.

In February of 1813 Oliver Hazard Perry, a young naval officer stationed at

After the Battle of Lake Erie and using his Navy cap for a pad, Commodore Perry wrote the following message to General Harrison.

We have met the enemy and they are ours. Two Ships, two Brigs one Schooner & one Sloop.

Yours, with great respect and esteem

O H Perry.

Newport, Rhode Island, received orders to take command of a fleet on Lake Erie. He traveled across the state of New York in a sleigh to Sackett's Harbor. Early in the spring at Erie, Pennsylvania, he put his men to work chopping down trees and sawing lumber to build the fleet he was to command. Five vessels arrived from Black Rock near Buffalo. Then when the boats were completed, he lacked men to sail them. When a hundred recruits arrived early in August, Perry ventured out on the lake. On the evening of the nineteenth General Harrison came on board the flagship, *Lawrence,* for a conference with Perry and his officers on a campaign to recover Michigan.

Perry cruised with his little fleet in search of the British patrol. On the morning of September 10 the sentinel watching in the maintop of the *Lawrence* shouted, "Sail, ho!" a signal that he had sighted the British squadron. The battle began at noon and was still in progress when the moon rose. When the *Lawrence* had been riddled with shot and only one mast remained, Perry was rowed to the *Niagara* amid a spray of bullets, arriving safely to direct the battle from the new flagship. When victory was assured, Perry wrote his famous message to General Harrison. At nine o'clock in the evening, the captured ships of the British fleet joined the American squadron sailing into Put-in-Bay near Sandusky on the southern shore. After the Battle of Lake Erie, Perry assisted Harrison in retaking Detroit which was recovered later in the year 1813.

IN THE SOUTH

THE SURRENDER OF Hull and loss of territory around the Great Lakes had encouraged the Indians to join the British, who promised to give back their lands taken from them by settlers in the United States. Tecumseh went south to stir up revolt among the tribes living in the region of the Gulf of Mexico. The leaders of the southern confederacy of Indians were the Muscogees, whom the first Europeans called Creeks because their country abounded in little streams.

The Creeks had attained skill in building houses, barges, canoes, arms, and fortifications. They cultivated the land, wove carpets of rushes, and made pottery for cooking purposes. As settlers moved westward into Tennessee and occupied the hunting grounds of the southern tribes, the Creeks grew restless. Then Jefferson purchased Louisiana which included territory that the tribes had occupied to escape the settlers. Both Spain and the United States claimed the region known as West Florida. The Creeks now felt impelled to resort to war in an effort to hold their lands. In August of 1813, shortly before Perry's victory on Lake Erie, Creek warriors attacked Fort Mims on the Alabama River. Of three hundred persons in the garrison at the time of the attack, only about twenty escaped with their lives. The women and children, seeking refuge on the top floor during the battle, were burned to death when the Indians fired the buildings of the fort.

After this massacre at Fort Mims the legislature of Tennessee voted to borrow a sum of money, not exceeding $300,000 to pay and supply an army of not more than 3500 men, to fight the Creek nation. The troops were gathered almost immediately and placed under the command of Andrew Jackson, the Indian fighter from Nashville. With added forces from East

Tennessee under General Cocke, from Georgia under General Floyd, and from Mississippi under General Claiborne, Jackson waged a war of extermination upon the Creeks. He destroyed their fields, burned their villages, and shot them on sight. The broken nation sued for peace. The Creeks lost most of their territory in the treaty signed by thirty-six of their chiefs. Reduced to starvation, the Creeks who survived the war were furnished with food and necessities by the Government until the next corn crop was harvested. Some Creeks fled to join their kindred, the Seminoles, who were hiding in the Florida swamps.

The defeat of Napoleon released British troops and ships for the war in North America, and threatened an invasion of the Atlantic coast. A force from British vessels landed in Chesapeake Bay. They advanced upon Washington, scattered the American troops who tried to stop the invaders, and burned the government buildings of the new capital. President Madison and his Cabinet fled across the Potomac into Virginia. Although a carriage stood waiting at her door, Mrs. Madison did not leave until the fire of British soldiers was heard. She took along valuable state papers, silver tableware, and Stuart's painting of Washington which she cut from its frame with a carving knife, as there was not time to remove it all. After destroying the capital, the British returned to their ships.

Upon leaving the burning capital late in August of 1814, the British took with them Dr. Beanes, a prominent physician. Francis Scott Key, a lawyer in Georgetown, gained permission from President Madison to board the flagship of Admiral Cochrane and plead for the release of Dr. Beanes. Key and a leading citizen of Baltimore went out to the fleet, massed near the mouth of the Potomac River for an attack upon Baltimore, next city on the list for capture after Washington. The Americans went out in the *Minden* under a flag of truce. Admiral Cochrane, although agreeing to release the doctor, held him, his attorney, and friend on board the *Minden.* He feared that they would reveal the plan of attack on Baltimore upon their return to shore. The three men watched during a whole night the bombardment of Fort McHenry, wondering if the morning would reveal the white flag of surrender or the Stars and Stripes on the flagpole.

In the dim light of the early morning, through glasses, they saw the nation's flag still waving over the fort. The firing had ceased. Overjoyed, Key, who was also a poet, scribbled The Star Spangled Banner on the back of a letter he had in his pocket. Set to the tune of an old English song, the poem later became the national anthem. When the British fleet was ready to sail away, the prisoners were sent ashore.

ON THE SEA

WITH FEW EXCEPTIONS, Americans lost the battles on land but they won most of the engagements on the water. The War of 1812 was essentially a naval conflict. The small United States Navy won more than its share of victories on lakes and at sea. Two months after war was declared, the United States frigate, *Constitution*, met the British ship, *Guerrière*, off the coast of Nova Scotia. Isaac Hull, captain of the *Constitution*, withheld fire until at close range to save ammunition. After forty-five minutes of close fighting the *Guerrière* was a total wreck and struck her flag. After the

Americans had taken off the British seamen who survived the battle, Hull ordered their vessel burned. His victory cheered Americans who were alarmed by his uncle's surrender at Detroit a few days before. Congress voted thanks and $50,000 to Hull and his crew. His ship was nicknamed *Old Ironsides.*

When war broke out between Great Britain and the United States, few persons in either country realized that it would develop into a conflict on the sea. When war was declared by Congress on the eighteenth of June, 1812, this nation had only seven well-manned, seaworthy frigates — *Constitution, President, United States, Congress, Constellation, Chesapeake, Essex* — with a total 278 guns. Great Britain had over a thousand ships and most of these were cruising the seas. Hopelessly outnumbered in warships, the Government of the United States turned to privateering to cripple British sea power.

A week after war was declared, Congress passed an act encouraging private ship owners to apply for letters of marque to fit out vessels as privateers. The act stated:

Prize money to accrue only to the owners, officers, and crews of the privateers, to be distributed according to any written engagement between them. Two percent of the net amount of prize money to be paid over to the collectors as a fund for widows and orphans and disabled seamen.

Hundreds of seamen, long out of work because of the embargo, enlisted for duty on privateers. The risk and adventure of chasing and capturing the British merchant vessels, as well as the chance to win a small fortune, lured them back to the seas. While defending their country they might also fill their own pockets. The immediate response to the act, passed

June 26, 1812, can be judged from a news item appearing in a Halifax paper under a date line of July 20, 1812:

American privateers are swarming round our coast and in the Bay of Fundy. Hardly a day passes but we hear of some captures by them. — Indeed, so numerous are the privateers around the coast that we consider it very imprudent for any vessel to sail from this port unless under convoy.

News of captures were published by newspapers everywhere, and eagerly read by citizens, anxious to keep track of the number of vessels taken to date. In October of 1814, the twelve hundredth capture was recorded in Niles Weekly Register as follows:

Brig, *Nancy,* from Liverpool for Halifax laden with dry goods, captured by the Portsmouth, of Portsmouth, New Hampshire, divested of 318 bales and packages of goods invoiced at 27,000 pounds sterling, and ordered in. This is a great prize well accounted for, as the privateer with her rich spoils has safely arrived.

The privateersmen, actually licensed pirates, had their own code of honor. The owners of the ship *Benjamin Franklin* learned that the British ship, *Industry,* laden with about two thousand dollars worth of pickled salmon, belonged to a poor widow and her family. They ordered the captain of their privateer to return the captured vessel and its cargo to the woman.

Ships and cargoes worth many millions of dollars were captured or destroyed by privateers, roving singly or in groups. These armed raiders were actually men-of-war, taking the place of the battleships that usually belong to a navy. In some encounters with the enemy these privateers were captured or scuttled and many sea-

James Madison, President of the United States of America,

TO ALL WHO SHALL SEE THESE PRESENTS, GREETING:

BE IT KNOWN, That in pursuance of an act of congress, passed on the *eighteenth* day of *June* one thousand eight hundred and twelve, I have commissioned, and by these presents do commission, the private armed *Schooner* called the *Leonidas* — of the burden of *one hundred thirty five Tons* tons, or thereabouts, owned by *J. W. Brune, B. I. Vonkapff, Jams Williams, Jams Bosley, Henry Didier & I John A. Darcy of the City of Baltimore in the State of Maryland*

mounting *one* carriage guns, and navigated by *nineteen* men, hereby authorizing *John Chase* captain, and *Thomas W. Jencks* lieutenant of the said *Schooner Leonidas* — and the other officers and crew thereof, to subdue, seize, and take any armed or unarmed British vessel, public or private, which shall be found within the jurisdictional limits of the United States, or elsewhere on the high seas, or within the waters of the British dominions, and such captured vessel, with her apparel, guns, and appertenances, and the goods or effects which shall be found on board the same, together with all the British persons and others who shall be found acting on board, to bring within some port of the United States; and also to retake any vessel, goods, and effects of the people of the United States, which may have been captured by any British armed vessel, in order that proceedings may be had concerning such capture or recapture in due form of law, and as to right and justice shall appertain. The said *John Chase* is further authorized to detain, seize, and take all vessels and effects, to whomsoever belonging, which shall be liable thereto according to the law of nations and the rights of the United States as a power at war, and to bring the same within some port of the United States, in order that due proceedings may be had thereon. This commission to continue in force during the pleasure of the president of the United States for the time being.

GIVEN under my hand and the seal of the United States of America, at the City of Washington, the *Twelfth* day of *December* in the year of our Lord, one thousand eight hundred and *fourteen* and of the independence of the said states the *Thirty ninth.*

BY THE PRESIDENT,

James Madison

Jas. Monroe Secretary of State.

From original in National Archives

LETTER OF MARQUE ISSUED BY
PRESIDENT JAMES MADISON DURING THE WAR OF 1812.

BE IT KNOWN, That in pursuance of an act of congress passed on the eighteenth day of June one thousand eight hundred and twelve, I have commissioned, and by these presents do commission, the private armed *Schooner* called the *Leonidas* — of the burden of one hundred thirty five tons, or thereabouts, owned by . . . of the City of Baltimore in the State of Maryland

mounting one carriage gun, and navigated by nineteen men, hereby authorizing John Chase captain, and Thomas W. Jencks, lieutenant of the said *Schooner Leonidas* — and the other officers and crew thereof, to subdue, seize, and take any armed or unarmed British vessel, public or private, which shall be found within the jurisdictional limits of the United States, or elsewhere on the high seas, or within the waters of the British dominions, and such captured vessel, with her apparel, guns, and appertenances, and the goods or effects which shall be found on board the same, together with all the British persons and others who shall be found acting on board, to bring within some port of the United States; and also to retake any vessel, goods, and effects of the people of the United States, which may have been captured by any British armed vessel, in order that proceedings may be had concerning such capture or recapture in due form of law, and as to right and justice shall appertain. The said John Chase is further authorized to detain, seize, and take all vessels and effects, to whomsoever belonging, which shall be liable thereto according to the law of nations and the rights of the United States as a power at war, and to bring the same within some port of the United States, in order that due proceedings may be had thereon. This commission to continue in force during the pleasure of the president of the United States for the time being.

GIVEN under my hand the seal of the United States of America, at the city of Washington, the Twelfth day of December in the year of our Lord, one thousand eight hundred and fourteen and of the independence of the said states the Thirty ninth.

BY THE PRESIDENT   James Madison

Jas. Monroe Secretary of State

men lost their lives. Part of their code was to defend their country, first and last. Few, if any, rendered as much service as the *General Armstrong*, which was owned by a group of merchants in New York.

In September of 1814 this privateer sought refuge in a harbor of the Azores Islands, which belonged to the neutral country of Portugal, to get water and other necessities for the men on board. In violation of international rules of warfare three British men-of-war entered the neutral port of Fayal to attack the American vessel. Captain Lloyd, commanding the squadron, intended to add the *General Armstrong* to his unit on the way to join a fleet assembling in Jamaica for an attack on New Orleans. He dispatched boatloads of men to board the privateer and capture it. At their approach Captain Reid fired upon them. It was a bright moonlit night. Crowds from the town gathered on the shore to watch the battle that raged for forty minutes. With his ship badly damaged and escape blocked by the British squadron, Captain Reid ordered his men to scuttle the ship and flee to shore.

The engagement was costly to the British who had over three hundred casualties. However, the loss of time amounted to a major defeat of the British. The fleet at Jamaica waited ten days past the scheduled sailing date for the arrival of Captain Lloyd's squadron. This delay gave General Jackson time to gather forces for the defense of New Orleans. In the public mind the captain of the privateer shared honors with a general in the army for saving the city of New Orleans from capture.

Why did the British want to take New Orleans? The reason was stated by the editor of the London Courier in his paper dated June 17, 1813:

If Great Britain will only take New Orleans, she will divide the States. By shutting that outlet to the fruits of western industry, she will make herself known and respected by those States, in spite of the power of the rest of the Union. If in the war of 1755, France had been as superior at sea, as Britain then was, we should never have heard of the United States of America. The back country would have been as well settled before this with Frenchmen, as it now is with the descendants of Britons.

Jamaica became the gathering place for British troops and ships for the invasion of the coastal region of the United States. About the first of December, 1814, a military force of about 10,000 men, including sailors and marines, embarked on forty ships and sailed from Jamaica for New Orleans. The army was placed under the command of Sir Edward Packenham, a veteran of the Napoleonic Wars. The small United States Navy was represented by a few squadrons of gunboats under Lieutenant Jones, who could do little more than fight a delaying action against the invading fleet.

The British troops were safely landed and prepared for the attack on the key city of Louisiana. Jackson delayed the battle until militia arrived from Kentucky. His men completed fortifications of logs, cotton bales, and mud. Behind this crude bulwark ranged a battle line of strange fighting men, enrolled under the banner of the Stars and Stripes. There were regulars of the United States Army, free Negroes, French dragoons, frontiersmen in homespun shirts, and sailors from boats in the river. In the midst of them was Jean Lafitte, who had guided his swarthy pirate gang over miles of secret trails through swamps to join the forces of General Jackson. Packenham's well-trained soldiers advanced across level country in the face of deadly fire. They were met by expert marksmen who had learned to use a rifle in boyhood, hunting turkeys, deer, and squirrels in the woods surrounding their frontier farms. About seven hundred British lost their lives and twice that number were wounded before they deserted the field of battle. General Packenham was killed in the rout.

The Battle of New Orleans on the eighth of January, 1815 was fought two weeks after peace had been signed on Christmas Eve in Ghent, Belgium. The news could not reach the armies until a sailing ship brought it across three thousand miles of ocean and through the Gulf of Mexico.

The war had been unpopular both in Great Britain and the United States. British merchants complained about the losses due to privateers and American traders missed their foreign markets. Although the war aims were not mentioned in the treaty, the results of the conflict were far-reaching. With foreign trade cut off by the British blockade, Americans built their own cotton and woolen mills and other factories to produce the things they needed. In this way the War of 1812 helped the United States to become an industrial nation. However, the real victory was on water, not land. The conflict coming so soon after the Revolutionary War has been called the Second War for Independence, because, by it, the United States won the freedom of the seas.

Pirates who long had robbed American ships in the Mediterranean were finally defeated, and that great waterway was free to commerce. Several years before Washington was inaugurated, the captain of a British vessel brought the news that the Algierians had declared war on the United States. They were building eight ships to prey on American commerce. This captain knew of two merchant ships from Boston that had been captured. Their crews had been sold into slavery on the auction block by the pirates of Algiers.

During Jefferson's term, Lieutenant Stephen Decatur boldly entered the harbor of Tripoli in a small row boat with a few sailors, set fire to the *Philadelphia* which pirates had taken from Americans, and escaped unhurt to his ship under heavy bombardment from shore batteries. To reward Decatur for his gallant service in the wars with the Barbary States and the war with England, James Monroe, Secretary of State in Madison's cabinet, promoted him to the Board of Navy Commissioners.

A few months later, his new duties took him to Norfolk, Virginia, his wife's birthplace, where they were entertained at a dinner by old friends. The guests responded to this toast in honor of Decatur:

"National glory! A gem above all price, and worthy every hazard to sustain its splendor."

To this praise for his part in defending national glory, Decatur modestly replied:

"Our country! In her intercourse with foreign nations, may she always be in the right; but our country, right or wrong."

The War of 1812 was the last armed controversy between Great Britain and the United States. Ever since, the two English-speaking nations have been allies in war and in peace. Before the treaty was signed, however, other wars for independence in the Spanish colonies of the Americas threatened to involve this country in another European conflict.

REVOLUTIONS IN SPANISH AMERICA BRING FORTH THE MONROE DOCTRINE

SOUTH AMERICA was also affected by Napoleon's rise to power in France. In the year following the decree forbidding trade with Great Britain, Napoleon's army marched into Portugal. The royal family of that little kingdom fled to their South American colony of Brazil under the protection of a British fleet. Rio de Janeiro became the capital of Portugal instead of Lisbon. Queen Maria was insane and her son, Prince John, ruled the country as regent. Immediately he opened the ports of Brazil to foreign ships; freed industry and encouraged trade; established the Bank of Brazil; started a printing press; and founded a royal library open to all readers. These measures made Prince John popular with his former colonists. With the royal family on the throne in Brazil, that nation escaped the revolutionary upheavals which started in the Spanish colonies when Napoleon invaded Spain the following year, 1808. Napoleon placed his brother Joseph on Ferdinand's throne.

However, the seeds of revolution had been planted in South America before Napoleon began his conquest of Europe. Four years before our War for Independence started at Lexington, Francisco de Miranda, a young man twenty years old, left his native country of Venezuela, and sailed for Spain to seek a military career denied him in his homeland. His father, a Spaniard of Basque origin, had migrated from the Canary Islands to Venezuela, where he became a wealthy man, owner of a cacao plantation and a fine house in Caracas. Francisco was refused entrance to the Royal Cadet Corps, reserved for the sons of the first families,

direct descendants of the conquistadores. With injured pride young Francisco left for Spain to continue his studies in language, mathematics, and military tactics. In 1772 he entered the service of Spain with a commission of captain in a favored regiment. This was gained through his influence at court and a payment of money.

During the Revolutionary War, Miranda had been transferred to a regiment leaving Spain to fight the British in the West Indies. Since France and Spain were then allies and France was helping the American colonies to win their independence, the King of Spain was forced to declare war on Great Britain although he was not in favor of it. Miranda's arrival in the West Indies was a turning point in the history of the Americas. Here he joined his French allies to whom he rendered a service as he was able to speak the language fluently. After a military base was established in the islands, Miranda went along with the expedition of French and Spanish forces to capture the town of Pensacola, Florida, held by the British. In his diary, Miranda reported the capture of the Florida fort:

On May 9, 1781, at seven A.M., Sergeant Major Campbell came to our camp with full powers to conclude a capitulation; and at two P.M., all was terminated as regards the arrangements. At three, General Galvez left with two companies of Grenadiers to take over the city, and they were well received by the inhabitants.

Upon his return to Havana, Miranda was sent to Jamaica to arrange with the British governor for the exchange of prisoners. Next he joined a combined force of French, Spanish, and United States naval units in an attack upon the Bahama Islands. On this expedition Miranda served side by side with soldiers and sailors, mostly men from the southern states, who explained to him the principles of the Declaration of Independence, based upon the idea that the human rights of man are above the rights of government. Miranda was keenly interested in the "something new" germinating in the Western Hemisphere and he wanted to learn more about it.

After the capture of the Bahamas and the surrender of the British garrison, Miranda returned to Cuba expecting to be well received. His general had officially cited him for merit and commended him for his part in making the campaign a success. Instead, he faced a series of charges that he had been too generous to the British commander in Jamaica when exchanging prisoners. Although the Governor-General of Cuba defended Miranda, his enemies pressed the charges against him and threatened to bring an end to his military career. While inactive in Cuba, Miranda rendered a service to the cause of independence in the United States by using his influence with the Governor-General to secure a loan of 35,000 pounds from the Cuban treasury for purchasing supplies for the French fleet. This financial aid, secured by Miranda, hastened the departure of the French fleet under Admiral de Grasse who sailed up Chesapeake Bay in time to block the escape of the British army by sea. This resulted in the surrender of Cornwallis at Yorktown.

When word came to Miranda that orders had been issued for his arrest and return to Spain, he paced the terrace of his lodgings and watched the lights on the ships riding at anchor in the bay. He made a fateful decision during the night. Because he was also an American he would go to the United States to learn more about the new freedom in that

FRANCISCO DE MIRANDA 1750-1816

Francisco de Miranda visited France, England, and the United States, seeking advice and arms to free Venezuela, his birthplace, from the rule of Spain. Being a military man, he took part in the wars of these four countries. On July 5, 1811, a congress made up of delegates of seven provinces declared they were "by act and right, free sovereign, and independent states." Real independence, however, was won only after a long and bloody war, following the death of Miranda in 1816. He spent the last four years of his life in prison on the island of Leon near Cadiz, Spain.

On a monument to Miranda in Caracas, Venezuela, these words are inscribed:

He took part in three great political movements of his age: the independence of the United States of America; the French revolution; and the independence of South America.

country. When the Spanish fleet sailed from Havana for Cadiz, Miranda was not aboard. In his diary for June 1, 1783, he wrote:

I went many times to the Court of Justice. I really cannot express my pleasure and satisfaction at seeing the admirable system of the British Constitution in practice. — What a contrast to the Spanish system of Government!

In Philadelphia he met George Washington and discussed military affairs. In touring battlefronts in New York and Massachusetts he became friendly with Alexander Hamilton and General Knox who had served on Washington's staff. Miranda, coming from a country where promotions in the army and the government were open only to persons of wealth and influence, was somewhat surprised to learn that General Knox whom he admired as "one of the best informed military men in theory and in practice of war" had been a bookseller before he joined the militia. Miranda often visited legislative assemblies to learn how laws were made by representatives of the people. In Boston he was a little disturbed that a tailor, an innkeeper, a porter, and a blacksmith were members of the state assembly. This way of providing government by the governed was so new to him.

Before leaving the United States for England in December of 1784, Miranda acquired an estimate of the cost of supplying an army of 5000 men for one year. The next four years were spent traveling through the countries of Europe. There he studied the various forms of government. He also contemplated the pattern best suited for South America when that continent would gain its freedom from Spain. He returned to New York in the autumn of 1805 to organize an expedition intended to liberate his native country, Venezuela. Although it failed, Miranda continued his efforts to promote revolution in the Spanish colonies of the Americas. But Napoleon, not Miranda, touched off the spark that kindled the flame of war.

NAPOLEON INVADES SPAIN

WHEN NAPOLEON deposed Ferdinand VII, King of Spain, and placed his brother, Joseph Bonaparte, on the throne, the Spanish Americans revolted as a gesture of loyalty to their monarch. This event was a good excuse for the general outbreak of revolutions smoldering in the Spanish provinces since the United States had declared its independence. However, independence was not so easily won in Spanish America as it was in British America. Although Great Britain and Spain had the same idea, that colonies existed for the benefit of the mother country, the British colonials gained a large measure of self-government. While still subjects of Great Britain they learned to enjoy freedoms and to fight for them. Therefore, the struggle for independence in the United States was more a general uprising of the people and less the vision of their leaders.

The Spanish colonies were ruled almost entirely by officials sent over from Spain. These viceroys had mounted guards, fine carriages, and the trappings of royalty. In the villages the people had a small voice in local affairs, but not enough for them to learn how to govern themselves in a separate nation. Therefore, the independence movement in Spanish America was like a game of "follow the leader." It rose and fell with the success and failure of the military chiefs who led the uprisings. Today in cities of the Americas, statues in public places honor the memory of these leaders whom the people call, affectionately, the "libertadores." The only one who rose to power in the revolutionary movement was another Venezuelan, Simon Bolivar.

Bolivar was born in the capital, Caracas, in 1783 the same year that Miranda sailed from Cuba for a tour of the United States. Like Miranda, he was the son of wealthy parents, but Bolivar's family belonged to the aristocrats who had refused to admit Miranda to their cadet corps. The two men, however, were destined to meet in later years on common ground, fighting for the independence of South America. At the age of nine Simon was orphaned. Like most sons of rich colonials he was sent to school in Spain when sixteen years of age. He had already served two years in the battalion where his father had once been a colonel. In 1802 he married the daughter of a Spanish nobleman and returned to Venezuela, intending to spend his days on his father's estate. But the death of his wife started him wandering with his former tutor as a companion. His teacher, Rodriguez, had fled from Venezuela after serving a prison sentence for stirring up a rebellion against Spanish authorities there. From Rodriguez, no doubt, the young Bolivar gained encouragement to liberate South America, according to a remark made in a letter to his former instructor after the country was freed from Spain and Simon Bolivar was the national hero:

Do you remember when we were together at the Holy Mount in Rome to swear upon that sacred earth the liberty of our country?

In 1807 Bolivar visited the United States to learn something about government in that country. Then, when Napoleon invaded Spain, Bolivar cast his lot with the revolutionaries who refused to accept Napoleon's brother as their monarch. In 1810 Miranda returned from Europe to his home country of Venezuela to foment another revolt. The following year, on the fifth day of July, he joined the patriots in a declaration of independence made by the American Confederation of Venezuela. It stated:

These united provinces are, and ought to be from this day forth, in fact and of right, free, sovereign, and independent states.

The Spanish governor was expelled from the country along with his associates. A constitution similar to the one in the United States was adopted, but the newborn republic did not last long. A year later Miranda surrendered to a loyalist Spanish army under a treaty agreement that persons and property of Venezuelans would be respected, but the nation's freedom was sacrificed. A storm of criticism fell upon Miranda. When he tried to escape on a British ship, several patriots, one of whom was Bolivar, captured him and threw him into prison where he was later found by the Spanish governor. After serving time in jails in the West Indies, he was transported to Spain where he died in a dungeon in July of 1816. His place as leader of the revolution had been taken by Simon Bolivar.

THE REVOLT SPREADS IN SPANISH AMERICA

DURING PRESIDENT Madison's administration, revolts broke out here and there all over Spanish America. While Miranda had been gathering recruits in

Venezuela, Hidalgo had been organizing an army in Mexico to overthrow the Spanish regime. Although the revolution started as an Indian uprising on September 16, 1810, Mexicans of Spanish blood joined Hidalgo's forces in their triumphal march into the country west of the capital. The revolutionaries, lacking arms and discipline, were defeated by the drilled and well-equipped regulars of the Spanish army.

Hidalgo was traveling north through friendly country with only a few com-

HEROES OF THE MEXICAN REVOLUTION

MIGUEL HIDALGO Y COSTILLA 1753-1811

It was Sunday morning, September 16, 1810. Hidalgo, a priest in the village of Dolores, Mexico rang the church bell. The people knew this was the signal to start the planned revolt for independence. Although thousands of Mexicans joined the ranks of Hidalgo's army, they lacked weapons of war and army discipline, and were defeated by the well-trained Spanish forces. Hidalgo was shot as a traitor, July 30, 1811 in Chihuahua. Today, in Mexico, September 16 is a national holiday — Independence Day.

JOSE MARIA MORELOS 1765-1815

Morelos, also a village priest, joined the army of Hidalgo in 1810, and became the leader of the revolution after Hidalgo's execution. Morelos was a successful general. Within two years, he controlled most of the southern part of Mexico. He summoned a congress to meet in Chilpancingo to draft a constitution giving the people the right to vote and to share in their government. His government soon fell. As more soldiers arrived from Spain, his armies were defeated. Morelos was shot as a traitor on December 22, 1815.

232

panions to seek refuge in Louisiana when he was captured through the treachery of one of his own officers. In less than a year after the uprising on September 16, now celebrated as Independence Day, the Father of Mexican Independence was executed by a firing squad.

One of Hidalgo's followers, Morelos, then became the leader of the revolution. He recruited soldiers and gathered an army that drove royalist soldiers from the district south of Mexico City lying between Acapulco and the capital. He summoned a congress, which met at Chilpancingo in the province of Guerrero. On November 6, 1813, seven of the eight delegates signed the first declaration of independence for Mexico. About a year later a constitution was adopted, but the document had little force because Spanish soldiers patrolled large sections of the country. The new government soon fell when Morelos was captured and shot as a traitor. Others took up the cause of the revolution, and fought until Mexico was free from Spain. Today two provinces of that country are named for Hidalgo and Morelos who gave their lives for Mexican independence.

After Napoleon's defeat in 1814 the King of Spain regained his throne. Immediately, Ferdinand dispatched troops to quell the rebellions gaining ground in the Spanish colonies of the Americas. His first concern was to save his empire in the New World. The largest number of soldiers was landed in the northern provinces of South America. There the wars for independence began, raged with the greatest fury, and lasted the longest time. There, the leader of the revolutionaries was General Bolivar, a rich landowner, who freed the thousand slaves he had inherited, used his fortune to equip his soldiers, and devoted his life to winning independence for the southern continent. There, the struggle was a long story of battles lost and won; freedoms granted and denied; towns pillaged and burned; women and children massacred; prisoners shot on both sides; congresses called and disbanded; and constitutions proclaimed and discarded. At times it was a war of extermination.

These wars for independence enlisted the sympathy of freedom loving peoples everywhere. Hundreds of volunteer troops from England, Scotland, and Ireland joined the ranks of revolutionaries in Spanish America. Among the officers were such names as Cochrane, MacGregor, and O'Leary. A Frenchman who lived in Baltimore became known as the Lafayette of the Spanish American revolutions. Many adventurous westerners in the United States joined the patriot armies of Mexico, Venezuela, Colombia, and the provinces farther south. Since the papers and magazines printed news from every battlefront and articles about the countries and the people, citizens of the United States learned about their southern neighbors with whom they strongly sympathized.

In 1817 James Monroe became President of the United States. Monroe, who had fought with Washington in the War for Independence, inherited the diplomatic problems of the South American revolutions. The events in South America during Monroe's term created anxiety in the United States where Henry Clay was advocating recognition of the revolutionary governments established in Mexico, Central and South America. In election parades in Mexico pictures of Washington and Franklin were carried along with those of the candidates for

MONUMENT TO SAN MARTIN
AND HIS ARMY OF THE ANDES

On a peak overlooking the city of Mendoza in western Argentina, this monument commemorates the daring crossing of the Andes by General San Martin and his army. The extraordinary feat of taking both infantry and cavalry from Mendoza and through a snowy, unmarked pass in the high mountains caught the Spaniards in Chile by surprise. The royal army was defeated at Chacabuco. Both Chile and Argentina were free. The figure of an angel holds aloft the broken chain that had tied these countries to Spain.

office. A short time after Monroe was elected, this note was published in the papers:

The supreme congress of the Mexican Republic have voted to Henry Clay, the speaker of the House of Representatives, their thanks for the disinterested, manly and generous sentiments he expressed on the floor of the house, for the welfare of that infant republic.

The feat of San Martin opened the passage through Peru for uniting the armies of the north and the south. Jose de San Martin was born in an Indian mission in Uruguay where his father was an army officer. When Jose was seven years old, his family returned to Spain. At eleven the boy enlisted in the Spanish army and grew into manhood fighting the wars of his King. He was thirty-four when he arrived at Buenos Aires, after an absence of twenty-seven years. He joined the revolutionary armies and fought to free the southern provinces in South America.

While governor of Cuyo, a province at the foot of the Andes, San Martin decided to cross the mountains and free Chile. Although the people of Cuyo were poor, they provided horses, mules, slaves, soldiers, arms, ammunition, blankets, food, and money for this daring expedition. In January of 1817, during the warmest summer weather, the army of 5,200 men and 10,000 horses and mules started on this journey. Along narrow ledges the mules trudged single file, carrying their loads of arms, food, and firewood. It kept three hundred men busy shoveling snow to clear a path for men and beasts. Five thousand pack animals were lost but only a few men perished in crossing the mountains. On the Pacific slope of the Andes, San Martin took the Spaniards by surprise, defeating the loyalist army at Chacabuco.

Soon Chile had a constitution modeled after that of the United States. The Chileans furnished soldiers, arms, and money to enlarge San Martin's army for freeing Peru. With the help of a fleet commanded by Admiral Cochrane formerly of the British Navy, Lima fell to the revolutionaries. Most of the country outside the capital was held by loyalist troops.

To free Peru, General San Martin on July 28, 1821 in company with representatives of the University of San Marcos, public officials, and many nobles marched in

Painting by Don Tito Salas. Bank of Venezuela

BOLIVAR'S ARMY CROSSING THE ANDES

After establishing the Republic of Venezuela, Bolivar decided to take Bogota on the other side of the mountains and add that territory to what he had taken from Spain. On May 23, 1819 the General called a meeting of his officers in a shabby hut on the bank of the Agure River that flows into the Orinoco. For chairs, the men sat on the skulls of cattle bleached white with sun and rain, all that was left of a herd slaughtered to feed the Spanish soldiers who had fled. Bolivar's men agreed to cross the Andes and take Bogota by surprise.

The army marched through flooded lands and swam raging streams to the foothills of the towering Andes. On June 22, the army, pelted by rain, hail, and icy wind, began the treacherous ascent to the cold heights. Men, horses and mules died on the way, but the army won enough skirmishes to enter Bogota. The surprise maneuver was a success. On the tenth day of August, Bolivar rode up to the palace of the Spanish viceroy who fled disguised as an Indian. He changed the name of the country. New Granada became Colombia, but borders were not settled for many years.

235

SIMON BOLIVAR — EL LIBERTADOR
1783-1830

People in South America call Bolivar "the Liberator."

triumph to the great square of Lima. There, San Martin unfurled, for the first time, the flag of another independent nation. Dramatically, he waved the banner three times, while the cheering crowd echoed his words, "Long live the country! Long live liberty! Long live independence!" Cannons fired salutes, the church bells rang, and the people shouted for joy. Peru was free.

A year later San Martin, the hero of the South, met Bolivar, the hero from the North, at the port of Guayaquil in the present nation of Ecuador. What happened when the two great men met remains somewhat of a mystery. Soon after the conference San Martin retired as protector of Peru and became a voluntary exile in Europe. He left the glory of Libertador to his rival, Simon Bolivar, in order that their ambitions would not clash and injure the united cause of independence. At this crucial time, the United States threw a protecting arm around the infant republics of Spanish America.

THE MONROE DOCTRINE

WHEN EUROPEAN MONARCHS met in 1822, both North and South Americans feared that the monarchs might help the King of Spain regain his lost provinces in the Western Hemisphere. Moreover, Russians were creeping down the Pacific coast from Alaska. Their trading posts extended five hundred miles south of the Columbia River, only thirty miles from the Spanish settlements in California. Every year, Russian ships laden with American furs sailed from the northwest coast. How long could the United States remain free and independent if rulers in Europe and Asia were able to conquer the nation's neighbors?

For the answer to this puzzling question Monroe consulted his friend and teacher, Thomas Jefferson, and his capable Secretary of State, John Quincy Adams.

Monroe considered asking Great Britain to join with the United States in declaring that any attempt to take any part of the Americas by force of arms would be resented by both countries. John Quincy Adams wanted this nation to stand alone and not "come in as a cockboat in the wake of the British man-of-war." In fact, the Monroe Doctrine was largely the work of John Quincy Adams. It was a rather simple statement but it startled the world.

On December 2, 1823, President Monroe informed Congress that the Western Hemisphere was no longer open for further colonization by powers in the Eastern Hemisphere. His statement was blunt, declaring "that the American continents, by the free and independent condition which they have assumed and maintain, are henceforth not to be considered as subjects for future colonization by any European powers." President Monroe added an explanation, stating the necessity for this opinion because the political systems in European countries were different from those in the Americas:

We owe it, therefore, to candor and to the amicable relations existing between the United States and those powers to declare that we should consider any attempt on their part to extend their system to any portion of this hemisphere as dangerous to our peace and safety.

The bold message struck the European diplomats like a bolt of lightning. Some spoke out against it and others ignored it. Among the new South American nations, the doctrine was most enthusiastically received in Chile. Congressmen, although approving the Monroe policy, were fearful that it might involve the United States in war. The people, however, were enthusiastic about the Monroe Doctrine which appealed to their national pride.

Monroe's Secretary of State, largely responsible for the document, won the next Presidential election. John Quincy Adams was the son of John Adams, the second President of the United States. As a little boy, holding tightly to his mother's hand, he had watched the Battle of Bunker Hill. He grew up with the nation. His term marks the end of a period when the Government had been guided by men from the original thirteen states and by citizens who had taken some part in the War for Independence. During that forty years the nation had paid its debts and restored credit; established business and become self-supporting; defended itself in war; and aided others fighting for freedom. The United States of America had won the respect of the world. Then "something new" came out of the West.

MAPS:

WA12r, WA18r, WA19r
Atlas of American History by Edgar B. Wesley

PART FIVE

The Nation Adjusts
to a Moving Frontier

To The West

With spirit

To the West! To the West! To the land— of the free, Where might-y Mis-sou-ri rolls down to the sea. Where a man is a man, if he's will-ing to toil, And the humb-lest may gath-er the fruit of the soil. Where chil-dren are bless-ings, and he who hath most, Has aid for his for-tune and rich-es to boast. Where the young may ex-ult, and the a-ged may rest, A-way, far a-way, to the land— of the West.

poco rit.

CHORUS:
a tempo

mf To the West! To the West! To the land— of the free, Where might-y Mis-sou-ri rolls down to the sea. Where the young may ex-ult, and the a-ged may rest, A-way, far a-way, To the land of the West!

To the West! To the West!
  Where the rivers that flow
Run thousands of miles
  spreading out as they go;
Where the green waving forests
  shall echo our call,
As wide as all England
  and free to us all.
Where the prairies like seas,
  where the billows have roll'd,
Are broad as the kingdoms
  and empires of old.
And the lakes are like oceans
  in storm or in rest,
Away, far away,
  to the land of the West.

To the West! To the West!
  There is wealth to be won,
The forest to clear
  is the work to be done;
Where the Stars and the Stripes
  like a banner unfurled,
Invites to its regions
  the world, all the world.
Where the people are true
  to the vows that they frame,
And their pride is the honor
  that's shown to their name;
And away! far away!
  let us hope for the best,
And build up a home
  in the land of the West.

Songs of Yesterday by Philip D. Jordan and Lillian Kessler, Doubleday and Company, Inc.

Chapter 13

The West Comes into Power

WHERE IS WEST?

DURING THE Revolutionary War settlers began to cross the mountains through the Cumberland Gap and to follow the Wilderness Road into Kentucky. Many were Scotch Irish from the middle and southern colonies. Their pack trains were loaded with precious salt, wallets of seed corn, bundles of bedding, a favorite rocker, a chest of drawers, a spinning wheel, and other prized possessions. The feather beds were tied in front, almost on the horses' necks, where the babies could ride in safety and comfort. Cooking kettles and long-handled spoons dangled from the pack saddles, fashioned from the fork of a hickory tree. At the end of a day's travel the emigrants "camped out." Over an open fire the women broiled venison, roasted turkeys, parched corn, boiled greens, and baked hoe cake. Rolled in their blankets the weary travelers slept under the stars beside the trail. In rainy weather they built a "lean-to" shelter of poles and bark. The way was long and hard but packed with adventure and filled with hope. At the end was a farm and a home for every one willing to work. Land was the magnet that pulled the train of settlers over the mountains into Kentucky and Tennessee.

Many settlers bound for Tennessee followed the valleys of the Powell, Clinch, and Holston Rivers. They loaded furniture, seed, and livestock onto flatboats and floated down the streams as far as they could and then went overland. Many of the early settlers used dugout canoes to ride the rapids of the Tennessee River. The most dangerous spot was Muscle Shoals in the great bend of the Tennessee River. In early days these shoals were covered with mussels. The first white men found Indian villages scattered the full length of the shoals so that the natives could feed upon the shellfish. For some unknown reason, perhaps because they did not know how to spell correctly, the first white men called the spot "Muscle Shoals." The name has clung to it. The most treacherous places were named Boiling Point, the Suck, Frying Pan, the Narrows, and Tumbling Shoals. A boatman's fear of these shoals can best be told in the words of a man who led a party of settlers down the Tennessee River.

It was during the Revolutionary War. Shortly after the British had captured Savannah, Donelson's boat *Adventure* led a flotilla of flatboats and dugout canoes down the river from the fort at Kingsport,

Tennessee. After reaching the shoals, Donelson wrote in his diary:

Sunday, March 12, 1780: Set out, and after a few hour's sailing we heard the crowing of cocks, and soon came within view of the town. Here, the Indians fired on us again. About ten o'clock, we came in sight of the Muscle Shoals. — When we approached them, they had a dreadful appearance to those who had never seen them before. The water being high made a terrible roaring, which could be heard at some distance among the driftwood heaped frightfully upon the points of the islands, the current running in every possible direction. Here we did not know how soon we should all be dashed to pieces, and all our troubles ended at once. Our boats frequently dragged on the bottom, and they warped as much as in a rough sea. — I know not the length of this wonderful shoal. It had been represented to me to be twenty-five or thirty miles. If so, we must have descended very rapidly, as indeed we did, for we passed it in about three hours.

The settlers drifted down the Tennessee River into the Ohio. Then they headed for the Cumberland, going up that river to found a settlement. In this party was a little girl who grew up to become the wife of Andrew Jackson. Her name was Rachel Donelson.

People like those in the Donelson party made a new and different life for themselves in their frontier homes. When they crossed the Appalachians, they put a mountain barrier between themselves and their past. Old ties were broken and they turned their faces toward the West. English, Scotch, Irish, German, Swiss, French, Swedish, and other Europeans lived as neighbors and friends. Their children and their grandchildren intermarried. They did not think of their neighbors as English or Germans but as Americans.

On the frontier, no one was rich and no one was poor. When a newcomer arrived, families in the neighborhood gathered to help him build his house. The men cut down trees, sawed logs, and erected the cabin, while the women roasted pork, beef, and venison in a barbecue pit. When the roof was on, the floor was laid with hewn logs, and the cabin was ready for the housewarming. This meant a party. A fiddler seated himself in a corner and the workers danced 'til sun up. Families rode horses and mules for thirty miles and more to take part in this lograising. Helping each other was fun for all. No one was ever too busy to aid in the harvest, to take care of the sick, or to attend a funeral. Here a neighbor was a "friend in need."

Frontier life was family life. Mother, father, and children went together to sermons, to picnics, to cornhuskings, to lograisings, and to funerals. It took large families to succeed in a wilderness where many hands were needed for many kinds of work. Mixed nationalities worked together, worshipped together, and played together. They built their own homes, raised their own food, and made their own clothes. They had little money and little need for money. They were independent, resourceful, and free. Every little town had its political club where the citizens of the surrounding country gathered to talk over new laws, to select candidates for office, and to squelch any attempt to rob them of personal liberty.

In August of 1786 a major in the United States Army stopped overnight in Danville, Kentucky, on his way to the falls of the Ohio to pay some western troops guarding the frontier. In his diary, he wrote:

Very much disturbed by a Political Club which met in the next house where we slept and kept us awake till 12 or 1 o'clock. — It is composed of members of the most respectable people in and near Danville, who meet every Saturday night to discuss politics. Some pretty good speeches and some tolerable good arguments were made use of last night. — A very long debate took place.

(From Filson Club Publications.)

On the frontier, a man was judged for what he was himself, and not for what his family had been before him. Where life was so real, people lived in the present, and looked forward to the future with hope, trust, and confidence. Again, "something new" was growing up in the New World.

A PRESIDENT MOVES INTO THE WHITE HOUSE

WHAT MAKES A self-made man? The story of Andrew Jackson is one answer. Andrew Jackson was the son of Irish emigrants from the north of Ireland. His parents landed at Charleston, South Carolina, ten years before the Battle of Lexington. They settled on a claim in the uplands of South Carolina, along the Catawba River near the border of North Carolina. (Since the line between North and South Carolina was uncertain at the time, both states claim Andrew Jackson). After cutting down trees and clearing about six acres of land, they built a cabin and planted corn. In 1767, after two short years in the new cabin home, the father died suddenly. About two weeks later his third son was born and was named Andrew Jackson for him.

During his childhood the fatherless lad lived with an uncle in a nearby settlement where children had the advantage of a one-room school. At the age of nine, young Andrew was invited to read aloud a copy of the Declaration of Independence printed in the first Philadelphia paper that reached the frontier settlement after July 4, 1776. Standing on the porch of his uncle's store, he pronounced every word of the document for the forty pioneers who had gathered at the village center to hear the latest news. (Many frontiersmen were unable to read.)

Following the death of his oldest brother in the Revolutionary War, Jackson, then thirteen years old, took part in a few skirmishes in the South. He and another brother were captured by the British and thrown into prison. Their mother won their release because they were so young and both were ill with smallpox. Only Andrew survived the terrible disease. Shortly after the surrender at Yorktown, his mother volunteered to nurse the ailing American soldiers released from British prison ships where they had suffered from starvation and neglect. She contracted yellow fever and died.

At fourteen, Andrew Jackson had lost his father, his mother, and his two brothers. He had to depend upon himself to make his way in the world. He learned to make saddles and to mend harnesses. While teaching school he managed to study enough law to pass the bar examination in North Carolina when he was twenty years old. The following year he joined an emigrant train of about sixty families headed west to the frontier settlements on the Tennessee River. Jackson rode horseback with two pistols in his saddle holsters, another in his belt, and a brand new rifle by his side. A pack mare trailed behind, carrying his clothes, blankets, law books, ammunition, tea, salt, and other personal belongings.

The young lawyer settled in Nashville where he and his partner began to practice law in a two-room log cabin with their office in the front room and their bedroom in the rear. In this frontier town Jackson began to fight the Indians. Tennessee had long been the hunting grounds of the southern tribes who resented its occupation and raided the settlements. When Indians attacked, Jackson closed his law office and led a band of frontiersmen against them. He soon held an officer's rank in the militia.

There was little money in the new settlements. Lawyer's fees were paid in land and livestock, as a rule. Jackson once said that he had been paid enough land in fees to make a county if he had it all in one place, and enough cattle and horses to stock the farms of a county. In this way, Jackson had his start as a plantation owner and a stock breeder.

At heart he was a farmer. He liked to see crops growing and he took great pride in his fine cattle and horses. But his countrymen did not let him spend much time at home on his large plantation.

Jackson helped to write the state constitution when Tennessee was admitted to the Union. Afterwards he was elected as the state's first Representative in Congress. Later he was appointed judge of the supreme court in Tennessee. Then came the War of 1812 and the officer of Tennessee's militia was appointed a general in the regular Army of the United States. The Battle of New Orleans, in which his straight-shooting backwoodsmen defeated a crack British army, made him a national hero. He invaded Florida without the permission of Congress to pacify that territory. Then it was ceded to the United States by a treaty with Spain in 1819.

Every year, all over the country, his admirers celebrated the anniversary of the Battle of New Orleans with Jackson Day dinners. The general was as popular in New Hampshire as he was in Tennessee. In 1828 Andrew Jackson was elected President of the United States. The westerners rejoiced. He was their man, one of them. (Six American Presidents had come from old states on the Atlantic seaboard where the first British settlements had been made — Virginia and Massachusetts. The seventh President came from the new state of Tennessee, out West, beyond the mountains.) The election was well received in Spanish America. Mexico City was illuminated and celebrations took place all over that republic. The westerners had supported independence for the colonies of Spain because they wanted to trade with these countries.

THE "JACKSONIAN ERA"

ANDREW JACKSON, a new kind of President, was swept into office on a wave of new ideas, new improvements, and new visions. However, the "Jacksonian Era" had been developing way for a quarter of a century and Jackson was only a part of it.

The prosperity of the westerners depended upon transportation to carry their produce to the markets in New Orleans. In August of 1807, after his first successful trip from New York to Albany on the steamboat, *Clermont,* Robert Fulton wrote to a friend:

Steam will give a quick and cheap conveyance to merchandise on the Mississippi, Missouri, and other great rivers which are now laying open their treasures to the enterprise of our countrymen.

The first frontier President of the United States was a passenger on a steamboat leaving Nashville, Tennessee, on the

ANDREW JACKSON
President of the United States 1828-1836

seventeenth of January in 1829. Jackson traveled by boat down the Cumberland River to the Ohio, up that stream to Pittsburgh, and overland by coach on the National Road to Washington. The journey took twenty-eight days. He traveled alone without a "First Lady" for the White House. A few weeks earlier, three days before Christmas, Mrs. Jackson had died at The Hermitage, their home in Nashville.

Since water transportation was the cheapest, the westerners wanted canals connecting rivers and lakes where natural waterways did not exist. Of these the best-known was the Erie Canal connecting the Great Lakes and the Atlantic Ocean by way of the Hudson River. Great crowds gathered to see the first canal fleet from Buffalo on its way down the Hudson to the port of New York. As part of the celebration the governor of New York State emptied kegs of water from Lake Erie into the Atlantic Ocean. It took eight years to dig the "big ditch," forty feet wide and four feet deep, for 363 miles across the state of New York from Buffalo on Lake Erie to Albany on the Hudson River. Although horses walking a path along the bank pulled the barges only four miles per hour, this canal became a highway of commerce from east to west. Another canal linking Lake Champlain with the Hudson River increased the boats on that northern body of water from twenty to two hundred. This was the canal era.

The demand grew in the West for good wagon roads where canals, lakes, and rivers could not provide transportation to markets. The Cumberland Pike began in Maryland and ended at Wheeling on the Ohio River. Later it was extended across Ohio, Indiana, and Illinois to St. Louis. The cost averaged about $13,000 per mile and tolls were charged to pay for it. In Pennsylvania a man on horseback paid four cents a mile at a tollgate and the driver of a "coach-and-four" paid eighteen cents. Many famous men traveled over this scenic road, including Lafayette, who visited the "Hero of New Orleans" in Tennessee on a tour of the United States in 1825. However, it was the wagon freighter, hauling manufactured goods to the West and farm products to the East, that paid for the Cumberland Road. These were the tavern days when hotelkeepers along the highways boasted of their lodgings, their meals, and their famous guests.

In the year of Jackson's election Baltimore celebrated the opening of the railroad age and tried to outdo Philadelphia with a big parade. Cloth woven on a float in the procession was presented to Charles Carroll, the last living signer of the Declaration of Independence. He was given the honor of breaking the ground for the building of a railroad line from Baltimore to the Ohio River. In winter the railroads could haul passengers and freight when the canals were frozen and closed to traffic.

The promise of more transportation to haul produce to market led to wild speculation in western lands. Men with money bought large tracts from the Government at $1.25 per acre, expecting to sell at huge profits when a wagon road or a railroad line went through their territory.

This period of rapid change was the setting for a President who toppled so many traditions that his term of office came to be known as the "Jacksonian Era." Traditions were broken on inauguration day. Andrew Jackson did not call on the outgoing President and John Quincy Adams did not attend his successor's inauguration. The plain people, who had elected Jackson, crowded into Washington by the thousands for his inauguration. Some wore homespun clothes and looked as if they had walked all the way from Tennessee. At the reception so many crowded into the White House to shake the hand of the new President, that Jackson was forced to escape through a window. The mob, in the excitement of congratulating "Old Hickory," as Jackson was called, broke dishes and glassware, and damaged fine furniture. The day was mild and in order to get the crowd out of the White House, servants carried tubs of punch onto the lawn and passed it around freely. Many inside were unable to get out when they tried to leave.

In his inaugural address, Jackson said:

The recent demonstration of public sentiment inscribes, on the list of executive duties, in characters too legible to be overlooked, the task of reform.

What did Jackson mean by reform?

JACKSON INTERPRETS THE WILL OF THE PEOPLE

THE FARMERS of the West and the planters of the South voted for Jackson, and he intended to give them what they wanted. The manufacturers of New England voted for John Quincy Adams and Jackson remembered that fact. For the first time, New England was not represented in the President's Cabinet. John C. Calhoun, the elected Vice President, hailed from South Carolina. The northern leader of the newly formed Democratic Party, Martin

CONESTOGA WAGON

In 1830, John Studebaker built this Conestoga wagon entirely by hand in his blacksmith's shop near Gettysburg, Pennsylvania. In this wagon, he moved his family to Ashland, Ohio in 1835, and to South Bend, Indiana in 1851.

This type of covered wagon with a deep, roomy bed was the rolling house on wheels for both passengers and freight going west.

Studebaker Corporation

Van Buren of New York, became the new Secretary of State.

To Jackson, a man of strong feelings, those who voted for him were his friends and those who voted against him were his enemies. Being intensely loyal, he wanted his friends to share in his success. "To the victor belong the spoils." Jackson discharged hundreds of government employees appointed by former Presidents, and gave their jobs to friends who had voted for him. Such wholesale "firing" had not been done by any President before him. Later, to check the abuses of this "spoils system," the Civil Service Act was passed in 1883. Under this law men and women take examinations for government positions. They cannot be removed as long as their work is satisfactory.

The northern manufacturers wanted a high tariff to make foreign goods cost as much or more than the articles they produced in their mills. The southerners, who did little manufacturing, wanted the tariff lowered to make the foreign goods they bought cost them less money. At first the southerners, too, had favored a protective tariff. Slave labor, successful in the field, proved to be unprofitable in the factory. Therefore, the high tariff protected the northern manufacturers and forced the southern planters to pay higher prices.

Out of this argument over tariff, there arose again the dangerous doctrine of nullification — the doctrine that a state had the right to nullify a law passed by Congress if a majority of its citizens agreed it was unfair and harmful to their interests. This doctrine (which threatened the Union) was the subject of the celebrated debate between Robert Hayne of South Carolina and Daniel Webster of Massachusetts in the Senate of the United States. Webster's answer to Hayne, delivered in the Senate on January 26, 1830, is considered to be a great oration.

A large forehead, heavy eyebrows, and deep-set eyes gave Webster a commanding appearance. When he stood and faced the Senate chamber, packed to the doors, a sudden silence fell upon the audience, like the hush before a storm. The Union itself was at stake. Webster was a master of reasoning. Slowly, he developed his subject, speaking in a deep, musical voice that wooed his listeners to agree with him. No state had the right to disobey a law passed by Congress. Nullification was unconstitutional. The oration finally ended with a masterful plea for the preservation of the Union and won for Webster the title, "Defender of the Constitution." Webster's final words became a slogan: "Liberty and Union, now and forever, one and inseparable!"

Although both the President and Vice President were staunch defenders of states' rights, they did not agree on nullification. Shortly after the reply of Webster to Hayne, both Jackson and Calhoun attended a dinner celebrating the birthday of Thomas Jefferson. Jackson sat, fuming with anger, while after-dinner speakers linked the doctrine of nullification with the Democratic Party. When invited to make his toast, his tall thin figure unrolled to its full height, tense and erect. The President was in a fighting mood. Looking Calhoun straight in the eye, Jackson spoke defiantly:

"Our FEDERAL Union. It MUST BE PRESERVED."

This was not the toast printed in the program, but words Jackson had scribbled in pencil on the back page of it. Calhoun felt obliged to reply. He lifted his glass and flung back this challenge:

"The Union — next to our liberty the most dear! May we all remember that it can only be preserved by respecting the rights of the States and distributing equally the benefits and burdens of the Union."

Calhoun resigned as Vice President and was elected to the Senate from South Carolina where he became the great champion of states' rights. When a state convention in South Carolina declared that the Tariff Act was "null, void, and no law, nor binding upon this state," Jackson dispatched a fleet to Charleston harbor and prepared to enforce the laws of the Union. The threat of secession was averted when Congress voted to lower the tariff to please the southerners.

Henry Clay helped to make this compromise but he made a political error when he forced the issue to recharter the Bank of the United States. The constitutionality of the bank had been questioned more or less ever since it had been established during Washington's Administration. In 1818, the legislature of Maryland passed a law to tax all banks, including the Bank of the United States. When the case was appealed to the Supreme Court, Chief Justice John Marshall ruled that Congress had the power to charter the Bank with branches in any state, and that these branches could not be taxed by state law.

Although the bank had restored credit, stabilized currency, and aided prosperity, many people claimed it was dangerous to liberty for government funds to be placed in an institution owned by approximately 250,000 stockholders, one third of whom were foreigners. Jackson shared the opinion of westerners, who owned less than two percent of the stock, that the Bank of the United States amounted to a monopoly of the few who might use their power to influence government policy. Under Clay's guidance Congress passed a bill to recharter the bank before the old charter expired. This made the bank a campaign issue in 1832. Jackson promptly refused to sign the bill and it was not passed over his veto. Henry Clay ran against Jackson as the champion of the bank and was defeated.

Jackson interpreted his reelection as a mandate from the people to destroy the bank. He began to withdraw deposits to pay the national debt but the bank was able to pay out this money. Then he adopted the policy of depositing government money in state banks which his enemies nicknamed "pet" banks. Without deposits the Bank of the United States suffered big losses, and caused many failures in business. Since the small banks that received the government deposits were not accustomed to handling such large sums of money, some loaned it unwisely for get-rich-quick schemes that failed. The United States Treasury did not suffer immediately from this speculation because such large sums were pouring in from the sale of public lands. The speculation in land created problems for Jackson.

THE TRAIL OF TEARS

WHEN DE SOTO marched into the mountain homeland of the Cherokees in search of gold in 1540, the long struggle began between the red man and the white man. Each wanted possession of the country east of the Mississippi River and south of the Ohio. As the land along the Atlantic coast was being occupied, settlers started across the mountains to stake their farms in the area which had long been the

**A SEMINOLE INDIAN AND HIS WIFE
MOVING TO A NEW CAMP**

The Seminoles living in the Florida Everglades are the descendants of tribesmen who fled into this swampy land to escape General Jackson's campaign against the southern Indians, and the forced migration to lands west of the Mississippi River.

home of Cherokees and Chickasaws. They went farther south and west to the lands of Choctaws, Creeks, and Seminoles. These tribes adapted themselves to the white man's way of life. They planted the same crops, reared the same breeds of cattle, and built the same kind of houses. The Indian women carded, spun, and wove into cloth wool clipped from their sheep and cotton grown in their fields. Many sent their children to the schools and churches of Christian missionaries. Thus they came to be called the Five Civilized Tribes.

Long before Jackson was elected, the yearly crops of cotton and tobacco had sapped the strength of the soil in the coastal region of Georgia and the Carolinas. The planters from the coast lands cast longing glances at the fertile fields of the

Creeks in Alabama and of the Choctaws in the rich bottom lands along the Mississippi River. This was cotton country. The tribes appealed to the "great white father" for protection when bands of armed men stole their horses and cattle and drove them from their farms. Many Indian families, of their own free will, moved to the prairie lands west of the Mississippi to get beyond the grasping reach of the white settlers. Most of the tribesmen clung to their ancestral homes, hoping to gain the right to stay through treaties with the government. Both Henry Clay and Daniel Webster spoke in Congress in defense of the right of the southern Indians to remain on their lands.

When Jackson the Indian fighter was elected, the southerners and westerners renewed their efforts to gain the lands of the Five Civilized Tribes. A bill was proposed to move the Indians from their ancestral holdings east of the Mississippi to new country on the western prairie. The eloquent plea of Clay and Webster failed to prevent the passage of the Indian Removal Bill by Congress. Jackson signed it. Four years later in 1834 Congress created the Indian Territory, lands beyond the Mississippi, for Indians ONLY. The forced removal was under way. The actual removal was carried out by the United States Army. Soldiers surrounded the Indian homes and ordered the families out. Cattle and horses were left grazing in the pastures, and meals left uneaten on the tables. The soldiers who herded the families into stockades to await the long trek west considered their military duty painful and sympathized with the Indians.

The government promised to provide food, shelter, and transportation for the entire journey with funds realized from the sale of tribal lands. The removal of 60,000

THE

FIRST

INTER-TRIBAL COUNCIL

OF THE

FIVE CIVILIZED TRIBES

1950

The five Civilized Tribes are Cherokee, Chickasaw, Choctaw, Creek, and Seminole.

persons was a large undertaking, however. The government was sometimes unable to keep its word, because men who had been engaged to have supplies waiting at stations along the line of march failed to arrive on time. It was a case of good intentions and bad management. In bitter winter weather a group of Indians had only one blanket for each family. Army officers had to halt the march six and seven times a day to build fires to warm the crying children. A kind-hearted farmer invited a party of hungry Indians into his turnip field and they ate the entire crop, raw, in one meal. Nearly two hundred and fifty Creeks drowned when a chartered steamboat

United States Department
of Interior National Park Service

THE GREAT SMOKY MOUNTAINS IN
NORTH CAROLINA AND TENNESSEE

This beautiful mountain country with streams and waterfalls, flowers and forests, is commonly called, "Land of the Sky." The Indian name for this region of misty mountains and heavy rainfall was "Unega" (White Land). Part of this area is now a national park. Adjoining is the Cherokee Indian Reservation where 3000 tribesmen live today, descendants of those who escaped the forced migration to the Indian Territory.

collided with another vessel at night on the Mississippi River. About six hundred Chickasaws died of smallpox, contracted when crossing Arkansas. Thousands died in this forced migration from exposure, accident, and disease. The Indians named this painful journey "The Trail of Tears."

Those who survived the hardships of this western trek settled down to making a living in their new lands on the prairie. The government furnished farm tools and seed for their first crops and food for their families while they awaited the harvest. Friends and relatives, who had gone West before the forced removal, greeted the newcomers kindly, and life was not unbearable. They were soon joined by other tribes who were forced to leave the country north of the Ohio River and to migrate to the Indian Territory.

Of all the tribes none fought removal more than the Cherokees, the mountain people of the South. On the way to the stockades and along the march some escaped and returned to their native hills. The fugitives lived in secret caves and ate wild roots. One group in North Carolina finally gained permission to stay because they had bought their farms from white settlers. This was the same land that had belonged to their forefathers before white men heard of the New World. Their descendants, and those of the runaways, are living today in their old home country, where a blue haze like ghostly smoke from ancient Indian fires still lingers in the valleys. In winter the frosty air still wraps the mountain peaks in fluffy cloaks of fog. This is "Unega" — white land — ancestral home of the Cherokees.

FUR TRADERS LEAD
THE WESTWARD MARCH

THE TREK of the Five Civilized Tribes to lands beyond the Mississippi was only a part of the westward march started years before by colonial explorers, hunters, and trappers. At the close of the French and Indian War, a royal charter from the King of England had given the Hudson's Bay Company the sole right to the fur trade in the territory acquired from France. Thus, English buyers found their way to trading posts scattered along the western rivers. French and half-breed trappers living in the territory brought their furs to the new buyers from the English firm.

When Lewis and Clark were exploring

the Louisiana Purchase for President Jefferson, they spent a winter at one of these fur posts. The post was located among the Mandan Indians on the upper Missouri, near the present town of Bismarck, North Dakota. It was here that Sacajawea joined the expedition, leading the explorers across the mountains to the Columbia River. American trappers and buyers followed close at the heels of this exploring party. They wanted to get some of the business from the Hudson's Bay Company. In less than ten years after the purchase of Louisiana, a number of these small companies were merged into one, the Pacific Fur Company. The president of the American company was a German immigrant in New York City. He was John Jacob Astor, destined to be one of the nation's first millionaires.

Following the plan of the rival British firm, Astor hired experienced French Canadian "voyageurs," some of the most daring and skillful canoe men in the world. A party of these woodsmen came down the Hudson River in bark canoes, attracting much attention all the way. The rollicking songs of these voyageurs brought crowds to line the river as the Canadians, with feathers in their caps, paddled their craft into New York.

The crowds at the dock gasped in

CANADIAN VOYAGEURS

When hunters and traders came to rapids in a stream, they unloaded their bundles of furs and carried them on their backs to a spot above the swift currents in the river. Then, the hardy woodsmen lifted their canoes to their shoulders and carried them over the same portage to the same place, where they reloaded their bundles and continued the journey.

Currier and Ives

wonder when these brawny boatmen from the north lifted the heavy canoes to their shoulders and walked off with them. A mutual understanding exists between a voyageur and his craft. The canoe carries the man over the water and the man carries the canoe over the land. After loading the canoes on a vessel in the harbor, the trappers sailed out of the port of New York for the long voyage around Cape Horn and up the Pacific Coast. At the mouth of the Columbia River in 1811 the party built a trading post and named it Astoria, after the founder of the company.

In a short time American vessels, loaded with pelts, were sailing for the Orient. In China the furs were traded for teas, silks, beads, cotton cloth, embroideries, art objects, and luxuries of an old and cultured civilization. These return cargoes were brought around Cape Horn to the Atlantic seaboard. They sometimes netted a profit of a thousand percent. In this way the fur business of the Northwest opened up new trade lanes across the Pacific. When the first American trappers landed at the mouth of the Columbia River, a new republic of the West faced an old empire of the East. Their interests became entwined through mutual profits in trade.

Great Britain and the United States were not the only nations competing for the rich fur business of the Northwest. Russia had trading posts extending south from Alaska to Fort Ross, near San Francisco.

Russia's claim to this territory was based

MINK TRAPPING

Trappers trailed the streams through forests, searching for the valuable pelts of mink and beaver. These furs brought the highest prices in St. Louis, the leading fur market in the United States.

Currier and Ives

upon her fur hunting expeditions into Alaska, whose boundaries had not been set. Russian trading posts, creeping down the Pacific coast, helped to invoke the Monroe Doctrine. In 1824 Russia agreed to give up all claim to territory south of 54 degrees, 40 minutes north latitude, leaving the United States and Great Britain as rivals for the possession of Oregon. A British naval officer, George Vancouver, sailed up the Columbia River soon after it had been discovered by an American, Captain Gray, and named by him. Lewis and Clark had followed the stream from the mountains to the sea. British fur traders were established in Oregon before Astor started his post at the mouth of the Columbia River. Astoria was captured by the British in 1812 and was not returned until after peace had been signed. About a hundred miles up the Columbia, the Hudson's Bay Company built Fort Vancouver, which became an English settlement with a trading post, farms, and sawmills. Who would win Oregon? Believing that those who lived on the land would gain the country, the American government encouraged emigration to Oregon. Meanwhile Great Britain and the United States agreed to let their citizens share the disputed territory until some permanent settlement was made.

MISSIONARIES
FOLLOW THE TRAPPERS

THE FUR TRADERS blazed the trail for missionaries who followed in their footsteps. With the French Canadian and half-breed trappers of the Hudson's Bay Company were members of the Iroquois and other eastern tribes. These Indians had become Christians. From them tribes of the Northwest learned something of the Christian religion. In 1831 four Indians from the Salmon River Valley of Idaho paddled their canoes almost 3000 miles down the Missouri River to St. Louis to ask that Christian teachers be sent to their tribes. Upon arrival the Indian leaders called upon General Clark of the Lewis and Clark Expedition, who made their request known. The story of these four brave men who endured the hardships of such a long journey to seek Christianity fired the missionary zeal of churches throughout the nation.

Fur traders leaving the Missouri frontier soon boasted of a minister or two in their parties. Among the first to answer the call was Dr. Marcus Whitman.

In March, 1836 Dr. Whitman and his bride left Steuben County, New York, to establish a mission in Oregon. At Pittsburgh they met another young minister and his bride on their way to start a mission among the Osages on the plains. They persuaded the couple to join them in the trek to Oregon. At Liberty on the Missouri frontier the two couples joined a hunting party of Astor's American Fur Company. It was not safe for small parties to travel alone. The wives of the two ministers were the first white women to cross the plains and the first the Indians had seen. Mrs. Whitman rode sidesaddle, which was strange to Indian women who rode astride. In her diary Mrs. Whitman wrote:

We ladies are such a curiosity to the Indians. They come and stand around our tent, peep in, and grin to see such looking objects.

At the trappers' rendezvous in the Green River Valley of Wyoming, the Whitmans met Indians from the tribes they hoped to Christianize. The rendezvous was the big

FORT VANCOUVER OF HUDSON'S BAY COMPANY

The Hudson's Bay Company was granted a charter by Charles II, King of England, on May 2, 1670 "for the finding some Trade for Furrs Mineralls and other considerable Commodityes" in the region of Hudson Bay. When the Northwest Fur Company joined the Hudson's Bay Company, western headquarters were established in 1824 with the building of Fort Vancouver on the Columbia River. John McLoughlin crossed the mountains to take charge of the new fur trading post where he came to be called a king of the Oregon country.

The fort stockade was 750 feet long and 600 feet wide. On a farm of 1500 acres around the post, grains, vegetables, and fruits were grown. Pastures were stocked with cattle, sheep, and horses. The McLoughlins entertained visitors like royalty in their frontier home.

event of the year, a gathering time for old friends. Around the evening fire they talked far into the night. They told of chasing bison, fighting grizzly bears, and swimming rivers. There were stories of quarrels with Indians over setting traps, of days of hunger without food of any sort, and of the many dangers and escapes in the daily life of a trapper. Yet, few of these hunters were willing to give up this free life in a wilderness. Indians came in large numbers to these meeting places and brought their families. While the men bartered their pelts of beaver, marten,

otter, fox, and mountain goat to the fur buyers, the women and children danced, visited, and feasted at the trappers' party. Mrs. Whitman wrote of her meeting with Indian women at this rendezvous:

As I alighted from my horse, I was met by a company of native women, one after another shaking my hands and saluting me with a most hearty kiss. This was unexpected and affected me very much. After we had been seated awhile in the midst of the gazing throng, one of the chiefs whom we had seen before, came with his wife and very politely introduced her to us. They say they all like us very much and are glad we have come to live with them.

At this trappers' rendezvous on the Green River, Dr. Whitman removed an arrowhead from the back of Jim Bridger, the noted scout for whom Fort Bridger was named. Indians from the Flathead and Nez Perces tribes in Oregon watched with awe. They were much impressed with Whitman's surgical skill and invited the doctor to live among them. He accepted the invitation.

Near the middle of September the missionaries arrived at Fort Vancouver, the Hudson's Bay settlement on the Columbia River, where they were hospitably received by Dr. McLoughlin, manager of the British post and actual governor of the Oregon Territory. After living for weeks at a time on dried buffalo meat it was a treat to be served a real dinner. There was vegetable soup with rice, roast duck, boiled pork, fresh salmon, potatoes, bread and butter, and tea with milk and sugar. The dessert was a great surprise – APPLE PIE.

An English fur buyer started the apple industry in the Northwest. In 1824 before leaving for the United States, his friends invited him to a farewell party in London, at which apples were passed around to the guests. To get rid of the seeds the man dropped them into his vest pocket. After a long sea voyage around Cape Horn he arrived at Fort Vancouver, wearing the same vest with the apple seeds in the pocket. He planted the seeds in the garden of the trading post. Here grew the first apples in the Pacific Northwest.

The big fur companies cultivated farms to furnish wheat, vegetables, fruits, poultry, milk, cheese, pork, and all kinds of food for their trappers. On the fourth day after arrival at the mouth of the Columbia, the Astor party planted potatoes and garden seeds. Indians and halfbreeds did most of the farm work for a share of the produce they raised.

Four years later Father De Smet, a Jesuit from Belgium, answered the request of the Indians for Christian teaching. He traveled by steamboat from St. Louis to Westport, now Kansas City, where he joined a hunting party of the American Fur Company. The traders hunted and trapped as they worked their way to the yearly rendezvous in the Green River Valley, arriving in time with bundles of pelts, salted and dried. There, in the summer of 1840, Father De Smet held a religious service for Indians, French Canadians, half-breeds, European immigrants, and citizens of the United States. The cathedral was a mountain meadow with logs for an altar and the sky for a roof.

This missionary zeal for Oregon played an important part in our history, not because of the number of Indians who were converted to Christianity, but for quite another reason.

COVERED WAGONS CROSS THE PLAINS TO OREGON

THE TRADERS AND TRAPPERS spent years amid the scenic beauty of the Northwest, but they had little to say about it. They were occupied with the fur business. It was the missionaries who spread the news in letters to their relatives back home. The wagon trek to Oregon was promoted by what the ministers' wives wrote to sisters, aunts, and cousins living in little towns in New England and the country east of the Mississippi.

Every letter told of the beauty of the country – the evergreens in the dense forests, the white cone of Mt. Hood, and

A WAGON TRAIN CROSSING THE PLAINS

Oxen were used more than horses and mules by the early western emigrants, because these animals could endure more hunger and thirst, and were more patient in wading the rivers. The driver of oxen, called a bullwhacker, walks beside his teams and drives with a long whip.

the waters of the Columbia, "clear as crystal and smooth as glass."

The mountains were covered with timber and the rivers were stocked with fish. Cherries were found along the streams and berries grew wild in the woods. Roast duck was an everyday dish and salmon was common fare. Anything would grow in the rich soil of Oregon valleys, where land was plentiful and free. New England farmers struggling on worn-out land cast their eyes westward. To jobless workers in the factory towns, Oregon became the promised land when the Panic of 1837 threw them out of employment.

Andrew Jackson's popularity had helped elect his former Secretary of State, Martin Van Buren, to succeed him in the White House. In a phaeton, made of wood from the famous frigate *Constitution* and drawn by four gray horses, the two had ridden down Pennsylvania Avenue to the Capitol on the fourth of March in 1837. The tall, white-haired President, seventy years old, sat erect and smiled but he looked thin and tired. Beside him, a whole head lower, sat "Little Van," Jackson's choice to take his place. It had been a time of peace and prosperity when only a few had been aware that a financial storm was gathering on the horizon.

People did not agree on the causes of the Panic of 1837. The opposing party, the Whigs, blamed Jackson's Administration. They declared that government funds removed from the Bank of the United States and distributed among many state banks, unaccustomed to handling such large deposits, were loaned too freely for speculation. Men borrowed money when it was so plentiful for speculating in land. When they could not sell quickly at a profit, they could not pay back the money when it was due. Many of these small state banks issued paper money that they could not redeem with gold nor silver upon demand. To check this speculation in land, Jackson had instructed his Secretary of the Treasury to issue the specie circular, instructing banks to accept only gold and silver money in payment for public land. The payment of the national debt during Jackson's Administration had increased the credit of the United States and brought in a flood of foreign capital to invest in real estate, canal and railroad stocks. The reckless gambling had continued. In 1815 land in Buffalo, New York was traded for forty dollars worth of candles and sold in 1835 for two million dollars. In the same year a hundred and fifteen acres near Louisville, Kentucky sold for $275,000, although it was purchased for $675 in 1815. This reckless speculation was probably the underlying cause of the Panic of 1837, although many reasons were given from many sources.

During the depression money became scarce, prices soared, business firms failed, banks closed doors, and factories shut

BUNCH GRASS ON PLAINS OF CENTRAL OREGON NEAR MAUPIN

This native grass still grows on the unbroken plain about twenty miles from a branch of the old Oregon Trail leading through Barlow Pass. Growing in tufts, clumps like these were commonly called bunch grass. The stringy clusters with long roots were high in food value for the teams pulling the wagons, but riding was rough for the people in the wagons. One woman who crossed the plains in 1849 wrote in her diary:

In our train were four bachelors who had a wagon drawn by four oxen with two milk cows following behind. These men gave many a cup of milk to children in the train. The evening's milk was used for supper, but that milked in the morning was put into a high churn. And the constant jolting that it got all day formed delicious butter by night. We were all glad to swap some of our food for butter and buttermilk.

Alfred A. Monner

down. In the cities riots occurred among the unemployed who demanded food and fuel. In such a time of want, people turned to the land for a living. The great migration to Oregon followed the Panic of 1837.

After Father De Smet had spread the news of Oregon in Europe, where he solicited funds for his Indian missions, families came from Belgium, France, the Netherlands, Germany, and Switzerland around Cape Horn to settle in the Pacific Northwest. However, most of the migrants were Anglo American. These people went overland in covered wagons. Some of the immigrants came from New England where their forefathers had settled in colonial days. Many were restless pioneers whose fathers and grandfathers had gone "West" over the Wilderness Road into Kentucky and down the Ohio in flatboats to farm the land in the Northwest Territory. The sons and daughters of one frontier pushed west to become the pioneers on another frontier.

The way to Oregon was long and hard. The route, starting at Independence, Missouri, followed the trail of trappers along the Kansas, Little Blue, Platte, Sweetwater, Snake, and Umatilla rivers to the Columbia. The immigrant trains crossed the Continental Divide at the easiest point, South Pass, discovered by early fur traders. At the rate of ten to twenty miles a day the clumsy covered wagons jolted across the plains, climbed over the mountains, and forded streams that were sometimes flooded or filled with quicksand. On the prairie the wind blew hot and cold, with clouds of sand, driving rain, and pelting hail. Women wept when family heirlooms were dumped into the sandy bed of a river to lighten the load of teams grown weary from the long haul. Oxen puffed for breath as the white-topped caravans climbed the gradual ascent of South Pass in Wyoming.

Diaries show that some of the immigrants complained of the hardships in crossing the plains, while others reveled in them with the spirit of adventure. A minister wrote:

Sunday, May 13, 1838 — Hoped it would rain so we could rest on the Sabbath. Strong appearance of rain, but the order was to start. Left the west branch of the Blue and rose from the bottomland on the prairie. Took our course for the Platte. Most of the way was on a level plain, the distance 25 miles without sight of wood or water. Made the whole distance without any stop. Much fatigued with the journey. How different from the manner of spending the Sabbath at home in New England!

Applegate, leader of a caravan in 1843, describes a day's journey in the same valley:

It is four o'clock A.M. The sentinels on duty have discharged their rifles, the signal that the hours of sleep are over. Every wagon and tent is pouring forth its night tenants, and slow-kindling smokes begin to rise and float away in the morning air. Sixty men start from the corral, spreading through the vast herd of cattle and horses that make a semi-circle around the encampment. — By five o'clock, the herders begin to contract the great, moving circle, and the well-trained animals move slowly towards camp. In about an hour five thousand animals are close up to the encampment, and the teamsters are busy selecting their teams and driving them inside the corral to be yoked. The corral is a circle formed with wagons, the one in the rear being connected with the wagon in front by its tongue and ox chains.

From six to seven is a busy time. Breakfast is to be eaten, the tents struck, the wagons loaded and the teams yoked ready to be attached to their respective wagons. All know when, at seven o'clock, the signal to march sounds, that those not ready to take their places in the line of march must fall into the dusty rear for the day.

It is on the stroke of seven. The rush to and fro, the cracking of whips, the loud command to oxen, and the confusion of the last ten minutes has ceased. The clear notes of a trumpet sound in the front; the pilot and his guards mount their horses; the wagons move out of the encampment and take up the line of march.

While a party of young hunters scoured the plains for buffalo and other game to provide the evening meal, scouts rode ahead to find the next camping spot with water, fuel, and grass, if possible. In the late afternoon the lead-wagon turned to the right, the next one to the left, and the others alternating to the right and the left until the wagons formed a tight circle. Inside this corral the sleeping tents were pitched. Outside the circle the cooking fires were kindled. Applegate's diary continues:

It is not yet eight o'clock when the first watch is to be set. The evening meal is just over, and the corral now free from cattle and horses. Groups of children are scattered over it. — Before a tent near the river a violin makes lively music, and some youths and maidens have improvised a dance upon the green. It has been a prosperous day; more than twenty miles have been accomplished of the great journey.

Hope lured on both old and young — free men, in a free country, on the way to free land. To OREGON!

MAPS:

WA16r WA21r WA19r
Atlas of American History by Edgar B. Wesley

Chapter 14

New Lands and New Ideas

THE WESTWARD MIGRATION LEADS TO WAR WITH MEXICO

THE OREGON TRAIL passed through the northern tip of Mexican territory. The immigrants on this trail aroused no active hostility from that country because the land being trespassed was not settled. Migration to the southwest, to Texas in particular, however, was a different story. It increased the tension between Anglo Americans and Latin Americans that had been brewing since the two peoples first met on the borders of their territories. Immigrants to this area before 1821 faced the displeasure of Spanish officials of Mexico. In 1821 the Mexicans finally succeeded in gaining independence from Spain. The new Mexican officials resented the invasion of traders and settlers from the United States just as much as the Spanish had resented it when they had governed Mexico.

In 1797, the year that Washington had retired from the Presidency, Philip Nolan, a young Irish immigrant from the United States had gained permission from the Spanish governor of the northern province of Mexico to hunt wild horses on the plains of eastern Texas. He sold the captured mustangs for cavalry mounts to General Wilkinson of the United States Army, stationed in the territory of Mississippi.

Several years later Philip Nolan returned to Texas with a party of twenty frontiersmen on another mustang hunt. He built pens to hold the wild horses and then erected a blockhouse for protection. This bold venture annoyed the New Spanish governor of the province. He sent soldiers to drive out the party. The Irishman decided to fight and was killed by the first cannon shot that struck his blockhouse. After a battle of several hours the rest of the hunters surrendered on the promise that they would be free to return to the United States. Instead, they were marched to San Antonio, capital of the province, and then across the Rio Grande to pass weary years in wretched Mexican prisons.

One of these prisoners was an adventurous frontiersman named Ellis Bean. At the age of sixteen Bean left his farm home in Tennessee with a flatboat load of flour, tobacco, hams, and other items to sell in New Orleans. His boat capsized in the treacherous Muscle Shoals in the Tennessee River. Bean lost his produce, escaping with only the clothes on his back. On a neighbor's boat he continued the journey. At Natchez on the Mississippi, he met Philip Nolan recruiting a party to hunt wild horses in Texas. This smacked of adventure and appealed to the farm lad. Bean joined the hunters. In the blockhouse fight he was in command when the group was forced to surrender.

Like most farm boys on the frontier young Bean was a jack-of-all-trades. When he was moved from jail to jail, he managed to get liberty by practicing his trades. In one town he made shoes; in another, hats. While in jail at Acapulco, the Mexican port on the Pacific, Bean learned that the town officials were looking for a man to blast rocks for improvements planned in the harbor district. He sent word that blasting was his specialty, although he really knew little or nothing about it. He figured he could learn to do anything that would win his freedom. Being ingenious he succeeded in blasting the rocks. He also escaped from his guard during the confusion. He hid away in a barrel on a vessel in the harbor, but the Portuguese cook betrayed him and he was returned to jail.

When revolutions broke out in Mexico, a Spanish officer promised Bean his freedom if he would join the loyalist army. A man who could blast rocks into bits might prove useful in quelling the revolt against Spanish authority. Bean snatched this opportunity for freedom but soon deserted to join the revolutionary forces of Morelos. He made guns and ammunition for Morelos who promoted him to the rank of colonel. Bean commanded the rebel troops that captured the port of Acapulco where he had been so long in prison. He treated his captives so kindly that he made friends out of enemies.

The aid given by citizens of the United States to Mexicans fighting for independence created a bond of sympathy between the two peoples. This tie was weakened when enterprising Yankees began to appear almost everywhere in Mexican territory.

A party of trappers from the states found beaver plentiful along the Colorado River. Their load became so heavy that they buried hundreds of skins on a hillside above the stream, intending to return later with more. They would take the furs north to the summer rendezvous. The trappers chanced upon some Mexican soldiers who arrested them and took them in to San Diego for trial. After six months in jail the trappers were freed with a warning to leave Mexican territory. Returning to the cache of beaver pelts, the trappers found that while the stream looked the same as when they had last seen it, the precious furs were soaked and ruined under a coating of slimy mud. During their imprisonment, the Colorado River had flooded in the spring as it annually did.

A large percentage of these Yankee tradesmen headed for the city of Santa Fe, now the capital of New Mexico. At that time it was the seat of government and the trade center of this northern province of Mexico. Before United States traders were on the scene, Santa Fe received its merchandise from Chihuahua in Mexico. Merchants put their goods on the backs of mules and traveled 230 miles from Chihuahua to El Paso, where they crossed the Rio Grande, and 320 miles farther to the northern capital. This long hard route through desert country, where both man and beast suffered from hunger and thirst, made the goods expensive. Common brown muslin sold for $3 a yard. When Lewis and Clark were on their way into the Northwest, a French Creole packed the first goods from the states to Santa Fe. The traders from the states were eager to compete with their Mexican neighbors for the flourishing business in Santa Fe.

By 1822 caravans of pack mules were leaving the frontier post of Independence, Missouri. They traveled southwest along the Arkansas River and blazed the Santa Fe Trail.

By 1824 a company of traders used wagons for the first time on this trade route into Mexican territory. With the usual train of pack mules were twenty-five wagons and carts, hauling $30,000 worth of goods. The heavy wagons were drawn by eight mules each. The canvas tops were padded with blankets to protect the merchandise from the wind and rain. During the twenty years of this overland trade $3,000,000 worth of goods was transported across the plains and sold in Santa Fe and other Mexican towns as far south as Chihuahua. On the return trips the wagons were usually loaded with gold and silver bullion from Mexican mines. To prevent robbery, well-armed guards rode in front and behind the caravans. Every man slept with his gun at his side. Sometimes, a prairie fire licked the heels of a wagon train in a wild race to short-grass country where the flames would die out.

In spite of all the harships and dangers, the prairie traders liked the life. After retiring to his old home in the East, one man wrote:

I am ashamed to confess that scarcely a day passes without a pang of regret that I am not now roving at large upon those western plains. The wild, unsettled, and independent life of the prairie trader makes perfect freedom. He knows no laws, save those of his own. His own conscience is court and jury. He lives in no society which he must look up to and please. The exchange of this independence for a life in civilization, — commends itself to few who have known the freedom of the great western prairies.

The Yankees were shrewd traders and built a big business. In 1846, 375 wagons, 1700 mules, 2000 oxen, and 500 men were on the Santa Fe Trail. In the same year war began with Mexico. However, the actual fighting was not in conflict with the carefree traders who came, bought and sold, and went on their way. The trouble began between the Mexicans and the colonists from the United States who had moved into Mexican territory, plowed the land, built their homes, and STAYED.

THE NATION STRETCHES WEST AND SOUTH

THE FIRST COLONIZATION of Texas by United States citizens occurred under the leadership of a New England family by the name of Austin. Moses Austin, the father, owned the first factory in the United States for making shot and sheet lead. Learning of rich lead deposits in the West he took his family to Missouri shortly before 1800. After he made a fortune in his new lead mines, a bank failure in St. Louis almost bankrupted him. He then had the idea of starting all over again in Texas.

At this time Spain still governed Texas. Austin journeyed from Missouri to San Antonio, Texas, to petition the Spanish governor there for land upon which he could settle three hundred families. Since his request had to be referred to many Spanish authorities, Austin did not wait in San Antonio for an answer. He left, intending to return to the city at a later date. On the way back to Missouri he was robbed by his traveling companions and was then deserted. In spite of the hardships he managed to reach his daughter's home, but only to die shortly after his arrival.

His son, Stephen Austin, founded the settlement. It lay between the Brazos and the Colorado rivers. Meanwhile, Mexico had declared her independence from Spain and established a republic. Desiring to abide by the laws of the new republic, Stephen Austin rode horseback 1200 miles to the capital of Mexico, arriving near the end of April in 1822. He found the Mexicans fighting among themselves for control of the government. He had to wait one long year in Mexico City before a Congress was able to confirm his land grant and declare the Mexican colonial policy.

When Stephen Austin finally returned from his 2400-mile journey on horseback, he found his colonists scattered and discouraged. Fortunately, newcomers made the colony grow and prosper. In July, 1823 Mexican officials set the date for laying out the capital of Austin's settlement. They named it San Felipe de Austin, now plain Austin, and still the capital of Texas. The generous colonization laws of the Mexican Republic attracted thousands from the United States into Texas. Cheap land in Texas enticed westerners and southerners to sell out and move into Mexican territory.

According to one law, promoters, called "empresarios," were allowed 23,040 acres of land for every hundred families they brought into Texas, receiving their fee in land for themselves. However, no one, not even a Mexican citizen, was permitted to own more than eleven leagues, or about 50,000 acres. A family arriving alone, and not under an empresarios contract, could purchase 4428 acres of pasture land for $30; and 174 acres for cultivation for as little as $3.50 if the land could be irrigated.

Difficulties soon arose between the Anglo American settlers and their Mexican authorities. The settlers became impatient with Mexican ways of governing. They wanted to make their own laws. When the Mexicans were under Spanish rule, they had little or no opportunity to practice self-government. Now that they were an independent country, they found it hard to make laws and harder still to abide by them. When a party in power displeased enough of the people, that party would be overthrown. Consequently, they had frequent revolts.

This lack of a stable government irritated the Anglo Americans, who had inherited a tradition of self-government. During the hundred and fifty years as English colonists the Anglo Americans practically governed themselves. The settlers in Texas felt they would be better off if their governing body was like that of the United States.

The Texans, unwilling to wait while the Mexicans learned, proceeded to make their own laws and govern themselves. Texas was cotton country. The settlers who came from the southern states brought along their slaves. This meant that they were defying the government because Mexico had abolished slavery. This disobedience to law annoyed the Mexican authorities. They felt they must discipline this unruly colony of at least 20,000 inhabitants. In 1836 a new Mexican constitution deprived the colony of any self-government and forbade further immigration from the United States. The Texans refused to accept the decrees. They adopted the slogan "Texas and Liberty!" They raised armies to defend their settlements. Posters appeared in Cincinnati, Louisville, and other western towns, promising large grants of land, free, to settlers in Texas. One line may have discouraged some. It read:

Come with a good rifle, and come soon.

THE ALAMO IN SAN ANTONIO, TEXAS

The city of San Antonio acquired its name from the mission, San Antonio de Valero, founded nearby in 1691 to bring Christianity to the Indians. After moving twice to seek a better location, the Spanish missionaries built a larger San Antonio de Valero on land now in the center of the city.

When the missions in Texas ceased operations in 1794, the mission was used for barracks by Spanish soldiers from Alamo de Parras in Mexico. The name was shortened to Alamo.

After winning independence from Spain, Mexico claimed all of Texas. Meanwhile, some people from the United States had moved into Texas. When Santa Anna, leader of Mexico, marched his army north in 1836, he found the Alamo guarded by a small army of newcomers, including David Crockett, James Bowie, and Colonel William Travis. After a siege of thirteen days, all the defenders had died in the Alamo, but the delay gave General Sam Houston time to gather an army at San Jacinto to defeat Santa Anna. Texans cherish the Alamo as a shrine of liberty.

San Antonio Chamber of Commerce

When Santa Anna, the new President of Mexico, marched soldiers into Texas, a short but bloody war began. In all, it is claimed, 188 Texans fought and died in the Alamo, the old fort in San Antonio. Forty-six days later Santa Anna was defeated at the Battle of San Jacinto, near the eastern border, by a little army of Texans under General Sam Houston of Tennessee. Texas became a republic with a constitution permitting slavery. Sam Houston, a former governor of Tennessee, was elected the first president of the "lone star" republic. This happened in 1836 during the last year of Jackson's Administration and the year that the Whitmans crossed the plains to Oregon.

Since most of the Texans had come from the United States, they wanted to reacquire their American citizenship. They asked the United States Government to annex Texas as a state. The United States Congress then had to decide whether or not to admit Texas to the Union. Many people in the country wanted to live in the West as citizens of the United States. Some of these people were southern planters who had worn out their land by planting the same crops year after year. Others were merchants and farmers made bankrupt by the Panic of 1837. They wanted to make a fresh start in the West. These groups rallied behind the Democratic Party, which openly advocated annexation of Texas in the Presidential election of 1844.

The people opposing the annexation felt that this move would involve their country in a war with Mexico. Many of them did not want to see Texas as a part of the United States because it would mean that slavery would spread. These groups voted for Clay, the Whig party leader, because he did not include annexation in his campaign promises.

Barker Texas History Library

GENERAL SAM HOUSTON,
First President of Texas,
The "Lone Star" Republic

James K. Polk, the Democratic candidate for the Presidency, won the election. A few weeks before he took the oath of office, Congress voted to admit Texas. President Tyler, on the last day of his term, sent a message to the Texans, inviting their "lone star" republic to become the twenty-eighth state of the Union. The war with Mexico came in the spring of 1846. President Polk sent United States troops to the Rio Grande to protect the United States claim that Texas extended to that river. The Mexicans insisted that the Nueces River, farther north, was the boundary line. The fighting began when a Mexican force crossed the Rio Grande. As soon as Congress received news of the skirmish, a formal declaration of war was voted. With war imminent, John C. Fremont's Third Expedition to explore and survey Mexican

territory, took on a military mission. He crossed the Sierras to Sutter's Fort, and in January of 1846, visited officials at Monterey. When asked to leave, Fremont refused, and made camp for his men armed with "guns, rifles, and pistols." Americans living north of San Francisco captured the town of Sonoma on June 14, 1846. They organized the "Republic" of California with a "Bear Flag." On July 7, 1846, after receiving news that war had been declared on Mexico, Commodore Sloat raised the flag of the United States at Monterey, and issued a proclamation declaring California annexed to the United States. Fremont arrived with his forces on July 19, and started south to join Kearny on his way from Ft. Leavenworth. Commodore Stockton appointed Fremont Governor of California, but his term lasted only about fifty days.

President Polk was anxious to send United States troops into California before winter set in and closed the trails through the mountains. Colonel Stephen W. Kearny, stationed at Fort Leavenworth, was made Commander of the West. Needing recruits quickly, Kearny dispatched Captain Allen to Iowa where bands of religious refugees were camped all the way across the state from Council Bluffs to the Missouri River.

Soon after the Mormon Church was organized by Joseph Smith in 1830, missionaries left the founder's home in Waterloo, New York to win converts on the frontier, preaching as they went. In a short time Joseph Smith and his followers were also on the way west to escape the opposition that developed against them in New York. The Mormons wandered to Kirtland, Ohio, to Jackson County, Missouri, and to Nauvoo, Illinois without

265

finding a congenial home among people friendly to Mormonism. When Joseph Smith was killed by an angry mob in Carthage, Illinois, Brigham Young succeeded him as president of the Mormon Church. The new leader held a council of his followers in Nauvoo. The Mormons decided to settle in the Far West beyond the Rocky Mountains where they could be alone and live in peace.

Their first wagon train crossed the Mississippi River early in February in 1846. Others followed day after day as families were ready to join the migration. It was a large undertaking to move between twelve and fifteen thousand people and about 30,000 head of live-stock. The refugees traveled in small companies and were scattered across Iowa. However, with snow, wind, and cold they did not leave that state until the following year.

On June 26, 1846 at Mount Pisgah near the Missouri River, Captain Allen read a circular explaining why Colonel Kearny was asking Mormons to enlist in the Army of the West to march into Mexican territory. Recruiting was encouraged by offering help in the westward migration. Allen stated:

This gives an opportunity of sending a portion of their young and intelligent men to the ultimate destination of their whole people, and entirely at the expense of the United States, and this advanced party can thus pave the way and look out the land for their brethren to come after them. Those of the Mormons who are desirous of serving their country, on the conditions here enumerated, are requested to meet me without delay at their principal camp at Council Bluffs, whither I am now going to consult with their principal men and to receive and organize the force contemplated to be raised.

I will receive all healthy, able-bodied men from 18 to 45 years of age.

Colonel Kearny asked for an enlistment of twelve months. He assured the Mormon recruits that they would be permitted to keep their guns and all other army equipment when their year of service was ended. At Council Bluffs Brigham Young advised young men to join the United States Army as their patriotic duty, although all hands were needed by the Mormons for the long trek westward. After a farewell dance on the open prairie, the Mormon battalion, numbering more than 500 men, marched away with Captain Allen to be outfitted at Fort Leavenworth for service in the Mexican War.

When the Mormon battalion arrived in Santa Fe, the soldiers found no war. The frontier town had surrendered to Kearny without firing a shot and he was on his way to the southern part of California. The Mormon battalion followed him. In the autumn of that same year Father De Smet, a missionary priest to Indian tribes in the Far West, stopped over at Council Bluffs on his way back to civilization. He wrote:

I found the advance guard of the Mormons, numbering about 10,000 camped in the territory of the Omahas, not far from the old Council Bluffs . . . . They asked a thousand questions about the regions I had explored, and . . . the basin of the Great Salt Lake pleased them greatly from the account I gave of it.

Early in April of 1847 Brigham Young led his followers with a party of 143 picked men, three women and two children. He blazed the trail of the great migration by following the route of hunters and trappers along the Platte River. In this lead train were 72 wagons, 93 horses, 52 mules, 66 oxen, 19 cows, 17 dogs, and some chickens.

On a tributary of the Green River,

George Smith, a scout, was riding ahead when he chanced to meet the famed mountain man, Jim Bridger, who had discovered the Great Salt Lake. With two companions Bridger was on his way to Fort Laramie to get a supply of goods for his trading post. He talked with Young and other Mormon leaders and advised them not to settle in the arid region around the lake. Instead, he suggested the country along the Bear River.

Young still headed for the basin of the Salt Lake, stopping over for several days at Fort Bridger to mend wagons, rest the animals, and trade a little with the Shoshone Indians camping at Bridger's store in the western wilds. On July 12 the party crossed the Bear River. Although the banks of the stream were lined with willows, the water was clear, the grass was high, and strawberry vines grew wild, Brigham Young ordered the party to go on.

At the start of the migration in 1846 Brigham Young appointed William Clayton to keep a journal day by day. In this diary for Friday, July 23, 1847 Clayton wrote, after arriving in the Great Salt Lake basin:

The soil looks indeed rich, black and a little sandy. The grass is about four feet high and very thick on the ground and well mixed with rushes . . . . The brethren immediately rigged three plows and went to plowing a little northeast of camp; another party went with spades, etc., to make a dam on one of the creeks so as to throw the water at pleasure on the field, designing to irrigate the land in case rain should not come sufficiently.

During the Mexican War more families came over the Mormon Trail to settle in the basin and to make the desert bloom. There they plowed the fields and built homes while waiting for the return of the Mormon Battalion.

These soldiers in the United States Army learned about life in the desert during their march of 2000 miles from Santa Fe to San Diego. With heavy knapsacks on their backs, they often had to pull wagons with long ropes to help their mule teams go forward when the sand was deep. This march was a rehearsal for their new venture when they joined their families in the valley of the Great Salt Lake.

Meanwhile, emigrants were going to the Mormon settlement there. One company came from Liverpool, England. Before leaving Council Bluffs for the long trek across the plains, a leader advised the ladies not to wear their skirts so long, and to cover their heads with very large sunbonnets. For the men, he suggested heavy beards to protect their faces from the sun and wind of the prairie. His advice to all was to take only things needed on the road and for use when their journey ended.

When the pioneers arrived, they found a dry and treeless valley with mountains on the rim, and populated by jack rabbits and rattlesnakes. They unloaded hoes, rakes, plows, axes, and shovels and went to work to change the place. One of their first tasks was to dig ditches to bring water from the mountains. Every street in the new village had two of these ditches running the length of it, one on each side. This abundant water supply turned the desert green with crops. It was "the promised land."

A year later, after the first harvest, one settler wrote in a letter to his brother "back home" that he lived in a lonesome place and liked it. Scarcely any news reached his ears. He led a busy, happy, peaceful life. The drums beat for merrymaking, not for a march to war. "How free from excitement we live!"

BUFFALO IN THE FOOTHILL COUNTRY OF THE "GREAT AMERICAN DESERT"

Old geographies labeled the dry area of the West, the "Great American Desert." Before entering this arid region, emigrants cut and dried grass and carried it on pack animals to feed their teams. Water was scarce, brackish with alkali, and hardly fit to drink. Yet, buffalo managed to survive.

The war with Mexico dragged on for nearly two years. The main battles were fought south of the Rio Grande where the Mexicans put up a strong defense. General Zachary Taylor invaded Mexico proper from the north. General Winfield Scott followed the route of Cortes from Vera Cruz to Mexico City.

The terms of peace were dictated by the victorious Anglo Americans. By the Treaty of Guadalupe Hidalgo in 1848, the United States gained territory west to the Pacific Ocean and south to the Rio Grande (except the Gadsden Purchase). That area included the present states of New Mexico, Arizona, Utah, Nevada, California, and parts of Wyoming and Colorado. The United States agreed to pay all claims charged to the Mexican Government for damages to property of its citizens and to give Mexico $15,000,000.

Polk missed the honor of annexing Texas. However, the people expected him to settle the Oregon question, and he did, but without a fight. In the uneven contest of trapper versus settler, the homebuilder won. British statesmen realized that the country could not be held with a handful of traders after the plowmen had taken possession of the land. Great Britain proposed the same compromise, offered years before by John Quincy Adams, dividing the disputed territory on the forty-ninth parallel. The United States accepted it. By a treaty signed in June of 1846, the United States gained the present states of Idaho, Washington, and Oregon, and a coast line of 2730 miles along the Pacific Ocean.

The settlers who migrated from Europe to North America won the main continent from the Atlantic to the Pacific, not because they got there first, but because they plowed the ground, planted the crops, and lived on the farms. They loved the soil. To one of these "sod-eager" pioneers it was thrilling to crumble a clod of rich black earth in his strong brown hands and say to himself, "This is mine! ALL MINE!"

AND THEN CAME GOLD!

IT HAPPENED ON Sutter's Ranch in California, nine days before the Treaty of Guadalupe Hidalgo ended the Mexican War. John Sutter, of Swiss origin, was tired of roaming and settled down to the easy-going life of a rancher on a 97,000 acre land grant from the Mexican Government, for which he pledged himself to protect the northern border of Mexico. Near the junction of the American and Sacramento Rivers, he built an adobe fort. It was armed with forty cannon which he had bought from the Russians when they abandoned Fort Ross north of San Francisco. Here the Swiss emigrant ruled over a little empire which he called New Helvetia, after the Roman name for his homeland. The world might never have heard of the globe-trotter, John Sutter, if he had not engaged John Marshall to work in his sawmill.

On Monday afternoon, the twenty-fourth of January in 1848, Marshall strolled down from the mill to the lower end of the tail race. There his eye caught the glitter of something bright in the crevice of a bare rock a few inches under water. He sent an Indian back to get a plate from his top sawyer, the man in the mill yard.

"What does Marshall want with a tin plate?" the man asked.

The Indian shook his head. He did not know. The workman jumped down from the saw-pit, went into his shack, and handed a plate to the Indian. That evening, Marshall came to the shanty and told two of the men to shut down the head gate in the morning and to throw in saw dust and rotten leaves to make it water-tight. These men had belonged to the Mormon battalion, mustered out at San Diego. They were working for Sutter while waiting for the snows to melt in the spring so they could cross the mountains to Utah, their new home. Bigler, one of them, wrote in his journal what happened on the next day:

The next morning we did as Marshall directed and while doing so, we saw him pass through the mill yard and go on down the race. We went in for breakfast and had scarcely commenced our day's work in the mill yard — I was busy preparing to put a blast of powder into a boulder that lay in the tail race near the utter wheel — when Marshall came carrying in his arms, his old slouch white hat. With a wise grin, he said "Boys, I believe I have found a gold mine," at the same time setting his hat on the work bench that stood in the mill yard. In an instant all hands gathered round, and sure enough, on the top of his hat crown, knocked in a little, lay the pure stuff — the most part of an ounce from the size of very small particles up to the size of a grain of wheat.

FORT SUTTER ON THE SACRAMENTO RIVER

This fort was built in 1840 and 1841. The walls were adobe, 15 feet high and 2 feet thick. Walls were 4 feet thick in the towers at all four corners. Sutter's house inside was comfortable for those days.

In December of 1841, the Russian American Fur Company sold the properties at Bodega and Fort Ross, north of San Francisco, to John A. Sutter who transported the livestock and supplies to his large ranch in the Sacramento Valley. Sutter acquired 1700 oxen, cows and calves; nearly 1,000 horses and mules; 900 sheep; plows, rakes and carts for farming; and a number of boats. This sale removed from California the thirty-year-old foothold which Fort Ross gave Russia in Mexican territory.

Marshall asked his workmen to keep the secret until he could go on horseback to notify Sutter at the fort some miles away. Sutter returned with Marshall and the two men found flakes of gold all along the stream. Sutter dug a little nugget of the metal from a rock with only his pen knife for a tool. He shuddered at the thought of what would happen to his rancho if the news leaked out. Just then, one of his Indian laborers rushed up, shouting, "Oro! Oro!" and displayed a nugget nestling in the palm of his hand. Some whispered and others shouted, "There's gold on the Sacramento!" The secret could not be kept. Sutter's business was ruined. His herders left their sheep and cattle unguarded in the pastures; his mill hands left bins of corn and wheat untouched; his workmen deserted and left tons of hides rotting in the vats of his tannery.

Then came the onrushing host of goldseekers from all over the world. They killed his cattle and sheep; dug up his

COMPANIONS OF MARSHALL WHEN HE DISCOVERED GOLD

Henry Bigler wrote the journal of the discovery of gold on Sutter's Ranch. With him were Johnson, Smith, and Brown. The four men belonged to the Mormon Battalion in Kearny's army.

fields and pastures; and pitched their tents all over his rancho. Hundreds of American soldiers, mustered out of the army in California at the end of the Mexican War, spent their last pay for a pick, a shovel, a pan, a kettle, and flour for flapjacks. They were off to the gold fields. In May of 1848 a captain at the army base in San Francisco wrote:

Last night about 18 men deserted for the purpose of working in the gold mines — nine of them from my company.

The same captain, when mustered out, also went to dig for gold along the Sacramento. In October of the same year, an army paymaster wrote to his chief in Washington from his headquarters in Monterey:

Nearly all of the men of company F, 3rd, artillery, have deserted. We have the *Ohio, Warren, Dale, Lexington,* and *Southampton* in port; but they cannot land a man, as they desert as soon as they set foot on shore.

Soldiers and sailors were not the only deserters. Tradesmen closed their shops and merchants locked their stores. "Gone to the Sacramento" became a familiar sign in the village of San Francisco. Disturbed by such wholesale desertion of army men, the War Department asked the first United

271

States governor of California to investigate and report on the gold rumors sweeping over the nation. He made a tour of the gold fields to see for himself. He reported:

A small gutter, not more than a hundred yards long by four feet wide and three feet deep, was pointed out to me as the one where two men had obtained $17,000 in gold. These men employed four white men and about a hundred Indians. At the end of one week, after paying the workers' wages, the two men had left $10,000 in gold.

The news of gold in California flashed around the world with amazing speed. Guidebooks with advice to emigrants flowed from the presses in the United States and Europe. They were quickly sold to eager buyers. In one of these, published in New York, a steamship company advertised fares from New York to San Francisco around Cape Horn for $350, the time, 130 days. However, the voyage around Cape Horn usually took a longer time because the overcrowded vessels were often delayed for repairs. A dealer advised emigrants to take along a supply of his pickles and sauerkraut to prevent scurvy on the long sea voyage. Another firm guaranteed that its hard ship bread would not mould in the damp sea air. Many voyages were made during the

CALIFORNIA GOLD DIGGERS

In this sketch of mining life during the gold rush, some men are panning for gold in a mountain stream. Others are digging into the river bank in the narrow canyon. A sentence in the "Miner's Creed" relates the hardships of a gold digger, with a bit of humor:

A miner believes in big vegetables, because he sees them; but wonders if there is any other kind of fruit than dried apples, dried apples scalded, and dried apples with the strings left in.

California Historical Society, San Francisco

winter of 1848, when it was summer south of the equator.

Emigrants from the Gulf States, and others in a hurry, crossed the fever-ridden isthmus of Panama. They traveled the Gulf in Indian canoes paddled by the natives. They went over the narrow mountain trails on the backs of surefooted burros. From Panama to San Francisco, a steamship line advertised fares of $250 for a trip of twenty days. The great land migration had to wait until the summer of 1849. Many of the covered-wagon emigrants were hardy western pioneers whose forefathers had rolled the frontier back over the first mountain barrier to the Mississippi River.

When pleasant camping grounds were found, with spring water and good grass, the caravans sometimes rested on a Sunday. Amid the rub-a-dub of wash-boards and the clang of the wagon-mender's hammer, the people managed to listen to a sermon preached by a minister standing in the center of the wagon corral. One caravan celebrated the Fourth of July in 1849 on the western prairie. A woman wrote in her diary:

After dinner we decided to celebrate. We sang patriotic songs, repeated what we could remember of the Declaration of Independence, fired a few guns, and gave three cheers for the United States and California, and danced until midnight to the music of a violin and Jew's harp. Indians came and looked on mystified at the dances of the pale faces.

After crossing the Rockies through South Pass the real hardships began. The emigrants could make some preparation for this part of the journey at Salt Lake. From the Mormons in the Salt Lake Valley, they were able to buy some supplies.

Brigham Young had refused to join the gold rush. When the gold-seekers passed through his settlement, the Mormons had corn meal to sell them at $60 per hundred pounds. One forty-niner traded a horse, for which he had paid $110, to a Mormon farmer for a hundred pounds of flour. One emigrant chanced upon a fur trader who sold him five tin cups of flour for $5.

In spite of this brief respite, many of these travelers did not reach the coast. Water and grass were scarce, teams died from exhaustion and hunger, and wagons with their contents were abandoned on the trail. One man wrote in his journal, "Counted 46 dead oxen in today's march." The suffering was greatest in the long stretch of desert country between Salt Lake and the Sierras in California. When the people living in California heard of the sufferings of emigrants stranded in the Sierras, they collected money to buy food, medicine, clothing, and horses and mules to bring them down from the mountains. Small children were carried in deep leather pockets dangling from pack saddles. Their tousled heads bobbed up and down with every step of the steeds. John Sutter donated flour from his mill, stock from his range, and cowboys from his ranch. No one man rescued as many emigrants as did Sutter, who lost all he had in the gold rush and died a poor man.

Who joined the gold rush? Gold was discovered in California during a period of hard times. Men who had failed in business and farmers who could not pay off the mortgages on their land, made up a good part of the forty-niners golden fleece. To them, mining $10,000 in one week was a tale of magic. On the Sacramento, perhaps, they could find enough gold to pay their debts and then start all over

A PROSPECTOR OF THE GOLDRUSH DAYS

The prospector founded the mining industry of the West. With burros hauling mining equipment, he tracked across deserts, climbed over mountains, and waded in streams. His first bag of gold dust paid for a "cradle," like the one on the burro's back. With this rocking device, he could wash more gravel and find more gold nuggets between sunrise and sunset than with a pick and pan. If he found little on some days, he was content. His needs were few, his hopes were high, and the gamble was thrilling.

again. A famine in Ireland in 1846 and a revolution in Germany in 1848 brought thousands from these countries.

Among the citizens of San Francisco, five years after the gold rush of '49, were merchants from New York, a farmer from Pennsylvania, a ship captain from Massachusetts, a gold miner from Vermont, a sheriff from Missouri, and a minister from Kentucky. The German immigrants, the largest number from any foreign country, were butchers, bakers, brewers, cabinet makers, jewelers, engravers, and musicians. Among the French, the next largest number from a foreign

land, were a sculptor, an actor, a bookbinder, an artist, a gardener, a watchmaker, a restaurant keeper, a baker, a cook, a florist, and a hairdresser. A language teacher from Mexico, a stock dealer from Chile, a cook from Hungary, a peddler from Poland, a tailor from Switzerland, a mariner from Norway, a sailor from Denmark, a sea captain from England, a policeman from Scotland, and a cook from China made their homes in San Francisco. The population of this village grew from 2,000 to 20,000 in a single year.

It was not enough to "live and let live." To survive the slogan had to be "live and

HELP live." People recognized the needs of fellow pioneers because those needs were the same as their own. This awareness erased lines of class distinction and developed a new social consciousness. People began to feel that it was their duty to share their freedom and opportunity with their fellow men. Again, "something new" took root in the New World.

WAGON WHEEL GOVERNMENT

WHEN EMIGRANTS crossed the Mississippi River to pass through unsettled country, they left the law of the land behind them. Each caravan was an independent community, a little nation in itself. Success or failure depended upon its citizens.

When enough wagons had arrived to make a train large enough to venture across the plains, a bugle call summoned all the men to a meeting where laws were drawn up to govern the caravan enroute. Although these rules were as varied as the men who made them, the regulations for safety were much the same. The most dreaded chore was guard duty at night. The men stood two, three, or four hour vigils from which no man was excused except for serious illness. Watching alone on dark nights with only the stars for light, what did men think about? One wrote in his diary:

Was on guard last night. The endearments of my home and family and friends occupied my thoughts nearly all the time. Ah! It is a hard fate to be thus separated from all that is dear to one on earth. And why? For the purpose of making a sudden fortune, all is forsaken in the beloved land of our fathers, – thousands upon thousands rushing over to the land of gold. – Doubtless every soul now traveling expects to realize his ten thousand ere he returns. But alas! The tale is yet to be told.

Even the stoutest hearts grew homesick on the journey. This created a problem for the leader who shouldered the responsibility of getting the train to its destination. After the rules were voted upon and a majority agreed, the leader was chosen. The job was an honor, without pay. When several men were nominated, the emigrants sometimes voted by standing in a line behind their choice. The candidate with the longest line won the election. Ever after, he was called captain, major, colonel, or some other military title that clung to him all of his life.

Although the people in a wagon train agreed to obey the rules, they did not always live up to their promises. The troubles of the journey were often too much to endure with patience. An ox died; a horse was stolen; a wagon broke down. The prairie wind seared their faces; the pelting hail tore holes in the wagon tops; the mountain cloudbursts flooded the streams. Men grew irritable and despondent and quarreled among themselves. Sometimes, in a sudden fit of anger, one emigrant killed another. Along the trail were graves with markers like the following:

Sam'l A. Fitzsimmons died from effects of a wound received from a bowie-knife in the hands of Geo. Symington, Aug. 25, 1849.

In case of murder or any crime the men of the train elected a judge and a jury to try the accused. Each evening, after a day's travel, the trial proceeded with witnesses testifying, lawyers arguing, a jury listening, a judge presiding. If guilty, the man was held as a prisoner and turned over to the first sheriff they met. If the jury agreed that the murder was in self-defense, the prisoner was freed. No court of law reversed the decision of a wagon train judge and jury. As hardships increased, men and women lost their tempers over trivial matters. A successful captain of an overland caravan was really a leader of men.

A little calf, born on the journey, became the pet of one particular wagon train. When his feet got sore from walking over the rough ground, an emigrant bought a buffalo hide from an Indian and made shoes for the animal. The calf looked very funny capering over the prairie in his seven-league boots. He needed them. He was bound for Oregon, a long way off. One night a wolf attacked the calf and mangled it badly before a guard could rescue it. Some argued that the animal should be killed to end its suffering. Others objected to killing their pet. Finally, a man shot it. Feelings ran high and the emigrants took sides, refusing to speak to each other. The wise leader stopped the train one noon hour, declaring the party could not go on with such ill feeling. He asked the men to sit down together, talk things over, and settle their differences, for the common good. They did and the wagon train went on.

When the caravans reached their destination, mining camps grew into towns almost over night. Citizens formed committees to keep order until elections could be held and laws passed. In San Francisco in 1849 such a committee sentenced several young rioters to terms in jail but they went free. There was not a jail in the whole territory of California.

In the wagon trains were men from all walks of life. Southern gentlemen left cotton fields behind, took along a few slaves, and started west to dig for gold along the Sacramento. On the prairie where every man did his share or was left behind, the landed aristocrat and day laborer rode side by side. In the "diggings" the college graduate from eastern states and the raw frontiersman who could neither read nor write panned for gold in the same streams, bunked in the same shack, and cooked over the same fire. The rich and poor of this country shared the discomforts of a miner's life with immigrants from Europe, Asia, and South America.

This frontier friendliness born of necessity, seeped into all phases of American life. It inspired a new sense of social justice. People began to question, to criticize, to demand.

CHANGES IN THE WAY OF LIVING

BY 1830, ALTHOUGH THE nation was still agricultural, people began to realize that an industrial era was dawning and that it was necessary to adjust to it. People began to think differently. When a family worked at home, parents and children toiled long hours, often from daylight to dark. They did not complain because they were working in their own little business. When industry moved from the home to the mill, everyone went with it, including the children as young as ten years of age. However, when they worked for wages instead of profits, they began to complain about the long hours of labor. Agitation began for a ten-hour day. To win it, workingmen joined trade societies or unions, sent petitions to state legislatures, called strikes, operated community shops, and started a political party. When people began to feel that the way of working on a farm and living in the country was not successful when applied to working in a factory and living in a city, they began to experiment. They sought a new life-pattern to fit their new way of earning through wages.

The thirty years preceding the War Between the States was a heyday for reformers with many ideas for adjusting society to an industrial era. Some ideas were practical and succeeded; some were impractical and failed. Most people agreed that young children should not work in the mills. The first laws forbidding or limiting child labor were passed. A group of manufacturers met and voluntarily agreed not to hire anyone under twelve years of age. Better working conditions, shorter hours, and higher wages became the goal of labor reformers. Progress was slow because working conditions were so much better in the United States than in Europe at the time.

About forty experiments were tried of living in groups where each man worked for the benefit of the community and not for his own personal profit. The first of these was established at New Harmony, Indiana by Robert Owen, a wealthy Scots manufacturer. On the Brook Farm near Boston, another group tried living on a dairy farm where men worked for the community without private profit. In a free country where every man with a spark of ambition could get ahead and possibly earn a fortune, these socialistic schemes failed, one after another.

In the age of social reform, the temperance movement became a great crusade, supported by churches of all denominations. In an address to the Boston Young Men's Total Abstinence Society in November of 1846, the minister of Federal Street Church said:

Young men of America! The future history of this republic must be determined by you. — A people among whom intemperance prevails can never accomplish an honorable destiny. Freedom is but an empty word where virtue is lost. Hear ye then the appeal which is made to you in the name of your country and all that you love within its borders. Patriotism calls to you from its fields of toil and its altars of sacrifice. Humanity waits for your decision. The hope of the world looks imploringly to you. Young men! Do your duty.

Dorothea Dix exposed the inhuman treatment of insane persons, many of whom were chained in the cells of city and county jails. She campaigned for real hospitals where those suffering from mental illness could have proper medical care and a chance to recover.

Some states passed laws to improve prisons and to outlaw imprisonment for debt. The first Women's Rights Convention met in Seneca Falls, New York, where a movement was organized to demand property rights for women, permission to vote and hold office, and equality with men before the law. More states gave men who did not own property the right to vote. It was a struggle to accomplish this, especially in Rhode Island where the property question almost caused a civil war. For nearly two hundred years no one had been allowed to vote for town or state officers unless he had property and was a freeman of the town in which he resided. Since the Statute of 1723, no person could be a freeman unless he owned a freehold estate of the value fixed by law or was the eldest son of such a freeholder. Under these antiquated laws thousands of men who worked for wages in mills and factories were denied the right to vote. There was trouble when property owners voted down their request for suffrage. Before 1850 nearly all men could vote. Women did not gain national suffrage until 1920.

Few of the crusades starting in the 1830's and 1840's accomplished as much as did the reforms in education. The idea of public schools took root in Massachusetts. In 1647 the colony passed a law that every town of fifty householders must hire a person to teach reading and writing to the children who came and asked to learn. Nearly two hundred years later Massachusetts took the lead again when Horace Mann, a young Bostonian lawyer, was appointed secretary of the first State Board of Education. Although Massachusetts had passed a law establishing public high schools ten years before Horace Mann was appointed, there were only about a dozen in the entire state. Yet, Massachusetts had more than any other state. Addressing a group of honor students at Harvard University in 1850, a speaker made this remark:

If there be any single trait by which the historian will distinguish the present from all past ages, it is the rage for *reform*. It agitates every nation and all classes; and it comprehends nearly every subject of thought and action. Everywhere on every matter, and in all ways, the great heart of humanity throbs for reform.

Class distinctions had little chance to rise on a fast-moving frontier where rich and poor shared alike in the struggle for food, shelter, and comforts in an undeveloped country. The labor system in the South came under attack from all sides during this age of reform and reformers. Slavery became the burning question of the day.

MAPS:

WA16r WA21r WA19r
Atlas of American History by Edgar B. Wesley

PART SIX

Disunity Upsets the Nation

ABRAHAM LINCOLN
President of the United States of America
1861-1865

JEFFERSON DAVIS
President of the Confederate States of America
1861-1865

Chapter 15

Slavery Gains a Foothold

SLAVERY AND FREEDOM MEET IN THE WESTERN HEMISPHERE

ON A MILD OCTOBER day in 1492, the first known black man to enter the Western Hemisphere set foot on a little island in the West Indies. He went ashore with the crew of Columbus. The natives who had never seen either a black man or a white man, gazed in wonder at the stranger with dark skin. Five hundred years before Columbus came to the New World, the first Negroes from Africa were sold in Europe. In fact, slavery is older than recorded history. No one knows when it began. For centuries the buying and selling of human beings was a respectable business. Columbus, himself, shipped five hundred natives, whom he called Indians, to be sold in the slave market.

A short time after the Spaniards came, only a few natives were left on some of the islands in the West Indies. The long hours of toil spent in searching for gold brought an early death to many. Others succumbed to white men's diseases. Then the Spaniards began buying Negro slaves from English, Portuguese, Dutch, and Spanish sea captains. Vessels made regular trips from Africa with their cargoes of men, women, and children. Today the descendants of these slaves form almost the entire population of some of the West Indies islands.

The same thing happened in Mexico and South America wherever the conquistadores went. Long before the English founded Jamestown in 1607, thousands of Negro slaves were owned by wealthy families in the Spanish and Portuguese colonies of the Americas.

In 1619, a year before the Pilgrims came to Massachusetts, a Dutch vessel had landed twenty Negroes at Jamestown. They were sold to Virginia planters who needed laborers in their tobacco fields. In that same year the Virginians had elected men to represent them in the first self-governing assembly in the English colonies. At this first meeting of the House of Burgesses the members boldly stated their rights. Yet, it did not occur to these men that persons held in bondage might be entitled to the same rights. Slavery had existed so long that it was generally accepted without question.

The profit people made in the slave trade held the Negro race in bondage in the Americas for a long time. From the lowly slave hunter in the African jungle to kings and queens on European thrones, thousands made a living, and some reaped fortunes in this business. King Philip of Spain and Queen Anne of England owned stock in a company formed to buy Negroes in Africa and sell them in the Spanish, Portuguese and English colonies of the Americas. In New England where lumber was plentiful, shipbuilders became rich by launching "slavers" for the African trade. Sailing on the slavers brought good pay to seamen and big money to captains. Between 1680 and 1688 the Royal African Company landed about 47,000 Negroes in the Americas.

The Caucasian (white man) and the Negro came together to the New World; one as the master and the other as the slave. Both took part in the discovery and the conquest. Both shared the dangers and labor of settlement. Each race has left its mark on the ever changing way of life on both continents of the Western Hemisphere.

However, opposition to the system of slavery began early in colonial days. The first written protest against slavery was read at a religious meeting of Mennonites in Germantown, Pennsylvania about seventy years after the first Negroes arrived in Jamestown. In part, it read:

Here is liberty of conscience, which is right and honorable; here ought to be likewise liberty of body, except of evildoers. But to bring men hither, or to rob and sell them against their will, WE STAND AGAINST.

When Lord Oglethorpe was vice president of the African Company, a British slave-hunting firm, he met a young prince who had been captured by a neighboring chieftain in Africa and sold to one of the company agents. After hearing the young man's story, Oglethorpe ordered the black prince returned to his own kingdom in Africa. Ever after, Oglethorpe refused to have any part in the slave business. When he founded his colony in Georgia, he made a law which prohibited slavery in any form. It was not long until his colonists began to look with envy at their neighbors across the Savannah River. The Carolina planters had slaves to do their work while the Georgia farmers plowed their own fields and harvested their own crops. After the benevolent founder surrendered his charter to the King and returned to England, his colonists imported slaves. Oglethorpe's settlement, founded to give freedom to the poor debtors in English prisons, became a powerful slaveholding state.

An advertisement appearing in the *Boston News-Letter* for September 26, 1754, explains in a few words why slavery did not gain a foothold in northern states:

TO BE SOLD, A LIKELY NEGRO BOY between 12 and 15 years of age, is handy about any sort of work, and is not sold for any fault, but only as his Master has no particular business for him to do.

Slave labor was profitable in the South where the climate permitted outdoor work for more months in the year than in the North. It also cost less money to clothe and house the laborers. The South depended upon agriculture, largely an outdoor occupation in which slaves were useful. Although some slaves became skilled workmen in factories, the majority were better adapted to work on the farm than in the mill. Since slave labor was not profitable in the manufacturing states, there were few bonded Negroes in the New England states except for house servants. Therefore, slavery died a natural death in the northern states. The system might have gradually disappeared in the South if a New Englander had not invented the cotton gin.

INVENTION OF COTTON GIN MAKES SLAVERY MORE PROFITABLE

IN A NEW ENGLAND farmhouse during the Revolutionary War a boy, Eli Whitney, carved, whittled, and tinkered to make little housekeeping tools for his step-mother. The war prevented the colonists from importing goods from England. They had to depend upon the work of their own hands for the tools they needed. The chips of wood from Eli's knives, augurs, and bits spurted into flame over the backlog, simmering in the fireplace. In cold weather boys of the neighborhood gathered in the Whitney kitchen to learn how to make everything from a nail to a fiddle. In the long summer twilight they crowded into Eli's little shop, apart from the house, to mend their hoes, rakes, and plows for work in the fields. While still a lad, too young to join the army, Eli's fame as a mechanic spread to distant towns in Massachusetts.

After eight years of fighting, the War for Independence came to an end. With peace came boatloads of goods from across the sea — glass, clocks, tinware, furniture, and tools. These articles from Europe sold for less money than it took to make them by hand in the little factories of New England.

Eli put away his tools and packed them in tallow to prevent rust. With a lock of his own making he bolted the door and left for Yale University to study law. There was no longer any need for mechanics. It was the time to win justice for all men, to right wrongs such as slavery, and to prove to the world that a free people could work out a better way of life. Eli Whitney would serve his country and his fellow-men as a lawyer, pleading in the courts, and not as a mechanic.

Upon graduation Eli agreed to teach the children of planters living in the uplands of Georgia, near Athens, while he continued reading law. Enroute to Savannah he met two passengers on the boat who soon changed his plans and the course of history. They were Mrs. Greene, widow of Nathanael Greene, a general in Washington's army and Eli's old college chum, Phineas Miller, manager of the Greene plantation. This large estate was Georgia's gift to General Greene for his victories in the South during the Revolutionary War. Although a rice plantation, it was called Mulberry Grove. The early colonists on this land had tried to raise silkworms and failed. The mulberry trees they had planted still grew on the old plantation.

It was early autumn when Eli arrived in Savannah. The air was warm and moist. A boat crew of slaves rowed the party up the Savannah River to Mulberry Grove. While waiting to get a horse or mule for the trip to Athens, Whitney was the guest of Mrs. Greene.

One evening the serious young lawyer-teacher returned from a walk to find the house ablaze with candlelight and filled with men, laughing and talking. The unexpected guests were Georgia planters, former army officers who had served under General Greene. Slaves were busy carrying trays of food from the kitchen behind the house. The long dining table was soon laden with platters of ham, dishes of crabs and oysters, and bowls of steaming rice. During the meal the conversation turned to cotton.

"It takes twenty slaves, working from sunrise to sunset, to clean twenty pounds of cotton."

"Slavery is dying out. The planters in Virginia are selling their slaves to plantation owners in the rice country farther south. Costs too much to keep them."

"The mills of New England, with new power looms, are ready to buy more cotton than we can raise."

"Good times would come to the South if the seeds in cotton bolls could be removed by machinery. We need mechanics down here — men with brains —."

Whitney listened while the planters discussed their cotton problems. He did not buy a mule. He did not leave Mulberry Grove to teach school in the uplands. In a workshed on the Greene plantation he invented a machine which would gin the cotton. To gin means to comb the sticky green seeds from the fluffy blossom of the cotton plant. Using Whitney's machine, a man could clean ten times more cotton than he could before.

Whitney and his friend, Phineas Miller, went into business to manufacture cotton gins. A fortune would be theirs, they thought. When their sign was hung over a shop door in a narrow street in New Haven, it attracted little attention. New England was turning rapidly to manufacturing and shops were opening everywhere. In a short time cotton gins were in use in Georgia. Most of them were not made by the firm of Miller and Whitney. All over the South planters built their own gins on their own plantations and paid nothing to the inventor. Miller spent most of his time in the courts, arguing that Whitney had invented the cotton gin; that he had a patent and

that every man who built a cotton gin should pay a royalty to the inventor.

In the sixth year after the patent in 1794, the cotton crop had increased from 8,000,000 pounds to 35,000,000 pounds. The planters bought more land to plant more cotton and more slaves to raise the crop. As the demand for cotton grew, the price of slaves rose higher and higher. Good field workers sold for $1,000 and as high as $1,500. At such prices the slaveowners in Virginia and the border states sold their Negroes in large numbers to the planters farther south. Thus it happened that a whittling boy who hated slavery chained the South to this system of labor by inventing the cotton gin. Whitney's invention brought new prosperity to the South, but not to himself.

THE SLAVERY PROBLEM STALKS WEST

FROM THE BEGINNING, slavery had troubled the new nation. In the first draft of the Declaration of Independence Jefferson had accused George III of promoting slavery in the American colonies. On the whole the "Fathers of the Constitution" were opposed to slavery and would have abolished it by law if possible. Some of the strongest arguments against slavery in the Constitutional Convention came from Luther Martin of Maryland and George Mason of Virginia, who both owned slaves. During the debate over the compromise to count three-fifths of the slaves as population, Luther Martin said that "it was inconsistent with the principles of the Revolution and dishonorable to the American character to have such a feature in the Constitution."

In the Constitutional Convention on August 22, 1787, George Mason made a long speech on the subject in which he said:

Slavery discourages arts and manufactures. The poor despise labor when performed by slaves. They bring the judgment of heaven upon a country.

Madison declared he "thought it wrong to admit in the Constitution the idea that there could be property in men." He also was a slaveholder.

In both the north and the south, during the state conventions called to accept the Constitution, voices were raised against slavery. In North Carolina, James Iredell, a soldier in the Revolutionary War who was, later, a Judge on the Supreme Court of the United States, told the Convention of his state:

When the entire abolition of slavery takes place, it will be an event which must be pleasing to every generous mind, and every friend of human nature.

Northern men realized that their southern neighbors were forced to depend upon slave labor. At the time, there were not enough free men for hire on the big plantations. Washington once had complained that he was forced to buy laborers for his fields although he preferred to hire them. His last will and testament leaves no doubt as to his own personal feelings about slavery. He wrote:

Upon the decease of my wife it is my will and desire that all the slaves which I hold in my own right, shall receive their freedom. — And whereas among those who will receive freedom, there may be some, who from old age or bodily infirmities, and others who on account of their infancy, will be unable to support themselves; it is my will and desire that — they shall be comfortably clothed and fed by my heirs while they live. — And I do

hereby expressly forbid the sale or transportation out of the said Commonwealth, of any slave I may die possessed of, under any pretense whatsoever.

As the United States moved westward, the slavery problem was solved peaceably east of the Mississippi River. Ohio, Indiana, Illinois, Michigan, and Wisconsin, the states formed from the Northwest Territory where slavery had been forbidden, were admitted as free states. The states south of the Ohio River were admitted as slave states.

Two great men, opposed to slavery, became the unwilling agents for its spread beyond the Mississippi. One, Eli Whitney, invented the cotton gin; the other, Thomas Jefferson, bought Louisiana. They knew each other and were friends. Whitney's invention made cotton the money crop of the South. Since cotton wears out land rapidly, the planters kept moving farther west where fresh new land was cheap and plentiful. The planters crossed the Mississippi into the Louisiana Territory to the rich farmlands of Arkansas, Louisiana, and Texas. They took their Negroes with them.

This westward migration brought the slavery question to a crisis point. The northerners did not want slavery to spread into the western lands. The southerners felt entitled to take their slaves with them when they moved west. Each side was anxious that its representatives in Congress not be outnumbered. If this happened, then Congress would be able to pass laws that favored one group over another. Some plan had to be found for admitting the new states to the Union.

When Missouri had enough settlers for a state, the people voted on a constitution, sent it to Congress, and asked admission to the Union. When the clause providing for slavery was read in Congress, it brought forth heated debates in both houses. If Missouri became a slave state, would slavery spread over the entire Louisiana Purchase? Henry Clay and his committee came forward with a compromise which both sides accepted. The famous Missouri Compromise of 1820 provided that Missouri would be admitted to the Union as a slave state, but that all other territory in the Louisiana Purchase, lying north of the southern boundary of Missouri, should be forever free. The South gained another slave state. At the same time Maine was admitted as a free state. For the time being this kept both slave and free states equally represented in the Senate.

When the United States gained more western territory at the end of the Mexican War, the slavery feud broke out again with renewed fury. The same question — slave or free — was debated in Congress when California applied for admission to the Union.

"We are obliged to take sides on the great question of questions — THE RIGHTS OF MAN" spoke a representative from Wisconsin. "If we properly appreciate the destiny of this republic, we shall become the emancipators of not only our own enslaved countrymen, but the liberators of the world."

Daniel Webster, a Senator from Massachusetts, tried to convince his fellow members of the Senate that nature had turned the scale against slavery in the territory acquired from Mexico. In a speech he described the country to prove his point:

California and New Mexico are composed of vast ridges of mountains of enormous height, with broken ridges and deep valleys. The sides of these mountains are barren; their tops capped with snow. — What is there in New Mexico that could induce any body to go there with slaves? There are some narrow strips of tillable land on the borders of the rivers: but the rivers themselves dry up before midsummer is gone. All that the people can do in that region is to raise some little articles, some little wheat for their tortillas, and all that by irrigation. And who expects to see a hundred black men cultivating tobacco, corn, cotton, rice, or anything else on lands in New Mexico? I look upon it, therefore, — that both California and New Mexico are destined to be free; — free by the arrangement of things by the Power above us.

The people on both sides became so angry that they could no longer think clearly. The great compromisers arose again in Congress to calm the storm.

THE COMPROMISE OF 1850

ON A COLD winter night in 1850, Henry Clay trudged through a snowstorm to call on his rival, Daniel Webster. The slavery issue was tearing the Union apart. The southern states were threatening to secede from the Union if Congress passed a law forbidding slavery in California, New Mexico, or any territory acquired from Mexico. Clay, deeply troubled, felt it was his duty to find a way out of war. The great peacemaker was seventy-three years old and near the end of his life. His compromise was a plan to settle the slavery problem forever, but he needed the support of his powerful rival.

In Congress the two men had often been at odds. Webster believed that the Union must be preserved at all costs. Clay, the great compromiser from Kentucky, thought it was better for each side to give up something than to risk a war where brother fought brother. In the library of the great Daniel's home, history was made on that stormy January night. Clay did most of the talking. Webster listened. His

Reading left to right: Henry Clay, author of compromises; Daniel Webster, foe of nullification; John C. Calhoun, defender of states rights.

forehead wrinkled and his lips tightened as he pondered his rival's words. War seemed imminent. Webster, like Clay, was near the end of his public life. It was late when Henry Clay trudged home through the falling snow, a happy man. Webster, the mighty orator, would speak in favor of Clay's latest compromise with slavery in an effort to save the Union.

On the seventh of March the Senate chamber was filled to overflowing with an eager, excited crowd. The halls and stairways were jammed with people who could not get inside. They had come to hear Webster speak in support of Clay's latest compromise with slavery. They wondered if he had deserted the cause of the Union. A silence, tense with feeling, gripped the audience when the stocky Senator from Massachusetts strode across the platform. His heavy eyebrows were drawn forward over his deep-set eyes. His voice was low and calm.

287

"I wish to speak today," he said, "not as a Massachusetts man, nor as a northern man, but as an American — I speak for the preservation of the Union."

After the speech had begun, a tall, thin man tottered to his seat. He was John C. Calhoun, the Senator from South Carolina. Three days before, Senators had listened to his last speech, read by a friend, in which he asked the question, "How can the Union be preserved?"

"That this government claims, and practically maintains the right to decide in the last resort, as to the extent of its powers, will scarcely be denied by any-one . . . . That it also claims the right to resort to force, to maintain whatever power she claims against all opposition," Calhoun said.

"Now, I ask," he continued, "what limitation can possibly be placed upon the powers of a government, claiming and exercising such rights? And, if none can be, how can the separate government of the States maintain and protect the powers reserved to them by the Constitution, or the people of the several States maintain those which are reserved to them, and among them, their sovereign powers, by which they ordained and established, not only their separate State constitutions and governments, but also the Constitution and government of the United States?"

Calhoun and Webster, born in the same year, had been political enemies for a lifetime. Although ranged on opposite sides, they admired each other. Both staunchly defended the Constitution, although they did not agree on the meaning of it. The great southerner was a champion of states rights; the great northerner, of nationalism.

Aware that his words might kindle the flames of war, Webster was the calm debater and not the fiery orator in this speech. He declared that the southerners were neither selfish nor dishonest in their views. He spoke:

All that has happened has been natural. The age of cotton became the golden age for our southern brethren. — There soon came to be an eagerness for other territory, a new area, for the cultivation of the cotton crop. In 1802 in pursuit of the idea of opening a new cotton region, the United States obtained a cession from Georgia of the whole of her western territory, now the rich and growing state of Alabama. In 1803 Louisiana was purchased from France, out of which the states of Louisiana, Arkansas, and Missouri have been framed as slaveholding states. In 1819 the cession of Florida was made, adding more slaveholding territory. — And lastly, Texas, great and vast and illimitable Texas, was added to the Union as a slave state in 1845.

Then he explained why the geography of California and New Mexico forbade slavery. Throughout his long address, which lasted for three hours and eleven minutes, Webster coaxed his listeners into the mood of compromise. Jefferson Davis, the Senator from Mississippi who was to become the President of the Confederate States of America, heard him say:

To break up this great government? To dismember this great country? To astonish Europe with an act of folly? No, sir! No, Sir! THERE WILL BE NO SECESSION.

After months of debate Congress accepted the Compromise of 1850. The most important terms were:

1. California was admitted as a free state.
2. New Mexico and Utah were organized as territories, with permission to enter the Union as slave or free states

according to the vote of the people.

3. A fugitive slave law was passed permitting runaway slaves to be captured in any state or territory of the Union and returned to their masters.
4. The slave trade was abolished in the District of Columbia.

Thus the northerners won California as a free state and the abolition of the slave trade in the national capital. The southerners won popular sovereignty for New Mexico (the people of the state could vote whether to be a free or slave state) and a law to force the return of runaway slaves.

The compromise did not settle the slavery feud over western territory. The demand for an established government in Kansas and Nebraska continued the battle over lands in the West. Should they be slave or free? In 1854 the Kansas-Nebraska Act was passed, providing for popular sovereignty in Kansas and Nebraska. By the Missouri Compromise Congress had forbidden slavery north of the southern boundary of Missouri. Now it was allowing the settlers in this territory to decide for themselves. The political storm broke with renewed fury, not only in the halls of Congress but in the towns and villages across the nation.

Instead of solving the slavery question, the Kansas-Nebraska Act led to actual war in Kansas. Emigration societies of free men were rushed into Kansas by people who wanted the territory to be free. Slaveholders from the neighboring state of Missouri crossed the border in large bands, determined to win the country. Two governments were set up, one slave and one free. This led to such violent fighting that the territory became known as "Bleeding Kansas." If the slavery question had been

"BLEEDING KANSAS"

Settlers moved into Kansas from both slave and free states trying to gain control of the new territory. This sketch depicts a "massacre" on May 19, 1858.

The Kansas State Historical Society, Topeka

argued only on the floors of Congress, there might have been more compromises. After the passage of the Kansas-Nebraska Act, the pressure of public opinion overwhelmed the lawmakers.

The Dred Scott decision handed down by the Supreme Court in 1857 increased the tension that the Kansas-Nebraska Act had been intended to ease. Dred Scott, a Negro slave, belonged to a surgeon in the United States Army. In 1834 the doctor was transferred from the state of Missouri, slave territory, to the military post at Rock Island, Illinois, free under the Ordinance of 1787. Scott sued for his freedom upon the grounds that his residence in free territory made him a free man. For over twenty years the case dragged through the courts until it reached the highest court in the nation. The Supreme Court judges decided that the Ordinance of 1787, which preceded the Constitution, "could not operate of itself to confer freedom or citizenship within the Northwest Territory on Negroes not citizens of the United States." This decision, a victory for the South, incensed the North where anti-slavery agitation was gaining ground.

OPPOSITION TO SLAVERY INCREASES

THE FUGITIVE SLAVE LAW of the Compromise of 1850 turned thousands of law-abiding citizens into law-breaking citizens. Some northerners hid escaping slaves in haystacks, barns, and cellars during the day. They sent the runaways out at night to travel to another protector until the fugitives reached the Canadian line. This plan for aiding runaway slaves was known as the "underground railroad."

At a meeting in Boston, Wendell Phillips said to his audience:

We will, ourselves, trample this accursed Fugitive Slave Law under foot.

Societies had been formed to abolish slavery before the United States became a nation. However, the abolitionists did not become a serious threat to the slave system until the time of the great compromises to preserve the Union. Sometimes, near riots occurred when meetings were held even in private homes. Magazines appeared such as *The Emancipator* in Tennessee, *The Liberalist* in Louisiana, *The Weekly Emancipator* in New York, and *The Liberator* in Boston. There were many abolitionists in the South as well as in the North. William Lloyd Garrison, who published *The Liberator,* became the leader of the antislavery movement.

Poets also joined the abolitionists and wrote poems against slavery. John G. Whittier's verses exposing the abuses of slavery won many members for societies of abolitionists. Since the Negroes in Virginia and the border states lived in dread of being sold farther south to work in the flooded rice fields, Whittier wrote:

Gone, gone, — sold and gone,
To the rice-swamp dank and lone,
From Virginia's hills and waters;
Woe is me, my stolen daughters!

Copies of the song, "My Darling Nelly Gray," had a place on reed organs and square pianos. It was a popular song on moonlit hayrides and summer picnics. Who did not pity Nelly Gray?

Of all the books written on slavery, *Uncle Tom's Cabin* by Harriet Beecher Stowe was the one most widely read.

Although it was a novel, the people who read it thought of it as a true story and not fiction. The furor created by this book fanned the flame of indignation that finally took the slavery problem out of the lawmakers' hands. The issue went to the people. As the breach widened between the North and the South, war loomed again on the horizon.

THE REPUBLICAN
PARTY IS STARTED

FINALLY THE PEOPLE in the North grew weary of talking and writing against slavery. They wanted to VOTE against it. In many towns from Boston to Chicago citizens met to form a party opposed to the extension of slavery. In 1856 this new party, called "Republican," held its first national convention in Philadelphia, Pennsylvania. All of the free states, except California, sent delegates who voted for a platform pledged to prevent the spread of slavery. John C. Fremont, the great western explorer, was nominated for President, and accepted by letter, July 6, 1856. His opponent was James Buchanan of Pennsylvania, nominated by the Democratic Party at its national convention in Cincinnati, Ohio. Buchanan won the election although the new Republican Party showed unexpected strength.

Six years before the South had lost its strongest champion, John C. Calhoun. He had fought in Congress for what he thought was right and just under the Constitution. Defiant to the end, he had struggled to his seat in the Senate to hear Webster's famous Seventh-of-March speech in 1850. A few weeks later the great southerner was dead. Both Webster and Clay walked beside his coffin, their heads bowed in grief and respect. In two more years the famed compromisers were gone and no men rose to take their places. The days of compacts with slavery were also gone.

In 1860 the northerners wanted a President who would openly oppose the extension of slavery and vow to preserve the Union. Who? There were a number of learned men in the East from whom to choose a candidate. The new Republican Party, however, nominated Abraham Lincoln, reared in poverty, and educated without schools. While still a lad, Lincoln had migrated from the slave state of Kentucky to the free state of Indiana. Later he moved into Illinois and settled in Springfield where he practiced law. His neighbors nicknamed him "Honest Abe" and elected him to represent them in the state legislature.

Not until 1858 did the lawyer from Springfield, Illinois become a national figure. In that year Lincoln was a Republican candidate for the United States Senate. Stephen A. Douglas was the Democratic nominee. Lincoln challenged his opponent to a series of debates on the slavery question, to be held in towns of northern, central, and southern Illinois. The two men were opposites. Douglas was short and stocky, less than five feet tall. Lincoln, towering over six feet, was lean and gawky. Douglas was a master of oratory and debate and a Congressman of note. Lincoln had a friendly way of chatting, neighbor to neighbor, that won the confidence of his listeners. He was little known outside his own home state.

Traveling in wagons over dusty prairie roads, on horseback through narrow woodland trails, and on railroad trains from nearby towns and neighboring states, the people gathered to hear these two men debate the question of the hour. When Lincoln accepted the Republican nomination for the Senate on June 16, 1858 in Springfield, he spoke to the convention:

A house divided against itself cannot stand. I believe this Government cannot endure permanently half slave, half free.

Douglas used this statement as a slogan. He argued that Lincoln advocated a war of the North against the South, to be carried on until one or the other won and every state in the Union was either all slave or all free. Lincoln did not back down. He cited the failure of the doctrine of popular sovereignty when public opinion did not support it in actual practice.

Douglas put on a big show that pulled in the crowds to hear these debates. He traveled on a private train from Chicago to Springfield. Cannons were mounted on flatcars. The coaches were filled with companies of militia and dozens of admirers. Welcoming committees escorted him into towns while guns fired salutes to announce his arrival. Editors of the big eastern newspapers sent reporters to cover the debates. Their copy was printed under such headlines as "The Little Giant Triumphant." They wrote about the great crowds — ten thousand at Bloomington, eighteen thousand at Galesburg, twenty thousand at Ottawa — crowds too large for any town hall. The meetings were held in public squares and in shady picnic groves. Wherever Douglas went, his trains, hacks, and hotels were swathed in banners labeled "Popular Sovereignty." Stephen A. Douglas, the popular hero, gathered the throngs that also heard his little known opponent, Abraham Lincoln..

The dapper Senator was a forceful orator with years of experience in public speaking. The lanky frontiersman was ill at ease on the platform. His voice was somewhat shrill and his gestures were often awkward. However, as the debates continued, people began to realize that Douglas had met his match in the "six-footer" from Springfield. Lincoln punctured the theory of popular sovereignty. He cited the failure of the Kansas-Nebraska Act which had been framed by Douglas. By permitting the citizens of a territory to vote a state slave or free, the act had led to chaos and bloodshed.

At that time Senators were chosen by state legislatures. (Not until 1913, when the Seventeenth Amendment went into effect, were Senators elected by the direct vote of the people.) In 1858 fifty-four members of the Illinois legislature voted for Douglas and forty-six for Lincoln. Although "the Little Giant" went back to the Senate, these debates made Lincoln a candidate for a higher office. The new Republican Party, casting about for a leader who could win the people's trust, selected Honest Abe.

When the votes were counted in November, 1860, Abraham Lincoln, farmer, rail-splitter, grocery clerk, river boatman, lawyer, was chosen as the next President of the United States, to succeed James Buchanan.

The nomination and election of the Republican Party's candidate sent panic through the southern states. They felt that the new party would have no understanding of the needs of the South. The Republicans had declared they would forbid further uses of rich western land for slave labor. Once Lincoln was in office, the southerners knew they could never muster enough votes in Congress to get laws passed that would preserve their way of living. They felt that the only thing left for them to do was to get out of the Union.

On the fourth of February, 1861, representatives from South Carolina, Florida, Mississippi, Alabama, Georgia and Louisiana met in Montgomery, capital of Alabama, to proclaim a new nation, THE CONFEDERATE STATES OF AMERICA. Jefferson Davis of Mississippi was chosen President, and Alexander H. Stevens from Georgia, Vice President. On February 18, in front of the Capitol in Montgomery, Alabama, Jefferson Davis made his inaugural address:

Our present political position has been achieved in a manner unprecedented in the history of nations. It illustrates the American idea that governments rest on the consent of the governed, and that it is the right of the people to alter or abolish them at will whenever they become destructive of the ends for which they were established.

On the last day of February, 1861, the Committee on Permanent Constitution made its report. The new government for the new nation was modeled on the Constitution of the United States, framed in 1787:

THE CONSTITUTION OF
THE CONFEDERATE STATES OF AMERICA

We, the people of the Confederate States, each State acting for itself, and in its sovereign and independent character, in order to form a permanent federal government, establish justice, insure domestic tranquillity, and secure the blessings of liberty to ourselves and our posterity — to which ends we invoke the favor and guidance of Almighty God — do ordain and establish this Constitution for the Confederate States of America.

After debate in the Confederate Congress, this Constitution was adopted on March 11, 1861, only a week after Lincoln was inaugurated as President of the United States. When Lincoln laid his right hand on the Bible and repeated his oath of office, he became the head of "a house divided against itself." The country was divided into two separate nations. The Union did not exist.

What would Lincoln say in his speech? Crowds blocked the streets in front of newspaper offices in towns and cities. Messengers astride fleet ponies gathered at stations out west, ready to carry his words to remote places in Oregon, Texas, and California. The whole country waited breathlessly for Lincoln's inaugural address. What would he tell the southerners? He said:

In your hands, my dissatisfied fellow countrymen, and not in mine, is the momentous issue of civil war. You have no oath registered in heaven to destroy the government, while I shall have the most solemn one to preserve, protect and defend it.

Both Lincoln and Davis were born in log cabins on Kentucky farms, about eighty miles apart. Both left the state as small children, one going north, and the other going south. The Lincolns moved to Indiana and then to Illinois. The Davis family, which had come to Kentucky from Georgia after the Revolutionary War, went first to Louisiana before settling on a cotton farm in Mississippi. Although both started their schooling in log cabins on the frontier, Lincoln was self-taught and Davis was graduated from the United States Military Academy at West Point. Both fought in the Black Hawk War. As a Colonel in the United States Army, Davis fought in the Mexican War and was wounded in the Battle of Buena Vista. Both Lincoln and Davis served in the House of Representatives. Stephen A. Douglas defeated Lincoln for a seat in the Senate, another of which was won by Davis, who resigned when his home state of Mississippi seceded from the Union. These two Kentuckians, born in log cabins, were now rival presidents of two nations on the verge of war in 1861.

MAP:

WA23r
Atlas of American History by Edgar B. Wesley

Chapter 16

North and South Disagree

THE CONFLICT WAGES ON LAND AND SEA

THE FIRST SHOT in the War Between the States was fired at daybreak, on the ninth of January, 1861. The *Star of the West* crossed the bar of Charleston harbor with supplies for Major Anderson and his troops. They were holding Fort Sumter for the Union after South Carolina had seceded. When the vessel was less than two miles from the fort, a hidden battery on Morris Island opened fire. One shell struck the ship. The captain turned around and went back to New York with his cargo.

War really began when a former student sent a message to his former teacher at West Point, demanding the surrender of Fort Sumter:

> Headquarters Provisional Army C.S.A.
> Charleston, S.C.
> April 11, 1861, 2:00 P.M.
> Maj. Robert Anderson
> Commanding at Fort Sumter
> Charleston Harbor, S.C.
> SIR: The Government of the Confederate States has hitherto forborne from any hostile demonstration against Fort Sumter, in the hope that the Government of the United States, with a view to the amicable adjustment of all questions between the two Governments, and to avert the calamities of war, would voluntarily evacuate it.
> I am ordered by the Government of the Confederate States to demand the evacuation of Fort Sumter. My aids, Col. Chestnut and Capt. Lee, are authorized to make such demand of you. All proper facilities will be afforded for the removal of yourself and command — together with company arms and property, and all private property — to any post in the United States which you may elect. The flag which you have upheld so long, and with so much fortitude, under the most trying circumstances, may be saluted by you on taking it down. Col. Chestnut and Capt. Lee will, for a reasonable time, await your answer.
> I am, sir, very respectfully, your obedient servant.
> G.T. Beauregard, Brig. Gen. Commanding

On the same day, Major Anderson sent his reply:

> Headquarters Fort Sumter, S.C.
> April 11, 1861
> To Brig. Gen. G.T. Beauregard
> Commanding Provisional Army C.S.A.
> GENERAL: I have the honor to acknowledge the receipt of your communication demanding the evacuation of this fort, and to say in reply thereto that it is a demand with which I regret that my sense of honor and my obligation to my Government prevent my compliance.
> Thanking you for the fair, manly, and courteous terms proposed, and for the high

295

compliment paid me, I remain, General, very respectfully, your obedient servant,

Robert Anderson,
Major U.S. Army, Commanding

The two men had long been friends at West Point, the United States Military Academy, and Anderson had chosen Beauregard to be his assistant there. After another exchange of notes between them came the last word, dated April 12, 1861, 3:20 A.M.:

Major Robert Anderson, United States Army, Commanding Fort Sumter

SIR: By authority of Brigadier General Beauregard, Commanding the Provisional Forces of the Confederate States, we have the honor to notify you that he will open the fire of his batteries on Fort Sumter in one hour from this time.

We have the honor to be, very respectfully, your obedient servants,

James Chestnut, Jr.,
Aide-de-Camp
Stephen D. Lee,
Captain, C.S. Army and Aide-de-Camp

When the small remaining stock of cartridges allowed a gun to be fired only every ten minutes, and the troops were almost overcome with heat and smoke, Major Anderson hoisted a white flag. A messenger arrived soon after to arrange the terms of surrender. Major Anderson accepted them, as follows:

All proper facilities for the removal of yourself and command, together with company arms and private property, to any point within the United States you may select.

BOMBARDMENT OF FORT SUMTER

Fort Sumter, built on a sand bar in Charleston Harbor, was named in honor of Thomas Sumter, a hero of the Revolutionary War. Sumter waged guerrilla warfare upon the British in the Carolinas.

Although under frequent bombardment, the Confederates held Fort Sumter until forced to evacuate it when General Sherman approached Atlanta.

Currier and Ives

Apprised that you desire the privilege of saluting your flag on retiring, I cheerfully concede it, in consideration of the gallantry with which you have defended the place under your charge.

G.T. Beauregard

After a bullet-riddled flag had been saluted and lowered, Major Anderson and his troops boarded the Confederate vessel, *Isabel*, where they spent the night. A report from an Army engineer briefly stated the end:

April 14. — The *Isabel* went over the bar and placed the whole command on board the steamer *Baltic*, which started to New York. April 17. — Arrived in New York.

Soon after the surrender of Fort Sumter, Virginia seceded, followed by North Carolina, Arkansas, and Tennessee. The mountain people of Virginia remained loyal to the Union. In 1863, they formed the new state of West Virginia. The states of Kentucky, Maryland, and Missouri on the border, where opinion was divided, did not secede.

Forts, arsenals, stores of ammunition, and buildings of the Federal Government were taken over by the Confederacy. Although war had actually begun, neither side realized that the struggle would last four years. Lincoln asked for 75,000 volunteers. Jefferson Davis, President of the Confederate States of America, issued a call for 100,000 volunteers. Both sides began training their armies. Many officers in the Confederate army were graduates of West Point and had served in the Mexican War, an advantage for the South initially. Robert E. Lee, son of "Light Horse" Harry Lee, who fought under Washington in the Revolutionary War, wrote a letter to General Winfield Scott, under whose command he had served in the Mexican

War. Lee asked Scott to accept his resignation as Colonel of the First Regiment of Cavalry, United States Army. He closed his letter, written in his home in Arlington, Virginia with these lines:

Save in defense of my native State, I never desire again to draw my sword. Be pleased to accept my most earnest wishes for the continuance of your happiness and prosperity, and believe me,

Most truly yours,
R.E. Lee

General Robert E. Lee led the Confederate forces during the War Between the States, his main work being the defense of Richmond, Virginia, the capital of the Confederacy which was moved from Montgomery Alabama; and drawing the plans to repel the invasion of Union forces throughout the southern states.

Early in July of 1861, Congress of the United States voted for an army of 500,000 men. Anxious to settle the war before it really gained headway, raw recruits under General Irvin McDowell met the Confederate forces under General G.T. Beauregard and General Joseph E. Johnston at Manassass, about thirty-five miles from Washington. The fighting took place along a little stream called Bull Run, and the engagement is commonly known as the Battle of Bull Run. By the evening of July 21, the untrained recruits of the Union army were fleeing back to Washington in panic. When untrained Confederate troops were also fleeing the battle, an officer pointed to the well-drilled brigade of Thomas J. Jackson, shouting:

"Look! There is Jackson standing like a stone wall!"

After this taste of war, both sides spent the remainder of the year training their soldiers. George B. McClellan, a stern drillmaster, took over the Army of the Potomac. Except for skirmishes in the border states, the largest being at Wilson's Creek, Lexington, and Milford in Missouri, little progress was made on land. Ft. Hatteras in North Carolina and Port Royal in South Carolina were captured by the Union. However, by the end of 1861, both sides had developed plans for carrying on the war.

The Union plan was to blockade the ports of the southern states; to open the Mississippi River and divide the Confederacy; to separate the Gulf States from the Atlantic States; to capture Richmond. War began in earnest in 1862 when these plans began to operate.

Defense was the only plan of war possible for the Confederates, since their country would be invaded. With farming as the main industry, the people of the South largely depended upon the North and Europe for their manufacturing needs. While gradually building some small factories for producing arms, after war broke out, supplies were gathered elsewhere. The Confederates gleaned guns and shells from battlefields and prisoners. But the main supply of munitions was smuggled through the Union blockade by the low, small, compactly built blockade runners which carried cotton to the West Indies to be traded for these necessities.

THE BLOCKADE

SOON AFTER the firing on Fort Sumter, Lincoln declared a blockade of southern ports. He intended to prevent the sale of cotton, rice, and other products in foreign countries and the purchase of ammunition, cloth, and other supplies that the South needed to carry on the war. In northern shipyards armed cruisers were built to patrol the sea lanes. These cruisers had orders not only to sink and capture the blockade runners, but to protect the merchant marine of the Union from the plucky privateers and well armed raiders.

At Norfolk the Confederates raised a sunken frigate, the *Merrimac.* After repairing this wooden vessel, they covered it with iron plates four inches thick. On a spring day in 1862 this monster steamed into the mouth of the James River to attack the Union warships. The ironclad rammed and sank the *Cumberland* and fired the *Congress,* a frigate with fifty guns. During the battle, shells from the batteries on shore peppered the ironclad, but failed to sink it. In the early evening, hampered by the tide, the *Merrimac* withdrew, intending to return at daylight the next morning to continue the attack on the Union fleet.

That night, another ironclad, guided by the light of the burning *Congress,* steamed quietly into Hampton Roads. It was the *Monitor,* designed by a Swede, John Ericsson, for the Union Navy. Confident of victory, the *Merrimac* returned the next day. A surprise was in store for the Confederate crew. Coming out to greet them was a queer little ship which looked "like a cheesebox on a raft." Soon, heavy gunfire began to spout from the turret. The gunners on the *Merrimac* answered with a broadside. After a battle of several hours the duel of the ironclads ended in a draw. The side of the *Merrimac* was caved in and the captain of the *Monitor* was wounded by a shell that struck the pilot house. Although not a man was killed, this naval battle was one of the most important in history. It sounded the death knell of

BATTLE BETWEEN THE IRONCLADS, MONITOR AND VIRGINIA
(MERRIMAC), MARCH 9, 1862, HAMPTON ROADS, VIRGINIA

Although the Confederates changed the name of the remodeled *Merrimac* to *Virginia*,
the original name clung to the vessel. Neither vessel lasted long after the famous battle.
The Confederates blew up the *Virginia* when they evacuated Norfolk two months later. In
the following December, the *Monitor* sank in a storm off Cape Hatteras, North Carolina.

wooden warships and put all the navies of
the world out of date. Nations had to begin
to build new fleets with ships of steel.

Unable to build a strong navy, the
Confederacy resorted to privateering to
get supplies through the blockade. During
the War Between the States, fortunes were
won and lost in the dangerous and
exciting venture of privateering.

SALLIE TURNS PRIVATEER

SALLIE WAS A SMART clipper, built
on Long Island in 1856 and christened the
Virginia. The name was changed when the
new owners asked the President of the
Confederate States of America for a letter
of marque, giving them the authority to
seize any armed or unarmed United States

vessel, public or private. On October 9,
1861, the privateer, trim and fleet, left the
dock in Charleston harbor. The skipper was
Captain Henry S. Lebby. It was six o'clock
that evening when the vessel crossed North
Edisto bar and sailed into the open sea. No
Union blockaders were in sight. The forty-
odd men on board were patriotic pirates
defending the Confederacy. The first day
out, not a single sail hove into view.

Sometimes, however, luck came day
after day. The following items were copied
from official government records:

On October 1, 1861, the brig *B.K. Eaton* of
Searsport, Maine, — W.C. Nichols, master, was
captured by the privateer, *Sallie.* Crew and captain
were carried to Charleston, thence to Columbia,
and to Richmond, and were prisoners with others
until sent on to Washington. Brig *B.K. Eaton* sailed
from New York loaded with lime and cement, in
employment of the government.

Captain Pettengill made a report of the capture of his vessel, *Granada*, of Portland, Maine, bound for New York:

On night of October 2, I fell in with and was taken possession of by the privateer *Sallie,* Captain Lebby, three days out of Charleston; and from her transferred three days later to the British schooner *Greyhound.* We arrived at New York today. The *Sallie* sailed southeast after leaving us, in search of coffee vessels from Rio.

In a little over three weeks the privateer captured six merchant vessels with valuable cargoes, without being fired upon by a northern blockader. One black night the *Sallie* had a narrow escape. It was Halloween and the wind was high. A steam frigate of the enemy, on patrol in southern waters, passed so near in the darkness that a watchman on the privateer heard the ship's bell strike seven and the Union sentinel call out, "All's Well!"

The privateer's first voyage ended when a United States cruiser gave chase. The captain of the *Sallie* outran the man-of-war and reached the shallow bar ahead of capture. Several times the vessel almost stuck in the sand, only to be washed afloat again by heavy billows crashing into foam on the hidden shelf. The *Sallie* reached safety in Charleston harbor, leaving her pursuer outside, beyond the choppy bar, in the open sea. The owners of the privateer agreed to divide the big profits of the first trip and sell the boat for $3200 rather than risk capture on a second venture.

As a blockade runner, carrying on foreign trade, and not as a privateer, capturing ships at sea, the *Sallie* sailed out of Charleston harbor with a cargo of cotton, turpentine, and rice. Sneaking through the Union blockade, her captain delivered the produce to a British freighter waiting at a port in the West Indies. For the

UNION VESSELS CHASING A BLOCKADE RUNNER
Built low and long, these fleet ships challenged the Union blockade. In the West Indies, they traded cargoes of cotton for arms and supplies to support the war effort in the Confederacy.

return trip through blockaded waters, he took on a cargo of guns, ammunition, and bolts of cloth. In this way southern cotton reached the mills of Manchester and Birmingham. British-made goods supplied some of the needs of the Confederacy. The plucky little clipper running the blockade survived the four years of war and escaped capture by Union patrols.

The blockade of southern ports was a powerful weapon in the hands of the North. It hastened the defeat of the Confederate States. As the war progressed, the blockade tightened its grip on the South. Fewer products were exported and fewer articles were imported. Prices rose to dizzy heights, even on common articles of food. In the *Mobile Tribune* of May 9, 1863, lard was advertised at $1.15 per pound; vinegar at $1 a gallon; and mustard, $5 a bottle.

Early in August of 1864, Admiral Farragut with twenty-six ships and a land force attacked Fort Gaines and Fort Morgan guarding Mobile Bay, a harbor for blockade runners bringing supplies for the Confederate war effort from ports in the West Indies. After a fierce naval battle with Confederate ships blocking entrance to the ship channel, and the firing from land, the forts surrendered. This Union victory sealed off Mobile from blockade runners and was a blow to the Confederacy.

While Union gunboats were operating south from Cairo, Illinois, Flag-Officer David Glascoe Farragut, commanding the West Gulf Blockading Squadron, received word that a squadron of bomb-vessels under Commander D.D. Porter would join his fleet. When these vessels arrived, his orders were to attack the forts guarding New Orleans — Ft. St. Philip on the eastern bank of the Mississippi River, and Ft. Jackson opposite on the western bank.

On a dark night with a haze over the water, Farragut gave the order to advance up the Mississippi River, blocked with heavy chains. The fleet was soon discovered and the battle began. Guns on Union mortar boats engaged in a duel with guns in the forts. Confederate warships shelled and rammed the invading fleet. Fire rafts floated dangerously among the vessels. Through the debris of a fierce battle, Farragut reached New Orleans on April 24, 1862 and demanded the surrender of the city. The mayor defiantly refused to lower the Confederate flag on the City Hall, although troops under General Lovell had departed to escape capture. With Union soldiers, General Benjamin F. Butler occupied New Orleans, closing the port to blockade runners and supplies from foreign countries. However, the capture of New Orleans still left most of the Mississippi River under Confederate control between that city and Cairo.

When Lincoln became President, the United States Navy had forty-two ships carrying one hundred and eighty-two guns with which to start a blockade immediately. In December of 1864, the Navy had nearly 700 vessels and others being built. Of these, the fastest ships-of-war were divided into four squadrons: the North Atlantic, the South Atlantic, the Eastern Gulf Squadron, and the Western Gulf Squadron. To outrun the Union fleet, the long, narrow, low-in-the-water and swift blockade runner, painted a dull gray, was built in British shipyards for the Confederate Navy. This naval war gradually reduced supplies for the South and hastened the end of the conflict, not only on the sea but also on the inland rivers.

OPENING THE MISSISSIPPI RIVER
(THE WESTERN CAMPAIGN)

THE GOAL IN THE WEST was to gain control of the Mississippi River and cut off supplies, especially food, coming from Texas, Arkansas, and Louisiana to maintain the Confederate Army. Early in February, 1862, A.H. Foote, commanding gunboats, and Ulysses S. Grant, in charge of an army, left Cairo to attack Fort Henry on the Tennessee River. Foote's gunboats won a victory, and Fort Henry was taken. While Foote was moving his small fleet back to the Ohio River and up the Cumberland to Fort Donelson, Grant marched his men overland through mud, sleet and snow. After a number of Confederates had escaped down the river and over flooded roads, General S.B. Buckner asked Grant for terms of surrender. He replied:

"No terms, except an immediate and unconditional surrender, can be accepted. I propose to move immediately upon your works."

Thus, Grant acquired the nickname of "Unconditional Surrender Grant."

After the fall of Fort Donelson, Union armies pushed south in Tennessee to meet the Confederate defenders in one of the bloodiest battles of the war at Shiloh Church in Pittsburg Landing. The South lost General Albert Sidney Johnston in this battle in which able leaders of both armies were engaged. The Confederates included Beauregard, Bragg, and Johnston. On the Union side were Grant, Sherman, and Buell.

NAVAL COMBAT OFF FORT WRIGHT IN THE MISSISSIPPI RIVER
MAY 8, 1862

This sketch of the battle between Union and Confederate gunboats at Fort Wright, north of Memphis, Tennessee is typical of the combats on the Mississippi River from Cairo to New Orleans. Union men in row boats are rescuing Confederates from their sinking ship, the *Mallory*, after it was rammed by the Union ironclad, the *St. Louis*.

Harper's Weekly, 1862

In opening up the Mississippi River from the north, Union forces were busy clearing out pockets of resistance behind them on the west side of the river. Grant met his first gunfire at Belmont, Missouri, in November of 1861, after leaving Cairo, Illinois. Then followed the battles of Pea Ridge, Missouri; New Madrid, Missouri; Pea Ridge, Arkansas; Island No. 10, Tennessee; Memphis, Tennessee; and six months later, closing the year of 1862, Prairie Grove, Arkansas.

Soon after Shiloh, President Lincoln appointed Grant commander of Union forces in Tennessee and Mississippi. Grant mapped a campaign to capture the strong Confederate base closing the Mississippi River at Vicksburg.

As the campaign in the West slowly progressed, Lincoln considered the drastic measure of freeing the slaves in the seceded states in order to win more northern support and hasten the end of the war.

LINCOLN'S EMANCIPATION PROCLAMATION

MANY CONSCIENTIOUS PERSONS, strongly opposed to slavery, felt it would be a great injustice to the Negroes to free them all at one time, when they had no place to go. During the 1830's and 1840's when the spirit of reform was sweeping over the nation, the American Colonization Society supported a plan to solve humanely the problem of slavery. The plan was to return the Negro to his homeland, from which he had been taken against his wishes. The slaves would be sent to the African republic of Liberia. There they would be free men and both slavery and the slave trade would be forbidden by law.

Children all over the country saved their pennies and brought them to Sunday schools to support this project. Hundreds of Negro families were transported to Liberia with these funds. There they could start life all over again in their own republic in their native Africa. In the *Norfolk Herald* in 1850 this news item appeared:

The ship, *Liberia Packet* from Baltimore, has arrived in Hampton Roads, where she received on board yesterday the colored emigrants who have been collecting here for some days previous. They amount in all to 141 persons — 59 from North Carolina, 49 from the Valley of Virginia, and 33 from Lower Virginia. A large part of them are children and young persons. Most of them were emancipated for the purpose of emigration; the rest were born free.

Lincoln's plan was to free the slaves gradually, a few here and there. He would allow the planters time to find other laborers for their fields and industry time to find jobs for the new freedmen. To the end, he believed that slaveholders should be repaid for their losses. With a pencil and pad Lincoln figured that all the slaves in the loyal border states could be purchased for $400 a head, and the total sum be no more than the cost of 87 days of war. No bloodshed, no destruction, no heartaches.

In the summer of 1862, the second year of the war, Lincoln invited prominent leaders in Missouri, Kentucky, Maryland, and the mountain region of Virginia (West Virginia in 1863) to come to Washington to talk over this plan. The men from the border states told the President that soldiers from their states were giving their lives on the battlefields to save the Union and not to free the Negroes.

In the states which had seceded, slaves were toiling to support the war against the North. They raised food for the soldiers

303

Free Negroes boarding ship to settle in the Liberian Republic on the western coast of Africa.

and erected fortifications on the battlefields. Some Negroes carried guns and followed their masters as soldiers of the Confederacy. With his wartime powers as Commander-in-chief of the Army and Navy, the President had the authority to do anything that would hinder the enemy and shorten the war. As a war measure, then, he issued the Emancipation Proclamation, declaring:

That on the first day of January, 1863, all persons held as slaves within any state or designated part of a state, the people whereof shall then be in rebellion against the United States, shall be then, thenceforward, and forever free.

This act freed the slaves in the rebellious states. It did not free the slaves in the border states nor in loyal sections of seceded states. It won the abolitionists to stronger support of the war and made many people in other countries the friends of the North. The aim of the war was now two-fold: preserve the Union and abolish slavery.

The news of the proclamation leaked through to remote plantations of the South and created a problem. Many Negroes packed their few belongings in any old cart or homemade wagon they could get and started down the road. They did not know where they were going nor how they were going to get there. They only knew that they wanted to work for "Massa Link'un." These homeless families were a burden to the Union armies who were obliged to provide them with food, clothing, and medicine. Most of them, however, were willing workers and did chores around camp. Some officers organized Negro regiments.

Many slaves, when freed, chose to remain on the plantations of their owners where they had something to eat, a place to sleep, and a master's family to take care of them. The thousands who deserted their homes had their freedom but they often suffered from cold, hunger, and neglect. As Lincoln had hoped, the emancipation of the slaves hampered the war effort in the South. With the master gone to war and no slaves to do the work, plantation after plantation fell into ruin. The crops withered in the fields. There were few jobs for the new freedmen because their former owners had little or no money to pay them wages. Both whites and blacks suffered alike in the upheaval. The Emancipation Proclamation was a blow to the Confederacy.

FALL OF VICKSBURG

THE COMBINED MANEUVERS of Grant and Sherman prevented General Joseph E. Johnston, Confederate commander in the West, from joining forces with Lieutenant General John C. Pemberton who was defending Vicksburg. The Union armies on land and gunboats on the Mississippi River laid siege to Vicksburg.

While the Battle of Gettysburg was being fought in Pennsylvania, the long siege of Vicksburg was ending in Mississippi. For six weeks the river town had been shut off from the world. Grant's army guarded the land approach and Porter's gunboats shelled the river front. The townspeople were near starvation. The only meat left was mule flesh. Other foods on hand were rice, sugar, molasses, and a little corn.

About eight o'clock on the morning of July 3, 1863, a white flag was raised above the Confederate fort. In a short time two officers in Confederate gray were led, blindfolded, into the Union lines. They carried a message from their commander, Lieutenant General Pemberton, asking for terms of surrender. Grant replied with the same terms offered to the commander of Fort Donelson on the Cumberland River, in 1862, when he acquired the nickname of "Unconditional Surrender" Grant. Then he paid this compliment to the enemy:

At the same time, myself and men, and officers of this army testify to the distinguished gallantry with which the defense of Vicksburg has been conducted.

At three in the afternoon Pemberton and Grant met in a grove of peach and fig trees. After shaking hands they sat down on the grass. The two men were friends. They had fought together at Buena Vista and Monterey in the Mexican War. Pemberton, somewhat embarrassed, pulled up blades of grass while Grant puffed on his long cigar. The commanders talked for more than an hour while both Union and Confederate soldiers looked on from a distance — and wondered. Would the terms be harsh?

The next day was the Fourth of July. After the Confederates had stacked their arms and surrendered their ammunition, Union bands led their regiments into the city of Vicksburg. The musicians played southern songs as well as northern airs to the delight of the crowds that jammed the sidewalks. Under Rear Admiral Porter the Union Navy paraded on the Mississippi River. Gay pennants and signal flags trimmed the ironclads from stem to stern. Dressed in white the sailors lined the railings and waved their hats to the crowds on the steaming levee. The day was hot and humid. Everyone appeared to be excited except Grant. Riding through the streets he calmly puffed his cigar as if the victory was nothing more than another day's work.

Grant's victory at Vicksburg caused the fall of Port Hudson, north of Baton Rouge. It opened the Mississippi River to the Gulf of Mexico, cutting the South in two. There was great rejoicing in the North. In *Harper's Weekly* a poem appeared, celebrating the event beginning with these lines:

> The Opening of the Mississippi River
> Hail! mighty river!
> Free from thy springs to the sea forever,
> From thy mountain springs to the Southern Sea.
> Free heritage of the millions free.

TO DIVIDE THE CONFEDERACY AGAIN

AFTER THE FALL of Vicksburg and the opening of the Mississippi River, a new campaign began to divide the Confederacy by driving a wedge between the Gulf States and the Atlantic seaboard. Plans for both

the Union attack and the Confederate defense centered in eastern Tennessee where deposits of coal, iron, and nitrate were being used in manufacturing guns and ammunition for the Confederate armies. The focal point was Chattanooga.

With General Burnside approaching Knoxville through Cumberland Gap on the east, and Sherman ready to move from the Mississippi River on the west, General Braxton Bragg evacuated Chattanooga to escape the danger of being cut off from supplies. On September 19 and 20, 1863, after General James Longstreet arrived with troops from Virginia, Bragg faced the Union army under General William S. Rosecrans at Chickamauga in northern Georgia. Although General George H. Thomas held his section of Union troops on the field until dark on the last day, the Confederates won the battle. For his stand, Thomas was named, "The Rock of Chickamauga," and soon replaced Rosecrans.

A month later, after closing the Mississippi campaign, Grant arrived in Chattanooga to take command of all the Union forces. When Sherman reached Chattanooga with more troops, Grant made plans to break out of the city, walled in with mountains and occupied by Confederates. He dispatched Hooker with soldiers outnumbering the enemy six to one, to Lookout Mountain. In a dense fog, about five hundred feet from the top, a fight took place, known in history as "The Battle above the Clouds."

On the same day, with the same advantages in numbers, Grant sent Sherman to Missionary Ridge, but the decisive battle was not fought until the next day. When Sherman's advance was repulsed, Grant sent Thomas to capture the rifle pits at the bottom of the ridge. To the surprise of the Union officers in charge, the men started climbing the rugged face of the mountain and kept on climbing although the Confederate defenders rolled rocks and cannonballs down the steep slope. After Missionary Ridge was taken on November 25, 1863, Bragg's army retreated, leaving Chattanooga to the Union. President Davis replaced him with General Joseph E. Johnston.

After the victory at Chattanooga, Grant sent reinforcements to relieve Burnside under seige by Longstreet's Corps in Knoxville. A few days before these Union troops arrived, after failing to take the city in a final assault, Longstreet retreated to the North Carolina border and later joined Lee in Virginia. The way was opened into Alabama, Georgia, and South Carolina.

Lincoln summoned Grant to Washington. On March 9, 1864, in the White House, the President promoted Ulysses S. Grant to the highest rank in the United States Army, giving him command of all the armies. Grant took the field in Virginia and appointed General William Tecumseh Sherman to his former command in the West. Sherman outlined a plan to take Atlanta, and after many skirmishes, entered the city on the second day of September, although the Confederates under General Nathan Bedford Forrest and General John H. Morgan continued the fight behind him and threatened his supply lines.

After destroying railroads, machine shops, factories, munitions, and food stores in Atlanta, Sherman divided his army into four parts. The four sections followed four separate routes, cutting a path of destruction forty to sixty miles wide through the state of Georgia. His orders to his soldiers were: "Forage for your food." What did this mean to the people living in the path of the invading army? In his report to military headquarters at Washington Sherman wrote:

We have consumed the corn and fodder in the region of country thirty miles on either side of a line from Atlanta to Savannah, as also the sweet potatoes, cattle, hogs, sheep, and poultry, and have carried away more than ten thousand horses and mules, as well as a countless number of slaves. I estimate the damage done to the state of Georgia and its military resources at one hundred millions of dollars; at least twenty millions of which has been to our advantage, and the remainder is simple waste and destruction.

Sherman's march from Atlanta to Savannah enraged the southerners more than any other event of the War Between the States. It was a harsh measure but it hastened the end of the war by destroying the main sources of supply for the Confederate armies.

With only about 15,000 poorly equipped soldiers to defend Savannah, General William J. Hardee arranged for surrender, and then left the city, taking his troops to join the Confederate army of General Joseph E. Johnston in North Carolina. A few days before Christmas, 1864, Sherman's Army occupied Savannah, five weeks after leaving Atlanta. A few weeks later, these Union soldiers started north through the Carolinas toward Virginia, living off the country and destroying property. Sherman was on his way to join Grant in Virginia, the main battleground of the war.

THE VIRGINIA CAMPAIGN

THE WAR BETWEEN THE STATES began and ended in Virginia. For four years, armies advanced and retreated within the borders of the state while Confederate soldiers tried to reach Washington, and Union soldiers tried to capture Richmond. Although the contending armies met first at Manassas, the Battle of Bull Run, in 1861, the organized campaign in Virginia did not get under way until the spring of 1862. George B. McClellan, leader of the Army of the Potomac, decided to transport his troops to Fortress Monroe and attack Richmond by moving up the peninsula between the James River and the York River.

After losing a month in the siege of Yorktown, which gave the Confederates time to build defenses of their capital, General McClellan advanced to Fair Oaks and fought a battle about eight miles from Richmond. Meanwhile Stonewall Jackson's raids up the Shenandoah Valley were a constant threat to Washington. Between June 25 and July 1, 1862, the combined forces of Generals Robert E. Lee, Stonewall Jackson, and James Longstreet defended Richmond in the Seven Days' Battle at Mechanicsville, Gaines' Mill, Savage Station, Glendale or Frazer's Farm, and Malvern Hill. In seven days of fighting, the Confederate loss in killed and wounded doubled that of the Union, but McClellan lost seven to one in prisoners. Total casualties for the South were nearly 21,000, and for the North, almost 16,000.

With the peninsular campaign a failure, McClellan retreated to be nearer Washington. After driving back the Army of the Potomac to the defense of the national capital, Lee marched with Stonewall Jackson through Frederick, Maryland on his first invasion of the North. They fought the Battle of Antietam, and recrossed the Potomac River into Virginia. A few days later, on September 22, Lincoln called his

cabinet to a meeting and read his Proclamation of Emancipation – to become law on January 1, 1863, if the war continued. Early in November of 1862, Lincoln removed McClellan and gave the command of the Army of the Potomac to General Ambrose E. Burnside. The people in the North had lost their confidence in McClellan who, they thought, moved too slowly – they wanted fewer defeats.

Burnside planned to capture Richmond by advancing due south. After crossing the Rappahannock River on pontoon bridges, he met Lee's army at Fredericksburg on the thirteenth of December, lost the battle, and retreated across the river. Thus ended 1862, without victory for either side, and the war continued, not only in Virginia, but also in the West. On the last day of the year, General William S. Rosecrans checked the advance of a Confederate army under General Braxton Bragg near Murfreesboro, Tennessee.

Six weeks after Burnside's defeat at Fredericksburg, Lincoln appointed General Joseph Hooker, the "fighting general," to his command. After reorganizing his army, Hooker advanced toward Richmond. On the first of May a battle developed at Chancellorsville, which lasted several days. In a flank attack, Jackson helped Lee to defeat the Union army, and forced Hooker to retreat across the Rappahannock River. It was a costly victory, however. During a lull in the battle, Jackson and some of his staff were riding in front of the Confederate lines at dusk to observe the Union moves. Thinking the men on horseback were enemy scouts, Jackson and his party were fired upon by their own men. Jackson was seriously wounded and died a few days later. Lee wrote to his son:

"You will have heard of the death of

General Jackson. It is a terrible loss. I do not know how to replace him. Any victory would be dear at such a cost . . . . "

After Chancellorsville, both Hooker and Lee rested their armies. Lee had received recruits and decided to invade Pennsylvania. Since many enlistments in Hooker's army would end in June, Lincoln issued a proclamation on June 15, calling 100,000 state militia into the Union armies. When Lee's army headed toward the Shenandoah Valley, Hooker started north. At Frederick, Maryland, Hooker was replaced by General George C. Meade. Lee's army was crossing the border of Pennsylvania and the people had no faith in the man who had lost the Battle of Chancellorsville. Meade marched north to keep the Army of the Potomac between Lee's Army of Northern Virginia and the city of Washington. Neither Lee nor Meade chose Gettysburg for a battlefield. They merely happened to meet there.

The little town of Gettysburg nestles in a mile-wide valley formed by two ridges, shaped like a horseshoe. Upon these ridges the two armies struggled for three days in one of the bloodiest battles of the war. The fight began on the morning of July first. It ended during the night of July third after Pickett's brave but disastrous charge up Cemetery Ridge. Almost half of the 15,000 men who charged the Union lines did not return. During that night Lee's troops retreated into Maryland. They left their dead and wounded on the field of battle.

The next morning General Meade, in command of the Union Army, prepared his weary men for another attack. None came. Instead of fighting, the Union soldiers observed the Fourth in carrying off the wounded and burying the dead. The peaceful little village of Gettysburg was one vast hospital. After three days of hiding in cellars from shells that toppled chimneys and wrecked houses, the citizens came out to care for the wounded, both Union and Confederate. The casualties at Gettysburg were frightful, with over 43,000 men killed, wounded, or missing. Never again did a Confederate army invade the North. The Fourth of July in 1863 marked the turning point of the War Between the States. Lee's defeat at Gettysburg uncovered Richmond and opened the railroad lines of Virginia to enemy attack. Grant's victory at Vicksburg cleared the Mississippi River to the Gulf of Mexico.

LINCOLN SPEAKS AT GETTYSBURG

ON THE NINETEENTH of November in 1863, the little town of Gettysburg was crowded with visitors. They had come from many states to see the dedication of a national cemetery. It was the last resting place of the Union and Confederate soldiers who had fallen in the Battle of Gettysburg.

The speaker for this important event was Edward Everett, a brilliant man and a famous orator. After the opening prayer Everett stepped to the front of the outdoor platform to face the huge crowd, standing on the same ridge where so many men had died. Everett began to speak:

Overlooking these broad fields now reposing from the labors of the waning year, the mighty Alleghenies dimly towering above us, the graves of our brethren beneath our feet, it is with hesitation that I raise my poor voice to break the eloquent silence of God and Nature. But the duty to which you called me must be performed.

It was. He spoke for two hours in the polished language of a learned man. Behind him on the platform sat the President, Cabinet officials, state governors, and army officers. Once during the long speech Lincoln drew two small sheets of paper from a coat pocket and glanced at them. When Everett finally sat down, a glee club from Baltimore sang an ode composed for this occasion. Then Lincoln rose slowly from his seat. He had two slips of paper in his hand. Because he was President of the United States, Lincoln had been invited to attend. The committee in charge felt obligated to ask him to make a few remarks after the speaker of the day had delivered his oration.

The President's face was lined and care-worn. Two years of war had aged him. A news photographer busied himself getting his camera ready, poking his head under the black hood and out again. He was going to take the President's picture while he spoke. There was plenty of time. Lincoln spoke slowly and thoughtfully:

Four score and seven years ago our fathers brought forth on this continent a new nation conceived in liberty and dedicated to the proposition that all men are created equal. Now we are engaged in a great civil war testing whether that nation or any nation so conceived and so dedicated can long endure. We are met on a great battlefield of that war. We have come to dedicate a portion of that field as a final resting place for those who here gave their lives that this nation might live. It is altogether fitting and proper that we should do this. But in a larger sense we can not dedicate — we can not consecrate — we can not hallow this ground. The brave men living and dead who struggled here have consecrated it far above our poor power to add or detract. The world will little note nor long remember what we say here but it can never forget what they did here. It is for us the living rather to be dedicated here to the unfinished work which they who fought here have thus far so nobly advanced. It is

rather for us to be here dedicated to the great task remaining before us — that from these honored dead we take increased devotion to that cause for which they gave the last full measure of devotion — that we here highly resolve that these dead shall not have died in vain — that this nation under God shall have a new birth of freedom — and that government of the people, by the people, and for the people shall not perish from the earth.

The world did note and does still remember what he said. One of the reporters wrote in his paper:

The oration by Mr. Everett was smooth and cold. The few words of the President were from the heart to the heart. It was as simple — and earnest a word as was ever spoken.

Everett's two-hour oration is scarcely known, but Lincoln's five-minute speech has been memorized by millions of Americans. The photographer, taken by surprise, tossed off the black hood and stared blankly at the platform. The speech was finished and he had failed to get the President's picture.

LINCOLN'S REELECTION AND THE END OF THE WAR

AFTER GETTYSBURG, the governments of both the United States of America and the Confederate States of America drafted more men into their armies. Yet, the war lagged in Virginia while decisive battles in the West were engaging many troops on both sides after the fall of Vicksburg. Early in March of 1864, with the Mississippi River opened to the Gulf of Mexico and Union soldiers moving eastward in the Tennessee Valley, Grant commanded the armies of the

United States, with his headquarters in the field. That final field was Virginia and the final goal, Richmond.

The people of the North were shocked when Union casualties in thirty days numbered nearly 54,000 men in three battles — Wilderness, Spottsylvania, and Cold Harbor. The long siege of Petersburg cost the Union over 24,000 men — killed, wounded, captured, or missing. While Grant was pounding at Richmond, General A.J. Early of the Confederacy and General Philip H. Sheridan of the Union were raiding the Shenandoah Valley, destroying crops, livestock, and property that might provide supplies for their rival armies.

According to the Constitution of the United States, an election occurs every four years, during war and peace, giving the citizens the opportunity to choose a President and members of Congress. In November of 1864, Lincoln was re-elected. On March 4, 1865, he was inaugurated to serve a second term as President of the United States. The day began with a violent storm of rain, wind, and hail, making the unpaved streets of Washington almost impassable with mud. The weather failed to hold back the crowd that gathered in the open park in front of the Capitol. Umbrellas gave scant protection to the wide skirts worn by the ladies. After a sudden shower silks and satins hung in limp folds over the bulging hoops and water dripped to the ground from the full, deep flounces. Men in rainsoaked suits and mud-spattered boots edged closer to the President's stand. The weather! Who cared? The crowd had come to hear Lincoln's second inaugural speech. What would he say to the secessionists?

About noon when the procession wheeled into Pennsylvania Avenue, the

GENERAL ULYSSES S. GRANT AT COLD HARBOR, VIRGINIA

During the summer of 1864, Grant's goal was the capture of Richmond, the Confederate capital. The city was strongly defended by the main Confederate army under General Lee. At Cold Harbor, northeast of Richmond, Grant ordered his whole army to attack the Confederate works. Although the battle was decided in a short time, the Union army was defeated and suffered heavy losses.

clouds had scattered and the sun was shining. Closed umbrellas were used for canes by tired spectators. Although the crowd was as large as in 1861, it was not so jubilant. Even with bands playing, bells clanging, and guns firing, the second inauguration of Lincoln was a rather solemn affair. Four years of war cast its shadow upon the ceremonies. When the President began to speak, the people listened in tense silence. The closing lines of his address brought hope to the South and tears to the eyes of many in the throng. Lincoln said:

With malice toward none; with charity for all; with firmness in the right, as God gives us to see the right, let us strive on to finish the work we are in; to bind up the nation's wounds; to care for him who shall have borne the battle and for his widow, and his orphan — to do all which may achieve and cherish a just and a lasting peace among ourselves, and with all nations.

Perhaps, the President's kind words, "with malice toward none," encouraged General Lee to ask for terms of surrender a month later.

The two commanders met in a farmhouse at Appomattox Court House, near Richmond, Virginia. Ulysses S. Grant and Robert E. Lee shook hands. At first they talked briefly not of surrender but of their campaign in Mexico. Perhaps Grant recalled the time when he was only a lieutenant in charge of wagon trains and Lee was a captain, the engineer who had built the road through marshy land into Mexico City. Maybe he thought of the day when his loaded wagons rumbled over the lava-bed road and Lee reined his horse to ride with him, jogging along behind the mule-carts. Then the conversation shifted to terms of surrender. Grant wrote the terms as the two men talked. The orders

GENERAL ROBERT E. LEE ON "TRAVELLER"

Valentine Museum

were most generously written. Grant handed them to the Confederate general:

Appomattox Court House
April 9, 1865
General R.E. Lee, Commanding C.S.A.

— I propose to receive the surrender of the Army of Northern Virginia on the following terms, to wit:

Rolls of all the officers and men, to be made in duplicate, one copy to be given to an officer designated by me, the other to be retained by such officers as you may designate. Officers to give their individual parole not to take up arms against the Government of the United States — and each company or regimental commander sign a like parole for the men of their commands. The arms, artillery and public property to be paraded and stacked, and turned over to officers appointed by me to receive them. This will not embrace the side arms of the officers nor their private horses nor baggage. This done each officer and man will be allowed to return to their homes not to be disturbed by the United States authority so long as they observe their parole, and the laws in force where they may reside.

Very Respectfully,
U.S. Grant, Lieut. General

The Confederate officers were delighted to learn that they were not to be paraded in Washington and humiliated. Grant added that cavalrymen who furnished their own mounts should take them home "for the spring plowing." Twenty thousand rations of bread and meat were issued for the Confederate soldiers, who had been reduced to eating parched corn. Enough supplies arrived the next day to add sugar, coffee, and salt to these rations. After the surrender had been arranged, General Lee rode away on his iron-gray horse, "Traveller." Grant stood in the doorway and saluted in silence. As Lee passed through the Confederate lines, soldiers vied for the honor of marching by his side.

The next day, General Lee dispatched a farewell to his army, closing with these lines:

You will take with you the satisfaction that proceeds from the consciousness of duty faithfully performed; and I earnestly pray that a merciful God will extend to you His blessing and protection. With an increasing admiration of your constancy and devotion to your country, and a grateful remembrance of your kind and generous consideration of myself, I bid you an affectionate farewell.

In a few days the joy of the people changed to sorrow. On the evening of April 14, 1865 the President and Mrs. Lincoln attended a performance of the play, *Our American Cousin,* at Ford's Theater in Washington. Shortly after ten o'clock John W. Booth, an anarchist, slipped into their box unnoticed and fired the fatal shot. Booth jumped down to the stage, waved a dagger, and shouted the state motto of Virginia, "Sic Semper Tyrannis" (Thus be it always to tyrants). In the excitement he escaped through a back door, mounted his horse, and rode away into the night before the audience realized what he had done. Lincoln's assassination turned joy into grief. The southerners, too, mourned his loss.

Four years of war ended at Appomattox. From 1861 to 1865, approximately 4,000,000 men had carried arms in defense of their views of states rights under the Constitution of the United States. Can a state secede? The War Between the States answered that question by force of arms. Yet, a hundred years later, citizens in all parts of the country were still debating the meaning of states rights under the Constitution. A military victory does not always change the minds of men.

Slavery, a cause of disputes from the beginning of the nation, was abolished forever by the Thirteenth Amendment to the Constitution:

Neither slavery nor involuntary servitude, except as a punishment for crime — shall exist within the United States, or any place subject to their jurisdiction.

Although the wounds of war heal slowly, people living in the North, South, East, and West began to feel that they belonged to one another. A new spirit of nationalism took root and began to grow.

THE MONROE DOCTRINE IS TESTED

DURING THE FIRST fifty years of its independence, the republic of Mexico had not been able to maintain a stable government for any length of time. Ambitious leaders seeking political power kept the nation in turmoil. While revolutions followed revolutions and leaders rose and fell, taxes became a burden to the Mexican people. Their rulers borrowed money from European bankers in the name of the Mexican Government, although they had reason to suspect they might not be in office long enough to repay the loans.

In 1861, the year that the War Between the States began, Benito Juarez, President of Mexico, stopped payments on these debts for a time. The following year, Great Britain, Spain, and France joined hands and captured Vera Cruz to compel payment of money owed to the citizens of these three countries. Napoleon III, Emperor of France, wanted the three powers to occupy Mexico City in defiance of the Monroe Doctrine.

Great Britain and Spain withdrew. Napoleon III went ahead, alone. During the summer of 1863 French troops took possession of the capital, Mexico City, overthrew the republic, and established a monarchy.

Napoleon III persuaded Maximilian, younger brother of Francis Joseph, Emperor of Austria, to accept the throne of Mexico. This good natured archduke was deceived into believing that the Mexican people wanted him to rule. In 1864 Maximilian and his beautiful young wife arrived in Mexico. They were welcomed by Mexicans who were weary of revolutions and were willing to try a monarchy. However, the Mexican people resented a foreigner whose throne was upheld by foreign soldiers. Troops were organized under Porfirio Diaz and Benito Juarez to drive out the French.

When the War Between the States ended in 1865, the United States had an army of one million war veterans. William H. Seward, Secretary of State, was in a position to remind the French Emperor that the Monroe Doctrine was still part of the nation's policy. Seward's reminder must have been rather firm. Napoleon III suddenly ordered the withdrawal of French troops from Mexico, declaring "I spontaneously decided upon the recall of our army." At the same time this message was dispatched to the French Minister in Washington:

> The Emperor has decided that the French troops shall quit Mexico in three detachments. You will please inform the Secretary of State, (Seward) officially of this decision.

The withdrawal of the French troops was a diplomatic victory for Seward, but a death sentence for Maximilian. He was shot by Mexicans at Queretaro on July 19, 1867. His tragic end discouraged European princes from ignoring the Monroe Doctrine and seeking thrones in the Western Hemisphere.

MAP:

WA23r
Atlas of American History by Edgar B. Wesley

Chapter 17

The Old South Begins a New Life

THE SHARECROPPER SYSTEM DEVELOPS

A YOUNG CONFEDERATE officer in his gray uniform rode up a long lane of moss-covered oaks to the big white house which he called home. No servant waited to take his horse to the barn and no loved one crossed the porch to welcome him. After the fall of Vicksburg in 1863, his family had fled to Carolina to escape the Union armies which swept over the Mississippi. The shutters were closed. The door was locked. The place was deserted.

The officer walked around the house, stumbling through his mother's flower beds where weeds occupied the berths of hyacinths and jonquils. A few yards behind the house he found the kitchen of home-burned brick and nearby, the log house where slaves had done the family washing. A little farther on he came to the smokehouse. Hams and sides of bacon had been cured there in hog-killing time. He poked his head inside sniffing for the old familiar smell of smoking pork and burning wood. The rafters were empty.

Through weeds waist-high he stomped a path to the poultry yard, the pigeon roost, and the dove cote. He stood still, listening for the quaint call of the guinea hens and the startled warning of the peacock at the approach of strangers. Well he knew the fowls had been roasted and eaten by the invading army that lived off the land. He passed the barn without hearing a neigh of a horse or the bray of a mule. The stock had been taken to pull the supply wagons of a Union army or as mounts for Union cavalry. A few vines of beans clung to the fence of the vegetable garden where okra, peppers, cabbage, onions, eggplant, peas, and squashes were grown to feed his family and the hundred slaves his father had owned. In the orchard hard green knobs on the branches of peach trees brought a ray of hope. Something was still growing.

Walking back to the house he pondered what to do. He had nothing left but land. As he gazed down the tree-lined lane, he saw a mule cart driving up to the carriage entrance of the old mansion. In the cart was one of his former slaves with his wife and children. The soldier smiled and stepped forward to greet him. Both were bankrupt — the former master and the former slave. One was a landowner without labor to cultivate his fields. The other was a farmer without an acre to plow. The two men made a deal.

315

"How about planting cotton on shares?" the owner asked. "I'll borrow enough money to feed us until we sell the crop. Then you take half and I'll take half."

The freedman gladly moved into his cabin on the old home ground. The sharecropper system aided former masters and former slaves in making a difficult adjustment. This plan partially restored agriculture all over the South. The sharecropper would get from one third to one half of the value of the crop.

White families, too poor to own land, also farmed plots of ground on the shares. After the War Between the States, the sharecropper system largely replaced slave labor because the freedmen preferred it. They were working for themselves. In 1875 a planter in Arkansas told a Congressman who had gone down South to investigate conditions that cotton picking was more successful with free labor than with slaves:

During slave times we never got through picking so early or saved the whole crop in such good order as now. Sometimes the cotton was not all gathered before March. Now the fields are usually stripped clean before frost comes.

COTTON LEADS THE WAY TO PROSPERITY

THE NEGROES, reared on the land, knew how to plant, chop, and pick cotton. When freed they turned first to the only work they knew how to do well enough to earn a livelihood. In the mild climate they could find some kind of field work nearly every month in the year. With farming on the share the desolate plantations slowly took on new life. Many tracts of land remained idle because the owners waited for better times. Progress was slow during the first ten years after the war when the southerners were hampered by the troubles of the reconstruction period.

By 1880 a new spirit took root among the people. On the level lowlands of the southern states fields burst into fluffy blossoms as before the war. Negroes sang as of old to lighten the load of the long white picking bags which they dragged behind them down the rows of cotton plants. Mule-drawn wagons waited in line at busy cotton gins. As prosperity increased with the years, levees and docks groaned under the weight of cotton, baled with burlap and bound with metal tape. At Savannah, New Orleans, and Mobile deckhands heaved the bales of precious fiber on board the freighters to the rhythmic chant of the work song, "Roll The Cotton Down."

After the war the southerners knew they must find a way to reestablish themselves. What was the way? It was to build factories for turning cotton into cloth on or near the same plantations where it was grown. The planters could then sell their cotton near home. This would save the expense of hauling it long distances for shipment to the textile mills of Massachusetts, Connecticut, Rhode Island, and across the seas in Europe. Any country, to be independent of other nations, needs to manufacture enough products to supply its own people. Long before the War Between the States, far-seeing men had realized that the South, to become self-supporting and independent, must develop manufacturing and not depend entirely upon agriculture. The small plantation factories began with a Whitney gin which combed the sticky seeds from the cotton bolls. Little by little machines were added to spin the fiber.

Four years before the war began, one inventor advertised that his machine could gin and spin into yarn 100 bales of cotton, each one weighing 500 pounds, between the first of September and the first of March. His sales argument emphasized the fact that his machine could be operated by five little girls, eight to twelve years of age; by one girl twelve to fourteen; and by three older men and women too crippled or too feeble to toil in the fields. It was not necessary, the inventor declared, to use the strong young slaves needed for the hard labor of planting, chopping, and picking cotton. Thus, before the war, did child labor begin in the cotton mills of the South.

In 1860 there were about 160 cotton mills in the South. Their yearly output sold for more than $8,000,000. During the war these mills were worked so hard that the machinery wore out. Some were destroyed by invading armies. In 1870 there were fewer mills operating than in 1860. After the war when a number of the large plantations began to break up into smaller farms, factories moved into towns and villages. However, the growth was slow because people long accustomed to farm tools had to be trained to handle machinery. Then, too, there was little money to be invested. In some communities people invested their savings on an instalment plan to gather capital for mills. The subscriptions to the stock amounted to fifty cents or a dollar a week, and it took two to four years to pay for a single share. Since this sum was enough to pay in part for the machinery and the buildings, the factory equipment was often purchased on the instalment plan. In this way the southerners were able to develop industry to provide employment and raise their standard of living.

To establish a mill, some town boun-daries were changed to reduce taxes on a factory site. Sometimes, taxes were not assessed upon mills until they were operating on a paying basis. This same plan had been used in New England after the Revolutionary War to start manu-facturing and relieve the hard times that followed that war.

PREWAR CROPS CONTRIBUTE TO POSTWAR RECOVERY

WHILE COTTON LED the way toward a new industrial South, many people clung to the security of the land, earning their living in agriculture. To rebuild their broken fortunes the southerners started with the land, growing the same crops on the same plantations as before the war. From the early colonial days rice had been the leading crop in the lowlands of Georgia and South Carolina. With the invention of Whitney's gin, cotton had become the leading crop.

Twenty-five years before the Declaration of Independence, the first sugar cane had been planted in New Orleans. A transport with two hundred French soldiers on board had made a stopover for supplies at a port on San Domingo, an island in the West Indies. The vessel was bound for New Orleans. Jesuits living in San Domingo had asked the captain to take along some cane for the Jesuits in New Orleans. They also sent a few Negroes who knew how to make sugar from the plant. The Jesuits of New Orleans planted the cane in their garden and cultivated it with great care. French planters, out of curiosity, had accepted cane from the priests to try out on their own plantations. It took years to develop a variety of cane that would thrive in the climate of Louisiana and to develop a process for making sugar from the sweet syrup. Nearly fifty years after the first cane was planted in the Jesuits' garden, a Spanish planter proudly presented two loaves of white sugar to a Spanish official. At a grand dinner the official had displayed the little loaves of sugar and then dropped them into a pot of coffee. He gave each guest a sip of the sweetened drink. However, it took years to perfect a process for making white crystals which could be shipped long distances without spoiling.

After the War Between the States, sugar mills were built in the cane-growing region of Louisiana. This was the southeastern part through which the Mississippi River meanders to the Gulf of Mexico. Year after year, for centuries, flood waters of the great river had washed over this flat land, leaving a film of fresh earth washed down from upstream. In this rich black soil of the delta region where the climate was hot and humid, the sugar cane grew thick and tall.

However, while rice, cotton, and sugar were big plantation products, small crops did more to bring a new way of life to the South than did the big crops. When fruits and vegetables were produced, many of the large plantations began to break up into small farms and garden tracts. These products had been grown on the old plantations for household use but not much for the market. A Mississippi planter of pre-war days wrote in his diary:

March 4, 1844 — Received a lot of fruit trees from a nursery in Tennessee, 30 varieties of apple, 6 of plum, and 3 of pear.

April 9, 1845 — Ridging up one acre, intending to plant sweet potatoes. Planted squash on the 5th and the 8th.

April 24, 1845 — Planted my watermelon patch today.

February 14, 1854 — Sowed cabbage, lettuce, and celery yesterday, and peas, parsnips, and beets today. Planted 2 barrels of Irish potatoes on the 11th.

March 27, 1855 — Began planting cotton today.

April 9, 1855 — Planting rice near the creek.

April 18, 1855 — Sowed two acres of corn yesterday. Plowed one acre of millet today. Finished planting cotton on the 16th. Thermometer was 94 degrees yesterday.

April 20, 1855 — Planted two dozen hills of Chinese sugar cane received from Atlanta, Georgia.

June 27, 1855 — Magnificent rain; began this eve and rained about one half an hour. Glorious! GLORIOUS!

The Mississippi planter who raised fruits and vegetables to feed his family and his slaves, depended upon cotton, rice, and cane to bring in the money. Little did he dream that the day would come when hothouse gardeners in his neighborhood would sell their fresh vegetables daily, for cash, in northern states covered with snow. The warm Gulf States gradually became the winter gardens of Minnesota, Illinois, Ohio, New York, and Massachusetts. Fast transportation made this possible. The Railroad Act, passed by Congress during the war, provided for the building of the first continental railroad. Later, the railroad "boom" struck the South, opening new markets for new products from new farms and new factories. With more in common the two sections of the country grew closer together.

In increasing numbers Negro farm hands left the fields of Alabama and Mississippi to work in the growing industrial cities of Pennsylvania, Michigan, and Illinois. Northerners moved down South to establish mills and to go into business. Southerners went West. Some sold their fine plantations for two to ten dollars an acre. Some advertised their holdings for fifty cents an acre. A few returned

Confederate soldiers had sold out and migrated to Mexico and Brazil. General Lee, beloved southern leader, advised his countrymen to remain and "share the fate of their respective states. The South requires the aid of her sons now more than at any period of her history." Most of them stayed, enduring the stormy period of reconstruction. During this time perplexing problems arose that had not been solved even a hundred years later.

THE POSTWAR ADJUSTMENT WAS DIFFICULT FOR ALL

BEFORE ALL of the Confederate soldiers had surrendered, Lincoln was dead. The Vice President, Andrew Johnson, took over his high office and tackled the difficult problems of reconstruction in the seceded states. Although Johnson attempted to carry out Lincoln's plans, "with malice toward none," he failed. The confusion that existed was well expressed in an editorial appearing in the *North American Review*:

There is hardly a Senator or member of Congress now who does not think that he has hit upon a sovereign remedy for the southern ill, if he can only secure its adoption, but there is no general agreement on anything.

Objecting to the President's lenient policy, Congress demanded the right to deal with the southern problems.

Thaddeus Stevens, a lawyer elected to the House of Representatives from Pennsylvania, stirred the spirit of revenge in Congress. "Old Thad," in his seventies, was a bitter enemy of the South. Under his powerful leadership, Congress passed the Great Reconstruction Act on March 2,

1867, and two additional acts establishing military governments in the seceded states. All three acts were vetoed by President Johnson but were passed over his veto.

The seceded states were divided into five military districts, each of which was governed by a military officer. This officer supervised the registration of voters in his district. All men who had taken part in the war in any way were denied the right to vote. This ruling prevented most of the educated men and property owners from holding office or selecting any one for office. All male citizens "of whatever race, color, or previous condition" were allowed to vote and choose delegates to a constitutional convention where a new constitution would be framed to be submitted to the registered voters. If this constitution was ratified and accepted by Congress and the legislature ratified the Fourteenth Amendment, the state would belong to the Union again. The states would again send Representatives and Senators to Congress. The Fourteenth Amendment finally read:

All persons born or naturalized in the United States, and subject to the jurisdiction thereof, are citizens of the United States and of the state wherein they reside. No state shall make or enforce any law which shall abridge the privileges or immunities of citizens of the United States; nor shall any state deprive any person of life, liberty, or property, without due process of law; nor deny to any person within its jurisdiction the equal protection of the laws.

The main purpose of the Fourteenth Amendment was to protect the freed Negroes in their rights, including the vote. Other articles excluded former Confederates from the right to hold office until Congress restored their citizenship and outlawed the debts of the Confederacy.

The educated, planting families were not allowed to vote or hold office. With few exceptions, they had taken part in the war. For generations, the members of these families had been the governors, congressmen, judges, army officers, and legislators. The governments of the southern states were then operated by Negroes and poor whites, many of whom could neither read nor write. Unscrupulous men from the North settled in the South to take advantage of this situation. Although some may have been interested in helping to rebuild the South, the majority were there to make money for themselves and by any means.

In this period it was the fashion to carry traveling bags made of Brussels carpet in bright, flowery designs. Because many of these adventurers owned little except what they carried in their suitcases, they were nicknamed carpetbaggers.

Since the President objected to this injustice under military rule, "Old Thad" welcomed any opportunity to strike down his foe. On March 2, 1867, along with the Reconstruction Act, Congress passed the Tenure of Office Act, denying the President the right to discharge any member of his cabinet without consent of the Senate. Johnson removed his Secretary of War, Edwin M. Stanton, his enemy in the cabinet and a friend of Stevens. (According to the Constitution, a President of the United States can be impeached by the House of Representatives for failure to execute the law.) Johnson declared he had not failed to obey the Tenure of Office Act because Stanton had been appointed by Lincoln. In fiery speeches, "Old Thad" accused the President of "high crimes and misdemeanors" and called for his impeachment.

By a two-thirds vote of the House of Representatives, Johnson was impeached.

The Constitution provides that the Senate shall hold the trial of an impeached President, with the Chief Justice of the United States presiding. With the South under military rule, there were fifty-four Senators, and a two-thirds vote was necessary to convict Johnson. After nearly two months of the trial, the vote was taken on May 26, 1868. Chief Justice Salmon P. Chase, asked each Senator the same question:

"Is Andrew Johnson, President of the United States, guilty or not guilty of a high misdemeanor, as charged . . . . ?"

Each Senator rose from his seat and stood to answer.

"Guilty," said thirty-five.

"Not guilty," replied nineteen.

Johnson escaped removal from office by only one vote, and completed his term of office.

In 1868 Ulysses S. Grant, hero of Vicksburg and Appomattox and the most popular man in the nation, was elected President of the United States, to succeed Johnson. Grant, elected on the Republican ticket, supported the Congressional plan of reconstruction, which resulted in carpetbag rule in the South. Unscrupulous politicans spread the story that freedmen who voted the Republican ticket would receive "forty acres and a mule." Some Negroes came to the polls carrying a halter to take home the mule General Grant was to give them. Other swindlers sold, red, white, and blue sticks for one dollar each, for Negroes to use in staking off the forty acres the Government had in store for them. All freedmen were not so easily fooled. Many saved their meager earnings to buy land for themselves, sometimes forty acres from their former masters. They continued to live in the same neighborhood that was home to them. As a general rule the freedmen who chose to stay on their old plantations, earning wages or sharing crops, suffered less in making the adjustment from slavery to freedom than did those who uprooted themselves, and wandered from place to place looking for a free mule.

Under the protection of United States soldiers, elections were held to select delegates to conventions to form new constitutions. Most of the voters and candidates were Negroes or carpetbaggers, since all who had taken any part in the war were disfranchised. Because they were enjoying their privileges the delegates sometimes took many months to make a constitution. Then, when legislatures were chosen under the new constitution, the legislators extended the time of the sessions for the same reason. In South Carolina in 1873 three-fourths of the state legislature were Negroes, inexperienced in government. The public debt swelled to enormous proportions through unwise spending. In refurnishing the state house, five-dollar clocks were replaced by new ones costing $600; $4 looking glasses by $600 mirrors; and $1 chairs by new ones at $60 each. Taxes paid for a free restaurant for members where hams, oysters, and champagne were served. The rich state of Louisiana probably suffered more from carpetbag rule than any other.

Although many southerners had been pardoned by Congress and allowed to hold office, general amnesty was withheld. In May, 1872 an Act of Congress restored the right to vote and hold office to all former Confederates, except certain leaders like Jefferson Davis, President of the Con-

federacy, and Generals Joseph E. Johnston and G.T. Beauregard of the army. Not until June 6, 1898, was full amnesty granted to all southerners, except a few leaders, who had taken part in the war.

Although Grant was reelected in 1872 for another four years, the people were generally dissatisfied with his Administration by the end of his second term. Grant was a soldier rather than a statesman. Being honest himself, he failed to detect dishonesty in officials he selected for office. His Presidential years were marred with widespread corruption in government circles. Congress voted to raise the pay of the President, Cabinet officers, and Congressmen when the country was in the throes of a depression following the Panic of 1873. It was discovered that a "Whiskey Ring" had been cheating the Government out of millions of dollars in taxes and that Grant's own secretary was involved in the scandal.

Money was scarce and times were hard but Grant was still a popular man. Fearing he might decide to run for a third time, the House of Representatives passed a resolution that any departure from the two-term precedent set by Washington "would be unwise, unpatriotic, and fraught with peril to our free institutions."

In 1876 the Republicans nominated Rutherford B. Hayes, governor of Ohio, as their Presidential candidate at their convention in Cincinnati. The Democrats assembled in St. Louis and nominated Samuel J. Tilden of New York. Tilden was well known for his part in destroying the "Tweed Ring" that had ruled New York City with a political machine. Boss Tweed and his associates had stolen many millions of dollars from the taxpayers of New York by various schemes. Tilden was in the public eye while Hayes was little known outside his home state at Ohio. The vote was so close that the election was contested in four states, Oregon, South Carolina, Florida, and Louisiana. It was decided by a commission of five Representatives, five Senators, and five Associate Justices of the Supreme Court selected by the two houses of Congress. On March 2, Hayes was declared elected. He was secretly sworn into office the following day because the fourth of March was on Sunday in the year 1877.

Although the Democrats were disgruntled, the public soon learned that the new President was a fair-minded man. He knew how to choose strong and capable men for his Cabinet. He asked a former Confederate officer from Tennessee to be Postmaster General in his Cabinet. He even considered appointing the Confederate General, Joseph E. Johnston, as Secretary of War. The Republican Party would not approve that. President Hayes determined to bring the southerners back into the Union, in spirit as well as in form. He ordered the return of United States troops from the former seceded states where the carpetbag governments soon tottered and fell. The southerners themselves recovered control of their governments to begin the task of meeting the public debt piled up by the carpetbaggers; to restore business and find markets; and to rebuild their war-torn land. The year 1877 marks the end of an era when the South turned its back upon an old way of life to build a new way in the future.

EDUCATION BEGINS
ANEW AFTER WAR

ON MARCH 3, 1865, before Lee surrendered, Congress passed a bill establishing a "Bureau of Refugees, Freedmen, and Abandoned Lands," under the War Department. This Freedmen's Bureau was intended to aid the newly-freed slaves in adjusting to their new way of life. Hundreds of Negro families wandering from place to place had been a great burden to the Union armies. Some willingly chopped wood, dug trenches, and picked cotton in abandoned fields, and others did not understand why they should work when they were free.

BOOKER T. WASHINGTON SPEAKING IN SHREVEPORT, LOUISIANA

Born a slave in Virginia, Booker T. Washington was seven years old when the Emancipation Proclamation freed him, and his family moved to West Virginia. After receiving an education at Hampton Institute, he devoted his life to the education and betterment of his own people. He traveled widely, advising Negroes to save their money to buy farms, to go into business, and to be self-supporting and independent. For his great service, his bust was placed in the New York University Hall of Fame, a long road from a slave cabin on a plantation.

Tuskegee Institute

322

TOMPKINS HALL, TUSKEGEE INSTITUTE, TUSKEGEE, ALABAMA

Tompkins Hall is one of the buildings on the campus of Tuskegee Institute, the famous school founded by Booker T. Washington in 1881 for Negroes. This school started in a small shanty with about forty students, all adults. Booker T. Washington began with teaching freedmen how to earn a living in new ways as carpenters, bricklayers, blacksmiths, cooks, farmers, and many trades, along with general schooling. Today, the school provides courses for college degrees.

Education was necessary. It was the only way the freedmen could learn to take care of themselves. As the Union armies advanced, a number of schools were started in churches and old barracks. Here reading and writing were taught by Northern volunteers, ministers, and women from the neighboring plantations, where some of the freed Negroes had stayed on.

It was not uncommon to see children and white-haired grandfathers spelling out loud in a class on a wide front porch, or outdoors under magnolia and live oak trees.

After the war ended, the state legislature of Florida passed resolutions to "establish schools for freedmen when the number of children of persons of color, in any county or counties will warrant the same." Other states did likewise. However, laws for education were only a small beginning, and results were disappointing. Schools for both black and white children were few in number and the teachers were poorly trained. Under the Freedmen's Bureau, favorites of the carpetbaggers, some of whom could barely read and write, at times were hired to teach school. Negroes lost interest in poor schools, and the better teachers quit. When the Reconstruction period ended, property

323

owners were so burdened with debts piled up under carpetbag rule, that little money could be spared for education. Yet, as fast as possible, schools were built for both black and white children to give them the best education possible.

Learning to read and write was not enough. It took time for colleges and universities to recover from the ravages of war. In 1874, a professor in Louisiana University wrote in his diary:

GEORGE WASHINGTON CARVER IN HIS LABORATORY AT TUSKEGEE INSTITUTE

George Washington Carver, born of slave parents on a farm in Missouri near the end of the War Between the States, came to be known as "The Peanut Wizard." In his laboratory at Tuskegee Institute, he developed foods, beverages, medicines, cosmetics, dyes, paints, and numerous household products from peanuts. From the sweet potato he made about forty products. Dr. Carver received many medals, scrolls, and honorary degrees for his scientific experiments that included soil building, cotton-growing, and plant diseases.

Tuskegee Institute

Many a time during the year have we been doubtful of rations one and two days ahead — even sometimes of a morning we did not know that we could have anything for dinner. And this is a state school.

Private colleges also promoted education after the war. Among these schools was Tuskegee Institute in Alabama, founded for Negroes by Booker T. Washington. Although born a slave in 1856, Washington was educated at Hampton Institute in Virginia, an American Missionary Association school for training Negroes and Indians to be teachers and farmers, and to be self-supporting. At the age of twenty-five, Washington left Hampton Institute where he had been teaching, to become principal of a school in Tuskegee, Alabama. When he arrived, he learned that the school had not yet been built. On July 4, 1881, he opened his school in a shanty and enrolled forty students. Books and tools shared their time as they worked together. From this poor beginning grew Tuskegee Institute in which thousands of Negroes acquired skills in the trades and learned to make a living in new and better ways.

In 1896, Booker T. Washington invited the Negro scientist, Dr. George Washington Carver, then teaching at Iowa State College, to join the faculty of Tuskegee Normal and Industrial Institute, as director of the Department of Agriculture. Dr. Carver, also born in slavery, brought fame to Tuskegee where he developed many new products from sweet potatoes and peanuts. George Washington Carver — scientist, artist, and musician, and Booker T. Washington — teacher, author, and lecturer, are buried on the campus of the college where they gave years of their lives to educate their own people.

In a hundred years, with education and

ambition, the Negro has won a high place in the professions, sports, arts, and in many other phases of American life.

IN THE MOUNTAIN REGIONS

THE SOUTHERN mountain people, largely of Scotch Irish and English ancestry with a sprinkling of French, are the descendants of the first American settlers. Their forefathers weathered Atlantic gales in sailing ships bound for the Carolinas. On rugged hillsides in a wilderness, they cleared a few acres and planted corn. From trees chopped down to clear the land, they erected log cabins and fashioned their furniture. The woods were full of game and the streams were stocked with fish. Their hogs roamed in the forest to fatten on acorns and their cattle grazed on wild hay. These first Americans were a proud and independent people who raised their own food, wove their own cloth, made their own laws, and created their own fun. Most important, they fought for their rights as free men. Their descendants are living today in the valley of the Tennessee River which has its headwaters in the mountains of eastern Tennessee, northern Georgia, and western regions of Virginia and North Carolina.

To a mountaineer, a "foreigner" was anyone who was not born on the ridge. Back in the hills a woman turned her spinning wheel while her children played about her feet. She had time to think about many things while her hands were busy with spinning. Sometimes, her back was bent over a washboard, while her hands rubbed clothes up and down, stopping now and then to smear homemade soap – soft, brown, and slimy – over the soiled knees of homespun trousers. She distrusted a little the new ways and new notions which drifted in from the outside, that world beyond the mountains. In living apart, the everyday language of these descendants of early Americans still retains words and phrases from the time of Queen Elizabeth I.

The mountaineer plucked his home-made dulcimer and sang the "lonesome tunes" of the backwoodsman who led a lonely life and liked it. These ballads were often sad, telling a story of hardship on that first frontier.

In performing these tunes, which can still be heard today, the singer slides his voice from phrase to phrase, holds a long note like a sigh, and catches a breath when and where he needs it. The "lonesome tune" is slow, with long-held notes that echo down in the "holler." The verses are many in ballads and they tell a long story. Why hurry? There is plenty of time.

Of necessity, the early settlers were hunters. It was every boy's ambition to learn to shoot straight and to own a "huntin' houn'." The sun filtered through the blue-gray mist that wrapped the hills in a smoky haze. The tang of autumn was in the morning air. It was a good day for squirrel huntin'. The porch may sag and the door may creak but chores can wait for another day – tomorrow and tomorrow. Shortly after sun-up the mountaineer, with a gun on his shoulder and a hound at his heels, was trailing through the timberland where the trees were red and gold.

For generations these rural dwellers earned their living on the land. The men walked behind the plow; the women picked cotton; and the children pulled green and white striped worms off the leaves of tobacco plants. In time, the land wore out.

325

The soil did not supply enough food for healthy, growing plants. Heavy rains washed away the top dirt, and left worthless clay, and dug gullies through the fields. Some moved west to fresh land, but the time came when farms in new country were neither cheap nor plentiful. Then the hill farmer tried to stay on his home plot and earn a living through new methods of farming that gradually redeemed his land. Some succeeded, and others failed.

In recent years the tourists have begun to bring new prosperity to the mountaineers. When the summer days are hot and the air is stifling in the lowlands, the trees and streams of the Blue Ridge and the Great Smokies invite the vacationist to linger in the highlands. The tourist takes home a water jug fashioned from clay in a farmer's pit; a rag rug braided by hand or woven on a hand loom; a candlewick bedspread homemade in a mountain cabin. A cherished souvenir of a vacation trip is something real and personal. In meeting tourists, the mountaineers are becoming less suspicious of the "foreigner." However, jobs in industry are doing more than anything else to raise the living standards of people now living in the mountain region of the South.

TEXTILES LEAD THE WAY

BEFORE THE WAR Between the States, much of the South was plantation country. Manufacturing with hand tools was done on these estates to supply the family and servants with clothing and other necessities. After the conflict had ended in 1865, the region began to build a new way of life with new industries. Since cotton was the leading crop, textiles came first. The weaving of cloth is still the major industry although much yardage is produced from other fibers as well as from cotton.

Twenty years before Lee's surrender at Appomattox, William Gregg had established a cotton mill in Horse Creek Valley, South Carolina. For this Gregg is remembered as the "father of southern cotton manufacture." Like many farseeing men in the South, he believed that cotton should go from the field to the factory instead of being shipped to the northern states to be manufactured. His mill was still doing business a century later, weaving in one year enough cloth to encircle the earth twice at the equator.

In 1895 the Massachusetts Cotton Mills of Lowell erected a factory near Rome, Georgia, which has grown to great size. Other mills from New England moved into the South where labor was plentiful and cotton was near at hand. By the middle of the twentieth century three-fourths of the textiles produced in this country were woven in southern mills. Over a period of a hundred years these mills had been operated by water, steam, and electric power.

The by-products and various new processes shared in the output of these mills. A young veteran of World War I started a cotton mill when he was released from military service. He decided to try to make rayon, processed from wood pulp and cotton linters, left over when the seeds were crushed for oil. There was a time when plantation owners were quite discouraged with the cotton crop because it took the time of so many slaves to pick the seeds from the fluffy white lint. They welcomed Whitney's gin that combed out the worthless seeds. The early planters little dreamed that the sticky little seeds would some day become so valuable that scientists would actually be working to develop a plant with more of them.

Textiles once meant woolens, cottons, linens, and silk. During the 1920's rayon became a staple fabric and its use increased for clothing, tire-cord, and carpeting. Rayon ushered in a feverish period of experiment in which textiles moved out of the plant and animal kingdoms into a fabulous world of chemistry. New chemical fabrics, known as synthetics, created a revolution in the textile industry. Sheep ranchers and cotton growers were worried. They wondered if their products of ancient lineage were doomed by modern science.

Gradually, manufacturers of synthetics began using wool and cotton to strengthen some chemical fabrics. Blends became popular. The cloth in a dress or suit may be made from air, natural gas, coal, petroleum, corn, wood, varied chemical compounds, cotton, and wool.

When synthetics cut into the cotton market, many plantation owners sowed their cotton fields with grasses to provide year-round pasture. They went into the cattle business. The wooden shacks and the fenced "patches" of the sharecroppers began to disappear in the rolling country of Alabama and other states. Instead of farms averaging a hundred acres, the "ranches" took in as much as 3000 acres. The small farmer and the tenant farmer then sought employment elsewhere. Some migrated to the northern states. Others stayed to work in the new mills developing all over the South. The same revolution is taking place in the South that occurred in the North — but a hundred years later. People are leaving the farms to work in the mills. Rural life is declining but not so rapidly as it did in the North.

Although cotton mills began moving from New England soon after the War Between the States, the South remained rural. The synthetic industry began in the South. It started with a southern pattern. Chemical industries need water, air, and space. The South has all three in abundance. Electricity can be obtained from both hydroelectric plants at river dams and from steam plants operated with coal from mines in the Appalachians. Since electric power can be carried for miles by wire, the new mills were located in the country where land was cheap. Today, one story buildings, simplest and cheapest to operate, sprawl over acres of ground, and give comfort in light, air, and space. Automatic lint eliminators protect the lungs of the employees. In a mild climate these one-story mills can be adequately heated in winter and air-cooled in summer. The grounds are landscaped with grass and flowers. There is plenty of parking space for cars.

Workmen for these mills are largely recruited from the displaced farmhands in the neighborhood. Cotton pickers, thrown out of work by cotton-picking machines, were grateful for employment in these mills sprouting along the country roads. Families still clinging to their small farms were glad to work for wages at a mill within driving distance of their homes. They did not ask for a raise in pay when assigned to night duty. The night shifts gave them the opportunity of spending a few daylight hours in their fields and gardens. A southern workman, owning a few chickens, a garden, and a cow, could afford to work for lower wages than were paid for the same job in a northern industrial center.

Southern mill owners with lower operating costs were able to sell their textiles for a lower price. They took the

327

business from northern mills. By the middle of the century mill hands were being laid off in Fall River, New Bedford, and Lawrence, Massachusetts, and in other textile centers throughout New England. In 1951, when more than 35 woolen and worsted mills went out of business or moved away, 40,000 jobs were lost. Unable to compete, these mills were gradually closing doors and moving South, to join the manufacturers of cottons and synthetics. In order to save the mills which provided employment and payrolls, workmen in some towns agreed to surrender benefits and accept reduced wages. These stop-gap measures cannot long hold the mills by the river banks. Textiles are headed South to streamlined, air-conditioned electric plants in the open country. Some mill owners have found it necessary to build houses nearby for the mechanics who have followed them to new locations in the South.

The textile industry has gone through three revolutions in this country. Before Eli Whitney invented the cotton gin, about seventy-eight percent of the cloth was woolen. When seeds were removed by machinery, cottons swept woolens out of first place. This was the second revolution. Although rayons came into the market during the 1920's, the third revolution did not get into full swing until 1938, when chemists evolved a new fabric, nylon.

The Du Pont Company spent ten years and $27,000,000 on the first pair of nylon stockings. When the textile industry was occupied with carding, spinning, and weaving, cloth was steadily manufactured as soon as the machinery was installed. A mill could operate on a small capital. With synthetics, as much as $40,000,000 is invested in research laboratories and chemical plants before a single yard of a new fabric can be sold. Fields of fleecy white cotton still spot the southern landscape, but Old King Cotton's throne is tottering.

BUSINESS EXPANDS

TEXTILES ALONE did not provide the South's break-through from agriculture to industry. World War II had a large share in it. New defense industries located in the South during the war. They continued to operate during the uneasy peace. Much of the South's industrial growth is still rooted in the soil. The processing of cotton seed, soybean, and peanut oils for margarines, shortenings, and salad oils is a growing industry in a region where food production still holds a leading place.

Since the settlement of Virginia, tobacco has been a favored crop in the southern states. The farmer hauls his product to a neighborhood warehouse. There it is sold by the droning chant of the tobacco auctioneer. Ninety-five percent of the men and women employed in the tobacco industry live in North Carolina, Virginia, and Kentucky. Tobacco is a major source of taxation with a revenue stamp on every package, box, and can.

Although the South is farming country, over half of the land has some trees on it. A description of the Carolinas, published in London in 1732, encouraged settlers to migrate to that colony. It stated:

The lands will not be difficult to clear because there are neither stones nor bushes, but only great trees which do not grow very thick. The custom of the country is, that after having cut down these great trees, they leave the stumps for four or five years to rot, and afterwards easily root them up, in order to fertilize the ground.

All of the stumps were not uprooted. Saplings sprang up to replace the fallen trees where the land was not plowed and cultivated. Timber products, ranging from turpentine and resin to furniture and pulp, add to the industrial wealth. Since most of the battles of the War Between the States were fought in southern territory, soldiers in the Union armies tramped through the woods and learned about the valuable lumber. Among them was an officer from New England who returned to the North Carolina woods and established a furniture factory. Today the manufacture of furniture is a profitable industry in the forested regions of the mountain states. The big wood product is pulp, used for making paper of every kind — from gray newsprint and tan cardboard to white tissue and tinted stationery.

Along the Gulf Coast of Texas and Louisiana an abundance of oil lies under the tidelands. Southern Louisiana has valuable beds of sulfur. Texas boasts that its cow country in the southern part of the state has a growing chemical industry in potash, soda, and chlorine. Nitrate beds in Alabama are ground into fertilizer in the plant at Muscle Shoals.

The city of Birmingham, Alabama, is an example of how natural resources affect a community. The region has an abundance of coal, iron ore, and limestone, the basic ingredients of steel. Birmingham became one of the steel centers in the nation. In this city, stoves, wire, rails, castings, bars, bolts, pipe, machinery, and numerous articles of iron and steel are produced.

THE SOUTH GOES INDUSTRIAL

THE SOUTH, once boastful of its leisurely plantation life, is seeking industry to give employment to field hands whose jobs have been taken by machinery. Machines have been invented to pick cotton, cut cane, and harvest rice. To attract manufacturing, some towns in the southern states offer to erect buildings with public funds. They rent them on favorable terms to business men who are willing to install machinery and hire the citizens to operate it. Louisiana agreed to exempt some new industries from taxes for ten years. Free water, free sites, and cash grants are sometimes voted by communities to get new factories. To lure manufacturers into the mid-South, state officials and business men advertise the resources of the lower Mississippi Valley. The region has timber, oil, and natural gas; soda ash, lime, and silica; cotton, sweet potatoes, and sugar cane; an abundant supply of willing workmen; and cheap transportation to New Orleans, the gateway to Latin America.

The South, always rich in natural resources, is busy converting its raw materials into manufactured goods — at home. Buildings on the courthouse squares of sleepy towns have new and modern fronts. The latest styles are displayed in the store windows. More southerners are wage earners and have more money to spend. Houses and barns glow with fresh paint, here and there, along a country road. The lightning rod is being replaced with aerials for television. Farms have electric lights. Perhaps no improvement is noticed more than the new, modern school buildings in the villages and out in the country. With increased income, local and state governments can pay for better educational opportunities. With new prosperity, combining agriculture and industry, the South is acquiring a new look.

PART SEVEN

Settlers Win the Central Plains

Uncle Sam's Farm

St. Lawrence marks our Northern line
  As fast her waters flow;
And the Rio Grande our Southern bound,
  Way down to Mexico.
From the great Atlantic Ocean,
  Where the sun begins to dawn,
Leap across the Rocky Mountains,
  Far away to Oregon.

While the South shall raise the cotton,
  And the West the corn and pork,
New England manufactures,
  Shall do up the finer work;
For the deep and flowing waterfalls,
  That course along our hills,
Are just the thing for washing sheep,
  And driving cotton mills.

Our fathers gave us liberty,
  But little did they dream,
The grand results that pour along,
  This mighty age of steam;
For our mountains, lakes and rivers,
  Are all a blaze of fire,
And we send our news by lightning,
  On the telegraphic wires.

Yes! We're bound to beat the nations,
  For our motto's, "Go ahead."
And we'll tell the foreign paupers,
  That our people are well fed;
For the nations must remember,
  Uncle Sam is not a fool,
For the people do the voting,
  And the children go to school.

Songs of Yesterday by Philip D. Jordan and Lillian Kessler, Doubleday and Company, Inc.

Chapter 18

The Path of Shining Rails

NEED FOR A CONTINENTAL RAILROAD

THE OUTBREAK OF WAR between the northern and southern states had convinced the Government that a railroad across the continent was an urgent necessity. It could not be delayed. It was a matter of national defense.

The first great westward migration to Oregon and California did not settle the plains area. The United States stretched west to the Pacific, with little means of defending the west coast from outside attack. The only route open for heavy military equipment and large numbers of troops was by way of Cape Horn, a voyage of 18,000 miles. Any naval power at war with the United States could easily close this water route. On a continental railroad within the country, soldiers and supplies could be shipped if an enemy threatened to invade the Pacific coast. Important mail could be transported by rail faster and cheaper than by stagecoach and pony express.

Also, such a railroad would increase the possibilities of trade with Asia where cheap labor supplied silk, tea, spices, and other luxuries for the people of the United States. The teeming millions of the Orient wanted hardware, engines, and machinery from our eastern factories. The continental railroad would be a link in the route to India, sought in vain by Columbus, Cabot, and Cartier.

With a rail line to carry grain and cattle to eastern markets, settlers would move into that vast territory lying between the Missouri River and the Sierra Nevada Mountains. A great agricultural empire would grow up on the western prairie. When people began to talk about a railroad all the way to the Pacific coast, their imaginations ran wild with excitement.

Furthermore, there were facts and figures to measure the value of such a railroad to the mining industry. In fourteen years the mines of the Pacific region had added millions to the treasury of the world. Indeed this horde of gold and silver helped to finance the War Between the States and was paying a share of the national debt. By 1862 nearly everyone realized that the war would be long, bloody, and costly. The Government needed to encourage the mining industry. Why did the miners want a continental railroad?

In the camps, living expenses were so high that only the best grade ores were worth

ABRAHAM LINCOLN AND GRENVILLE M. DODGE, COUNCIL BLUFFS, IOWA, 1859

On a warm August day, Lincoln arrived in Council Bluffs from St. Joseph, Missouri after a 200 mile trip in a steamboat up the Missouri River. He came to look over land on which a friend had asked him to loan money. There he found two families, old neighbors from Illinois, who called him Abe. One took him sightseeing to a bluff where he could get a good view of the river and the surrounding country. Today, a granite monument marks the spot where they stood.

In the hotel where he stayed, he met a young engineer from Massachusetts, Grenville M. Dodge, who had gone west to survey lands for railroad companies. Lincoln and the engineer talked about the best route for a rail line to the Pacific. Dodge wrote about the meeting:

After dinner, while I was sitting on the stoop of the Pacific House, Mr. Lincoln came and sat beside me, and in his kindly way and manner was soon drawing from me all I knew of the country west and the result of my surveys.

A few years later, while Dodge was an army officer fighting under Grant in the Mississippi Campaign, President Lincoln signed the bill for a railroad to start west from Council Bluffs. He did not live to see his dream come true — to travel on that line — but General Dodge returned from the war to build the Union Pacific Railroad.

Union Pacific Railroad

working. Food and machinery and sometimes water, had to be carried into remote places on the backs of little burros. With every new "strike" prices soared upward as crowds swarmed into the new camp. In 1849 emigrants who bought eggs for 2½ cents a dozen and chickens for ten cents each from Iowa farmers paid $1 for an egg and $10 for a chicken in Sacramento. In San Francisco, with only ships to bring in food, a meal might cost eight dollars, according to a menu from the Ward House, a well-known eating place in the goldrush days.

With a railroad to bring in supplies, living and operating expenses would be lower. This would mean that mines of lower grade ore would be profitable to work. There would be more jobs and more men would come to seek work in the mines. They would bring their families. Towns would grow up along the railroad line and around the mines. Homes, stores, schools, and churches would be built. Farmers and ranchers would settle on the land when towns provided a market for their grain, vegetables, fruit, eggs, butter, milk, and meat. In time factories would be built to make what the people needed, wanted, and had the money to buy. The vast new territory on the Pacific would be safe from enemies with Americans living in it and prepared to defend it.

In country stores, at the crossroads, and in the halls of Congress in Washington, men talked of a path of shining rails from the Atlantic to the Pacific. A continental railroad became the dream of a nation. The Railroad Act of 1862 was passed by Congress. It reads as follows:

An Act: TO AID IN THE CONSTRUCTION OF A RAILROAD AND TELEGRAPH LINE FROM THE MISSOURI RIVER TO THE PACIFIC

333

OCEAN, AND TO SECURE TO THE GOVERNMENT THE USE OF SAME FOR POSTAL, MILITARY, AND OTHER PURPOSES.

In this Act Congress gave authority to two corporations to build this line. One was the Union Pacific Railroad Company, starting west from Council Bluffs, Iowa and laying tracks, "between the south margin of the valley of the Platte River, in the territory of Nebraska." The other was the Central Pacific Railroad Company of California, authorized "to construct a railroad and telegraph line from the Pacific Coast at or near San Francisco, or the navigable waters of the Sacramento River, to the eastern boundary of California, –

COPY OF SIGNATURES ON THE RAILROAD ACT SIGNED INTO LAW July 1, 1862

Union Pacific Railroad

Thirty Seventh
Congress of the United States,
At the Second Session
Begun and held at the City of Washington in the District of Columbia
...Monday the second day of December one thousand eight hundred and sixty one.

AN ACT To aid in the construction of a railroad and telegraph line from the Missouri river ... the Pacific ocean; and to secure to the government the use of the same for postal, military, and other purposes.

Be It Enacted by the Senate and House of Representatives of the United States of America in C...
... Walter S. Burgess, William P. Blodget, ...
...; Augustus Brewster ...

... Taylor, Alvin
... Evans, of Colorado; together with five commissioners
... be appointed by the Secretary of the Interior, and all persons who shall or may be
associated with them, and their successors, are hereby created and erected into a body
corporate and politic, in deed and in law, by the name, style, and title of "The Union
Pacific Railroad Company;" and by that name shall have perpetual succession,
and shall be able to sue and to be sued, plead and be impleaded, defend and be
defended, in all courts of law and equity within the United States, and may
make and have a common seal; and the said corporation is hereby ...
and empowered to lay out, locate, construct ...
continuous railroad ...

... which whole shall be ...

... the Secretary of the Treasury on or before the first day of July in ...

Galusha A. Grow
Speaker of the House of Representatives.

Solomon Foot,
President of the Senate pro tempore

Approved, July 1. 1862.
Abraham Lincoln

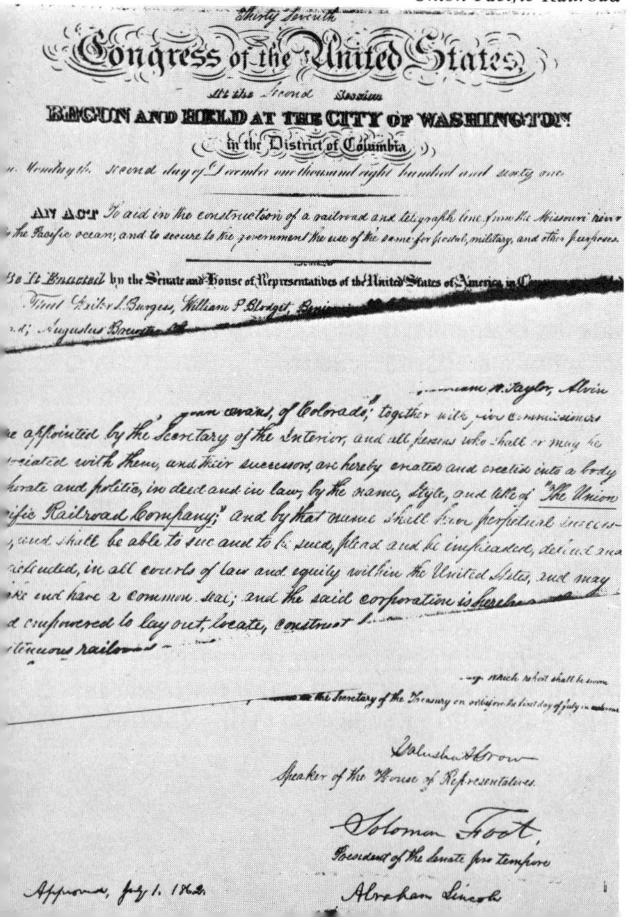

and to meet and connect with the first mentioned railroad and telegraph line."

The War Between the States had hastened the passage of the bill for a continental railroad by removing the southern congressmen who had insisted that the line pass through slaveholding states. The actual construction of the railroads was not started until after the war ended, except for a small beginning made by the Central Pacific heading eastward from Sacramento. In the summer of 1865 the Union Pacific started to build westward from Council Bluffs. When and where would the two lines meet?

PROBLEMS FOR THE RAILROAD BUILDERS

THE FIRST PROBLEM was money. That had to be borrowed by selling bonds to the public. To the average American of that day, wealth was measured in acres of land. To encourage the sale of the railroad bonds and provide cash to purchase materials and to pay wages, this Act of 1862 granted 6400 acres of land to each company for each mile of completed road. Still men were wary of investing their money in bonds to send an iron horse snorting across the prairie. The sale was slow. Two years later the land grant was almost doubled. The two companies were allowed the timber on this land but were not given the mineral rights. This land allotment, 12,000 acres per mile of track, was granted "upon condition that said companies (Union Pacific and Central Pacific) shall keep said railroad and telegraph line in repair and use, and shall at all times, transmit dispatches over said telegraph line; and transport mails, troops,

and munitions of war, supplies and public stores upon said railroad for the Government; and that the Government shall at all times have the preference in the use of the same for all the purposes aforesaid, — at fair and reasonable prices, not to exceed the amounts paid by private parties for the same kind of service."

Materials presented a problem to the Union Pacific. West of the Missouri River there were few trees except cottonwoods and willows along the streams. Most of the ties for the Union Pacific came from Ohio, Michigan, and Pennsylvania. Some were hauled overland by mules and oxen at a carrying charge of $2.75 per tie. It cost $135 per ton to deliver rails from Pennsylvania mills, when shipped by train to St. Louis and thence by steamboat to Omaha. Most of the rails, timber, cars, and engines for the Union Pacific went by boat down the Ohio to St. Louis and up the Missouri River to Omaha.

A boom struck the little river village of Omaha after the first rail was laid in July of 1865. Supplies were costly. Second-hand shovels cost $10 and were scarce at that price. Fuel for the wood-burning engines cost $100 a cord; grain for the horses and mules, $7 a bushel; and wild hay, cut from the river bottoms, $34 a ton. When the rail lines were completed between shipping points, supplies became more plentiful and cheaper.

On the open prairie food was an important item. The first continental railroad was built by hand labor. Such hard work, out-of-doors in all kinds of weather, created large appetites among the Irish immigrants who laid the rails and tamped the ties. To furnish meat for one construction crew, the Union Pacific hired the expert rifle shot, William F. Cody, at

$500 a month. Early each morning "Buffalo Bill" rode away from camp to shoot the ten or twelve bison needed for one day's meat supply. When the line was completed, Cody moved his family west and settled on a ranch in Nebraska, where his cattle grazed on the old buffalo range.

Military officers were employed to boss the laboring crews. They used army methods, with each worker going at top speed. When the ties were in place, horses pulled a car of rails to the end of the track. At a signal from the foreman five men on each side seized a rail. "Down!", the foreman shouted, and two rails hit the ties. Every fifteen seconds nine yards of the Union Pacific were finished.

The crew laid about six miles of track in a day. It was not unusual for the men to get up the next morning and find that Indians had come during the night and torn out their work. In an effort to keep on good terms with the red men, the crews invited them to ride on the "iron horse." The Indians were fed and given trinkets when they visited the construction camps. Wise men among the Indians knew that the puffing engine would haul more white men to shoot more buffalo. More Indians would be cold and hungry, without tepees for shelter and meat for food. Every workman, if not guarded by soldiers, took both shovel and rifle to the job. In case of Indian attack he put down his shovel and picked up his rifle. Much of the time the construction crews were guarded by soldiers under the command of General William T. Sherman, who had led the march to the sea through Georgia. Finally in 1868 the Government made a treaty with the Indians to give them lands where no white man could go, in exchange for the railroad lands. This treaty, like others, did not last long. The plains

LARAMIE, WYOMING IN EARLY DAYS

Laramie was founded in 1868 when the Union Pacific chose the site for a supply center. This photograph shows the shops constructed of rocks picked up nearby; a water tank; a windmill that cost $10,000; and a little steam engine with a big smokestack.

West of Laramie, the Union Pacific Company faced the task of building the railroad over the Continental Divide at an altitude of 8,000 feet. This pass was named for General William T. Sherman who commanded the soldiers sent to guard the line while under construction.

tribes had watched the trains of covered wagons cross enroute to the Pacific. Would this iron monster, whose sides no arrow could pierce, bring another westward migration to plow the buffalo range? The Indians knew the answer and fought to stop the white man from coming.

The problems of the Central Pacific, building east, were different. The land grant of 12,000 acres per mile gave this company forests with fine timber. In 1868 near the present site of Truckee, twenty-four sawmills were kept busy furnishing ties for tracks, timber for trestles, and lumber for snowsheds. Rails, engines, and other supplies came by boat around Cape Horn. Thousands of Chinese immigrants poured into San Francisco to work on the railroad. The California Indians were docile and gave little trouble to the railroad builders. The problems of the Central Pacific were rolled into one word — MOUNTAINS.

Not many miles from Sacramento, the starting point of the Central Pacific, the Sierras begin to rise and form a barrier nearly 150 miles wide. Many people thought a railroad could not possibly be built through these mountains. They proposed a line to the foothills only, with a wagon road to transport freight and passengers over the range. The Central Pacific was built through the mountains and in record time. With glycerine and dynamite, roadbeds were blasted from the walls of the cliffs; trestles were erected to bridge the canyons; and tunnels were bored through peaks of solid rock. With plenty of timber, a seaport for supplies, cheap Chinese labor and friendly natives, the Central Pacific Railroad Company completed a line through the Sierra Nevada Mountains and continued building toward the east. The wonder of this feat can best be told in the words of a forty-niner, who took a pleasure trip on the new railroad in 1868, as far as it went. He recalls experiences in the "dreaded American desert":

From the Truckee River to the sink of the Humboldt is a sandy desert of 40 miles, dry and arid, where neither water nor grass could be obtained. On this terrible waste, hundreds of teams gave out, and cattle perished. Now, on a train, I make a pleasure trip in a few hours over ground which it took many weeks to pass, with great suffering. Like one recovering from a trance, I gaze around in doubt, wonder, and surprise.

As the two lines approached each other, an exciting race began, with one company trying to build farther west, and

A WOODEN TRESTLE ON THE CENTRAL PACIFIC RAILROAD

Chinese laborers used wheelbarrows and carts to make this fill in a gorge near Colfax, California.

Southern Pacific Railroad

FIRST RAILROAD THROUGH THE SIERRA NEVADA MOUNTAINS

This old photograph tells better than words what a task it was to build the first railroad through nearly 150 miles of mountains. Two wood-burning engines chug up the steep grade. The passenger train looks like a huge caterpillar crawling along a ledge.

the other, farther east. Crews worked from sunrise to sunset. In the race against time the Central Pacific made a record, but many Chinese coolies dropped by the tracks from exhaustion.

D-O-N-E

ON MAY 10, 1869, the lines met at Promontory, Utah, in the desert country of sand and sagebrush, north of the Great Salt Lake. The spring day was bright and pleasant. During the morning a passenger train arrived from Sacramento with officials of the Central Pacific. Another came with men of the Union Pacific and invited friends. From Salt Lake City a crowded excursion train arrived with a Mormon band and the army band from Fort Douglas to furnish music for the gala event. Pioneers who had never seen a railroad train came long distances in wagons and on horseback to join the crowd of track-layers, uniformed soldiers, and well-dressed railroad officials and politicians.

It was nearly noon when General Dodge lifted his hand to silence the crowd. The ceremonies opened with a prayer. Then the last two rails were laid, one by Irish immigrants working for the Union Pacific and the other by Chinese laborers for the Central Pacific. Thus did

Europe and Asia grasp hands across the continent of North America. Thus did a path of shining rails take the place of the mythical "Northwest Passage" long sought by the early explorers.

Congressmen, governors, and leaders from the western states were there to present spikes of precious metals for these last two rails and to praise the feat of the railroad-builders.

The speeches lasted over two hours while Utah, Arizona, Nevada, and Montana presented spikes of gold and silver. California's token was a spike of pure gold, worth over $400 at that time. The last tie of polished laurel was cut from a tree in a California forest. A citizen of Sacramento, where the Central Pacific started, presented the tie and the spike from his home state.

"From her bosom was taken the first

MEETING OF THE RAILS — PROMONTORY, UTAH — MAY 10, 1869

Montague, chief engineer of the Central Pacific shook hands with Dodge, chief engineer of the Union Pacific, while each one stood nearest the engine of his company. The Central Pacific engine with the funnel-shaped smokestack made the run from Sacramento, California. The engine with the tall, slender smokestack made the longest run across Nebraska, Wyoming and into Utah, all the way from Omaha on the bank of the Missouri River.

Today, a monument stands on the spot where the rails met. Late in 1942, the last rails of the old line north of the Great Salt Lake were hauled away and sold for scrap to be made into war materials.

Union Pacific Railroad

soil," he said, "so let hers be the last tie and the last spike."

To Leland Stanford, president of the Central Pacific, went the honor of driving the last spike with a silver-headed hammer. A telegraph operator tapped in Morse code, the word D-O-N-E. The officials of both lines signed this telegram which was sent to President Grant in Washington:

The last rail is laid, the last spike driven. The Pacific Railroad is completed. The point of junction is 1086 miles west of the Missouri River and 690 miles east of Sacramento City.

After the golden spike had been driven, the two engines were uncoupled and sightseers scrambled aboard for a ride. Slowly Jupiter from the West and One-Nineteen from the East crawled toward each other until the engines met. The crowd cheered wildly. News of the event touched off celebrations in towns and cities throughout the nation. In New York the bells of Trinity Church pealed an invitation to prayer while guns in City Park fired a military salute. In honor of the achievement the new building of the Chicago Tribune was lit that night. On this memorable tenth of May a shipment of tea from Japan left San Francisco for St. Louis over a path of shining rails.

SLAUGHTER OF BISON ENDS A WAY OF LIFE

EARLY ONE MORNING IN 1869 a military scout in Kansas was awakened by a dull and steady roar like the rumble of distant thunder. He and other scouts in his company mounted their ponies and rode in the direction of the rolling thud of tramping hooves. From the safety of a bluff they gazed for hours upon the mighty herd, a moving mass about twenty miles wide and sixty miles long, heading northwest across the prairie. How many bison were in this herd? They could not guess.

In that same year the first continental railroad was completed. As the Indian had foreseen, the iron horse became his deadly enemy. As fast as the rails were laid, settlers followed the line to farm the land in Nebraska. They scared away the buffalo. From car windows of slow moving trains, passengers shot buffalo for sport. Expert marksmen, shooting with rifles which fired bullets a half mile, were known to kill one hundred and twenty bison in forty minutes. When one buffalo was shot, others gathered around their fallen comrade, pawing the ground and uttering a cry. This habit made the animals easy prey for the sharpshooters. The hunters took the skins, and left the flesh to wolves and buzzards.

The railroads carried trains of box-cars filled with buffalo hides to be made into lap robes in eastern factories. The fashion of buffalo robes in sleighs and carriages almost wiped out the "hunchback cows" on the western plains. The hidehunters, a rugged group of men, made their headquarters in Dodge City, Kansas. From this town in one year, a single firm shipped almost 130,000 hides. The high-powered repeating rifle and the railroad lines doomed the bison.

Ten years after the completion of the first continental railroad, only a few of these shaggy animals could be found anywhere on the plains. At stations along the railroads, buffalo bones were stacked higher than a two-story house. From these stations they were shipped east to be ground into fertilizer for worn-out farms in New England. For years the skeletons of slain bison bleached on the prairie. Bone-gathering was a regular, recognized business among the poor. While collecting bones in Oklahoma, a frontier poet using a bullet for a pencil scribbled this verse on the shoulder blade of a buffalo.

I pass by the home of the wealthy,
And I pass by the hut of the poor,
  But none care for me
  When my cargo they see,
And no one will open the door.
O think of the poor bone Pilgrim.
  Ye who are safely at home;
No one to pity me, no one to cheer me,
  As o'er the lone prairie I roam.

Scott Cummins

Currier

THE ROAD — WINTER

The fad of buffalo hides for sleigh robes caused the ruthless slaughter of the western bison on which the Plains Indians depended for food, clothing, and shelter.

This ruthless slaughter of the bison left the Plains Indians in a starving condition. These tribes had always been hunters. They depended upon the buffalo for their living. They ate the meat, made clothing and tepees from the hides, and fashioned the bones into tools. The end of the bison brought an end to their way of life. Their loss, swift and sudden, left the Indians dazed and confused. They fought the hidehunters with fury. However, Indian arrows were no match for the rifles, six-shooters, and knives carried by these tough and bloody killers. The once-proud Indian hunters turned to bone-gathering to eke out a miserable existence.

Trains of covered wagons and miles of shining rails snaked across the plains, bringing emigrants to settle in the old hunting grounds of the Indians. The Indians tried to stop them but on they came in an endless procession, these palefaced people with a longing for land. A territory, called Oklahoma, which means "land of the red men" was set aside by the Federal Government as an Indian Reservation. Some of the tribes of the plains the Pawnees, the Poncas, the Iowas, the Omahas, the Kiowas, the Osages and others — found it necessary to follow another "Trail of Tears" to the Indian Territory.

THE CLASH OF TWO CIVILIZATIONS

WHEN INDIANS SOLD their land, they did not realize that they bartered away their rights to hunt in the forests and to fish in the streams of their old hunting ground. To an Indian, the birds, the beasts, the trees, the flowers, and the streams were not a part of the land. These belonged to everyone, but the European had another idea of ownership. When he owned land, everything on the ground — plants, animals, rivers — belonged to him.

The European who settled in this country did not clearly understand the Indian principle of tribal law, "All for one and one for all." When Indian buffalo hunters returned from a chase, the meat was divided among the families of their village. The widows, the aged, and the sick shared the spoils of the hunt with those who had killed the bison, skinned the animals, and cut up the meat. In the Indian code there was less private ownership of the necessities of life than in the European way of living. Although each family raised corn, melons, squash, and pumpkins on little plots of ground, the land itself was owned by the tribe as a whole. The red man did not understand the white man's greed for personal gain. If an Indian had shelter, food, and clothing, though meager, he was satisfied. If ten acres of corn provided enough meal for his family, why plant twenty acres? Because of this character trait, the white man thought the red man was lazy. On the other hand the Indian was at a loss to understand why his European neighbors should want more land to plant more corn to make more money, with which to buy more land to

plant more corn to make MORE money. The red man thought the white man was greedy.

At heart the native Indian was deeply religious. He was a nature-worshipper like most primitive peoples. His belief in the Great Spirit was akin to the Christian idea of God. The Indian's religious services were rituals performed in dance, song, and pantomime because he spoke to the Great Spirit through music. The actors in these sacred dramas painted their faces and wore costumes. The buffalo dance was a thanksgiving for a successful hunt. The harvest festivals, in honor of the giver of corn, were elaborate rituals which lasted for days. H'atira Hu Weta Arioso is a prayer that is always sung. It is part of a religious drama of the Pawnees in which the Indians ask for children and corn to feed them, and that their race may live on and never die. The

BUFFALO ON A RESERVATION IN OKLAHOMA
The American bison is not extinct. Herds exist on a number of western reservations where they are protected.

Oklahoma Historical Society

four words, a poem in the Pawnee language, state that corn gives life, like a mother. There is an unseen spirit which gives life to the corn that the corn may give its life that the Indian may live.

The red man's religious rites were not like the services in the white man's church. The European, not understanding these ceremonials, dubbed the Indian "a painted savage."

The Plains Indians were hunters. Under the guidance of Sitting Bull, the Dakotas, Sioux, and Cheyennes rallied the tribes in a last desperate attempt to hold their hunting grounds. Thinking the Indian forces numbered not more than a thousand warriors, General George Armstrong Custer met them in battle near the Little Big Horn River in Montana, June 25, 1876. His small band was surrounded by over four thousand warriors armed with rifles and plenty of ammunition. Every man was killed, including General Custer. It was the Indian's last stand except for raids here and there upon settlers.

From the beginning the two ways of life clashed because they were so different. Thinking his way of living the better one, the white man sought to impose it upon the red man. The Indian, proud of his heritage, clung to his customs, his religion, and his tribal law. The result was feud, war, and massacre until the tribes, outnumbered and defeated, were moved to reservations under the protection of the Federal Government. Agents of the Government were stationed in the Indian country to persuade the tribes that they should settle down on the reservations allotted to them and till the soil. It took time for the hunter to trade his rifle for a plow. After the Custer Massacre, the Indian tribes on the Central Plains were scattered on reserva-

tions from Canada to Oklahoma. Many kindly citizens believed it was better for the Indians to live apart from the Europeans. They welcomed the removal of the tribes to the Indian Territory. They hoped these native Americans would find peace and happiness in a land all their own. The tribes had scarcely settled in this territory for red men ONLY, when they found themselves living again among white neighbors — the cattlemen of the Southwest.

For many years before Oklahoma was made the Indian Territory, this area had been a hunting ground for the Indian tribes and an open range for the cattlemen of the Southwest. Along the streams the Indians had trapped beaver; in the woods they hunted deer and quail. It was also a stockman's paradise as the grass grew tall and thick and the streams were full of water. The Indian hunted and the cattleman used the pasture. Both were satisfied.

LONGHORNS TO HEREFORDS

THE LONGHORNS WERE distant cousins of cattle brought by the Moors from Africa to Spain during the eighth century. When Columbus made his second voyage in 1493, his ships carried a cargo of these "Moorish" cattle to Santo Domingo in the West Indies. Every vessel bringing colonists from Spain had a shipment of cattle and horses for their ranchos in the New World. Wherever the Spaniards settled, livestock went with them. When Coronado made his journey north in search of the Seven Cities of Cibola, he took along five hundred cattle to feed the men in his expedition. This was less than fifty years after the first voyage. The cattle industry, founded by Columbus, grew rapidly and is

LAYING TRACK 300 MILES WEST OF THE MISSOURI RIVER
KANSAS-PACIFIC RAILROAD, OCTOBER 19, 1869

Ranchers in Texas wanted a railroad on which to ship their cattle to eastern markets. In the same year that the Union Pacific met the Central Pacific in Utah, the Kansas-Pacific Railroad was being pushed westward in Kansas. The prairie town of Abilene became a shipping point for cattle and buffalo hides. It was the end of the "Chizzum Trail."

still big business throughout the Americas.

Since there were no fences, cattle wandered from the large Mexican ranches and were lost to their owners. From these strays, herds of wild cattle grew up to roam over the plains of the Southwest. These animals were really wild, with the keen sense of a deer and the fighting pluck of a grizzly bear. When a pack of wolves broke into a herd, the cows quickly bunched their calves and formed a tight circle to protect their young. Facing a solid wall of long horns the hungry wolves howled in vain.

Other imported breeds mixed with the wild cattle. The Spaniards were fond of black cows and this strain, too, found its way into the herds on the plains. Thus came into being the famous breed, the longhorns. With a mixed ancestry the longhorns were brindled-blue, mouse-colored, creamy-tan, reddish brown, pale red, or black with spots of white, red, and tan. In addition to horns with as much as a nine-foot spread, these animals had long legs, long tails, and long backs that sometimes swayed in the middle.

Many a future cattle baron of Texas made a start by capturing the best specimens of the wild herds. These cattle were free for the taking but the taking was not an easy matter. When chased by men on horseback, the wild creatures switched their long tails, snorted their anger, and battled for their freedom.

The longhorns survived droughts in summer and blizzards in winter. In hard months they ate the prickly pear on the thorny cactus plant and quenched their thirst with the juice of the fruit. When grass dried up, they nibbled brush like deer and chewed the leaves of withered trees. Sensing a storm in the air a longhorn herd instinctively headed toward the south, stringing along in a thin line. When a blizzard overtook them, they lowered their heads, turned their tails to the driving snow, and drifted with the wind. These animals were weather-wise in all seasons of the year. The longhorn inherited the plains from the buffalo. This hardy breed with flat ribs, lanky bodies, and hunched shoulders founded the great cattle industry of the Southwest.

ON THE OLD CHIZZUM TRAIL

AFTER THE FALL of Vicksburg in July of 1863, the Mississippi River was under the control of the Union armies. The cattlemen in the seceded state of Texas lost their markets in towns along the river from St. Louis to New Orleans. By the end of the War Between the States in 1865 there were about 3,000,000 cattle on the range in Texas. In the northeastern states the demand for beef boosted prices. How could the cattlemen get their stock to market?

A cattle buyer finally persuaded a railroad company to lay a track as far west as Abilene, Kansas. Then the longhorns could be driven through unsettled country and loaded into cars for shipment to the meat packing centers of Kansas City and Chicago. Ranchers from southern Texas had tried driving their cattle to St. Louis. They lost much of their stock going through the Indian Territory where the Five Civilized Tribes fought both herds and herders. The bloodsucking ticks

LOADING LONGHORNS AT ABILENE, KANSAS, IN 1871

Kansas State Historical Society

carried in by the tough longhorns attacked other breeds owned by the Indians and the animals died of tick fever.

The first herd, driven to Abilene two years after the war, followed a trail marked

JESSE CHISHOLM

Jesse Chisholm was a trader, not a cattleman. His father was a Scotch Irish frontiersman in Tennessee, and his mother was part Cherokee Indian. As a boy about ten years old, Jesse journeyed over the "Trail of Tears" to the Indian Territory.

As a young man, he began to mark trails to trade with the Indian tribes of the prairie. They trusted him in business and sought his advice in trouble.

The first herd of longhorns driven north tramped over his main trail in the Indian Territory. Ever after, the full length of the route from San Antonio, Texas to Abilene, Kansas was called the "Chizzum Trail." The following spring, Jesse Chisholm died. Little did this quiet, honest, and kind frontiersman dream that his name would find a place in history and be celebrated in song.

Oklahoma Historical Society

by the storekeeper and trader, Jesse Chisholm. This route of the longhorns from San Antonio to Abilene became known as the "Chizzum Trail." Many a boy in Texas longed for the day when he could "hit the trail." Driving cattle to the railroad line in Kansas was an adventure, not a job. The salary was $30 a month for beginners, with food furnished from the chuck wagon.

From the wild herds of mustangs the cowboys captured horses for their work on the range. The mustangs, free for the taking, were as daring as the cowboys who roped them and broke them to the saddle. The stocky ponies would dash into the thick of a wild stampede or plunge into a swollen stream to swim with the herd. With all its hardships the cattlemen clung to the adventurous life of the open range. He spent his days jogging in the saddle over a vast domain, wild and free. At night, when not on watch, he made a cocoon of his blankets and slept on the ground.

The dangers and hardships of the cowboys were many but so were the thrills. Life on the old Chisholm Trail can best be told in the words of those who traveled it:

When I was sixteen years old, the son of a cattleman asked me to go up the trail with him. Of course I was willing, but my mother objected. It took a good deal of persuading on the part of Pete and myself to get her to consent for me to go. She gave in, however, and I went with Pete to a shoe shop where he ordered a pair of boots made for me. These boots cost $14. He also gave me a pair of bell spurs, a Colt's cap and ball six-shooter, and a rim-fire Winchester, as well as a pair of leather leggins which cost $12. This was the first time in my life that I had been rigged out, and you bet I was proud.

We started with the herd about the middle of March, 1871, with 2500 cattle. — We reached our destination, Kansas, where Pete sold out, and we came back home together.

DODGE CITY, KANSAS, IN THE 1880'S

This town grew up at the place where the Western Trail from San Antonio, Texas to Ogallala, Nebraska crossed the Santa Fe Railroad. From this center cattle, hides and bones were shipped to eastern markets.

One of the great hazards of this journey was swimming the herds across the rivers. There were no bridges. One cowboy tells of crossing the Red River, swollen with recent rains:

Several of us boys tried to swim across. None were successful but another fellow and myself, and I only upon second trial, as my first horse drowned under me and I was forced to get another. We two had our hands full, as we had to sing to about six thousand cattle to keep them together.

The trail drivers used music to quiet their cattle when the animals became restless and nervous. If the herd became frightened by thunder and lightning or some unfamiliar sound, it might stampede. During the night the cowboys kept watch in four shifts. When young steers refused to lie down and milled around in circles, the cowboys sang lullabies to quiet them. Sometimes the cowpunchers played tunes on fiddles, guitars, and harmonicas. One wrote:

BAREBACK BRONC RIDING

In early days on the plains, cowboys captured wild mustangs and tamed them for their riding horses. It was exciting and dangerous work. Today, on western ranches cowboys still break untamed horses (broncs) to the saddle. At rodeos and fairs, they display their riding skill for sport, prizes, and championships, under strict regulations. Rules for bareback bronc riding are printed in a program of Cheyenne Frontier Days:

This is strictly a one-hand contest, with rigging attached to a surcingle, which is grasped with one hand. In short – no saddle, no halter, no rein, just the flat, slippery deck of a dynamite-laden bronc ... Naturally, the rider is not permitted to "tightleg" or hold with his knees and he must keep raking his spurs fore and aft across the horse's flanks for the whole eight seconds of the ride.

Often I have taken my old fiddle on herd at night when on the trail, and, while one of my companions led my horse around the herd, I reeled off such oldtime tunes as "Shake That Wooden Leg," "Arkansaw Traveler," and "The Unfortunate Pup." And say, brothers, those old long-horned steers actually enjoyed that old-time music.

The women who lived on the frontier were as brave as the men. One woman who went with her husband on a trail trip tells of her experiences:

In the early spring of 1871, my husband rounded up his cattle. We started north in April with about ten cowboys, mostly Mexicans, the cooks, and a thousand head of cattle. The cattle were driven only about ten miles a day, so they would have plenty of time to graze and fatten along the way. — Our herd was stampeded one day, supposedly by Indians. It was a horrible, yet fascinating sight. Frantic cowboys tried to stop the wild flight, but nothing could check it. The men gathered the cattle in about a week's time. After a stampede, the men would be almost exhausted. I felt so sorry for one of them, a young tenderfoot. The boy lay down and was soon sleeping so soundly that he did not hear us breaking camp, and we forgot him when we left. The boy overtook us late in the evening, and said that he would not have awakened then if an approaching herd had not almost run over him.

Young men liked the excitement and adventure of driving cattle to the railroad line in Kansas and the stayover in the lawless frontier towns of Dodge City and Abilene.

The cattlemen whose herds roamed the prairie had a profitable business. During the twenty years following the War Between the States millions of cattle were driven over the trails to Kansas. It cost only about fifty cents to raise a longhorn steer for market and that was the cost of branding him. The animals foraged for their food and took care of themselves.

Like the Indians before them, the cattlemen were driven from their empire when the plowmen invaded the open range. Barbed wire brought an end, too, to the reign of the Texas longhorns. The master of the trail and king of the plains now cooped on ranches behind fences, was no longer profitable for cattlemen. They turned from this lean, lanky-framed stock to the meaty Hereford, with short horns,

348

HEREFORDS BEING DRIVEN IN FROM THE RANGE IN WYOMING

These white-faced, short-horned, broad-backed Herefords are good rustlers, steady grazers, and can be fattened on grass. The breed is popular today in the ranch country of the Central Plains where the longhorn vanished as did the buffalo.

short legs and round bodies. Today these gentle, white faced cattle have replaced the ill-tempered, nervous, untamed longhorns that have all but vanished, along with the buffalo.

The path of shining rails had brought a new way of life to the Central Plains.

MAP:

WA 24r
Our United States by Edgar B. Wesley

Chapter 19

Homesteaders Invade the Great Plains

SETTLERS SEEK NEW LANDS

THE BANNER YEAR for the West was 1862. In that year, while burdened with the War Between the States, President Lincoln had signed the two congressional bills which started the frontier on a westward march across the Great Plains. These were the Railroad Act to build a line to the Pacific and the Homestead Law to give free land to settlers. During the Presidential campaign of 1860 people in torchlight parades had carried banners with the slogan, LINCOLN AND FREE HOMESTEADS. Born in a log cabin on one frontier, Lincoln was a friend of the pioneer.

Under the Homestead Law a man was entitled to 160 acres of land if he lived on it, improved it, and made it his home for five years. A head of a family or anyone twenty-one years of age was eligible providing he was a citizen of the United States or had declared his intention of becoming a citizen. Free land for all! A railroad to carry products to market! What more could anyone want? In a popular song with a rollicking tune, Americans of the day boasted of their land of liberty with FREE farms, FREE votes, and FREE schools.

"Come along!" they said, inviting the world to share freedom and opportunities.

Agitation began in Congress to open the Indian country for settlement. Homeseekers wanted the land for farms and this land was public domain. The men who fought to open Oklahoma Territory for settlement were nicknamed "boomers." Sometimes, these land-hungry boomers moved their families into the territory and helped themselves to farms, declaring they had as much right to plant crops on government-owned land as did the cattlemen to graze their herds on it. They claimed this right under the Homestead Law.

When the Cherokees had been moved to the Indian Territory from the East, the tribe had been given a narrow strip of land lying between the northern border of Oklahoma Territory and the southern boundary of the state of Kansas. This strip provided an outlet for the hunters to reach the buffalo range farther west. It was first known as the Cherokee Outlet and later as the Cherokee Strip. The Cherokees were farmers, not hunters, and did not use this land. In 1883 cattlemen organized the Cherokee Live Stock Association and leased the 6,000,000 acres for pasture. The price paid was $100,000 a year for five years, payable six months in advance. This money was divided among the Cherokees who considered the rental a good business deal. The pleasant and profitable arrangement for Indians and cattlemen was doomed for an early end.

It irked the homesteaders to see the cattlemen pasturing their herds on land where they could plant wheat and corn. A feud developed between the two factions and this led to violence. The cattlemen argued that this land was better suited to grazing than to farming. The fight reached the halls of Congress, and the plowman won. In 1889 President Harrison opened the first section of Oklahoma under the Homestead Law. A few years later President Cleveland issued a proclamation opening the Cherokee Strip, for which the Government had paid the Cherokees $8,500,000.

WILD RIDES FOR FREE LAND

THE FIRST RUN for staking claims was made on an April day in 1889. It was warm and sunny. In covered wagons, in high-wheeled buggies, and on horseback, the homeseekers lined up along the border of the "Promised Land." They came from nearly every state in the Union, these farmers, lawyers, mechanics, laborers, cowboys, gamblers, adventurers who formed this human wall. The knowing ones were the cowpunchers who had herded cattle all over Oklahoma and had driven steers to market over the Chisholm Trail. Under wide-brimmed hats they slouched in their saddles and waited for the signal to start. They knew where they were going and the shortest way to get there. Weeks before they had selected their claims in the bottom lands where the soil was rich, the

A "BOOMER CAMP" ON THE BORDER OF THE "PROMISED LAND"

Settlers camped in the open, awaiting the day set by Congress to ride in a race for free land.

OKLAHOMA RUN
To the fleetest belonged a prize — 160 acres of land — a free farm.

grass was tall, and the timber was heavy. The cow ponies were fast runners and the cowboys were good riders. To the fleetest belonged the prize.

Only one railroad passed through this country. On the morning of the land opening fifteen passenger trains left Arkansas City for the tract. About ten thousand people tried to board the first train, leaving at daylight. When no standing room was left in the coaches, men sat on the tops of the cars, on the cowcatchers of the engines, and on the steps of the open vestibules. The crowded trains also lined up at the border to await the signal for the run. Noon was the appointed time. A tense silence crept over the restless mob as the hour approached. Army buglers sounded the get-ready warning. The last faint echo had scarcely died away when a soldier in

each guard rode out in front of the line, turned his horse around, and faced the anxious crowd. He raised his six-shooter and pointed toward the sky, with his finger on the trigger. At exactly twelve o'clock each trooper fired into the air. The race was on.

A mighty shout arose as the horses dashed across the line. On the unbroken prairie, the rumbling noise of horses' hooves and creaking wagons sounded like a herd of bison on a wild stampede. The men rode ahead on fast horses. Women drove teams of horses and mules hitched to covered wagons, bringing up the rear with food, bedding, cooking utensils, and supplies for the new home. On the floors behind the wagon seats, the babies were cradled in feather beds to cushion the jar as the wheels bumped over the lumpy ground. Whistles blew shrieking notes and funnels

352

belched smoke and cinders as the railroad engines chugged their way into this race for free land. Now and then, with the trains running, men were seen to drop from the steps of coaches, roll down the bank of the right-of-way, and sprint across the prairie to stake their claims.

When the sun set on the twenty-second day of April, 1889, a hundred thousand people had entered Oklahoma. On that first night the prairie was aglow with the light of their campfires. A land which had known only the heavy thump of buffalo herds and the gentle pat of grazing cattle was now consigned to the plow. On a warm spring day the homesteaders came and the land was theirs.

More Indian lands were opened to settlement in 1891 and 1892. The crowds came as in 1889. The cattlemen had built houses and barns in the Cherokee Strip. It was a sad day when the order came for them to vacate. The settlers in nearby Oklahoma helped themselves to miles of barbed wire, tons of fence posts, piles of lumber, and anything else on the ranches that could be hauled away. With heavy hearts the cowmen left their belongings where they were and drove their herds south to the open range in Texas.

The summer of 1893 was hot and dry. Every breeze was dust-laden, and water was scarce in the Cherokee Strip. The drought did not discourage the landseekers who

SOD SCHOOLHOUSE IN WESTERN OKLAHOMA

This photograph was taken in the 1890's soon after Oklahoma was opened to homesteaders. In one-room schoolhouses with sod walls and sod roofs, the children of farmers who broke the prairie learned to read, write, spell and cipher.

Courtesy, Muriel H. Wright

came to the opening. About 50,000 people raced into the strip from the Arkansas border. As in the other runs some sneaked in ahead of time to be first on a claim. These were called "sooners," and usually lost out in the courts to the rightful owner who had won in a fair race. Sometimes the "sooners" sold for a small sum and left.

The opening of the Cherokee Strip marked the last time that any man won free land in a horse race. In later days men drew lots for farms, but the old excitement was gone. The adventurer found waiting for numbers in a lottery a tame affair. It was not the thrill of sitting in a saddle with a fleet horse under him, waiting for the crack of a gun.

The homesteader turned the sod in the cowman's pasture and planted his crops of maize, wheat, cotton, alfalfa, and broom corn. Barbed wire fences criss-crossed the prairie like designs in a crazy quilt and closed the cattle trails forever. The open range shrank in size, as year by year, more acres of the western plains came under cultivation. The cattlemen, too, settled on ranches and plowed the ground to grow hay and grain to fatten their stock for market.

FARMERS FROM EUROPE

WHILE WASHINGTON WAS President of the United States, Alexander I, Czar of Russia, had invited German farmers to settle on the steppes of southern Russia. The Czar wanted the Germans to show his people better methods of farming. To induce the sturdy German farmers to migrate, the Czar offered religious freedom, exemption from military service, no taxes to pay for ten years, and the gift of a hundred acres of land to each family. Each colonist was required to be a good farmer or a skilled tradesman, to be of good character, to have a family or children, and at least $120 in money or property. Thousands of German families, mostly from the province of Wurttemberg, migrated to Russia.

Gradually, these families lost their freedom in Russia. By 1874 compulsory military service became a law in Russia and the colonists of German descent were not exempt. In a mass migration nearly a million Russian Germans left their adopted country to become colonists in North and South America. Thousands of families came direct from the Black Sea region to the prairie states of North and South Dakota. These farmers who had grown wheat on the Russian steppes knew how to raise wheat on the Great Plains of the United States. The children and grandchildren of these Russian Germans live today on wheat farms in North and South Dakota and neighboring states.

In the latter part of the nineteenth century Finns, too, were leaving their homes. Since Finland was then a Russian province, freedom was denied to these people as well as to the Russian Germans. Thus many Finns joined the migration to the United States. They settled on the northern plains and in the lumbering regions of the Northwest.

Their neighbors, Swedes and Norwegians, came for economic reasons. When a former emigrant returned to his native home in Norway and Sweden, he wore new American clothes and jingled American money in his pockets. He boasted of his big farm of 160 acres, given to him by Uncle Sam. His kinsmen stared in amazement and gasped. In the old country 160 acres were a rich man's

ARRIVAL OF RUSSIAN-GERMANS AT EUREKA, SOUTH DAKOTA
November 13, 1892

These immigrants were the descendants of Germans who migrated to Russia about the time of the American Revolution. A hundred years later, their move to the United States began. These Russian-Germans settled mainly in the Dakotas where they bought and homesteaded land, and became wheat farmers. The women wore shawls and the men wore fur caps, as was the custom in Russia.

holdings. Such a visitor, glowing with prosperity, was enough to start an "America fever" in a whole district. Sometimes, villages and countrysides in Norway were almost depopulated by the mass migration.

Northern Europeans were not the only foreign settlers on the Great Plains. From Central Europe came Germans, Slovaks, Bohemians, Moravians, Poles, Ukrainians, and Hungarians, seeking farms. They brought along their folklore, songs, dances, language, and customs to add color to the growing nation. They were law-abiding citi-

zens who appreciated the opportunity to earn a better living for themselves and their children.

These thrifty, hard-working emigrants from Europe lived peacefully with other Americans whose forefathers had come to the New World in colonial times. Many of the Plains settlers were the grandchildren and the great grandchildren of the first pioneers who had moved into the Northwest Territory and Kentucky after the close of the Revolutionary War. Each generation pushed farther west to open up a new

355

frontier. As the Union Pacific pushed westward, mile by mile, settlers came and turned the sod in the Platte River Valley. The railroads could not prosper without passengers and freight. They advertised their lands for sale. Farmers were encouraged to buy land along the railroads to be near markets and thus save the freight costs of long hauls. The railroads published guide books, free, to sell their lands. They offered time payments, one-fifth as a down payment and the remainder in five years. On the cover page of one of these folders was the following quotation from a poem by Whittier:

I hear the tread of pioneers
Of nations yet to be,
The first low wash of waves, where soon,
Shall roll a human sea.

These guide books warned immigrants to beware of swindlers and gave advice on many matters — the kind of clothes needed, what seed to bring, the nature of the soil, climate, and scenery. Stout-hearted men and women sometimes faltered at the task of beginning life anew in a sod shanty on the lonely prairie. In the railroad folders were words of encouragement, like the following:

It is better to be poor for a few years on your own land than to be moderately poor as a tenant for others.

Never fear failure at farming your own land if you live economically, work hard, and select your place well.

This clever advertising was aimed at the home-seeking immigrants with a longing for land. The railroads played a big role in developing the West and that settlement is still in progress. As more dams are built to irrigate more land, more people find ways of earning a living on the broad central plain of North America. There is little free land left now for the courageous homesteader.

THE PRAIRIE WIND — FRIEND AND FOE

THE PRAIRIE WIND was a nuisance to the traveler but a boon to the settler. Without the stiff breeze to turn the windmills, the plains might not have been settled for a long time. Streams were few and far apart on the western prairie. The farmers depended on deep wells for a water supply. The windmill pumped water to fill the barnyard trough, to irrigate the vegetable garden, and to supply the household needs.

Before the sod was broken, a tough, coarse grass covered the prairie. Without this nutritious grass, the ox and horse teams of the emigrants could not have survived the long journey to Oregon and California. For centuries bison had fed upon the blue-stem bunch grass and the short green buffalo grass of the western plains. Then cattle grazed on the prairie, grew fat, and went to the slaughter pens of Omaha, Kansas City, and Chicago. Finally the homesteader came. He turned the sod and uprooted the ancient grasses of the Great Plains. Unknowingly, he allowed the friendly gale, which turned his windmill, to become a vengeful foe.

Through the years that followed, more ground was plowed, harrowed, and cultivated, until the soil was powdered into dust. By the early 1930's the prairie wind was scooping up the loose top soil and swirling it into the air. In blinding blizzards of dust, boys rode horses hitched to plows in an effort to guide the animals across a field. The furrows were soon filled with "blow dirt"; seed was whipped out of the shallow turf and blown away; houses and fences were partly buried under drifts of sand and loam. Congressmen came from Washington to see the black blizzards which choked livestock and human beings and drove farmers from their homes. It was a national calamity. Thousands of farm families, "blown out" of their homes, were forced to seek any kind of a job, anywhere, to earn a living. The plight of these people became the concern of the nation. The "Dust Bowl" had to be redeemed to produce food for people at home and abroad.

Man had destroyed the native grasses with their long, stringy roots that held the soil against the wind. Perhaps the stockmen were right when they argued that the plains were grasslands, unsuited to cultivation. The plowman held on to the land and made a deal with the prairie wind. The friendly breeze would turn his windmill, but the avenging gale would not destroy his farm.

The first emigrants to Oregon had told of the endless prairie without a tree in sight. If they made the same journey today, they would find lanes of trees planted for windbrakes along the fences between fields. When the sod of the prairie was first turned over, the wind did not blow away the soil because the long tough roots of the native grasses matted the dirt. Now, the plains farmer plows his wheat stubble like a "sod-buster" and leaves part of the straw above the ground to hold the soil when the March wind blows. Instead of plowing in straight rows, he writes the letter "S" in furrows up and down the field, planting his crops in strips at right angles to the wind. In dry areas on the northern plains some farmers use a

United States Department of Agriculture

DUST STORM IN SOUTHEASTERN COLORADO

This black cloud of dust swirling over Highway 49 south of Lamar, Colorado is loaded with topsoil scooped up by prairie winds from drought-stricken farmlands in neighboring states.

lister which builds little dams every few feet. It makes a field look like a checkerboard. When the winter snows melt, each little square is turned into a puddle of water. The same thing happens when it rains. A field, tilled in this way, will store about 56,000 gallons of water per acre if the soil is not too sandy. Damp dirt will not "blow." The prairie farmer plants some of his land in cover crops like clover and alfalfa to feed his livestock. Admitting the plains are grasslands, both stockmen and farmers in the dry regions are trying to restore the rich native grasses, so nutritious for cattle and sheep, and so valuable for holding the soil.

Three timely inventions were convenient allies of the homesteader on the western prairie. The repeating rifle killed off the buffalo and drove the Indian tribes to reservations. The windmill pumped water from deep wells to supply human needs and to fill the boilers of steam engines on the early railroads. Barbed wire made a cheap and useful fence to enclose a farm of any size. Through a compromise with nature, settlers turned grasslands into farmlands. The homesteader invaded the Great Plains and he was there to stay. Neither wind nor water could dislodge him.

"FATHER OF WATERS"

THROUGH THE AGES the Mississippi River ran free and untamed from Lake Itasca in Minnesota, 2350 miles to the Gulf of Mexico. Along the way the Missouri, the Ohio, and many tributaries poured their spring floods into the ever-widening stream. The swollen Mississippi spread the surplus over the waiting lowlands and pursued its way serenely to the goal of all great rivers — salt water. Flowing through the heart of North America, the big river drained two-fifths of that continent. The river accepted the floods from its numerous tributaries as a paternal responsibility. The Mississippi was the "Father of Waters" the Indians said.

Then Europeans discovered the new country with the mighty river. Some came to trap otter, mink, and muskrat in the marshes left by the overflow in the spring of the year. Others arrived, tillers of the soil, to view with envy the vast lowlands and the delta coated with layers of silt deposited by the river in times of flood. On the broad delta were thousands of acres of the richest soil to be found any place in the entire world. Settlers had determined to plant their cotton, corn, and sugar cane in this delta at the mouth of the river. They also planted the lowlands skirting the banks as far inland as they wanted to go. Thus began the long and bitter feud between man and the Mississippi.

In 1717 De la Tour, a French engineer, laid out the city of New Orleans on a site selected by Bienville, who was commandant general of the fever-ridden settlements. At a bend in the river where huts of voyageurs sprawled over a knoll, New Orleans was founded. Each settler was given a plot of ground if he agreed to dig a canal all the way around it to drain off the overflow during high water. The engineer also asked the landowners to build an embankment along the river front.

Ten years later Governor Perrier proudly announced that a levee 5400 feet long and 18 feet wide had been completed to protect the capital of Louisiana from floods. The year 1727 marks the beginning of levees erected to change the region of the Lower Mississippi. As more colonists arrived, settlements stretched up the river from New Orleans. The owner of each plantation was required to build his own levee on his own river front. In 1743 a law required all landowners to complete strong levees to protect their own land and that of their neighbors or to forfeit their property to the Crown.

After the United States purchased Louisiana in 1803, the inhabitants were disappointed to learn that the new Government would follow the policy of the French and Spanish before it. The policy was that the floods on the Mississippi were problems for the people who live on the river and were not the concern of the nation. However, Congress willingly appropriated money to improve navigation on the stream which became an inland highway of commerce during the steamboat era. Trade benefited all the people.

In 1845 John C. Calhoun presided over a meeting of Mississippi Valley leaders in Memphis, Tennessee. He spoke in favor of the Federal Government doing more to control floods. The majority of the leaders still held the opinion that the states should pay for their own internal improvements. In 1848 Abraham Lincoln spoke on this subject in the House of Representatives:

The next most general object I can think of would be improvements on the Mississippi River and its tributaries. They touch thirteen of our states — Pennsylvania, Virginia, Kentucky, Tennessee, Mississippi, Louisiana, Arkansas, Missouri, Illinois, Indiana, Ohio, Wisconsin, and Iowa. Now I suppose it will not be denied that these thirteen states are a little more interested in improvements on that river than are the remaining seventeen . . . . Nothing is so *local* as not to be of some *general* benefit.

It was customary, at the time, for states to levy a tax upon every ton of freight carried on a canal or river. The tax was used to pay for improvements on these waterways. Knowing that most of the Congressmen approved tonnage duties and did not favor using federal funds for flood control, Lincoln told this story about an Irishman and his new boots.

"I shall niver git 'em on," says Patrick, "till I wear 'em a day or two, and stretch 'em a little."

Lincoln added, "We shall never make a canal by tonnage duties, until it shall already have been made awhile, so the tonnage can get into it."

Lincoln's idea of advancing federal funds to make internal improvements that would enable the states to pay for them was not generally accepted for a long time. Meanwhile states levied more and more taxes to build levees all the way from Cairo, Illinois, to the Gulf of Mexico. In 1879 Congress passed an act creating the Mississippi River Commission. The act put the United States into flood control work. Levees were raised and channels were dredged in a vain effort to confine the Mississippi within its manmade banks. When "Ol' Man River" charged these barriers they crumbled for miles and fell into the brown torrent. Towns and farms on the lowlands were under water as the river returned to its former flood basin.

Through the years the combined efforts of the state governments and the Federal Government failed to conquer the Mississippi. The floods became more destructive. In March, 1916 the Committee on Flood Control in the House of Representatives conducted hearings to which experts were summoned to give their advice. General Arsene Perrilliat, who had devoted twenty years to a study of flood control, defined the basic problem in his testimony:

The floods of the present time are higher than the floods of the past for two reasons. The first reason is that originally the river in flood time used to flow from Cairo to the Gulf over a waterway which might be in some places fifty miles wide extending from hills to hills. It was a wide channel with a sluggish flow of current. But, because of the ever-increasing population and because of the demands of commerce and agriculture, the confinement of the river between levees has been found to be necessary. Therefore, the water which used to flow to the Gulf through this very wide channel is now flowing to the Gulf through a very much restricted channel of perhaps not more than two to three miles in width confined between the levees. The result necessarily has been that the flood height has been increased. It is now a swift, rapid, constricted river instead of being, as formerly, a very wide, shallow, and sluggish stream.

Since the Mississippi River carries so much sediment, engineers must plan to make it flow between the levees at a speed which will keep it roiled and muddy. If the water moves slowly enough for silt to drop on the bottom, the river will fill up its own channel and spread over the cultivated lowlands.

General Perrilliat told the committee that the floods on the lower Mississippi were caused by rivers flowing from the eastern regions of heavy rainfall, such as the Tennessee Valley with as much as ninety inches of rain per year in some places. Congressmen inquired if reservoirs on the Missouri River would remove floods. The experienced engineer replied that such reservoirs would help, but that the big offender was the Ohio River where floods came in the early spring. High water on the Missouri came later, in May and June, when the channel of the Mississippi was better able to handle it.

Meanwhile, engineers built levees higher, broader and deeper, trying to force the stubborn river to go a way it did not want to go. When man appeared to be gaining the upper hand, the Mississippi would assert its authority with power and vengeance. In the spring of 1927 the Mississippi River rose higher than at any time in its history. It was a wet year throughout the entire basin. No one suspected disaster was imminent because the levees had been strengthened all the way from Cairo to the Gulf. As the water crept higher and higher, these dikes began to crumble in Arkansas and all the way to the Gulf of Mexico in a number of spots. By the middle of April, the levees around New Orleans began to weaken. To save the city, the farmers and townsmen in two counties had to be evacuated and the levee protecting their homes shot into holes with dynamite. Herbert Hoover, Secretary of Commerce, rushed to the region to render aid to the victims of this major disaster. In a radio broadcast from Memphis, Hoover said:

There are thousands of persons still clinging to their homes where the upper floors remain dry, more thousands needing to be removed in boats and established in great camps on higher ground, and yet other thousands camped upon broken levees.

The Mississippi took a terrific toll. Four hundred lives were lost, seven hundred thousand persons were made homeless, thirteen million acres were flooded, and three hundred million dollars worth of property was destroyed. The floods of 1927 convinced engineers, governors, and congressmen that levees alone would never hold the mighty river within the banks made by man. Yet, redeemed land worth many millions of dollars could not be returned to the Father of Waters.

The argument between state and national governments over who is responsible for the conduct of rivers was the subject of a poem printed in the *American Lumberman* early in the century.

> To Whom Does the River Belong?
> The river belongs to the nation;
>   The levee, they say, to the State;
> The Government runs navigation
>   The Commonwealth, though, pays the freight.
> Now, here is the problem that's heavy,
>   Please which is the right or the wrong?
> When the water runs over the levee,
>   To whom does the river belong?

THE TENNESSEE VALLEY AUTHORITY

TO PREVENT flood waters from entering the Ohio River and the Mississippi some Congressmen persistently urged that dams be built in the tributaries of the Tennessee River. After raising levees for over two-hundred-years, only to have them cracked by the mighty river, both engineers and politicans agreed that flood control of the Mississippi must start miles from that waterway.

On May 18, 1933 Congress passed the Tennessee Valley Authority Act, suggested by President Franklin D. Roosevelt. It stated that the Tennessee Valley Authority (called TVA) "was established for the purpose of maintaining and operating the properties now owned by the United States in the vicinity of Muscle Shoals, Alabama. It was created in the interest of the national defense; and for agricultural and industrial development; and to improve navigation in the Tennessee River; and to control the destructive flood waters in the Tennessee River and Mississippi River Basins."

Under TVA, reservoirs were built to store the flood waters of the Tennessee River, and those of the Powell, Clinch, and Holston Rivers which rise in the western part of Virginia and flow through a hilly region of heavy rainfall. The entire project was planned, financed, executed, and operated by the National Government, the cost being paid by all taxpayers in the United States, rather than only by people living in the region — a plan followed generally. For flood control and navigation, the Tennessee Valley Authority acquired over a million acres of land, an area one and one-half times the size of the state of Rhode Island. As some of this flooded land was in the bottoms it was rich farm soil.

If Donelson's flotilla of thirty boats could make the same trip today as in 1780, the pioneers would scarcely recognize the Tennessee River. Boiling Point, Frying Pan, and the treacherous rapids that frightened them would lie harmless on the bottoms of lakes behind dams, and their boats would be taken from one level to another through

Tennessee Valley Authority

A FLOOD ON THE CLINCH RIVER IN EAST TENNESSEE

According to an old record, a hunter in the early days almost drowned in swimming this river. "Clinch me! Clinch me!" he yelled to his companions who came to his rescue. The hunters named the stream the Clinch River. Another source claims that Clinch was the name of the man who almost drowned.

The Clinch River has played a leading role in East Tennessee. Daniel Boone left his family in a stockade near the stream for safety from Indian attack, while he guided the first band of settlers into Kentucky and founded Boonesborough. Later, pack trains with settlers on foot and horseback trailed this river to its junction with the Tennessee.

locks in the river. Their flatboats would not scrape the rocks nor lodge on a sandbar. In summer, when the river is low, water flows down from the artificial lakes behind the dams to deepen and widen the streams for boat traffic. Through a system of dams, locks, and reservoirs, the Tennessee River is open to traffic with a deep water channel from Paducah, Kentucky to Knoxville, Tennessee, a distance of 650 miles.

Under the Tennessee Valley Authority, farmers are advised on ways to prevent soil erosion in a region of heavy rainfall. Tourists are attracted by boating, camping, and fishing. Indus-

361

NORRIS DAM ON THE CLINCH RIVER

The Norris Dam stretches across the Clinch River to store flood waters in a mountainous region where rainfall is heavy. During the summer months, the water pours over the spillway into the Clinch River and on into the Tennessee River. Each large river in this area is blocked by a dam to hold back the flood waters, to fill channels for boats to navigate the Tennessee River, and to generate electricity for homes and factories.

tries are encouraged by cheap electricity to locate in the Tennessee Valley.

Today the Tennessee Valley Authority is owned and operated by the Federal Government in Washington. Since electricity can be bought for less money from TVA's dams and steam plants than from privately owned, taxpaying power companies, the project is popular with people living in the Tennessee Valley. However, many people who feel they are sharing the cost of this cheap electricity, and live elsewhere, do not approve of TVA.

BIG MUDDY

THE RESERVOIRS that stored the rain where it fell in the Tennessee Valley lowered the flood waters pouring in from the Ohio to the Mississippi. It was not enough to remove the threat of high water below Cairo, Illinois. Then attention was turned to the largest tributary from the west, the Missouri River.

One day in June, 1673, Father Marquette and his Indian guides were paddling their birchbark canoes down the Mississippi. Suddenly they were startled by the frightful sound of rushing water. Soon they were gazing upon a raging torrent swirling into the river in front of them. Large trees with roots, branches, and leaves drifted with the speed of the current. This was the "wild Missouri" during the June rise. Marquette was the first white man to see it. In describing the river, he wrote:

The agitation was so great that the water was all muddy and could not get clear.

To Indians, explorers, trappers, traders, and pioneers, the Missouri was the "Big Muddy." The name still clings to the river. Sioux Indians living along the stream called it "Muddy Water," with a word that sounded something like Missouri in their language. To boatmen, "Big Muddy" was a term of affection, meaning the water was high enough to take them upstream for many miles if they were skillful enough to dodge the floating logs and edge around the submerged islands. In dry seasons the upper Missouri is a vagabond, strolling from pool to pool, disappearing behind sandbars, and slyly detouring down a lane of cottonwood trees.

This unpredictable river, the highway of adventure, has been celebrated in song and story. Daring and courageous men, whose deeds are recorded in history, share their fame with the Missouri. In the spring of

1804 soon after the purchase of Louisiana, President Jefferson had sent Lewis and Clark up the Missouri during the high water, to explore the new possession. They had been given up as lost when they returned to St. Louis in the fall of 1806. Their return caused great excitement among the fur traders. When Manuel Lisa, a Spanish trader from New Orleans, heard the explorers tell how plentiful beaver were on the Yellowstone and on branches of the upper Missouri, he formed a company to hunt and trap in this region.

In the spring of 1807 Lisa's party of fifty-two trappers started up the Missouri to catch the spring flood. He had only one keel boat fitted with a square sail. Other craft included a number of dug-out canoes paddled by French-Canadian voyageurs. The boatmen scouted the river ahead to locate navigable channels around the dangerous sandbars in the shifting stream. Lisa established posts along the tributaries of the upper Missouri. The Spanish explorer led the way and others followed to make the Missouri River the highway of trappers and traders, a venturesome breed of men.

To the pioneers in covered wagons an important event of the westward journey was a boat ride on the Missouri River. All the travelers crossed the stream somewhere. If they did not have a boat, they forded or waded across at spots where shallow channels streaked through wide sandy islands that filled the river bed during low water. Some of these families looking for rich farmland found it along the Missouri. They settled there on the fertile lowlands covered with silt from the early summer freshets. These farmers soon learned the tricks of the fickle river. No one was greatly surprised to get up some morning and find the stream in his front

yard and to see his corn field on the other side of the Missouri.

As settlers moved into Iowa, Nebraska, and the Dakotas, steamboats plied the Missouri to take their products to market. During the steamboat era, demands came from states bordering the river to improve the stream for navigation. The Federal Government was willing to spend money for navigation on the Missouri as on the Mississippi, because these rivers were inland highways of trade which benefited the whole nation. However, the prankish Missouri played hide-and-seek with the engineers. Old steamboat pilots figured the river would not be the same on each trip, perhaps not even in the same place.

With the coming of railroads the colorful steamboat practically disappeared from the inland rivers. New cities and towns grew up along the banks as industry moved westward with population. Land became valuable along the river front and levees were erected to stave off the floods. Sometimes these barriers cracked and fell apart under the weight and force of the strong current and flooded acres of farmland and blocks of city buildings.

THE MISSOURI RIVER BASIN

THE MISSOURI RIVER BASIN covers one-sixth of the area of the United States, and is thirteen times larger than the Tennessee Valley. The winters are cold, with temperatures twenty degrees below zero and lower. The summers are hot with temperatures soaring to one hundred and ten degrees and sometimes higher. The area has water problems, ranging from drought to floods. When Congress passed The Flood Control Act of 1944, work on these problems began in earnest by the Corps of Engineers and the Bureau of Reclamation.

In 1945 Senator James E. Murray of Montana, the state where three clear mountain streams join to form the Missouri River, introduced Bill S555 in Congress. This bill sponsored a Missouri Valley Authority giving the Federal Government full rights to develop the region through which the Missouri River flows.

The Murray Bill was long debated. Some Congressmen approved it and others opposed it. Strangely, much of the opposition came from the people living near the Missouri River. As the debate progressed, telegrams poured in to the Senate Committee Hearing on S555, and most of them came from farmers and stockmen. On April 25, 1945, Charles Y. Thompson from the Nebraska Farm Bureau, who was appearing to protest passage of the Missouri Valley Authority, read some of these telegrams to the committee:

You are authorized to speak for the Minnesota Farm Bureau Federation to the extent that we want full and complete development of the water resources of the Missouri River Valley region for irrigation, flood control, and navigation. But we believe that States rights must be protected and for that reason we are absolutely opposed to administration by any regional authority.
Minnesota Farm Bureau Association

The Agricultural Council of Wyoming composed of State Farm Bureau, Wyoming State Grange, Wyoming Stock Growers, Wool Growers, and Beet Associations are opposed to Senate bill 555, and insist that all reclamation work be done by Army Engineers and the Reclamation Bureau. H.J. King
President, Wyoming Agricultural Council

A long telegram from the Chamber of Commerce in Butte, Montana made the same kind of statements, that complete federal authority was an invasion of the

rights of states; that the government agencies then handling flood control and reclamation were competent and were cooperating with local agencies. However, the telegram from Butte contained another objection to the Murray Bill:

The plans of this bill, in our judgment, will eventually make it imperative for the United States Government to go into business in the State of Montana, and we are opposed to such entry by the Federal Government into the field of business where it can be avoided.
Butte Chamber of Commerce

The people wanted a program shared by local agencies, not federal ownership and federal control. When S555 failed to pass, development of the Missouri River Basin followed the plan approved by Congress in 1944 and in former years. About 90 dams have been planned for flood control, irrigation, hydroelectric power, recreation, and navigation. These projects have been built as fast as money has been available. Fort Peck in Montana, Garrison in North Dakota, and Fort Randall in South Dakota

KERR DAM ON THE FLATHEAD RIVER IN NORTHWESTERN MONTANA

This dam is owned and operated by The Montana Power Company, formed by investors who bought stock in the company. As the dam is on the reservation of the Flathead Indians, the company pays rent to the tribe for the use of this land.

Montana Power Company

belong to this huge project. A disastrous flood in 1952 reminded the engineers building the dams that this long western river is still the "Wild Missouri."

THE MAGIC OF BLACK GOLD

NEAR BEAUMONT, TEXAS, was a small hill rising twenty feet above the marshy coastal plain. Trees crowned it in the shape of a spindle top. Springs, oozing from the side of the hill, contained so much gas that picnickers delighted in setting the water on fire. Where there is gas, there is oil, as a rule. After spending thousands of dollars, promoters found no oil. They abandoned the shaft dug into Spindletop.

Others tried a new method of sinking pipes through the quicksands and met with success. The day was January 10, 1901; the hour, 10:30 A.M. A worker was perched high in the derrick when the earth began to tremble beneath him. The spidery framework shook like a leaf in the wind. Frightened, he slid down the rope barely in time to miss tons of pipe hurled up from the hole. The gusher roared in, shooting a black fountain a hundred feet into the air. Fifty thousand barrels of oil a day and all wasted. It took seven days to cap the well. Thousands of sightseers came from long distances by train to see Spindletop running wild. It was a great show. This well started the oil boom in the Southwest.

In the northern part of Texas the March winds had scooped the soil from plowed fields and piled it into drifts along the fences. The summer drought which followed the dust storms had withered the cotton and burned the corn. The farmers were selling out and moving farther south to the part of the state where rain fell and crops grew. One man, however, clung to his parched land, hoping for that chance in a million. Sometimes, the water in his well had the smell and taste of kerosene. This was a ray of hope. Maybe a pool of oil lay under his farm.

On borrowed money he built a derrick and began to drill. Weeks later, during the night, the well came in. The excited driller banged on the door to awaken the family.

"The tanks are full," he shouted, "and the oil is running through the cotton field!"

In a short time the well was gushing three thousand barrels of oil a day, worth $6750. The cotton field blossomed in derricks, rooted in the greasy black mud. From this beginning developed the rich strike in the Burkburnett oil fields near the town of Wichita Falls.

The farmers near Oklahoma City settled down to a peaceful rural life after oil men had solemnly declared there were no pools of flowing gold beneath their red soil. They planted lilacs, zinnias, and honeysuckle in their yards, and corn, alfalfa, and strawberries in their fields. They would escape the oil craze which had upset the lives of so many country people all over the Southwest. Then a company was formed to explore for oil and to dig deep enough to find it.

At one time Mary Sudik was a little-known farmer's wife in Oklahoma. All at once her name was known to millions, not only in this country, but in Europe and Asia. It all happened because of "Wild Mary." For weeks the drillers had been boring a hole into the ground on the Sudik farm. On a March morning in 1930, the well came in with a roar heard for miles. The gusher was christened "Mary Sudik" after the pleasant smiling farm woman who lived on the land. The pressure of underground gas tossed a foamy black mass of oil into the air. The wind of the prairie carried the spray for miles and miles to wash the countryside in liquid gold. Mary went "wild" and spouted oil, destroying crops in the fields, driving farmers from their homes, and wasting money in huge sums. When no one was able to cap the well, the name was changed to "Wild Mary." For eleven days the Sudik well raged and spouted before the output was under control and flowing into pipe lines.

Derricks sprouted in the barnyards, in the chicken pens, and in the flower beds of neighboring farms to end the quiet peace of the countryside. Like an invading army, towers of wood and steel crept up to the city limits, and then, brazenly marched into the capital. The oil craze struck Oklahoma City. Derricks, a hundred and twenty-five feet high, were planted in backyards, on front lawns, and in driveways. Night and day the engines chugged and the pumps clinked, making the air foul with the stench of fresh oil and stagnant water.

Oil booms strike suddenly in the most unexpected spots and they suddenly change a way of life. Tulsa was once a cowtown and a trading center for the Indian tribes. Now, it is a city with skyscrapers, traffic jams, and millionaires. It boasts the title, "Oil Center of the World." After the oil boom in the eastern part of Texas, Houston was a contender for Tulsa's title. In East Texas an operator drilled wells on land without a sign of oil. He was a "wildcatter" (prospectors who seek oil in out-of-way places). The wildcat

OIL INVADES THE CAPITOL OF OKLAHOMA

When the oil boom struck Oklahoma City, derricks were erected on the grounds of the State Capitol Building.

Meyers

THE HOUSE BOAT "LITTLE EVA" IN A BAYOU OF LOUISIANA

The men who live on this boat travel back and forth in motor launches to work an oil well surrounded by water. Once upon a time, pirates sailed into these bayous to hide their loot. Unknowingly, their boats skimmed over a buried treasure worth more than all the gold coins they had captured from all the Spanish ships.

wells punctured one of the largest pools of oil ever found any place in the world. Before this happened, Houston was only another cotton town. Now, half the people in this growing metropolis earn a living, directly or indirectly, from the oil business. Oil built the skyscrapers, enlarged the suburbs, and paid for the yachts in the harbor at Galveston. Houston, fifty miles from the gulf, became a seaport when Buffalo Bayou was dredged and deepened to bring ocean liners and freighters to the city's doorsteps. Now, sleek tankers glide down this channel to carry Texas oil around the world.

OIL DID IT

THE PRAIRIE STATES of the Southwest — Texas, Oklahoma, and Louisiana —

were originally settled by tillers of the soil who came from New England, the Midwest, and the old South. Women in frilly sunbonnets brought eggs, butter, and cream to the country village to trade for coffee, sugar, and tea. Men in blue overalls and wide straw hats unloaded their farm wagons at shipping centers where they sold the products of their fields, orchards, and gardens. The sidewalks of the cowtowns resounded to the clack of high-heeled boots and the rattle of spurs. The Southwest was rural and content to remain that way.

Then came the oil men! Derricks mingled with the windmills and sticky oil sloshed over the fields. Skyscrapers sprouted on Main Street and sleepy towns grew into bustling cities. The agricultural Southwest started to become an industrial empire. Oil did it. A gusher of flowing gold brought the oil men, swarming like a hive

367

of bees. The topless auto with flapping fenders and the closed limousine with hooded tires crept chummily over the dusty roads to a new oil find.

Shacks rose overnight along a prairie lane and a town was born. There was no time to pave the streets. In hip boots the "roustabouts" slogged through the oily slush. An enterprising lad hitched a horse to his sled and charged a dime to ferry new arrivals across the soggy road. Main Street wallowed in mud when it rained. Trucks bogged down in the mire. In a hotel lobby from morning until midnight there was excitement. Tobacco ashes and chewing gum wrappers rolled in front of the cleaning brigade. Excited men crowded around the telegraph office and the telephone booths. They were nervous and impatient. Couldn't wait. Huge sums of money were made and lost in a minute.

When hotel rooms were available at all, they had to be shared with other guests. Cots lined the halls and filled the porches. Many, unable to find a bed, slept in their cars, in the park, and by the side of the road. Food was scarce and high in price. The green lawns of trim white cottages were splotched with hamburger stands and soft drink bars. The oil boom was on! Milling crowds! Money talk! Choking dust!

Who were these oil men? Some were well-dressed with leather brief cases under their arms. These were the lease men, the lawyers, the promoters. Others went about in greasy overalls and rubber boots — the rig builders, the drilling crews, the pipe liners. These fortunehunters were the conquistadores of *our* day.

Long years ago Spanish conquerors roamed over the plains of the great Southwest, searching for a yellow metal. The silent prairie kept its secret from them. The hidden treasure was BLACK gold!

MAPS:

WA 24r, WA 30r
Our United States — Its History In Maps
by Edgar B. Wesley

PART EIGHT

Climate and Resources
Pace Western Growth

ZUNI RAIN DANCE
"COME, LET US GO TO OUR PEOPLE AND DANCE AND MAKE RAIN FOR THEM."

The rain-making ceremonies of the Zuni Tribe are long and elaborate, and sometimes last for days. The men who impersonate the rain gods wear masks because clouds hide the faces of the rainmakers in the sky.

When the dancers arrive, the people gather on the roofs and in the courtyards, and watch with quiet reverence. The dance is a prayer. A flute plays ceremonial tunes, and choirs chant the sacred ritual, — one long, solemn prayer for rain.

"Let the heavens be covered with the banked-up clouds.
Let the earth be covered with fog; cover the earth with rains.
Great waters, rains, cover the earth. Lightning cover the earth.
Let the thunder be heard over the earth; let the thunder be heard.

* * *

Rainmakers come out from all roads, that great rivers may cover the earth;

That stones may be moved by the torrents;
That trees may be uprooted and moved by the torrents.

* * *

That my children may have all things to eat and be happy,
That the people of the outlying villages may all laugh and be happy.

* * *

May all my children have corn that they may complete the road of life."

Translation of verses from a Zuni Rain Ritual (Bureau of American Ethnology)

Chapter 20

In the Land of Little Rain

THE RAINMAKERS

IN ZUNI LEGEND the rainmakers were water spirits who roamed over the world collecting showers from the four encircling oceans. They dwelled in the white cumulus clouds that crown the mountain peaks rising from the mile-high plateau of their homeland. Creatures on earth could see their breath — it was mist — but no mortal could ever look upon their faces. They wore clouds for masks.

There was great rejoicing among the Indians when the fluffy clouds began to roll into white puffs like snow and hover over the mountain ranges. The rainmakers were at home and their jars were filled with water from the four encircling oceans. Great were the holy men of the tribe, who, with their fasts, dances, and songs were able to coax the rainmakers down from the mountain to sprinkle the thirsty fields of corn. Their prayers were answered when the clouds turned gray, drifted across the sky, and cast their shadow upon the ground. Then the natives knew the water spirits were coming to empty their jars, pouring rain on the baked earth.

Since maize was the "staff of life," the natives could live only where there was water for their fields of corn. Historians are inclined to agree that a long drought dried up the streams before Columbus came and forced the ancient cliff-dwellers from the safety of their canyon homes. Drought forced them to settle in the river valleys where melting snows in the mountains fed the streams with water with which they could irrigate their fields. Here in the river valleys Coronado found Indians, although a few still lingered in canyons where streams trickled through the narrow floors of the gorges. One of Coronado's exploring parties found beans growing along the banks of a creek winding through the bottom of a canyon. They were more surprised to discover that the bean farmers lived in the caves that looked like pockmarks on the face of the canyon wall. They named the stream El Rito de los Frijoles — the Little River of the Beans.

Slowly, white men trickled into the Indian country to establish trading posts and missions. They brought in new ideas for watering the corn. The Indians in their ceremonials waved sticks tipped with downy feathers, a symbol of lifting the moisture-laden clouds over the mountain barrier to spill their precious contents on the thirsty plain. The white men knew that

ZUNI WATER JAR

In symbolic designs, Indians in the semi-desert country expressed their awe of sun, moon, stars, rain, and the wonders of nature all around them. This ancient jar, beautiful in form and design, is a rare work of Indian art. The need for water influenced religion and the arts of native peoples in the Southwest.

the clouds dropped their moisture in crossing the mountains. Raging torrents rolled down the dry arroyos after a cloudburst in the hills. The sudden, roaring flood took with it trees, logs, houses, cattle, sheep — anything in its path. Little by little the palefaces began to store the water in reservoirs where it fell. They brought it down in canals to irrigate the crops when needed. In times of drought when water is low in the ditches, the Indians still chant their rainmaking ceremonials as in days of old.

Yet, if Coronado returned today to lead his expedition over the same route he followed in 1540, he would find much of the country little changed. Away from the paved highways, the irrigated farms, and the lighted towns, the cacti and the sage-

brush still struggle for life in the desert. In the warm sand the spotted rattlesnake curls, unseen by the passerby until he sounds a warning with the rattles on his tail. On hot summer days long-tailed lizards doze in the scanty shade of soapweed plants. The sharp yip of the coyote may disturb the quiet of the night. The noise and bustle of modern civilization have lightly touched this land of Coronado. Water still is king and dictates the way of life in this land of little rain.

ZUNI WATER JARS
DECORATED WITH RAIN SYMBOLS

After a heavy rain, dragon flies hovered over the mud puddles where frogs croaked and tadpoles wiggled. Indian mothers told their little ones that these creatures were the rainmaker's children who brought water from the clouds to earth. Two of the jars are decorated with designs of tadpoles and dragon flies.

The Deer Clan had a special part in rain-making ceremonies. The dancers who impersonated the rain gods fasted for 24 hours. At the end of the ritual, women of the Deer Clan brought cool water to the thirsty men. Other women trailed them, carrying bowls of food for the feast that followed the long fast.

On the large jar, deer are standing in a cloud design with a background of the falling-rain pattern: \\\\ Today, as in olden times, a lonely gray cloud can be seen pouring water on a small area in the Zuni country. The rain streams down in a veil so thin that the sun shines through, and the bluish mountains can be seen through the sheer downpour. Did the Indians get the pattern of falling rain from such freakish little cloudbursts?

All three jars have these familiar cloud designs:

THE PASTORAL ERA
CAME FIRST

WHEN CORONADO RETURNED to Mexico from his land expedition, he learned that Cabrillo, a Portuguese navigator in the service of Spain, had been sent by sea to explore the coast line of the unknown land lying to the north. In September of 1542 Cabrillo and his sailors sought shelter from a storm in the Bay of San Diego. Here the natives told them about other palefaced men who had been seen inland a few days journey away. The bearded strangers whom the Indians described with signs and gestures probably belonged to Alarcon's expedition, dispatched by sea to carry added supplies to Coronado. With the help of friendly Indians, some of Alarcon's men traveled in small boats quite a distance up the Colorado River, but failed to find any trace of Coronado's party traveling overland.

Following the coast line of California, Cabrillo discovered the Bay of Santa Monica which he named the "Bay of Smokes." Probably, natives had started brush fires to drive rabbits from their holes and a haze of burning chaparral and manzanita veiled the surrounding hills. Continuing the voyage north, Cabrillo explored the coast almost as far as San Francisco Bay. Plagued by fog and violent winds, in which one of his two ships was lost for days, he decided to turn back. He took refuge from the ocean storms in the Bay of Monterey. With a sick and starving crew he sought a warmer climate. They spent the winter in a sheltered harbor of an island off the coast of Santa Barbara. Here, early in January of 1543, Cabrillo died and was buried. His pilot became captain and continued the exploration of the shore line until provisions were almost exhausted. He then returned to Mexico. Upon this voyage of Cabrillo Spain based her claim to California.

It was more than two hundred years before Spain made any effort to colonize the country discovered by Cabrillo. Meanwhile Russian hunters had crossed the narrow strait separating the continents of Asia and North America to get furs. Not content with only Alaskan seal they worked their way farther and farther down the coast to trap beaver, otter, and mink along the rivers flowing into the Pacific Ocean. When the King of Spain heard that Russians were establishing trading posts in or near his territory, he became alarmed and ordered the Viceroy of New Spain "to guard that part of his Dominions from all invasion."

To carry out the King's request two expeditions were planned. One was to be by land and one by sea, under the direction of Jose de Galvez, commissioner of the King. To hold the country it had to be occupied by Spaniards. Captain Gaspar de Portola was given the military command and instructed to erect forts for defense. Junipero Serra, a Franciscan friar, was placed in charge of the missionaries who were to establish settlements and convert the natives to Christianity.

Galvez immediately began the task of recruiting both soldiers and friars and gathering supplies for the new country. Two vessels sailed first for San Diego with tools and necessities to sustain life in an unsettled land. The cargo included ornaments and vestments for the chapels of the missions. Since Spain and California lie in the same latitude, Galvez figured that the same crops could be grown in both countries. He loaded the vessels with an ample supply of all kinds of seeds, grains for food, flax for linen, and flowers for the patios. On board, also, were bundles of tree cuttings for orchards and gardens. Junipero Serra was at La Paz on the eastern coast of Lower California when the *San Carlos* sailed on the ninth of January, 1769, for San Diego. Galvez accompanied the explorers as far as Cape San Lucas on the western tip of the peninsula. Here he found the *San Antonio,* buffeted by storms which had prevented the ship from reaching the harbor of La Paz. After supervising repairs of the vessel, Galvez ordered the captain to sail for La Paz to get supplies.

With the ships on their way Galvez turned his attention to the land expedition. He sent messengers throughout the peninsula to collect cattle, horses, and mules for the new settlements and to persuade soldiers, friars and settlers to join the caravan for California. The necessary supplies were gathered for man and beast, as the explorers traveled north from mission to mission in the peninsula. From the northernmost outpost of civilization, the expedition proceeded in two sections. The first went ahead to drive the cattle and the second traveled behind with soldiers under Portola and missionaries under Junipero Serra. It was the middle of May when the second party left the last mission to cross unknown country, proceeding to San Diego to meet the men who had gone by sea. Misfortune upset the well-laid plans of Galvez.

The *San Antonio* sailed a month after the *San Carlos*, but arrived first at San Diego April 11, 1769 after fifty-nine days at sea. About half of the men on board were suffering from scurvy. After being lost in storms for 110 days, the San Carlos reached the port of San Diego later in the month of April, 1769. Only a few men of the crew were able to stand and handle the boat. Both soldiers and sailors were gravely ill from scurvy and thirst. A number of the seamen died after reaching San Diego, although the ship's doctor had searched the country nearby and found herbs from which he made tea in an effort to cure the scurvy.

By the first of July the land expeditions arrived at San Diego. The combined sea and land parties numbered only a little over a hundred men. The land parties traveled through desert country and some of the livestock perished on the way. These marchers suffered less than the sea voyagers. It was decided to send the *San Antonio* back to San Lucas to report what had happened and to ask for more sailors to man the *San Carlos* which was to proceed north to Monterey. Junipero Serra waited in San Diego with the sick men expecting the *San Jose*, a supply ship, to arrive any day with men and supplies.

On July 14 with sixty-six men, a fourth of whom were friendly Indians, a military expedition under Portola started north from San Diego to occupy the country and erect forts to defend it. Two days later Junipero Serra founded the first mission at San Diego.

Meanwhile, Portola's explorers made their way inland, through valleys and over mountains. They were looking for the place marked on a map made by an early explorer in 1602 and named after the Count of Monte-Rey, Viceroy of New Spain. On November 2, 1769, Portola dispatched Sergeant Ortega and a squad of soldiers to explore the region near his camp. They had orders to return in three or four days. On that same day a few men from camp went deer hunting, and returned that evening with the exciting news that they had seen a huge inland sea not far from the ocean. The next day Ortega returned with the same news, stating that he and his companions had tried to go around the great body of water, but that their way had been blocked by a narrow outlet leading into the ocean. Four days later Portola and the missionaries viewed this "arm of the sea." What would they name it?

Before leaving Lower California in 1769, Junipero Serra had been given a list of names for the missions he was to start in California, the northernmost province of New Spain. Disappointed that one was not named for St. Francis of Assisi, founder of his order, Serra had asked, "Is there to be no mission for our father St. Francis?"

Galvez had replied, "If St. Francis wants a mission, let him cause his port to be discovered, and it will be placed there."

Another bay had been charted by an early explorer in that region and called by him, St. Francis Bay of Cermeno (probably Drake's Bay). Thinking the enclosed harbor was part of this body of water, the friars named it, San Francisco Bay. Provisions were running low and the natives who had been so kind and brought them food were becoming unfriendly. After a few more days of exploring, Portola decided to turn back, hoping to discover Monterey on the

THE GOLDEN GATE

Great mariners failed to find this narrow strait leading into San Francisco Bay. Cabrillo missed it in 1542, and so did Francis Drake thirty-seven years later. It was discovered by a landlubber who stumbled upon it by accident. He was Jose Francisco Ortega, a sergeant, whom Portola had sent with a squad of soldiers to explore the coast as far north as Port Reyes. A gateway to the "arm of the sea" barred his way. On the fifth of August in 1775, the Spanish supply ship, San Carlos, sailed through this uncharted strait, opening the Golden Gate to the trade of the world.

Courtesy, Californians Inc.

way south. He hoped to find either the *San Jose* or the *San Antonio* anchored in the harbor with much needed supplies.

The retreat began on the eleventh of November, and on the twenty-eighth, Portola unknowingly camped on the site of Monterey. After waiting there for twelve days for provisions he headed south, having only a few sacks of flour to feed his men. It was necessary to kill twelve of the pack mules to provide meat for the party, which arrived in San Diego on the twenty-fourth of January in 1770. There, Portola learned that most of the men who had been sick with scurvy had died but that Junipero Serra had recovered from the disease.

Before leaving Lower California, it had been agreed that the explorers were to return if ships carrying supplies failed to arrive by the nineteenth of March. The despondent men watched anxiously for a sail as the March days slipped by. Neither the *San Jose* nor the *San Antonio* appeared in the harbor. As the day approached to abandon the settlement, Junipero Serra went aboard the *San Carlos* lying helpless in the bay without a crew. He went to inform the captain that he and Father Crespi would remain to preach the gospel when the expedition returned. Serra refused to desert the mission.

On the nineteenth of March farewell religious services were held in the morning. The expedition was packed and ready to leave on the morrow. Portola, the commander, decided to wait one more day for help to arrive. On the afternoon of the nineteenth a sail was sighted in the distance. Captain Perez of the *San Antonio* enroute to Monterey had turned back from Santa Barbara Channel when he learned from natives through their sign language that Portola had returned to San Diego. The expedition waited four days for the *San Antonio* to anchor in the harbor with provisions for the land forces and sailors for the *San Carlos*. Serra's first mission was saved.

With only twenty men Portola left San Diego on the seventeenth of April to make another search for Monterey which he had not recognized the first time. His orders were to build a fort there to defend the territory from invasion by the Russians or any other settlers. Two days after Portola started overland to Monterey, Junipero Serra sailed on the *San Antonio* for that northern port. The fort was erected at Monterey. The mission where Junipero Serra labored was located at nearby Carmel where the land could be irrigated from a mountain stream.

The Bay of San Francisco was fortified with a garrison of soldiers in a district still called the Presidio, and still an army post. The missionaries looked around for a mission site not far away; a place with water handy and a view of the surrounding country. One of the friars, Juan Crespi, wrote in his journal describing the spot that was selected:

From this mesa one enjoys a most beautiful view — a good part of the bay and its islands — and a view of the ocean. In fact, although, so far as I have traveled, I have seen very good places and beautiful lands, I have yet seen none that pleased me so much as this. I do believe that, if it could be well populated, as in Europe, there would be nothing more beautiful in the world. This place has the best accommodations for founding on it a most beautiful city, inasmuch as the desirable qualities exist as well on the land as on the sea. The port is exceptional and large for dockyards, docks, and whatever would be wanted.

Five days before the Declaration of Independence was signed in Philadelphia, a mission for St. Francis of Assisi was founded near the tip of the peninsula which separates the ocean from the "arm of the sea" destined to be known as the Bay of San Francisco. The first religious service was held in an arbor fashioned of boughs. This crude shelter was the first church. Soldiers with their families and servants and the native Indians made up the congregation. Thus in the year of independence, the future city of San Francisco started with a fort and a mission. If the early missionary could return today, he would see his dream fulfilled.

MISSIONS – RANCHOS – PUEBLOS

UNDER SPANISH LAW all colonial territory in the New World belonged to the King. He could give this land to anyone for any purpose. He was generous with land grants to missionaries who pushed the Spanish frontier north into California and induced settlers to occupy the country. Since land was plentiful, these grants included thousands of acres with scarcely any limit at first. The friars sought to convert the natives not only to Christianity but also to a civilized way of life. Indians were trained in agriculture, trades, and handicrafts, and the talented ones were taught the arts. The Christian Indians who lived at the missions worked in the fields, molded adobe bricks, cut wood, hauled water, herded cattle and sheep, took care of horses, erected buildings, cobbled shoes, and fashioned tiles. The women washed wool, carded, spun, and wove it. Most of the young women worked at grinding wheat and corn into coarse flour and meal by rubbing the grains between rocks. A large stone served as a bread board and a small one as a rolling pin. Mush made from these grains was the main dish.

All the natives did not come to the missions to work, even though they frequently starved in their wild surroundings. Some who accepted Christianity ran away from food and care to escape toil and discipline, preferring to live in the mountains and eat berries, roots, and game. When ill and in need, however, many runaways returned to the missions, which became self-supporting communities for both the natives and missionaries. When soldiers were garrisoned in presidios near missions, the friars were expected to contribute both food and clothing for their support, although each fort was allotted land for cultivation and pasture. Thus in the early days the missions bore the main burden of extending the outposts of civilization into California.

How the missionaries met the problems of establishing settlements in new country was observed by an English visitor to the mission in San Francisco. In November of 1792, George Vancouver, Captain of the British ship *Discovery*, anchored in the Bay of San Francisco to find wood and water. He had been exploring the western coast of North America and searching for the mythical Northwest Passage. The Spaniards received him cordially. The soldiers at the Presidio vied with the friars at the mission in making him welcome and comfortable. In the journal of his travels Vancouver described the Mission of St. Francis on Dolores Creek.

One of the missionaries boarded the *Discovery* to invite the captain to dinner on Sunday, the eighteenth of November. Since he was the guest of the commander at the Presidio, he was escorted by officers on horseback from the fort to the

CALIFORNIA INDIANS DANCING AT THE MISSION OF ST. FRANCIS

mission, not quite three miles distant. Vancouver wrote of the mission and the Presidio:

While dinner was preparing, our attention was engaged in seeing the several houses within the square. Some we found appropriated to the reception of grain, of which however they had not a very abundant stock; nor was the place of its growth within sight of the mission. One large room was occupied by manufacturers of a coarse sort of blanketing, made from the wool produced in the neighborhood. The looms, though rudely wrought, were tolerably well contrived, and had been made by the Indians under the immediate direction of the fathers. The produce resulting from this manufactory is wholly applied to the clothing of the converted Indians. The garden contained about four acres, was tolerably well fenced in, and produced some fig, peach, apple, and other fruit trees, but afforded a very scanty supply of useful vegetables.

On our return to the convent we found a most excellent and abundant repast provided of beef, mutton, fish, fowls, and such vegetables as their garden afforded. The attentive and hospitable

behavior of our new friends amply compensated for the homely manner in which the dinner was served; — After dinner we were engaged in an entertaining conversation, in which, by the assistance of Mr. Dobson, our interpreter, we were each able to bear a part.

Vancouver arranged for cattle, sheep, poultry, and some vegetables to be taken aboard the *Discovery* to feed his crew. When he called at the fort to pay for these supplies, the commander refused to accept any money. Wishing to show his appreciation, Vancouver presented the commander with a few kitchen pans and dishes, some bar iron, and decorations for the churches, asking that these small gifts be divided between the Presidio and the mission. Vancouver wrote:

Thus we quitted San Francisco highly indebted to our hospitable reception, and the excellent refreshments, which in a few days had entirely eradicated every apparent symptom of the scurvy.

In time, however, the famed hospitality of the ranchos surpassed that of the forts and missions. Soldiers in the presidios also wanted land for themselves on which to pasture their flocks and herds. Their pay was small and life was dull and idle in the forts. Only a few disturbances occurred to break the monotony of the pastoral way of life. On the whole the natives were peaceful and docile. No enemy came to invade and conquer the country. Soldiers pastured their stock on land allotted to the fort or nearby missions until their herds grew too large and more space was needed for grazing. Portola's men, nicknamed "leather-jackets" because they wore vests padded with layers of deerskin and carried shields of raw bullhide,

petitioned for land. They had endured the dangers and hardships of exploring and occupying the country for Spain.

In 1784 Pedro Fages, a leather-jacketed captain under Portola who was appointed governor, made the first land grants to three corporals in his command and thus founded the rancho system. Jose Dominguez received about 75,000 acres lying along the ocean front. He named his grant the Rancho San Pedro. When Jose Verdugo, stationed at the San Gabriel Mission, heard about the grant to Dominguez, he asked the governor for the same favor, and received 36,000 acres of wooded hills bordering the mission tract. Upon retirement from the army Verdugo lived on his Rancho San Rafael which

MISSION SANTA CLARA

Santa Clara Mission was founded in 1777 in a valley south of San Francisco. This painting by Andrew Hill tells the story of Spanish California during the pastoral era. Less than fifty years after its founding, this mission owned 6000 cattle, 13,000 sheep, 760 horses, 20 mules, and 20 hogs.

Title Insurance and Trust Company Historical Picture Collection, Los Angeles

extended into the foothills. The third corporal was Manuel Nieto whose grant for the Rancho Santa Gertrudes was the largest — 300,000 acres — but it was cut in half shortly because the grant overlapped the tract assigned to the Mission San Gabriel. Thus began the rancho system which spread throughout the province of California.

Pueblos were part of the Spanish plan to populate California and towns were founded along with the missions and the ranchos. Sites for these pueblos, or towns, were also grants from the King of Spain. They usually contained about 17,500 acres, although a few amounted to about 70,000 acres. Land was always reserved for a plaza, or central square, a church, and public buildings. To encourage settlers in the pueblos, each head of a family was given a place to build his house with ample space for an orchard and a garden. Each pueblo had a communal pasture where all the colonists could graze their livestock. Still the Viceroy of Mexico, charged with the responsibility of populating California, had a hard time persuading colonists to venture north into the new country.

Before Felipe de Neve left Lower California to become the first governor in the new capital, Monterey, he and the viceroy had talked over plans for establishing towns in the territory. San Jose was the first pueblo, founded in November of 1777, not far from the capital. For the second pueblo de Neve selected a site in the southern part, near the Mission San Gabriel, where a river provided water to irrigate the fields. Two years after the founding of San Jose, de Neve sent his lieutenant-governor to northern Mexico to recruit fifty-nine

soldiers for a fort at Santa Barbara and twenty-four families to start a town near San Gabriel.

In a year and a half the leader of the expedition enlisted the soldiers but secured only half the quota of settlers. He took a few soldiers with him and joined the party going overland to drive the cattle and horses for the new pueblo. The colonists and most of the soldiers crossed the Gulf of California and then marched north through the peninsula. This party reached the Mission San Gabriel on the eighteenth of August after traveling for four months, only to learn that their leader and his small party had been massacred by the Yuma Indians while camping on the bank of the Colorado River.

On September 4, 1781, Governor de Neve proudly led the procession from the San Gabriel Mission to found the pueblo which grew into the city of Los Angeles. Soldiers and friars joined the march, adding Indians to swell the number escorting the settlers to their new home. The founders of Los Angeles, now one of the largest cities in the United States, consisted of eleven men, eleven women, and twenty-two children. The adults were two Spaniards, nine Indians, one mixed Spaniard and Indian, eight mulattoes, and two Negroes. Not one could read or write and only one had a trade. He was a tailor. They went to work digging their irrigation ditches and erecting their mud-roofed huts.

Towns also grew up around the presidios and missions. However, the ranchos set the pattern of living as more and more settlers came. The huge grants of land were divided into smaller plots through inheritance and purchase. Life on a rancho was quiet and peaceful, except when the daily routine was broken by social gatherings. There were fiestas with dancing and music, picnics in the groves of oak trees, and bullfights in the corrals. Strangers and invited guests were welcomed on the ranchos where they were fed, housed, and entertained as if they belonged to the family. They stayed as long as they pleased. Such courtesies won for the ranchos their far-famed reputation for hospitality.

Luxuries were acquired by selling hides and tallow, the main products of both ranchos and missions. During the pastoral days in California trade was largely carried on by barter. Smuggling was general since there was only one custom house and that was at Monterey. Many a captain from New England found shelter and security in the smuggler's den on Catalina Island, beyond the reach of Spanish officials who might order him to sail north and pay duty on his cargo.

When sails appeared in the bay off San Pedro, oxcarts were soon rumbling over the dusty road. Some hauled bundles of hides and others, bags of tallow. This poor harbor, where ships could not anchor near the shore, became the hide and tallow port of the Pacific. From a ship captain one ranch owner received supplies of tobacco, rice, knives and forks, dishes, hooks and eyes, cotton cloth, colored prints, gingham, shoes, slippers, thread, linseed oil, glass bottles, corks, hammers, nails, and numerous small items for his household, amounting to $1196.20. For each cartload the captain issued a hand-written receipt like the following copied from his personal records:

Ship Alert — April 14, 1841
Received from Don Abel Stearns Sixty-two Bullocks' hides, being for his own account. Received — nine bags weighing 164 lbs. — tallow.

Carts arrived with hides and tallow until the rancher's credit equalled the amount of the bill. Debts were also paid with produce instead of money, according to the handwritten order of a rancher, requesting an employee to deliver:

One hundred and thirty-one hides — if there is not that number in the warehouse, make up the amount in tallow. November 16, 1835.

The pastoral life of the missions and the ranchos was not as easy-going as it appeared to be on the surface. The major problems were water, politics, and gold. It was semi-desert country. In years of drought the missions suffered because in both good and bad years the same requests for corn, beans, soap, shoes, blankets, stockings, and woolen cloth were received from the California governors to supply the soldiers and their families. In June of 1822, a friar from Mission San Jose wrote to the governor:

I do not know what we shall have to do since this year through lack of water, scarcely any corn and beans will be grown. Everything is dried up and ruined. — If all that is demanded must be furnished, the Indians will have to go hungry.

Although sites for missions and ranchos were selected near rivers, these streams were torrential in winters when rainfall was normal and dried up entirely during summers of drought. By digging wells to tap the underground supply of water stored by winter rains, early Californians managed to get enough water to maintain a pastoral way of life which brought them a measure of prosperity. In rainy seasons their cattle fattened on wild oats; in times of drought, their herds dwindled in number.

In 1821 the Mexicans declared their independence of Spain and took over most of the Spanish territory in North

America, including California. Years of revolution followed in Mexico with governments that rose and fell in rapid succession. Politicians passed new decrees and were out of office before their laws had time to be enforced. The missions suffered heavily in this political upheaval. At the close of the year 1832 the twenty-one missions of California owned 151,180 cattle, 137,971 sheep, 1,711 goats, 1,164 hogs, 14,522 horses, and 1,575 mules. Two years later the lands and herds of the missions were taken over by the Mexican Government. The missions gradually fell into ruin. (In recent years, a number of these old buildings have been restored by private funds and are used for church services.)

In 1848 following the war between the United States and Mexico, politics interfered again to change the way of life. By the Treaty of Guadalupe Hidalgo the United States gained the present states of California, New Mexico, Utah, Nevada, nearly all of Arizona, and parts of Wyoming and Colorado. The United States recognized the property rights of former Mexican citizens living in this vast territory. It was gold, more than war and politics, that sounded the death bell for the pastoral era.

Gold was discovered in California shortly before the treaty was signed. The rush of immigrants from all over the world brought a period of prosperity to the ranchers who sold their cattle, sheep, and horses to the goldseekers passing through on their way to the "diggings" in the Sacramento River Valley. However, it was not long before hundreds of disillusioned miners were abandoning the pursuit of gold and were settling upon the land. Although ranch owners tried to defend their property in the courts, they gradually lost their vast estates. They were forced to sell them piece by piece to pay the costs of years of court trials over titles and boundaries. Again the plowman replaced the herder. Little by little the pastures were turned into farms by means of irrigation.

Water ended one era and ushered in another. Drought completed the destruction of the old Spanish land system of the ranchos. During the dry years of 1856 and 1857 over 100,000 cattle were lost in Los Angeles County, alone. Scarcely had the remaining ranchers recovered from this blow when the drought of the early 1860's practically destroyed their herds. In Santa Barbara 60,000 cattle were sold for 37½ cents a head as there was neither green grass for the animals to eat nor water for them to drink. Thousands of cattle, so starved that even their hides were worthless, were driven to ocean cliffs and crowded over them to drown in the surf that washed their bodies out to sea. After this disastrous drought the large ranchos began to break up. The pastoral era in the Southwest faded into memory as scientists and engineers put water on the land. They made the desert bloom.

THE FEDERAL GOVERNMENT ENCOURAGES RECLAMATION

RECLAIMING THE ARID LANDS of the West became the dream of a cowboy who was born in New York City. In 1883 after serving in the state legislature at Albany, Theodore Roosevelt took over a partnership in two cattle ranches, Chimney Butte and Elkhorn, on the Little Missouri River. Like other cowboys, the man from the big city shared the duties of the spring roundup. He crawled from his bedroll before daybreak at the cook's call; rode the long circle to cut out calves and yearlings for branding; and kept the lonely night watch to quiet the restless herd. Jogging in the saddle on the open range gives a man time to think. Roosevelt pondered the future of the dry sagebrush country if water could be found to irrigate the land. Years later he was in a position to make his dream come true.

In 1900 Theodore Roosevelt was nominated for Vice President on the Republican ticket with William B. McKinley for President. They won the election. Six months later McKinley was shot by a young Polish anarchist at the Pan American Exposition in Buffalo, New York. The Vice President succeeded McKinley in office. Roosevelt, in his first message to Congress, presented his plans for conservation and reclamation. The program was planned to protect national forests, to irrigate dry lands, and to improve inland waterways. He wanted to enlist the cooperation of the states with the Federal Government in this work.

On June 17, 1902, Congress passed the Reclamation Act which allotted money from the sale of public lands in western states to a reclamation fund. The money would be used for "the storage, diversion, and development of arid and semi-arid lands in the said States and Territories." This act was a long legal document covering many problems that would arise in carrying out the projects. In general the act provided "that the settlers would reimburse the Government for the actual cost," with payments extending over a number of years.

About a month after the Reclamation Act was passed, surveys were being made to estimate the cost of constructing a dam in the Salt River of Arizona. Since the desirable land in the Salt River Valley was privately owned by farmers who had been using water from the stream, there were no public lands of value to be sold to defray the costs of a dam. The four thousand individual landowners who would be benefited by the project formed the Salt River Valley Water Users' Association in February of 1903 for these purposes:

To establish a central organization to represent the individual water users in dealing with the Secretary of Interior under whose direction the dam would be erected.

To maintain this central organization to guarantee payment to the Government for the costs of the irrigation project.

To use this organization for operating the irrigation works, distributing the water to the landowners, and insuring members that water rights and assessments would be equally allotted.

Under a contract with the Salt River Valley Water Users' Association, the Federal Government financed the construction of the Theodore Roosevelt Dam, the first to be built under the Reclamation Act. The members of this Association repaid the Government for the cost without interest on the money borrowed. To reduce the cost per acre for water, the Association erected power plants to sell electricity to nearby towns. As more and more people wanted water and power, the same plan was used to build three more dams in the Salt River and three in the Verde River. The soil is rich and the climate is mild. Although cotton is a main crop, vegetables and fruits are being planted or harvested the year round in the valleys of the Salt and Gila Rivers flowing through desert country in Arizona, redeemed by irrigation.

INDIAN LABOR

With a team of horses hitched to a shovel, an Apache Indian scoops out dirt and rocks for the dam site in a remote canyon, sixty miles from a railroad. The Apaches fought fiercely to hold their bleak dry homeland. Water on the desert brought settlers and defeat to the Indians.

SQUARING THE FIRST STONE
SEPTEMBER 20, 1906

Skilled masons were brought from Italy to shape blocks of stone cut from the mountainside to erect the wall. Hydro-electric power was generated at the mouth of the canal diverting the Salt River around the dam site. This power was used to manufacture 350,000 barrels of cement that fitted the stones into a solid wall 184 feet thick at the base, tapering 284 feet above bedrock to 16 feet at the top.

THEODORE ROOSEVELT
SPEAKING AT DEDICATION
MARCH 18, 1911

A salute of eleven guns reverberated through the canyon as Theodore Roosevelt approached to dedicate the dam named for him. He told the crowd:

If there could be any monument which would appeal to any man, surely it is this. You could not have done anything which would have pleased and touched me more than to name this great dam, this great reservoir site, after me, and I thank you from my heart for having done so.

IN OPERATION

The sum borrowed from the federal government to erect this dam at the junction of the Salt and Tonto Rivers has been repaid, without interest, by the Salt River Water Users' Association. The project is operated by this organization.

The Theodore Roosevelt Dam is still the tallest masonry dam in the world.

HEAD GATE

Water stored behind the dam flows through the countryside into a system of canals. Along the way, head gates are lifted and water pours into ditches to irrigate the fields of farmers who order the water and pay for it.

IRRIGATING A FIELD

Water flowing in the farmer's ditch is turned down the rows of plants to water land that was a desert not long ago.

In the dry country of the West, the value of a farm depends upon the water rights per acre for the land. Water sets the price.

What this country was before irrigation can best be told by the emigrants who crossed the southwestern desert during the gold rush days. Among the forty-niners was the artish and naturalist, John Woodhouse Audubon, who joined a wagon train to make sketches on the way. In passing through the valley of the Gila River, he wrote in his diary:

Broken wagons, dead shrivelled-up cattle, horses and mules as well, lay baking in the sun, around the dried-up wells that had been opened in the hopes of getting water. Not a blade of grass or green thing of any kind relieved the monotony of the parched, ash-colored earth.

As a naturalist, Audubon forgot thirst, heat and dust in his enthusiasm for the wild life in the desert. He wrote:

For lizards this country cannot be surpassed; one little beauty with a banded tail runs before us and across our path by dozens. It makes frequent stops, and each time curls its tail on its back, and waves it gently four or five times most gracefully, finally retreating to some hole in the sand, or to a thicket of cactus which abounds.

About 300 B.C., Indians settled along the Salt River. By hand, they dug canals to water their little fields of corn, squash, beans and cotton. They came to be called Hohokam (Hoe-Hoe-Kom), a word in the Pima Indian language meaning "The People Who Went Away." Mysteriously, they left the valley about a hundred years before Columbus came, leaving only canals to prove their triumph in irrigation. Modern engineers found traces of these old channels so well placed that they followed the shadowy beds in surveying some of the new irrigation ditches.

In Egyptian mythology the Phoenix was a *large* bird that lived five hundred years, was consumed by fire, and then rose again from its ashes to be young again. In 1868 Darrell Duppa, an early pioneer, was living in a village near the Salt River. He predicted that a modern city would rise on the spot, "Phoenix-like," from the ashes of ancient civilizations. Duppa named the largest city in Arizona.

IMPERIAL VALLEY
OASIS IN THE DESERT

THE GILA EMPTIED into the Colorado River that emigrants crossed to enter the dreaded Colorado Desert in California. Wagon trains followed a trail blazed by Anza, a Spanish explorer, and later by trappers and traders from the United States. This path across the sandy waste was known as the Sonora Road, the Colorado Road, the Emigrant Trail, and the Butterfield Route.

A long time ago, geologists claim, the Imperial Valley was under water, part of the Gulf of California. Through the ages silt dropped from the muddy waters of the Colorado River and built a delta at the head of the gulf. Sediment carried yearly by this stream, before dams were built, amounted to a square mile of dry earth 125 feet deep. At flood time each year, May to July, the river spread over this lowland, deposited layers of mud, and formed a valley as level as the page of a book. Then the fickle Colorado cut another channel farther east, leaving its former flood bed to wither into desert. During the Mexican War General Kearny marched through this valley enroute to San Diego. Forty-niners on their way to the gold diggings crossed the barren land, rich with the soil deposits of the ages. It was farmland and the best, but worthless without water.

Then came the irrigation engineers to turn the Colorado desert into a garden spot, the fertile Imperial Valley. The Imperial Dam was erected in the Colorado River to divert water into the All American Canal. The "big ditch" flows into the thousands of acres of vegetables. With large crops of lettuce, the region has become the nation's salad bowl.

The Imperial Irrigation District was organized under the reclamation laws of the state of California. The All American Canal is publicly owned by the people living in Imperial Valley. They control the use of the water through their votes at the polls. Without this man-made river, the lush Imperial Valley would soon dry up into a parched wasteland.

If Audubon returned today to the irrigated desert lands of Arizona and California, he would need tubes of green oils and water colors to paint the fields of vegetables, grains and cotton. Acres and acres of the valleys of the Gila, Salt, and Colorado Rivers would be bluish-green with alfalfa, the farmer's standby in a dry country. It is water from the rivers, stored in lakes behind dams, that makes the desert bloom.

THE COLORADO RIVER IS HARNESSED BY MAN

MELTING SNOWS on the western slopes of mountain ranges in Colorado and Wyoming feed streams of water into the

THE DESERT — BEFORE AND AFTER

An early aerial view of the All American Canal in the Imperial Irrigation District. From this man-made river, water from the Colorado River is distributed through 2000 miles of canals to farmers in Imperial Valley. The ground on the left is a patchwork of green fields watered from the big ditch. On the right lies the gray, barren, thirsty desert.

Spence Air Photos

COLORADO RIVER AQUEDUCT

Barren desert country of 25,000 square miles was surveyed to chart the route of this aqueduct, bringing water from the Colorado River to the coastal region of Southern California. The total length of the aqueduct system is almost 700 miles. The aqueduct is able to carry a billion gallons of water per day.

The cost of building and operating this aqueduct is paid by The Metropolitan Water District, composed of the thirteen cities that joined together originally and other districts that joined later.

Metropolitan Water District

PARKER DAM

Parker Dam halts the flow of the Colorado River to make a reservoir 55 miles long, named Lake Havasu after a nearby Indian tribe. A few miles down the river, water from Lake Havasu backs up behind Headgate Rock Dam to store a supply of water for Indians living in that area.

WHITSETT INTAKE PUMPING PLANT

From Lake Havasu, Colorado River water is lifted nearly 300 feet to start on its long journey of 242 miles to Lake Mathews, the storage reservoir. The pumping plants are mainly operated by electricity generated at Hoover Dam and Parker Dam.

ON THE WAY

Where the aqueduct crosses level desert land, the water flows in concrete-lined canals, 55 feet wide and 12 feet deep, protected by high steel wire fences. This aqueduct carries 1,000,000,000 gallons every day to supply 70 percent of the water used by 10,000,000 people living in Southern California.

LAKE MATHEWS

The main aqueduct flows into Lake Mathews, the storage reservoir, from which water is distributed through a network of canals to the wholesale customers who, in turn, sell it to retail units serving home needs. A citizen turns on a faucet and the Colorado River pours out.

Colorado River, flowing 1700 miles from the Rocky Mountains to the Gulf of California. Down through the ages this torrent had not been checked. It has been jokingly said that water in the Colorado River was "too thick to drink and too thin to plow." In tumbling down the mountains, streams feeding the great river gathered heavy loads of silt. In fact, the river was named Colorado, Spanish word for red, because of the reddish-brown soil washed into it.

Every spring as snow melted in the mountains, the flood waters charged through the narrow canyons and spread over the lowlands. Sometimes the wild river changed its course and cut new paths through the delta to the Gulf. This winding river drains an area of 244,000 square miles, extending from the western slope of the Rocky Mountains to the plateau on the eastern slope of the Sierra Nevada Range. Much of this vast territory is land with little rainfall or semi-arid country like the coastal region between the mountains and the Pacific Ocean. It was a bold undertaking to harness this stream and force it to serve the needs of mankind.

In Nevada where the treacherous stream flows through Black Canyon, Hoover Dam now blocks the waterway. Spring floods rolling into this gorge strike a concrete barrier a seventh of a mile high and fall back to fill Lake Mead. Below this dam the Colorado River flows serenely on its way, halted here and there by other dams. Its wild free days are gone. Since floods have been checked by dams, the delta of the Colorado River is shrinking. Without the tons of mud dumped yearly on the upper rim, the Gulf of California is cutting back into the delta and washing away the land — not much, as time goes, but enough to be measured.

In the land of little rain, every project to bring water to dry land and thirsty people costs millions and millions of dollars. The Reclamation Act of 1902 was based upon the idea that the Bureau of Reclamation would build dams to provide water, but the people who used the water would repay the cost to the Government. President Herbert Hoover refused to sign the bill passed by Congress to erect a dam in the Black Canyon of the Colorado River until contracts had been signed by users of water and power to repay the cost *with interest* in fifty years. Hoover Dam enjoys the distinction of being the only one in the West built without cost or risk to the taxpayers of the nation.

ELECTRIC POWER CROSSING THE MOJAVE DESERT IN CALIFORNIA

Over these wires, high voltage is transmitted across the rugged terrain of mountain and desert from Hoover Dam to Los Angeles, 266 miles away. The spiny plant is the rare Joshua tree.

Department of Water and Power, Los Angeles

The sale of electricity is paying the largest part of the bill. The same water that stores the flood and irrigates the land, turns the wheels in the power plant. Public and private water and electric companies, in the early years, were required to pay for more electricity than they could use, under their contracts to pay for Hoover Dam in fifty years. The Boulder Canyon Project Act, passed by Congress in 1928, ushered in a new way of life in the thirsty Southwest. The Colorado is the only river with tributaries entirely within the United States which travels for the greater part of its course through desert country. With electric power from Hoover Dam, industry moved into the cattle country of the original Spanish settlers. Towns and cities competed for the grazing lands of the old ranchos. With water from Lake Mead, crops thrive in a former desert, trees line the curbs of city streets, and flowers bloom in June and January.

THE CENTRAL VALLEY PROJECT

THE CENTRAL VALLEY PROJECT is for California. The states of Connecticut, Rhode Island, and Maryland could be neatly tucked away in the long basin of 12,000,000 acres running north and south between the high Sierra Nevada Mountains and the lower coastal ranges. The Sacramento River runs south from the northern half, and the San Joaquin River runs north from the southern half. The two streams flowed through the broad, swampy delta into San Francisco Bay until engineers arrived to change their ways to suit the needs of man.

The problem of reclamation in the central valley was varied. The area

Central Valley Project

IRRIGATING GRAPES

A farmer in the San Joaquin Valley of central California soaks his vineyard with water from the Friant-Kern Canal, part of the huge Central Valley Project. He uses a system of earth checks and dams to insure proper moisture to the roots.

included both desert and swamp. Rains fell in the wrong places and at the wrong time. In the north the Sacramento Valley receives two-thirds of the rain and snow but has only one-third of the farmlands needing irrigation. In the south the San Joaquin receives only one-third of the rainfall, but has two-thirds of the farmlands needing water. Farmers in the dry country wanted water on their lands during the long hot summers. In the delta region where rich land had been drained and planted, farmers wanted fresh water from the two rivers to wash out the sea water creeping into their fields from San Francisco Bay.

This immense project to irrigate dry land, to store flood waters, to build power plants, to protect fish and fowl,

391

Central Valley Project

**AN ALMOND ORCHARD
IN BLOOM IN THE CENTRAL VALLEY**

The main ditches in orchards curve among the trees, following the contour of the land. Earth dikes are thrown up around the trees, forming pools of water to insure the deepest penetration into the soil.

and to provide recreation will take many years to complete and will cost many millions of dollars. The key structure of the project is Shasta Dam in the Sacramento River at the northernmost tip of the Central Valley of California. Behind this dam lies Shasta Lake which stores enough water to provide a thousand gallons for nearly every person living in the United States. This project is being carried out gradually because the cost is so great, and these improvements are expected to pay their own way, eventually, according to the Reclamation Law. Water is expensive in the semi-desert region of the Southwest.

THE WAY OF
THE RIO GRANDE

THE RIO GRANDE rises in a soggy meadow near timberline on the Continental Divide in southwestern Colorado. The clear, cold water of the little creek runs white in a wild dash down the canyons to cross the Colorado line into the high plateau of New Mexico. The stream flows gently for 465 miles to El Paso, Texas. There it starts a winding course of more than 1200 miles to the Gulf of Mexico. This river marks the boundary between the United States and Mexico.

To whom did the Rio Grande belong? The United States or Mexico? Which nation had prior rights to its life-saving water? In 1906, the two nations made a treaty whereby the United States agreed to deliver, for all time, 60,000 acre-feet of water per year in the Rio Grande. Then, the three states through which the river flowed began to ask which state had prior rights to the water in the stream. There was not enough water for each state to irrigate all the arid lands, but each state could get more water if a plan was made to store the spring floods that sometimes washed away villages and flooded farms. How much water should each state get? To answer this question, Colorado, New Mexico and Texas would have to reach an agreement that would be acceptable to Congress. The Rio Grande Compact was approved by the legislatures of Colorado, New Mexico, and Texas; passed by Congress; and signed by the President into law on May 31, 1939.

This agreement stated:

The State of Colorado, the State of New Mexico, and the State of Texas, desiring to remove all causes of present and future controversy among these states and between citizens of one of these States and citizens of another State with respect to the use of the waters of the Rio Grande above Fort Quitman, Texas, and being moved by considerations of interstate comity, and for the purpose of effecting an equitable apportionment of such waters, have resolved to conclude a

Compact for the attainment of these purposes, and to that end, through their respective Governors, have named their respective Commissioners.

The Rio Grande Compact is a long legal document on how to operate it within the existing treaties made with Mexico and the Indian tribes by the Federal Government.

The middle Rio Grande Valley in New Mexico is the oldest area in the United States to be farmed continuously. Before white men came, natives irrigated their fields with water from the river. Indians living today in New Mexico need more irrigated land to raise food. With their numbers increasing, fewer families can be supported by herding sheep. A long-range plan is being developed for flood control, irrigation, and power to aid all peoples living in the Rio Grande Basin, and to supply the defense projects located in New Mexico.

The Federal Government will advance the money to build the dams and canals. The people who benefit from this reclamation will pay back the costs through the sale of water and power, but not the interest on the borrowed money. For levees on the river itself, dredging and like improvements, the Federal Government pays the costs. Before the Rio Grande Compact was made, the Middle Rio Grande Conservancy District under the State of New Mexico had built and operated a system of storage reservoirs and irrigation ditches.

With each new source of water tapped, little valleys fringed with reddish bluffs turn green with fields of corn and alfalfa. On holidays and at fiesta time Indian tribesmen still don their ceremonial garb and perform the old dances for rain. In this land of Coronado the search for water goes on without ceasing.

WATER PACES GROWTH

WHEN A FARMER living on irrigated land needs moisture for his crops, he calls the water clerk of his district on the phone.

"I want forty-eight hours of water on my cabbage patch in the northwest quarter," he says.

"Heavy or light?" the clerk inquires.

"Heavy for twenty-four hours, and then light for a day," the farmer replies.

"Your water will begin at eight o'clock tomorrow morning," the clerk assures him. "Be at your water gate on time."

The water flowing through the gate is carefully measured, and the landowner pays accordingly. This is the way of farming where rain comes from a ditch more often than from the sky. The miracle of the Southwest is irrigation. The gray desert wears patches of green and gold wherever water flows in the little man-made rivers from the main canals. How many farms? How many towns? How much industry? How many people can earn a living in the semi-arid region of the Southwest? The answer to these questions is summed up in one word — WATER. Here, as in ancient Arabia, "water is the fount of life. We have made of water, everything living."

CITRUS FRUITS
ARE OLD — YET NEW

IN THE MILD climate of the Pacific Southwest — on land under irrigation — oranges, lemons, and grapefruit found a new home. Citrus fruits were first grown in the Orient and were eaten as a healthful food. Although grapefruit is 4000 years old, it was little known in this country before 1880 when Florida growers began shipping the fruit to New York markets. Today, the United States supplies more than half the grapefruit grown in the entire world. Most of it comes from Florida, Arizona, California, and Texas.

It is generally believed that lemon culture began with wild trees, native to the northwestern provinces of India. Arabs brought lemon trees into Spain about 800 years ago. Along with cattle, sheep, and horses the early Spanish settlers brought lemon, orange and lime trees to plant in the New World.

The orange came from China. Portuguese sailors first brought the fruit to Europe and orange groves were planted in the warmer regions of Spain. Orange trees were growing in the West Indies before Cortes conquered Mexico, according to a story told by one of the explorers who went with Grijalva to Yucatan the year before he joined the expedition of Cortes. In 1518 Grijalva led a band of explorers from Cuba to Yucatan. At a spot where the party landed on the coast, one of the explorers climbed to the roof of a native temple to escape the swarms of mosquitoes that infested the region. He rested and slept soundly on the roof. When he awoke he wondered what he could do to show his appreciation of the peaceful slumber away from the blood-sucking pests. Fumbling in a pocket he discovered eight orange seeds that he had brought from Cuba. At the foot of the temple he planted the orange seeds, hoping the native priests would take care of the little trees.

After Mexico had been conquered by Cortes, this same explorer returned to the same spot, out of curiosity, and found the orange trees growing. The native priests had taken good care of the plants. He dug up the trees and transplanted them on his rancho in the valley of the Guacasuleo River where many of the conquistadores had settled. It was fine country for cattle and sheep and good farming land. Thus it happened that in 1518 the first orange trees were planted on the mainland of North America. When English colonists, 250 years later, were forging a new nation on the Atlantic Coast of North America, Spanish Franciscans were planting groves of orange and lemon trees in their mission gardens on the Pacific Coast of North America.

However, it was packing and shipping more than growing that enabled the industry to grow in California.

In the fall of 1830 a hunting party of thirty men left Taos, New Mexico, to trap beaver in the central valley of California. It was winter when they reached the Sierra Nevada and the snow was too deep to cross the mountains. The party followed the eastern slope of the range, heading south and crossed the San Bernardino Mountains through Cajon Pass to reach the Mexican settlements in the coastal region. In the little village of Los Angeles, some of the hunters traded their Indian blankets from Taos for mules to ride on their way home. William Wolfskill, a Kentucky trapper and leader of the party, remained and married the daughter of Jose Lugo, a wealthy Spanish landowner.

One day, Wolfskill was strolling on a wharf in San Francisco when a schooner arrived with a cargo of oranges from the Sandwich Islands (Hawaii). Much of the fruit had spoiled during the voyage and men were throwing it overboard. Suddenly, the Kentuckian got the idea of buying the rotten fruit for seed. The cost was little. He shipped the fruit to his southern home and

Lyon Museum

THE WOLFSKILL ORANGE GROVE

Wolfskill, the trapper from Kentucky, planted this grove of orange trees from which the first carload of fruit was shipped to an eastern market. These trees grew on land now covered with business blocks in downtown Los Angeles.

had the seeds extracted. From the seedlings obtained, he set out thirty acres of orange trees near the Los Angeles River. This grove was enlarged until it had over 1600 trees bearing oranges. From this grove in 1877 the first carload of oranges was shipped by rail to a market in St. Louis, and the citrus industry was on its way to big business.

Today the former Wolfskill grove is covered with buildings in the downtown section of the city of Los Angeles that grew from the little village founded by Felipe de Neve in 1781. The old church still stands at the plaza, in the heart of the city, on the El Camino Real. Monks in brown robes and barefoot sandals once strode this path of the missions from San Diego to San Francisco. Teams of oxen, hitched to lumbering carts with high wooden wheels,

hauled the early settlers to Sunday worship along this dusty road. Now the traffic hums and snorts its way past the humble mission and the drowsy plaza. It is Main Street, not the Highway of the King.

MOVIE MAKE-BELIEVE

AS MORE WATER became available, more industries moved into the Southwest. Those needing a mild dry climate were among the early arrivals. In November, 1913, a producer, Jesse L. Lasky; a director, Cecil B. De Mille; and a Broadway star, Dustin Farnum, left New York City and headed west to start a movie studio in Flagstaff, Arizona. According to weather reports filed in Washington, this town boasted the most hours of sunshine per year. Since sunlight was necessary for making motion pictures, Flagstaff was the place. It read well in print but the men from New York failed to grasp the meaning of altitude. The town is in the mountains, a mile and a third high.

Three surprised men from a city at sea level stepped off the train at Flagstaff in a raging blizzard. The ground was white with snow and the wind hurled icy mist into their faces. On the wintry day the little mountain town seemed lonely and forlorn to the men from a big city. They acted quickly and stepped back to the car platform. When the conductor drawled "ALL A-B-O-A-R-D," the producer, the director, and the actor were seated again in the same coach they had just left. They had decided to ride to the end of the line.

On the way the train halted at a station called Bagdad, with a water tank and a few dwellings, some being box-cars. The sandy desert stretched westward into the barren hills, sparsely covered with thorny cactus and spiny yucca. A great place for staging two-reel westerns with gun-toting sheriffs and cattle thieves, but the director had something else in mind. He was going to make feature pictures which told long stories like the plays on the regular stage.

With the help of two puffing steam engines, one pulling and the other pushing, the passenger train climbed to Cajon Pass on the crest of the San Bernardino Mountains where trappers and traders had crossed the barrier between the desert and the coast before the railroad was built. With ease, the train descended the western slope of the range into a warm and pleasant valley where the scene changed. From the car window fences of red geraniums, lanes of palm trees, and groves of orange trees greeted Lasky, De Mille, and Farnum. The train stopped at Los Angeles, the end of the line. The winter day was clear and mild and the sun was shining. Why not start a studio here?

Out in the country a few miles from the city, the strangers rented half a barn in a lemon grove for $25 per month. This room was the office. In a clearing among the trees they erected a small platform. Movable frames with canvas were the walls and the sky was the roof. On this crude outdoor stage was filmed THE SQUAW MAN, the first stage play used in movies. The picture was a big "hit." From that time on there was never any doubt that movies would succeed as entertainment. With mountains, deserts, and beaches nearby for scenery, the motion picture industry grew from a spot in a lemon grove to the land of make-believe, called Hollywood.

IN THE AIR

AVIATION AS WELL as motion pictures, found the mild climate of the Pacific Coast from Canada to Mexico suited to its needs. However, mere chance had a share in establishing the aviation industry here as it did with motion pictures. In the early twenties when movies were well on the way to big business, aviation was only beginning with a few sheds scattered over the bean fields and truck gardens between the foothills and the ocean. Some of the pioneers of aviation happened to be living in Southern California. They started their small airplane factories near their own homes.

When war was declared in December of 1941, these plants were taken over by the

Government. Walls of buildings were raised and planes rolled off the assembly lines with little more than a roof overhead. This amazing volume of production was accomplished by air-minded pioneers, who a few years before had leveled runways in the bean fields and constructed little planes in sheds at fence corners.

To fly has been man's dream through the ages.

In 1783 Benjamin Franklin was in Paris arranging the peace treaty at the close of the Revolutionary War. Although busy with duties of state, he found time to witness the first ascent of a balloon, inflated with hydrogen. Franklin was both scientist and diplomat. Two months later in a letter to a friend he predicted airborne invasion:

It appears a discovery of great importance may possibly give a new turn to human affairs. Convincing Sovereigns of the folly of wars, may perhaps be one effect of it . . . Five thousand balloons, capable of raising two men each, could not cost more than five ships of the line. And where is the prince who can afford so to cover his country with troops for its defense, as that 10,000 men descending from the clouds might not in many places do an infinite deal of mischief before a force could be brought together to repel them?

The airborne invasions came, as Franklin predicted, but not in balloons. Not content with lighter than air inventions, men began to wonder if a machine heavier than air could be made to fly. For the first time — on December 17, 1903, at Kitty Hawk, North Carolina — a man flew in a gasoline engine plane, and lived to tell the tale.

A chill wind swept the beach at twenty-seven miles an hour. The sky was murky overhead. Orville Wright climbed into the heavier-than-air machine for his first ride. The plane rose but came down again in twelve seconds about a hundred feet from the starting point. He and his brother, Wilbur, took turns at the controls. Wilbur made the fourth flight, covering 852 feet in 59 seconds before the plane began to pitch like a bucking bronco and drop to the sands along the shore. With this experiment the air age began. Man had learned to fly.

How surprised would Cabrillo be if he could stand today on the deck of his little sailing ship and watch the airplanes flying like huge birds to and from the Los Angeles airport behind the natural harbor which he named, "Bay of Smokes." With the invention of heavier-than-air flying machines man took to the air in a way that Franklin could not foresee when he watched the first balloon ascent in Paris.

Man seems to want to go places with the greatest speed. He once was satisfied with a fleet riding horse or a fast team. In turn, overland travel was by stagecoach with four horses in harness; in railroad trains with steam-driven engines; in automobiles with gasoline motors. Today, fast travel is in the sky. No longer content with conquering air around the earth, man is exploring the realm of outer space. In July 1969, three American astronauts, Neil A. Armstrong, Edwin E. Aldrin, and Michael Collins, made the first trip to explore the moon.

WATER CONTROLS GROWTH OF INDUSTRY

VAST AREAS in the Southwest will probably never be irrigated and will remain sparsely settled. The centers of population are in irrigated country. Water attracted the people, farms, and industry that gradually took over the old ranchos of the early Spanish settlers. As more factories are built, more people migrate westward to find more jobs, to make their homes, and the need for water increases.

A city in a semi-desert buys a mountain stream and brings it home in an aqueduct. A river fed by melting snows in the high Sierras no longer finds the sea. The normal flow is checked and stored upstream, filling a reservoir. With only puddles here and there, the river bed is a sandy waste. Old mines, deserted towns, winding roads, fossils of dinosaurs, and wonders of nature slip out of sight as lakes spread behind dams in western rivers.

Industry continues to invade the agricultural empire of today's ranchers and farmers. Orange groves are uprooted by bulldozers to use the land for factories, houses, and apartments. Smoke and steam rise above the treetops from a steel mill where the odor of burning coke replaces the scent of orange blossoms. Stubby oil well pumps draw up a sticky, greasy treasure from pools beneath the pastures where cattle once grazed on wild oats. Acres are covered by refineries with mazes of pipe lines in fantastic designs and domes that glisten in the sunlight.

In the swamps, a few long-legged cranes still wade among the rushes as in the days when Jose Dominguez sat on the long veranda of his adobe house to watch the smugglers' ships and the spouting whales. In ox-drawn carts his Indian servants hauled hides and tallow down to the soggy shore. Thus did commerce begin in a mud hole destined to become one of the busy ports of the world.

If the old soldier who came with Portola could sit on his porch today, he would look down upon a lively waterfront where Rattlesnake Island used to be. The spot was once infested by rattlers washed down from the foothills during the winter rains. Freighters, tankers, and passenger ships would be nosing around the breakwater of this man-made harbor, and heading for the channels dug from the mud flats of his Rancho San Pedro. Noisy trucks would be speeding over the network of highways, streaking through his pastures to and from the Port of Los Angeles. The land of the herder is now an industrial area with storehouses, canneries, factories, docks, and cargo sheds. Today, there would be neither peace nor quiet for the retired leather-jacket on his land grant in the bustling harbor district.

Yet there is still a common bond between the early rancher and the later industrialist — a water problem. For every newcomer, water must be stored, not only for the present but also for the future. Eleven western states have formed a Western States Water Council to study existing and future water projects. How can states with ample rainfall share their surplus water with dry states without depriving their own citizens at any time? How can flood waters in Oregon and Northern California be channeled south to arid lands before the raging torrents wash away houses, fields, and cause damage amounting to millions of dollars? Since the Colorado River does not carry enough water to satisfy demand, what would be the cost of digging a canal to bring water from the Columbia River to the Colorado to increase the flow in that stream? Transporting water all the way from Alaska is a daring topic of conversation. Like the rainmaking gods in the ancient Indian legend, modern engineers are expected to fill the water jars "from the four encircling oceans."

Chapter 21

In the Pacific Northwest

RIVAL NATIONS COMPETE IN THE NORTHWEST

AFTER CORTES had conquered Mexico, Spanish explorers ventured farther and farther north along the Pacific Coast. Ferrelo in 1543 discovered and named Cape Mendocino on the point farthest west. The daring English buccaneer, Sir Francis Drake, was sailing off the coast of the present state of Washington in 1579. After plundering Spanish towns farther south, he steered the *Golden Hind* into northern waters to elude capture by Spanish captains who were searching for him. Unable to find a water route back into the Atlantic Ocean, Drake headed westward, crossed the Pacific, and returned to England by sailing around the globe.

Following the voyage of Vizcaino in 1603, Spain did little more than lay claim to land bordering the Pacific. Then a rival appeared, over a century later, to threaten the nation's possessions. In 1724 Peter the Great, Czar of Russia, sent a personal letter in his own handwriting to Vitus Bering, a Dane, serving as an officer in the Russian Navy. He instructed Bering to proceed to Kamchatka, to build one or two boats, and then to sail north to learn whether or not the continents of Asia and North America were joined by land.

Although the Czar died five days after writing the letter, his heir carried out his orders. In the summer of 1728 Bering's vessel, christened the *Gabriel,* sailed on the momentous voyage through the strait which bears his name. This proved beyond doubt that the two continents were separated by this narrow body of water. Thirteen years later the Russian Government called Bering from retirement on his farm in Finland to take charge of another expedition into the North Pacific. Early in June in 1741 Bering sailed from Avacha Bay, Kamchatka, in command of the *St. Peter.* His partner, Cherikov, was captain of the *St. Paul* with a crew of seventy-six men, one more than Bering had on his vessel. In a stormy gale the two ships became separated and the captains never met again. Cherikov drifted to the island where Sitka is now located. After losing two boats and their occupants in attempted landings, Cherikov turned homeward. He arrived in Avacha Bay early in October of the same year. No word had come from Bering.

On the sixteenth of July in 1741 Bering sighted a high mountain on the mainland of North America. He named it St. Elias.

Hampered by fog and an ailing crew, the explorer turned homeward. His supplies were running low. On the voyage two invalid sailors who still had use of their legs supported sick steersmen at the helm. Finally, after being lost at sea for weeks, snow-covered hills, which the captain thought was the peninsula of Kamchatka, were sighted. The land was only an island. The crew beached the ship and prepared to spend the winter in caves dug in the sandy shore. Here on this lonely island Bering died. The place was named for him. Half the men in the crew were saved by the German scientist, Steller. He dug roots and boiled them to cure scurvy, killed sea cows for meat, and fur-bearing animals for clothing. In the spring the survivors built a crude boat from the wreckage of the *St. Peter* and started home with bundles of valuable furs. Late in August of 1742 the party reached Avacha Bay.

The appearance of these seamen clad in the remnants of luxurious furs started a rush of emigrants into the new country and the islands of the North Pacific. In the scramble for sudden wealth many hunters ventured into the cold waters on clumsy rafts and lost their lives. In 1790 Baranov was appointed manager of the Russian company which was granted a monopoly of the fur business in the new lands. Nine years later he traded articles to an Indian chief for land upon which to erect a trading post, named Sitka for the tribe inhabiting the island. The town became the center of the fur trade which had lured Russians to establish posts in scattered regions throughout the Northwest.

As Russian traders moved farther south, the King of Spain became alarmed. He ordered the occupation and settlement of California. He also sent more explorers to chart the coast farther north and to try to hold that country for Spain. In June of 1774 the *Santiago* commanded by Perez, sailed from Monterey to explore the northern coast and report on the natives he found. A diary of this voyage was kept by a friar, Juan Crespi, a friend of Junipero Serra.

The native Indians proved interesting to the Europeans. Crespi wrote much about them — their actions, their dress, and their wares. While anchored in a harbor on the western shore of a large island, now called Vancouver, singing and shouting Indians paddled out in long, bark canoes to trade with the strangers. They brought well-tanned beaver skins, finely stitched fur blankets, and neatly woven mats to trade for knives, cloth, and beads. The natives prized highly any scraps of iron. A souvenir-minded sailor traded his knife for an Indian hat with a conical crown and a small brim fashioned of rushes with leather thongs to tie it on under his chin. Along the route, while charting the coast, Perez landed and erected wooden crosses at many places, claiming the country for the King of Spain. The next year Heceta left San Blas on the western coast of Mexico to explore the inlets of the northwest coast. The voyage was a disappointment. Indians murdered his landing parties and scurvy spread among his men.

In July of 1778 Spain's great rival appeared in the person of Captain Cook. Great Britain entered the race for territory and the fur trade of the northwest country. Captain James Cook was a successful explorer because he took care of the health of his men. He forced his sailors to take a daily ration of vinegar, molasses, sauerkraut juice, lime juice, or sassafras tea to prevent scurvy.

He charted the coast line of Alaska and sailed through Bering Strait into the Arctic Ocean until ice blocked his way. He was searching for the mythical Northwest Passage. His splendid job of exploration gave Great Britain a claim to northwestern America at a time when the British colonies on the Atlantic coast were fighting for independence. Little did Russia, Spain, and Great Britain — world powers in that day — realize that the new nation rising on the opposite shore of North America would some day own most of the territory which they were exploring.

In 1787, the year of the Constitutional Convention, six merchants in Boston loaded two vessels with merchandise to trade for furs in the Northwest. The *Columbia* was commanded by Captain John Kendrick, former master of a privateer which had raided British commerce during the Revolutionary War. Captain Robert Gray, another Revolutionary sailor, took the helm of the smaller ship, the *Washington.* The Bostonians hoped to establish a trade like that of the Hudson's Bay Company of Great Britain. On October 1, 1787 the two ships sailed out of Boston harbor. They arrived nearly a year later in Nootka Sound where Perez had anchored on the western shore of the island, later named for Vancouver.

For nearly nine months the Americans bartered for furs and hunted for new lands with more furs. Upon Gray's return to Nootka Sound after sailing through the Strait of Juan de Fuca, the two captains exchanged boats. Gray took command of the *Columbia* with a cargo of precious skins and sailed for China. In Canton he traded the furs for a cargo of tea. Returning home by way of the Cape of Good Hope, Gray arrived in Boston on the tenth of August in 1790. He had completed the first voyage

Provincial Archives, Victoria, British Columbia

SIR ALEXANDER MACKENZIE

Alexander Mackenzie was a fur trader at Fort Chipewyan, located at the head of Lake Athabasca in western Canada. In 1789, he led a party in canoes down a large river, looking for a new waterway to the Pacific Ocean. A few notes from Mackenzie's journals tells a story of hardship and adventure on this river named for him:

Clouds of mosquitoes — saw a black fox — large flocks of geese; kill many of them — the hunters kill reindeer — view the sunset at midnight — obliged to tow the canoe — come to rapids — land among the Esquimaux Indians.

The river flowed into the Arctic Ocean. Mackenzie returned to Fort Chipewyan after traveling 1600 miles in 102 days. Disappointed that he had not found the Pacific Ocean, he made another hazardous journey, more for business than for exploration. In 1792-93, he led a party across the Rocky Mountains to the western sea where Russian hunters were gathering furs. Whenever possible, the British traveled by canoe, stopping at Indian villages on the way to make friends for future trade. On this journey, Mackenzie's journal deals with business:

Abundance of animals — see some bears — saw beaver — kill a red deer — make preparations to build a canoe — meet with some of the natives — saw two otters in the river — met trading party of Indians carrying skins of otter, marten, bear, lynx, and dressed moose skins.

401

around the globe under the flag of the new nation, the United States of America.

Although Captain Gray returned to Boston with a damaged cargo of Bohea tea, Governor Hancock gave a reception in his honor. Arm in arm, Gray and a chief from Hawaii, marched up State Street to attend the party. This first native Hawaiian to visit the United States wore a priceless robe of rare feathers to Governor Hancock's reception.

Although this initial voyage was not a financial success, some of the merchant adventurers decided to risk another trip. Captain Gray bought some shares in the venture from two merchants who were too discouraged to invest money in a second trial. After only seven weeks in port, Gray sailed again from Boston in the *Columbia* on another trading expedition. In less than nine months he was back again in the sheltered harbor of Vancouver. Canoes swarmed around the ship. Native chiefs, clothed in rich otter skins, were welcomed when they came on board. The Bostonians were looking for such furs. Captain Gray led the first party ashore to gather greens for members of his crew who were ill with scurvy. When all had recovered, Gray left this place to find new and unworked territory where more furs could be had for less goods. However, the second voyage of Captain Gray is famous for discovery and not for trade.

Late in April while cruising southward for summer trading with Indians who brought their winter catch to the coast to meet the ships, two great explorers passed at sea. They did not meet. They were Captain Robert Gray of the *Columbia* and Captain George Vancouver of the *Discovery.* One was American and the other was British. Vancouver describes the event in his journal:

At four o'clock (A.M.), a sail was discovered to the westward standing in shore. This was a very great novelty, not having seen any vessel but our consort (the *Chatham,* supply ship), during the last eight months. She soon hoisted American colors and fired a gun to leeward. At six we spoke her. She proved to be the ship *Columbia,* commanded by Robert Gray, belonging to Boston, whence she had been absent nineteen months. Having little doubt of his being the same person who had formerly commanded the sloop *Washington,* I desired he would bring to, and sent Mr. Puget and Mr. Mensies on board to acquire such information as might be serviceable in our future operations.

During the conversation Lieutenants Puget and Mensies told Captain Gray of finding fresh water flowing into the sea about the latitude of 46° 10′. Gray told them that he had waited nine days on the way up the coast to enter that river, only to be balked in every attempt by the current and the breakers. Gray courteously followed the *Discovery* and the *Chatham* to be certain that Vancouver found the Strait of Juan de Fuca which he was seeking. Then he turned southward again in search of furs he hoped to find plentiful along the unexplored river. The bar outside had frightened mariners and kept the mighty stream a secret.

On May 11, 1792 during the spring flood, Gray discovered a channel between the breakers. With a favorable wind and high tide he crossed the choppy bar and sailed into the great river of the Northwest which he named Columbia after his ship. Boit, in his log of the famous voyage, wrote:

We directed our course up this noble river in search of a village. The beach was lined with natives, who ran along shore following the ship. Soon after, about 20 canoes came off, and brought a good lot of furs and salmon which last they sold two for a board nail. The furs we likewise bought cheap, for copper and cloth. — At length we arrived opposite to a large village, situated on the north side of the river, — the river at this place was about 4 miles over. We purchased four otter skins for a sheet of copper; beaver skins, two spikes each; and other land furs, 1 spike each.

Captain Gray, as on the first voyage, crossed the Pacific Ocean and sold his furs in Canton, China. His cargo brought the sum of $90,000. Gray's second voyage was a financial success. This encouraged more and more Americans to invest their money in the maritime fur business. Thus developed the triangle of trade in the Pacific. Trinkets were brought from eastern ports of the United States to exchange for furs on the northwestern coast. The furs were taken to China to be bartered for tea. The tea was sold in eastern United States ports at a profit.

However, it was the entrance to the Columbia River, and not the trading expeditions, that brought fame to Captain Gray. Upon his discovery of the Columbia River the United States based its claim to the Oregon country drained by that stream and its tributaries. In less than twenty-five years this claim was strengthened by the overland journey of Lewis and Clark, who traveled down the Columbia River in canoes to reach the Pacific Ocean.

After Captain Gray had courteously escorted Vancouver to the Strait of Juan de Fuca, the British captain began to explore the region inside. Thinking he was the first European to chart the shores of the numerous gulfs, bays, straits, shoals, and islands of the jagged coast line, he named the places seen and visited. On the last day in April the third lieutenant called Vancouver's attention to a snow-covered mountain in the distance. The captain promptly named it for the young officer, Mt. Baker. For a base of operations Vancouver selected a sheltered harbor which he called Port Discovery after his ship. The spot of land guarding the entrance was named Protection Island.

Vancouver took particular pleasure in naming places for his friends. Today, maps list more names conferred by Vancouver than by any other explorer in this region. Port Townsend was named for the marquis of that name; Hood Canal, for Lord Hood; Mt. Rainier for Rear Admiral Peter Rainier; Howe's Sound for Admiral Earl Howe; Port Gardner for Admiral Sir Alan Gardner and Port Susan for his wife. After spending two weeks examining a waterway, Vancouver named it Admiralty Inlet in honor of the Board of Admiralty which directed operations of the British Navy. Vancouver was generous in giving recognition to his officers who assisted him in carrying out a thorough, scientific job of exploration. Port Orchard was named for the clerk of the *Discovery*; Whidbey's Island after Joseph Whidbey of the *Chatham* who found the island and went around it; and Puget Sound for Lieutenant Peter Puget, whose careful work of charting and exploring was deeply appreciated by Vancouver.

Under a date line of June 4, 1792, Captain Vancouver wrote in his journal:

On Monday, all hands were served as good a dinner as we were able to provide them, — it being the anniversary of His Majesty's birth; on which auspicious day, I had long since designed to take formal possession of all the countries we had lately been employed in exploring, in the name of, and for His Majesty, his heirs and successors.

Accompanied by several officers, Vancouver went ashore to take formal possession of the country while gunners on board the ships fired the royal salute. About three weeks later, while rowing to

403

land to cook breakfast, Vancouver spotted two small vessels at anchor nearby. The commanders, Galiano and Valdez, belonged to the Spanish Navy. They were engaged in exploration to continue charting the inland waterways which had been partly surveyed by Spanish explorers the year before.

The Spanish and British officers, strangers in strange lands, entertained one another on their ships, examined one another's charts and traded information. They went off together to continue exploring. The Spanish vessels were too slow to keep up with the *Discovery* and the *Chatham.* Vancouver had to go ahead because he was due at Nootka to take possession of territory surrendered by Spain through a treaty made with the British Government.

CLAIMS ARE
SETTLED WITHOUT WAR

BY RIGHT OF DISCOVERY and exploration four nations — Russia, Spain, Great Britain, and the United States — held valid claims to the northwestern coast of the continent of North America. Yet, a situation which might easily have led to war was settled peaceably over a period of years.

Spain claimed possession of Nootka on the western coast of the present Vancouver Island because Perez had discovered it in 1774. Great Britain did not accept Spain's claim to lands washed by the Pacific Ocean. Sir Francis Drake and Captain Cook had also skirted the Pacific shores. A diplomatic difficulty arose when an Englishman sailing under the Portuguese flag attempted to plant a Chinese colony at Nootka. The Spanish officer in the port seized some British trading vessels. The controversy was settled when Spain signed a treaty in October, 1790, agreeing to restore the British buildings at Nootka and pay damages. Spain sent Quadra, marine commissioner, to Nootka and Great Britain sent Captain George Vancouver to arrange the transfer of property and territory.

The two men met and became good friends. Quadra explained that much of the difficulty was due to a misunderstanding

SPANISH FORT, NOOTKA SOUND, 1793

Sketch of the Spanish fort with guns mounted on a hilltop to guard landings on Nootka Sound, Vancouver Island. This was drawn at the time the British arrived, according to treaty, to take possession of the fort.

Provincial Archives, Victoria, British Columbia

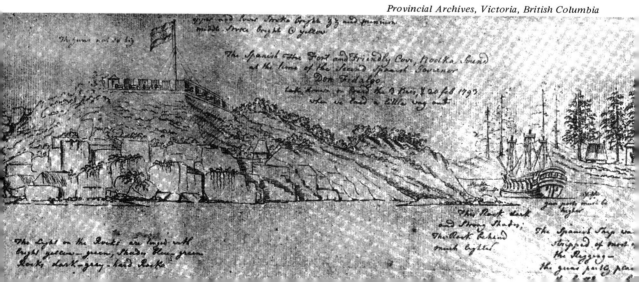

but that he had repaired the houses, and was ready to turn over the property, including cattle, hogs, and chickens, as well as the gardens which the Spaniards had planted. Quadra renamed the island Quadra-Vancouver to commemorate the historic event. Vancouver did not complete the negotiations and the British did not actually take possession until several years later. The Spaniards gradually retreated from the northern coast as far south as California and made no further claim to northwestern America.

Russia's claims receded with the fur trade. Russian trading posts extended farther inland and down the coast until competition cut into the profits. American traders, more than the British, broke the monopoly of the Russian American Company to whom was entrusted the extension of the Russian influence on the North American continent. Baranov, the director of the company, was an empire builder. Under his capable leadership Russian trading posts by 1812 were extended as far south as Fort Ross, about fifty miles north of San Francisco. The company was required under the charter from the Imperial Government of Russia to establish agricultural settlements around their trading posts wherever soil and climate were favorable. Fort Ross was to render a double service for hunting sea otter and supplying grains and meat for trading posts farther north. Since most of the inhabitants of Fort Ross were hunters from the Aleutians, where farming was unknown, little wheat was harvested.

In an effort to make Fort Ross a paying venture, Baranov resorted to doing business with the Spaniards. Although officials from the Presidio called regularly upon the Russian commander of the fort and asked him to leave California, both Spaniards and Russians remained on friendly terms. It was against the law to trade with any country except Spain but the Californians openly bartered with the Russians. Ranchers and missionaries were glad to exchange grains, peas, tallow, meat, flour, and hides for bulk iron, copper kettles, cloth, wax candles, tobacco, and sugar brought into ports by Russian ships. Many a sweet-toned bell tolling in a mission belfry was cast in the Russian foundry which Baranov established in Sitka, Alaska. Russian hunters paddled their boats through the Golden Gate, past the Presidio, to catch sea otter in San Francisco Bay, and to trap beaver on a stream which still is called the Russian River. They tried boatbuilding to make Fort Ross pay but the post's revenue never equalled the cost of maintenance. It was too far away from the posts in the north and the British and Americans were gaining control of the country in between. Meanwhile, California became Mexican territory.

In 1838 the Russian American Company had asked permission of the Imperial Government to abandon the post in California. It was 1842 before the hundred inhabitants — men, women, and children — departed in a rickety old boat for Sitka. Captain John Sutter, the Swiss immigrant who had received a land grant of thousands of acres in the Sacramento River Valley, purchased their cattle and other livestock, guns and fort equipment, and other movable property. He needed guns for Fort Sutter, since he had received his huge grant from the Mexican governor of California by promising to protect that part of the province. The Russians gradually abandoned their trading posts in territory worked by Americans and British where competition was too keen for them. They

ST. MICHAEL'S CHURCH, RUSSIAN ORTHODOX CATHEDRAL IN SITKA, ALASKA

This church with an Oriental dome and spire consoled isolated Russians living in a bleak land far from home.

retreated into the northern Pacific to hunt for fur-bearing animals on the numerous islands and the mainland of Alaska. The Indians soon became shrewd at bargaining and sold their furs to the highest bidder.

Following Gray's second voyage Americans entered the maritime fur trade of the Northwest in ever increasing numbers. The ships of the Boston traders were floating department stores. They had many articles to tempt an Indian hunter to part with a precious sea otter skin. The cargo of a Yankee trading vessel consisted of plenty in weapons — muskets, powder, pistols, flints, shot belts, leather powder flasks, shot and ball articles that always caught the eye of a native hunter. Bars of iron, iron pots, brass rings, sheets of copper, knives, scissors, hatchets, brass and copper tea kettles, pie pans, buckets and spoons, and anything made of metals sold well. Cloth, blankets, trunks, combs, looking glasses, pewter

jugs, and buttons attracted the Indian women.

The retreat of the Spaniards south into California and of the Russians north into Alaska, left Great Britain and the United States competing for the territory lying between. In 1818 the United States and Great Britain agreed that citizens of both countries could occupy any of this country without being asked to leave by the governments of either nation. In 1824 and 1825 the United States and Great Britain made treaties with Russia, agreeing that 54°40′ would be the southern boundary of Russian territory, and that British and Americans would not advance beyond that line. Thus 54°40′ became the northern boundary of the disputed Oregon country. By the Florida treaty with Spain in 1819 the northern boundary of Spanish territory had been defined as the forty-second parallel, which became the southern boundary of Oregon.

Although "Fifty-four Forty or Fight" was a slogan of the election in 1844, when James K. Polk was elected President on the Democratic ticket, the United States did not gain fifty-four forty, nor did the nation fight for it. By this time so many citizens of the United States had moved into the southern part of the disputed Oregon country, that the region was practically occupied by them. The British held the trading posts of the Hudson's Bay Company. Again territory was won by settlers who tilled the soil and lost by traders who trapped for furs. In June, 1846 the Oregon controversy was settled by dividing the country on the forty-ninth parallel "to the middle of the channel which separates the continent from Vancouver's Island; and thence southerly through the middle of said channel, and of

Fuca's Straits, to the Pacific Ocean." A later dispute over which country should claim San Juan Island was settled peaceably by arbitration. San Juan now belongs to the state of Washington. Great Britain's share of Oregon became British Columbia. The portion allotted to the United States was divided into Washington and Oregon.

"SEWARD'S ICE BOX"

AFTER THE Monroe Doctrine had been announced in December, 1823, the feeling grew among citizens of the Western Hemisphere that it would be an advantage if no part of the Americas were possessions of European nations. Although the Monroe Doctrine was not officially mentioned in negotiating the purchase of Alaska, it probably influenced the deal. During the terms of President Van Buren and President Polk there was some talk among Congressmen about buying Alaska. Not until the War Between the States, when the Confederate vessel, the *Shenandoah,* was raiding Union commerce in the North Pacific, did the need arise for naval posts in that region. William H. Seward, Secretary of State in Lincoln's Cabinet, seriously considered the purchase of Russian territory. Soon after the end of the war the opportunity came.

Russia had reasons for wanting to sell the country. That nation's navy was not large enough to defend the long and jagged Pacific coast. Since Alaska was a hunting ground, not actually a colony, and the valuable sea otter was being pursued to extinction by traders of three nations, the distant country ceased to be worth defending. The British and especially the Americans could afford to pay the native

Courtesy of the Bancroft Library

DOG SLED IN ALASKA

Travel by dog sled was common in "Seward's Ice Box" before the airplane took over transportation.

hunters higher prices for skins because they could sell them where they brought the most money. The Russian American Company, favored with a government monopoly, had to sell furs at home. It could not meet this competition. Russia permitted the fur trader to exploit the new country and leave it. It neglected the settler who would have stayed and defended it.

A Russian ambassador arrived in Washington in February, 1867 and hinted that Alaska might be bought. Seward immediately discussed the matter with President Johnson. Since the purchase would need the approval of the Senate, the Secretary of State quietly consulted a number of Senators who agreed to support the measure. Seward was so anxious to get the agreement signed that he asked the Russian agent to urge his government for approval of the price, $7,200,000. The two men were together on the evening of March 29th when the message of acceptance arrived. They

SITKA, ALASKA SOON AFTER TRANSFER TO THE UNITED STATES

Sitka, founded by Alexander Baranov in 1804, was headquarters for the Russian-American Fur Company. About 600 half-breeds and civilized natives from the Aleutian Islands lived in huts on the slope rising from the waterfront. For these hunters and fishermen, the fur company built a small church on a hill at the end of the palisade separating them from 300 Russians commanding the post. The larger buildings on the other side of the high fence provided living quarters for company officials, their offices, and the warehouses where furs were stored.

worked on the treaty that night, completing it by four o'clock in the morning. On the ninth of April the Senate ratified the treaty by a vote of 37 to 2.

On October 18, 1867 the transfer of the territory was made at Sitka, the Russian headquarters. At three o'clock in the afternoon one hundred Russian soldiers in full dress uniform formed in front of the Governor's castle. Two hundred United States soldiers, also in full dress uniform, paraded opposite the Russians. Salutes were fired from Russian batteries on shore and from the United States ship in the harbor. The flags were changed. Then the Russian captain stepped up to the American general and said:

General Rousseau, by authority from His Majesty the Emperor of all the Russias, I transfer to the United States the Territory of Alaska.

Some of the Russian inhabitants returned to their native land. Some remained to become citizens of the United States. The territory was ceded before it was paid for, since only the House of Representatives can appropriate money. Not until July 14, 1868 did the appropriations bill pass in the House and Russia receive payment. Many citizens opposed the purchase. They ridiculed the deal by calling it "Seward's Folly" and spoke of Alaska as "Seward's Ice Box." They did not foresee that the time would come when Alaska would be the strategic outpost of defense for the entire continent of North America. The purchase price of $7,200,000 is a small figure when compared with the sum realized from the yearly output of minerals, oil, lumber, fish, and furs in this area one-fifth the size of the United States.

In the end the United States gained most of the territory in the northwestern part of North America through negotiation. The nation held it by populating it. Under the form of government existing in the United States, all citizens had the privilege of going into any territory belonging to the country; of engaging in any business or following any profession that they wanted; and of selling their products and services wherever they brought the highest price. Under freedom of enterprise Americans by the thousands crossed the plains and rounded the Horn to develop the vast resources in the Northwest.

LOGGERS FELL THE TREES

IN THE SPRING OF 1792 when Captain Vancouver had sighted the mainland of North America through a misty rain, he wrote in his journal, dated April 18:

The shore appeared straight and unbroken, of a moderate height, with mountainous land behind, covered with stately forest trees.

On nearly every page of his journal kept while exploring the Northwest, there is some mention of the wonderful trees. The British were a seafaring people with an eye on timber for building their ships.

The lumbering industry of the Northwest began with a tiny sawmill erected by the British Hudson's Bay Company at Fort Vancouver on the Columbia River in 1827. The first missionaries who journeyed to Oregon with trappers in the 1830's expressed surprise at finding several sawmills along the great river.

A small party of immigrants, who had come overland in a covered wagon to Portland, decided to seek new homes farther north in the timbered wilderness. On the schooner *Exact* they arrived at a point which they first named New York, visioning a great city there, like the metropolis of the Atlantic seaboard. Since this city was only a dream, the place was called Alki, which, in the Indian language, meant bye and bye. In November, 1851 twelve adults and twelve children landed on the beach in a cold drizzling rain. These settlers had barely finished crude log huts for shelter when the brig *Leonesa* arrived from San Francisco, seeking a cargo of pile

PACKERS ON CHILKOOT PASS NEAR SKAGWAY, ALASKA, 1898

In July of 1897, sixty-eight miners returned from the Klondike in northwestern Canada to Seattle with over a million dollars in raw gold. They started a gold rush. Fortune hunters crowded ships from Seattle bound for Skagway, the northernmost port on the Inland Passage to Alaska. During the spring of 1898, thousands of goldseekers and packers, their backs loaded with supplies, toiled up Chilkoot Pass. At the top, they crossed into Canada for the long trek of 570 miles to Dawson in Yukon, entrance to the Klondike Gold Region.

Courtesy of the Bancroft Library

EARLY LOGGING IN MASON COUNTY OF WASHINGTON

Teams of oxen drag huge trunks of trees over log roads to the lumber mills. Cuttings lying on the hillside show the wasteful methods of early logging in the great forests of the Northwest.

timber for building docks in the harbor of the fast-growing port of the gold rush. The pioneers felled trees near the water's edge to fill the order. They found it difficult to load 35,000 board feet of logs in the shallow water of Alki Point. Several families moved to the east side of the bay. There the hills sloped down to a deep-water shore line, making a natural harbor on their doorsteps. They named their settlement Seattle after the friendly Indian chief of the Duwamish tribe, who, as a boy of six, had gazed in wonder at the

Discovery anchored in Puget Sound.

The rapid growth of the lumber business may be judged by advertisements appearing in *The Columbian,* the first newspaper in the state of Washington. Its first edition was published in September of 1852 in Olympia. Seven weeks later the following advertisement appeared:

TO SHIP OWNERS AND MASTERS OF VESSELS: The undersigned is just completing an excellent new DRY DOCK three miles below Olympia on the west side of the Harbor, which will soon be ready for the accommodation of

410

**SEATTLE, CHIEF OF THE
DUWAMISH AND OTHER TRIBES
LIVING ALONG PUGET SOUND**

Dr. Henry A. Smith, early settler of Seattle which was named for the great chief, wrote about him:

Old Chief Seattle was the largest Indian I ever saw, and by far the noblest looking. He stood nearly six feet in his moccasins, was broad-shouldered, deep-chested, and finely proportioned. His eyes were large, intelligent, expressive, and friendly, when in repose, and faithfully mirrored the varying moods of the great soul that looked through them. He was usually solemn, silent and dignified . . . .

ship owners and masters of vessels for the repair of their vessels. — Cargoes for spars for the China or English markets will at all times be furnished at the docks.

In 1853, the first shipment from Puget Sound to a foreign country was a cargo of ship spars to China. From such small beginnings grew the lumber industry of the Pacific Northwest. Stands of Douglas fir, 200 to 500 years old, were common on the rainy side of the mountains in Washington and Oregon. In the fog belt farther south in California grew redwood trees 1000 to 2000 years of age. The fur hunters trapped animals in these forests but did not cut down the trees except for cabins and fuel. After settlers arrived in large numbers companies were formed to purchase thousands of acres of mature trees. Logging began on a wholesale plan. At one time nearly half of the nation's lumber supply, one-fifth of its wood pulp, and half of its plywood came from the Northwest.

Finally, the reckless cutting alarmed the public and laws were passed to regulate it to prevent the timber from being exhausted in a generation or two. Mountains, once covered with straight pine, tapering Douglas fir, and bluish-green spruce were barren except for stumps and snags. A bald range, shorn of its glory, makes a silent and moving appeal. Now, the lumbermen have rules for rotated forest cutting and tree planting to insure a steady supply of timber, and state and federal laws regulate the industry.

JOB CARR'S CABIN
Job Carr built his log house in a forest where the land was cleared later for the city of Tacoma.

FISH THRIVE IN NORTHWEST WATERS

SALMON LIVE ALONG the northwest coast where the geography of the region suits their way of life. The adult fish live in salt water but salmon spawn in fresh water. Their eggs are laid in little lakes and sluggish streams miles inland from the ocean. The fish need larger rivers to ascend to these spawning grounds in fresh water.

Salmon was big business before the white man came into the Northwest. Sometimes several thousand Indians gathered at The Dalles and in the long narrows of the big bend in the Columbia River when salmon were running. Men speared the leaping fish. The women and children dried and salted them for the winter food supply. With plenty of fish to feed the crowds, the Indians carried on trading at the same time. The Plains tribes brought buffalo hides and beaver skins to trade for shells and dried salmon. However, the natives gathered along the rivers during the salmon runs for fun as much as for fishing. They sang, danced, and made merry.

The diaries of adventurers and mission-

FORT LANGLEY ON THE FRASER RIVER, BRITISH COLUMBIA

On June 28, 1827, James McMillan of the Hudson's Bay Company left Fort Vancouver on the Columbia River with two boats and 24 men to build a fur-trading post on the Fraser River. A month later, he chose the site on the south bank of the Fraser River below the mouth of the Salmon River, and named it Fort Langley after a manager and stockholder of the company.

Fort Langley was built to regain the coastal fur trade for the British company whose business was suffering from the competition of the "Boston Peddlers." After Captain Robert Gray returned from voyages to the Northwest and reported a wealth of furs, merchants of Boston loaded ships with cloth, hardware, trinkets, guns and ammunition to trade with the Indians for furs. These Yankees cut into the profits of the British and Russian traders.

Archibald McDonald, who succeeded McMillan, turned to fishing and farming to increase business. In a letter written in 1831, he wrote that "the loss in skins was more than made up by 220 barrels of salmon." Barrels for shipping salmon were made at the post. He planted potatoes, grains and vegetables, and raised pigs, cattle and horses. The great salmon industry of the Northwest began at Fort Langley, a fur-trading post.

Provincial Archives, Victoria, British Columbia

aries who crossed the plains to Oregon tell in glowing terms of the abundance of salmon and of how they enjoyed the fresh fish after living for weeks on dried buffalo meat. One scientist told of seeing salmon so numerous in headwaters of streams that the Indians waded into the pools and killed the fish with cedar paddle boards.

The early settlers also salted and dried salmon as the Indians did. They depended on it for winter food. Before the arrival of the pioneers who occupied the land, hunters and trappers carried dried salmon in their packs wherever they went. The fishing industry was established about 1800 by the Northwest Fur Company, which later merged with the Hudson's Bay Company. Salmon was salted and cured to supply the company men who were tracking through the wilderness. By 1835 the Hudson's Bay Company was shipping about 4000 barrels of salted salmon per year to the Hawaiian Islands. In 1836 over 67,000 salmon were sent to the company's trading posts along the upper Fraser River. In the year that the first settlers came to Elliott Bay, Chief Seattle, for whom their village was named, brought Dr. Maynard from Olympia to start a fishing business and give employment to members of his tribe. Barrels of salmon were packed in brine and shipped to San Francisco. Although the fish spoiled enroute, the venture established the fishing industry as the second commercial enterprise on Elliott Bay.

The Fraser River with its many tributaries and its chain of lakes is the greatest sockeye river in the world; and sockeye salmon know it. So do fishermen who caught over 195,000,000 of this species in the Fraser River between 1894 and 1917. It was in 1863, during the War

SALMON FISHING ON THE FRASER RIVER

Simon Fraser, a clerk in the Northwest Company, was sent from eastern Canada to western Canada to establish new fur-trading posts among the Indian tribes west of the Rocky Mountains.

On May 22, 1808, an exploring party led by Simon Fraser left Fort George to paddle canoes down a large river not yet traveled by white men. Was this great river the Columbia? It was a hazardous voyage over treacherous rapids, through narrow rock-walled canyons, and with encounters with unfriendly Indians. In the swift current of the stream, canoes sometimes gathered speed of thirty miles per hour. The party sighted the Georgia Strait on the second day of July, proving that the river was not the Columbia. It was named for Simon Fraser. The river became famous for fish, not furs. It was the favorite waterway of salmon.

Between the States, that the first salmon was canned on this river in northern Washington. Three years later the first cannery was built on the Columbia River. It was the canning process, more profitable than salting or drying, that made fishing a leading industry in the Northwest.

Salmon are caught going up the rivers because the adults never go back down to the sea again. They lay eggs and die. When hatched the young fry remain in these quiet waters until they can swim freely.

413

They then work their way to the ocean. The young of sockeye and king, or chinook salmon, may stay in fresh water until their second spring. Those starting to the ocean as yearlings have a better chance to survive; but their real growth takes place in salt water. The king salmon, largest of the five common species, likes to spawn in deeper and swifter waters. The average weight of king salmon is twenty-two pounds but fish have been caught weighing sixty pounds and more. Being strong and heavy the chinooks like the wide Columbia River with its large tributaries and sometimes lay their eggs in the main channels of streams. This large species, a deep pink color, brings the highest price in markets. As a result many have been trapped for the fisheries on their upstream runs and too few have reached the spawning grounds. Their numbers are declining.

The rivalry between fishermen from Canada and the United States damaged the sockeye industry in the Fraser River country. In 1937 the two nations made a treaty to work together in guarding the sockeye from over-fishing and to build ladders to aid the salmon in getting over dams and other unnatural barriers in streams. Some years before, another treaty rescued halibut from over-fishing and restored the normal supply to fishermen of both nations. The future of this business, like lumbering, depends upon conservation.

In some places logging has destroyed the watershed and the streams where salmon spawned have dried up. However, the greatest hazard to the fish are the dams blocking the rivers to store water for irrigation and to generate electric power. Sometimes, the struggling salmon are lifted to the top of a dam by elevators which operate like canal locks. Salmon have a homing instinct which leads them to the spawning grounds of their forefathers — to die. To get there, many are forced to accept the aid of man's invention.

FARMING IS VARIED
IN THE NORTHWEST

THE CASCADE MOUNTAINS divide the states of Washington and Oregon into two kinds of climate, moist and dry. On the ocean side where rainfall is plentiful, the forests are dense, the soil is rich, and the crops are abundant. On the eastern side the rainfall is light because few clouds blowing in from the sea can cross the range without dropping their moisture. Seattle, on Puget Sound, has an average yearly rainfall of thirty-four inches; while Spokane, in the eastern part of Washington, has less than half that amount, sixteen inches. The rodeo town of Pendleton, Oregon, east of the mountains, has an average yearly rainfall of only fourteen inches; while the rose city of Portland, near the seacoast, has three times as much rain, forty-two inches in all. This variety of climate accounts for the variety of crops in the Northwest. On the rainy side of the mountains the farmers specialize in fruits, vegetables, and dairy cows. On the eastern side they depended upon wheat, forage, and beef cattle until irrigation, in some places, enlarged their production.

For irrigation and power the Northwest has its own great river, the Columbia. This stream rises in the Canadian Rockies and flows about 200 miles northwest before turning south for the 500 mile run to the United States border. The Columbia enters this country in the northeastern corner of the state of Washington.

GOLD MINERS — AURORA CLAIM ON WILLIAMS CREEK — 1867

When gold was discovered among the headwaters of the Fraser River in Canada, mining was added to the leading industries of the northwestern part of North America.

Miners working the Aurora Claim on Williams Creek were averaging $20 a day in September of 1867. Some of the ground on bedrock of this stream yielded $2.25 to the pan.

Ninety miles west of Spokane, in Columbia Canyon, the river is spanned by the Grand Coulee Dam, containing enough concrete to pave a four-lane highway from Seattle to New York City. Behind this barrier twice the height of Niagara Falls, the river backs up to form a reservoir, named Lake Roosevelt for President Franklin D. Roosevelt. This body of water extends almost to the Canadian border, a distance of 151 miles.

The Grand Coulee Dam, costing about $225,000,000 was constructed by the Bureau of Reclamation. As water reaches a vast area through an irrigation system with 4000 miles of canals, the settlers will begin to pay a certain amount per acre for the water to repay the Government for the costs of construction. That will take a long time. In the meantime electric power, generated by the falling water, is being sold to private companies and for defense projects to make payments.

The Bonneville Dam, below Columbia Gorge, was the largest until the Grand Coulee was built. Both have large powerplants. However, much of the power generated at the Grand Coulee must be used to pump irrigation water up to the desert land because the million and more acres to be irrigated are at a higher altitude than the dam. The Northwest needs more electricity for its industries and more dams are being constructed in the Columbia River.

415

Who owns the Columbia River? What state has prior right to the water in the stream? On July 16, 1952 Congress approved the Interstate Compact Commission drawn up by representatives from Washington, Idaho, Oregon, Wyoming, and Montana to settle by agreement the use of water in interstate streams. In October of the same year, at a committee meeting in Yakima, Washington, a permanent organization was formed with headquarters in Boise, Idaho. The States of Nevada and Utah did not join the compact. At this meeting, however, these states and the Dominion of Canada were invited to send representatives to meetings of the Interstate Compact Commission.

Since the days of the first settlers, water from the Columbia River has been used for irrigation, but for land near the stream. The Wenatchee Valley on the eastern side

HOOD RIVER VALLEY IN OREGON

Hood River Valley rises gently from the Columbia River to the base of Mt. Hood, an extinct volcano, rising to the height of 11,245 feet. This land was a forest of evergreens when the first settlers came over the Oregon Trail. Today, dairying and fruit farming are leading industries.

Al Monner

of the Cascade Mountains was a semi-desert. A missionary, Father De Grassi, taught the Indians to irrigate the valley with water from the Columbia River. In 1872 Philip Miller, a homesteader, planted the first apple trees in this valley. More settlers came and planted apple trees where the soil was rich, the days were sunny, and the nights were cool. The apple industry, however, waited for the railroad, the Great Northern, in 1892. The first carload of apples was shipped from Miller's ranch in the fall of 1901. Now the Wenatchee Valley, thirty-five miles long, claims to be the "Apple Capital." The orchards are watered from the Columbia River and small tributaries that flow down from the mountains.

Farther east and south are the rolling wheat lands of Washington. The soft white wheat grown in the Pacific Northwest makes a moist flour preferred for cakes and fancy pastries. As more land gets water, more orchards and more fields spread over the landscape. Many of the crops that flourish on the rainy side of the Cascades can be grown on the dry side east of the mountains with irrigation.

The stockman is still secure on the plains of eastern Oregon where no great river flows to be harnessed for irrigation. To cowboys riding the range and herders minding their sheep, the Pendleton Roundup is the big event of the year. It is ranch country east of the Cascade Mountains in Oregon. Without irrigation the farmer will not arrive to run his plow through the stockman's pasture.

MAP:

WA17r
Our United States by Edgar B. Wesley

Chapter 22

In the Mountain Regions

THE LURE OF
GOLD AND SILVER

MANY OF THE richest gold finds were made by accident. Late in the spring of 1850 a small band of Mormon emigrants camped on the Carson River in Nevada to wait for the snow to melt in the high country so they could cross the Sierras. To pass away the time, some of the men did a little prospecting in a canyon nearby. In washing the first pan of gravel they found gold. They named the place Gold Canyon. Although the men earned from $5 to $8 a day, they did not stay. When the snow melted, the party crossed the mountain range to the "diggings" in the Sacramento Valley and left a fortune behind them. They had camped near a big bonanza, the famous Comstock Lode.

Nine years later two Irishmen, Pete and Pat, were prospecting in the same region. They dug a pit in a small mountain stream to bury their tool for washing gravel. Just out of curiosity they washed through their rocker some of the dirt from the bottom of the pit. They knew they had made a strike when they found flakes of glittering gold. They were much annoyed with heavy black chunks that clogged

their rocker and hindered the washing of gold dust. They tossed the black metal aside, thinking it worthless.

Late in the afternoon of the same day, Henry Comstock, searching for his mustang pony, happened along. He saw the gold. Instantly he declared that the land was his claim and threatened to have the Irishmen arrested. To settle the matter, Pete and Pat took in Comstock as a partner, although he knew as little about mining as they did. However, Comstock's loud boasting about HIS mine attached his name to the bonanza. Samples of the "black stuff" were sent to Nevada City to be assayed. It was pure silver.

The news spread like a prairie fire. Miners, gamblers, and adventurers swarmed over the Sierras to seek new fortunes in Washoe County, then a part of Utah but soon to be in the state of Nevada. It was summertime. Tents dotted the hillsides but many slept on the ground without shelter of any kind. The ore was rich but it took expensive machinery to tunnel into the mountain and dig it out. Pete, Pat, and their bluffing partner sold out to men who could finance the project. The wealth from the famous Comstock Lode helped Lincoln to fight the War Between

TONOPAH, NEVADA IN 1902

This street scene in Tonopah was typical of new mining towns during boom days. A teamster is on the way to nearby camps with a load of cots, bed springs, and food for miners. The wagon freighter carries a barrel of water for man and beast in the desert country. Trunks and suit cases of new arrivals are piled high on the board walk in front of a little hotel with a sign advertising: A NICE NEW BED, $7.50 a month, 50¢ a night.

the States and made a number of millionaires. More than $40,000,000 in gold and silver was taken from this district. Some mines around Silver City, Nevada, are still producing with profit.

Ten years after Marshall discovered gold in the tail race of Sutter's mill, prospectors were panning in the South Platte, Cherry Creek, and other streams of the Colorado Rockies. "Pike's Peak or Bust" became the slogan of another gold rush and another westward migration. One "Pike's Peaker" wrote in a letter to the folks back home:

418

Camped for the night. There are 60 men and 12 wagons in the company, all well provided with food, clothing, and ammunition. There is no house in sight or sign of civilization, — but prairie — boundless, endless. I feel first rate — free, free as air! We live by the side of our wagon and sleep in the tent. I do the washing, Charlie washes the dishes, and Dunton drives the team and attends to the oxen and wagon . . . . While I am in my tent writing by the light of a lantern, the Germans are singing, and the others are fiddling and dancing. We have merry times out here.

A donkey discovered the rich Mizpah vein in Nevada which yielded $150,000,000 in gold and silver ore and made Tonopah a mining town. In 1900 a Nevada rancher loaded four burros with supplies and went prospecting. One evening he camped near a place which the Indians called Tonopah, their word for little water. The next morning a dust storm was blowing and the burros were nowhere in sight. After a search the rancher found them huddled behind a big dark rock that provided a little shelter from the wind and the dust. While waiting for the storm to blow over, the prospector chipped off pieces of the rock to take with him to be assayed. This chunk of black rock on a lonely desert proved to be the outcropping of a rich vein of silver ore. It was named Mizpah. Not having the capital to develop the mine, the rancher sold his holding for some cash and shares of stock in the Tonopah Mining Company. He retired to a quiet ranch life, a rich man.

Gold was the magnet that drew thousands across the plains, through mountain passes, and over sandy wastes to establish the mining industry in that vast region lying between the Missouri River and the Pacific Ocean. Today, western mines furnish a variety of minerals, from gypsum to gems, for a variety of

PANNING FOR GOLD IN COLORADO

With pick, pan and shovel, rich and poor, old and young, lawyer and laborer worked side by side, independently and alone. Panning for gold was democratic and adventurous for fortune seekers, and inspired verses in the newspapers.

THE GOLDSEEKER'S SONG

"Take up the oxen, boys, and harness up the mules;
Pack away provisions and bring along the tools;
The pick and the shovel, and a pan that won't leak;
And we'll start for the gold mines. Hurrah for the Peak!

We'll cross the bold Missouri, and we'll steer for the West,
And we'll take the road we think is the shortest and the best;
We'll travel o'er the plains, where the wind is blowing bleak,
And the sandy wastes shall echo with — Hurrah for Pike's Peak!

We'll sit around the campfire when all our work is done,
And sing our songs, and crack our jokes, and have our share of fun;
And when we're tired of jokes and songs, our blankets we will seek,
To dream of friends, and home, and gold. Hurrah for Pike's Peak!

(Hannibal Messenger, April 28, 1859)

Title Insurance and Trust Company, Los Angeles

MAIL STAGE TO GOLDFIELD, NEVADA, 1905

Stage coaches were used for hauling mail and passengers until railroads were built into the mining camps. Goldfield enjoyed a story-book boom during the early days of this century. As the veins of rich ore were exhausted, the yield of gold and silver became less and less. The camp is a lonely town, sprawled over a saddle between two barren peaks, more than a mile high. Some of the old-timers remain, confident that new ores will be found in the bleak hills to bring a new boom to Goldfield.

industries all over the nation. This kind of mining is a money-making business but it lacks the lure of gold and silver.

WESTERN MINES SUPPLY MANY MINERALS FOR MANUFACTURERS

NO ONE KNOWS how long prehistoric man used copper before he learned to mix it with tin to make bronze. Pieces of bronze have been found in Egyptian tombs nearly 6000 years old. The isle of Cyprus in the Mediterranean was an ancient source of copper and from this island the metal took its name. It was first called cyprium, then cuprum, and finally copper. No other metal has served man so long and so well.

Butte, Montana, boasts of being the greatest mining camp in the world. Copper did it. The city is built over a maze of tunnels and underground workings that pierce the "richest hill on earth" to a depth of almost a mile. Miners go down in cages to dig the valuable ore in these shafts. The product is brought to the surface in huge elevators. In Utah along the western shore of the Great Salt Lake, an unusual copper mine exists where no one digs for ore. The miners simply cut away the mountains with big electric shovels. It is necessary to scoop up 450,000,000 tons of ore to get 8,000,000 pounds of copper. Some gold, silver, and molybdenum are also found in this lowgrade copper ore. The minerals are extracted in mills and smelters in Garfield, nearby, on the lake shore. Arizona is another copper-producing state where mines were worked by the Spaniards before this territory belonged to the United States. The Rocky Mountains from Canada to Mexico yield copper ores.

Zinc, the non-rust metal, is usually present in ores containing copper, silver, and lead. Primitive man discovered that a mixture of copper and zinc made brass. At Great Falls, Montana, a mining company operates a zinc plant, the largest of its kind in the world. Although the brass industry is still zinc's biggest customer, this non-rust metal has come to have more varied uses than any other except iron.

Like copper and zinc, lead is one of the oldest metals known to man. The Pharaohs of ancient Egypt made solder from lead to glaze their pottery. The Babylonians used lead to fasten iron bolts into stone bridges. Nearly 4000 years ago, the Chinese had lead coins before silver money came into use. The Romans had lead water pipes in their private homes and public baths. Since the metal is found in ores containing copper, zinc, and silver, the Rocky Mountain states have lead smelters.

However, the mining industry of the West owes much of its success to plain black coal. It warmed the miner's cabin, cooked his food, and fired the furnaces that smelted the ores. Colorado, Utah and Wyoming have thousands of acres of coal lands.

From the Indians, early pioneers heard of "rocks that burn" and often saw outcroppings of coal deposits. Little was done to develop these coal beds until the first railroad was built across the continent. In 1869 the first ton of coal was mined at Rock Springs, Wyoming. The basin of the Green River is rich in coal deposits from its source in the Wind River Range to its junction with the Colorado in southeastern Utah. With the completion of each new railroad in the mountain states, coal mines were opened to supply fuel for the engines. In turn these coal mines brought business to the railroads.

Although electricity and oil are strong competitors of coal in industry, this fuel will probably not be replaced entirely for heating in a long time. When winter winds howl and heavy snow fall, man likes the warmth of glowing red coals in the home grate and the cabin stove.

The basic minerals, such as gold, silver, copper, zinc, iron, lead, and coal are the bread and butter of the mining industry. The miner is ever on the lookout for new minerals to serve the needs of manufacturers. In processing the basic metals, new and valuable minerals are found. This never-ending search keeps the spirit of adventure alive in the business.

Utah has whole mountains of gypsum and enough salt to supply the world for a long time. California has the largest known supply of borax now being mined for commercial purposes. Idaho has eighty-five percent of the phosphate rock known to exist in the United States. When the soil of our nation becomes less productive, this bed of phosphate rock underlying 268,000 acres of ground may revive the farmland. Both Nevada and California have large deposits of magnesite ore and the salt that is needed to process the ore.

Leadville, Colorado in the gold rush of 1860 was a roaring camp. A few years later the town was almost deserted. Silver brought another boom that swelled the population to 30,000 in 1875. When that bubble burst, the mining camp, situated about two miles above sea level, again became a ghost town. Now a new metal is bringing new prosperity to the old mining village in the Rocky Mountains. It is molybdenum, which is used like starch in making tool steel. Most of it came from a mountain of ore near Leadville. The steel industry's demand for both molybdenum

COPPER MINE — BINGHAM, UTAH

This mine of the Kennecott Copper Corporation is the largest surface copper mine in North America, covering over 1000 acres of excavated ore — rich earth. About 177 miles of railroad tracks are moved from terrace to terrace as the mountain is being slowly demolished to supply smelters at Garfield with ore.

Courtesy, Salt Lake Chamber of Commerce

and vanadium has led to the discovery of these silver-white metals in other places.

From Paradox Valley in western Colorado, in the basin of the Dolores River, yellowish carnotite ore was shipped to France for the experiments which led to the discovery of radium by Mme. Curie. This same carnotite ore that produces radium to cure man's ills also contains uranium to make that frightful weapon of modern warfare, the atomic bomb. Before its tremendous power was known, a world-wide search began for the nickel-white metal that had been used in making steel, stainless silverware, and pottery.

Gems found in mountain regions of the West are made into jewelry in factories of the East. A jet mine near Zion Canyon in southern Utah produces the shiny black stone from which beads, buckles, and buttons are made. Idaho furnishes opals for New York jewelers. In 1896 a sheep herder discovered sapphires in Yogo Gulch in the Little Belt Mountains of Montana. The claim that he sold for $1600 has produced $10,000,000 worth of sapphires.

Miners and manufacturers walk hand in hand, depending upon each other for prosperity. Steel is dipped in molten zinc to make a galvanized metal that will not rust. This coating of zinc was probably one of the first known methods of preventing rust. Zinc has been used for flashlight batteries, lids for canning jars, gutters on houses, rubber tires, hardware, paints, automobiles, washing machines, and many other articles. Because zinc serves with other metals in alloys and is often covered with paint, the public is not always aware of this important non-rust metal in the world of industry. Over one hundred industries use lead in manufacturing their products. Among these are aircraft, automobile, building, canning, chemical,

dyeing, explosives, electrical, gasoline, glass, paint, printing, plumbing, radio, and rubber. As a metal, magnesium is used in photographer's flashlights, signal lights, and fireworks. As a compound it is used in medicines, tooth powders, silver cleaners, electric batteries, textiles, bleaching solutions, paper, and furnace linings.

The polished silver in knives, forks, and spoons made by silversmiths in New England may come from ores buried for centuries in the hard hills of the East Tintic Mountains of Utah, or from mines in Idaho. Gold from western states may be melted into bullion and stored at Fort Knox, to guard the face value of our paper money. Molybdenum from Colorado may be shipped to steel mills in Gary, Indiana, and Pittsburgh, Pennsylvania, to harden the steel used by manufacturers of tools in Hartford, Connecticut.

Although mining is adding new minerals with long names that send us scurrying to the dictionary and counts production in dizzy millions, the industry began with a pick, a pan, and a shovel. To find new deposits and new minerals, mining now depends upon geologists, mineralogists, metallurgists, and other scientists. Where is the mining man who does not greet an old prospector with a hearty handshake? When they meet in the desert and the mountain, the scientist shares the prospector's coffee and beans and sleeps by his campfire. Of what do they dream?

FARMING AND STOCK RAISING COMPETE WITH MINING AND LUMBERING

THE MINER AND THE LOGGER followed the trapper and the hunter. Then came the stockman with his herds and the farmer with his plow. The miner who

HOMESTEADERS GOING WEST ON THE OVERLAND TRAIL — 1882

This photograph was taken on a trail across Wyoming. The wagon caravans continued long after trains were running. Many homesteaders could not afford to travel by rail. They had horses, cattle, wagons, furniture, and clothing, but little ready cash. In going overland by wagon, they had teams to plow the ground and plant their crops, and cattle for a start in livestock.

pockmarked the hills with holes in the earth welcomed meat on the hoof in mountain meadows and fruits in bloom on valley floors. The time came when the crops of the soil brought more money than the ores in the hills. Even in Colorado, "the mining state," the value of farm products exceeds the value of minerals. Fruit trees flaunt their blossoms in the valleys when the peaks are topped with snow. Utah celery, Colorado peas, and Idaho potatoes find a waiting market in many states. On the wide, high plateaus approaching the mountain ranges, sugar beets are a paying crop. Alfalfa is everywhere because stock-raising is important in the mountain states.

It is generally believed that Columbus brought the first sheep to the Western Hemisphere. These animals were the ancestors of the Mexican sheep on which was founded the wool-growing industry of the Southwest. Because sheep have a herding instinct, they can be handled successfully with little help in open country without fences. Sheep will eat weeds and shrubs that cattle will not touch. They can survive in the semi-arid plateau regions of the West. In summer shepherds drive their flocks higher and higher as the snow melts, until they are above timberline. The summer hiker on vacation in the mountains sees flocks of sheep grazing in meadows carpeted with fragile white primroses and brilliant blue lupine.

Not so long ago, the range was free. Some still is free, but for the most part stockmen now lease much of the grazing land for their horses, cattle, sheep, and goats. In a number of western states land was set aside to provide support for schools

423

and other public institutions. This land can be leased by stockmen. Wyoming has the most state-owned land because a law prohibits the sale of any state land for less than $10 per acre. Wyoming, the stockman's paradise, is the state of wide open spaces, jingling spurs, high-heeled boots, ten-gallon hats, and cowboys.

By carefully obeying grazing rules, stockmen can secure permits to graze their herds in national forests. Although they pay so much per head of stock for this privilege, many people object to the plan. They claim the domestic animals eat the forage needed to feed the wildlife in these protected areas. The mountain state of Idaho has over 20,000,000 acres of forest preserves while Kansas, a prairie state, has none.

Westerners live and toil with mountains in their scenery, in their work, and in their hearts. The fisherman trolling his net on Puget Sound predicts the weather by looking toward the east to see if Mt. Baker's white crest is clear. The cowboy rounds up his cattle on high plateaus hemmed in by mountain ranges that are blue in the distance. The herder watches his sheep feeding in timberline meadows above the clouds where the sky is purple at noon, gold at sunset, pink at dawn, and the air is thin and clear.

No mountains are more cherished, perhaps, than the first range of the Rockies rising from the central plain. Pike's Peak and Long's Peak are landmarks for the people who live on the western fringe of the prairie. Snow on these peaks means water in the ditches and crops in the fields. The farmers plant potatoes, cut alfalfa, and top their sugar beets. Their lives cannot escape the changing moods of the mountains, their everyday companions in a workaday world.

RAISING SHEEP IS A BIG INDUSTRY IN MONTANA

Sheep graze during the summer in high mountain meadows nestled among snowy ranges in Montana.

Montana Highway Commission

A LITTLE CAMPFIRE
INSPIRED A BIG IDEA

WHEN LEWIS AND CLARK led the first expedition into the Northwest in 1804, they took along sturdy outdoorsmen who knew how to survive in a wilderness. Among the first to enlist as a private was a frontiersman, John Colter. He joined Lewis as a hunter when the captain's keelboat tied up at Maysville, Kentucky, on October 15, 1803. Nearly three years later on the return trip from the Pacific, Colter asked for his discharge to join two trappers, Dickson and Hancock of Illinois, whom he chanced to meet on the way. They had offered him a third of their fur business if he would join them. Officers and men in the expedition gave Colter knives, powder horns, hatchets, and enough supplies to maintain him in the wilderness for two years. Passing through the Mandan villages, Lewis and Clark bade farewell to Sacajawea and Colter. They tied their canoes together and headed for home.

It was a long cold winter for the three trappers on the Yellowstone River. By spring the men had quarreled. Colter left to trap alone and took his beaver skins along in a canoe. As soon as the ice broke in the Yellowstone River, Colter paddled down to the Missouri and on down that swollen river to the market in St. Louis to sell his furs. At the junction of the Platte River he was surprised to see several keelboats tied to trees. Rising above the grove of cottonwoods was the smoke of campfires. He had come upon the fur hunting expedition of Manuel Lisa. The solitary figure paddling through the swirling waters toward the river bank attracted men from Lisa's expedition. They hailed their welcome to Colter. Colter met several

National Park Service

**CLIMBING EAGLE CLIFF,
ROCKY MOUNTAIN NATIONAL PARK**
Mountain climbing is a popular sport in the national parks of the West. The peaks in the background of the mountaineer are Mt. Meeker, Long's Peak, and Lady Washington.

friends from the Lewis and Clark expedition. They had joined Manuel Lisa's newly formed company to trap beaver on the upper Missouri.

Lisa persuaded Colter to join his fur company. Again, on the way back to civilization, Colter halted to return to the wilderness. He guided Lisa's party to the junction of the Yellowstone and Big Horn Rivers. Here the men erected a log cabin consisting of two rooms and a loft. This trading post was the first permanent building in the present state of Montana. It was known as Manuel's Fort. The next step was to notify the Indian tribes of this post and to invite them to bring in their furs.

425

Lisa dispatched Colter into unexplored country to get business from tribes.

Alone with a thirty-pound pack on his back and a rifle in his hand, Colter started on a long journey into an unknown wilderness which the Indians called "Land of Burning Mountains." He was probably the first white man to see Wind River Range, the Grand Teton, Jackson Hole, and the headwaters of the Green River and the Snake River. The wonders of nature unrolled before his eyes. Geysers spouted into the air, mud boiled in paint pots, and hot springs bubbled over colored rocks. When he returned to Manuel's Fort and told about this strange

LONG'S PEAK — ROCKY MOUNTAIN NATIONAL PARK — COLORADO

In 1819, Congress voted money to send an engineer, Major Stephen H. Long with 300 men to explore the territory of the Louisiana Purchase lying north of the Red River between the Mississippi River and the Rocky Mountains. The party went up the Missouri River to Council Bluffs in a new sternwheeler with the bow in the form of a serpent's head. To impress the Indians, smoke escaped from the nostrils of the snake instead of the usual funnel on a steamboat.

After a disastrous winter at Council Bluffs and the loss of one third of the men, Congress ordered all the troops to return except a few. The party finally consisted of six soldiers for protection, scientists, a surveyor, and an artist, nineteen in all to complete the journey on horseback.

The group followed the Platte River to the junction of the North and South Forks, and then turned south. While camped on the site of the present city of Denver, Colorado, the men "were greatly impressed by a lofty peak, square-topped, rising from the mountain range." On his map, Long marked it "Highest Peak" but the name was changed to Long's Peak in his honor.

In 1915, this spectacular region of 405 square miles with fifteen peaks above 13,000 feet, many lakes, and several glaciers became the Rocky Mountain National Park.

National Park Service

wonderland, the traders laughed at him.

Twenty-seven years later another trapper, Jim Bridger, for whom Fort Bridger was named, told the same story. His listeners shrugged their shoulders and laughed at another of old Jim's yarns. Making fun of the mountain man, who was a master storyteller, his friends wrote his epitaph — Here LIES Bridger. For sixty years people refused to believe these fantastic tales though hunters and trappers verified them again and again.

Finally in 1870 an official expedition, composed of ten prominent men whom the public trusted, was organized to investigate these rumors and separate truth from fiction. The leader of the expedition was General Henry D. Washburn who had served in the War Between the States and had been elected to Congress for two terms. All ten were from Montana: a president of a bank, an assessor of internal revenue, leading merchants, and Judge Cornelius Hedges, a highly esteemed lawyer. The men entered the "Land of Burning Mountains" believing nothing they had ever heard, only to be astonished by the wonders they saw with their own eyes.

On the chilly evening of September 19th, the explorers made their campfire at the junction of the Firehole and Gibbon Rivers. The time was nearing for their return. They began to wonder what people would say when they told of seeing pink and lavender mud seething in holes in the ground; jets of steam spouting from pits and crevices; petrified wood buried for ages under lava and ashes belched from craters of volcanoes long extinct; a river tumbling over a waterfall 310 feet high; and a canyon twenty miles long and over a thousand feet deep, with tinted walls of volcanic rock. Would they too, be ridiculed?

Montana Highway Commission

GLACIER NATIONAL PARK — MONTANA

This park is well named with 60 glaciers perched upon rocky ledges, all that is left from the ice age, and glacial lakes numbering 200 in the valleys. An early French explorer called this region, "the land of shining mountains" because the snow-capped peaks with patches of glacial ice glistened in the sunlight.

Although Lewis and Clark mentioned these mountains, little was known about them until engineers seeking a route for a railroad entered the region. Surveyors, to establish the border between the United States and Canada on the 49th parallel, tramped over the mountains in 1861.

In 1910, President Taft signed the bill making this scenic area a national park. Glacier National Park covers 1500 acres, touching Waterton-Lakes National Park in Canada. In 1932, the two were joined in the firm belief "that it will forever be an appropriate symbol of permanent peace and friendship."

All of this territory was public land. Seated around the fire, the men talked of homesteading the wonderland, with some taking the geysers, some the hot springs, and others the canyon of the Yellowstone River. During this conversation Hedges, the

427

Judge from Helena, remained silent. He stared thoughtfully at the sputtering logs of the campfire. When he did speak, however, his words echoed around the globe. He declared that such a wonderland of nature should remain forever, untouched, to be enjoyed by all the people in all the world. There and then, by the light of the campfire, the explorers solemnly pledged themselves to work unceasingly to have this region set aside as a national park, for the citizens of the United States and visitors from other lands.

Two years later in 1872 an act of Congress established the Yellowstone National Park, the first in the world, as a "pleasuring ground for the benefit and enjoyment of the people." Nathaniel Pitt Langford, one of the Washburn Expedition, was appointed to be the first superintendent of the first national park. He held this office for five years without either salary or expenses. He refused any remuneration to prevent the job from being given to a man who might allow the region to be commercialized and the natural beauty ruined. Langford successfully prevented all attempts of men to obtain leases and the right to build fences around the wonders and to charge admission. No concessions were granted. Later it was necessary to provide accommodations for the millions of sightseers who came from all over the country to view the wonderland but

The famous campfire scene re-enacted as it happened, September 19, 1870, at the junction of the Firehole and Gibbon Rivers in Yellowstone Park, Wyoming.

the area remains a national park for all the people.

The national park idea spread over this country and over the entire world. Big ideas are born, sometimes, in unexpected places. It is fitting that an invitation to enjoy the beauties of nature should come from a campfire group in a wilderness. The old West still lives because a lawyer from Montana suggested to his fireside companions that they share with their fellowmen, the thrills they had experienced in an outdoor wonderland.

RECREATION IS BIG BUSINESS

EVERY YEAR, millions of vacationists play pioneer in the national parks covering more than 6,500,000 acres west of the Mississippi River. Like fur trappers, wagon immigrants, and mining prospectors, they fish in mountain streams, cook over a campfire, and sleep in tents. They ride over scenic trails, ski down the slopes of mountains, and climb to rocky pinnacles.

Most of the vacation pioneers are city dwellers seeking escape from the noise and the speed of their everyday lives. For nearly fifty weeks of the year they drive bolts and rivets on assembly lines; write letters and operate office machines; and serve customers with everything from a ham sandwich to a diesel truck. The people of the United States support a tourist business in which many millions of dollars are invested. They go sightseeing for fun as did adventurers in the early days. A scientist who rode horseback with a party of trappers from St. Louis to Oregon in the 1830's kept a diary of his experiences in the western wilderness. It is packed with thrilling escapes. He wrote of one experience:

June 10, 1836: In the afternoon, one of our men had a perilous adventure with a grizzly bear. He saw the animal crouching his huge frame in some willows which skirted the river. Approaching on horseback to within twenty yards, he fired upon the bear. The beast was only slightly wounded by the shot, and with a fierce growl, rushed from his cover and gave chase. The horse happened to be a slow one. For the distance of half a mile, the race was close, with the bear frequently snapping at the horse's heels. The terrified rider, who had lost his hat at the start, used whip and spur, frequently looking back at his rugged and determined foe. His wild shrieks, "Shoot him! Shoot him!" brought hunters in the party to his rescue, and the bear was killed. The man rode in among his fellows, pale and haggard, but cured of meddling with grizzly bears.

Today, in the national parks and forests where wildlife is protected, tourists hunt bears and other animals with a camera, not a gun. The shy grizzlies are scarce and are seldom seen by summer vacationists, but black and brown bears are rather tame, and at times, a little too familiar. Signs are posted with the warning, "Feeding, Molesting, Teasing, or Touching Bears Is Prohibited." Sometimes a tourist has difficulty explaining to a friendly bruin that the candy box is empty. Beavers build their houses in streams without fear of traps; striped chipmunks sit up and beg for peanuts; curious pack rats carry off small articles that are bright and colored. Birds, too, find the national preserves a haven of delight and safety. The trumpeter swan, once thought to be extinct, has chosen Yellowstone Park for a nesting place.

The forests are practically untouched. Trees are cut down only to provide shelter and roads for the throngs of visitors. Wild flowers grow in abundance and tourists are requested not to pick them. The waterfalls, unharnessed for electric power, tumble into frothy rivers not drained by irrigation. This conservation is profitable for man's purse as well as his pleasure as it protects the watershed. In uncut forests the snow melts slowly, thus preventing floods and maintaining a steady flow of water in the streams.

States, too, have set aside recreation areas and parks where their citizens may relax and play at pioneering. In our modern world, recreation is considered to be a necessity. Work hard and play hard is the slogan. Many corporations, employing large numbers of men and women, provide gymnasiums, baseball fields, swimming pools, reading rooms, and other opportunities for play after working hours. Labor unions have clubhouses for their members. The members who rush through the morning traffic to punch a time clock are the people who turn the wheels of our complex industrial civilization. They promoted recreation and made it big business. When vacation rolls along, they hit the tourist trail to seek a change, to play at pioneering, and to see the continent. Our push-button civilization of speed, efficiency, and production began on the eastern coast of North America, where the nation began, and grew up with the country. When? How? Why?

MT. RAINIER IN WASHINGTON

Captain George Vancouver of the British Navy was sailing along the northwest coast of North America during the term of Washington as first President of the United States. He named a lone white mountain for his friend, Admiral Rainier.

To the Indians, the mountain was Tahoma, a god. It was probably 16,000 feet high before the top was blown to bits by an explosion, described in Indian legends. Today, the peak rises 14,408 feet above sea level. This national park is scarcely more than a mountain, containing less than 240,000 acres. The space, though not large, abounds in beauty for nature lovers and with thrills for skiers and mountaineers.

National Park Service

YOSEMITE NATIONAL PARK — CALIFORNIA

During the ice age, glaciers gouged out the U-shaped valley with sheer granite walls rising to the height of almost a mile in some places. Streams dropping into the valley break into frothy spray, creating a number of waterfalls.

One day an Indian boy was walking to Mirror Lake below the falls to spear fish. On the way he met a grizzly bear, also going fishing in Mirror Lake. In the fight that followed, the Indian lad was wounded and the bear was killed. The tribes living in the sheltered basin called it Ah-wah-nee, or grassy valley. After the brave boy won the fight, both the tribe and the place were called Yosemite, Indian word for grizzly bear.

PART NINE

Manufacturing Centers
in the Northeast

SAMUEL SLATER
"FATHER OF AMERICAN MANUFACTURES"

In the old Slater Mill, seen through the window, the first water-powered machinery was used to produce cotton yarn. In 1791, the site overlooking the Blackstone River was purchased for 350 Spanish milled dollars. In 1793, Almy Brown and Slater, the owners, began spinning on machines in Pawtucket, Rhode Island. The old mill is now a museum where water-powered machinery is being exhibited in operation to show visitors the crude beginning of the factory system in the United States.

Chapter 23

A New Way of Life

IRON WAS THE FIRST MINERAL INDUSTRY

IN THE TIME of Queen Elizabeth I, laws were passed that trees could not be chopped down for fuel within fourteen miles of the sea or any navigable river; and that nowhere in England could oak, beech, or ash be used for making charcoal. The timber was needed to build ships for the growing commerce of the little island kingdom. Since the British ironmasters depended upon charcoal for smelting iron ore, these laws were a hardship. With interest they read Hariot's report (page 50) of one of the exploring expeditions that Walter Raleigh sent to the Carolina coast. America was a land of forests and "in two places of the countery" he stated, "wee founde neere the water side the ground to be rockie, which, by the triall of a minerall man, was founde to hold iron richly." The English explorers, like the Spaniards, were looking for gold and did not take back a sample of the iron ore.

After iron was discovered in Virginia, a group of men called the Southampton Adventurers formed a company and sent over skilled workmen and their families to erect the first ironworks in America. The site chosen was on Falling Creek, sixty-six miles up the river from Jamestown, where iron ore had been found in bogs. On March 22, 1622, when the furnace was fired, Indians attacked. They destroyed everything and killed the workmen and their families. The young son of the superintendent, who escaped by hiding in the woods, made his way back to Jamestown and reported the tragedy. Perhaps the Indians thought the furnace, belching fire and smoke, was a monster that would devour them. The works were not rebuilt because the "adventurers" ran out of money. They had lost all they had invested.

Although a little iron was shipped to England by the London Company, the first really successful ironworks were built by another company of English adventurers. They were built on the Saugus River near Lynn, Massachusetts, where iron, washed down by rains, was fished from swamps and bogs with long tongs. The ironworkers named their village Hammersmith, where one of their houses still stands. Men employed at the ironworks were exempt from paying taxes and were excused from the tiresome chore of watching for Indian attacks. Since the colonists paid for kettles,

COOKING POT WAS FIRST
PRODUCT OF SAUGUS IRONWORKS – 1644

The ironworkers decided their first product would be something useful. Joseph Jenks, a skilled ironworker from England poured molten metal from the furnace into a mold he had made in sand. When the iron was solid, he broke apart the mold and held up this cooking pot, still in existence and cherished by the descendants of the man who sold the land for the ironworks.

anchors, and scythes with beaver pelts, bags of grain, and Indian wampum instead of money, the English adventurers realized little or nothing on their investment. The colonists, however, were provided with cooking utensils and farm tools.

The success of iron encouraged an attempt to make steel from a portion of the output. In 1655 a man living in Southold, Long Island, informed the General Court of New Haven of his "abilitie and intendment to make steele" if certain privileges were granted to him. The court encouraged him by agreeing that his property would not be taxed for ten years.

However, he was warned not to take clay and wood from private grounds without the owner's permission, as the court was unwilling "to meddle with any man's proprietie." It is not known for certain whether or not this man succeeded in making steel. The credit for the first steel manufactured in this country probably belongs to another man from Connecticut. Two smiths declared in writing:

This may certify all concerned that Samuel Higley of this town of Simsbury came to the shop of us, being blacksmiths, some time in June in the year one thousand seven hundred and twenty-five, and desired us to let him have a pound or two of iron. – He desired that we take notice of them that we might know them again, for, said he, I am going to make Steel of this Iron, and I shall in a few days bring them to you to try for steel. Accordingly he brought the same pieces which we let him have, and we proved them and found them good steel, which was the first steel

RESTORATION OF EARLY
IRONWORKS, SAUGUS, MASSACHUSETTS

In 1948, the still-existing ironmasters's house, erected in 1646-1647 on the Saugus River north of Boston, determined the site of the first ironworks in Massachusetts. Where were the works? Digging through layers of earth, the remains of the furnace, the forge, and the slitting mill were discovered. Surprisingly, after 300 years, a section of a wooden water wheel was found buried 22½ feet under the pavement of Central Street. The old ironworks has been restored, and water again splashes over the water wheels as in colonial days.

that ever was made in this country that ever we saw or heard of. As witness our hands this 7th day of May, 1728. Timoth Phelps John Drake

William Penn, who owned ironworks in England, looked for ore in his colony and soon found it. Although he tried to induce his colonists to dig the ore and use it, this was not done until two years before his death when a Quaker blacksmith in Berks County made iron in his forge. To satisfy the demand for articles of iron, little forges and furnaces sprang up wherever families settled in new country. Sometimes farmers, who knew something about the iron trade, built small furnaces, where wood was plentiful, to smelt the iron they needed for pots, nails, hinges, hoes, and many items. When neighbors needed these same articles, the farmer left the plow for the furnace. Some large ironworks were started in this way.

Captain Augustine Washington, father of the first President of the United States, was an iron manufacturer as well as a plantation owner when his famous son was born. When iron ore was discovered on one of his big farms along the Potomac River below Mount Vernon, he traded the 1600 acres of land for one-sixth interest in Principio Company. This was the largest ironworks in the colonies. A furnace was built on Washington's plantation and others at the head of Chesapeake Bay. From these ironworks with direct water transportation, bars of the metal were shipped to England. Their products sometimes brought a higher price than Swedish or Russian iron.

The iron plantations of Pennsylvania were much like the cotton plantations of the old South, except that the laborers were miners, woodchoppers, charcoal burners, and teamsters as well as farmers. These communities were self-supporting, raising their own food and weaving their own cloth. However, most of the labor in the field and at the loom was performed

HOPEWELL IRON PLANTATION NEAR BIRDSBORO, PENNSYLVANIA

Mark Bird, the owner of this iron plantation, outfitted 300 soldiers for Washington's army at his own expense. Products from Hopewell farms and iron from Hopewell's furnaces were generously supplied to fighting men in the Revolutionary War. Since the Continental Congress was unable to pay for all of these goods, Bird went bankrupt, and his iron plantation was sold by the sheriff.

United States Steel Corporation

The National Society of the Colonial Dames of America
in the Commonwealth of Pennsylvania

A "LIBERTY" FIREPLACE

This iron fireplace was made on the Hopewell Iron Plantation near Birdsboro, Pennsylvania. The design on the front plate shows an angel blowing a trumpet, announcing "BE LIBERTY THINE."

by the women and children while the men were busy in the woods and the mines. Life centered around the mansion house where the owner lived and the general store where eggs, butter, milk, vegetables, and labor were traded for sugar, molasses, shoes, medicines, and coffins. The woodcutters and charcoal burners greatly outnumbered the miners and ironmasters because one blast furnace, in a single day, consumed all the timber on an acre of ground. Some of these iron plantations, located in heavily forested regions, covered as much as 10,000 acres of land. Others were small, only a few hundred acres, like Valley Forge.

The British Parliament became alarmed at the growth of the iron industry. They were afraid that the colonists would make all the kettles, Dutch ovens, nails, shovels, tongs, anchors, and other articles they could use and would cease to buy from British merchants. The Act of 1750 of Parliament encouraged the production of American pig iron and bar iron as many British manufacturers preferred it to Swedish iron because it did not rust so quickly. This same act declared that after June 24, 1750, the colonial governors had the duty "to prevent the erection of any mill, or other engine, for slitting or rolling of iron, or any plating-forge to work with a tilt-hammer, or any furnace for making steel in any of the said colonies." Since many ironworks were tucked away in forests, where wood was plentiful for charcoal, this act could not be enforced.

By 1775 when the Revolutionary War broke out, the colonies had more forges and furnaces than England and Wales

MAKING NAILS AT HOME IN COLONIAL DAYS

Neighborhood merchants stocked narrow strips of iron from slitting mills, along with food, clothing, hardware, tools, and anything they could sell to customers in town and country. On long winter evenings, these iron rods were heated in tiny forges in chimney corners and cut in a vise to the proper length. Farm families, including children, pounded broad tops on the warm pieces of iron. These hand-hammered nails were returned to the storekeeper and traded for articles the farmers needed and could not provide for themselves. Manufacturing began at home.

United States Steel Corporation

combined. The colonies were producing fourteen percent of the world's iron. Cannon, muskets, shot, shells, bayonets, axes, camp kettles, and swords were made in 80 blast furnaces and about 175 forges scattered throughout the colonies.

Steel emerged as the metal of war in the struggle for independence. During the Revolutionary War some states offered premiums for steel, needed for swords and bayonets. North Carolina, where the first iron ore had been discovered by Raleigh's explorers, offered the sum of nearly $500 to the first man who, within eighteen months, succeeded in making steel equal in quality to British steel. A reward of over $2000 was offered in South Carolina to the first three works producing 500 pounds of steel.

Although men employed in iron and steel works were exempt from military service, so many enlisted in the patriot armies, that it was necessary to use prisoners of war in iron and steel manufacture. Many of the Hessians stayed after the war was over and kept the same jobs they had had as prisoners. Five signers of the Declaration of Independence were in the iron business. Two more became generals, Nathanael Greene from Rhode Island and Daniel Morgan, a charcoal burner for his father's furnace in Pennsylvania. The ironworks making guns and ammunition for the American armies were targets for British attack. Many were burned. A detachment of soldiers from Howe's army, retreating to Philadelphia to spend the winter of 1777-78, burned the Mount Joy Iron Works, better known as Valley Forge. On this iron plantation Washington spent the same winter drilling his ragged Continentals.

COAL COMPETES WITH CHARCOAL

FIVE HUNDRED YEARS before Columbus found the New World, the Hopi Indians of Arizona were using lignite, a variety of coal, to fire their pottery. As far as is known, this was the only use made of the mineral by any tribe except for ornament. The common use was crushing it into powder to blacken their faces for ceremonials.

In North America when trees were plentiful everywhere, wood cooked the food and heated the houses; charcoal fired the forges in the blacksmith shops and smelted the ore in the furnaces of ironworks. Blacksmiths were the first to use mineral coal in place of charcoal. In 1702 a Huguenot living on the James River about fourteen miles above Richmond sent his request to the Colonial Council of Virginia:

David Menestrier a black smith and one of ye french Refugees Inhabiting Luciana Petitions his Excellency that he may have leave to use ye coal mines lately discovered there for his forge.

The request was granted for the French blacksmith "to take what coales he shall want out of ye said coal mine for ye use of his forge."

Coal discovered along the James River above Richmond did reach colonial markets. These mines had the advantage of cheap water transportation. Although explorers noted coal deposits in many places, most of this supply was out of reach because there was no way to get it to market. Both Joliet and La Salle mentioned finding coal along the Illinois River. Dr. Walker wrote frequently about coal in the diary of his journey into Kentucky. When their shoes wore out, Walker and his party were forced to seek shelter in a huge cave in Rockcastle County while they made new moccasins out of the hide of an elk they had killed. Walker thus describes the cave in his journal:

May 12, 1750 — Under the rock is a soft kind of Stone almost like Allum in taste; below it A Layer of Coal about 12 Inches thick and white clay under that. —
May 13, 1750 — The Sabbath.
May 14, 1750 — We wrote several of our Names with Coal under the Rock, —

Five years before the War for Independence, George Washington trailed through the wilderness to the Ohio River, paddling down that stream in a canoe as far as the mouth of the Kanawha River. He was busy surveying land to pay off the Virginia officers who had served in the French and Indian War. In his journal of this tour Washington mentions coal:

Oct. 14, 1770 — At Captain Crawford's all day. Went to see a coal mine not far from his house on the banks of the river, (Youghiogheny, near Connelsville, Pennsylvania); The coal seemed to be of the very best kind, burning freely, and abundance of it.

The coal seen by Joliet, La Salle, Walker, and Washington was bituminous, or soft coal. Anthracite, or stone coal, was first used in the forge of the Gore Brothers, blacksmiths who settled in Wilkes-Barre, Pennsylvania about 1769. They discovered that the hard coal, so plentiful all around them, made a hotter fire than charcoal and lasted longer. During the Revolutionary War anthracite from this region was floated on barges down the Susquehanna River to Harrisburg. It was taken overland in wagons to stoke the furnaces of the armory at Carlisle where guns were made for Washington's soldiers.

Charcoal continued to be used in the

Bituminous Coal Institute

STRIP MINING THE PITTSBURGH SEAM IN EASTERN OHIO

The Pittsburgh Seam is a layer of coal near the surface, found in Pennsylvania, Ohio, West Virginia and Maryland. In some places, layers of rock and soil must be removed to uncover this rich deposit of bituminous coal. In other places, like this strip mining operation near St. Clairsville, Ohio the seam rises to the top of the ground where the coal can be scooped up in huge buckets, loaded into trucks, and hauled to a preparation plant to be cleaned and sized for sale. Early explorers reported finding coal throughout the Appalachian region.

iron furnaces until the scarcity of trees forced operators to turn to coal. Then for some time buyers favored iron produced in charcoal furnaces. It was the invention of the steam engine that made coal a great commercial product. Coal became the fuel to fire the boilers that created the steam to operate the numerous inventions ushering in the machine age.

MACHINERY AIDS THE GROWTH OF INDUSTRY

WHILE THE COLONISTS in North America were quarreling with England over trade and taxes, industry in the British Isles

439

was being moved from the home to the factory by the invention of power machinery to do the work of hands. This movement during the latter part of the eighteenth century so changed the pattern of living that it was called the Industrial Revolution. A few inventors led the way.

James Watt was a frail and studious boy who wanted to be an instrument-maker, not for music but for science. His father sent him to school in London where he could learn this trade. At the age of twenty he returned to his home town of Greenock, Scotland, with a kit of tools and a craftsman's skill. A few months later he was employed by the College of Glasgow to clean some instruments, purchased in the West Indies for use in the department of astronomy. Later a professor asked him to repair a model engine that had failed to operate successfully in his classroom. Watt discovered that a waste of steam caused the engine to stop after a few strokes. How could he save this steam to provide the energy to keep the engine going? On a pleasant day in May of 1765 while strolling on the Glasgow Green, the plan suddenly popped into his mind for condensing steam without cooling the cylinder, a principle still in use today in steam turbines. Watt's invention of the separate condenser so improved the steam engine that it soon was used to pump water from British mines and to operate machinery in British mills.

Meanwhile the invention of textile machinery in England was creating a future market for the improved steam engine. James Hargreaves, a poor weaver in Lancashire, invented a machine with a number of spindles placed upright, side by side, all spinning at the same time. He tried to keep it a secret, but the news leaked out that he was operating a spinning machine in his own home. Fearing this device, neighbors, who depended upon hand work to earn a living, broke into the inventor's house and smashed his spinning jenny. Hargreaves managed to make a few of these machines privately and sell them for enough money to buy clothes for his many children and the family fled to Nottingham.

At about the same time Richard Arkwright, a barber and hair dyer with a knack for tinkering, was also at work on a spinning machine. The youngest of thirteen children in a poor family, Richard had little schooling. He could barely write but he was a natural mechanic. Fearing that mobs would destroy his invention, Arkwright also fled from his home town to Nottingham. There, two bankers advanced the money to manufacture his machines for a share of the profits. Samuel Need, a partner of the ingenious farmer, Jedediah Strutt, joined the bankers in business. Strutt had perfected a frame for making ribbed stockings.

In Derbyshire they built a mill where the wheels were turned by water. Ever after, Arkwright's spinning machine was called the "water frame." Since Hargreaves' jenny made a soft thread for woof and Arkwright's frame spun a hard thread for warp, British manufacturers used both inventions and other labor-saving devices. With the new machinery the British could make cloth faster and sell it cheaper, and so increased their sales everywhere. Therefore, every effort was made to keep other countries from copying the machines; but the new inventions crossed the Atlantic.

William Slater, an independent farmer who owned his land, was a neighbor of Jedediah Strutt in Derbyshire, England. He helped the three manufacturers to find and purchase the land with water privileges on which they erected the mill. Strutt offered to accept Slater's oldest son as an apprentice and to teach him the cotton spinning trade. The father suggested that he take Samuel, his fifth son, who had a "mechanical turn, and was good at figures." The lad was not quite fourteen. During this probation the boy's father fell from a load of hay and died soon after the accident. Since Samuel's work had been satisfactory, Strutt accepted the fatherless lad as an apprentice in his factory and took him into his own home to live with his family.

In the paper of indenture Samuel Slater promised to serve his master for six and a half years. He agreed not to:

contract matrimony within the said term, play at cards, dice, or any unlawful games, haunt taverns or play houses, nor absent himself from his master's service day or night unlawfully, but in all things as a faithful apprentice to behave himself toward his master during the said term.

Jedediah Strutt signed the indenture, agreeing:

in consideration of the true and faithful service of the said Samuel Slater, his apprentice in the art of cotton spinning, — to teach and instruct him, — finding unto the said apprentice sufficient meat, drink, washing and lodging during the said term.

Offers of prizes by some American manufacturing societies and state governments to inventors and machinists encouraged the young apprentice to seek his fortune in the New World when he had learned his trade. He told the secret to no one, not even his mother and older brothers. When Samuel had completed his apprenticeship of six years and six months, his master was so pleased with his progress that he hired him to oversee the construction of a new mill. When it was completed, the young man decided to go to the United States and enter into business for himself. How could he get out of England?

Early in September, 1789, Samuel Slater, then twenty-one years of age, asked his mother to pack his clothes as he was leaving on the stagecoach for London. Because he had worked with the Arkwright machines, he dared tell no one that he was bound for the United States. Export of the new inventions in whole or in part and drawings of them were forbidden by law. Machinists who operated them could not leave the country. Every ship and every passenger on board was searched before sailing from a British port. Fortunately Samuel Slater was a country boy and looked like a farmer. Disguised as a field hand he took nothing to identify him as a machinist except his indenture, which he hid in his old work clothes. The searchers did not find it. Just before the vessel sailed, he mailed a letter to his mother with the news that he was going to try his luck in the New World.

After a voyage of sixty-six days he arrived in New York and went to work in a small factory. He stayed there only three weeks because the machines were poor and the neighborhood did not have a single stream to furnish water power. During this time Slater chanced to meet the captain of a sloop carrying cargo between Providence and New York. From him he learned that Moses Brown, a manufacturer in Rhode Island, was looking for a factory manager. Slater wrote a letter to Brown, explaining that he could build the Arkwright machines. Brown had tried water power unsuccessfully and was using horse power. He answered Slater's letter in his Quaker way, offering the young man a share of the profits, "if thou wilt come." Slater went to Pawtucket where he began building the Arkwright water frames entirely from memory. He put into operation the first successful water mill in the United States. For this achievement he earned the title, "Father of American Cotton Manufacture."

As in England the introduction of power machinery began to change the way of life in the United States. Laborers were moved from homes to factories where machines did the work of hands.

Soon after the new machines were introduced by Slater, the water wheels of cotton mills were turning in the short, swift rivers of New Hampshire, Connecticut, and Massachusetts. At first these factories produced cotton yarn, which was sold to weavers in the neighborhood to be woven into cloth on their hand looms at home. Gradually new items were manufactured. One day Samuel Slater showed his wife some unusually fine smooth yarn spun from long staple cotton in his mill. She twisted it into thread on an old fashioned spinning wheel. Testing it on seams, she found it to be stronger than the linen thread she had been using. In the mill of Almy, Brown and Slater the first cotton sewing thread was made.

The industrial revolution moved more slowly in the United States than in England. For years after carding and spinning were done in factories with machinery, weaving continued to be done in homes by hand. Farmhouses of New England were miniature mills. When a single machine could produce more in a day than many hands, the home manufacturer could no longer compete with the mill

owner. Weaving moved into the factory.

Lowell, Massachusetts, became one of the first factory towns. Before the English had settled on the shores of Massachusetts, the site of Lowell at the junction of the Concord and the Merrimac Rivers was called Wamesit. It was the capital of the Pawtucket Indians who gathered there to catch salmon, shad, and many kinds of fish in the waters around the Pawtucket Falls. About eight years before the Pilgrims landed, a mysterious epidemic almost annihilated the tribes living in that part of the country. Daniel Gookin, a magistrate of the Massachusetts Bay Colony, in charge of Indian affairs, wrote in his history of the New England tribes:

I have discoursed with some old Indians that were then youths, who say that the bodies were exceeding yellow, describing it by a yellow garment they wore, both before they died and afterward.

Only about one-tenth of the 3000 men in the Pawtucket tribe survived the fatal sickness. The small number of survivors were unable to resist the English settlement of their lands. Thirty-three years after the arrival of the Pilgrims, about forty settlers in Woburn and Concord sent a petition to the General Court of Massachusetts. They asked for a land grant extending six miles along the Merrimac River and six miles along the Concord River, near the junction of these two streams. This area of thirty-six square miles included Wamesit, the ancient capital of the Pawtuckets. Rev. John Eliot, defending the tribe, sent another petition to the court, asking that the land lying around Pawtucket and Wamesit Falls be reserved for his "praying Indians" whose wigwams stood on the site. The Massachusetts court settled the dispute with a compromise. The court gave the settlers the land they wanted except for 2500 acres along the river banks near the falls where the Indians lived.

However, as more and more settlers came to fish in the rivers and to cut timber from the forests, the Pawtuckets were crowded out of their old home. The big demand for ship timber in England and in the colonies made lumbering profitable for the early settlers. Rafts of logs cut from the forests along the Merrimac were floated down the river to Newburyport on the seacoast. The logs were used in shipbuilding there or sent across the sea.

In 1792 during Washington's term as President, a company was formed to dig a canal around the falls. Five hundred shares of stock were sold at $100 a share to raise the sum of $50,000 to dig a canal a mile and a half long. The canal started at a spot above Pawtucket Falls and dropped thirty-two feet through four locks to flow into the Concord River. Five years later a big crowd gathered to see the first boat pass through the first canal to be opened in the new United States. When the boat entered the canal which was jammed on both sides with sightseers, the sides caved in. The spectators plunged into the canal and doused the passengers on board the boat. No one was drowned.

After the Middlesex Canal was opened in 1804, connecting the Merrimac River with the Charles River in Boston, lumbermen floated their rafts to that town. Business dwindled on the Pawtucket Canal. Although it was a poor investment for the stockholders, the old canal inspired the founding of the first big manufacturing city in the United States — Lowell, Massachusetts.

In 1810 Francis Cabot Lowell took a voyage to England for his health. Because he was a manufacturer he visited mills in England to observe new machinery being used in producing cotton cloth, especially the power loom operated by steam. Although the steam engine was invented by a number of men, James Watt is generally credited with making many improvements that made it practical in cotton manufacture. In 1785 the Rev. Cartwright of Kent invented a power loom to be operated by steam. Many improvements were necessary before the machine came into general use in British mills.

The growth of cotton manufacture was slow until Lowell returned from England shortly before the War of 1812. As in the case of Hargreaves' jenny and Arkwright's water frame, the secret of Cartwright's power loom was guarded by the British Government. Like Slater, Lowell depended upon his memory.

When the War of 1812 cut off British imports, Americans were forced to manufacture goods to supply their own needs. Lowell discussed the idea of starting a cotton mill with a relative, Patrick Tracy Jackson, who was familiar with the process in the Slater mills. Needing power looms for weaving, they bought an ordinary loom and began to experiment. Lowell had a knack for mechanics and finally succeeded in building a power loom much like the Cartwright model he had seen in England. Then Lowell and Jackson asked their friends to invest money in a company to make cotton cloth. The two men raised a capital of $100,000, purchased water power at Waltham, Massachusetts, and hired a skilled mechanic and inventor to install the machinery. The mechanic found it necessary to invent a number of devices to make the power looms work. Then, when the power looms were put into operation, the yarn purchased from spinning mills could not be used on the new looms. They sold the yarn to hand weavers in the neighborhood and constructed special spinning machines in their own mill.

Before the new factory had produced a single yard of cloth for sale, the War of 1812 ended. The $100,000 had been spent. After the peace was signed, cheap cotton yardage from England and India flooded the American market, forcing factories to close their doors. Mechanics out of work went West beyond the mountains, to seek farms in the Ohio Valley where they could raise enough produce to feed their families. Yet, in spite of the loss, another $100,000 was invested in the Waltham mills. Lowell spent much time in Washington where he pleaded with Congressmen to pass a tariff law, placing a duty on imported goods, and thus save American manufacture from ruin. He convinced John C. Calhoun of South Carolina that a protective tariff would enable the southern planter to sell his cotton to northern mills for cash to purchase his manufactured goods in this country. This would keep American dollars at home for American prosperity. The Tariff of 1816 placing a duty on foreign goods was passed. This law increased employment in the mills and slowed down the westward march that was draining off the population of New England. The following year Lowell died, leaving the responsibility of the Waltham factories to his partner, Jackson.

One day in 1820 Ezra Worthen from Amesbury called on Jackson to suggest that the Waltham Company start factories in a new place and put him in charge. Jackson was willing to consider the proposition if good water power could be found. As a boy Worthen had fished at Pawtucket Falls and he knew the country well. With a piece of chalk he sketched a map of the location on the floor, convincing his friend that the old canal could furnish the water power for many mills. Jackson sent his superintendent with Worthen to examine the land at the junction of the Concord and Merrimac Rivers. The site was chosen for a new manufacturing town.

The Waltham Company bought the 500 shares of canal stock and nearly 400 acres of farm land for about $100,000. Five hundred men were employed to widen the mile and a half long canal to sixty feet and to deepen it to eight feet at a cost of $120,000. In 1822 on the bank of the river the foundation was laid for the first cotton mill, the Merrimack Manufacturing Company. Ezra Worthen was made superintendent. As more and more manufacturers came, lateral canals were dug to provide water power for their mills. In 1826 the little village of factories was incorporated as the town of Lowell in honor of the man who had done much to establish manufacturing in New England. Ten years later Lowell was the "Spindle City" where 9,000,000 pounds of cotton were turned into 30,000,000 yards of cloth by six mills.

When manufacturing moved from the home to the factory, home laborers sought employment in the mills. Since most of these operators were country girls skilled in handicraft, they soon learned to handle machinery. The labor of young men, however, was scarce. With land cheap and plentiful in unsettled country, the young men went West. Few returned to marry the girls they had left behind. The American urge to own land slowed down the industrial revolution in the United

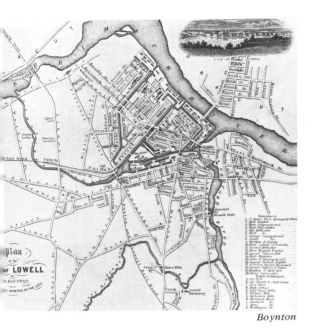

Boynton

EARLY MAP OF LOWELL, MASSACHUSETTS — CITY OF MILLS

This map shows how an industrial city was laid out when factories depended upon water power. Mills were huddled along the Merrimack and Concord Rivers, and along the branches of the main Pawtucket Canal.

The sketch in the upper right hand corner shows the boarding houses where the mill girls lived. Twenty churches are listed in the lower right hand corner. Church attendance was required by mill owners, as a rule.

Lowell, Massachusetts, built for the textile industry, became known as the "Spindle City."

States, where many preferred profits in agriculture to wages in manufacturing.

In Lowell the mill girls lived in three story brick boarding houses, provided by their employers and managed by a house mother who supervised the care of the girls. Everyone had to be in by ten o'clock at night when the doors were locked. This type of boarding house was a unique institution that did not become the living pattern in other factory towns. In 1845 the matron of a boarding house for the Merrimack Manufacturing Company made this report in a survey:

Kept house on Merrimack six years; twenty-eight boarders now; two hundred in all; seventy-five have been married, having kept account; two have died; four gone home sick; three dismissed for bad conduct; very little sickness.

The efforts of both employers and employees to make Lowell a model factory town drew visitors from all over the United States and from foreign countries. Many praised the place as a model industrial community and others criticized it. There were thirty-three churches in Lowell when the population was under 30,000. The town had thirty-three mills. To get operators for machines, manufacturers found it necessary to assure parents that their daughters would be provided with both religious and educational opportunities. Rules like the following were posted in the mills:

All persons are required to be constant in attendance on public worship, at one of the regular places of worship in this place. Persons who do not comply with the above regulations will not be employed by the company.

Labor was scarce during the summer when many girls went home to help on the farm. Since the work day was from daylight to dark, as a rule, they returned in the winter when the days were shorter to attend the evening schools provided by the churches. Out of 300 illiterate employees in one factory, all but 30 learned to read in these evening schools. There were lectures at the Lowell Institute where great men, including Ralph W. Emerson, spoke. Girls formed clubs to study languages, literature, and music. One of these "Improvement Circles" published a magazine called "The Lowell Offering" in which stories, poems,

445

and articles written by the mill girls were printed. Some of the best stories were published in a book, *Mind Amongst The Spindles.* The editors of this magazine favored laws for a ten-hour day. They suggested that the employees save to buy stock in the companies where they worked. The hours of labor drew the most criticism from visitors. The running time of the mills throughout the year averaged twelve hours and ten minutes, with time out for meals.

The overseers and officials were men with families for whom the manufacturing companies provided houses at reasonable rentals if they did not own their own homes. To this permanent but small population were added the immigrants who lived with their families and not in the boarding houses. A discharge book of one of the factories contains a report of a typical immigrant girl working in the cotton mills of Lowell and other New England towns:

Oct. 14, 1844 — Mary — , worked nine years, discharged to go on Lowell Corporation. She and her sister, who left a short time since to be married, had worked for us over ten years. They are Irish. Their father died about nine years ago. They have since entirely supported their mother, having built her a house costing $600, in which they have kept house together. They own a pew which cost them $125, and they have from $100 to $200 each at interest.

In this way the mill towns of New England became centers of foreign populations and the way of life changed. In Lowell the mansion of one manufacturer was converted into a hospital where sick employees received medical care at their company's expense, if they could not pay the fees. One corporation donated the land and others the hall, where the Middlesex Mechanics Association met and discussed

the problems of the mill hands. The experiment at Lowell, based on the Waltham system, was a preview of a dawning industrial society with its problems in hours, wages, health, housing, and employment. With freedom of opportunity gained through a political rebellion, the nation met the challenge of an industrial revolution.

COAL BECOMES A COMMERCIAL PRODUCT

AFTER THE Revolutionary War more deposits of glassy anthracite were discovered in eastern Pennsylvania. In 1791, a hunter accidentally found a rich bed of coal near Mauch Chunk (Bear Mountain) in the Lehigh Valley. He tells the story:

One day, after a poor season, when we were on short allowance, I had unusually bad luck and was on my way home, empty-handed and disheartened, tired and wet with the rain — when I struck my foot against a stone. It was nearly dusk, but light enough remained to show me that it was black and shiny. — When I saw the black rock I knew it must be stone coal. On looking round, I discovered black dirt and a great many pieces of stone coal under the roots of a tree that had been blown down. I took pieces of this coal home with me, and the next day carried them to Colonel Jacob Weiss at Fort Allen.

Shortly afterwards, the Lehigh Coal Mine Company was formed. Digging began in an open-cut mine on the top of Summit Hill, near the spot where the hunter had stumbled over the chunk of anthracite. Eastern Pennsylvania was rich in coal, but how could it reach the markets? The only transportation was on the Susquehanna, Lehigh, and Schuylkill Rivers when the streams were swollen with rains and navigable for many miles. Who would buy the coal? Anthracite had a hard time winning the favor of a public that had been using bituminous coal in both homes and factories.

A nail manufacturer experimented with anthracite in his factory and in his home. For his fireplace he fashioned a grate from hickory wood and had a blacksmith copy it in iron. With proper drafts he succeeded in burning anthracite in this grate in his fireplace. When he invited his neighbors to witness the feat, only a few came. They could not believe it. Those who basked in the warmth of his grate fire on that cold night in February, 1808, spread the news that "stone coal" was better for heating than wood.

Four months before, two brothers had gone down the Susquehanna River as far as Columbia. No one would buy the black rocks so they dumped their load. After seeing "stone coal" burning in a grate, the brothers tried again the following spring. This time they took along an iron grate to prove to customers that the shiny black stones would heat their homes. Today the main use of anthracite is to furnish fuel.

When the War of 1812 broke out, delaying shipments of bituminous coal from the James River fields in Virginia, an enterprising mine owner in Pottsville, Pennsylvania, started for Philadelphia with nine wagonloads of anthracite. On the way he sold one load to the proprietors of a rolling mill. The foreman complained that the stones would not burn in the furnace. The mining man persuaded one of the millowners, who was a mechanic, to go with him early the next morning to fire a furnace before the workmen arrived. The two men kindled a fire with wood and piled the black stones on top. Anthracite

burns slowly; so when the fire was started, the mining man closed the furnace doors and suggested to his partner that they leave to eat breakfast. When they returned, the furnace glowed with a white heat. Workmen put in iron ore, watched it heat more quickly than usual, and pass through the rolls with greater ease. All were convinced.

On hearing of this success, a wire and nail manufacturer bought a wagon load and tried it in his furnace. The miner from Pottsville made no profits, having sold the coal for the cost of transportation. Hoping for better luck, he went on to Philadelphia with the seven remaining loads. Here and there he sold a few bushels to blacksmiths, but gave away most of his coal to persons who said they would try it. Not only was his business venture almost a total loss, but a writ was secured for his arrest as a swindler, selling black stones for coal.

During the War of 1812 more and more manufacturers tried "stone coal" because it was near at hand. The demand grew for the product. The big problem was transportation. To transport the coal to customers on schedule, rivers were dredged and a network of canals was built all over eastern Pennsylvania and north into the state of New York. One of the first navigation companies was organized by Josiah White, the wire and nail manufacturer at the falls of the Schuylkill who had purchased a wagon load of coal from the Pottsville miner. This company undertook to make the Lehigh River navigable for barges of coal from Mauch Chunk to the Delaware. In the early days of industry the proprietors were often skilled mechanics, themselves, and did hard labor by the side of the men they employed. White directed the work in the difficult spot at the Schuylkill Falls. He wrote in his memoirs:

As our work was generally in the water seven or eight months in the year, and my portion of it being to lay out the walls and channels in the river, pile stones as marks, etc., I dressed in clothes suitable — a red flannel shirt, roundabout coat, cap, strong shoes with holes cut in the toes to let out the water; our clothing being made of a coarse cloth and buckskin tanned in oil to turn the water. In the summer, during the day I was as much in the water as out of it, for three seasons, allowing the clothing to dry on my back, — sleeping at night in one of our boats in a bunk, in the same manner as the workmen.

With this improved navigation 365 tons of anthracite came down the Lehigh River in 1820. The coal business began in earnest. Twenty years later a million tons of anthracite went to market over a network of canals and rivers, large and small. Long after railroads were built, coal barges slipped quietly through this maze of waterways, supplying fuel for homes, factories and mills. However, the great bituminous deposits of the Appalachian Mountains, and not the beds of anthracite in eastern Pennsylvania, put the crown on "Ole King Coal." Anthracite was scarce but the United States had enough bituminous coal to last 3000 years. The market for coal increased as steam engines furnished the power for operating machinery, especially in the field of transportation. Then the fur-trading posts, located on navigable rivers in the coal land, soon began to feel the throb of industry.

HOW COAL CHANGED
LIFE IN PENNSYLVANIA

DURING THE Revolutionary War Jonathan and Ruth Slocum, with their seven sons and three daughters, moved west from Rhode Island to the Wyoming Valley in northeastern Pennsylvania. Shortly after the family settled on land where the city of Wilkes-Barre now stands, the father was killed in an Indian raid, known as the Wyoming Valley Massacre. Later, two of the Slocum brothers, Ebeneezer and Benjamin, settled in a bowl-shaped valley a little north of Wilkes-Barre where they built a forge, a grist mill, and a saw mill to supply new settlers with iron, grain, and lumber. After an early, cold winter when crops had frozen, a Dutch blacksmith employed at the forge named the little settlement Slocum's Hollow, because he said, only a Slocum would have the courage to seek a living in such a poor place. Slocum's Hollow is now part of the industrial city of Scranton. The name of Slocum Hollow was changed to honor George W. Scranton who moved there from New Jersey in 1840 and erected new furnaces to burn anthracite coal. However, bituminous coal rather than anthracite promoted the great iron and steel industry of the Appalachian region. The rise of manufacturing made coal a valuable product. As factories bought more and more coal to operate the increasing number of steam-driven machines, mining grew into a big industry.

PITTSBURGH PROFITS
FROM A STRATEGIC LOCATION

SETTLEMENT AND INDUSTRIAL growth in the United States depended upon transportation to carry pioneers to western lands and to haul their products to market. However, both occupation and business began in the days of pack horses, wagon freight, and river flatboats. The trader went first and settlers followed

FROM FARMING TO MINING IN THE WYOMING VALLEY OF PENNSYLVANIA

FIRST CLEARING IN THE WILDERNESS

In 1762, about 200 sturdy New Englanders, mostly from Connecticut, settled in the Wyoming Valley of northeastern Pennsylvania. Mothers and little children rode in ox carts with chicken crates and farm tools. Fathers and older sons drove a few cattle, sheep, and hogs to provide milk, wool, and meat. On the way, some of the animals were devoured by wolves.

In the sketch above, the chimney of the log cabin is a hole in the roof; the door is a hide or two; and the window may not be glass. The barn is a crude log shelter with a brush roof. Although snow covers the ground and the brook is frozen over, the pioneer is busy chopping down trees, enlarging the clearing for the spring planting.

THE SAME PLACE — A FEW YEARS LATER

The clearing is larger. Corn, potatoes, and pumpkins are growing among the tree stumps. The lone settler now has neighbors who are helping him to pile logs for future use. The log cabin has a chimney plastered with mud, a plank door with wooden hinges, and a window with four panes of glass. Vines shade the doorway, a "worm" fence protects the house and garden, and a log bridge spans the creek.

Wyoming Valley was a land of trees which the pioneer had to chop down before he could plant a crop. The logs were used for houses, barns, bridges, fences, furniture, and for cooking and heating in fireplaces. On the frontier, neighbors helped one another in the hard labor of settlement in a wilderness.

THE SAME CLEARING A GENERATION LATER

The settler's son, now the owner, hauls a load of hay to the barn. His daughter dips a bucket of water from the well in the orchard. His son walks down the lane carrying a bucket in each hand.

The original log cabin is now a wing of the new house built of squared logs shaped in the farmer's sawmill a little distance upstream. Paneling on the front door, shingles on the roof, boards in the barn, lumber in the straight fence, and planks on the bridge are products of the sawmill.

More land has been cleared, and more crops are growing, and a garden flourishes in the side yard. Beyond a grove of trees stands the one-room schoolhouse where children living on farms study the three R's — "readin', 'ritin', 'rithmetic."

THE OLD HOMESTEAD

At the dawn of the industrial era, a big house stands on the spot where the first settler built his log cabin in a wilderness. A few trees on the hilltops are all that remain after farmers had cleared the land for planting. The landscape is a network of fields and orchards, with a village where the farmers sell their produce and buy the things they need. Gone are the "worm" fences, the wooden bridge, and the tree stumps.

Smoke streaming from the funnel of a railroad engine is an omen of the future when the quiet countryside will hum with industry. Coal will take the place of corn as shiny beds of anthracite lure more and more miners into the river valleys of eastern Pennsylvania.

close behind. The triangle formed by the junction of the Allegheny and Monongahela Rivers to form the Ohio was a strategic location for a settlement. Pittsburgh began as a frontier post for the Indian trade and grew up to be a large industrial center, the celebrated city of steel.

In December, 1758, a merchant in Philadelphia had wagons loaded with lead, shot, powder, knives, hatchets, cloth, saddles, kettles, pipes, and tobacco. He was enroute to Pitt's Borough where he hoped to trade the articles for valuable furs brought in by the Indians. At Cumberland the merchandise was transferred from wagons to pack horses — 34 in all — for the journey over Braddock's Road to the frontier post. When icy streams were too deep for fording, the bundles were ferried across in canoes while the horses swam to the opposite shore. The leader of the pack train was a Quaker. In his diary he tells of the hardships of this mid-winter journey across the mountains:

My horse lame & ye snow balling his feet made his passing something doubtful, but I lead him along & got safe across, but in swimming ye creek ye water got into my boots & saddle-bags. I emptied ye bags & walked until I was warm. — It being late, and about four or five miles further (to a farmer's house), I began to look for a lodging place, which I found under ye side of a great mountain in a hollow stump. After I cleared ye snow out & made a floor of bark & a great fire at ye door, I lodged with more comfort than I expected & slept some.

At night, wolves chewed the hide tongs that tied his bundles of goods; a keg of knives fell into a stream and the leader had to scour off the rust and oil them; dried apples and hard biscuit were soaked with water; rolls of wet blankets were spread out to dry; horses strayed at night, were lost or stolen, and some died on the way. On the last day of April after a trip lasting five months, the merchandise reached Pittsburgh. During the summer Indians wandered into the settlement with pelts to trade for these articles. Finding Colonel Mercer and 280 men in the fort disturbed the Indians. They feared the soldiers would be the advance guard of white settlers who would occupy their lands.

The settlers followed upon the heels of the traders. On the way back to Philadelphia in the early autumn with 9000 pounds of valuable furs, the trader met others going west, as related in his diary:

Sept. 14, 1759

Ye South Branch of Pottomock people are in droves along ye road, going to Pittsburgh, some with flower and some with corn, oats, butter, cheese, etc. The day I overtook ye wagons, I met Col. Burd of Pennsylvania & a party with wagons and pack horses going to ye mouth of Redstone Creek to build some storehouses, in order to have ye carriage on this road to go from thence down ye Monongahela to Pittsburgh.

EARLY PITTSBURGH
A FRONTIER SETTLEMENT

This small village at the junction of the Allegheny and Monongahela Rivers became the supply center for settlers traveling down the Ohio River to settle in the Northwest Territory. With coal, iron, and water transportation, Pittsburgh became the "City of Steel."

Chamber of Commerce of Pittsburgh

The early storekeepers of Pittsburgh lived in constant fear of Indian raids. They were kept busy moving their goods in and out of the protected enclosure of Fort Pitt. In 1763 Pontiac, the brilliant chief of the Ottawas, organized the Indian tribes from Lake Superior to the Gulf of Mexico in an all-out attempt to prevent the British from settling the country in the Ohio Valley.

After a year of savage war Pontiac's conspiracy failed. White men crossed the mountain barrier to build their cabins and plant their corn in the western country. The first written description of the village of Pittsburgh appeared in the journal kept by Washington of his trip down the Ohio to the Kanawha River. Washington wrote in 1770:

We lodged in what is called the town, distant about three hundred yards from the fort. The houses, which are built of logs, and ranged in streets, are on the Monongahela, and I supposed may be about twenty in number and inhabited by Indian traders.

During the Revolutionary War soldiers had been stationed at Fort Pitt. Carpenters and sawyers had been sent there to build six boats, each one carrying a cannon, to aid the garrison in defending the place. The soldiers were sometimes hungry and cold because the hunters and woodchoppers were easy targets for Indians and Frenchmen who lurked in the woods. When the garrison complained of freezing, with tons of coal only half a mile away, the commander of the western district ordered that "the coal pit be occupied by turns day and night," while some kept guard.

After the War for Independence ended, the United States gained territory to the Mississippi River. The frontier village at the headwaters of the Ohio began to grow.

When the Ordinance of 1787 opened up the Northwest Territory for settlement, Pittsburgh became the supply center for western emigrants going down the Ohio River to settle in Kentucky, Tennessee, Ohio, Indiana, and Illinois. It was a dangerous route. Slow-moving keel and flatboats were easy targets for attack by Indians still trying to hold the country against the inroads of settlers.

General Rufus Putnam, who had served in both the French and Indian War and the War for Independence, took out the first emigrants of the Ohio Company to found the first permanent settlement in the Northwest Territory. After crossing the mountains in winter, when it was sometimes necessary to haul their belongings on sleds because the snow was too deep for wagons, Putnam's party of New Englanders reached the Youghiogheny River. At Simrall's Ferry, about thirty miles above Pittsburgh, the emigrants built the *Mayflower,* a galley 45 feet long and 12 feet wide, with a roof over part of the deck. To carry all the baggage of the party, it was necessary to build a flatboat and three canoes, also. On a spring day the little flotilla pushed out into the Youghiogheny, dodging sand bars and shallow water. It then drifted down the wider and deeper Monongahela to Pittsburgh.

The frontier town of log houses and about 400 to 500 inhabitants looked like a city to the New Englanders who had spent weeks in a wilderness. They enjoyed shopping in the stores for clothing and tools to take to their new homes. On April 7, 1788, Putnam's party arrived at the mouth of the Muskingum River, unloaded the boards they had brought along, and began to erect the first crude huts in a little town they named Marietta, after the Queen of France.

A month later Colonel May from Boston, another Revolutionary officer, arrived in Pittsburgh where he was delayed seventeen days waiting for a boat down the Ohio to the colony on the Muskingum River. He, too, did some shopping in Pittsburgh. In a letter to his wife, dated May 1, 1788, he wrote:

I dined today on bacon that was good which I bought by the quantity. — I have laid in four barrels of excellent flour.

During his stay in Pittsburgh, Colonel May purchased many useful items, including a grindstone, axes, hoes, and tools. To his food supply he added a bushel of salt and two bushels of potatoes. Enroute down the Ohio with twenty-seven men on board, two cows, two calves, seven hogs, nine dogs, and eight tons of baggage, he bought more supplies from farmers living along the shore. May's purchases included 300 pounds of smoked hams, more seed corn, potatoes, butter, a barrel of pickled pork, young plants and trees, and as many cows with calves as he could crowd on board the boat.

Revolutionary officers of the Society of Cincinnati and soldiers from the ranks settled in Belpre, Cincinnati, and other places where streams flowed down through fertile valleys to empty into the Ohio River. Forts had been erected to protect them. Fort Harmar was at the mouth of the Muskingum River and Fort Washington was near the Miami in Ohio, opposite the Licking River in Kentucky. However, the area protected by these forts was small because the Indians fought desperately to hold their farms and their hunting grounds. Boatloads of immigrants were captured, scalped, and carried away into captivity; farmers were shot from ambush while plowing in their fields; frontier cabins were burned to the ground and the torch was applied to crops of corn. After General St. Clair, the first governor of the Northwest Territory, had been defeated in Indian warfare, Major General Anthony

MARIETTA, OHIO IN 1792

Marietta, oldest town in Ohio, was founded in 1788 at point where the Muskingum River flows into the Ohio.

Wayne, known as "Mad Anthony," took over the campaign against the Indians.

After the Indians were defeated in the Battle of Fallen Timbers, near Fort Miami, in 1794, their power was broken. In straggling bands, dispossessed and disheartened, the tribes of the Northwest Territory began the westward trek to prairie lands beyond the Mississippi. Among them were Shawnees and other tribes who had lived near the Atlantic seaboard before the white man came to North America.

Freed from big Indian raids, the settlers came in ever-increasing numbers. With them came industry, boatbuilding, forges, furnaces, saw mills, grist mills, and factories to make the many articles needed by emigrants in a new country. Coal, plentiful in and around Pittsburgh, was delivered to the doors of homes and factories for five and six cents a bushel. In 1807 about 200,000 bushels of coal were burned in Pittsburgh. Travelers called it the "Smoky City."

When the use of steam made river travel safe and profitable, Pittsburgh became an inland port. Since early industrial growth in this country depended largely upon water transportation to carry the goods to market, inventors began to experiment with steam engines to propel boats. Robert Fulton visioned a future with steamboats hauling the products of farms and factories on the western rivers and, he was willing to invest money in a steamboat on the Mississippi River. In 1809 two years after the *Clermont* steamed up the Hudson to Albany, Nicholas J. Roosevelt and his bride journeyed overland to Pittsburgh to investigate the possibilities of steamboat navigation on the western rivers. They were to report to Fulton and Livingston in New York.

Upon arrival in Pittsburgh, Roosevelt had a flat-bottom boat built with two small houses on top, like boxes, one for himself and his wife, and the other, for the crew, which included the cook who prepared the meals with the aid of a fireplace. This flatboat was home for six months while Roosevelt tested the current and measured the depth of the Ohio and Mississippi Rivers from Pittsburgh to the Gulf of Mexico. From New Orleans the Roosevelts took a ship home, arriving in New York after an absence of nine months. Fulton and Livingston were so pleased with Roosevelt's report that they agreed to furnish the money for him to build a steamboat at Pittsburgh and test it on a river trip.

On a September day in 1811 the residents of Pittsburgh lined the banks of the Monongahela River and shouted farewells as the first steamboat chugged down the stream on its epoch-making voyage. On board the *New Orleans* were the builder and his wife, a captain, a pilot, an engineer, six hired hands, two women servants, a waiter, a cook, and a big Newfoundland dog, named Tiger. At a speed of about ten miles an hour, the steamboat reached Cincinnati on the second day. The whole town turned out to see it. The hardy river men who had poled the flatboats and the keelboats down the Ohio shook their heads in doubt. The steamer would never get back against the current of the Mississippi River.

At the Falls of the Ohio, opposite Louisville, Kentucky, the *New Orleans* had to wait for the river to rise enough to carry the boat across the rocky barrier. On the way down in the flatboat, Roosevelt had taken time to explore along the banks, searching for coal lands. He had found some deposits on the lower Ohio. He had coal dug and piled on the bank of the river to burn in case he returned in the steamboat. This fuel came in handy. When all he loaded had been used, the steamboat was forced to tie up along the bank once every day while the crew cut wood to fire the boiler. At about that time there had been an earthquake which shook the region where the Ohio River empties into the Mississippi. Many Indians were afraid of the "fire canoe," and thought the paddles stirring the water had caused the earth to tremble under their feet. Well might the Indians fear the "fire canoe" as it was to bring both settlers and industry westward to drive them from their hunting grounds along the inland waterways.

The *New Orleans* reached Natchez in safety where it served for years carrying passengers and freight back and forth between that town and New Orleans. It cost about $38,000 to build. The boat was designed, built, and delivered by Nicholas Roosevelt, the grand-uncle of a future President, Theodore Roosevelt, and a distant relative of a later President, Franklin D. Roosevelt. Thus began that colorful and romantic period of American history, known as the Steamboat Era, which developed the river ports of Pittsburgh, Cincinnati, Louisville, St. Louis, Memphis, Vicksburg, Natchez, and New Orleans into centers of trade and manufacture.

In 1824, a famous decision by the Supreme Court promoted steamboat traffic on the rivers all over the country. The legislature of the State of New York had granted Robert R. Livingston and Robert R. Fulton special rights of navigation on the Hudson River. John Marshall, Chief Justice, stated that navigation on the Hudson River involved interstate commerce that only Congress had the power to regulate, according to the Constitution. This decision made all rivers free to all boatowners who obeyed the laws passed for navigation.

The South Americans, too, were interested in steamboat navigation for their rivers. In the late 1820's a German immigrant tried to establish a steamship line on the Magdalena River, the highway of commerce in Colombia. The Magdalena, winding through a tropical country, was a treacherous river with a strong current, shifting channels, and deep and shallow water according to seasons. Although Simon Bolivar rode on one of the German's steamboats, and encouraged the project, it was not a success. Revolutions that upset the government and natives who refused to cut wood hindered the operation of the line. Natives who were employed to paddle canoes in the Magdalena River, some carrying as much as eighteen tons of freight, were not anxious to cut down trees to fuel a steam engine that would take away their jobs.

Soon after steamships were tried on rivers, the commander of the *Clermont* took the first steamship out into the ocean on a voyage from New York to the Delaware River. Later he was captain of the *Savannah,* the first steamboat to venture across the Atlantic Ocean, but not without the aid of sails. On May 22, 1819, this vessel steamed out of the port of Savannah, Georgia, arriving in Liverpool twenty-six days later, but much of the voyage was under sail. The first vessel to cross the Atlantic under steam power only was the *Royal William,* built in Canada in 1833. This steamship made the voyage from Quebec to the Isle of Wight in nineteen and a half days, "with seven passengers, a box of stuffed birds, some household furniture, 254 chaldrons of coal (a chaldron being at that time 3456 pounds), and a crew of 36 men." In London the *Royal William* was chartered to the Portuguese Government for a transport. Later it was sold to Spain for a war vessel, as it was the first steamship from which a hostile gun was fired. Pittsburgh, Cincinnati, and Louisville became the building centers for steamboats navigating the western rivers, and New York, Philadelphia, and Baltimore for ocean-going steamers.

Some ocean-going vessels were built in Pittsburgh and loaded with cargoes for foreign countries. The town boasted of being a world port. In the House of Representatives, Henry Clay of Kentucky told an amusing anecdote. When a boat from Pittsburgh arrived at Leghorn (Livorno), Italy, the captain presented his papers to the custom house officer, who refused to accept them.

"Sir, your papers are forged," the Italian said. "There is no such place as Pittsburgh in the world! Your vessel must be confiscated."

The captain laid a map of the United States before the customs officer. Beginning at the Gulf of Mexico, he traced with his finger the Mississippi River to the Ohio, and thence up that stream to Pittsburgh.

"There, Sir, is the port whence my vessel cleared out," the captain claimed with pride.

Pittsburgh soon acquired two rivals for the Ohio River trade, the towns of Louisville, Kentucky, and Cincinnati, Ohio.

In 1815 Cincinnati was manufacturing the same articles as Pittsburgh, except some made of iron. The town early acquired a large number of skilled craftsmen who made clocks, jewelry, pottery, carriages, and fine furniture. Hides brought up the Mississippi and Ohio on boats were tanned and manufactured into saddles, boots, and shoes. Lead was imported from the Missouri Territory and Cincinnati became well-known for white lead products. From surrounding farms, grains and fruits for which there was not a market, were made into liquors that were shipped in barrels to New Orleans. However, flour was the chief article of export from the Miami country. A book, published in Cincinnati in 1815, lists the exports of this river port:

After flour follow pork, bacon, and lard; whiskey, peach brandy, beer and porter; pot and pearl ash, cheese, soap, and candles; hemp and spun yarn; walnut, cherry, and blue ash boards; cabinet furniture and chairs; to which might be advantageously added, kiln dried Indian meal for the West Indies.

Five years later when steamboats were plying the inland waterways, a merchant from Cuba wrote a letter to the editor of *The Cincinnati Directory*, suggesting that the people of the Ohio country ship their produce to his country, direct, "receiving in return the coffee, sugar and other articles common to the Island of Cuba."

At this time revolts were brewing in the Spanish colonies, seeking their independence from Spain. The westerners, whose market was New Orleans, wanted the trade of the Latin American countries. Rifles, cannon, shot and shell, made in the little iron furnaces and lead factories of the Ohio Valley, were shipped down the Mississippi and smuggled into the southern countries to aid the revolutionaries. The friendship between the westerners and the insurgents in Spanish America resulted in trade gains when the colonies became independent nations, according to a dispatch in a Pittsburgh newspaper in 1845:

Four Mexican gentlemen arrived in our city yesterday, by the Steamer *Bertrand*. They brought with them over $40,000, the greater portion of which they will leave in our city, for articles of Pittsburgh Manufacture. The value of our trade with Mexico is very considerable. Every spring and fall, large orders are furnished to our mechanics and Manufacturers for Iron and Glass Wares, Harness, Saddlery, Wagons, Ploughs, etc. These articles are mostly taken by the Santa Fe route, from whence they are distributed over the Northern Provinces of Mexico.

Steamboats carried merchandise to the Missouri frontier, where it was loaded into covered-wagon freighters and was strapped on to pack saddles for the trek over the prairie to Santa Fe, the trade center of northern Mexico. As markets were extended westward, towns on the inland waterways began to grow in size and importance, with the combined aid of coal, iron, and steam.

Before the steam engine came into general use, factories were erected near streams where falls and rapids furnished water power to operate the machinery. Then the manufacturers were forced to lay out a town and to build houses for their employees, as was the case in Lowell, Massachusetts. Real estate agents selling business sites in Pittsburgh proudly advertised the advantages offered to manufacturers in the town where mechanics had settled and workmen provided their own living quarters. Where coal was so plentiful, steam power was cheap, and one could start a little factory with a small amount of money. Markets were assured because Pittsburgh was the supply center for western emigrants. Steamboats plied the inland waterways of

C. & O. O. EVANS,

FOUNDERS,

Plough Manufacturers and Millers,

Stone Steam Mill, Water Street,

2 squares west of Market st.

PITTSBURGH,

Respectfully inform their friends and Correspondents, that having re-built their Foundry and Works, are now prepared to fill orders to any extent for

Crane Ploughs,—Cotton Ploughs—Wood's Ploughs—Prairie Ploughs, large and heavy ploughs expressly made for breaking up *prairies, new clearings, roads, &c.*—Hill-side Ploughs, for ploughing on sides of hills, throwing the furrow all one way, True American Ploughs, Half Patent Ploughs, Peacock's Ploughs,—Eagle Ploughs,—Miller's Ploughs,—Shovel Ploughs, and Cultivators; and Trucks for Stores and Steam Boats.

Their much approved *Farmers' Mill*, for grinding Grain, Corn in the Cob, Plaster, &c. propelled by the most modern and simply constructed horse power in use, which can also be applied to Threshing, Straw Cutting Machines, &c.

Corn Shellers, Threshing and Straw Cutting machines, Mill Irons, Wagon Boxes and Castings of all kinds.

They are also making arrangements for manufacturing *Stoves*; the patterns selected will be of the newest and most approved kind.

They also have just received the following Eastern Manufactured articles, so indispensable to Farmers:

Hand mills, for grinding Grain, Coffee, Spices, &c.; Hay Knives of different descriptions; Corn Cutters, for taking stalks from grain fields; manure forks, made from plate steel, and other kinds; and Grain Shovels.—Also, the following Pruning Implements: Pruners, Handled Slide; Gentlemen's Pruning Knives and Saw Cases; Heavy Bill Hooks, Fancy Slide Pruners, &c.; Edging Knives, &c. &c.

☞ *Fresh Family Flour always on hand.* ☜

Henry E. Huntington Library

ADVERTISEMENT FROM HARRIS' PITTSBURGH DIRECTORY FOR 1837

the Ohio River and its tributaries, carrying the products made in Pittsburgh to river towns all the way to New Orleans, and thence to foreign ports.

With the coming of railroads the steamboat gained a rival in the steam locomotive. In less than twenty-five years after the first boats were propelled by steam, the first steam locomotive in the Western Hemisphere actually ran over three miles of track at Honesdale, Pennsylvania.

457

FIRST STONE OF BALTIMORE AND OHIO RAILROAD

To restore western trade taken from Baltimore by canals and toll roads, a group of business men decided to invest money in a railroad. On July 4, 1828, in Baltimore, Charles Carroll of Carrollton, last living signer of the Declaration of Independence, took part in laying the cornerstone of the first railroad to the Ohio River.

The engine was called the "Stourbridge Lion" because it had been built in Stourbridge, England, and had the head of a lion painted in red on the front of the boiler. The rails had been laid and the engine imported by the Delaware and Hudson Canal Company to haul anthracite coal sixteen and a half miles from their mines at Carbondale to the head of their canal at Honesdale. The same man who had gone to England to buy the engine was the passenger, the engineer, the brakeman, the fireman, and the conductor when the little engine chugged around a curve on a rickety trestle crossing Lackawaxan Creek and disappeared in the woods beyond. On the eighth day of August in 1828, this brief run of the "Stourbridge Lion" opened the railroad era. In August of the following year, the first American-made steam locomotive, the "Tom Thumb," hauled thirty-six passengers in a coach a distance of thirteen miles on the Baltimore and Ohio Railroad. Although the engine broke down on the return trip in a race with a horse, and the gray steed won, the trial of Tom Thumb was a success.

Railroads could penetrate regions of rich coal and farm lands in the hilly country where canals could not be dug, and operate in winter when the canals were frozen lanes of ice. The directors of the Baltimore and Ohio Railroad offered a prize of $4000 for the best coal-burning locomotive delivered to them by June 1, 1831. A man from New York won the money. Although wood was long burned in locomotives hauling cars of coal from mines to markets, coal became the railroad fuel. In both steamboats and locomotives, bituminous coal could be used in engines made to burn wood. Special engines had to be built for anthracite.

Little country villages dreamed of a future with factories, population, and payrolls when a rail line passed through. No longer were the river towns the only locations for industrial plants when rails streaked across the country hauling products to market. The railroad era increased "the grand results" of the "mighty age of steam."

Chapter 24

Inland Waterways Spread Industry

INDUSTRY WENT WEST
WITH THE PIONEERS

THE WESTWARD MARCH to the inland waterways really began when George Washington stood for the first time on the triangle of land where the Allegheny and Monongahela Rivers join to form the Ohio. This perilous journey to deliver Governor Dinwiddie's message to the French commander marked the beginning of Washington's adventures in this western wilderness where a county was named for him. Fur traders entered the country first, ahead of the land pioneers who pushed their clearings westward over the mountains to the Ohio Valley. Ironmasters soon followed.

After the War for Independence the iron industry along the seaboard went into a decline. The prewar British market was gone and money was scarce. Forges and furnaces were in need of repair. New inventions like the steam engine and the nail-cutting machine rendered the old equipment scarcely worth replacing. Ironmasters from New Jersey and nail makers from New England joined the returned soldiers in the westward trek to the Northwest Territory and Kentucky

and Tennessee. Their simple methods of smelting ore and cutting nails were welcomed by settlers opening up a wilderness.

Before the tenth anniversary of the surrender of Yorktown, a German immigrant was erecting the Bourbon Furnace on Slate Creek, a branch of the Licking River that flowed through his land in Bath County, Kentucky. Armed guards kept watch to ward off Indian attacks while workmen dug ore from surface mines, hauled it to the furnace, cut down trees, burned charcoal, and hammered at the forge. Early settlers in Kentucky were supplied with kettles, warming pans, bake ovens, stoves, and flatirons from this ironworks. Cannon balls and grape shot made in the Bourbon Furnace went by flatboat down the Licking to the Ohio, and on down the Mississippi. They were used against the British regulars by General Jackson's frontiersmen and pirate recruits in the Battle of New Orleans.

In the 1790's furnace smoke curled above the treetops in the mountain wilderness of eastern Tennessee where Daniel Boone had hunted as a lad. Customers were the settlers going west, following the valleys of the Wautaga,

United States Steel Corporation

A PIONEER FURNACE IN THE WILDERNESS

Since charcoal was used for fuel to smelt the iron ore, pioneer furnaces were located where trees were plentiful. In this sketch, a charcoal burner tends a turf-covered pit in which cords of wood are being slowly burned into sticks of carbon to fire the furnace. Air is forced into the furnace with a foot-operated bellows.

Holston, Clinch, Powell, and Tennessee Rivers. Traders went down these streams in flatboats and canoes, peddling their iron wares in frontier settlements. Some traders went all the way to New Orleans. With streams for water power, trees for charcoal, and ore for furnaces, the industrial pioneers under primitive methods made one or two tons of iron per day. This supplied the neighborhood blacksmiths who turned it into horseshoes, wagon rims, and harrow teeth for the soil pioneers. Bar iron was the same as money for paying taxes and buying salt, sugar, coffee, calico, and shoes at the country store.

In the Hanging Rock District iron ores were discovered on both sides of the Ohio River near the present towns of Ashland, Kentucky, and Ironton, Ohio. Early settlers in Michigan were supplied with potash kettles and stoves by forges and furnaces in northeastern Ohio near the shore of Lake Erie. Ironmasters and

plowmen walked side by side, pushing the frontier westward to the Great Lakes and the Mississippi River. The little charcoal forges and furnaces of the iron pioneers were the advance guard of the conquering legions of mills and factories that followed them when industry marched westward to the inland waterways under the triple banner of coal, steam, and steel.

THE GREAT LAKES BASIN FORMS A NATURAL SETTING FOR INDUSTRY

INDUSTRY DEPENDS upon transportation. The farmer and the manufacturer without easy access to markets actually have little to sell. From the beginning, industry in the Great Lakes region was harnessed to the waterways. The first known white men to enter this country were French explorers and

"BOUND DOWN THE RIVER"

In early America, inland waterways were highways of commerce. Farmers in the Ohio Valley went down the Mississippi River in flatboats with bundles of furs, bushels of grain, and hickory-smoked hams to sell in New Orleans. Steamboats plying the rivers added tools and utensils made in frontier furnaces to cargoes of farm products. Families moving west needed cooking pots, frying pans, hoes, rakes, shovels, hatchets and plows. Plantation owners in Louisiana needed big boiling kettles to make a salable product from their sugar cane. Steamboats moved both passengers and merchandise westward on the rivers, and industry followed close behind.

Currier & Ives

missionaries who traveled mainly by water. Close on their heels followed the trapper and the fur trading business. The villages of Indians and half-breeds, with a sprinkling of Frenchmen, that clustered around the mission centers were little more than wayside camps for the swaggering voyageurs, coming and going on fur hunting expeditions.

The actual settlement of the Great Lakes region did not get under way until plowmen came to turn the sod after most of the territory was ceded to the United States by the Treaty of Paris in 1783. After the War for Independence pioneers paddled down the Ohio River to settle in the Northwest Territory. Others came later, filtering into the back country along the tributaries of the Ohio. They reached the shores of Lake Erie and farther north to the prairie strip of southern Michigan. During the War of 1812 supplies were furnished to soldiers and sailors from farms along the Erie shore. In August, 1813 six farmer boys rented an old French boat, loaded it with melons, beans, cucumbers, corn, butter, and other produce from their farms. Hearing that Perry's fleet was near Sandusky, they set out in the unseaworthy vessel to find it. Not knowing there were any settlements nearby, Perry was astonished when the boatload of fresh food arrived. The boys wanted to give the food to the crews, but Perry insisted on paying for it, asked for more, and gave the boys a better boat. Their boat was leaking.

After they returned, one of the lads rode horseback from farm to farm, collecting potatoes, vegetables, smoked meat, and homemade pickles for Perry's sailors. The day after the victorious battle on Lake Erie, the farmer boy hastily gathered a crew from the neighborhood and left the

shore with a boatload of potatoes. Rowing through the floating litter of broken spars and torn rigging, he came alongside Perry's flagship, the *Lawrence.*

In the beginning of settlement the basin of the Great Lakes showed signs of becoming the great food-producing center that it is today. As early as 1796 a ship captain, who had once been General Washington's gardener, delivered to a farmer in Windsor, Canada, a shipment of apple trees purchased in Montreal. The captain, a skillful grafter, took specimens from these trees across the border to improve the fruit growing in an orchard that then stood on land now covered with buildings in downtown Detroit. A traveler, going west by boat, wagon, and horseback, described the country along the Raisin River in southern Michigan:

> Monroe Michigan
> Dec. 3, 1833
> It would delight an eastern farmer to see the magnificent pear trees which, tall as the trees of the forest, extend through orchards for miles along the stream. Here, too, are apple trees that were brought by the French in 1731. The grapevines, also, from which the river takes its name constitute a beautiful feature in the level landscape, as they hang in rich festoons along the banks of the stream, and climb wherever it is wooded to the tops of the loftiest elms.

In that same year of 1833, two pioneers bought fruit trees, berry bushes, and flowering shrubs in Rochester, New York, shipped them by way of the Erie Canal, across the lake, and overland by wagon to stock their nursery near Ypsilanti. Today Michigan is a fruit raising state, and famous for cherries growing along the shores of Traverse Bay. The miller and the sawyer trailed close behind the plowman in a new country. They came to grind the farmer's wheat into flour for his bread and to saw the lumber for his house and his barn.

Since boats were needed to carry settlers and products over the inland waterways, the ship-building industry began to grow. The first steamboat upon Lake Erie was *Walk-in-the-Water*. When completed, the vessel lacked enough power to push its way against the current of the Niagara River where it was built. It took sixteen yoke of oxen to pull it out of the stream and launch it in the lake. When the steamer entered the Detroit River, Indians swarmed along the banks and gazed in wonder. What paddled it? When the boiler blew off steam, the natives ran frightened into the woods. *Walk-in-the-Water* launched steam navigation that played so large a part in building an industrial empire along the shores of the Great

WALK-IN-THE-WATER IN HARBOR OF DETROIT

The first steamboat on the Great Lakes was named WALK-IN-THE-WATER for the chief of the Wyandot Indians whose name was Mier, meaning turtle. His tribe lived on the bank of the Detroit River in Michigan. The chief's totem or signature was the figure of a turtle walking in the water.

WALK-IN-THE-WATER, built in the Niagara River at Black Rock had to be towed to Lake Erie for launching, May 28, 1818. Boats anchored in the Niagara River and were pulled through the rapids by oxen until Buffalo developed a harbor. The sailors jokingly called this towing process, the "horn breeze."

In 1820, and again in 1821, this boat transported United States Army soldiers to forts defending frontier settlements. Among the notable passengers was a young officer who later gained fame as General Winfield Scott in the Mexican War.

WALK-IN-THE-WATER met an untimely end in a gale on Lake Erie on the first night out from Buffalo, bound for Detroit, October 31, 1821. Through high waves, strong winds, and heavy rain, the captain steered the battered, leaking boat to the shore not far from the lighthouse in the harbor. He wrecked the boat, but saved the lives of the passengers.

Buffalo and Erie County Historical Society

LIGHTHOUSE, STEAMSHIP "BUFFALO," AND HARBOR AT BUFFALO

After opening a harbor in 1820, Buffalo, New York became a port city in time to serve the people going west by way of the Erie Canal, completed in 1825. New Englanders traveled by stage to Albany, Erie Canal to Buffalo, and boat to Detroit and settlements along the shores of the Great Lakes.

At one time, the steamship BUFFALO was the fastest boat on the Great Lakes.

Lakes. Passenger vessels did a thriving business during the years of the westward migration. In July of 1835 the following news item was printed in the *Erie Gazette:*

No one who does not witness it, can have any just idea of the immense throng of people who are wending their way, by the route of Lake Erie, to the West. The steamboats and the schooners plying between the various ports on the lakes, are constantly crowded. More than 200,000 settlers will go west during the present season, and take up their abiding places on the fertile lands which border on the Great Lakes and their tributary streams.

The wharves at Buffalo were piled with barrels, boxes, and bundles for shipment to Cleveland, Detroit, and a frontier village, called Chicago, whose population grew from 54 in 1832 to 4000 in 1835. So many New Englanders were going west by way of the Erie Canal in 1837, that one editor declared: "the fever for emigration pervaded the whole region from Rhode Island to Vermont." Popular songs of the day advertised the states bordering on the Great Lakes, with verses like the following:

We here have soils of various kinds
To suit men who have different minds,
Prairies, openings, timbered land
And burr oak plains, in Michigan.

You who would wish to hunt and fish
Can find all kinds of game you wish;
Our deer and turkey they are grand
Our fish are good in Michigan.

By 1840 Buffalo, western terminal of the Erie Canal, was a port of call for most of the fifty-three steamboats on Lake Erie. In July of that year the steamboat *Erie* made a record run of 1200 miles from Chicago to Buffalo in four days, "carrying a large number of passengers and 300 barrels of flour and pork." One of these steamers consumed, on an average, three cords of wood per hour. To provide this fuel, woodchoppers went into the forests, and lumbering began in a small way. Another industry was then added to the Great Lakes region and a new kind of ship appeared on the inland seas — the lumber schooner.

LUMBERMEN INVADE THE WHITE PINE FORESTS

THE RAPID SETTLEMENT of the rich farm lands in the basin of the Great Lakes and the prairie beyond opened up a greedy market for timber. Poles for masts, lumber for hulls, pilings for docks, ties for railroads, boards for boxcars and siding for houses in town and country were in constant demand.

Trees growing near the rivers and lakes were the first victims of the woodsman's ax because water transportation was handy. The pilots who guided the log rafts down the Mississippi River were viewed with awe and wonder — so great was their skill! One slight error might cause a break-up that would crush and drown dozens of raftsmen maneuvering a float of logs around a treacherous bend in the river. These daring pilots, dressed in red flannel shirts, flowing black ties, and wide slouch hats earned $500 a month and more during the busy rafting season. This sum was a fabulous salary in those days. The reign of the rafting pilot was colorful, but brief. The steamboat took over his job.

During the War Between the States the first steamboat rafter towed a shipment of timber from the Chippewa River in Wisconsin to a sawmill in St. Louis, Missouri. The largest raft ever towed down the Mississippi River by a steamboat was one third of a mile long, 270 feet wide, and contained 9,000,000 feet of lumber. More logs could be handled at a time by a small steamboat crew than by pilots and their gangs. The daredevil raftsmen, with their fiddlers and cooks, faded out of the lumbering scene. As soon as the ice began to thaw in the rivers of Wisconsin and Minnesota, captains of the steamboat rafters headed north in the annual race. Each wanted to be the first to nose into the current of the Mississippi with a float of logs.

Sawmills in towns and villages along the Mississippi and its tributaries were busy slicing logs into boards to build houses for the western immigrants. The huge migration to the prairie state of Iowa in 1854 can be traced in the local newspapers.

The Keokuk Dispatch: No one can travel up and down the Mississippi without being astonished at the immigration pouring into Iowa from all parts of the country, especially from Indiana and Ohio. At every ferry on the river, crowds are waiting to cross. The land offices all over the state are unable to meet the demands upon them by those who are eager to enter lands.

The Burlington Telegraph: 20,000 immigrants have passed through the city within the last thirty days, and they are still crossing at the rate of 600 to 700 a day. We have these facts from the ferry folks. About one team in a hundred is labelled "Nebraska." All the rest are marked "Iowa."

There was plenty of government land selling at $1.25 an acre. Town lots were often donated to men willing to improve them. For about $2.50 per acre the settler could hire a man to "break the prairie" with a heavy plow, pulled by five yoke of oxen. This plow, which was ten feet long and turned a furrow two feet wide, was able to cut through the stringy roots of the native grasses on the buffalo plains.

Each new settler was a new customer for lumber. By 1854 the town of Davenport, Iowa, was becoming a lumber depot, with six sawmills cutting about 20,000,000 feet of lumber a year to supply the needs of settlers in the surrounding territory. A spacious eddy in the river made it easy for rafters from the northern pineries to halt at Davenport. The loggers bartered with the sawmill owners for the sale of their logs. The cost of rafting timber from the Chippewa River to Davenport or to Rock Island on the opposite bank of the river amounted to only a dollar per ton for the lumber sawed from the logs. In all, about 50,000,000,000 feet of lumber, rafted down the Mississippi from the northern pineries, was used in building farm houses and city dwellings in the Middle West. This river output was only a part of the lumber industry. Another story of adventure and production was written in the woods of Michigan and on the timber schooners plying the waters of the Great Lakes.

The race for timber land on sale by the Government lured many a fortune hunter into forests where no white man had been

LAST STAND OF WHITE PINE SOUTH OF GRAYLING, MICHIGAN. ABOUT HALF THE TREES IN THIS PHOTOGRAPH ARE NORWAY PINE.

Michigan Historical Commission

before. In the early 1870's two fishermen left a hamlet on the northern shore of Lake Michigan to search for unclaimed timber land on the upper peninsula which was wild country south of Lake Superior. It was midwinter. With packs on their backs, snowshoes on their feet, and a compass in one man's pocket, they plunged into the wilderness. Each night they chopped down a green maple tree, cut it into logs, and erected a shelter for their campfire. Rolled in blankets, they slept on a bed of balsam boughs in front of the fire. The bitter cold of the northern night settled down around them.

The fishermen located a forest of white pine well worth the government price of $5 to $10 an acre. The first man to file a claim on a specific section of land in a certain township became the owner of both the land and the timber on it. He must have the location correctly measured to hold his claim. In surveying with the aid of a compass the fishermen stumbled upon some snowshoe footprints in a swampy clearing. The tracks in the snow ran in a straight line. Only a timber cruiser walked like that and he was stepping off a claim. They followed the footprints until they turned toward Marquette on Lake Superior. The land office was there. These fishermen stepped off their claim as if no one had been there before. Their rival was at least a day ahead of them and they could not overtake him on land. He might travel slowly, stopping to hunt along the way, since he had seen no tracks in the snow. It was moonlight. In twenty-four hours the fishermen walked forty-five miles on snowshoes to reach the shore of Lake Superior, where they could travel faster on ice than on land. Here they parted. One man turned toward home. The other raced over the ice, reaching Marquette ahead of his rival. The winner's feet were covered with painful blisters and bleeding cuts from walking on the jagged ice along the frozen shore.

The key man in the lumber industry was the timber cruiser. With only a compass for a guide, he trailed through the primeval forests, stepping off the sections of land and counting the number of white pine giants on every single acre of it. In following his compass in a straight line, the cruiser hacked his way through briars and brush and waded through swamps and streams. So keen was his judgment, he could glance at a tall tree and measure with his eye the number of board feet of lumber in it. He wrote down the amount in a pocket notebook. The successful timber cruiser was an uncanny mixture of surveyor, woodsman, and mathematician – strong, fearless, and efficient. Upon the reports of the timber cruisers the lumber companies based their logging operations.

By 1850 lumberjacks were trudging westward from the logging camps of Maine, to chop white pine in Michigan's upper peninsula, along with the French Canadians. Immigrants arrived from Europe – Irish and Germans, and later, Finns, Swedes, and Norwegians. In the heyday of lumbering 140,000 men were employed during the winter months cutting down the forests of Michigan, Wisconsin, and Minnesota.

The logger's workday was from daylight to dusk. His home was a bunkhouse, a rambling shack of logs with a sloping roof. His bed was a straw-filled bunk nailed to the rough, unplastered wall. In the center of the shelter was an open fireplace, a pavement of stone and sand in a wooden box about eight feet square and a foot

Michigan Historical Commission

WHITE PINE TREES IN MICHIGAN

A student of forestry uses calipers to measure a white pine tree, four feet in diameter, as the timber cruisers did during the great lumbering days in the state. The last stand of original white pine trees was cut in the summer of 1910.

high. There was a funnel of slabs for a chimney sticking through a hole in the roof. The smoky air reeked with the wooly smell of socks and shirts drying on hooks and wire clotheslines strung around the fire. Buried in the hearth under glowing embers was the everlasting beanpot, day and night, around the clock.

The lonely men, marooned in a frozen wilderness, hungered for amusement. An unwritten law of the lumber camps provided the only entertainment between paydays. A new logger, a timber cruiser, a mining prospector, and any passing stranger found a hearty welcome in any bunkhouse of a lumber camp. He must pay for his beans, bread, molasses, and coffee with a song or a story. He who could neither chant a ballad nor spin a

467

yarn was tossed in a blanket. Thus came into being the shanty-songs of the lumber camps and the fanciful tales of the Finnish comic, Big Matt, and the superman, Paul Bunyan. Many legends reflected the superstitions of the men to whom danger was merely a habit, like eating and sleeping. Who would cut down a poplar tree, change his bunk, or his place at the table? What teamster would change his horses? Bad luck! A tree might crash in the wrong direction, an ax fall from a partner's hand, or logs jam on the river drive. The everyday life of the lumberjack crept into the lore of the northern woods.

Timber from the woods of Michigan and Wisconsin went into homes and factories of the industrial cities rising on the shores of the Great Lakes, where lumber was king. Some of the square timber used in Chicago's first breakwater was cut in a forest that once stood on the streets of Escanaba. Special vessels had to be constructed to deliver the heavy piling on

Chicago's waterfront, where winter gales dashed waves upon the doorsteps of houses at the foot of Lake Street. Timber from the same woods went into ships that carried lumber and other products to ports on the lakes, and into ties for the railroads that transported grains and meats from the western prairie to the shipping centers.

When the trees were gone, the way of life changed in the northern country. The lumberjacks burned out the dead stumps, plowed the land, and planted beans, potatoes, oats, barley, and fruits. Many of the Scandinavian loggers became farmers and stayed in Michigan, Wisconsin, and Minnesota. Others moved on farther west to fresh, uncut forests in the Pacific states of Washington and Oregon. The prospector for ore and the cruiser for timber trailed through the same forests at the same time. Long before lumbering began to wane, mining stepped in to take its place as the backbone of industry in the Great Lakes region. Then came steel, like magic, creating new industries, new cities, and new patterns of living along the waterways, where the trapper and the trader once paddled their canoes with the murmer of the forests ever ringing in their ears.

A FIELD OF STUMPS
IN NORTHERN MICHIGAN

Like tombstones in a graveyard, stumps mark the spots where trees were felled in a forest that covered the land before the lumberjack arrived.

Haines

STEEL ENTERS THE MARKET

DURING THE Revolutionary War, prizes were offered to increase the production of steel needed for armaments. This encouragement continued after the peace treaty that ended the war. In April of 1783 the state legislature of Pennsylvania lent a manufacturer about $1300 for three years, to aid him in making steel from bar iron, "as good as in

England." The steel industry of this country grew out of experiments by Americans to make from native iron "as good" steel as the British made from Swedish iron.

Since it was easier and cheaper to manufacture articles from iron than from steel, the iron industry continued to prosper for half a century following the war before steel loomed on the horizon as a strong rival for business. In 1832 near the close of President Jackson's first term of office, two English emigrants, brothers, made crucible steel in Cincinnati, Ohio. One of the brothers, William Garrard, was a bricklayer, not an ironmaster, which explains why he succeeded in being a steelmaker. In West Virginia he found clay like the famous Stourbridge variety used by the British steelmakers. From this clay he made molds into which he poured a poorer grade of steel, first converted into the metal from iron ore in his own furnaces. The clay purified the steel. The process of making steel in clay molds, or crucibles, was probably invented by some unknown Hindu in ancient times, long before the Christian era. The famous swords of Damascus were forged from crucible steel made in Persia and India.

In the Cincinnati Steel Works the Garrard Brothers made a tool steel from Missouri and Tennessee charcoal iron. Manufacturers declared that this steel was "as good as in England" for saws, springs, chopping axes, files and tools of all kinds. With blades shaped from Garrard steel, Cyrus Hall McCormick, the young inventor of the reaper, cut grain on his father's farm in Rockbridge County, Virginia. The Panic of 1837, following Jackson's second term, put the Garrard Brothers out of the crucible steel business and left McCormick with only the patent for his reaper.

A decade later, farther west than Cincinnati, a new day dawned for steel in a village near the Cumberland River in the western part of Kentucky. In 1846 William Kelly made a trip through Ohio, Indiana, Kentucky, and Tennessee, selling dry goods for a wholesale firm in Pittsburgh in which his brother had an interest. Late in that same year William Kelly persuaded his brother to quit the dry goods business and become his partner in an ironworks in Eddyville, Kentucky. They purchased an old furnace and 14,000 acres of ore and timber land. From chunks of ore picked up on top of the ground, the Kelly Brothers manufactured kettles for boiling sugar and ironware to supply the needs of their neighbors. The business prospered. Soon it became necessary to dig ore from underground where it was plentiful. However, this buried ore was different and caused trouble in the furnace.

Kelly began to experiment, hoping to find a cheaper and less troublesome way to refine pig iron than the process used by ironmasters of the time. One day he noticed that a small spot in his iron brew was white with heat, although there was no fuel near it. Then he discovered that a draft of cold air was blowing on the spot. He concluded that oxygen in the air was burning out the carbon, causing the intense heat. Kelly reasoned that if he could burn out nearly all the carbon, he could make steel out of this very same brew. After a number of experiments he constructed a crude converter, something like an iron barrel with perforated holes in the bottom. Kelly invited the ironmasters of the Cumberland River Valley to be in Eddyville on a certain day to see his new process in action. Out of curiosity a crowd gathered.

First, workmen filled the bulging barrel with molten iron. When a bellows pumped cold air into the sizzling brew, there came a roar like a muffled thunder. The converter, spouting fire and smoke, splattered hot iron like hailstones over two acres of ground. No one was hurt. The ironmasters had come to laugh at "Crazy Kelly" but went away wondering how his experiments would affect their future.

Kelly's product, however, was really more a soft, carbon-free iron than a finished steel, but it could easily be pounded into shape. Seldom is a great

THE KELLY CONVERTER

Kelly's converter was tested for the first time in a large ironworks in Johnstown, Pennsylvania, and found to be as usuable in a large plant as in a small one. This same converter has been preserved. The words identify it as follows:

KELLY
STEEL CONVERTER
used at
CAMBRIA IRON WORKS
1861-1862
The
PIONEER CONVERTER
of America

United States Steel Corporation

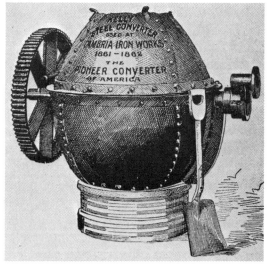

invention the work of only one man. Like the steam engine, perfected by a number of inventors and mechanics, the process of making steel by blowing drafts of cold air through molten iron was achieved by combining the discoveries of several men. In 1856 Kelly was busy continuing his experiments at an ironworks in Johnstown, Pennsylvania, when he read in a newspaper that Henry Bessemer had arrived in the United States from England to patent his discovery of a steel process. The formula was the same as Kelly's — hot iron and cold air. Since Kelly had failed to get a patent, he rushed to Washington and proved that his discovery had preceded Bessemer's. Although Kelly received a prior patent in 1857, lawsuits lingered in the courts for some time. As a matter of fact both men followed the same formula but Bessemer had invented the better machinery for making it. At about the same time another Englishman, Robert Mushet, discovered an alloy to purify iron brewing into steel. Since Kelly's process was not successful without Bessemer's machinery and neither one could make commercial steel without Mushet's alloy, the patents were consolidated. Steel men named the combination the Bessemer process, and the converter, Bessie.

In Wyandotte, Michigan, during the fall of 1864 occurred the first blow of Bessemer steel in the United States. In May of the following year, shortly after the death of Lincoln, the first steel rails produced in the Western Hemisphere were rolled in a Chicago mill from Bessemer steel blown at Wyandotte. The railroad boom that began to develop following the War Between the States created the first big market for steel. With the Bessemer process came mass production of steel, which lowered the price of the metal. Like the touch of a magic wand, new markets arose from new discoveries and new inventions until the race for steel became as dramatic as a play upon the stage. In fact the steel industry of the United States owes much of its success to a mistake in geography and to Benjamin Franklin who shrewdly took advantage of it.

WON BY A MAP

WHEN THE Revolutionary War ended, Benjamin Franklin had been one of the commissioners sent to Paris to arrange a treaty with Great Britain. Franklin had advocated taking possession of Canada during the French and Indian War. He had made the journey to Canada urging the people there to join in the fight for independence. Then he went to Paris, determined to get all the territory he could for the new United States. Both the British and American commissioners agreed to a water boundary by way of the Great Lakes as far as possible. This rule worked well until the line reached Lake Superior.

In 1783 maps of the Lake Superior region were few and faulty. The British and American commissioners agreed to accept, as the best available, a map sketched by a Virginian, John Mitchell, who had never seen Lake Superior. John Adams was most concerned with the Maine boundary and John Jay with the Mississippi River. This left Benjamin Franklin to barter for the mineral wealth in the western wilderness. Being a printer and publisher, Franklin was fond of books and read widely in both French and English. No doubt, he was familiar with the writings of French missionaries who told of finding great deposits of iron ore and copper in the region of Lake Superior.

Beside Franklin at the peace table in Paris sat a rough-and-ready fur trader from Milford, Connecticut. The trader had tramped through the northern woods and paddled a canoe along the shore of Lake Superior. Although he could not draw a map of the region, he knew the resources of the country. The British also knew there were mineral deposits near Lake Superior.

When they met at the peace table, the British commissioners wanted the line drawn through the middle of Lake Superior to the mouth of the St. Louis River, the present site of Duluth. This plan would have given to Great Britain the rich iron ranges that later supported the steel industry of the United States in supplying armaments for two world wars.

Since trappers and traders paddled their canoes on a curving line north of Isle Royal and Isles Philippeaux to Grand Portage, fur center of the Northwest, Franklin suggested that Lake Superior be divided on this familiar route. Also, Long Lake, as shown on Mitchell's map, afforded a better water route than the St. Louis River. The Treaty of Paris, signed in 1783, defined the western boundary, "thence through Lake Superior northward of the Isle Royal and Isles Philippeaux to Long Lake, thence through the middle of said Long Lake, and the water communication between it and the Lake of the Woods to the said Lake of the Woods." Herein occurred the error that gave to the United States the fabulous wealth of iron ore deposits in northern Minnesota. There was no such body of water as Long Lake and the Pigeon River extended inland only a short distance. The Isles Philippeaux, mythical home of the

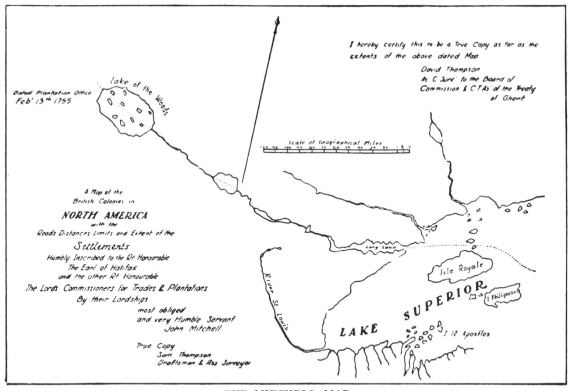

THE MITCHELL MAP

Had the border between the United States and Canada been drawn westward from the mouth of the St. Louis River, where the city of Duluth now stands, the United States would have lost the rich iron ranges of northern Minnesota.

The British agents in Paris in 1783 selected Long Lake for the border on Lake Superior, and this body of water was an error in the Mitchell map. In a later survey, the Pigeon River became part of the border between the two countries.

Great Spirit, existed only in Indian legend. The shadowy islands disappeared like magic, the natives declared, when they paddled their canoes in that direction.

Disputes soon arose over this boundary line. British trappers and traders complained bitterly because Grand Portage, the fur center, was in American territory and no longer free to them. Hoping to roll back this line, the British Government did not surrender posts in this northern country. Thomas Jefferson, Secretary of State in Washington's Cabinet, tried to settle the boundary dispute. He wrote to Benjamin Franklin to verify what map had been used at the peace table in Paris. Franklin, then 84 years old, replied in a letter from Philadelphia, dated April 8, 1790:

I am perfectly clear in the remembrance that the map we used in tracing the boundary was brought to the treaty by the Commissioners from England, and that it was the same that was published by Mitchell.

Not until 1842 was the boundary line between Canada and the United States definitely settled by Daniel Webster,

472

Secretary of State in President Tyler's Cabinet, and Lord Ashburton, Commissioner from Great Britain. Today, the northern border of Minnesota follows the same line that Franklin traced on Mitchell's map in Paris.

MINERALS ON THE SHORES OF THE GREAT LAKES

A JESUIT MISSIONARY to the Huron Indians wrote in his report for the year, 1653:

The earth contains iron ores, and certain rocks which melt like metal, with an appearance of having some vein of silver. There is a copper ore, which is very pure, and which has no need of passing through the fire.

In the records of the Detroit mission is the copy of a contract between a blacksmith and the director of the mission:

On the 16th of July, 1733, Father La Richardie and Jean Cecile entered into the following covenant: the said Cecile, toolmaker and armorer, binds himself to work at the forge of the said Reverend Father at Detroit, in the Huron Village, for all the needs of the French and of the natives, in all matters connected with this trade. The said Reverend Father will give the assistance of his servant, when he has one, to the said Cecile for chopping wood and building his charcoal furnaces.

The profits derived from the forge were divided between the mission and the blacksmith. Although this contract was for six years, with permission for Cecile to leave at will, after due notice, the blacksmith remained a longer time, expanding his ironworks.

One French missionary, skirting the shore of Lake Superior in a canoe, wrote about seeing a large mass of copper from which the natives cut chunks of the metal weighing from ten to twenty pounds. However, long before Indians inhabited this region, mound builders toiled in copper mines along the shore of this inland sea. Ten cartloads of their stone hammers, one weighing nearly forty pounds, have been found in mine pits they had abandoned centuries ago.

Commercial copper mining did not begin until after Michigan was admitted to the Union. To win statehood Congress demanded that Michigan cede a strip of territory along the southern boundary to Ohio, in exchange for the upper peninsula. A verse of a popular song told the feelings of the irate citizens:

But now the song they sing to us
Is — trade away that land,
For that poor, frozen country,
Beyond Lake Michigan.

A state geologist, Douglas Houghton, was one of the first appointments made by the first legislature of Michigan which convened in 1837. The discovery of

JACKSON PIT IRON MINE
NEGAUNEE, MICHIGAN — 1860

Iron ore found along Lake Superior was first mined with pick and shovel. In two-wheel carts drawn by horses, the ore was dumped into rail cars.

Michigan Historical Commission

valuable ores in "the howling wilderness on the shores of Lake Superior" might soothe the wounded feelings of the people over the loss of Toledo and surrounding territory. Houghton's report of copper deposits on the tip of the upper peninsula started a mining boom there in the early 1840's. In frail canoes and sturdy mackinaw boats the copper hunters searched the bays and inlets of Lake Superior.

Copper Harbor on the far northern tip of the peninsula was the meeting place of these eager adventurers in flannel shirts and slouch hats. The noise of blasting powder and clanging hammers echoed through the woods where mining was pushing aside the old-time quiet industries of hunting and fishing. Towns began to rise along the Eagle and Ontonogan Rivers and on the shore of Portage Lake. Canadian voyageurs sang as they rowed their boats, loaded with fortune hunters, over the waterways of the copper country. The Cliff Mine, discovered near the Eagle River in 1844, was the first in the United States to tap a vein of pure copper.

However, it was iron, more than copper, that turned the "poor frozen country" of the upper peninsula into a mint of wealth for the state of Michigan. Since the natives who used copper never learned to smelt iron, this metal was not mentioned in Indian legend. Although the French missionaries made some use of iron ore found near their settlements, the rich deposits of the northern ranges were unknown until 1844. In September of that year a surveyor for the Federal Government noticed that his solar compass, his own invention, was behaving in a strange manner. The queer antics of the needle denoted the presence of iron nearby. He showed the compass to the seven men in his party, two of whom were Indians.

"Boys," he said, "look around and see what you can find."

Within a mile of Teal Lake, with every turn of the sod the explorers found outcroppings of iron ore. The party went on its way surveying the country, making no attempt to realize any personal gains from the great discovery. Among the natives, to whom the surveyors spoke freely of finding ore, were a half-breed living at Sault Ste. Marie, and a Chippewa chief whose wigwam stood at the mouth of the Carp River. The following spring an adventurer from Jackson, Michigan, arrived at Sault Ste. Marie, looking for copper and silver in the upper peninsula. He chanced to meet the half-breed who told him about the Indian dwelling near the mouth of the Carp River where iron had been found.

The Indian guided the stranger and his party to two hills of iron ore, later called Jackson Mountain and Cleveland Mountain. Returning home with samples of ore, the adventurer organized the Jackson Mining Company. In February of 1848 in a forge on Carp River, this company produced the first iron made on the upper peninsula from Lake Superior ore. This iron was sold to a manufacturer who used it to make a ship's beam.

With cabins of miners, wood-choppers, and charcoal burners, a town sprouted around the Jackson mine and furnace. The people decided to give their camp an Indian name, Negaunee, meaning in Ojibwa, "I take the lead." The settlement around the Cleveland mine perched on the divide from which one could see the Carp River flowing toward Lake Superior and the Escanaba heading for Lake Michigan. It was named

Ishpeming, the Ojibwa word for a high elevation. The early French explorers were well remembered in naming the towns on the iron ranges. A little nest of log cabins and Indian huts was christened Marquette, after the Missionary who had explored the Mississippi River.

In 1852 it took four vessels to move a big shipment of iron ore, 152 tons in all, from Marquette to Sault Ste. Marie. Here, it was unloaded, hauled over the portage at the falls, and reloaded on other ships for the voyage to Erie, Pennsylvania. The ore was purchased by an iron works in Sharon, Pennsylvania, where it was made into bar iron, spikes, and nails of good quality. The freight cost was so high that it was almost prohibitive.

To get the Lake Superior ore to the furnaces in Ohio and Pennsylvania, a canal was needed to bypass the rapids in the St. Mary's River and to connect Lake Superior with Lake Huron. In 1852 Congress passed an act granting 750,000 acres of land in the state of Michigan to any company willing to build this canal 100 feet wide and 12 feet deep. Since land sold for as little as 25 cents an acre, bids would have been few without the privilege of selecting the allotted acres from any government lands offered for sale. The bid made by the St. Mary's Falls Ship Canal Company was accepted. On the first day of June in 1853, a young man only twenty-four years of age arrived at Sault Ste. Marie on a chartered steamer, the *Illinois* which was loaded with horses, lumber, tools, and supplies. His name was Charles T. Harvey, the man in charge of construction on the proposed canal. Three days later work gangs marched with their picks and shovels to the site. Harvey shoveled the first barrow of dirt,

wheeled it aside, and dumped it. The Soo canal had become a reality.

Labor was scarce in the wild unsettled country. The canal company dispatched agents to New York and other Atlantic ports to hire immigrants as soon as they landed, to buy railroad and steamship tickets for them, and to escort the laborers in gangs to Sault Ste. Marie. Sometimes as many as 2000 men were digging and hauling dirt within the space of a single mile. It took less than two years to hollow out a ditch 5700 feet long and 13 feet deep. On April 19, 1855, when Harvey opened the northern gate, the waters of Lake Superior gushed into the Sault Ste. Marie Canal. The brig *Columbia,* leaving Marquette on August 14, passed through this man-made waterway with the first shipment of Lake Superior ore. The cargo was delivered to a firm in Cleveland at a carrying charge of $2.75 per ton.

With cheap water transportation direct from the mines to the furnaces along the southern shores of Lake Erie and Lake Michigan, it proved to be more profitable to ship the ore than to smelt it into iron on the upper peninsula. The iron and steel works of the Great Lakes region and the Ohio Valley were near the coal fields of Pennsylvania, Virginia, and Kentucky.

Soon a network of railroads was built to transport ore to docks on Lake

LOCKS IN THE SOO CANAL, BUILT IN 1855

Michigan Historical Commission

**A HIGH SCHOOL BAND SERENADES
A WINNER AT SAULT STE. MARIE**

Since the "Soo" Canal was opened in 1855, captains of ore boats, from time to time, have vied for the honor of being the first skipper to navigate his ship through the Canal into the icy waters of Whitefish Bay in the spring of the year. Crossing Lake Superior and loading the first cargo of iron ore was a coveted title. The captain of the John T. Hutchinson, 14,000 ton ore carrier, won the race in 1949.

During World War II, 16,000 soldiers were sent to guard the "Soo" Canal through which passed most of the iron ore consumed by the steel industry manufacturing the tools of war.

Superior and from docks on Lake Erie and Lake Michigan in all directions to mills in Pennsylvania, Ohio, and neighboring states. As industry moved westward into the Great Lakes region, the demand grew for more iron to make more steel. Then came the greatest discovery of all, the immense iron ore deposits in upper Minnesota. The deposits were north of the St. Louis River in territory that had been won by Benjamin Franklin with the stroke of a pencil.

DULL RED DIRT
AND SHINY BLUE STEEL

LUMBERING PAVED THE WAY for mining in the Great Lakes region. The timber cruiser knew iron when he saw it and was usually able to fish a specimen of ore from his pocket at any time. Some of the richest mineral deposits were found accidentally by lumbermen.

During the severe winter of 1851, along the Escanaba River in the upper Michigan peninsula, a logger struck slate ore when shoveling dirt to coat an icy road. Where there is slate, there is probably iron not far away. Later, only a mile from this spot, the Princeton mine was located on a bed of ore lying near the surface of the ground.

In the lush forests along the Menominee River, separating Michigan from Wisconsin, a productive iron range was discovered by chance. It happened in the 1880's. Three prospectors, shouldering knapsacks with blankets and food, plunged into the wilderness one summer to search for ore. In crossing a dense cedar swamp one man became separated from his companions and lost his way. Emerging finally from the spongy bog, he climbed a hill and hallooed loudly. While waiting for his comrades to overtake him, he sat down on the knoll and began to probe the leaf mold with a small exploring pick. The point came out tipped with red hematite. Eagerly scraping away the leaves, he uncovered a vein of iron ore. Thus was discovered the rich deposits of the Menominee range in Michigan, extending across the border into Wisconsin.

On board the first vessel passing through the Soo Canal in 1855 was a sawyer from Chautauqua, New York, enroute to the head of Lake Superior to erect a mill. His name was Lewis H. Merritt. He settled with his large family of boys on a homestead near the place where the village of Duluth was soon to appear. Shortly after his arrival the sawyer made a trip into the woods to locate choice timber for his mill. Upon his return he told his sons that he believed there was iron on the Mesabi Range because his compass acted so strangely when he walked over the ground. During the summer months the Merritt boys sawed lumber in their father's mill. When snow covered the ground, they cruised the northern woods for timber, following their father's advice to keep one eye on the ground.

In the same year that President Lincoln was assassinated, the elder Merritt joined the gold rush to Lake Vermilion in the Arrowhead district of northern Minnesota. Over rough trails hundreds of miners and prospectors carried drills and supplies on their backs, only to learn that the yellowish mineral was "fool's gold." They had been deceived by pyrites, a compound of sulphur and iron ore that glitters like the precious metal. Thus was discovered another supply of iron ore, the Vermilion range deposit near the border of Canada. From this foolhardy gold rush Merritt returned with only a package of dull red dirt that he kept in his log cabin for many years. Every once in awhile he would open the box and sift the heavy grains of dirt through his fingers, wondering if the soil had iron in it. Not being a geologist, Merritt reasoned that iron might have been washed into the soil ages ago because the region had once been under water. His boys remembered what he had told them.

Ten years after their father's death, four of the sons and three nephews began prospecting for ore in the queer, rocky hills that the Indians called Mesabi. In thrusting a shovel only one length into the ground, they struck soft hematite, dull red in color, with only a mat of pine needles hiding it from view. Confident that they had made a great discovery, the Merritt Brothers, as they were called, set out to raise capital to mine the ore and to

A TRAIN OF LOADED ORE CARS ATOP THE DOCKS AT DULUTH, MINNESOTA

At the mines, iron ore was loaded into cars with huge shovels and then hauled by train to the docks in Duluth, a port on Lake Superior. There, the sandy ore was dumped from the cars into loading spouts to fill waiting carriers, long boats built for this trade on the Great Lakes.

Oliver-Iron Mining Company

transport it to mills in Pennsylvania, Ohio, Indiana, and Illinois. The public was slow to invest money in ore that was scarcely more than dust. Miners and geologists, sent to investigate the site, did not make favorable reports. The experts were looking for ore that was hard and firm, not soft and loose. They solemnly declared that the Mesabi ore was quite ordinary and at the time they were walking over millions of tons of sixty-six percent ore, almost as pure an iron as has ever been found.

In 1890 with little outside help, the Merritts opened the first Mesabi mine. Two years later, over their own railroad, the first shipment was hauled to docks on Lake Superior and shipped for trial in steel mills. When the reddish-brown dust turned out to be superior Bessemer ore, steel men rushed into the northern country to homestead and buy sections of land. The Mesabi Range, one hundred and ten miles long and one to three miles wide, has produced three times as much ore as the Marquette, Menominee, Gogebic, Vermilion, and Cayuna ranges put together. The place was well named by the Indians, Mesabi, the Chippewa word for giant, whence came the dull red dirt that made the shiny blue steel for industries established in the basin of the Great Lakes.

SUPPLIES AND MARKETS FOR STEEL

WITH RANGES near Lake Superior supplying iron ore, the southern shores of Lake Michigan became a natural setting for the steel industry and for manufacturers using the metal in their products. Steel became the main support of navigation on the Great Lakes. During the free season, a speck looming on the horizon might be an ore carrier bound for steel mills in northern Indiana and Illinois. In the distance, these long boats with smokestacks in the rear resemble Indian canoes with stovepipes.

Other ingredients needed to make steel were also found nearby. Limestone came from northeastern Michigan where cliffs of Dundee limestone hugged the shore of Lake Huron, from Kelly's Island in Lake Erie near the site of Perry's victory, and from Marblehead on the Ohio shore. Water transportation from mine to mill encouraged location of steel plants in the region of the Great Lakes. Coal, another necessity, was abundant in Pennsylvania, Kentucky and West Virginia, but much of it was shipped by rail to the mills.

Water played a large part in the developing industry. Steel works need plenty of water and acres of ground. A desolate waste of sand dunes and stagnant pools along the southwestern shore of Lake Michigan was redeemed by the steel producers. Swamps were drained, canals were dug, lake front was filled in, harbors were dredged, and the Calumet River was deepened for navigation of the huge lake freighters and ore carriers.

The labor supply, too, favored this location near the rapidly growing city of Chicago. As steel employees wanted to live within a reasonable distance and not spend too much time going to and from their work, towns grew into cities around the mills. In less than twenty years, the city of Gary, Indiana rose from the dunes and marshes along the Michigan shore. The suburbs of Chicago crept steadily southward.

Located in the heart of the continent,

the Chicago area attracted manufacturers of steel products wanting to locate near sources of supplies. Markets were easy to reach from Chicago, and this was an added inducement to manufacturers. The first steel plant in the area was built to supply rails for lines leading out of Chicago in all directions. Being a transportation center for boats and trains, the city was a natural place to make locomotives, coaches, freight cars, wheels and all kinds of railroad equipment. Trade on the Great Lakes was responsible for the growth of the shipbuilding industry in Chicago. Settlement of the rich prairie lands created a demand for plows, reapers, cultivators and every kind of farm implement from a hoe to a harvester. Hogs, cattle, and sheep from midwestern farms supplied the developing meat-packing industry in centrally located Chicago. The canning industry bought land for packing meats, fruits and vegetables.

Before long, structural steel was needed for skyscrapers rising along Michigan Boulevard, and for the factories being started in smaller towns in the Middle West. Then came an entirely new industry to patronize the steel industry. It was a new invention destined to revolutionize transportation — the automobile. The new business centered in Detroit and vicinity, near steel plants in Pittsburgh and on the shores of Lake Michigan.

Benjamin Franklin had predicted that the time would come when future generations of Americans would feel that his greatest patriotic service to the country was rendered at the peace table in Paris in 1783, where the new-born nation gained the rich iron deposits in northern Minnesota. Lake Superior mines furnished most of the iron ore that made the steel for armaments in two world wars. From 1940 to 1945 steel plants in the United States consumed 482,000,000 gross tons of iron ore from this northern mining area. Much of it came from the fabulous Mesabi Range, won through an error in the Mitchell map.

The nation's two world wars within twenty-five years cut deeply into the supply of high-grade iron ore left in the Lake Superior region. While new processes were being developed to use lower-grade ore, steel companies were searching for iron deposits elsewhere.

IRON DEPOSITS ARE DISCOVERED IN THE WESTERN HEMISPHERE

STEEL COMPANIES began to explore in other countries of the Western Hemisphere for new iron deposits. Iron of good quality exists in Labrador, where open-pit mining is possible for only about six months out of the year. Winters are

CERRO BOLIVAR — MOUNTAIN OF IRON ORE IN VENEZUELA

This dome of rich iron ore was located 150 miles east of the mouth of the Orinoco River. "Bolivar's Hill" is a rounded dome of reddish earth, six miles long, rising 1800 feet above grasslands in sparsely settled country. It is one of the richest deposits of high-grade iron ore ever found.

United States Steel Corporation

Orinoco Mining Company

OPEN-PIT MINING OF CERRO BOLIVAR

Huge electric shovels take big bites of iron ore from man-made cliffs to fill trains of cars on the railroad tracks winding around the mountain on man-made ledges.

long and severe in this far northern country. However, since the opening of the St. Lawrence Seaway, more iron ore from eastern Canada is being used in steel plants in the region of the Great Lakes. Much of this ore still enters through Atlantic ports.

Men searching for ore turned to South America. In 1939 a rubber tree hunter discovered iron ores six miles from the Orinoco River, near the place where the stream branches to flow through its wide delta to the Atlantic Ocean. Mining engineers and geologists hacked their way through country along the Orinoco never visited before except by native Indians and rubber hunters. The search in the grasslands with scattered trees was made by air. Pictures were taken with aerial cameras of an area of about 11,000 square miles in Venezuela. These photographs were divided into sections and enlarged for study of the rock formations and the rolling hills.

Engineers and scientists poring over these pictures of the landscape noticed a dark rounded hill which looked as if it might have iron deposits. Traveling in a jeep and on foot over rugged ground, two ore hunters reached the hill and climbed it on April 4, 1947. They found huge outcrops of iron all over the hill. When they reported their rich find, drills were moved in as fast as roads could be blasted out of the ore deposits. Deep drilling proved that the rounded dome was made of iron, more than half a billion tons of high grade open-pit ore.

After arrangements had been made to acquire the necessary amount of territory, and to pay taxes to the government of Venezuela, work began. To ship this ore to steel mills in the United States, it was necessary to dredge channels for ore carriers, span rivers with bridges, lay tracks of rails for hauling ore and supplies, construct good roads for trucks and tractors, and build an airfield for landing big planes. Permission was granted by the Venezuelan government to rename the dome-shaped mountain, "Cerro Bolivar" (Bolivar's Hill), in honor of the great liberator born in that country. His armies had camped in this area preparing for the daring march across the Andes to Bogota, Colombia. In 1951, construction began on a steel mill along the bank of the Delaware River near Trenton, New Jersey. Today, huge ore carriers unload the treasure of Cerro Bolivar on the docks of this steel plant, located for water transportation from mine to mill.

STEEL AFFECTS
THE PATTERN OF INDUSTRY

IRON WAS LITTLE BUSINESS. In places where trees provided charcoal for fuel and ore lay buried near the surface of the ground, it took only a small amount of capital to engage in the iron business. A new steel age arrived with the converters developed by both Kelly and Bessemer at about the same time, one in the United States and the other in England. What did the ironmasters do? Owners of large ironworks either financed their own steelmaking plants, or merged with other companies to raise enough capital to enter the steel business. The little man kept his furnace going as long as he could sell his wares, and then put out the fire, leaving his works to rust in the sun and rain.

Steel was big business. New inventions for making steel and new products to use the metal sometimes rendered a plant obsolete in a short time. Changes came so fast that steel became a race of "the survival of the fittest." By the year 1900, sixty-five percent of the 10,000,000 tons of steel was produced by the Bessemer process, and thirty percent of this amount was rolled into rails. Thirty-seven years later, when the output was 54,000,000 tons, only five percent was purchased by the railroads. Even the Bessemer process has been largely replaced by newer methods of making steel. Customers want a certain kind of the metal for a certain product. To please them, ingredients of steel are measured as carefully as a housewife mixes a cake. New inventions create new products that develop new industries that bring new customers to the steel mills. Factory orders may include anything from a toy to a truck. Industry in the United States is constantly renewed and expanded by new inventions.

PART TEN

The Nation Moves
Toward Industrialization

United States Immigration and Naturalization Service

ALIENS ENTERING ELLIS ISLAND STATION — 1900

MILLIONS OF EUROPEANS SOUGHT OPPORTUNITY IN THE UNITED STATES

Scandinavian farmers settled in the northern states of the Central Plains, and in the region of the Great Lakes. Others, including Finns, went farther west to cut timber in the forests of Washington and Oregon, and to enter the fishing industry of the Pacific Coast. Many families from Sweden, Norway and Denmark settled in Chicago, Minneapolis, and Seattle.

A large number of immigrants from Russia, Poland, Hungary and other countries of eastern Europe were Jews. Being a town people, they remained in the large cities, especially New York. Many Poles, Hungarians, and Bohemians sought jobs in mills and mines. Some of the farmers among them made their new homes on the prairie lands west of the Mississippi River.

Many immigrants from the Mediterranean countries — Italy, France, Portugal, Greece and Spain — settled in the manufacturing states of the North Atlantic Coast. Some found their way to regions in the United States where they could follow the same occupations they had in the old country. French and Italians planted vineyards in the wine-producing states. Portuguese fishermen found employment in the growing fish-canning industry of the Gulf region and the Pacific Coast. Greeks settled largely in cities like New York, Chicago, and Cleveland. Spaniards tended to seek places where their native language was spoken.

Chinese junks crossed the Pacific Ocean to North America before Columbus came, according to historians, and all of the Chinese sailors did not return to their homeland. After the Europeans arrived and claimed the country, not many Orientals were welcomed to settle among them. Asiatic peoples who came first as laborers to work the mines, build the railroads, and plant the crops, remained in the new land. Today, their descendants are citizens of the United States, living mainly in the Pacific region.

Chapter 25

Inventions Contribute to National Growth

MESSAGES BY WIRE

UNDER A FORM of government granting freedom of opportunity, men were able to dream, to experiment, and to produce. Men's dreams and work made this nation a land of invention. According to records in the patent office, inventors were numerous but only a few found fame and fortune. Among them were the inventors in communication.

Samuel F.B. Morse was born in 1791, in a house at the foot of Breed's Hill (where the battle of Bunker Hill actually took place). Though his curiosity about electricity was aroused when he entered college at the age of fourteen, a year later his talent and interest in art led him to decorate a room in his father's house, with a picture of the family. Samuel liked best to paint historical scenes, but no one would buy them. While visiting in the country towns of New Hampshire and Vermont he turned to painting portraits, and these he did sell for $15 apiece. Before long the demand for Samuel's portraits was so great that he could charge as much as $60 for a picture. In 1825 the authorities of New York City commissioned Morse to paint a full-length portrait of Lafayette

who was making a triumphal tour of the United States in that year.

While painting and teaching, Morse spent his spare time tinkering with a machine to send electric current along a wire and with an instrument to interrupt the current and make a spark. In this way signs could be made into an alphabet and messages could be transmitted. In fact Morse spent so much time with his invention that his art suffered and he became poor. It was a great disappointment, however, that turned him away from his profession and made him an inventor. Commissions were offered to American artists to paint pictures for panels in the capitol at Washington. Being president of the National Academy of Design, Morse felt he should be engaged as one of the artists to decorate the capitol. He was not among those selected.

From an old canvas frame, the wheels of a clock, three wooden drums, a pencil, some paper, carpet binding, a wooden crank, an electro-magnet, and a few more items, Morse put together his first telegraph instrument. He worked in a room of the University of the City of New York where he was a professor in design.

Not until one of his students, Alfred

484

Vail, managed to obtain for Morse some money in exchange for a one-fourth interest in the project, was Morse able to build an instrument to place on exhibit and try to prove its worth. Finally, he was able to present his plan in Congress. He asked for an appropriation to build the first telegraph line between Washington and Baltimore. At first the legislators were skeptical and insisted upon proof that messages could be sent over a wire. On the last day of the session on March 3, 1842, five minutes before Congress adjourned, the Senate voted $30,000 to build the first telegraph line. Morse, weary from waiting all day, had gone home at twilight, thinking that all hope was gone. As he came down to breakfast the next morning, the daughter of the Commissioner of Patents arrived to tell him that her father had stayed until Congress closed, and that the telegraph bill was the last one passed. Morse promised the young lady that she would have the honor of sending the first message when the line was opened officially.

Morse took advantage of the popular interest in the convention of the Whig Party meeting in Baltimore to prove the worth of the telegraph. In a letter to his brother, Sidney, dated May 7, 1844 he wrote:

"You will see by the papers that the Telegraph is in successful operation for twenty-two miles, to the junction of the Annapolis road with the Baltimore and Washington road. The nomination of Mr. Frelinghuysen as Vice President was written, sent on, and the receipt acknowledged back in two minutes and one second, a distance of forty-four miles. The news was spread all over Washington one hour and four minutes before the cars containing the news by express arrived."

Later, when the key clicked the choice of the Whig Party for President, the man was Henry Clay whose portrait Morse had painted. Although Henry Clay was the first man whose nomination for President came over a wire, his Democratic opponent, James K. Polk, won the election.

On the twenty-fourth of May in 1844, friends of Morse assembled in the chamber of the Supreme Court in Washington to witness the official test of the new telegraph. Miss Ellsworth, daughter of Morse's friend, was there with the first message, suggested by her mother — WHAT HATH GOD WROUGHT! At the station in Baltimore ten men and one boy sat silently and tensely, awaiting a signal. When the instrument clicked, the operator, Alfred Vail, touched his lips with his fingers and the watchers scarcely breathed. The message came in and Vail touched the key, sending it back to Washington. As the use of the telegraph spread to foreign countries, honors were poured upon Morse, as a benefactor of all mankind.

About two years before the first telegraph line was completed on land, Morse began to experiment with a cable to carry messages under water. On a moonlit night, October 18, 1842, he unreeled nearly two miles of wire, insulated with hemp coated with pitch, tar, and rubber, from lower New York City to a small island. The next morning a notice appeared in a New York paper that Morse would exhibit his telegraph by sending messages under water to a station on Governor's Island. The inventor arrived early to prepare for the event and found seven vessels lying along the line of his submerged cable. In testing the wire he was able to send a signal or two, but the messages suddenly ended. One of the ships in pulling up its anchor caught the

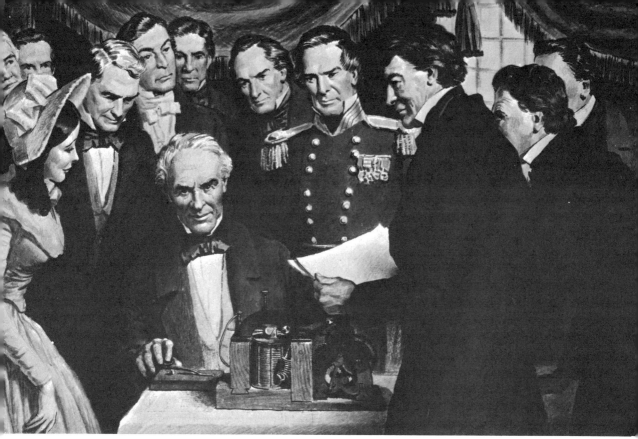

SAMUEL F.B. MORSE SENDS FIRST PUBLIC TELEGRAM

The inventor asked a few friends to witness the sending of the first public telegram from the Supreme Court Chamber in Washington to Alfred Vail, forty miles away in Baltimore.

The girl is Annie Ellsworth to whom was given the honor of selecting the first official message. With dots and dashes, Morse ticked the words she chose — WHAT HATH GOD WROUGHT. This practical use of electricity was made on May 24, 1844.

cable. Not knowing what the strange line was, sailors pulled in about 200 feet of it and then cut it off, carrying it away with them. The exhibit failed and the crowd jeered. This first attempt, however, stirred the idea of bringing Europe and the Western Hemisphere closer together with telegraph service.

The laying of an Atlantic cable was undertaken by a wealthy New York business man, Cyrus W. Field, who was neither a scientist nor an inventor.

Although he was not the first man to dream of laying an underwater cable from one hemisphere to another, he was the first one to make up his mind to do it. In 1856 the Atlantic Telegraph Company was organized "to continue the existing line of the New York, Newfoundland, and London Telegraph Company to Ireland, by making or causing to be made a submarine cable for the Atlantic." Field, himself, subscribed $500,000 of the $1,750,000 that had to be raised before work could begin on laying a cable from Trinity Bay in Newfoundland to Valentia in Ireland. The plan was outlined by Field, to haul the cable on two ships, to meet in midocean where they would splice the cable and then to go in opposite directions. After many breaks and disappointments, the *Agamemnon* headed west toward Newfoundland and the *Niagara* started east toward Ireland. There was great excitement when the cables were pulled ashore at both ends in August of 1858. It was a fleeting triumph. In a few weeks the cable stopped working and all was lost.

Before another effort was prepared, war broke out between the North and the South. However, during the conflict, Field was busy with plans to try again when he could get enough support. In January, 1863 Field wrote in a letter to a friend:

Some days I have worked from before eight in the morning until after ten at night to obtain subscriptions to the Atlantic Telegraph Company.

By the time the war ended in the spring of 1865, cable had been manufactured and the *Great Eastern* was chartered to lay it across the Atlantic. The English were as enthusiastic about the project of a telegraph line across the ocean as were the Americans. A news report from Valentia Island off the coast of Ireland was printed with the date line of July 24th. It read as follows:

Before this reaches the public, the *Great Eastern*, if all goes well, will already have laid some 300 miles of the Atlantic cable.

The crew published *The Atlantic Telegraph* on board the cable ship but the paper did not long survive. On the second of August while Field was on watch, the cable broke. Pale but composed, he announced to his working partners, "The cable has parted and gone overboard."

Several days later, he wrote to his family explaining the disaster:

Spent nine days in grappling; used up all wire, rope; nothing left, so obliged to return to England. Three times cable was caught and hauled up for more than three-quarters of a mile from bed of ocean.

In London another company was formed by ten men who sat around a table discussing help for Field. When each one put down 10,000 pounds, the Anglo American Telegraph Company took over the task of laying the cable.

Although the new company was formed only on March 1, 1866, the messages were speeding from continent to continent over the underwater telegraph about five months later. On the twenty-seventh of July, the western end of the cable was landed on the shore of Trinity Bay in Newfoundland and the eastern end on the Irish coast. The national rejoicing at the successful completion of the first ocean cable is expressed in a poem by John Greenleaf Whittier. The last stanza expressed the hope that new means of rapid communication would bring the people of the world together to live in peace:

And or e in heart, as one in blood,
  Shall all her peoples be;
The hands of human brotherhood
  Are clasped beneath the sea.

Both Morse and Field persevered through hardships and disappointments because they believed their work would benefit mankind.

TALKING OVER THE WIRE

ANOTHER MEANS of wire communication developed from the experiments of Alexander Graham Bell who taught deaf children with a method of "invisible speech" evolved by his father. Before migrating to the United States the Bell family of Edinburgh, Scotland had been known as elocutionists (public speakers). Alexander, like his father and grandfather, studied the human voice and taught the deaf to speak. Two well-to-do men, one a leather merchant and the other a lawyer, were so impressed with Bell's lectures, sponsored by the board of education in Boston, that they engaged him as a private tutor for their deaf children, a girl and a boy. With their encouragement Bell opened a school for the deaf in that city.

When not occupied with teaching, Bell was busy experimenting with sound, hoping to discover new ways of helping deaf children to talk and to understand speech. The fathers of his two private pupils took an interest in the young teacher's experiments and provided him with needed supplies for his projects. The grandmother of the small boy invited Bell to live in her roomy house in Salem. Here he could teach the lad in the evening after returning on the train from his school in Boston. Since Bell could not be satisfied away from his experiments, she kindly offered the basement of her house for his use as a laboratory.

As a boy Bell had played the piano and he had wanted to be a musician. He first experimented with transmitting the tones of the scale over a wire — a musical telegraph. Then it occurred to him that the spoken word might be sent over an electrical wire. Since Bell knew little about electricity, his two patrons hired a young mechanic for nine dollars a week to assist him and moved his laboratory to the attic of the electrical shop where the electrician was employed. Here Thomas A. Watson, the assistant, spent his evenings and sometimes most of the night with the inventor.

As the experiments progressed, Bell quit teaching and gave all his time to this endeavor. He rented two rooms in an attic for living quarters and laboratory combined, where he could work privately. In these stuffy upstairs rooms on a hot June day in 1875, a faint sound passed over the wire while Watson was sending in one room and Bell was receiving in the other. Though only a feeble wail, this was the birth of the telephone. After forty weeks spent in improving the invention, Bell spoke over a wire to his helper in the next room on the evening of March 10, 1876.

"Mr. Watson, come here. I want you!" he said.

Bell's voice was clear and natural, but there was such a note of alarm in it that the assistant rushed into the room. He discovered that Bell had spilled some acid on his clothes and was actually calling for help. The damage was soon forgotten, however, in the joy the men experienced talking over the wire.

It was the year when the United States was celebrating the one hundredth anniversary of independence with the Centennial Exposition in Philadelphia. Needing money for food and rent, Bell had returned to teaching deaf children in Boston. When he decided to show his "toy," it was too late to find space in the electrical building. Finally, the telephone was placed on a table under a stairway among the school exhibits from Massachusetts. Hubbard, the lawyer, whose daughter was Bell's pupil and later his wife, secured a patent for the inventor, barely in time to save his telephone. While at the exposition Hubbard sent Bell a telegram notifying him that the judges were scheduled to reach his exhibit on June 25. At the last minute Bell decided to go to Philadelphia although school examinations were at hand. He realized that his telephone would receive scant attention if he were not there to demonstrate it.

It was Sunday when the gates were closed to the general public, but distinguished visitors were admitted. On this day Dom Pedro II, Emperor of Brazil, his Empress, and their retinue were touring the buildings and grounds of the Centennial Exposition. The royal guests examined the products and inventions as eagerly as children and showed their enthusiasm to the judges. Late on the hot, humid Sunday, near closing time, the judges arrived at the exhibit next to Bell's. They announced that one would be the last for that day. As the judges turned to leave, Dom Pedro spied the teacher, whose school for the deaf he had visited in Boston. Greeting Bell with a hearty handshake, the genial emperor inquired why he was there. The inventor showed his instrument, explaining that he could talk with His Majesty over a wire, if he wished. Since Dom Pedro showed much interest in the apparatus, the judges were obliged to do likewise as a matter of courtesy to their royal guest. Aleck hurried to the transmitter, five hundred feet away. While the members of the party passed the receiver from ear to ear, Bell turned elocutionist and recited Hamlet's famous soliloquy, "To be or not to be."

Dom Pedro listened with astonishment.

"It talks!" he exclaimed.

"It is the most marvelous thing I have seen in America," remarked a British scientist.

The "talking wire" became a sensation. Although many inventions are combined in modern telephone equipment, the original idea of Alexander Graham Bell is still a basic principle in transmitting sound over wires. Like the telegraph which sent signals under water, the telephone crossed the oceans to make possible conversation between persons in remote corners of the globe.

SIGNALS THROUGH THE AIR

FEW ACHIEVEMENTS OF SCIENCE thrill people more than a new means of communication. Soon after the first message was sent over a wire by Morse, experimentors began to send messages without wires. Although several inventors made progress, Marconi was the man who made wireless telegraphy operate successfully. Unlike most inventors Guglielmo Marconi was born rich, the son of an Italian father and an Irish mother. As a boy, Guglielmo did not go to schools with other children. He was instructed by a private tutor, whether his family was at home on the country estate at Pontecchio or in the town house at Bologna, Italy.

It was at the Villa Griffone in the country, that Marconi carried on his experiments to send signals through the air. While he worked, the door of his shop on the third floor was locked to all except his mother, to whom he explained his experiments. Even when she did not know what he was talking about, she listened and encouraged him in his efforts.

489

Sometimes the sons of peasant farmers living on his father's estate were seen burying copper plates in the ground, climbing trees with strange apparatus, and erecting poles in odd places. His two brothers often helped him to string wires through the terraced garden, across the spacious lawn, and down into the chestnut grove. The elder Marconi was a bit perplexed because his youngest son spent so much time in the attic and so little in the family circle.

"What IS he doing?" his father asked his mother one evening.

"His idea," she answered proudly, "is to send signals, even voices, through the air."

One autumn day in 1894, when Marconi was twenty years of age, he invited his parents to his attic workshop to show them the progress he had made on his experiments. He pressed a button and rang a bell on the first floor of the house without the aid of connecting wires. As further proof the father asked his son to remain in the attic and send the Morse signal for the letter "S" to the receiver on the lawn, a distance from the house. When the machine outdoors tapped three dots, he was convinced that Guglielmo's experiments had resulted in wireless telegraphy.

On the twelfth of December in 1901 Marconi and his assistants were huddled in a station on Signal Hill, St. John's, Nova Scotia. Outside the wind was blowing a gale and a man was scarcely able to stand upright. Inside the anxious watchers could barely hear one another speak with the rattle of icy rain on the sheet iron roof. The masts stood against the storm and a kite remained aloft to catch the signal from the Cornish coast of England — if it came that way. The letter "S" was chosen because it is easy to transmit. Marconi sat tensely with an earphone clasped on his head for a long time past the hour set for the test of wireless across the ocean. Finally, he heard three dots — and again. When he was sure, he passed the earphone to his assistants. Although the signals died out from time to time, they were heard quite often on that day and the next, across 1700 miles of water. Later it was agreed among nations that the wireless distress signal for ships at sea would be SOS — three dots, three dashes, three dots.

Wireless telegraphy was one of the marvels at the World's Fair in St. Louis in 1904. It created as much excitement as the telephone when that invention had been exhibited in Philadelphia in 1876. In June of 1910, the United States Radio Act was passed, making it unlawful for any ship carrying more than fifty persons to leave port without wireless equipment and a trained operator, if the vessel was bound for a harbor two hundred miles away. Although wireless had been credited with saving lives at sea before the *Titanic* struck an iceberg in the North Atlantic in April, 1912, the dramatic rescue of 700 persons on that sinking vessel proved the value of Marconi's invention to the entire world. By 1914 the leading maritime nations had laws requiring even cargo vessels to carry wireless apparatus and a licensed operator for the safety of the crew. The outbreak of war in 1914 was flashed around the world by wire.

In that same year a few months before war began, two officers on separate vessels forty-five miles apart held a conversation by radio-telephone. Marconi predicted at the time that the day was near when the human voice would cross the Atlantic on the air waves.

INVENTIONS LIGHTEN LABOR

IN THE SAME YEAR that Samuel F.B. Morse sent his famous message over the first telegraph line, Elias Howe completed a working model of a sewing machine. Being one of eight children in the family of a farmer and miller, Elias began at the age of six to help with chores. He would stick wire teeth through leather straps used for carding cottons. When he was eleven years old, he tried farm work but failed because he was lame and not strong. He returned to his father's mill where he took an interest in machinery, when he was not busy grinding flour. A friend who had visited Lowell, Massachusetts, the first real industrial city in the nation, told Elias about the wonderful machinery he had seen in the mills there. Elias went to Lowell when he was sixteen and found employment in the mills where machines were doing the work of hands. When the Panic of 1837 struck, the mills were forced to cut down production. Elias found new employment in a machine shop in Cambridge, Massachusetts.

Since Howe's earnings were small, and there were three small children to support, his wife did sewing to add a little cash to the family income. Because this labor was poorly paid and his wife sewed late at night, Howe began to work on a machine which she could use to lighten her burden. Although he completed a working model in October of 1844, he lacked the money to buy the metals to make the kind of machine which he could exhibit to prove the worth of his invention. A coal and wood dealer in Cambridge, who had a little money saved, offered to give Howe's family board and room and advance $500 for materials to construct a sewing machine. In exchange the dealer would have half ownership in the patent if Howe succeeded in procuring one. By the middle of May in the following year, 1845, the machine was completed. Before the end of the year Howe secured his first patent and was ready to show his invention to the public.

Then followed years of disappointment. Tailors refused to buy the sewing machine. It would ruin their trade, they said. The more Howe improved it and the better it sewed, the more tailors resisted it. Few persons were willing to invest money to manufacture it. His partner became discouraged and withdrew, leaving Howe to return with his family to his father's house. He moved with his family to England, where he thought he could interest someone in helping him to market his invention. He soon sent his family back home while he stayed on hoping to gain financial help. Failing in this he arrived in Boston to learn that his wife was dying from tuberculosis. This was Howe's dark hour.

After his machine had been copied and manufactured by Englishmen and its value was established, Howe found men willing to advance money to defend his patent and force the manufacturers to pay him royalties. The demand for his sewing machine grew so rapidly, for both home and factory, that his royalties grew in six years from $300 to $200,000. Howe welcomed the inventions of other men to improve his machine and even helped some of them to obtain their patents. The invention of the sewing machine made possible the making of wearing apparel in factories. It gave rise to the garment industry which in turn provided employment for thousands of men and women.

While the sewing machine was finding

its way into farmer's homes, other labor-saving machines were being invented to lighten the burden of toil in the field. The westward migration created a demand for improved farm tools. In a new country where there was much work to be done and not enough workmen to do it, people were eager for any machinery that saved labor and speeded the production of food. In the New England states hundreds of families were leaving the country to work for wages in the mill towns. The rise of manufacturing in the East increased the demand for flour, corn meal, pork, cheese, and all kinds of farm produce. The simple tools that were good enough on the small, sandy farms of New Hampshire and Vermont became dwarfed and puny implements on the vast prairies of the Middle West.

In 1836 the lure of the West brought to this region a blacksmith, skilled in making shovels, hoes, and pitchforks, and in repairing all kinds of iron tools. He was John Deere. He came from Vermont, having traveled the length of the Erie Canal on a packet boat pulled by mules walking the towpath on the bank of the big ditch. At Buffalo he boarded a lake steamer for the voyage to Chicago. The blacksmith did not linger long in the marshy settlement with about 400 houses and 75 stores which sold clothes, food, and drink to travelers heading west. Deere continued his journey to settle among Vermonters in the frontier village of Grand Detour on the Rock River in northwestern Illinois. In his pocket he had $73.73 with which to go into business.

He built a forge from stones picked up along the river, using clay for mortar. He filled his first order, the repair of a broken shaft in a sawmill nearby. With the nearest blacksmith forty miles away, Deere, from the first, had all the work he could handle. Next door to his shop he built a five-room frame house and sent for his wife and five children. John Deere might have been any one of the thousands of unknown settlers who went west, had he remained a blacksmith and not become an inventor.

While shoeing oxen and mending chains, Deere overheard the farmers talk about their difficulties in plowing through the sticky soil of the prairie. The earth clung to the plow like balled snow, forcing the farmer to spend more time cleaning off the muck than turning furrows in his field. For the prairie they needed a plow that scoured. The blacksmith from Vermont began to fashion such a plow from a broken circular saw he found on the floor of a neighbor's sawmill. It was made of Sheffield steel. This metal was hard to obtain on the frontier. From this scrap of steel he shaped and reshaped the plowshare to cut through the black earth and slice the furrows without muck clinging to the blade.

The day came to make the test in a field while unbelieving farmers trudged behind the inventor. While the farmer, in whose field the trial was made, guided the horse pulling the steel plow, soil curled from the moldboard in a smooth furrow. One furrow was not enough to convince the watchers. Turning the horse, Deere guided his plow down another furrow, just as neat as the first one, proving that he had invented "a plow that scours." Then he gave the plow to the farmer who had furnished the land and the horse for the test. Others had taken a turn and felt the plowshare biting deep into the gummy soil. In the following year, 1838, the blacksmith from Vermont fashioned three steel plows in his spare time. In 1842 he sold nearly a hundred

JOHN DEERE TESTING HIS PLOW

**John Deere, a blacksmith, tested his plow in a field. He proved that he had shaped
a steel plowshare that could cut a clean furrow through the sticky soil of the prairie.**

implements by allowing settlers to take the plows to their farms to try them out before buying. The inventor of the first steel plow moved to Moline, Illinois, to take advantage of the steamboat traffic and started a factory. Plowmen followed, turning the buffalo range on the western prairie into fields of grain.

Inventions come when a need arises for them. From another blacksmith shop, this time it was in Virginia, came the reaper to cut the grain on the boundless prairie. In 1831 Cyrus Hall McCormick, then twenty-two years of age, completed a working model of a mechanical reaper in the blacksmith shop on his father's farm, Walnut Grove in western Virginia. On a hot July day young McCormick invited his neighbors to Walnut Grove for a demonstration of his wheat-cutting machine, destined to free laborers in the harvest from the sickle and the scythe. Although the grain fell in waves as horses pulled the reaper, the inventor saw the need for improvements before asking for a patent. Like John Deere, who made a

493

plow and set it outside his shop for passersby to see, McCormick built one reaper at a time and sold it to a neighbor. He also believed in field trials to prove the worth of his invention. He, too, went to the Middle West.

The reaper was not well suited to the rolling landscape of western Virginia but the machine performed successfully on the level lands of the western prairie. For a factory site McCormick selected the fast-growing village of Chicago which had less than one hundred inhabitants in 1832. It grew from three to four thousand only three years later. A news item of May 16, 1835, stated:

Chicago has one of the finest harbors on Lake Michigan, 20 to 25 feet of water in front of the town. The town will command the trade of the Illinois River and the Mississippi by means of the canal, and the west and east by the navigation of the lakes. It is destined to be the New Orleans of the west.

When McCormick moved to Chicago in 1847, the population of the town was 17,000. The place was uninviting. Broken plank roads threaded through the swampy townsite, few streets were paved, and the houses were small. The canal was about to be opened. Immigrants were flocking into the village, arriving by the hundreds on the lake steamers from Buffalo. Chicago was a place of opportunity, located in the heart of fertile lands awaiting the reaper for development. In a small brick factory a new industry was established in 1848. Thirty-three men were employed and ten of these were blacksmiths. The output was 778 reapers, but twice as many were built in 1849, the year of the California gold rush. When people were leaving their farms to try their luck in mining gold, McCormick advertised his reaper as a

labor-saving machine that would save the harvest of grain that might be lost for lack of men to swing the scythes. The mechanical reaper had a large share in making the central part of the United States one of the great wheat regions of the world. This invention was merely the beginning of labor-saving machines for use on the farm.

RUBBER PUT THE NATION ON WHEELS

WHILE JOHN DEERE was forging steel plows and Cyrus McCormick was building reapers, Charles Goodyear was seeking a way to "cure" India rubber. In time, Goodyear's experiments put tractors in the fields to pull disc plows and harvester-threshers which developed from the early inventions of Deere and McCormick. Today the treads of rubber tires trace a geometric pattern along the moist, black furrows on many farms.

Indians living along the Amazon River in South America tapped certain trees in the forests to obtain sap from which they made bottles and rough shoes. Hence, the gummy substance came to be called Indian rubber or India rubber. In 1823 a Boston merchant bought five hundred pairs of rubber shoes, made by the natives of Para, and sold them. The Portuguese settlers in Brazil, for some time, had been manufacturing waterproof shoes, boots, hats, and cloaks from rubber to afford comfort during the rainy season. However, the rubber shoes were not practical in a climate with extremes of heat and cold. The rubber hardened in winter and melted in summer.

A struggle, lasting twenty-five years,

began in 1834 when a hardware merchant in Philadelphia, out of curiosity, bought a life-preserver made of the substance. The storekeeper was Charles Goodyear, then in his thirty-fifth year and in poor health. He moved to Massachusetts to use the abandoned works of an India rubber company in Roxbury, where he succeeded in making articles with such a smooth, dry surface that he secured an order from the Government for a hundred and fifty rubber mail bags. The handles began to fall off before delivery as coloring matter had caused the gum to decompose.

While Goodyear was describing the merits of sulfur-cured India rubber to a few relatives and friends on a winter evening, a piece accidentally fell from his hand onto a red hot stove. It shrivelled like leather but did not dissolve. He nailed the sample outdoors in the cold. When it was still flexible the next morning, Goodyear knew that he had made a discovery. This happened in Woburn, Massachusetts, where the inventor had moved to use another factory for his experiments. Five years later, in 1844, Goodyear patented his process for vulcanizing rubber and started a factory in Naugatuck, Connecticut.

Like many other inventors he had difficulty holding his patent and was sued in the courts. Six years after patenting his process, shoe manufacturers depending upon it paid Daniel Webster, the famous lawyer and brilliant orator, the sum of $25,000 to defend the rights of Goodyear to his patent for vulcanizing rubber. Goodyear was cheated out of the fortune which might have been won by his discovery. He was not a good business man. During his lifetime he served jail sentences for debt and still a debtor, he died in July of 1860, leaving his great discovery for mankind.

Although factories sprang up in many towns to make garments, life preservers, and numerous articles from rubber, the product did not become a big factor in the business world until it was used in the field of transportation. First, wheels of carriages, buggies, and bicycles were fitted with rubber tires, but it was the automobile that built the big rubber industry.

While travelers were still depending upon vehicles drawn by animals, inventors were experimenting with the horseless carriage, propelled by steam. Although some steam cars were built in the United States and other countries, the real automobile waited for gasoline, rubber, and roads.

Shortly after Goodyear vulcanized rubber in 1839, an Englishman patented the principle of the pneumatic tire. Gasoline was developed soon after the Drake well in Titusville, Pennsylvania, began pumping oil in 1859. It took some years to discover its use for motor fuel. The first application for a patent on a gasoline motor to propel a road vehicle was filed in 1879. However, to the bicycle goes the credit for road improvement which prepared the way for the horseless carriage. The bicycle was a social vehicle and every town had its cycle club. On Sunday afternoons parties of cyclists pedaled miles into the country to enjoy the great outdoors. Rubber tires for bicycles and carriage wheels started the tire industry in a small way, by establishing plants that were in operation when the demand arrived for automobile tires. Cyclists wanted smooth tracks for their wheels and worked for the improvement of roads. The bicycle made highways more important to more people than ever before and a roadminded public welcomed the advent of the automobile.

Charles E. Duryea of Springfield, Massachusetts is credited with building the first American-made gasoline car that actually ran. He won the first automobile race held in this country on Thanksgiving Day, 1895, in Chicago. Many mechanics were tinkering with horseless carriages in backyard shops. One of these was Henry Ford, who awakened his neighbors on a rainy April night in 1893 as he drove his noisy, chugging gasoline buggy through the deserted streets of Detroit. Not until Ford acquired a special permit from the mayor was he allowed to drive freely about the city. The horse owners objected to the contraption which frightened their animals and caused accidents. At the time, Henry Ford claimed "the distinction of being the only licensed chauffeur in America."

It was March of 1898 before the first automobile was sold commercially, when a mechanical engineer from Carbon, Pennsylvania, bought a car from the Winton Motor Carriage Company in Cleveland. At that date only one automobile was completed, but three more cars were in production. These small beginnings at the dawn of the twentieth century marked the rise of the fastest-growing industry yet launched in the world. The rubber industry that furnished tires kept pace with the output of cars. Rubber put the nation on wheels, although rails and ships continued to share the responsibility of transportation.

INVENTORS IMPROVE
RAIL AND WATER TRANSPORTATION

JOHN ERICSSON, though born in Sweden, is usually listed among American inventors because he lived in this country for so many years and rendered such outstanding services to the nation. Although he invented many improvements for railroads, he is best known for screw-propellers on steamboats.

Captain Ericsson's name is linked with the sea and ships. At the time that Ericsson was working to improve water transportation, Abraham Lincoln was trying his hand at inventing. He actually secured a patent in 1849 for an apparatus to float river vessels over sand bars and other obstructions. Steamboats on the inland rivers were Lincoln's concern, and ocean-going vessels were Ericsson's major interest.

The Yankees, who excelled in building wooden vessels, had developed the fastest sailing ships afloat — the tall, slender and graceful clippers. These speedy merchant vessels, the pride of the seas, pulled down the curtain on the golden age of the American merchant marine. Although the steamship was gaining in popularity, owners of shipping companies in the United States clung to the sturdy sailing ships that had made money for them. Seamen have an affection for sails and the challenge of wind and weather that is not easily transferred to a steam engine that turns a propeller. However, it was after the War Between the States, and the sea battle between Ericsson's *Monitor* and the iron-plated *Merrimac,* that the death bell was sounded for wooden vessels and yards of wind-filled canvas. Shipbuilding began to decline when manufacturing turned the nation's interest to railroading for inland transportation. Following the War Between the States, after a century of colorful Yankee traders, the United States veered away from the sea. American cargoes were carried in foreign ships more and more, although the diminishing merchant marine still bravely carried the Stars and Stripes into ports all over the world.

During the canal era inland transportation was by water wherever possible, since barge freight was cheaper than wagon freight. Towns and cities grew up along the navigable rivers, lakes, and the canals between them. Not until the coming of the railroads in the 1830's did settlements grow and prosper away from the rivers. The frontier moved westward with the railroads. Any country, though rich in soil, timber, and minerals, is practically worthless without transportation. Since the opening of new territory depended largely upon rails, inventions to improve railroading were welcomed. They came as the need arose for them.

As more and more freight was hauled and trains grew longer, brakes became more important. When a long train was suddenly halted, cars bumped one another so hard that, sometimes, cattle were knocked down and trampled and the shipment was ruined. A vital improvement for railroads had its origin in a wreck. George Westinghouse was riding on a passenger train enroute to Troy, New York, when his trip was delayed by a collision ahead. One freight had rammed another because the engineer of the second train had not been able to stop quickly

GEORGE WESTINGHOUSE — INVENTOR

At the age of 15, George Westinghouse was experimenting with his rotary steam engine. For this invention, he received his first patent.

Westinghouse Air Brake Company

enough to avoid an accident. In the early days of railroading, brakemen ran from car to car on top, turning hand wheels to set the brakes. This procedure took considerable time. Viewing the damage done to merchandise, scattered and broken by the impact, Westinghouse realized the need for a brake that could be operated readily by the engineer in the cab of the locomotive. Not long afterwards he invented one which worked by compressed air.

At first railroaders showed little interest in this invention. Finally, an alert superintendent of one line persuaded his directors to equip one train with the new air brake and test it. Westinghouse and

CROWD AT BURLINGTON
TRIALS — 1887 — BURLINGTON, IOWA

Although Westinghouse patented his air brake in 1869, all railroads did not accept it. So many inventors were working on brakes for trains that railroad officials held tests every few years. These races were exciting. People came for miles to check the time it took to stop a train at high speed after the brake was applied.

In the trials held in Burlington, Iowa the air brake won again. This invention, with improvements through the years, came into general use on railroads.

Westinghouse Air Brake Company

the railroad officials boarded the train for the trial run between Steubenville, Ohio, and Pittsburgh, Pennsylvania. During the trip the engineer decided to gain some speed before he tested the brake. He waited for a straight stretch of road. Emerging from Grant's Hill tunnel at thirty miles an hour, he sighted a wagon crossing the track not far ahead. As the frightened driver lashed the team with a whip to clear the track quickly, the horses reared. With all his strength the engineer applied the brake. The train rolled to a full stop within four feet of the driver and a life was saved. Although the officials had skinned knees from the sudden bump, the air brake needed no further testing than this incident. A few months later, a group of far seeing railroad men met in Pittsburgh and organized a company to manufacture the safety device. They named the twenty-four year old inventor president of the Westinghouse Air Brake Company. Westinghouse patented his air brake in 1869.

Railroading has traveled far since Peter Cooper's engine ran a race with a horse in 1830 and lost it. The following year the first mail was carried on a railroad train in South Carolina. In 1858 the first sleeping car, named Pullman after the inventor, added comfort to long journeys by rail. The cars were elegant with red plush seats, paneled wood, gleaming mirrors, linen damask, and silver-plated cuspidors.

An item of news in a Denver paper, dated June 18, 1870, mentions the first train to that city on the Great Plains:

Nearly every tall building in Denver had someone on its roof yesterday looking at the inbound engine. It was first seen on Wednesday evening, June 15, from the roof of the First National Bank building by some officers of the road. Many in Denver have never seen an engine.

The Diesel engine, named for its German inventor, was developed by Alexander Winton, a Scotch immigrant, for use on ships. Winton first became famous as a builder of bicycles, then of the first automobile sold commercially. Later, Winton built Diesel electric-driven power plants for the United States Navy. The nation's first Diesel electric-powered streamlined train went into service between Denver and Chicago in 1934. Diesel engines have also been developed for trucks hauling freight. For mountain country some railroad operators prefer electric engines.

In a short time, the coal-burning steam locomotives, puffing smoke and cinders, lost out in competition with the powerful Diesels. The old work horses of the railroad era were driven from the tracks to the lonely pastures of museums as relics of the past.

THOMAS EDISON – INVENTIVE GENIUS

THE NAME OF Thomas Alva Edison, with more than a thousand patents to his credit, is linked inseparably with the electro-industrial progress of the push button age. When Edison was twelve, he was a newsboy on the Grand Trunk Railway running between Port Huron and Detroit. He became interested in telegraphy and secured his first employment as a telegraph operator at Port Huron when he was fifteen years old. He was soon experimenting during spare time in his office and invented his first successful telegraph instrument. He was discharged from the office in Louisville, Kentucky, when acid from one of his experiments dripped through the floor and ruined fine furniture in the private office of a bank official on the floor below. Edison landed in New York, penniless, in 1870. He walked the streets for three weeks before he found a job as a telegraph operator by repairing an instrument that no one else had been able to put in working order.

From New York he went to Menlo Park, New Jersey, where he established a laboratory and began work on varied inventions that came into his mind. By this time many men had discovered his genius and were willing to offer financial help. Edison foretold in 1878, the many uses that would be made of his inventions, such as:

Letter writing and all kinds of dictation without the aid of a stenographer – Reproduction of music – Preservation of language by exact reproduction of the manner of pronunciation – The family record, a registry of sayings.

Being an expert telegrapher, himself, he invented devices to improve wire communications, including the telephone. In August of 1879 Edison attended a meeting of the American Association for the Advancement of Science in Saratoga, New York. The following report was published in the *Popular Science Monthly:*

An exhibition of Edison's electro-chemical telephonic receiver was given before the Association in the Town Hall. Mr. Edison was present and he offered an explanation of his new instrument. Apparently it is simply a small box provided with a crank, and looking like a coffee mill.... The instrument exhibited was only an experimental model; nevertheless, it transmitted messages which were heard by the whole audience, numbering 1500 persons.

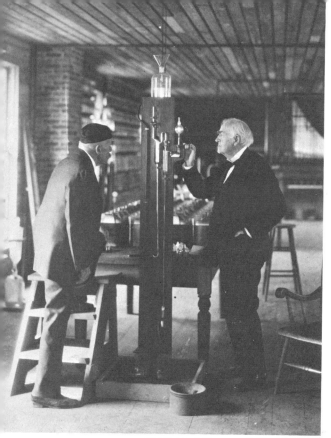
Henry Ford Museum, Edison Institute

CELEBRATING FIFTY YEARS
OF ELECTRIC LIGHTING

Thomas Alva Edison and his assistant repeated their original experiment in the same setting on the fiftieth anniversary of the inventor's electric light.

At the time, Edison was trying to produce a steady light with electricity, and to do it so cheaply that it could compete with gas for illumination. After costly experiments using platinum for a filament, the inventor began the search for a cheaper material. He tried almost anything at hand, including cotton sewing thread. He sealed a piece of carbonized thread in a glass bulb, after pumping out the air, and turned on a current of electricity. A steady light glowed without a flicker. How long would it burn? Edison and a few of his assistants kept vigil for forty hours and the lamp was still burning. Edison increased the current to see what would happen. The light flared brighter and then suddenly blinked out at two o'clock on October 21, 1879.

Two weeks later Edison filed application for a patent on an electric lamp with a paper filament, carbonized pasteboard baked in an oven. The scientists were skeptical. The public was curious. A reporter from a New York paper went down to Menlo Park to see for himself. The inventor was always news because readers expected almost any startling device to follow the phonograph, the wonder of the day. Edison promptly invited the public to Menlo Park on New Year's Eve to watch the old year out in the glow of electric lights. The invitation was a scoop for the reporter who made the most of it by whetting the curiosity of his readers. On December 21, he wrote, teasingly:

Edison's electric light, incredible as it may appear, is produced from a little piece of paper — a tiny strip of paper that a breath would blow away. Through this little strip of paper is passed an electric current. The result is a bright, beautiful light, like the mellow sunset of an Italian autumn.

The public did not wait until New Year's Eve. To accommodate the crowds, the railroad ran special trains from New York City to Menlo Park, where Edison staged a nightly demonstration of his lamps. On December 29, the reporter continued his story, describing the crowds:

All came with one passion — the electric light and its maker. They are of all classes, these visitors, of different degrees of wealth and importance in the community and varying degrees of scientific ignorance . . . . In the office the lights were all electric. In the library upstairs it was the same. Such volleys of questions as were pouring out! The visitors have been around to see the engine, the generators, the regulators . . . .

Satisfied about the electric light, they have asked about the tasimeter, the microphone, the phonograph and a dozen other things, as though they wanted to improve every instant before the train starts. At last they go in twos and threes down the hill to the railroad track, and it is all "wonderful! marvelous! wonderful! wonderful!" among them till the train takes them away and Menlo Park is left to itself.

New Year's Eve arrived. Snow was gently falling as trains pulled into the little depot. Eager guests hurried up the lighted lane to enter the buildings. Farmers came in wagons from the countryside and sightseeing parties arrived in carriages from nearby towns. Many guests were well-dressed. Edison wore his working clothes. The inventor was busy explaining how he regulated the supply of current at the central station, stopping now and then to inspect the apparatus. An electric motor pumped water and operated a sewing machine to the delight of the visitors.

NEW YEAR'S EVE PARTY AT MENLO PARK, NEW JERSEY

To greet the new year of 1880, Edison invited the public to his laboratories in Menlo Park to see an exhibition of electric lighting.

Henry Ford Museum, Edison Institute

Edison told his guests that electric motors would change the pattern of living in both the home and the mill. Edison had a keen sense of the value of publicity. In a dramatic way his New Year's party for 1880 announced to the public that the age of electric power was dawning. People came to see for themselves and were convinced by the "Wizard of Menlo Park."

Although water, steam, and gasoline operated machinery, electric energy was largely responsible for the age of power. Electricity helped to take the drudgery out of labor in this industrial nation and gave man more time to improve his education.

New inventions in printing increased the number of books, magazines, and newspapers. In 1825, at the age of fifteen, Richard M. Hoe went to work in his father's printing business in New York City. Printing with a flat-bed model in the press was too slow for him. He set type on a revolving cylinder to print with greater speed. Hoe's invention developed into the rotary or "lightning press," patented in 1846. The rotary press has made possible the printing of so many sheets of paper in a short time that the daily newspaper has become a necessity in American life. Books, also, could be printed at a price more people could afford to pay, and book shelves in homes, schools, and libraries added volumes for learning and pleasure.

New inventions create new industries and new markets. As factories grew in number and production of goods and services increased, more money was needed for investment and more workmen were needed to fill jobs. Emigrants came by the thousands from other countries to find employment and opportunity in the United States and other nations of the Americas.

501

Chapter 26

A Century of Moving

THE WESTERN HEMISPHERE SEEKS POPULATION

MAGNIFICENT OCEAN! I commit all my hopes to thee! A young family, in whose happiness centers my own, I trust to thy fickle, thy vanishing waves. May they live to inherit the land of promise, the land of hope and liberty!

Looking out upon a watery world as the sun went down, an English emigrant wrote this entry in his diary, May 22, 1818. For hours he had been on deck, silently watching until the coast of his native land faded from his sight. He was one of the millions of emigrants who crossed the Atlantic to the Americas in the nineteenth century.

During the early 1800's the armies of Napoleon swept over Europe, all the way from Paris to Moscow. The Americas needed population to develop the resources of the two continents and the tax-burdened peoples of war-weary Europe welcomed a place to go. Thus did the great migration to the western world get under way. The nations of both North and South America entered the race for population. The one winning the largest number of emigrants in the shortest time could develop its natural resources the

quickest. It could become the richest and most powerful nation in the Western Hemisphere. Land was the lure. From the North Pole to the South Pole governments offered free and cheap farms to settlers.

The British encouraged migration to Canada, Australia, New Zealand, and South Africa to populate these possessions. The British Government even agreed to pay part of the passage for farm workers, general laborers, and domestic servants, as well as for tradesmen and their families who wanted to settle in Canada. Since most of the British emigrants came from the big manufacturing towns and had never held a plow, they were advised to accept small wages as farm workers while they learned to work on the land. It took time for tailors, shoemakers, and weavers to become wood choppers, stock raisers, and tillers of the soil.

Typical of the British immigrants to Canada was the canny Scotsman who came to look things over before he moved his family. After a stormy voyage of six weeks in a sailing vessel, he landed at Quebec. There he talked with an agent of the Canada Company who advised him to look around a bit before choosing a place to settle. Traveling on a boat to Montreal, he passed through settlements of French Canadians, with "the bonny white farm houses in the middle of their orchards" and "the beautiful kirks, with tinned steeples glancing in the sun." On a sightseeing tour he continued his way to Toronto, thence overland to view the famous Niagara Falls. Hearing of a fair in London, Ontario, he went to the town to see the cattle and sheep on exhibit. He wanted to learn more about the crops raised in that part of the country.

Sauntering through the fair grounds he chanced to meet an old friend, Tam, from his home town in Scotland. Tam had come to Canada ten years before with only enough money to pay his passage. Now he owned a fine farm well-stocked with sheep and cattle. He advised the new-comer to buy an improved farm near his,

ADVERTISEMENTS IN A BRITISH EMIGRANT FOLDER

The British Government encouraged Englishmen to settle in Canada and develop that British possession. Emigrant folders notified farm laborers, tradesmen, and domestic servants that jobs awaited them there. Although jobs lured many to Canada and the United States, the real bait to catch emigrants was free land. In the countries of northern Europe, land meant more to the people than jobs. As farmers, they wanted to work for themselves.

soon to be auctioned at a sheriff's sale. The owner had gone to the United States. The Scotsman's bid was the highest, less than $500 for 100 acres of land. There were thirty cleared acres, a barn, an orchard, and a log house with broken windows and a leaky roof. Then he bought a yoke of oxen for $60. He arranged to pay Tam $2.50 a week for boarding himself and his team, while he felled trees, burned brush, and prepared the ground for planting wheat, oats, barley, potatoes, and turnips after the snow had melted. Early in the spring he sent for his wife and children. To his brother, a mechanic in Glasgow, he wrote in a letter:

Tell Mary I'll be sure to have the house sorted for her and the bairns. She should come in one of the earliest ships, go to the agent of the Canada Company in Quebec, get to the head of Ontario, then through the Welland Canal, and I'll meet her. Blythe will I be to see her and the bairns on the banks of Lake Erie, and take them to their own home with the wagon and ox team.

The countries of South America also entered the race for population. Brazil bid high for immigrants, offering land for as little as 44 cents an acre, and to some of the German Colonization Societies, only 22 cents an acre. Europeans coming to buy land and settle on it had their goods imported free, including farm tools and machinery; free board and room while they waited to be taken to the government colonies; free transportation for themselves and their belongings; free lodging and food for six months, if necessary, or until they were settled on a farm; and free seed for their first planting. Most of the government colonies were located in Santa Catarina and other provinces south of Rio de Janiero. Here the climate was more like that of Europe. A colony of Irish settled in Rio Grande de

Sul, the southernmost province of Brazil. However, most of the immigrants came from Germany, France, and Portugal.

Dom Pedro II, Emperor of Brazil, who was strongly opposed to slavery, used immigration to get rid of the system. His government made it easy for plantation owners to import all the help needed on their big estates. He proved to them that free labor was more profitable than slave labor. By encouraging immigration Brazil was able to abolish slavery without a war. The freed Negroes were hired by former masters to work for wages, especially in the tropical regions where the climate was hard on the white immigrants. The newcomers found employment as managers and overseers on the huge plantations.

Although the nations along the Rio de la Plata were torn with revolutions, they received their share of immigrants because the climate was so much like that of western and southern Europe. When Brazil guaranteed the independence of her southern neighbor, Uruguay, that nation offered land and privileges to foreign settlers. Big colonies of German farmers from the Rhine Valley came over to till the land left idle when slavery was abolished and the owners had no laborers for their fields. Montevideo and Buenos Aires grew up to be foreign cities. The region of the Rio de la Plata became a little Europe where Basques were vegetable gardeners, Italians were boatmen, Germans were farmers, English were merchants, French were shop owners, Portuguese were tavern keepers, and Irish were servants.

However, the mass migration of the nineteenth century descended upon the United States. A ticket cost less to New York City than to Rio de Janiero and this nation offered greater freedom of opportunity. The United States had industry as well as land to offer. There were mills and factories where people could work for wages if they had neither the means nor the desire to settle on a farm. The landseeker, with a little money to invest, could go to Canada or Brazil and get along well. The poor job-hunter, with only a ticket in his pocket, had little choice. He came to the United States. This comment was printed in the *Glasgow Chronicle* in 1830:

The manufacturing and commercial speculations which are fostered and encouraged by the tariff laws of America, have had the effect of draining our country of its improvements, and many of its productive population.

An Englishman wrote to a friend in this country:

Though some of the Hull and Yarmouth ships are bound for Quebec, the people are going to the United States, — Three millions of gold will, this very year, go from England to the United States, by means of emigration.

The editor of the *Mainz Gazette*, printed in the town where Germans were crossing the Rhine River to Atlantic ports, wrote in his paper on April 25, 1840:

At no period was emigration to North America so considerable as at present. The emigrants, in general, are families in easy circumstances, some even rich, and whole caravans are daily passing through this town. The Americans will be delighted with their new colonists — young, active men between twenty and thirty years of age.

This mass migration opened up the western lands for settlement and built the transportation to carry the products to market. The Germans usually settled on farms. The Irish dug the canals and laid the rails. The immigrant created his own market and industry grew to supply it.

Three events of the 1840's pushed the United States far ahead in the race for population. One happened in each of three countries. The potato, introduced by Sir Walter Raleigh in 1610, became the main food of the Irish people. When a blight caused the failure of the potato crop, famine spread over Ireland, taking the lives of about 300,000 persons in a short time. To escape starvation, the Irish fled from their native land. Most of them came to the United States to seek jobs as day laborers. Many young men sold themselves to ship captains, who sold them to foremen of construction gangs to work out their passage. Only a few had money enough to reach into the western country and settle on the land. The Irish settled largely in the cities of the Atlantic seaboard where their labor erected the buildings, installed the water systems, and paved the streets.

In 1848 a revolution in Germany drove thousands of that nation's best citizens to other lands. These people wanted more self-government, and not obtaining it, they left their homeland to seek freedoms in the Americas. With them came Bohemians and others escaping from the political turmoil of central Europe.

In that same year of 1848 gold was discovered in California. The cry, "there's gold on the Sacramento," echoed around the world, luring emigrants from nearly every country on the face of the earth.

By the middle of the nineteenth century the United States was thirty years ahead of the other American nations in the race for population. Although the rising tide of immigration alarmed some citizens, little was done to check it until a secret society was formed in 1853. To questions the members replied, "I know nothing," and it was called the "Know Nothing Party." There was some cause for alarm. Governments in Europe were known to pay passage of their paupers and criminals to the United States to evade supporting them in almshouses and prisons. An investigator in New York discovered that one third of the steerage passengers on two vessels became inmates of the city poorhouse. Persons unable to support themselves in their homelands found the task even more difficult in a strange new country. To stop this traffic, laws were passed forcing ship captains who brought immigrants physically unfit or undesirable to take them back at their own expense.

Between the years of 1850 and 1855 about 2,500,000 immigrants entered the United States. Guide books printed stories of the hazards for emigrants — smart swindlers, ship fever, crowded steerage, false advertisements, frontier hardships. There was advice ranging from what to wear to where to settle. The author of "The Emigrant Pocket Companion" stated in his guide book:

No man is fit for being an independent emigrant, or even existing at all in a new country, who is not both able and willing to work. He must have health, he must have strength, he must have perseverance, — and be able to turn his hand to many things.

Little heed was paid to these warnings by the onrushing horde, fleeing from hunger and poverty, war and military service, taxes and political persecution. America was a dream. Going up the St. Lawrence or the Rio de la Plata, they pursued the vision of the British emigrant who sailed up the Delaware River to dock at Philadelphia. It was June, 1818. Only a month before the emigrant had stood on the deck of the same ship, bidding a silent farewell to his native England. Gazing over the green countryside of Pennsylvania, he wrote in his diary:

Hail, land of liberty! I live to behold thy hospitable shores, the abodes of peace and plenty, and the sure refuge of the destitute, the persecuted, and the oppressed of all nations.

IMMIGRANTS ARRIVE FROM SOUTHERN AND EASTERN EUROPE

FROM THE CLOSE of the War for Independence to the year 1855, more than 14,500,000 foreign-born persons arrived to seek new homes in the United States of America. These immigrants came largely from Ireland, Germany, England, and France. Smaller numbers came from forty other nations, including islands like the Azores and the West Indies. Most of these foreigners, Irish, German, and English, had the same general ancestry as the native-born citizens whose forefathers had crossed the Atlantic in colonial times. On the whole these newcomers were welcomed, whether rich or poor, if they were able and willing to work.

The immigrants created a market for food, clothing, and many articles of manufacture, increasing commerce both at home and abroad. Between the years 1840 to 1855, exports increased 300 percent, and imports increased 200 percent. Although these immigrants brought in millions of dollars to invest in the United States, their labor was worth more to the nation than their money.

Industry, expanding rapidly to supply the needs of the increased population, was able to provide employment for most of the job-hunting immigrants except during hard times. Sometimes, there were more jobs than there were men and women to fill them.

During the War Between the States, the American Emigrant Company was organized "for the purpose of procuring and assisting emigrants from foreign countries to settle in the United States." Advertisements like the following one appeared in the newspapers. This one is from the *Missouri Democrat,* 1865:

LABORERS OF EVERY KIND SUPPLIED — The American Emigrant Company is now prepared to supply miners, puddlers, machinists, blacksmiths, moulders, and mechanics of every kind; also gardeners, railroad and farm laborers, and female help at short notice and on reasonable terms.

Agents of this company and others like it, stationed in foreign countries, were supplied with blocks of prepaid steamship tickets to transport laborers to this country. The immigrant signed a contract agreeing to work for a specified time at fixed wages and to repay the sum advanced for his passage and expenses in regular monthly payments. Small payments served to extend the time that the immigrant worked for the wages specified in his contract.

Since wages were higher in the United States than in Europe, these immigrants often agreed to work for less than was paid to native-born citizens. The labor unions protested loudly against the importation of cheap contract workmen. Congress passed a law forbidding the practice. However, societies, formed to aid immigrants, sent agents abroad with prepaid tickets to offer to laborers desiring to go to the United States without a labor contract. Then other agents in this country met these immigrants at the boat landings and found jobs for them. This insured the payment of the sum advanced for their steamship ticket. The foreign agents, who received a certain percent for each immigrant, did a profitable business in the over-populated and poverty-stricken countries of southern and eastern Europe.

In 1896 a government official in Rome wrote in an Italian magazine:

For Italy, emigration is a necessity. We should desire that some hundreds of thousands of our people should find annually an abiding place abroad. If twice as many left us as now leave we should not lament the loss of them, but rather rejoice that they find work outside.

In January of 1949 the President of the Italian Chamber of Deputies in Rome made this statement:

The problem of emigration is, for us, fundamental, — and this is generally known. We can never employ in Italy all the manpower which we have in overabundance.

About forty percent of the land surface of Italy is mountainous, swampy, and worn-out. On the remaining land enough food cannot be raised to feed the people. Although the Po Valley in the north is industrialized, the factories in the big cities cannot employ all workmen who apply. Many Italians for many years have been forced to emigrate or starve. By 1881 half a million persons from Italy had settled in Argentina. Early in that year at an exhibition in Buenos Aires, pianos, organs, furniture, jewelry, carriages, farm implements, steam engines, boilers, leather goods, and many other articles made by Italians were shown and admired. Some of

507

the states of Brazil gave prepaid steamship tickets to Italian peasant families who were farmers. In 1888 Brazil acquired 104,000 Italian immigrants. Three years later the number increased to 183,000.

However, under the "padroni" system, more Italians came to the United States than to any other country in the Western Hemisphere. The padroni were Italian agents who spoke English. They made a business of finding jobs in mines, mills, and on railroads and public works for immigrants from their homeland. These immigrants were obligated to work under the orders of their padroni until they had repaid the price of their steamship tickets in monthly payments of as little as $2.50.

IMMIGRANT RUNNER

During the mass migration, "immigrant runners" did a thriving business. With bundles of steamship tickets stuffed into their pockets, they arrived in European countries seeking emigrants to the United States. They offered workmen free passage across the Atlantic for themselves and families if they signed a wage agreement with the "runner" who agreed to get jobs for them in return for a part of their salary.

Since wages were much higher in the United States than in their homelands, the workmen accepted a much smaller part of the money, received for their labor, than the "runner," who collected their wages. The difference was the "runner's" profit. Some factory owners, needing help, hired "runners" who worked on a commission. Others operated independently.

New York Public Library

In a strange country with a strange language, these Italian workmen were often exploited by these agents who became rich at the expense of their less fortunate countrymen. Labor unions objected, declaring that this system differed little from contract labor and demanded an investigation. Immigrants were summoned to testify before a Congressional committee in the Fiftieth Congress. Among those questioned was an Italian laborer from a village near Naples.

Congressman:"What was your occupation in Italy?'
Immigrant: "Farmer."
Congressman: "What did you receive for farming?"
Immigrant: "Ten cents and meals."
Congressman: "Meals for yourself, or yourself and family?"
Immigrant: "No, sir, the meals were for me, and the family fed on ten cents."
Congressman: "When you landed in this country, were you in possession of any money?"
Immigrant: "Not a cent."
Congressman: "Or property of any kind?"
Immigrant: "Nothing, sir, no property."

Although many of the poorer Italian immigrants could neither read nor write, they had over 2000 years of civilization for a background. They appreciated the opportunities for education in their new homeland and made loyal American citizens. So many had settled in New York that a district of the city was called "Little Italy."

During the Middle Ages, Jewish people were expelled from countries of western Europe. They settled in eastern Europe, especially in Poland and provinces of western Russia. They had little freedom in these countries. Forbidden by law to be farmers and own land, they were forced to live in towns and earn their living in

COOLING OFF IN EAST HARLEM YEARS AGO

On hot days, city firemen flooded streets in crowded sections of New York City, giving the children a cool shower. These tenements were the first American homes for immigrants of many nationalities. Many of the houses were razed and replaced with large airier apartment buildings by the New York City Housing Authority.

trade and money lending. In the early 1880's anti-Semitic riots broke out in western Russia. The Jewish people were robbed, beaten, and killed, and their houses were stolen, plundered, and burned. Laws passed in 1882 made it almost impossible for them to live in Russia. A Jewish person could have no share in the government, could not hold office, could not assemble without a permit, could not do business on Sundays and Christian holidays, and could not leave his section of a town without permission. They were barred from universities and the learned professions. Then the mass migration of Jewish people began. Being a townspeople, few emigrated to South America where cities

were few and far apart. One-third of the Jewish people in Russia came directly to the United States, before laws were passed establishing quotas for each nation. Most of these immigrants remained where they landed in the neighborhood of New York, making that city and its suburbs the largest Jewish community in the world.

The Jewish immigrant had a "sweater," as the Italian had a padroni. Agents known as sweaters, who could speak English, Russian, and Yiddish, contracted with manufacturers to have ready-cut garments stitched and finished. Sweaters were busy carrying bundles of pants, vests, coats, skirts, dresses, and many articles of clothing to dingy flats and little factories where men, women, and children worked on them. Often, the factory was only one room in a damp basement or a stuffy attic. In these dirty, crowded, and poorly-ventilated "sweat shops," new immigrants toiled long hours for low wages. Earnings were so small that several families sometimes lived in a one-room flat, sharing the rent.

The sweating system was pointed out as the great evil of unrestricted immigration by those citizens beseeching Congress to limit the number of persons who could enter the United States from a foreign country in any year. In 1905 the Garment Workers of America voted in favor of limiting immigration to protect the foreign-born who were already here. Today, many of the descendants of these Russian emigrants still live in New York City, Brooklyn, and nearby cities and towns, and earn their living in the garment industry. But, the sweat shops have disappeared from the scene.

Since New York was the main port of entry and the poorest immigrants usually stayed where they landed, that city bore the burden of Americanizing most of the foreign-born immigrants who arrived each year. These new citizens were Americanized largely through their children who learned in schools the language and ways of their adopted country. Evening lectures for adults were held in the schools where stereopticon slides were shown of Niagara Falls, the Adirondacks, the Mississippi Valley, Yellowstone Park, and other places in the United States. Courses on how to use the secret ballot were given in Yiddish, Italian, Russian, Slovakian, Polish, and many languages to aid new citizens in learning to vote for the first time in a constitutional republic. Many of these immigrants had never voted until they became citizens of the United States. Large industrial cities like Pittsburgh, Buffalo, and Chicago promoted Americanization of their foreign-born through programs in schools, churches, libraries, lecture halls, and union meetings.

A Canadian declared that the right of property was the strongest motive for Americanization:

The possession of permanent property creates a tie between the emigrant and his adopted country. There (in the old country) he was dependent, but here independent; there he was a tenant, but here he is the proprietor — the lord of the soil.

The government of Argentina considered it a good investment to buy steamship tickets for farmers who were willing to settle on undeveloped lands away from the seacoast. In one year, 1888 to 1889, the export of corn in Argentina increased nearly 350 percent — more laborers, more crops, more exports, more business, more prosperity. Other nations in South America, especially Brazil, helped farmers to settle on land. The abolition of slavery in May of 1889 in Brazil had cost the planters one-third of their coffee crop. In that same year the government passed a bill to spend $5,500,000 to increase immigration and secure labor for the plantations.

In 1889 from three German ports, records show that 187,057 emigrants from Germany, Russia, Hungary, Austria, Bohemia, Denmark, Sweden, and smaller European nations boarded vessels to seek new homes in the following places: 179,142 to the United States; 2,522 to the Argentine Republic; 2,043 to Brazil; 816 to Australia; 490 to Africa; 426 to Asia; 328 to various countries in Latin

America; 200 to Chile; 107 to the West Indies; 53 to Mexico; 39 to Peru.

The German Government became alarmed at the loss of many citizens leaving the fatherland for the United States and taking their money with them. These German citizens were going forth to invest their money in the United States and with their labor, to develop the resources of that country. Perhaps the United States would become a rival of Germany for world trade and world power.

In 1880 commissioners at German ports requested emigrants bound for the United States to tell why they preferred that country to others throughout the world. From the answers of over 100,000 emigrants, the German Commissioner of Emigration made this statement in 1880. The emigrants chose the United States because:

There, an opportunity is afforded every one, by diligent work, in a comparatively short time, to gain possession of a house and land of his own, and to become independent of others and well-to-do.

Thus did the United States win the race for population, develop its resources the fastest, and become the richest and most powerful nation in the Western Hemisphere. The achievements of man are boundless when his spirit is set at liberty. To this land of the free came millions of men, women, and children from places all over the face of the earth. These immigrants pooled their talents and their labor and helped to build the greatest industrial civilization the world has ever known. In doing it most of the people earned for themselves that for which they had come to the New World — a more abundant life. Sometimes, their days were laden with hardships but their hearts were filled with hope. They were free men, carving their own destiny in their own way, and this was what they asked. They MADE history.

Chapter 27

Adjusting to Industrial Change

EMPLOYERS

THE NATION owes its rapid industrial growth to the fact that the nineteenth century was one long moving day. It was the mass migration to the United States that provided mechanics for mills, hired hands on farms, diggers of canals, lumberjacks in forests, and builders of cities. As more and more people came to depend upon industry for a living, new relationships between employers and employees began to evolve.

When industry was in the home, the same person was owner, manager, and workman. In a home factory, as a rule, employer and employees were father, mother, children, and any relatives living with them. When industry began to move from the home to the factory, owners, managers, and employees gradually became divided into three separate groups. The change came slowly because most factories were small in the beginning. A weaver, printer, shoemaker, tailor, or any tradesman who had saved enough money to go into business for himself could start a little factory. He was both owner and manager. His employees were few and he worked with them, as he was a skilled craftsman himself. Working together in the same room the owner-manager became well acquainted with the men he hired. They could easily talk over their common interests.

The machine age forced workmen to use tools so costly that they could not afford to own them. In early days, a canal digger brought his hand shovel to the job. He paid for it. The operator of a power-driven shovel cannot afford to buy such a tool. Therefore, others must furnish the money to buy his shovel before he can get a job digging a ditch. As machines became more and more costly, it took the savings of more and more people to create jobs. The amount of money invested to insure one job varies with the kind of industry, large sums being necessary where the risk is great and machinery is expensive. In some industries the cost is so great that corporations have more stockholders than jobholders. This system of sharing a business with investors wanting to own a part was used during Washington's first term as President of the United States.

In 1965, an estimate of the amount of money needed for investment to insure one job was approximately $25,000. Therefore, big corporations employing

Museum of the City of New York

UNDER A BUTTONWOOD TREE ON WALL STREET, NEW YORK CITY

On May 17, 1792, twenty-four merchants and auctioneers signed an agreement to meet daily under a buttonwood tree on Wall Street to buy and sell shares in business. They also handled the buying and selling of government bonds issued by Alexander Hamilton, the first Secretary of the Treasury, to pay the debts of the Revolutionary War.

The following year, this first "broker's office" moved indoors from the table under the buttonwood tree to cozy quarters in the new Tontine Coffee House nearby. From this humble beginning grew a world center of finance, the New York Stock Exchange.

thousands of men and women need thousands of stockholders to operate successfully. For example, approximately 2,500,000 shareowners maintain the telephone and telegraph companies serving millions of people. A large automobile manufacturer has over a million owners, and a steel company has more than half a million. How does a business with so many owners operate?

The stockholders elect a board of directors from their group, voting either at a meeting or by mail. These chosen members accept the responsibility of conducting the business for the owners. The directors, as a rule, hire trained managers to carry on the business for them, and the managers, in turn, hire employees to manufacture the products of the company, and sell them. The employees report to the managers who hire them, the managers to the board of directors who hire them, and the board of directors to the owners who elected them.

Most big corporations providing products now in everyday use began in a small way. New products and inventions create new industries. For example, let us examine the progress of a can opener business:

1. A man invents a new can opener.
2. He secures a patent on his invention from the United States Patent Office. Now no one can copy and manufacture his can opener without his permission.
3. He starts making can openers, perhaps in a shed in his backyard, and sells them to his neighbors.
4. The neighbors like his can opener. Soon he receives more orders than he can fill. From his local banker he borrows money to enlarge his plant and to buy a new machine to make can openers faster. He sells more, and hires a salesman.
5. More and more orders come in as distribution spreads. The inventor needs a little factory. Instead of borrowing again from his local banker, he goes to an investment banker who has customers with money to invest in any growing business. The inventor agrees to share his business with others by selling stock to get enough money to build a factory, buy new machinery, and hire more help. The investment banker sells shares in the can opener factory for a fee.
6. With the new factory, business grows rapidly. More salesmen are hired. The inventor, who is probably the president of the company and owns shares of stock, decides to incorporate under a charter from the state. To be granted this charter his company must comply with laws that protect people doing business with him. His incorporated business, under this charter, becomes a corporation and operates accordingly.
7. The corporation prospers. Additional money is needed to enlarge the factory and to buy newer machines to turn out more can openers in less time. By increasing production prices can be cut to meet competition. At this point, the business may be large enough to seek a listing on the stock exchange. The inventor applies to a stock exchange. Again, he has certain requirements to meet, one being proof that his company has many individual stockholders and that it is not owned by a few men who control nearly all the shares.
8. If accepted, shares in his company will be listed in daily newspapers. More people will buy them if the company is successful, continues to grow, and pays a fair profit to its stockholders, who really own the factory making can openers. Thus little business grows into big business.

In our highly industrialized society, business is carried on through a system of representation. As industries grow larger and larger, both employers and

A MEETING OF STOCKHOLDERS

The president of the board of directors of an electric company reports to a group of shareholders attending an annual meeting. Although reports are mailed to each one, some part-owners like to be present at a meeting to express their own opinions.

In this company, 150,000 shareowners have invested $221,000 per job to furnish electric power for 6,500,000 people. If any shareholder is not pleased with the progress of the company, he can sell his stock and invest his money elsewhere. It is a free market.

Southern California Edison Company

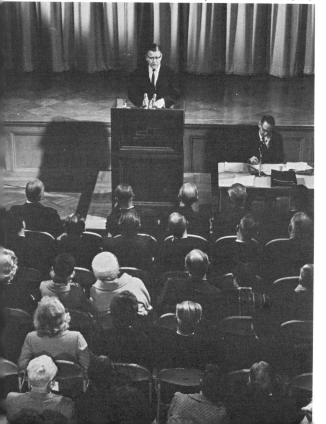

TRADING ON THE OLD NEW YORK STOCK EXCHANGE

A stock exchange is a market place where bonds and stocks are bought and sold. Bonds and shares are not the same. A person who loans money to a corporation, at interest, the sum to be repaid at a certain date, is a bondholder. A stockholder buys a share in a business and runs the risk of losing his money or making a profit on his investment. A bondholder is not a part-owner as is the share-owner.

As industry grew, the market place that started under the buttonwood tree had to be enlarged to keep pace with demand. After moving many times, a hall was built and seats were sold to brokers. A seat gave its owner the right to buy and sell there. Needing larger quarters, the present Exchange was built in 1903 to accommodate more brokers, but no chairs were provided for them. However, "seats" are still sold at prices that vary, since a "seat" means the privilege of trading in the market place. Brokers with orders walk among the trading posts seeking the best prices for their customers. The Stock Exchange does not buy, sell, or set prices. It is only the market place for buying and selling by brokerage firms who own "seats."

employees seek ways to speak to one another in a collective voice. Personal contacts are impossible because so many people are involved in so many ways.

EMPLOYEES

DURING THE TERMS of our first two Presidents, George Washington and John Adams, carpenters and shoemakers in

Philadelphia, tailors in Baltimore, and printers in New York were seeking the kinship of trade. In their meetings, they discussed conditions in their work. How many apprentices should a shop accept? Should the owner of a shop hire traveling journeymen? What should be the qualifications of a journeyman? (An apprentice who can prove he has mastered the skills of his trade can be "graduated" to journeyman.) Wages and hours were also debated. When craftsmen became wage earners producing for others in shops and mills instead of working for themselves in their own home factories, they felt the need to talk among themselves.

As little business grew into big business and both owners and employees were numbered in thousands, both groups were contacted through representatives. Labor organizations, generally called unions, began to grow in number and size.

ADVERTISEMENT IN CINCINNATI, OHIO NEWSPAPER

In early days it was the custom for parents to bind their children when quite young as apprentices to learn a trade. This advertisement offers a reward for the return of a runaway apprentice who had not served his full time. The apprentice system is still used but the boys are assigned under union laws, as a rule. Most laws make sixteen the age of a beginner, but many are older.

Members of these unions elected their officials who acted as their representatives and met with managers who represented the owners to discuss their working conditions. They met for the purpose of entering into mutually satisfactory contracts binding upon both parties.

These contracts establish wages, hours of work, paid holidays, paid vacations, safety, sanitation, and general work rules. Gradually, more personal services paid for by owners in whole or in part, have been added to union contracts. Among these benefits are medical care of employees and their families which includes hospital bills, doctors' fees, medicines, sick leave, dental care, and sometimes, psychiatric care. Many corporations, large and small, support pension plans for their employees at retirement age.

As this pattern developed in business and industry, men in various trades formed unions of their own crafts. The next step was to unite these craft unions. In 1886 at a labor conference held in Columbus, Ohio, the American Federation of Labor was organized. Samuel Gompers, an immigrant cigarmaker, was elected the first president. As industrialism advanced, more and more unskilled workmen were employed. In the early 1930's the American Federation of Labor set up a committee to organize these employees into unions for employees, no matter what their jobs were, according to industries instead of crafts. At a meeting in Pittsburgh in 1937 these industrial unions withdrew from the American Federation of Labor to form a new organization, the Congress of Industrial Organizations, known as the C.I.O. John L. Lewis, president of the United Mine Workers of America, was elected the first president of the C.I.O.

A MEETING OF RETAIL CLERKS UNION — LOCAL 770
Affiliated With Retail Clerks International Association, AFL-CIO

The people attending this meeting are clerks in food markets, drug stores, and discount centers. Such meetings are held to present new contracts for approval by members of the union. These agreements define working conditions, wages, paid holidays and vacations, apprentice-ships, medical and hospital benefits, and other items of common interest. Meetings are called by the secretary of the union when the need arises.

After being separated for about twenty years, the two joined to form a single group again.

As our industrial pattern becomes more complex, more emphasis is being placed on the human side. Jobholders are people. Managers are people. Stockholders are people. All three groups cooperate for the benefit of all concerned. No one group can succeed if one group fails. Industrial relations are human relations.

The big human problem of the machine age is to restore pride to workmen who can no longer provide their own tools, make their own products nor market them for their own personal profit. What can be done to get a workman on an assembly line to feel that he has a personal stake in the factory where he is employed? Managers give much time and thought to this question, and study the many factors to be considered.

517

What should be the basic wage for the average production of each workman? How can an employee be rewarded for better conduct, workmanship, and output? How can an efficient employee be encouraged to stay on his job? Since the industrial pattern is based upon mass production, the men and women who make products must be able to buy them, and to share in the services they provide for others. Therefore, basic wages need to be scaled to make consumers out of jobholders. If the workmen on an assembly line in an automobile factory were not able to drive their cars to and from their jobs, how extensive would the automobile business be? Jobholders represent the mass of consumers. Therefore, big mills and big markets demand products and services that most jobholders can afford. Small business also prospers by catering to buyers who can afford to pay more money for their products and services. Customers create business through their choice of products. This fact accounts for the American business slogan, "The customer is always right."

Employers have developed a variety of ways, generally called incentive plans, through which their employees may share in the profits earned from increased effort on their part. The employer wants to produce more goods. The employee wants to increase his income. This result may be achieved in different ways in different companies. There are many incentive plans operating in various industries in this country. All aim to encourage pride in workmanship and a personal interest among employees to aid productivity.

In some companies employees in the various departments share in a bonus award for increased production. At the end of a week, a month, or a year, they receive extra pay. Some factories operate on a piece plan. A seamstress in a garment factory may prefer to be paid by the piece since it would be a simple matter to measure her work at the end of a day. However, the piece plan would not be practical in a large steel mill where men work with coke ovens, blast furnaces, and cauldrons of molten metal. Employees in heavy industry and in large plants with thousands of men and women usually prefer hourly wages with medical and other services provided by owners in union contracts.

In recent years the profit-sharing plan has gained in popularity, but it is not a new idea. In some corporations, profits are shared by giving employees stock on which they receive dividends the same as any shareholder who bought his stock from a broker. Owners of some big retail stores include the employees who automatically become partners in the business when they have worked there satisfactorily for a specified time. Some corporations contribute a percent of profits to pension funds to which employees also contribute from their wages, and so provide a larger income for retirement. Seldom are any two profit-sharing plans exactly alike as each one is adapted to a certain situation. The varied incentive plans, as a rule, are benefits in addition to the customary wage agreements.

The cooperative corporation has been particularly successful in agriculture. Farmers form cooperatives both for buying and selling. In contrast to the ordinary corporation, the cooperative serves only as an agent for its members. The members serve only themselves. A farmer delivers his milk to the cooperative creamery which sells and distributes it for him. At the end of each month, usually, the farmer is paid for the milk the creamery sold for him, minus the operating expenses.

Variety is the keynote of "The American Way" for doing business. In this country during the rise of industry, there was no set pattern which could not be modified or changed for the greatest good of the greatest number. Only in a constitutional republic like the United States can there be such healthy disagreement and respect for the rights of others.

LAWS INFLUENCE INDUSTRIAL RELATIONS

With the rapid growth of industry came problems of adjustment which the Federal Government sought to solve by law. Interstate commerce drew the attention of Congress during the railroad era. Following the War Between the States so many railroads were built that competition for business resulted in rate wars and unfair charges for passengers and freight. Many lines traversed new country where the settlers were too scattered to support them. Sometimes two railroads served the same territory and each tried to take business from the other by lowering the rates. When these same companies had a monopoly, and farmers were forced to ship their products on the single railroad, freight rates were unreasonably high to make up for losses suffered under keen competition. In the late 1860's freight rates between Chicago and New York varied from 25 cents to $2.15 per hundred pounds. A few years later cattle could be hauled from Chicago to New York for $5 a carload.

In 1867 the National Grange of the Patrons of Husbandry, an organization to improve the lot of farmers, was formed in Washington, D.C. The Grange made a determined fight for laws regulating railroad rates and cheap transportation for farm products to markets. Although many Senators and Representatives introduced bills in Congress to regulate railroads and stop the rate wars which were harmful to the public, it took twenty years for the original Act to Regulate Commerce to win a majority of votes in Congress. The measure was signed on February 4, 1887 by President Grover Cleveland. This act established a commission to regulate commerce between the states.

From this small beginning grew the powerful Interstate Commerce Commission which controls transportation between states on railroads, inland waterways, and highways. The original act has been amended many times to fit new situations, and now includes truck and bus travel between states. In the public interest the Interstate Commerce Commission makes rules of safety for both employees and passengers; fixes rates on freight handled by any carrier; and requires insurance as a protection against loss of life or property.

Passage of the Act to Regulate Commerce has been generally interpreted as giving the Federal Government power to supervise industry. Later, Congress passed the Sherman Anti-trust Act, granting the Federal Government the authority to prevent industrial monopoly. President Benjamin Harrison signed this bill into law on July 2, 1890. The first section stated:

Every contract, combination in the form of trust or otherwise, or conspiracy, in restraint of trade or commerce among the several states, or with foreign nations, is hereby declared to be illegal.

According to this law, what is a trust? The word was interpreted to mean a person

519

or corporation, or combination owning or controlling enough industrial plants producing any certain article to be able to fix the price. People were disturbed about the way small companies refining oil, manufacturing sugar, tobacco, shoe machinery, steel products, farming implements, and other essentials were being absorbed into large corporations. The passage of the Sherman Anti-trust Act set off long and bitterly fought cases in the courts over what kind of combination constitutes a trust dangerous to the public interest. Both the Republican and Democratic parties favored anti-trust laws. On September 5, 1901, President McKinley was shot while attending the Pan American Exposition at Buffalo, New York. The Vice President, Theodore Roosevelt, was sworn in to succeed him in the office. The new President enforced the Sherman Act so vigorously that he gained the nickname of "trust buster." During the seven and one half years of Theodore Roosevelt's administration, forty-four cases were launched under the Sherman Act. In 1909 William Howard Taft, another Republican, followed Roosevelt in the Presidency. Taft's record for a single term of four years eclipsed that of the former President with a total of ninety anti-trust proceedings. During the first term of Woodrow Wilson, who followed Taft into the White House, thirty-four anti-trust indictments were filed. In fact court dockets seldom are cleared of cases to question any monopoly leading to price fixing not in the public interest.

Although the original Sherman Act has been amended a number of times with the passage of new laws, courts find it difficult to decide when a merger of companies becomes a trust exercising a dangerous monopoly. The United States holds the lead in scientific progress because large industrial organizations have been willing to invest capital in long, detailed, often unsuccessful experiments. Before a yard of cloth is offered for sale, $23,000,000 maybe spent to research and develop the fabric. If the fabric is enthusiastically accepted by the public, employment is provided for thousands — in garment factories, department stores, small owner-operated shops, defense plants and numerous industries. The question then asked is: If the cloth can be purchased by anyone at a reasonable price, does the corporation owning the patent on this new fabric constitute a harmful trust?

People generally do not become concerned about the size of any corporation unless it becomes powerful enough to set prices which they consider unfair. From the beginning, the average citizen of this country has harbored an innate fear of any kind of monopoly that would rob him of personal liberty, be it in business or government.

As industries grow in size and number, industrial laws are passed by local, state, and federal governments. Business firms hire attorneys to keep officials informed on these laws, changing from time to time. One may regulate the amount of smoke from a factory chimney, and another, safety devices on machinery. Child labor laws are general. A law in Vermont states:

No minor under 14 may be employed in or about any mill, cannery, workshop, factory or manufacturing establishment, or in any other gainful occupation except during vacation and before and after school.

The minimum wage law of California contains this clause concerning hours:

520

No woman or minor shall be employed more than eight (8) hours during any one day of twenty-four (24) hours, or more than forty-eight (48) hours in any one week.

In some states a fund is raised by a tax upon both employers and employees, to provide a weekly allowance for men and women who have lost their jobs. The amount of tax taken from the wages of employees and the operating expense of their employers depends upon the number of people who apply for unemployment compensation. Industrial laws differ from state to state, and legislatures add more as needed.

The United States Department of Labor, directed by a member of the President's Cabinet, was established to serve both employers and employees in adjusting to the ever-changing pattern of our complex industrial society.

Chapter 28

Mass Production Promotes Abundance

EDUCATION GREW
WITH THE COUNTRY

EDUCATION HAS BEEN considered important since colonial days. In 1636, just sixteen years after the landing of the Pilgrims, Harvard College was established in the British colonies. The story of its founding was written in a letter from Boston, dated September 26, 1642:

After God had carried us safe to *New England,* and we had builded our houses, provided necessaries for our livelihood, rear'd convenient places for God's worship, and setted the Civill Government: One of the next things we longed for, and looked after was to advance *Learning,* . . . dreading to leave an illiterate Ministery to the Churches, when our present Minister shall lie in the Dust. And as wee were thinking and consulting how to effect this great Work; it pleased God to stir up the heart of one Mr. *Harvard* . . . to give one halfe of his Estate towards the erecting of a College, and all his Library.

(Latin America's University of San Marcos in Lima, Peru, and the University of Mexico in Mexico City, are on record as being the oldest universities in the Western Hemisphere. Both were founded in 1551 by order of Charles V, King of Spain.)

In the Ordinance of 1787 for governing the Northwest Territory, Article 3 expressed the feeling of most citizens then and now:

Religion, morality, and knowledge being necessary to good government and the happiness of mankind, schools and the means of education shall forever be encouraged.

In early days, schooling for children was provided by parents in the home, church, and private school. Children on the large southern plantations had tutors who lived with the families. Not until a little over thirty years after the end of the War for Independence was the first system of schools started for every child at public expense. The reforms of the 1840's improved the public schools. However, the pattern of the present public school system was barely taking shape when war broke out between the states in 1861.

On July 2, 1862, Congress passed the Morrill Act, "an Act donating Public Lands to the several States and Territories which may provide Colleges for the Benefit of Agriculture and the Mechanic Arts."

By this law, public land was to be divided to each state — 30,000 acres for each senator and representative the state

522

had in Congress, under the census of 1860, except mineral lands. This Act stated:

That all moneys derived from the sale of these lands . . . shall be invested in stocks of the United States, or of the states, or some other safe stocks yielding not less than five per centum upon the par value of said stocks; and that the moneys so invested shall constitute a perpetual fund, the capital shall remain forever undiminished and the interest of which shall be inviolably appropriated . . . to the endowment, support, and maintenance of at least one college where the leading object shall be . . . to teach such branches of learning as are related to agriculture and mechanic arts . . . .

In 1862, during the war, Lincoln signed three bills passed by Congress to promote settlement of the West: the Homestead Act, the Railroad Act, and the Morrill Act.

When a settler in the frontier region had built a log cabin or a sod house, and planted a crop, he and his neighbors gathered to talk over ways to erect a schoolhouse, a church, and a courthouse, to provide for education, religion, and law. Sometimes a single log cabin served all three until separate buildings could be afforded. Having no factories, rural schools received taxes from land only and so often suffered from poor housing, lack of textbooks, and untrained teachers. A backwoodsman who could neither read nor write owned a country store and a boat at a ferry where the trail crossed the Cache River in Arkansas. When he wanted to go fishing for a few days he asked the country schoolmaster to write a notice to travelers that he tacked on the door of his log cabin trading post:

Ef anny boddy cums hear to git across the Rivver they kin just blow this here Horne, when my wife betsey up at the House heers the Horne a bloin she'll cum down and set across the Rivver, i'm a gwin fishin.

Education was so much appreciated in new settlements that a school could actually start a town. The first school in Denver, Colorado was opened on the third of October in 1859. It was only a log hut with a strip of wagon cover for a door and a hole in the gable end for a window. The teacher was a graduate of the University of Dublin, a newspaper man who had come to the West to write about the gold rush in the Rocky Mountains of Colorado. When a covered wagon train was sighted approaching on the plain, scouts rode out to meet it, telling the families, not about gold in Cherry Creek, but about the school in West Denver with a college graduate for a teacher. With attendance between twelve and sixteen per day and tuition only $3 per month for each pupil, the teacher could not have survived had he not received $20 a week for articles printed in eastern papers on the Colorado gold rush. Living expenses were high. Flour cost $20 a barrel and tallow candles sold for $1 apiece.

As a rule schools improved faster in industrial towns where factories helped pay the taxes that supported them. Since New England had the most industry, this section for a long time had the best schools, both public and private. Public schools for the children of all the people, were gradually established throughout the country, wherever industry located to share the burden of the cost. Today, even in rural districts, splendid graded schools offer instruction in many subjects to prepare children for abundant living in our complex industrial society. Education has traveled far from the one-room school with the three R's — "readin', ritin', rithmetic."

Education is a costly item in the budgets of town, city, county, state, and federal governments. Taxpayers are assessed to provide education from the nursery school to the university. In many communities schools are maintained at the taxpayers' expense for adults, especially evening schools. Although a citizen no longer attends classes, he may continue his education by reading books, magazines, and newspapers and listening to lectures in halls and over the air. There are day schools, evening schools, and correspondence schools; public schools, private schools and church schools; country schools, city schools, and state universities. A citizen of the United States has a wide choice in education.

FOUNDATIONS TO PROMOTE LEARNING

FROM EARLY DAYS, leaders in the nation encouraged learning. In 1732, Benjamin Franklin established the first circulating library in Philadelphia. Wishing to continue his support to education after his death, he set up the first foundation for training young men in crafts. During his lifetime, he had helped many skilled craftsmen from Europe to settle in Pennsylvania. Franklin stated in his will:

I have considered that among Artisans good Apprentices are most likely to make good Citizens, and having myself been bred to a manual Art Printing, in my native Town . . . I wish to be useful even after my Death, if possible, in forming and advancing other young men that they may be serviceable to their country . . . . To this end I devote Two thousand pounds Sterling, which I give, one thousand thereof to the Inhabitants of the Town of Boston . . . and the other thousand to the Inhabitants of the City of Philadelphia . . . .

With this fund, Franklin desired to help young married men take care of their families while learning a trade and starting a business. His will reads:

The said sum of One thousand Pounds Sterling, if accepted by the Inhabitants of the Town of Boston, shall be managed under the direction of the Select Men, united with the

FIRST CIRCULATING LIBRARY IN PHILADELPHIA
Benjamin Franklin welcomed readers at the first circulating library in Philadelphia in 1732. His idea helped to establish free libraries in the United States.

Franklin Institute of Boston

Franklin Institute of Boston

STUDENT AND TEACHER IN
FRANKLIN INSTITUTE OF BOSTON

In the early days, young men borrowed money from the Franklin Fund to learn trades of that time. According to the records, they wanted to be bricklayers, cabinet makers, tanners, silversmiths, blacksmiths, tallow chandlers (candlemakers), coopers, bakers, and hairdressers.

Today, graduates of the two-year programs find jobs as assistants in chemical research, civil engineering, architecture, electrical maintenance, electrical engineering, electronic research, mechanical engineering, automotive repair, commercial photography, and in factories requiring special skills.

Ministers of the oldest Episcopalian, Congregational and Presbyterian Churches in that Town; who are to let out the same upon Interest at five per cent per Annum to such young married artificers, under the age of twenty-five years, as have served an Apprenticeship in the said Town; and faithfully fulfilled the Duties required in their Indentures, so as to obtain a good moral Character from at least two Respectable Citizens, who are willing to become their Sureties in a Bond with the Applicants for the Repayment of the monies so lent with Interest according to the Terms . . . .

Among the "young married artificers" who borrowed money from this fund in May of 1791 were a bricklayer, a cabinet maker, a tanner, a silversmith, a blacksmith, a saddler, and a baker. They paid back their loans with interest.

According to Franklin's will, the fund was divided into two parts in both Boston and Philadelphia, the first to gather interest for one hundred years, and the second, for two hundred years. In Boston, after a hundred years, the 1000 pounds sterling amounted to $432,000 with which the Board of Managers established a trade school, the Franklin Institute. The second part of the fund available in 1991, after two hundred years, is now well over a million dollars.

In Philadelphia, Franklin requested that the city officials handle the money. He recommended that the hundred-year fund be spent "in bringing by Pipes the Water of Wissahickon Creek into the Town . . . I also recommend making the Schuylkill compleately navigable." Since these needs

FRANKLIN INSTITUTE OF BOSTON

In time, fewer "young married artificers" applied for loans from the Franklin Fund. The apprentice system of Franklin's day was no longer popular. The trustees pondered a way to carry out Franklin's instructions in the spirit of his will. In 1908, plans were made to spend the money for a trade school where students could learn skills needed in new industries. The school is now co-educational.

Franklin Institute of Boston

no longer existed, the Board of Trustees in Philadelphia turned over the first part of the Franklin Fund, a little over $133,000, to erect the Franklin Institute in that city. With good management and profits, the fund grew to over a million and a half dollars. At the end of two hundred years, the money on hand is to be "divided between the inhabitants of the city of Philadelphia and the Government of Pennsylvania" as stated in Franklin's will.

Franklin remembered children in the Boston schools. He left in his will "One hundred Pounds Sterling" to be "put to Interest, and so continued at Interest forever, which Interest annually shall be laid out in Silver Medals, and given as honorary Rewards annually by the Directors of the said Free Schools for the encouragement of Scholarship, . . . " Today, students in the Boston Public Schools still vie for the honor of winning a Franklin Medal.

Benjamin Franklin, one of the few rich men in the British colonies, lived to play a part in writing a constitution for a new republic, the United States of America. Aware that the new government needed informed citizens to survive, he provided a way for his lifelong interest in education to function after his death.

Many wealthy men in this country have followed Franklin's idea and established foundations to support art museums, music schools, symphony orchestras, colleges and universities. A foundation frequently reflects the interest or hobby of the man who gives his money to support it. For example, Henry E. Huntington collected rare books, manuscripts, paintings, and art objects as a hobby. Then he decided to share his treasures with the public, free of charge, and set up a

THE BLUE BOY
by Thomas Gainsborough

The BLUE BOY was Jonathan Buttall, the son of a wealthy ironmonger in London. His portrait was painted by Gainsborough about the time of the American Revolution.

Another great portrait painter, Sir Joshua Reynolds, who lived at the same time, made this statement: "that the masses of light in a picture ought to be always of a warm, mellow color, yellow, red, or a yellowish white, and that the blue, gray, or the green colors be kept almost entirely out of these masses, and be used only to support or set off these warm colors."

According to tradition, to refute Reynolds' remark, Gainsborough painted young Buttal's costume in shades varying from pale turquoise to deepest azure blue. The famous portrait was purchased by Henry E. Huntington in 1921 for his art gallery, open to the public and free of charge. During the year, thousands of children accompanied by their parents and teachers visit the Henry E. Huntington Library and Art Gallery to see the BLUE BOY.

Henry E. Huntington
Library and Art Gallery

foundation to maintain the Henry E. Huntington Library and Art Gallery in San Marino, California. Many Americans continue their education in some way during their leisure time, by taking advantage of opportunities offered free or at a small cost.

Thomas Jefferson planned to keep his book collection of about 10,000 volumes until his death, when it would be offered to Congress "at their own price." But after a British army burned all the public buildings in Washington, including the public library, Jefferson offered to sell the books to start a new library. He wrote to his friend, publisher of the Washington Intelligencer, on September 21, 1814, describing them:

I have been fifty years making it, and have spared no pains, opportunity or expense, to make it what it is. While residing in Paris, I devoted every afternoon I was disengaged, for a summer or two, in examining all the principal bookstores, turning over every book with my own hand, and putting by everything which related to America, and indeed whatever was rare and valuable in every science. Besides this, I had standing orders during the whole time I was in Europe, on its principal bookmarts, particularly Amsterdam, Frankfort, Madrid and London, for such works relating to America as could not be found in Paris . . . . Nearly all of the whole are well bound, abundance of them elegantly, and of the choicest editions existing.

With the letter, he enclosed a catalogue. His friend showed the letter to members of Congress, and a bill was passed to pay Jefferson $25,000 for his great and rare collection which became the nucleus of the Library of Congress. He kept a few books "chiefly classical and mathematical" until his death. Jefferson preferred to read books written in Latin and Greek in the original languages instead of translations.

After serving eight years as President of the United States, Jefferson returned to Monticello to take care of his farm. The big project of his later years was the University of Virginia which he planned, designed, built, organized, and cherished. At the age of 82, he frequently rode to Charlottesville, not far from Monticello, to see how the University was getting along.

From colonial times to the present, schooling has been a treasured goal of the people. Today, the opportunity to acquire an education in any chosen field is being constantly improved for anyone who wants it.

GOOD HEALTH

SAFEGUARDING HEALTH is part of the program for abundant living. In few nations is public health so well protected as

THOMAS JEFFERSON
1743-1826

Thomas Jefferson wrote his own inscription for his tombstone, listing three events which he considered to be the most important services to his country.

"Author of the Declaration of Independence, of the Statute of Virginia for Religious Freedom, and father of the University of Virginia."

Library of Congress

in the United States. Food and drugs must pass inspection and be properly labeled. Drinking water is treated to kill germs that cause disease. Restaurants and hotels serving the public are regularly checked for sanitation. Cities, counties, and states maintain health departments.

Great advances in medicine are made by foundations and organizations supported by private donations. These voluntary associations study cures for polio, tuberculosis, cancer, diabetes, arthritis, and many diseases while aiding people who are afflicted with these ailments. Health insurance is popular in this country. Large corporations maintain, or pay for, medical care of employees, and some have their own hospitals and doctors. Some labor unions also support these services. Nearly every factory with a large number of employees hires nurses to take immediate care of workmen who are injured or become ill on the job. Many union contracts include health benefits for workmen and their families. The average citizen has his physician or health consultant, in whom he has confidence.

For people unable to pay for medical care and without a health insurance plan of some kind, clinics and hospitals are maintained at taxpayers' expense. Church organizations also provide medical care for those unable to pay. On July 30, 1965, Congress passed bill HR 89-97, providing medical aid by the Federal Government, under specified rules, to persons 65 years of age and older. Again, in the matter of health and medical care, variety is the keynote of the American way. Both private and public health clinics are maintained.

Freedom of opportunity in this country has resulted in so many voluntary organizations that the United States is known as a nation of "joiners." Nearly every adult and school child joins some kind of club, lodge, or society. Whether these organizations meet for business or pleasure, most of them support some kind of program to assist their fellowmen. The average citizen of this nation considers it a privilege as well as a civic duty to donate part of his earnings and his time to helping others. Most citizens give time or money, sometimes both, to an orphanage, a home for the aged, a hospital for the sick, a research bureau to eradicate disease, a missionary society, a community chest, and pay dues to a lodge or society carrying on a program to help those in need. The spirit of human brotherhood expressed in action by these many groups contributes to abundant living in this country.

Americans are interested in sports for both health and fun. In many schools, a well-equipped gymnasium and large athletic field are considered as important as classrooms. In most cities, playgrounds are cheerfully supported by the taxpayers. Some states maintain picnic grounds in shady spots along the roads to encourage families interested in outdoor fun. Although more and more citizens are participating in sports such as swimming, hiking, boating, skiing, skating, horseback riding, and tennis, many enjoy being spectators at games and contests. This country affords many opportunities to enjoy good health for those who seek it, offered with or without cost to the individual. Health is a national goal.

MORE LEISURE FOR AMERICANS

LEISURE FOR AMERICANS is a product of the machine age. Before

Mayhew Photographers, Cincinnati, Ohio

MAY FESTIVAL IN
MUSIC HALL — CINCINNATI, OHIO

On a rainy afternoon, a woman who liked music talked with the conductor of the Cincinnati Symphony Orchestra about inviting the singing societies of the community to take part in a music festival. During the first week in May of 1873, the first concerts were performed. This date marks the beginning of the Cincinnati May Festivals, for which the chorus rehearses year after year to perform the works of great composers. Most of the singers are volunteers.

power-driven machinery came into use, a man usually toiled from daylight to dark to produce enough goods to supply his needs. He had little time for play. As machines did more and more of the work, a man was able to produce more and more per hour. The working day grew shorter, gradually, and there was time for the pursuit of leisure. How are Americans spending this leisure time?

Although sports are a favorite pastime for many citizens, a large number of Americans follow cultural interests in their leisure time. Music, long considered the privilege of the rich, is now universally enjoyed through phonograph records, radio and television, as well as in the concert hall. Those who enjoy playing a musical instrument join small orchestras which rehearse and perform for the fun of it. Those who like acting may join a drama club or little theater group. The study of art is a pastime for many who paint in oils and water colors, carve figures from wood and stone, mould objects in clay, draw with pen and pencil, and design patterns for clothes. Library shelves are filled with books on varied subjects to please most readers. Few citizens are without a hobby.

Leisure time grows in proportion to the speed with which power-driven machinery takes the drudgery out of labor and increases the rate of production. Now, education includes opportunities for students to discover how to spend their leisure time in a wholesome and profitable manner. In our complex industrial society communities shoulder the responsibility

JUNIOR HIGH FIGURE PAINTING CLASS
THE ART INSTITUTE OF CHICAGO

On Saturdays during the school year, students from seven years of age through high school may study drawing, painting, sculpture, design, and various forms of visual expression in The School of The Art Institute of Chicago, established and supported mainly by private contributions.

More than a million persons a year visit the galleries to see the paintings, sculpture, prints, bronzes, fabrics, pottery, and the famous miniature rooms, correct in every detail of French, English, and American interiors.

The Art Institute of Chicago

for preparing youth to earn a living and equally important, to learn to live abundantly.

Citizens of the United States have the highest standard of living ever known in the world. This country, which has contributed so many labor-saving devices, has reaped the benefits from these inventions through industrialization. Telephones, refrigerators, automobiles, gas and electrical appliances, plumbing, washing machines, radio, television, and numerous items for comfort and pleasure are common necessities to millions of Americans. To most people scattered throughout the world, such luxuries are practically unknown.

Why? This question can be answered in a few words — freedom of opportunity. The high standard of living in this country was founded upon the right of individual ownership. A citizen may own his home, his farm, his business. In this nation with a wealth of natural resources, free people, spurred by ambition, achieved success for themselves and for their country. Living in the United States is based upon mass production of goods and services at a price many people can afford to pay. This system operates under law. After free men have acquired food, shelter and clothing, they seek the better things of life and promote a cultural society.

PART ELEVEN

World Conflicts Involve the United States

TWENTIETH CENTURY WARS

World War I (Declared)

U.S. Army Photograph

**General John J. Pershing
leading American troops
Arch of Triumph, 1918**

World War II (Declared)

United States Navy

**USS Pennsylvania leading warships
into Lingayen Gulf,
Philippine Islands, 1945**

War in Korea (Undeclared)

United States Marines

**United States Marines
rest in the snow during move
south from Koto-ri, Korea, 1950**

War in Vietnam (Undeclared)

United States Air Force

**Flying F-4C Phantom jets
being refueled from KC-135
Strato tankers over Vietnam, 1967**

TWENTIETH CENTURY PRESIDENTS

Theodore Roosevelt
1901-1909

William Howard Taft
1909-1913

Woodrow Wilson
1913-1921
World War I

Warren G. Harding
1921-1923

Calvin Coolidge
1923-1929

Herbert C. Hoover
1929-1933

Franklin D. Roosevelt
1933-1945
World War II

Harry S. Truman
1945-1953
World War II
War in Korea

Dwight D. Eisenhower
1953-1961
World War II — General
War in Korea

John F. Kennedy
1961-1963
War in Vietnam

Lyndon B. Johnson
1963-1969
War in Vietnam

Richard M. Nixon
1969-
War in Vietnam

All photographs, Library of Congress

Chapter 29

The Spanish American War

CUBA'S ADVENTUROUS PAST

SINCE THE DAYS of John Quincy Adams and Simon Bolivar, statesmen throughout the Americas had been slowly developing a policy to make the Western Hemisphere a bulwark of freedom. Therefore, a threat from a foreign power became a matter of concern to all, especially to the nations situated near the disturbance. Cuba had belonged to Spain since the island was discovered by Columbus in 1492. His son, Diego, founded the first permanent settlement in 1511. Cuban soil felt the tread of conquistadores — Cortes, Balboa, de Soto, and many more. The island was used as a supply base for Spanish exploration in the New World.

Cuba suffered from piracy. Havana, founded in 1519 the year that Cortes launched his conquest of Mexico, was looted and burned by pirates in 1538.

In 1762 a British fleet captured Havana and all of Cuba. So many soldiers died of yellow fever while occupying the island that Great Britain was quite willing to return it to Spain the next year.

When the cultivation of tobacco and sugar cane began late in the sixteenth century, Negroes were imported from Africa to work in the fields. Native labor had almost vanished in the vain search for gold and silver. By the middle of the nineteenth century about half a million Negroes had been admitted to the island.

Toussaint L'Ouverture had organized a rebellion in Haiti and stirred slaves on Cuban sugar plantations to revolt for freedom. The riots were quickly suppressed by Spanish authorities. During the revolutions in the Spanish colonies Cubans formed secret societies to fight for independence from Spain. The members received sympathetic help from citizens in Mexico, Colombia, and the United States. However, when most of the Spanish colonies won independence during the first quarter of the nineteenth century, Cuba and Puerto Rico were left to Spain as a remnant of empire in the Western Hemisphere.

In 1868, three years after the end of the War Between the States, rebellion broke out in Cuba and lasted for ten years. Plantations were burned and commerce was halted. The Cubans demanded a constitutional government — the right of Cubans to hold office, permission to assemble, and local self-

534

government. The ten-year war ended in a deadlock rather than a victory. The Spanish Government promised to carry out the desired reforms, including the abolition of slavery, but insisted that the governor-general still hold supreme power. Spain had lost about 80,000 troops in the long struggle. More men were lost from yellow fever than from bullets.

The Cubans who wanted independence and not reforms gained enough strength with outside help to launch another revolt in 1895. President Cleveland adopted a "hands-off" policy, but newspapers in this country inflamed public opinion with blood-curdling stories of Spanish atrocities. Sometimes these harrowing tales were printed before the reports were checked to separate truth from fiction.

During President McKinley's term sympathy for the Cuban revolutionists increased to fever heat. To protect the property of United States citizens in Cuba, the battleship *Maine* was dispatched to Havana. A few weeks later, on February 15, 1898, the *Maine* was blown up in the harbor of Havana with a loss of 266 lives. Newspaper headlines, "Remember the Maine" stirred the anger of United States citizens to the point of intervention. A board of inquiry was not able to find what had caused the explosion. War hysteria swept over the United States. The easterners were inclined to consider war only as a last resort; the westerners, as in the time of Jefferson, wanted to extend the area of freedom in the hemisphere. Senator William V. Allen from Nebraska expressed this policy in a speech, "Cuba Must Be Free," in the Senate of the United States in March, 1898:

I believe it to be the true policy and the true doctrine of our country that whenever a people show themselves desirous of establishing a republican form of government upon any territory adjacent to us they should receive our encouragement and support. If our form of government is the correct one — and of that I have no doubt — then its recognition or establishment in other lands should be encouraged, and when an opportunity shall present itself to us to lend this encouragement, it should be promptly and effectually given.

BATTLESHIP MAINE PASSING MORRO CASTLE TO ENTER HAVANA HARBOR

United States Navy

President McKinley did not want war with Spain. The pressure of public opinion, however, forced him to ask Congress for authority to use the Army and Navy to establish peace in Cuba. War began soon after a joint resolution of Congress stated "that the people of the island of Cuba are and of right ought to be independent." However, the first major battle of the Spanish American War was in the Philippines in another hemisphere, not in Cuba.

IT WAS A BRIEF WAR

ON THE 25TH OF APRIL Commodore Dewey, commanding a squadron of warships anchored in the Bay of Hong Kong, received the following cablegram from the Secretary of the Navy in Washington:

War has commenced between the United States and Spain. Proceed at once to Philippine Islands. Commence operations at once, particularly against the Spanish fleet. You must capture vessels or destroy. Use utmost endeavors.

After a voyage of 600 miles, Dewey's six warships slipped into the Bay of Manila under cover of darkness. They lined up for battle at dawn on the first day of May. The American vessels had heavier armaments than the Spanish ships. During three hours of fighting the enemy fleet was practically destroyed. The naval victory electrified the public and made Dewey a national hero. He was promoted to the rank of admiral.

The *U.S.S. Oregon* was leaving drydock at Bremerton, Washington, when news arrived that the *Maine* had been sunk in Havana harbor. Orders came to proceed to San Francisco immediately and prepare for a long cruise. On the nineteenth of March, the *Oregon* steamed out of the Bay of San Francisco for a voyage of over 13,000 miles through the Strait of Magellan and up the eastern coast of South America. After a voyage of sixty-eight days at top speed the crew received a rousing welcome on that Sunday morning when the warship from the Pacific joined vessels of the Atlantic fleet patroling the northern shore of Cuba. Each ship in turn saluted the *Oregon*. Bands played "There'll Be A Hot Time In The Old Town Tonight." The next morning Admiral Sampson arrived on the *New York*. The *New York* and the *Oregon* joined the vessels lying off Santiago on the southern coast where a Spanish fleet was bottled up in the harbor. Five weeks later in the Battle of Santiago Bay, eleven warships under Admiral Sampson destroyed the Spanish fleet which was attempting to run the American blockade. The long voyage of the *Oregon* through the Strait of Magellan awakened the American public as no other event had done to the need of a canal across the Isthmus of Panama.

Two weeks after the naval victory in Santiago Bay, Major General William R. Shafter was negotiating for the surrender of Spanish land forces in the country surrounding the city of Santiago. United States troops were landed to battle Spanish troops wherever they could be found and to occupy the islands of Cuba and Puerto Rico. Convinced, after three months of fighting, that further resistance was useless, the Spanish Government sued for peace. An armistice was arranged whereby Spanish troops would be sent home as soon as transports came for them. The war ended so quickly that the United States scarcely knew what to do with the victory. It took a longer time to sign the peace than to win the war.

Peace negotiations in Paris were drawn out because even the American commissioners could not agree among themselves. George Gray argued against retaining the Philippines and many citizens agreed with him. He thought it proper to govern Cuba and Puerto Rico because these islands were so near the coast of the United States and their occupancy by another country might endanger the national safety. Gray objected to holding the Philippines so far away in another hemisphere. His reasons accurately foretold the happenings of the next fifty years. He declared:

Policy proposed introduces us into European politics and the entangling alliances against which Washington and all American statesmen have protested. It will make necessary a navy equal to the largest of powers; a greatly increased military establishment; immense sums for fortifications and harbors; multiply occasions for dangerous complications with foreign nations; and increase burdens of taxation.

The anti-expansionists argued that it was imperialism for the United States to demand the cession of the Philippines. The expansionists claimed it was "our duty to the world as one of its civilizing powers" to extend the area of freedom. President McKinley pondered what action to take. If the United States withdrew, France or Germany might annex the islands. McKinley was forced by circumstances of war to agree to annexation, in this statement:

The Philippines are ours, not to exploit but to develop, to civilize, to educate, to train in the science of self-government.

On the tenth of December, 1898, the Treaty of Peace was signed in Paris whereby Spain ceded to the United States, Cuba and Puerto Rico in the West Indies, Guam in the Mariannas, and the Philippine Islands for the sum of $20,000,000. The United States guaranteed the inhabitants of these territories the free exercise of their religion.

By this treaty the United States gained 120,000 square miles of territory and responsibility for about 8,500,000 persons in two hemispheres. Unexpectedly and unintentionally, as far as the average citizen was concerned, the nation emerged from the conflict as a rising world power with a colonial empire. The Spanish American War tossed the United States into the seething cauldron of world affairs.

WAR HASTENS THE ANNEXATION OF THE HAWAIIAN ISLANDS

VERY SOON AFTER the Anglo Americans settled on the Pacific Coast and started trading with the Hawaiians, the little island monarchy began to gravitate toward the United States. As commerce increased with the Orient, American vessels called enroute at the "Crossroads of the Pacific" for coal and other supplies. Among these ships was *Old Ironsides,* sailing in the island waters about the year 1846. An alert young naval officer on board recommended Pearl Harbor as a future naval base for this country in a report he wrote on the voyage.

In 1876, during the term of President Grant, the United States and Hawaii signed a trade agreement permitting raw sugar from Hawaii to enter this country free of duty. This favorable treaty brought an era of prosperity to the Islands. In exchange for this privilege, the King ceded Pearl

Harbor to the United States to be used as a coaling base for ships bound for the Orient.

Since business depended largely upon trade with the United States, agitation began in the Islands for annexation. However, revolts against the monarchy were not serious until the 1890's when the new ruler, Queen Liliuokalani, revoked the constitution in order to submit a new one. Revolutionaries took advantage of this incident to proclaim a republic. The newly-formed government sought annexation to the United States. This was granted by President Benjamin Harrison after an act of Congress. The annexation became a political issue with the Republicans favoring it and the Democrats voting against it. When Grover Cleveland, a Democrat, succeeded Harrison, a Republican, the treaty for annexation was withdrawn from the Senate, on the grounds that the Queen had been deposed because the landing of United States troops to protect American property had encouraged the revolutionary party.

Then, while the expansionists and the anti-expansionists were debating for and against annexation of Hawaii, the United States went to war with Spain. Troops enroute to the Philippines were entertained in Honolulu. Soldiers from the first three transports were guests at a banquet on the capitol grounds where bushels of potato salad, 10,000 ham sandwiches, 300 gallons of milk, 800 pineapples, and 500 oranges were included in the menu. All were free to men in uniform. Business prospered when American troop transports arrived enroute to the Philippines.

Hawaiian business men wanted annexation. The United States needed the Islands for a supply base and a coaling station for naval vessels operating in the Pacific. The fact that Japan was a rising nation in need of colonies convinced some Congressmen that Hawaii should be annexed by the United States for national safety.

About a month after Dewey's victory in Manila Bay, President McKinley remarked, "We need Hawaii just as much and a good deal more than we did California. It is Manifest Destiny."

Sixteen months after President McKinley was inaugurated, Hawaii was annexed by a joint resolution of Congress. On August 12, 1898, the Stars and Stripes was raised in Hawaii, and our nation "plunged into the sea." The Hawaiian Islands, with Pearl Harbor, became a bulwark of defense for the protection of the Pacific Coast of the continental United States and the Philippines in Asia.

TERRITORIAL EXPANSION PROVES EMBARRASSING AND EXPENSIVE

HERETOFORE THE NATION had expanded westward into territory practically unoccupied. The settlers, being citizens from other states, adapted old and familiar patterns of living to the new country. Not until the Spanish American War did the United States gain territory with large populations whose backgrounds were rooted in different civilizations. Although Cubans and Filipinos were fighting for independence, they lacked training in self-government. Spanish colonials had been ruled almost entirely by officials from Spain. Therefore, to maintain order the United States was placed in the embarrassing position of forcing a military regime upon foreign peoples, most of whom showed little interest in

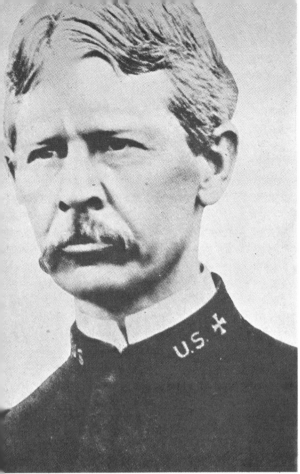

WALTER REED

Major Walter Reed of the Army Medical School was sent to Cuba during the Spanish American War when yellow fever was causing the death of many soldiers. With the aid of physicians, nurses, and persons who accepted mosquito bites in experiments, Dr. Reed, a surgeon, proved the theory that the bite of a certain mosquito spread the disease.

The United States Army General Hospital in Washington, D.C. was named for Walter Reed.

exchanging one master for another master.

Routine army reports told of the problems faced by American forces in restoring order where plantations were in ruin, business was disrupted, people were homeless and starving, sanitation was lacking, and laws were not enforced. As fast as possible the Army turned over to native Cubans all functions of government — courts, mails, customs, schools, sanitation, and health.

Cubans were grateful for the American army's program to improve the health of the people. For every American soldier killed in battle or dying of wounds, at least three had perished from tropical diseases such as malaria, dysentery, and yellow fever. After the Treaty of Paris was signed, the army of occupation under Major General Leonard Wood inaugurated a program of sanitation and health. Walter Reed, an army doctor, launched a campaign against yellow fever with Major William C. Gorgas, Department Surgeon of Havana, as one of his assistants. Dr. Carlos Finlay, a Cuban of Scotch and French ancestry, had read a paper before the Royal Academy of Havana in 1881 in which he stated his belief that yellow fever was carried by mosquitoes. He had not been able to prove his claim. Through experiments with soldiers, doctors, nurses, and civilians who allowed themselves to be bitten by inoculated mosquitoes, Walter Reed proved Finlay's theory to be true. Then Gorgas took over the task of ridding Havana of the dangerous insects. Since Gorgas had recovered from yellow fever years before, he was immune to the disease. He visited patients and studied yellow fever until he became an authority on it. In less than a year there was not a single case in Havana, a city scourged by the dreaded ailment for over 150 years.

The United States had promised to free Cuba and recognize the island as an independent nation as soon as the country was pacified and Cubans were ready to take over the reins of government. The pledge was kept on May 20, 1902. Many

Cubans regretted the early evacuation, feeling the need of more time for all segments of the population to learn self-government. Theodore Roosevelt was determined to avoid the taint of imperialism in the political campaign of 1902. Cuba was free! The densely populated island of Puerto Rico became a territory of the United States like Hawaii and Guam.

Although no promise of independence had been made to the Filipinos, they rather expected it. Under the leadership of Emilio Aguinaldo, they had been fighting for independence from Spain since war broke out between them and the mother country in August of 1896. The revolutionary government had framed a constitution patterned after the Constitution of the United States. When war suddenly began between the United States and Spain, Aguinaldo was at Singapore seeking foreign aid for his cause. Dewey invited him to return to Manila with the American squadron but Aguinaldo did not reach Hong Kong until Dewey had gone to sea. He was transported there later on an American ship. This attention led the Filipino leader to think that the Government of the United States intended to declare the Philippines an independent nation and to support him for the presidency. On June 12, 1898 Aguinaldo was chosen president of the revolutionary government. On December 21 of the same year, President McKinley declared that the United States was sovereign in the Philippines.

To Americans it seemed logical to restore order in the islands first and then decide what to do. The task proved to be difficult. On February 4, 1899, from his headquarters Aguinaldo issued this general order to his Filipino army:

Peace and friendly relations between the Philippine forces and the American forces of occupation are broken, and the latter will be treated as enemies, with the limits prescribed by the laws of war.

Guerrilla warfare followed this proclamation. The casualty lists from the Philippine war dimmed the clamor of expansionists. The conflict became a major issue in Congress. In 1900 the Democrats nominated William Jennings Bryan for President and made the Philippine question the main issue of the campaign. Bryan poked fun at the "manifest destiny" of Americans waging war with alien people who wanted independence. Republicans defended their policy of restoring order in the Islands as humanitarian and reelected McKinley to the high office. Fighting did not stop when Aguinaldo surrendered in April, 1901. A month later Major General Arthur MacArthur cabled Washington for 40,000 troops.

For the difficult task of establishing courts and civil government while the Army maintained order, McKinley appointed William Howard Taft as chairman of the Philippine Commission. Taft encouraged the residents to prepare themselves for independence, assuring them that "the Philippines are for the Filipinos, and the government of the United States is here for the purpose of preserving the Philippines for the Filipinos." Meanwhile the army of occupation at times became impatient with civil authorities who hesitated to take over certain districts and tried to govern them without military aid. The following reply to a request for a garrison to remain in a town explains the policy of the Army to evacuate troops as soon as a region was fairly peaceful:

Pangasinan is a pacified province and has been for some months under a provincial governor. It is believed that if the civil authorities are ever going to protect the people from themselves, now is a good time to begin. It is respectfully submitted that the United States troops cannot be expected to serve these people as policemen indefinitely.

It took real war — over 2000 combats in three years — to pacify the archipelago acquired from Spain. Then the problem was not solved. From the brief Spanish American War, the United States inherited commitments in Asia which cost billions of dollars to the taxpayers and took the lives of thousands of the nation's fighting forces.

TURN OF THE CENTURY
MARKS A TURN IN FOREIGN AFFAIRS

MOST CITIZENS OF THIS COUNTRY were not prepared to grasp the real meaning of the expansion into the Pacific. They had long taken for granted that the two great oceans were permanent barriers that would protect the Western Hemisphere with little effort on the part of the United States. Few Americans realized that the Atlantic Ocean was a barrier only as long as no European nation had a navy large and powerful enough to challenge Great Britain's supremacy of the seas. Soon Germany began to build a fleet. Did that nation intend to contest Great Britain's title as Queen of the Seas?

Alaska was a far-flung outpost that needed little or no protection because Asia had long been dormant. By the turn of the century Japan was rising as a naval power in the Pacific. Japan was only a few hundred miles from the Aleutian Islands. On July 8, 1853 Commodore Perry had steamed into Yedo Bay, Japan, with a squadron of four warships. He intended to make a treaty with the emperor. He delivered a letter from President Fillmore to the ruler of Japan. He also presented gifts such as a telegraph set and a miniature locomotive with a string of cars and rails. He was not received in a friendly way. Perry left, stating that he would return in the spring to learn the emperor's decision after that ruler had read the letter from the President of the United States. On the last day of March in 1854 Perry returned. He secured a treaty of friendship and trade that opened up commerce between the two nations. Japan signed similar treaties with many nations and developed industry capable of supporting a program for military might. Perry's treaty opened up a new epoch in Asia.

Before the end of the nineteenth century Great Britain and the United States agreed upon the "open door" policy for China. This meant that all nations have a right to trade with that country. Since the peoples of the East were generally suspicious of foreigners, a patriotic society, called Boxers, was formed in China to drive out the foreigners. Along with other nations the United States sent troops to China to put down the Boxer Rebellion.

For several centuries the little "hermit kingdom" of Korea had been coveted by neighboring states. In self defense Koreans had shut themselves off from the world. They, too, in the latter part of the nineteenth century had opened their ports to trade. The little peninsula became an object of rivalry among three Pacific powers — China, Japan, and Russia. In 1883 the United States had ratified a trade treaty with Korea which recognized the little kingdom as an independent country. However, these agreements did not mean much to the average citizen of

541

this country until the United States took possession of the Philippines.

In fact, acquiring the Philippines placed the United States at the geographical center of Eastern Asia. A circle with Manila as a center and a radius of 1700 miles would include the area containing most of the rich resources of the East Indies, Burma, Malaya, Indochina, China proper, the industrial area of Japan, and southern Korea. The eastern powers were not too pleased to have a western nation with western ideas in their midst. Since Japan had defeated China in a war in 1895, and had taken the island of Formosa from China by treaty, that nation did not want the United States for a neighbor in the Philippines. For this reason Japan strongly protested the annexation of Hawaii until the United States Government assured the Emperor's Government that the 25,000 Japanese living in Hawaii would be fully protected in their rights.

While under military occupation, many Filipinos continued to argue for independence. A petition from Manila, dated July 15, 1900, and signed by 2000 Filipinos, was submitted by Senator Teller of Colorado. It was read in the United States Senate where the Philippine problem was bitterly debated. It began thus:

TO THE CONGRESS OF THE UNITED STATES: . . .

The Filipinos steadfastly believe that their independence is their only salvation. Should they obtain it, they would be forever grateful to whomsoever shall have helped them in their undertaking . . . . America, consistent with her tradition, is the only one which could play that great role in the present and future of the Philippines . . . .

Such pleas carried great weight with citizens of this country whose forefathers had objected to being colonials and had fought for independence. Public opinion swung toward independence — but when? If the Philippines were granted independence immediately, would Japan gain control of the Islands before the people were able to defend themselves against aggression? Although both political parties came to agree, after a time, that the Philippines should become an independent nation, they disagreed on the date. The Republicans preferred to wait, as William Howard Taft explained, "long enough to give to the poor, the weak, and the humble a consciousness of their rights, and a certainty that they would be preserved under any government to which we might transfer sovereign power."

The United States Government maintained order; established courts; built schoolhouses and promoted education of the people; launched an extensive program for sanitation and health; and encouraged the erection of factories to provide employment and to increase commerce. While the Filipinos were learning how to govern themselves and were adapting to new ways, they continued the agitation for independence. In August, 1916, Congress passed a law establishing an all-Filipino legislature. In 1934, the independence law was passed, providing for a ten-year period as a commonwealth before becoming a free republic. During this time, the Filipinos could depend upon the United States for help if needed, while operating their own government. They wrote a constitution which was approved by a vote of the people and was accepted by the President of the United States.

It was necessary for the Filipinos to develop an army for defense before being cut loose as a free nation. To help in organizing and training this native army, the United States Government sent units of this nation's military forces under the command of General Douglas MacArthur, the son of General Arthur MacArthur who had served in the Philippines during the American occupation. The Filipinos had gone more than halfway toward final independence when war broke out in the Pacific in 1941.

THE PANAMA CANAL
LINKS THE OCEANS

THEODORE ROOSEVELT, who became President in September, 1901, inherited the foreign commitments resulting from the Spanish American War in which he himself had fought. He was aware of the responsibilities which expansion had thrust upon the nation. Having been Assistant Secretary of the Navy during McKinley's first term, Roosevelt realized the need for a two-ocean Navy. He began at once to ask Congress for large appropriations to build new and modern ships for the United States Navy, and to provide for two fleets, one in the Atlantic and one in the Pacific. To concentrate both fleets in one ocean in an emergency, a canal was needed across the Isthmus of Panama. Noting the rise of Germany to world power, Roosevelt was determined to build that canal as soon as possible. Although such a canal had been talked about for centuries, action could no longer be delayed when the nation had expanded in both hemispheres. The building of this canal also proved to be embarrassing and expensive.

The Isthmus of Panama was discovered by Bastidas who sailed from Cadiz, Spain, in October of the year 1500. With him on this voyage was a young man destined to fame as the discoverer of the Pacific Ocean. His name was Vasco Nunez de Balboa.

Balboa's discovery of the South Sea in 1513 intensified the search for a natural water route linking the two large bodies of water separated by a narrow strip of land. However, the Spaniards did not wait for the doubtful strait to be found. They began building a road across the isthmus in 1521. Although it was scarcely more than a track through swamps and jungles, the Spaniards proudly named it Camino Real (royal road). Over this winding trail went the pack trains laden with silver and gold from the fabulous mines of Peru.

While explorers were still looking for a natural waterway, Charles V, King of Spain, had surveyors hacking their way through the jungle and paddling on the streams to discover the best route for a canal. The Chagres River way was considered. The King ordered the stream cleared of logs and obstructions. Later, this course was followed during the rainy season when heavy shipments were hauled overland to the Chagres, and loaded on to boats for the completion of the journey from the Pacific to the Atlantic. However, the main thoroughfare across the isthmus continued to be the Camino Real, threading a path through the tangled vegetation from Panama City to Nombre de Dios.

Philip II inherited the throne of his father, Charles V, but not his enthusiasm for a canal which he feared would open up the country to the enemies of Spain. During his reign, pirates spread terror throughout the area. For several years, Sir Francis Drake and his followers joined with French corsairs in plundering barges on the Chagres River, waylaying the pack trains on the Camino Real, and raiding the ports where bars of gold and silver were stored awaiting shipment to Spain. Philip II did not want a canal to encourage more raids by these bold buccaneers. He forbade mention of such a waterway.

However, the idea of a canal persisted in the Spanish mind and found its way into the thinking of Frenchmen and Americans. Both Franklin and Jefferson had been interested in the project. Early in the nineteenth century, when Napoleon invaded Spain and the colonies in the New World flared into rebellion, the last chance was gone for Spain to build a waterway across the isthmus connecting the two continents.

Who would dig the canal? Where would it be? Across Tehuantepec, Nicaragua, Panama? Simon Bolivar, when president of Gran Colombia, was besieged with offers from European countries, but his Congress accepted none as practical. In 1825, when Henry Clay was Secretary of State in the Cabinet of John Quincy Adams, he asked a diplomatic official in Central America to investigate a proposed canal route through Nicaragua, but warned him not to give the idea "that the United States will contribute . . . to the work, because it is not yet known what views Congress might take of it." After the discovery of gold in California, new settlements rose on the Pacific Coast, increasing the need for the canal.

The triumphal opening of the Suez Canal, twenty years after the California gold rush, made Ferdinand de Lesseps the hero of the hour. If this Frenchman could divide the continents of Africa and Asia, why couldn't he separate North and South America? He had provided a shorter route to India by linking the Mediterranean and

the Red Sea. De Lesseps was the man selected to build the Panama Canal and connect the Atlantic and the Pacific. President Grant, in his first message to Congress, recommended that this waterway be constructed by the United States, and Congress appropriated the funds to investigate the possible routes. This decision stirred the French to action. Many thrifty French peasants as well as rich citizens and bankers, invested money in the Panama Canal project directed by the hero of Suez. A concession was secured from Colombia. In 1881, the contract was signed by the French company for work on the canal.

Panama was not Suez. The French had failed to reckon with the humid climate and yellow fever, the deadly scourge of the tropics. Although the French company sent excellent doctors and equipped fine hospitals, malaria and yellow fever actually broke out in clean, well-kept wards. To prevent ants from crawling into the beds of patients, the four posts of each cot were placed in small pans of water. Vases of flowers were in the rooms and on the porches to cheer the sick. At that time, it was not yet known that mosquitoes carried both yellow fever and malaria. Not knowing that stagnant pools in pans and flower pots were breeding places of the unsuspected enemy, the French doctors were unable to prevent epidemics of yellow fever and malaria. From 1881 to 1888, the death rate among employees averaged 63 per thousand. Nearly half of this number died from the two diseases carried by mosquitoes.

The French company had financial troubles, too. Although expert engineers advised a lock canal, de Lesseps insisted upon a sea level waterway. By the time he finally consented to locks, the company was practically bankrupt. After securing permission from Colombia to transfer its concession and property, the French company set the price at $109,000,000, hoping to sell. Congress authorized the President to pay $40,000,000 for the assets of the French company.

In 1903, during the term of Theodore Roosevelt, the Hay-Herran Treaty was proposed to Colombia, giving the United States the right to dig a canal across the Isthmus of Panama and perpetual control of a strip of territory on each side of the waterway. For these concessions, Colombia was to be paid $10,000,000. At the time, the President of Colombia was serving without a legal election and there was a danger of a military revolt occuring at any moment. To ratify the treaty, the Colombian Congress had to be convened and that body had not been called into session for five years. Thus the canal project became involved in Colombian politics. The Colombian Congress rejected the Hay-Herran Treaty after the United States Senate had approved it.

After the Congress of Colombia had rejected the treaty and blocked the canal, the province of Panama seceded from Colombia and declared its independence again as it had done several times before. This declaration of independence led to the formation of the Republic of Panama. President Theodore Roosevelt's hasty recognition of the new republic caused criticism in both Colombia and this country. The Republic of Panama accepted the offer rejected by Colombia for canal rights and received $10,000,000. Work began on completing the Panama Canal at a cost of $375,000,000.

Doctors and engineers were both necessary to make a success of the immense project of the Panama Canal. The officer in charge of sanitation was Colonel William Crawford Gorgas who had served in Cuba where he had been associated with Walter Reed in the study of yellow fever and malaria. Fresh from his triumph of ridding Havana of these dread diseases after the Spanish American War, Gorgas came to Panama. Often working against great odds, he succeeded in making the tropical region a reasonably healthy place for people to live and work. Engineering science could dig the canal and the United States Government could furnish the money if medical science could keep men on the job. Health was the responsibility of Gorgas, whose success is a dramatic human story even in the routine reports printed in the *Canal Record,* published weekly by the Isthmian Canal Commission:

September 11, 1907 – The Sanitary Department used about 160,000 gallons of oil during the last fiscal year . . . . All larva must come to the surface for air on an average of every two minutes . . . . This is where the Sanitary Department catches the mosquito. During the twelve days of their larval life before developing into adult mosquitoes, these babies are at the mercy of the man with the oil sprinkler.

January 15, 1908 – We had just one fourth as much malaria in December of 1907 as in the same month of 1906 . . . . It has been two years since yellow fever disappeared from the Isthmus.

Gorgas posted notices in all camps warning people to screen the windows and doors of their houses and always to use a mosquito bar at night; not to go out at night as mosquitoes bite principally after dark; and to drink boiled water and protect food from flies to avoid typhoid fever. With health carefully guarded, United States citizens working on the canal lived much as they did at home. There were churches, schools, libraries, gymnasiums, and hospitals. For recreation, there were band concerts, club meetings, lodge socials, bowling contests, rifle matches, tennis games, and a baseball league.

On March 30, 1910, the combined Canal and Panama Railroad employees totaled 38,676 – the largest labor force since work began on the waterway. The man in charge of the entire project was Colonel George W. Goethals, Corps of Engineers, U.S.A. He and his staff successfully met engineering and construction problems which involved changing the course of rivers, excavating troughs through low mountain ranges, and dredging sand from harbors. Lakes were filled, dams were built, and locks were constructed. Many difficulties beset the path of progress. A freshet on the Chagres River poured over the dam, flooding the valley and inundating the railroad line. Culebra Cut, that had defied the French, was a source of trouble to the Americans. At Cucaracha, the hillside began to slide as early as 1884 when the French company was working. It continued slipping after the Americans began excavating in 1905. These slides all along Culebra Cut sometimes buried steam shovels and tracks, filled up drainage

BUILDERS OF THE PANAMA CANAL

U.S. Army Photograph

William C. Gorgas (The Doctor)
Health and sanitation

Panama Canal Company

George W. Goethals (The Colonel)
Engineering and Administration

Both men attained rank of Major General in the United States Army.

CULEBRA CUT, RENAMED GAILLARD CUT

Massive slides in this area proved disastrous to the French Company. Under direction of the United States, Culebra was known as Gaillard Cut, after the engineer in charge. This section of the Panama Canal was dug through solid rock for eight to nine miles to take the waterway through the Continental Divide. To solve this problem, American engineers discarded the plan for a sea level canal and built a lock canal.

ditches, and blocked the canal itself. All these problems were finally solved, and the big ditch was completed.

On August 15, 1914, the Panama Canal was officially opened for commerce. On that day, the *Ancon*, a cement-carrying steamer, left Cristobal on the Atlantic at 7:10 A.M. Nine hours and forty minutes later, the ship steamed into the Pacific. A dream of four centuries had been fulfilled. A waterway linked the two great oceans. The voyage from New York to San Francisco was 5262 miles, less than half the distance by the old route through the Strait of Magellan. The great event was celebrated

in 1915 with the Panama Pacific International Exposition in San Francisco. The Panama Canal, open to the commerce of nations, was a gift to the world. None too soon was the strategic waterway put into service. When the *Ancon* was steaming through the canal on opening day, war was stalking over Europe. In a few years, the United States became involved in the conflict that swept over the world.

MAP:

WA 52ŕ

Atlas of American History by Edgar B. Wesley

Chapter 30

The Nation Joins World Wars

WORLD WAR I
BEGINS IN 1914

ON JUNE 28, 1914 an eighteen-year-old student shot the heir to the throne of the Austro-Hungarian Empire, Archduke Francis Ferdinand, as he drove away from a reception in the town hall of Sarajevo, Bosnia. The young Slav killed the prince of the ruling Hapsburg family and his wife because Austria had taken control of the province of Bosnia which belonged to his native country of Serbia. This incident was the spark that set off an explosion in the Balkans, called the "powder-keg of Europe."

Since nations, like individuals, want friends who will help them in time of trouble, they enter into alliances. When war threatens, a nation appeals to its allies either to intercede for peace or to furnish military aid if attacked. Russia, another Slavic country, was Serbia's friend. Fearing the rising might of Germany, both France and Great Britain had made treaties of alliance with Russia. These three countries formed the Triple Entente, called the Allies. Germany was the close friend of Austria-Hungary. These two nations in central Europe formed the backbone of the

Triple Alliance. Italy was a weak tail which might wag in either direction. Thus were the great countries of Europe lined up, three to three, in a balance of power.

Tension and fear gripped the capitals of the continent when the Archduke Ferdinand was murdered in the shaky Balkans. Officials of the Triple Entente and the Triple Alliance met to discuss the danger of war. Europeans breathed easier when the royal victims were buried privately in Vienna without the excitement of a state funeral to stir the wrath of the Austrians against the Serbs. Nearly a month passed before the clouds of war began to gather over Europe, lulled into a feeling of security by the weeks of silence.

On the twenty-third of July, the Austrian Government sent an ultimatum to Serbia. Serbia did not meet the stern demands of this note. Five days later, exactly a month after the fatal shots were fired in Sarajevo, Austria declared war on Serbia.

In a few days Russia, Serbia's friend, began to mobilize army and navy units. On July 31, Germany, Austria's friend, demanded to know why Russia was mobilizing troops. At the same time German soldiers were moving toward the frontier of France, an ally of Russia. The French grew nervous and started calling men to the colors on August 1. In the meantime Great Britain was busy trying to arrange a conference to halt the impending conflict.

Germany declared war on Russia on the first of August because Russia had failed to halt mobilization within the time limit of hours, set by the German officials in Berlin. On August 4, 1914, German soldiers crossed the border of Belgium. Great Britain was pledged to protect Belgian neutrality. Thus Great Britain declared war. The Triple Entente locked horns with the Triple Alliance (except for Italy) in a struggle for power.

Germany planned that it would be a short, swift campaign, with the fast-moving, well-drilled, and thoroughly equipped German armies marching into Paris within a few weeks. There, a victorious peace would be signed that would make Germany the master of the continent. The timetable was upset. Early in September the German armies reached the Marne River, almost within sight of Paris. Their drive was checked at the Marne by French soldiers, many of whom had been rushed to the battlefield in taxicabs. The contest lingered on. History has named the conflict World War I because it spread over the continents of the earth, dragging into the struggle more than thirty nations.

THE UNITED STATES ENTERS THE EUROPEAN WAR

ON THAT FATAL FOURTH of August in 1914 President Woodrow Wilson issued a proclamation of neutrality. He stated that this country would take neither side in the conflict among Europeans. The United States would stay out of their war. However, Americans soon learned how difficult it was to remain neutral when the deadly feud interfered more and more with their affairs at home and abroad.

Blockade is a common weapon with which warring nations try to starve one another into defeat. American overseas trade suffered when Great Britain declared food, clothing, and fuel as well as munitions and other war materials to be contraband and subject to capture if going to an enemy. The waters between Scotland and Norway were patrolled by British men-of-war to prevent merchant ships of any nation reaching German ports with supplies. Then Germany struck back with a blockade of British ports. Germany warned neutral nations that their vessels plying the waters around the British Isles were in danger from torpedoes. The torpedoes would be fired from submarines.

Ever since the War of 1812, by which the United States won the freedom of the seas, the policy of this country has been to defend the rights of its citizens to travel on the oceans, anytime and anywhere. Accordingly, William Jennings Bryan, then Secretary of State in President Wilson's Cabinet, warned the German Government against sinking American vessels and taking American lives. Bryan's warning went unheeded. On May 1, 1915 the German Embassy inserted an advertisement in New York papers, cautioning American citizens of the danger of traveling under the flag of Great Britain or her allies. On that same day the *Lusitania*, flying the Union Jack, sailed on schedule from New York harbor on a homeward voyage. There were nearly 2000 persons on board. A week later the vessel, zig-

A CAMOUFLAGED SHIP
Ships were painted in odd designs to confuse German U-boat commanders and to escape torpedo-attack at sea.

zagging through the war zone off the coast of Ireland, was hit by a German torpedo. The *Lusitania* sank in eighteen minutes. Over 1100 persons were lost, including more than a hundred citizens of the United States.

The sinking of an unarmed passenger ship without warning turned American public opinion toward the Triple Entente. About a year later the German Government promised not to sink unarmed vessels without warning and without saving lives unless the captains tried to escape or started to fight. This note pacified Americans after the torpedoing of the *Sussex* in the English Channel, although both passengers and mail from this country were lost. At this time

President Wilson addressed identical notes to the warring nations. He hoped to arrange a conference for a peace without victory and to end the war. The German Government hesitated to accept Wilson's offer as peacemaker and gambled on winning the war with submarines.

Meanwhile, a revolution on the eastern front favored Germany. Russia was the first nation to mobilize and the first to quit. Discontent, festering for years, had broken out in 1905 when Russia was defeated in a war with Japan. Although the Czar's government had put down the rebellion, revolutionaries kept the revolt simmering among the peasants on farms and among the workmen in factories. As the war beginning in 1914 went on and on, the government was not able to maintain the flow of supplies to soldiers on the long battle line. German armies were steadily advancing into Russian territory.

At this time, a revolutionary leader who had been exiled from Russia returned to his native land, after ten years. Nikolai Lenin, whose right name was Vladimir Ilyich Ulyanov, was living in Switzerland when a violent strike broke out in St. Petersburg in February of 1917. Factories and schools closed and mobs roamed the streets. Police fired on the mobs, trying to restore order. Long lines formed at bakeries as food became harder to get. Soldiers on short rations joined the peasants.

On March 15, 1917, Czar Nicholas II abdicated his throne, naming his brother Michael to succeed him, but the Grand Duke was also forced to abdicate. On March 18, the State Duma, the Russian Parliament, set up a provisional government and named a list of ministers to rule for the time being. The Soviet (council) of Workmen's and Soldier's Delegates elected Alexander Kerensky, a Socialist, to be the premier with full power. Kerensky tried to rally the army to fight and continue the war, but failed. A rival party, the Bolsheviks, who took their name from the Russian word meaning majority, steadily gained power and undermined the Kerensky government, but not until their leader had returned from exile.

How could Lenin cross German lines to get home? That was arranged by some officials of the German government. Thinking Lenin would use the revolution to take Russia out of the war, they secured permission to run a secret train across Germany. On April 9, 1917, Lenin and 32 of his followers left Zurich, Switzerland for the secret journey through enemy territory. The cars were not opened at stations, the running time was not scheduled in advance, windows were shaded, no passengers were seen, and no one knew, except the plotters, who was on the train. On April 16, Lenin and his party arrived at the Finland station in St. Petersburg, now Leningrad, and was met with a guard of honor, soldiers, sailors, and workmen from an arms factory. Standing in an armored car, Lenin made a short but fiery speech, closing with the slogan, "Long live the worldwide socialist revolution!"

From the railroad station, he went to the Bolshevik headquarters where he made another speech to his followers gathered there. In this speech he gave his revolutionary party a new name, "Communist," and outlined part of his program, closing again with the slogan, "Long live the worldwide socialist revolution!"

Early in 1917, with revolution sapping the strength of the Russian war effort, Germany resorted to unrestricted submarine warfare. President Wilson asked Congress for permission to arm merchant vessels. Since this country was unprepared for war and it would take a long time to get ready for it, the Germans figured that Great Britain could be starved into submission. They thought a victorious peace could be signed before the United States could send enough help overseas to turn the tide against them. The announcement of unrestricted submarine attacks upon shipping amounted to a German declaration of war against the United States.

On April 2, 1917 President Wilson addressed Congress on the world situation. He asked for a declaration of war. The President stated in his speech:

We shall fight for the things which we have always carried nearest our hearts — for democracy, for the right of those who submit to authority to have a voice in their own governments, for the rights and liberties of small nations, for a universal dominion of right by such a concert of free peoples as shall bring peace and safety to all nations and make the world itself free.

That the United States would not be suspected of seeking territory, the President declared:

We desire no conquest, no dominion. We seek no indemnities for ourselves — . We are but one of the champions of the rights of mankind.

On April 6, 1917, after Congress had voted for war by a large majority, President Wilson signed the resolution formally declaring war against Germany. The United States became an ally of Great Britain, France, and Italy. Italy was a part of the Triple Alliance but had remained neutral until May of 1915, when she denounced her treaty of alliance with Austria. Italy joined the Allies in order to regain control of former Italian provinces and other territory. By the time the United States entered the war, Russia was in the throes of revolution. The day April 6, 1917 is the historic date on which the United States abandoned its life-long policy of isolation from European entanglements as outlined by Washington in his farewell address:

'Tis our true policy to steer clear of permanent alliances with any portion of the foreign world.

In a little over a hundred years, the United States had grown to be a world power, sharing responsibility in world affairs. With grim determination, citizens of this country tackled the many problems involved in waging war on foreign soil.

THE NATION GIRDS FOR WAR OVERSEAS

ON THE DAY war was declared, the United States Army numbered less than 200,000 men, a puny force with which to enter a world-wide conflict. The first demand was manpower. On May 18, 1917 Congress passed a draft law summoning men 21 to 30 years of age for military service. The law was later extended to include men 18 to 45. In all, about 24,000,000 registered with draft boards between June, 1917 and August, 1918.

Men could be inducted into service only as fast as they could be provided with shelter, clothing, and food. Lumberjacks raided the forests for lumber to erect training camps that were hastily being built in every section of the country. Mill owners used their looms to weave yards and yards of woolen cloth for uniforms. Farmers kept busy sowing wheat, raising cattle, planting gardens, trimming orchards, and cultivating corn under the slogan, "Food will win the war."

For trench warfare fighting men needed helmets, hand grenades, and gas masks in addition to guns, shells, and bayonets. Since the output of munition makers was too small for such a large-scale war, manufacturers of peacetime products made weapons of all kinds. In an automobile plant sheets of steel were pressed into helmets. Shoemakers lined the metal headgear. An old New England firm of silversmiths turned from tableware to hand grenades. Manufacturers of rubber tires, tin cans, hardware, castings, and even a bread company, that baked charcoal in its ovens, had a share in producing gas masks. A laundry machine company furnished mortar barrels instead of washers and a harvester firm made the carts to mount the barrels. Industry prepared to make the necessities of war, anything from bullets to bombs, trucks to tanks, and pots to planes.

As men were drafted into the army, women took their places at desks and benches. In seaport towns gaunt frames of wooden ships stood in rows along the waterfronts. Citizens in all walks of life saved and scrimped to buy Liberty Bonds to pay for these Liberty Ships and the war supplies the vessels carried overseas.

By the time the United States entered the war, Russia's defeat had released thousands of German soldiers and their equipment for a determined attack on the western front. The Germans wanted to win the war before help arrived from the United States. British and French forces were pushed back in the German drive toward Paris. To brace their morale and prove that "the Yanks are coming," as well as to prepare for the arrival of American troops, General John J. Pershing sailed on the *Baltic* in May to confer with Allied leaders. He was the Commander in Chief of the American Expeditionary Forces. A month later the first American contingent of approximately 5000 soldiers landed in France. Late in October the first shots by Americans were fired from European trenches. By the end of December, 1917 there were more United States soldiers in France than were in the whole army when war was declared in April of that year.

At the same time, events in Russia were affecting the progress of the war. On the seventh of November of that year, the Bolsheviks had gained control of the Russian government after a bloody uprising costing many lives. Lenin, the new leader in power, wanted peace at any price to clear the way for extending his

The American Stock Exchange

THE OUTDOOR CURB MARKET ON A SUMMER DAY IN 1917 – NEW YORK

Brokers weave their way through the crowd gathered between the curbs of Broad Street near Wall Street buying and selling stocks and bonds for their customers. Here, Liberty Bonds were sold to buy armaments and supplies for World War I, then in progress.

In 1921, this outdoor market moved indoors to a spacious hall with tiers of comfortable telephone desks and eight-sided trading booths scattered over the floor.

control over more Russian territory, and for promoting the revolution in other countries. On December 15, 1917 the Bolshevik government had agreed to an armistice with the Central Powers – Germany, Austria-Hungary, Bulgaria, and Turkey. Three months later, a peace treaty was signed at Brest-Litovsk, releasing more German soldiers for fighting on the western

553

front. After the Treaty of Brest-Litovsk, the Bolsheviks, who had changed their name to Communists, moved the capital from Petrograd (St. Petersburg) to Moscow.

Early in the summer of 1918 troop trains were rolling to points of embarkation on the Atlantic seaboard. On many kinds of vessels, large and small, soldiers were crowded into every nook and corner. Troop transports and merchant vessels traveled in convoys. They were protected from submarine attack by warships of the United States fleet. Ships landed over 2,000,000 soldiers in Europe and more than 5,000,000 tons of supplies in the space of seventeen months. Although some vessels were torpedoed, the convoy system blocked success of the German plan to win the war with the submarine. The Yanks came.

When it was plain that the war would be decided on land, the Germans summoned all their strength for a final offensive to reach Paris. They realized after the second battle of the Marne in August that victory had slipped from their hands. As fresh troops from the United States took over sectors of the battle line from war-weary French and British soldiers, the Germans began a retreat. Veterans of World War I remember Chateau Thierry, Belleau Woods, the Meuse River, the Argonne Forest, St. Mihiel and other places in France. Thousands of Americans gave their lives and now lie buried in military cemeteries in France.

Finally, with the people alarmed and rebellious, the German Government asked for peace terms. The terms included Wilson's principle of settlement:

Compensation will be made by Germany for all damage done to the civilian population of the Allies and their property by the aggression of Germany by land, by sea, and from the air.

At five o'clock on the morning of November 11, 1918 the armistice was signed in a railroad car in France. A cease-fire order for eleven A.M. brought to an end the most destructive war in all history to that date. This conflict introduced new death-dealing weapons — tanks on the land, planes in the air, and submarines under the water. The United States Department of War estimated that approximately 65,000,000 men were mobilized by all nations. Over 8,500,000 were killed in battle or died of wounds or disease; over 21,000,000 were wounded; and over 7,750,000 were listed as prisoners or missing. The total casualties amounted to more than half the men called into military service. All over the world Armistice Day was celebrated with wild outbursts of joy. The war had ended but the shock of the global struggle lingered on to make the world a different place for almost everyone — everywhere.

TRUCE OR PEACE?

AFTER MORE THAN four years of war and a loss of life that saddened the world, peace was a cherished word. Men groped for a cure of war. Would it be possible for representatives of nations to meet and discuss their common problems? Such an idea had been suggested by a citizen of the United States in the early days of this Republic.

In a letter to a friend in the British Parliament, Benjamin Franklin had expressed his views on how to secure peace. He sent the note with John Adams who was going to London for treaty negotiations with the British Government after the War for Independence. The letter of October, 1783 read:

What would you think if I should make it, of a family compact between England, France, and America? What repeated follies are these repeated wars! You do not want to conquer and govern one another. Why then should you be continually employed in injuring and destroying one another? How many excellent things might have been done to promote internal welfare of each country — with the money and men foolishly spent during the last seven centuries by our mad wars in doing one another mischief? You are near neighbors, and each have very respectable qualities. —

In 1918, following a disastrous war in which Great Britain, France, and the United States fought together, another citizen of the United States voiced a similar appeal. He was Woodrow Wilson, then President of the United States, who wanted a league of all the countries in the world — a League of Nations. President Wilson arrived in Paris for the peace conference with a covenant for such a league in his mind as well as in his pocket. Nearly a year before he had issued fourteen points as a basis for peace. These included freedom of the seas, equality of trade among nations, reduction of armaments, evacuation of occupied territory by the enemy, and peaceful settlement of the claims of small countries to govern themselves. The fourteenth point was to be the cornerstone of the new league. It read:

A general association of nations must be formed under specific covenants for the purpose of affording mutual guarantees of political independence and territorial integrity to great and small states alike.

Wilson vainly hoped that the conflict of 1914 — 1918 would be the war that ended wars. Through a League of Nations, he thought, the basic causes of conflict between countries could be openly discussed and settled by agreement or com-

promise. War would be used only as a last resort. Wilson wanted a new kind of peace.

The first general session of the peace conference was held on January 18, 1919. It was exactly forty-eight years to the day after the German Empire had been proclaimed in Paris when France had been defeated in the Franco Prussian War. Now France was the victor over Germany. Although President Wilson favored a more lenient treatment for the losers, he was outvoted by the Allies who had suffered from the German invasions. In the war 1,300,000 Frenchmen had been killed, and over 4,000,000 had been wounded. The French peasant whose cow had been driven off by German soldiers wanted Germany to buy him another cow. The industrialist whose factory had been destroyed by gunfire, demanded that it be rebuilt by German money. The university president expected the German government to restore the library burned by the invaders. The sum of money required to repair the damage done by German arms was called reparations, which was to mean toil and taxation for Germans yet unborn.

The loss of territory and colonies, added to reparations, made the Treaty of Versailles a harsh document. The representatives of twenty-seven Allied Nations rose when the German delegates entered the room to receive the peace terms. They signed the treaty on June 28, 1919 in the Hall of Mirrors in the Palace of Versailles, former home of French kings. In less than fifty minutes over seventy delegates wrote their signatures. President Wilson signed for the United States. Some used traditional goose quills but Lloyd George, prime minister of England, preferred a fountain pen. The signing was a solemn affair, without the display of goldbraided uniforms and the colorful ceremony on like occasions in former days. Too many men had died. It was peace with a heavy heart.

It was not the new kind of a peace for which Wilson had hoped although he had won a covenant for a League of Nations. As in former years at other peace conferences, men gathered around a big table and changed the map of Europe. Europe was cut up into more nations than before in an effort to place disgruntled peoples under governments to their liking. As of old, diplomats juggled for balance of power to which they had long been accustomed. On the day the treaty was signed, crowds gathered in public squares throughout Germany to protest the back-breaking debt of reparations and the loss of Alsace and Lorraine. On that day a German editor printed on the front page of his paper:

The German people reject the treaty which its delegates are signing today − . Despite the fact that it is written on parchment, it remains a piece of paper.

At noon, the day after the signing, President Wilson sailed from Brest for home. He had won a covenant for the League of Nations. He pinned his faith in this plan to avert another war. However, his covenant had to be approved by the Senate since only this body has the right under the Constitution to ratify treaties. Opposition was growing in the Senate against the League Covenant.

Many citizens, including Congressmen, interpreted Article X of the document to mean that the United States would be obligated to go to war upon foreign soil if any nation belonging to the League suffered invasion or attack from any other nation. The nation's first and costly venture into the never-ending squabbles of Europe was still fresh in the public mind. Many citizens recalled Washington's advice in his farewell address:

'Tis our true policy to steer clear of permanent alliances with any portion of the foreign world.

Geography often determines the course of history. Protected by two oceans, the United States had been able to grow without fear of aggression. Citizens followed the pursuits of peace, not war. When the European conflict ended, the average citizen wished to pick up where he had left off. He wanted to go on as before, feeling secure with ocean barriers and friendly neighbors in the Western Hemisphere. For a hundred and thirty years the policy of the United States had been to evade "entangling alliances" abroad. Yet, some public opinion was strong for joining the League in the vain hope of ending war.

Determined to take the issue of the League to the people, President Wilson left Washington on the third of September to tour the country. He spoke in large halls in the big cities and from the rear platform of his train in the small towns. The President traveled over 8000 miles to deliver forty speeches before he made the last one of the tour in the western steel town of Pueblo, Colorado. When his special train arrived in Wichita, Kansas, on September 26, he was too ill to speak and returned to Washington. He never fully recovered from the breakdown suffered on this strenuous journey although he lived for four more years.

The war had shoved the United States into first place as the most powerful nation in the world. Great Britain had held this position before the catastrophe of 1914.

556

The average citizen was slow to realize that world leadership had saddled him with world responsibility.

In the next election held in November of 1920, people went to the polls to vote Wilson's Democratic Party out of office, and to elect Warren G. Harding, a Republican from Ohio, President of the United States. The League was defeated in the Senate. Although the United States did not officially join the League of Nations, the Government cooperated with the program outlined to promote peace. Americans were familiar figures at headquarters of the League in Geneva, Switzerland.

To help restore peace, the United States extended aid to the unfortunate victims whose homes and fortunes had been lost in the conflict. Among the 200,000 Americans stranded in Europe when war suddenly broke out in 1914 was the mining engineer, Herbert Hoover. In the emergency he organized the groups of panic-stricken tourists, arranged for a London bank to cash their checks, engaged ships, and sent them home. Then he accepted the responsibility of directing relief for the Belgians. From this beginning Herbert Hoover advanced to the position of Director of Relief for the Allied Governments. During the nine months following the armistice Hoover raised the money to deliver over 4,000,000 tons of food valued at more than $1,000,000,000. When the harvest of 1919 increased the food supply in many countries, Hoover organized another relief program to care for 10,000,000 children, victims of the war.

Over a period of ten years, from 1914 to 1924, there were few citizens of the United States who failed to make some personal sacrifice to feed and clothe the victims of war and revolution. This relief cost over $5,000,000,000 without including the huge sums of money spent by private charity. Americans opened their hearts and their pocketbooks when poverty and starvation stalked over war-torn Europe.

This generosity did not win the peace. Other forces were at work undermining it. Since the Treaty of Versailles changed the map of Europe, some peoples suddenly found themselves living in new nations with new names like Czechoslovakia and Yugoslavia. Many felt strange with their new neighbors who spoke different languages and were not always friendly. For a short time the future looked bright with more self-government spreading over Europe. Many peoples had long been more accustomed to rule by a few men than to rule by representatives of the people. They were bewildered with new forms of government and new patterns of living under systems of political liberty. Following the war, millions lost their newly acquired freedoms before they had time to become acquainted with them. On the battlefield the fight was won for government recognizing the human rights of man. In the chaos resulting from the war dictators rose to sabotage the victory. Young constitutional republics crumbled into dictatorships.

THE RISE OF DICTATORS

OUT OF THE TRAGEDY of world war, a new hunger for freedom emerged. As the old way of life disappeared during the conflict, the desire grew among peoples to have governments shared by the people. Since Russia was the first large nation to collapse under the impact of war, a feeble beginning toward personal liberty was made in that nation. When Czar Nicholas gave up his throne, the State Duma (the Parliament) formed the Provisional Government with a president and a cabinet elected by its members. On March 16, 1917 this emergency government announced its principles. A few of these are quoted from the official document, "Declaration of the Provisional Government:"

Freedom of speech, press, union, assembly and strikes, with extension of political liberties to persons in military service within limits consistent with military technical conditions.

Immediate preparation for the convention of a Constituent Assembly, which will establish the form of administration and the constitution of the country, on the basis of general, equal, secret and direct voting.

Replacement of the police by a people's militia with an elected administration, subordinated to the organs of local self government.

Elections to the organs of local self government on the basis of general, direct, equal and secret ballot.

* * *

The Provisional Government considers its duty to add that it does not intend to exploit military circumstances for any delay in the realization of the above outlined reforms and measures.

This document was signed by the President of the State Duma, President of the Council of Ministers, and eight ministers of the cabinet, including Alexander F. Kerensky, Minister of Justice.

A month later, Lenin arrived from Switzerland and announced some of his plans for a new government in Russia, as follows:

No support to the Provisional Government . . . .

Not a parliamentary republic, . . . but a republic of Soviets of Workers', Farmhands' and Peasants' Deputies in the whole country, . . .

Confiscation of all land belonging to landlords.

Nationalization of all land in the country, management of the land by local Soviets of Farmhands' and Peasants' Deputies . . . Creation out of every big estate of a model farm under the control of farmhands' deputies and at public expense.

Immediate fusion of all the banks of the country into one general national bank . . .

Many Russians favored a constitutional republic similar to the United States. The Communists who followed Lenin favored a socialist state. On November 8, 1917, the Congress of Soviets published a decree on land signed by "Vladimir Ulyanov," Lenin, as a temporary law:

The right of private property in land is forever abolished; land can be neither sold, nor bought, nor leased, nor pledged, nor alienated in any other way. All land, state, Crown, monastery, Church, which is owned by private persons, by public organizations, by peasants, etc. is taken away without compensation, . . .

All the mineral resources of the earth, ore, oil, coal, salt, etc., and all forests and waters which are of general state significance pass into the exclusive possession of the state.

Caught between two opposite kinds of government, the people formed groups to express their own personal opinions on what kind of government they wanted. Although all were revolutionaries, they fought one another over their differences. In the struggle, factories closed, transportation broke down, and famine swept over the country. It took four years of civil war, 1917 to 1921, to bring a cruel victory. The Communists won and Lenin became the first dictator of a new government in an old country with a new name, UNION OF SOVIET SOCIALIST REPUBLICS, the U.S.S.R.

In 1922 Benito Mussolini seized the government of Italy and became the dictator of that country. The following year Adolph Hitler organized an unsuccessful revolt in

Germany. Ten years later he became Chancellor and the short-lived republic in that nation fell. From the Arctic to the Mediterranean, dictators gained power over millions of people.

DICTATORS LEAD
TO AGGRESSION

WAR REFUGEES RETURNED to their desolate homes in the battle areas. In the aftermath of "the war to end wars" simmered revolts, bloody and bloodless, that halted liberty in its stride. Hungry and despairing men fell victim to dictators in bartering freedoms for bread.

In order to gain power, dictators promised employment and prosperity to starving peoples whose means of earning a living had been swept away in the war or during the years immediately following. To keep their word and their power, dictators embarked upon armament programs and prepared for aggression against their neighbors. Perhaps they thought they needed territory held by a border nation to provide farms for their loyal followers. Maybe a country nearby had rich deposits of iron and coal needed by manufacturers to provide steel for armaments. Large populations are always a temptation to an ambitious dictator who needs soldiers for his armies and laborers to support them by toil in field and factory.

With dictatorships established in the Union of Soviet Socialist Republics, in Italy, and in Germany, free peoples all over the world began to tremble with fear of another war. Since the dictatorships allowed only a single political party, the people had no opportunity to vote against the policies of the dictators. They could not vote them nor their parties out of office. Personal liberty withered away in the dictatorships where the people were being helplessly regimented. In countries where a few men have seized complete control of the government, few of their subjects risk arrest, imprisonment, exile, and death to criticize their all-powerful rulers. Freedom of speech, press, religion, and assembly were crushed under dictators whose will had been imposed upon the people.

Millions of people in the world had pinned their wishful hopes for peace on the newborn League of Nations. The United States took the lead in disarmament by inviting a number of countries to send representatives to discuss ways and means to cut down the production of war materials. The conference met in Washington in November, 1921 with delegates from Great Britain and the Dominions, Japan, France, Italy, the Netherlands, Portugal, Belgium, China, and the United States. About two months later the five large naval powers — United States, Great Britain, Japan, France and Italy — agreed to limit dreadnoughts and large cruisers. More important, perhaps, was the effort made at this meeting to maintain peace in the Orient. The nine-power treaty resulting from this conference bound the nations that were represented to maintain the policy of the Open Door in China, and not to take advantage of China's weakness to secure special privileges in that country.

In 1925 the nations that had defeated Germany met in Locarno, Switzerland, to ease the terms of the Versailles Treaty to which Germans so strongly objected. They hoped to keep peace. In 1928 sixty-three nations agreed to outlaw war by signing the Pact of Paris. The pact was drawn up by

France and the United States as the result of a remark made by Aristide Briand, French Minister of Foreign Affairs, to Frank B. Kellogg, American Secretary of State. Briand suggested that their two nations sign a pact of perpetual friendship and agree never to go to war with each other under any circumstances. When so many countries joined the Kellogg-Briand Pact, peoples all over the world rejoiced. War was outlawed and all disputes would be settled peaceably.

The following year the economic depression, creeping in the wake of the great conflict, struck the United States. It had gradually settled over the world like a pall of smoke. In all countries prices fell, banks closed, and many were unemployed and hungry. The Japanese looked with longing at the bread basket of Manchuria across the Sea of Japan. In September, 1931 Japan seized Mukden and gained a foothold in a country with vast plains for raising grains and soy beans. Rich mineral deposits were there as well. Although Japan was a monarchy ruled by Emperor Hirohito, a small group of military-minded men actually held the power. In the chaos resulting from World War I, they found the opportunity to extend Japanese authority in Asia where China was torn by revolution and too weak to resist aggression.

The Japanese Government ignored a strong protest made by the League of Nations over this violation of Chinese territory. The following year, Japanese troops invaded Shanghai. By 1933 the hopes for peace were fading fast. When the League of Nations asked Japan to end the conquest of China, Japan withdrew from the organization and invaded North China. The failure of the League to halt aggression in Asia encouraged dictators in Europe to consider military adventures. In that same year Adolph Hitler gained a dictator's power in Germany. When Hitler established a dictatorship, the Germans lost their right to vote against him. Hitler then took Germany out of the League, and outlawed all parties except his own Nazi Party.

In 1934 Japan conquered Manchuria. Japan installed a puppet emperor there and changed the name of the country to Manchukuo. Meanwhile, under Hitler's leadership, Germany was marching toward war again. The dictator wanted not only to regain territory lost in World War I, but to extend the nation's authority over neighboring countries. The rich Saar region was returned to Germany by the vote of its people. Hitler's demands only increased with each gain. He demanded the union of Austria with Germany and marched triumphantly into Vienna.

At the same time Italy, under the dictatorship of Mussolini, was engaged in the conquest of Ethiopia.

Italy sent troops across the Adriatic into Albania. Germany added a province of Czechoslovakia and was making demands upon Poland. Germany, Italy, and Japan signed a pact to fight communism, which the form of government in the Union of Soviet Socialist Republics was called. Japanese troops were digging deeper into China and threatening Mongolia on the Soviet border. While war was spreading in Europe, Africa, and Asia, what was happening in the United States?

THE COUNTRY ENDURES
A DECADE OF DEPRESSION

WHEN THE ARMISTICE was signed on November 11, 1918, about one-fourth of this nation's labor force was employed in war industries that supplied the 4,355,000 men enlisted in the armed services. Immediately, the Government cancelled orders for war materials. Men working in ammunitions were laid off; factories producing armaments shut down while changing over to make peacetime goods; and some offices in Washington closed suddenly. As soon as the war ended, the soldiers wanted to go home. Their families urged their release from service. At the rate of over 300,000 per month, almost the entire force was demobilized within a year. All of these men were not able to secure employment immediately upon their return, although the United States Employment Service set up bureaus for veterans in towns and cities.

No serious crisis developed for a number of reasons. The shipyards continued in operation, completing vessels that were started in the hope of restoring the merchant fleet of this country. Women who had worked in the war industries returned to their home duties. People who had left the country to enter war plants during the war emergency returned to their farms when they lost their jobs. Each soldier as he was mustered out of the service received his transportation home and $60. The purchase of civilian suits, when uniforms were put aside, aided employment in the textile industry. However, exports were largely responsible for the brief post-war boom. Since the Government of the United States was still lending money to the Allies, this sum was spent in this country mainly to purchase food. Farmers were prosperous for several years.

By 1921 a recession was beginning and unemployment increased. The following year, however, business began to recover and to expand. During President Coolidge's term of office there was an era of prosperity. New industries were creating many new markets for new products — automobiles, phonographs, radios. These products could be purchased on the installment plan. Advertising to create a popular demand for new products almost doubled the output of paper plants.

The assembly line, which speeded production, lowered the cost of automobiles and many luxury items, making their purchase possible by more buyers. More cars created a demand for better highways. A spurt in road building provided employment for many, including some farmers who worked on roads when not busy in the fields. With a car, a family could move from a crowded apartment district in the city to a house in a suburb, which then needed more stores to serve the newcomers. The construction business enjoyed a boom during the first half of the prosperous 1920's. New markets were found at home to replace, in a measure, those lost in foreign countries. Could this prosperity be maintained? For how long?

Farmers formed a large buying group and the prosperity of the nation in part depended upon their purchasing power. In the second year following the war, prices of farm products dropped because of overproduction. Spurred by the slogan, "Wheat will win the war," farmers had planted far too much wheat. In many parts of the South growers planted more cotton than they could sell and the price went down. People began to eat more fruits and vegetables and less bread and cereal and to wear more garments made of rayon fabrics instead of cotton goods. When farmers fed their surplus grain to

561

hogs, there were soon more pigs than could be marketed and the price of pork fell. The wider use of tractors and machinery made it possible for fewer farmers to raise larger crops. Many tenants and share-croppers lost their homes and their means of earning a living. Industrial prosperity is endangered when customers do not have the money to buy manufactured articles.

Even in prosperous years following the war coal was a sick industry. The fuel was still used for house heating but faced new competitors — oil and electricity — in manufacturing. Bituminous operators and miners suffered the most. As the demand for this kind of coal decreased, profits dwindled. Miners worked fewer days per month, earned less money, and were able to purchase less goods for themselves and families. Cotton and woolen manufacture declined. Cotton mills migrated from New England to the South Atlantic States, not only to be near the cotton fields, but to get cheap labor, a good supply of soft water, and a favorable climate. During the decade following the war the shoe industry began moving from Massachusetts into towns of the midwestern states. This western move was not to get cheap labor but to be nearer the center of population. The old basic industries such as coal, cotton, wool and leather failed to grow in proportion to new ones — petroleum, automobiles, textiles, and chemicals.

During the general prosperity of the 1920's citizens were not aware of the many events, at home and abroad, that were pushing this nation and the world toward a serious depression. If they had realized the danger, could they have prevented the disaster? The average level of living in the United States was the highest in the world. Large incomes, however, were increasing much faster than small incomes. The surplus, in part, was being used for speculating in land and stocks.

During Jackson's term as President, nearly a hundred years before, a similar speculation in land had helped to bring about the Panic of 1837. In the 1920's some people bought land, not to live on it, but to resell it quickly at a profit. Fortunes were made in the land booms of Florida and California where populations were growing rapidly. Both individuals and corporations bought shares of stock in business concerns, not intending to invest their money and wait for dividends, but only to resell in a few days or weeks when the price rose. This gambling was indulged in by wage earners and small business men as well as by millionaires and large corporations. By October of 1929 the price of stocks began to drop. Investors rushed to sell before the values of their stocks fell to lower sums. On October 24, 1929, "Black Thursday," nearly 13,000,000 shares were sold and prices experienced the widest drop in the history of the New York Stock Exchange. Although the loss in market value of stocks the day before had amounted to $4,000,000,000, the collapse of the stock market in 1929 was only a partial cause of the depression.

Herbert Hoover, who succeeded Calvin Coolidge as President, was in office when the depression came. Having lived for years in foreign countries, Hoover realized that the depression was world-wide. The President's first concern in meeting the situation was to help the farmers. He outlined a program to be carried out by the Farm Board. He objected to the Government buying and selling and fixing the price of farm products. Conditions did not improve much because farmers were still

562

producing more staples than could be sold profitably. The drought of 1930, which ruined many crops, actually helped to solve farming problems. Although Hoover did not approve of government interference, he thought it was necessary to offer federal aid in the emergency.

The President asked Congress to establish the Reconstruction Finance Corporation with a capital of $500,000,000, advanced from government funds, for loans to restore industry and provide employment. Although this bill was opposed by Democrats in Congress, the RFC finally was established. Hoover signed the act on January 22, 1932. Promptly, agencies of the RFC were opened in thirty cities to lend government funds to banks, building and loan associations, and insurance companies to protect the savings of people which would be lost if these institutions failed. Money was also loaned to railroads, to farmers, and other groups to prime the business pump and increase employment. The RFC did help to relieve the depression but could not cure it.

When so many men and women were unemployed, they were unable to buy more than necessities with their decreased incomes. They paid less money for taxes and government receipts declined. In 1932 tax collections amounted to less than half the sum collected in 1930. President Hoover called for more economy, stating, "We cannot squander ourselves into prosperity." He wanted to balance the budget, if possible, by spending no more money than could be raised by taxes.

In November, 1932 Franklin Delano Roosevelt, candidate of the Democrats, was elected President. In these times of distress the people wanted a change. Roosevelt asked Congress to appropriate large sums of money for public works in order to give jobs to unemployed men. For young men, the Civilian Conservation Corps was organized in the spring of 1933. With the C.C.C. the Government employed about 250,000 youths in outdoor work for "the prevention of forest fires, floods and soil erosion, plant pest and disease control, the construction, maintenance or repair of paths, trails, and fire lanes" and such aids to conserve the natural resources. The Works Progress Administration, created by act of Congress in 1935, appropriated almost $5,000,000,000 to provide jobs for everyone from transients to artists. The program of the WPA emphasized individual skills and talents. Jobs had to be found for plumbers, painters, and electricians; writers, musicians and artists; janitors, waiters, and cooks, where their employment would not conflict with private employment. Although millions of dollars were spent for direct relief, an effort was made to help people to help themselves through some kind of employment. The largest engineering project attempted by the Government during this period was the Tennessee Valley Authority.

The National Industrial Recovery Act, commonly called NRA, was a plan whereby Government, business, and labor would cooperate in trying to restore prosperity through regulations outlined in codes worked out for every industry. This proved to be such a complex procedure that NRA had already bogged down in confusion when the Supreme Court declared the act was unconstitutional. However, Section 7a was not declared unconstitutional. It stated:

That employees shall have the right to organize and bargain collectively through representatives of their own choosing . . . .

That no employee and no one seeking employment shall be required as a condition of employment to join any company union or to refrain from joining, organizing, or assisting a labor organization of his own choosing.

That employers shall comply with the maximum hours of labor, minimum rates of pay, and other conditions of employment, approved or prescribed by the President.

This clause was approved by both employers and employees when the National Recovery Act was framed. The same principles were later included in the Wagner Act and the Taft-Hartley Act, laws regulating procedures of both employers and employees.

The Agricultural Adjustment Act of May 12, 1933 was the rural relief program. It was a plan to limit production. For, example, too much cotton was grown so administrators of the AAA arranged to have about 10,000,000 acres of growing cotton plants plowed under. The farmers who destroyed their crops were paid by the Government for their cooperation in making cotton scarce. Under AAA over 6,000,000 pigs were killed in 1933. The cooperative farmers were reimbursed for their losses by the Government. Nature took a hand in the game and helped to create scarcity with severe droughts in 1934 and 1936. Nature limited production and increased prices of farm products more than did the agreements with farmers to destroy crops and livestock. The Government appropriated $500,000,000 yearly for paying farmers not to plant certain crops and for diverting part of their acreage to pasture.

Although taxes were greatly increased to raise money to operate the increasing number of welfare agencies of the Federal Government, it was necessary to borrow large sums of money. When Franklin Roosevelt took office as President in March of 1933, the federal debt amounted to $22,500,000,000 or about $180 per person. Eight years later the debt had more than doubled and amounted to $367 for each man, woman, and child. The system whereby a government operates on borrowed money is called "deficit financing." In the national emergency President Roosevelt felt the large increase in the debt was justified by the efforts of his Administration to provide jobs at government expense to relieve the depression. His policies are often spoken of as the "New Deal" because in his speech accepting the nomination for President on the Democratic ticket, he said:

I pledge you, I pledge myself, to a new deal for the American people.

In March of 1935 about 22,000,000 persons were receiving money from the Government. In November of that year the records showed that during the eighteen months preceding, $3,694,000,000 of tax funds had been spent for direct relief, in addition to vast sums aimed at helping people to help themselves. Although more and more government bureaus were created to spend more and more money, the actual depression lingered on. Finally, the President and Congress began to view the depression as a symptom of changing times. The cure was difficult.

It was a time of experiment in which some measures succeeded and some failed. Some families living on eroded land that was no longer fit to support them were moved to better soil by the Resettlement Administration. During drought years when dust blew on the plains, thousands of tenant farmers migrated west to California. They looked for employment picking fruit and harvesting vegetables. Since California ranchers could not give work to all who came, these migrant families created a relief problem in that state. The Federal Government decided it was better for these people to be aided in their home communities than to be moved. Soil conservation programs carried out at government expense helped them to make their land produce again. For an experiment in reclaiming eroded country, flood control, navigation, and electric power, the Tennessee Valley Authority was the boldest venture of the Federal Government into big business.

The Social Security Act of August 14, 1935, is the best known piece of legislation of the depression decade. The law instructs employers to deduct money from the pay checks of wage earners in order to provide a small income for them at the age of 65 years when they are retired from employment. Employers also contribute to this social security fund in proportion to the amount deducted from the pay envelopes of their employees. Each wage earner whose job comes under the Social Security Act is assigned a number when he is first hired, and he keeps that same number for life no matter how many times he changes his job.

The numerous welfare programs set up during the depression decade changed the pattern of taxation. As services rendered by the Federal Government increased in number and volume, more bureaus were established, more buildings were erected to accommodate them, and more persons were employed to operate them. To meet this added expense, it was necessary for all citizens to pay more taxes to the Federal Government. Before the depression citizens generally paid the largest sum for local taxes to support their town, city, and county governments; the next largest amount for their state, and the least to maintain the National Government. The welfare and defense programs called for such huge expenditures of money that the pattern of taxation was reversed. Citizens began to pay most of their taxes to the Federal Government and least to their local governments.

Yet the welfare program of the Government did not cure the depression, although it did relieve some distress of the period. Real recovery did not set in until war broke out in Europe. The unemployed were put back to work supplying the armaments needed for the conflict and for the defense program of the United States. Under a lend-lease plan whereby this nation supplied funds to warring nations to buy food, clothing, machinery, guns, ammunition, trucks, and all kinds of war materials, employment rose steadily.

MAPS:

WA26r WA27r
Atlas of American History by Edgar B. Wesley

Chapter 31

World War II Encircles the Globe

WAR SCURRIES OVER EUROPE FOLLOWING INVASION OF POLAND

ADOLPH HITLER rose to power in Germany by tearing apart the Treaty of Versailles and throwing it, piece by piece, into the faces of the winners in World War I. After adding Austria and provinces of Czechoslovakia to Germany, Hitler demanded the return of the narrow corridor which had been allotted to Poland by the treaty. He wanted Danzig for a port on the Baltic. This territory had formerly belonged to Prussia, one of the German states.

Since both France and Great Britain were allies of Poland, leaders of these nations objected to Hitler's demands. Hoping to keep these two nations from interfering while he conquered Poland, Hitler signed a non-aggression pact with the Union of Soviet Socialist Republics. The invasion of Poland began on September 1, 1939. Three days later Great Britain and France declared war on Germany. In less than two weeks Soviet armies invaded Poland from the east. Before the end of the month Poland was conquered and the territory divided between Germany and Soviet Russia.

Near the end of November, Russia attacked Finland, forcing that small country to surrender valuable territory. Within seven months the Soviet Government seized Lithuania, Latvia, and Estonia on the Baltic Sea and took a province from Rumania. Meanwhile, the German Army invaded Denmark, Norway, the Netherlands, Belgium, Luxembourg and France. On June 10, three days before the German Army entered Paris, Italy declared war upon France and troops crossed the border. By the end of the summer of 1940 Europe was aflame with war. The Italian Army had invaded Egypt, bringing the continent of Africa into the conflict.

What was happening in the United States during this time? When the German Army entered France in May, President Franklin D. Roosevelt asked Congress to appropriate billions of dollars for defense. Then, less than a week after the Italians invaded Egypt, he signed the first compulsory draft law for military service during peacetime. Canada and the United States announced a joint plan for defending both countries. The President approved lend-lease payments to Great Britain, enabling that country to purchase war supplies in the United States. Orders from overseas gradually increased employment in the United States for both men and women. This nation's preparedness program absorbed some of the unemployed in manufacturing and in the armed services.

Nearly all of Europe had fallen to the dictatorships of Germany, Italy, and the Soviet Union. Only Sweden, Switzerland, and Portugal escaped being drawn into the war, along with Spain, which had had its own bloody civil war at home.

In June of 1941 Hitler's decision to attack the Union of Soviet Socialist Republics extended the European war into Asia where China and Japan had already been locked in a struggle for ten years. About the middle of July, Great Britain and the Soviet Union signed a war pact. They agreed that neither one would make a separate peace with Germany. Early in November President Roosevelt pledged lend-lease of a billion dollars to the Soviet Union, now an ally of Great Britain. Meanwhile, war crept closer to the United States, moving west from Europe and east from Asia at the same time. When and where would the blow strike?

THE UNITED STATES IS DRAWN INTO WORLD WAR II

IN SEPTEMBER OF 1940, Japan formally joined the Axis powers, as Germany, Italy, and Bulgaria were called. Then Japan signed a five-year non-aggression pact with Russia in April, 1941. This secured the northern Japanese shores from attack and a move south was expected.

The grand prize of war included the East Indies, Malaya, and the Philippines. There, Japan could get the raw materials needed to carry on the war with China and any other nation opposing the Japanese advance. In this southern area were supplies of nickel, manganese, iron, gold, oil, 85 percent of the world's rubber, 65 percent of its tin, and 90 percent of its quinine. The loss of these materials to the Allies would greatly weaken the war effort in Europe. The one obstacle to carrying out the conquest of this region was the United States Fleet at Pearl Harbor in Hawaii.

Japan's basic war plan was divided into three steps. First, it was necessary to destroy or neutralize the United States Fleet and air bases in Hawaii; second, to seize the southern area rich with raw materials; and third, to capture the strategic areas and islands to establish a line of defense extending from the Kuril Islands north of Japan, through Wake Island, the Marshall, Gilbert, and Bismarck Islands, northern New Guinea, Timor, Java, Sumatra, Malaya, and Burma. Then, after seizing this vast area, plans were developed to defend it against attack until the United States, the only nation with power to challenge this conquest, gave up the fight.

On December 7, 1941, this plan was placed in operation with an air attack upon Pearl Harbor. About eight o'clock on that Sunday morning, bombs began to fall on the airfields where grounded American planes were perfect targets. Without advance warning, the armed forces were taken by surprise. At practically the same time, a dozen planes approached from the southeast to drop torpedoes on the battleships, cruisers, and all Navy vessels anchored in Pearl Harbor. More planes arrived with more destructive torpedoes. After the attack, lasting almost two hours, the Pacific Fleet had suffered a major disaster, with over 3000 men killed and missing and over 900 wounded.

Immediately Japan declared war on the United States, Great Britain and the British Dominions. In a few days Germany and Italy, Japan's allies, declared war on the United States. Our country announced that a state of war existed also with Germany, Italy, and Japan. Suddenly, the United States faced war on two fronts and across two oceans. The nation was not prepared. Army officers were sent from this country to train Filipino troops but progress was slow because funds were lacking. It was a part of Japanese strategy to gain control of the rich resources of these islands before the Filipinos were prepared to defend their homeland. The initial attack on Luzon was timed to follow the bombing of Pearl Harbor. It was another surprise which caught bombers and all types of planes on the ground. On the tenth of December, Japanese troops made their first landing on the main island, Luzon.

By the end of December, Japanese troops had captured the American islands of Wake and Guam. This blocked the regular sea lane for supply ships to the Philippines, the British possession of Hong Kong, and the little country of Thailand. By launching attacks at the same time in so many places, Japan was ready early in January in 1942 to begin the conquest of the richest prize, the Dutch East Indies. Although the United States attempted to send some supplies and reinforcements to the Philippines by way of Australia, American forces were obligated to get along with the men and materials on hand. On December 24, General Douglas MacArthur, commanding the American and Filipino soldiers, ordered the evacuation of Manila and a retreat to the peninsula of Bataan.

On this neck of land, thirty-two miles long and only twenty miles across at the widest part, Philippine and United States soldiers put up a heroic defense. They had only a few pieces of artillery and airplanes left to them. Starvation and illness sapped the strength of the defenders as rations were cut lower and lower for the 78,000 troops and 26,000 civilians crowded into the peninsula. Occasionally, a submarine arrived with a little food, but the cargo was usually much-needed drugs and ammunition. Realizing that help could not arrive in time to stave off defeat, President Roosevelt ordered General MacArthur to leave the island fort of Corregidor in a submarine on the night of March 11. He was transported to Mindanao and then flown in an American bomber to Australia where he established temporary headquarters as Supreme Commander of the Allied Forces in the Southwest Pacific.

On March 12, General Jonathan M. Wainwright took command of half-starved troops existing on one-third rations on the Bataan peninsula. Their position was under increased air attack by planes based on nearby Formosa. Japan had gained control of this large island off the coast of China in 1895 and was now using it as a base to assemble troops and planes for the conquest of the Philippine Islands. Early in April General Wainwright was forced to surrender the troops on Bataan. About 45,000 Filipino soldiers and over 9000 Americans were imprisoned in central Luzon. So many men died on the way from Bataan to the prison camp that the trek was named the "Death March." Not until May 6, after Japanese gunfire had destroyed artillery and even the water pipes, did the gallant defenders of Corregidor surrender the island fort in the harbor.

The Japanese strategy had been successful, although the timing had been upset by the heroic stand made by Filipinos who fought to the end with forces of the United States Army. By attacking at the same time at many points along the islands, Japan was able to fortify a line of defense from Wake Island to the East Indies. Early in March the Dutch Government had been forced to surrender the entire Netherlands East Indies to Japan. This gave the Japanese oil, food, minerals, quinine, copra, hemp, and other supplies needed for waging war. Malaya with large amounts of tin, rubber, lumber, and the excellent naval base at Singapore was in Japanese hands. However, the people of this region were the greatest asset since they were now working for Japan. The island of Java with 40,000,000 population was a prize. Great Britain, the Netherlands, and the United States at war with Germany and her allies, were not able, at the time, to defend their possessions in the East. Any nation that controls this southern area of vast rich resources and the islands around it is master of the Pacific and in a position to endanger the security of the United States. While our country was occupied in preparing to wage war on two fronts and across two oceans, Japan met with little opposition in Asia except from the Chinese. China kept up the fight with the meager aid that could be flown "over the hump." The hump meant across the lofty Himalayas, a distance of 500 miles between the province of Assam in India and the Yunnan Plateau in China.

THE UNITED STATES GOES TO WAR IN EUROPE, ASIA, AND AFRICA

In December of 1941, the Prime Minister of Great Britain, Winston Chur-chill, the Chiefs of the British Navy, Army, and Air Forces met in Washington with President Franklin D. Roosevelt and the American chiefs of staff. At this meeting, it was agreed that the war would be conducted by a group known as the Combined Chiefs of Staff. They would concentrate upon the defeat of Germany first, and Japan, second. Because of this decision the American defenders in the Pacific area had to wait for help in the initial phase of the conflict.

Two plans for attacking the German homeland were considered. One was to invade Europe through the Balkans, the other, to invade through France. In April, 1942 in London, an agreement was reached that the final blow against Germany would be made by a large force crossing the English Channel, invading France, and pressing forward over the plains of Western Europe into Germany itself. This decision meant provision must be made to transport 1,200,000 men, from the United States across the submarine-infested Atlantic Ocean; to build living quarters, hospitals, and supply centers for them; and, before anything else, to draft the men into the armed services and train them.

Many demands for all kinds of war materials increased employment. Again, as in World War I, thousands of women went to work in war factories. Three shifts were operated around the clock to fill orders for articles ranging from plastic combs to bombing planes. Tanks, instead of cars, rolled off the assembly lines in automobile plants. All over the country, manufacturers set aside their peacetime products and converted their machinery to make the supplies of war.

It was during the summer of 1942 that General Dwight D. Eisenhower was appointed Supreme Allied Commander of the British and American Forces. They were to land in Africa and drive out the German and Italian armies operating there and threatening the Suez Canal. The canal was the life line of the British for oil supplies in the Near East. The Allies were not yet strong enough to land in Europe to relieve the eastern front.

In the fall, Field Marshal Rommel, the German commander in northern Africa, was defeated. The following year an attack was launched against Sicily with the aim of eliminating Italy from the war. After several weeks of aerial bombardment the first landings were made in Sicily. The American forces were commanded by Lieutenant General George S. Patton. In the first two days of the invasion, more than 80,000 men with war equipment landed on the shores of Sicily. In thirty-nine days the island was cleared of enemy troops with an Allied loss of over 30,000 men killed, wounded, and missing. General Eisenhower's report stated the result of the Sicilian campaign:

Nine months after the first landings in North Africa, the Allied Force had not merely cleared its shore of enemy forces, but had wrested from him the Sicilian bridge to use as our own in an advance onto the Italian mainland.

The threatened invasion of Italy forced the Italian dictator, Mussolini, to resign his office. On September 8, 1943, the day after American troops landed on the shores of the Gulf of Salerno, the unconditional surrender of Italy was announced. German troops, however, were in possession of the country. It took nine months of bitter fighting for the American and British armies to get to Rome and capture the city. All the way up the peninsula progress was

slow and costly. Early in May of 1945, the German forces in northern Italy finally gave up the struggle.

The British and American campaigns in Africa and Italy pinned down thousands of German troops and much war equipment, relieving the German pressure on the Soviet Union. The German Army advanced as far as Stalingrad on the Volga River, where the Russians halted them with a long and stubborn defense. The defeat at Stalingrad and in northern Africa forced Germany into a war of defense.

Meanwhile, what was happening in the Pacific? While the Japanese were gaining control of the rich resources of the southern area and fortifying the island defense line, the United States was preparing bases in Australia, from which to launch attacks upon the Japanese line of defense. The Battle of the Coral Sea in May of 1942 checked a Japanese thrust at Australia. In the Battle of Midway in June, Japanese naval strength suffered a severe blow. Japanese troops landed on Guadalcanal in the Solomon Islands in July and began to lay out an airfield. Some action then had to be taken to prevent Japanese planes based on this island from severing the weak American supply line to Australia.

Eight months after Pearl Harbor, United States Marines and other troops landed on Guadalcanal from transports which had brought them from New Zealand under guard of naval warships. After almost 11,000 Marines had landed and captured the airfield, the Japanese began an air attack with planes based at Rabaul on the island of New Britain only 675 miles away. Since the American Marine landing on Guadalcanal was the first attempt to break into the enemy line of defense, the

LANDING ON NANUMEA IN THE ELLICE ISLANDS

Under the protection of destroyers, an LST is unloaded by United States Marines on Nanumea, an island in the Ellice group belonging to Great Britain. A shallow reef makes it impossible for the ship to hit the beach, and the cargo is unloaded and hauled ashore.

Japanese were able to concentrate both air and naval power on this spot.

Japanese planes strafing the landing beaches were attacked by American planes. On the morning of August 23, 1943 a reconnaissance plane spotted Japanese vessels approaching, about 250 miles away. The American fleet steamed north to meet the Japanese force, making contact northeast of Malaita Island, where the Battle of the Eastern Solomons was so bravely fought. Admiral Chester W.

Nimitz considered the encounter a major victory that turned away a large-scale reinforcement for Guadalcanal.

While another decisive sea battle was being fought near the Santa Cruz Islands, a battle was raging on land. In the dense, rain-soaked jungle of the mountainous island of Guadalcanal, Marines and soldiers were locked in a bitter struggle with the Japanese defenders. It took six months to dislodge the jungle-trained Japanese veterans from caves and dugouts and to clear the island of resistance. Meanwhile, American forces were landing on New Guinea, forcing Japan to use both land and naval forces, as well as aircraft, in scattered engagements. This relieved the pressure on Guadalcanal. The close teamwork between General Douglas MacArthur of the Army, and Admirals Chester W. Nimitz and William F. Halsey of the Navy initiated the successful offensive operations in the Pacific. Most of the credit for taking Guadalcanal, one of the decisive battles, belongs to the United States Marines.

The Pacific offensive was a slow, island-hopping campaign to gain control of the widespread line of defense around Japan. After operations in the Solomon Islands, landings were made in New Britain where the Japanese base at Rabaul was menacing the American advance. Landings were made in the Gilbert Islands where Tarawa was difficult and costly to take; on the Marshall Islands where forces took Kwajalein in January of 1944 and Eniwetok in February; and in the Marianas where Saipan was the first island invaded after the Navy defeated and scattered a Japanese fleet in the Battle of the Philippine Sea on June 19, 1944. Guam was retaken and Japanese strongholds in the Caroline Islands and the Paulau Islands were cleared out. In a gigantic game of leap-frog from island to island in the Pacific, American forces crept nearer and nearer to the Philippines. Japan was landing reinforcements there to hold the strategic islands. In keeping with the original plan to defeat Germany first, the long-awaited invasion of France preceded the final campaign in the Pacific region.

LANDING SUPPLIES ON GUADALCANAL

The battle of Guadalcanal in the Solomon Islands northeast of Australia was the first step in the tedious, island-hopping campaign in the Pacific.

Official U.S. Marine Corps Photo by Margun J.F. Leopold

DEVELOPMENTS OF 1944
ASSURE ALLIED VICTORY

ON JUNE 6, 1944, hundreds of craft, large and small, crossed the English Channel with troops destined for the invasion of France, which had been held by the Germans since the early months of the war. By nightfall, five divisions had landed on the beaches of Normandy with tanks, artillery, ammunition, trucks, and other equipment. The advance destruction of rail lines, highways, and bridges by the air force prevented the enemy from sending large reinforcements against the beachhead. The invasion was under the direction of General Eisenhower as Supreme Allied Commander.

Two days before, Rome had fallen to the Allies. British and American armies were pushing their way up the peninsula of Italy. Other British and American forces were driving across France toward the western border of Germany and Soviet armies were advancing toward the eastern border. By September 5, over 2,000,000 Allied troops had been put ashore in France, along with nearly 3,500,000 tons of supplies.

By the summer of 1944, industry in the United States was able to produce enough war materials to supply Eisenhower's invasion of France, the Allied advance north from Rome, and preparations for landings in the Philippines. Tanks, trucks, and planes moved along assembly lines of American factories on a twenty-four hour schedule. The same speed was maintained in the production of clothing, food, and necessities for troops. Transportation on the ground, across the seas, and in the air moved war supplies to all fronts in a steady flow, including the lend-lease shipments to Great Britain and the Soviet Union.

After the fall of Paris late in August of

U.S. Army Photograph

GENERAL DWIGHT D. EISENHOWER
Supreme Allied Commander in Europe

General Dwight D. Eisenhower issuing instructions to paratroopers in England before they boarded planes for the invasion of Europe.

1944, defeated German armies began retreating to defend their homeland. With the Allied campaign in Italy succeeding, and about 3,000,000 Allied troops on the continent of Europe, the defeat of Germany seemed assured. More attention could be given to Japan. Late in October of 1944, with the aid of air and naval forces General MacArthur was able to make surprise landings of troops at Leyte in the Philippines. In an effort to prevent Americans from retaking these islands, Japanese commanders committed their nation's grand fleet to a battle with the American fleet. The Battle of Leyte Gulf from October 23 to 26, which practically destroyed Japan's sea power, is considered one of the decisive engagements of World War II.

Early in January, protected by both air and sea support, ground troops landed on the shore of Lingayen Gulf to recover the key island of Luzon.

While MacArthur's troops were advanc-

GENERAL DOUGLAS MACARTHUR WITH INDIANS
— SIGNAL CORPS, UNITED STATES ARMY

The Indian soldiers in this photograph belonged to the following tribes (left to right): Pima of Arizona; Pawnee of Oklahoma; Chitimacha of Lousiana; Navajo of Arizona.

Indian soldiers received much praise from army officers for their skill in jungle fighting. In the Signal Corps they were particularly helpful, being able to talk in sign language and tongues unknown to the enemy.

ing on land, the carrier force of Admiral Halsey was occupied with destroying Japanese air power on Formosa and other islands. The fleet under Admiral Nimitz was protecting supply lines and bombarding positions slated for occupation. The airfields on Iwo Jima and Okinawa were strongly defended by the Japanese and were as strongly attacked by the Americans. The Allies were determined to gain the islands to use for bases for bombing the industrial cities of Japan.

More than 4500 Marines were killed in action. Before Okinawa surrendered, the war ended in Europe.

With Soviet troops approaching from the east and French, British, and American forces pushing forward from the west, the Germans were forced to give up the fight. Their cities where war industries were located had been reduced to rubble by long bombardment from both the east and the west. The repeated air attacks had sapped the will of the people to resist. On May 7,

1945, all land, sea, and air forces of the German Reich surrendered to the Allies at Reims, France, eleven months after the landings on the beaches of Normandy. Five days before, the commander of the German Army in Italy had surrendered. Only Japan remained in the war. Both the campaign in Italy and the advance from the English Channel had been slow-moving and bitterly contested. Soviet armies from the east and Eisenhower's armies from the west met in Germany. The conquered nation was divided among them for occupation. East Germany went to the Soviet Union and West Germany was shared by Great Britain, France, and the United States.

Berlin was occupied by all four powers.

However, the bombing of Japan began long before bases and airfields were established on Iwo Jima and Okinawa. On April 18, 1942, sixteen army bombers under the command of Lieutenant Colonel James Doolittle raided Tokyo in a surprise attack. The planes took off on this mission from the carrier *U.S.S. Hornet*, flew 600 miles to the capital of Japan, and made their way back to the China coast. Although gasoline ran out before any one of the planes reached the designated airfields in China, only two crews fell into enemy hands, when forced to land.

As United States forces crept closer to

APPROACHING IWO JIMA IN THE VOLCANO ISLANDS
The Fourth Marine Division men head toward the bloodiest, biggest, and toughest fight of their history, the fanatically defended island fortress, Iwo Jima.

Official U.S. Marine Corps Photo

Japan, American bombers began raids to destroy the industrial cities in which war supplies were manufactured. On the night of March 9, 279 bombers dropped incendiaries on Tokyo. The bombs burned out sixteen square miles in the heart of the capital. To date, this was the most destructive air raid in history, but one, more disastrous, was soon to come. The decision to introduce the atomic bomb to a startled world was made by President Harry S. Truman who took over the office after the death of Franklin D. Roosevelt.

On August 6, 1945, a superfortress released a single atomic bomb over Hiroshima, a military base. In the first use of this new weapon, sixty percent of the city was destroyed with a frightful loss of human life. Two days later, a second atomic bomb was dropped on another important industrial center, Nagasaki. On the eighth of August Russia declared war on Japan. The following day Russians smashed across the borders of Manchuria in several places to pinch off that rich country. Soviet troops occupied the southern part of Sakhalin Island, a Japanese possession, and moved forward rapidly to take as much territory as possible before Japan surrendered.

On the fifteenth day of August (fourteenth in this country), after three years and eight months of war with the United States, Japan accepted the terms of unconditional surrender. About nine o'clock on Sunday morning, September 2, 1945, the Japanese delegation of eleven men, diplomats and military officers,

SIGNING THE ARMISTICE ON DECK OF USS MISSOURI
September 2, 1945

Admiral Chester W. Nimitz signs the armistice on board the *Missouri*. Standing behind him are General Douglas MacArthur, Admiral William F. Halsey, and Rear Admiral Forrest P. Sherman.

Official U.S. Navy Photo

boarded the battleship *U.S.S. Missouri* in Tokyo Bay. They lined up on the slate-gray deck to sign the document of surrender before an impressive group of Allied military leaders who had brought about the defeat of Japan. Sailors, marines, and cameramen clung to vantage points on long-nosed guns and high platforms to view the historic ceremony. General MacArthur stepped up to the microphone, breaking the hollow silence with brief remarks:

We are gathered here representative of the major warring powers, to conclude a solemn agreement whereby peace may be restored. It is my earnest hope and indeed the hope of all mankind that from this solemn occasion a better world shall emerge out of the blood and carnage of the past — a world founded upon faith and understanding — a world dedicated to the dignity of man and the fulfillment of his most cherished wish — for freedom, tolerance, and justice.

Then he invited the Japanese delegates to sign the surrender first. Representatives of the Allies, following in order, stepped up to the green table to add their signatures for their own nations. In twenty minutes the signing was completed. The eleven Japanese departed in the same silence that marked their entry. There were no salutes. Thus ended the world conflict that took the lives of more than 22,000,000 persons, wounded nearly 35,000,000 and cost the staggering sum estimated at more than $1,000,000,000,000.

However, the end of the shooting war left the causes of the struggle in the minds of men. Two great world powers emerged from this mighty conflict of nations. The United States became the leader of governments based upon the idea that the human rights of man are above the rights of government. These privileges are defined in the first ten Amendments to the American Constitution. The Union of Soviet Socialist Republics became the promoter of the opposite idea, that the rights of the state precede the human rights of man. The former is a constitutional republic; the latter, a socialist dictatorship.

THE UNITED NATIONS

PRESIDENT Franklin D. Roosevelt invited the nations of the earth, except those on the list of enemies at the time, to send delegates to a meeting in San Francisco, but his successor, Harry S. Truman presided. This conference, called to write a charter for an organization through which countries could settle their quarrels without war, began on April 25, 1945 in the War Memorial Opera House.

Plans for world peace have been discussed down through the ages by many men, but their efforts failed to end war. In 1693 William Penn had advanced a plan for world peace based upon the theory that each nation has authority within its own borders, but that no nation should impose its will upon another without the free consent of the people living in that country.

Penn figured that peace was broken for one of three reasons: to keep what one has; to recover, when able, what had been taken away by force; and to increase power by adding neighbors' territory. The problems in 1945 were the same as in 1693. For two months the delegates from fifty nations labored to write a charter whereby these problems might be solved:

TO KEEP — How to prevent the invasion of an independent country.
TO RECOVER — How to provide a way for peoples who are living under governments not

their own, to be able, through a system of free voting, to select or establish a government of their own choice.

TO ADD – How to prevent large and powerful nations from conquering and enslaving weaker countries.

On May 15, 1945 Edward R. Stettinius Jr., the chairman of the United States delegation, told the 850 delegates from 50 countries:

As a nation which has been devoted through its history to the cause of liberty, the United States will continue to exert its full influence in behalf of all peoples to govern themselves according to their own desires, whenever they are prepared and able to assume the responsibilities of freedom as well as to enjoy its rights.

The United Nations was planned at a meeting of the "Big Three" in Yalta, Union of Soviet Socialist Republics, in February, 1945, although the idea had been considered earlier. In this conference, President Franklin D. Roosevelt represented the United States; Prime Minister Winston Churchill, Great Britain; and Joseph Stalin, with the title of Marshal, the Union of Soviet Socialist Republics. At this gathering, Stalin insisted that membership be given to the Bylorussian Soviet Socialist Republic and the Ukrainian Soviet Socialist Republic, along with the Union of Soviet Socialist Republics. This demand was granted and the Soviet Union won three votes in the General Assembly to one each for all other countries.

When this meeting of the United Nations closed on June 26, 1945, the following nations had signed the charter, except Poland, who was later listed among the original members.

NATIONS IN THE WESTERN HEMISPHERE		NATIONS IN THE EASTERN HEMISPHERE			
North America	**South America**	**Africa**	**Asia**	**Australia**	**Europe**
Canada	Argentina	Ethiopia	China	Australia	Belgium
Costa Rica	Bolivia	Liberia	India		Bylorussian Soviet
Cuba	Brazil	South Africa	Iran		Socialist Republic
Dominican	Chile	United Arab	Iraq		Czechoslovakia
Republic	Colombia	Republic	Lebanon		Denmark
El Salvador	Ecuador	(Egypt)	New Zealand		France
Guatemala	Panama		Philippines		Greece
Haiti	Paraguay		Saudi Arabia		Luxembourg
Mexico	Peru		Syria		Netherlands
Nicaragua	Uruguay		Turkey		Norway
United States	Venezuela		Union of Soviet		Poland
			Socialist Republics		Ukrainian Soviet
			(partly in Europe)		Socialist Republic
					United Kingdom
					Yugoslavia

In the beginning, 29 (or 58%) of the countries in the United Nations were in the Eastern Hemisphere; 21 (or 48%) were in the Western Hemisphere. The term "United Nations" did not mean agreement among the signers. With different forms of government, the organization was divided into hostile camps. Some nations defended the principle that governments exist to protect the human rights of man. Others argued that the state is supreme and may give or take away any rights, at will.

The United States took the lead in

complying with Article I, paragraph 2 of the United Nations charter:

To develop friendly relations among nations based on respect for the principle of equal rights and self-determination of people, and to take other appropriate measures to strengthen universal peace.

The United States abandoned the policy of colonialism by turning over the government of the Philippine Islands to the people living in that country.

INDEPENDENCE FOR PHILIPPINE ISLANDS

IN FEBRUARY, 1945 the Commonwealth Government of the Philippines returned to Manila to prepare for the establishment of an independent constitutional republic. The war did not end until the following August. In April, 1946 Manuel Roxas was elected President of the Republic of the Philippines. With a new constitution, the Filipinos were ready for independence as previously voted by the Congress of the United States.

The great day came on July 4, 1946. A large crowd gathered early for the ceremonies in an outdoor pavilion. General Douglas MacArthur, whom the Filipinos called "the Liberator," spoke to the people. He said:

Let history record this event in the sweep of democracy through the earth as foretelling the end of mastery over peoples by power of force alone — the end of empire as the political chain which binds the unwilling weak to the unyielding strong. Let it be recorded as one of the great turning points in the advance of civilization in the agelong struggle of man for liberty, for dignity, and for human betterment.

The United States High Commissioner, Paul V. McNutt, rose from his chair to face the microphones. The assembled throng of Filipinos listened breathlessly to the single sentence that meant so much to them. McNutt spoke:

I am authorized and directed by the President of the United States to proclaim the independence of the Philippines as a separate and self-governing nation.

Then he lowered the Stars and Stripes while the new President of the Republic of the Philippines hoisted the banner of the newborn nation. After the flag ceremony, President Roxas addressed his people:

MY COUNTRYMEN:
An historic drama has just been unfolded before our eyes. The American flag has been lowered from the flagstaffs in the land — not in defeat, not in surrender, not by compulsion, but by the voluntary act of the sovereign American Nation.

Filippinos were free for the first time since 1521 when Magellan had arrived to claim the islands for Spain. In a gala parade that followed the speeches, General Emilio Aguinaldo marched with a remnant of aging veterans wearing the old-fashioned uniforms of nearly fifty years before. In 1962, Independence Day was officially changed from July 4 to June 12. On that day in 1898 Filipinos had declared their independence from Spain. At the first celebration of the new Independence Day, Macapagal, President of the Republic of the Philippines told his people:

We shall be ready to fight on the side of America, as in the past, in defense of freedom and human dignity for ourselves and for all mankind.

579

In former years, signing peace treaties was often a dramatic event, and the place was a stately hall. Military men entered wearing colorful uniforms, their coats dripping with medals. Polished swords dangled at their sides. Diplomats in formal dress took their places of honor around the peace table. One by one, they advanced with solemn dignity to sign the treaty for their separate nations.

No such gathering followed World War II. No formal treaty was signed by all the nations taking part in the conflict. There is no peace. The struggle continues in shooting and debate, hot and cold, here and there around the world in a war of the minds of men.

MAPS:

WA33r   WA34r
Atlas of American History by Edgar B. Wesley

PART TWELVE

The World Is in Conflict

HOUSES OF PARLIAMENT
Ottawa

THE CAPITOL
Washington

PAN AMERICAN UNION
Washington

Chapter 32

Colonial Empires Crumble

OPPOSING FORMS OF GOVERNMENT

THE VOYAGE OF COLUMBUS in 1492 lured explorers westward from Europe to seek riches and adventure in an unknown hemisphere. After their discoveries, new maps were drawn showing the Western Hemisphere and the Eastern Hemisphere — the New World and the Old World — separated by oceans on the north, south, east, and west.

Down through the centuries, as a rule, the few had ruled the many in the Old World. Through war and conquest, families gained enough power to maintain their control over peoples, declaring they governed by divine right as princes, emperors, and kings. The thrones were passed down from fathers to sons, and sometimes, to daughters. Their loyal followers were granted land and privileges along with titles of count, lord, duke, earl and the like. These honors, being inherited, created a nobility as a ruling class. Gradually, as towns grew in size and number, merchants and tradesmen gained a voice in their governments in some countries. However, the pattern of the few ruling the many prevailed throughout the Eastern Hemisphere when Columbus sailed

from Palos, Spain, on his famous voyage.

Anxious to gain territory in the newly discovered Hemisphere, governments in Europe encouraged their subjects to seek new homes in distant places so they could hold the country. Although an effort was made to transfer the same pattern of living across the sea, the main goal was possession. Newcomers in a wilderness, far from home, learned that survival depended upon what each one did for himself — man, woman and child. When every family faced the necessity of acquiring food, clothing and shelter, a common bond held them together. People began to think for themselves and to share their ideas with their neighbors. To survive and prosper, they gradually developed government in which they shared responsibility for their safety, success, and happiness. In learning to govern themselves, they acquired the notion that they had the right to govern themselves. This idea, fostered strongly in the British colonies, gradually spread over the Americas, crossing boundaries like seeds in the wind. Leaders rose among peoples to champion the principle of government by the governed:

1765 — I say RIGHTS, for such men have, . . . RIGHTS that can not be repealed or restrained by human laws, . . . RIGHTS, from the great Legislator of the universe . . . .

JOHN ADAMS
President of the U.S.

1774 — . . . the experience of all states mercifully demonstrating to us that, when arbitrary power has been established over them, even the wisest and bravest nations that have ever flourished have, in a few years, degenerated into abject and wretched vassals.

JOHN DICKINSON
Signer of the Constitution

1788 — In a serene mind the sciences and virtues love to dwell. But can the mind of a man be serene, when the property, liberty, substance of himself and of those for whom he feels more than for himself, depend on a tyrant's nod?

JAMES WILSON
Signer of the Constitution

1811 — Let us fearlessly lay the cornerstone of South American liberty; if we hesitate we are lost.

SIMON BOLIVAR
Liberator of Spanish colonies in South America

1816 — . . . the way to have good and safe government, is not to trust it all to one, but to divide it among the many, distributing to every one exactly the functions he is competent to.

THOMAS JEFFERSON
Author of Declaration of Independence

After government by the governed became law through the Constitution of the United States, the idea spread in the Americas and crossed the Atlantic to Europe. In some countries, peoples gained more personal liberty during the nineteenth century. This march of freedom was halted in 1914 by the outbreak of war, involving so many nations that it was called World War I. The armistice, signed on November 11, 1918 officially ended the shooting war, the most destructive conflict in history to that date, and left to war-weary peoples the

turmoil resulting from the struggle. The way of life did not return to that of 1914.

Before the Treaty of Versailles was signed in Paris, a feud between two forms of government was brewing in the Russian revolution. After the Communists had gained control of the nation, their plans for government were enforced, and later written into a constitution to be the law of the United Soviet Socialist Republics, and to be promoted in other countries. A few samples from this document are quoted as follows:

ARTICLE 4

The economic foundation of the U.S.S.R. is the socialist system of economy and the socialist ownership of the instruments and means of production . . . the abolition of private ownership of the instruments and means of production . . . . "

ARTICLE 6

The land, its mineral wealth, waters, forests, mills, factories, mines, rail, water and air transport, banks, communications, large state-organized agricultural enterprises (state farms, machine and tractor station and the like), as well as municipal enterprises and the bulk of the dwelling-houses in the cities and industrial localities, are state property . . . .

ARTICLE 12

The principle applied in the U.S.S.R. is that of socialism: From each according to his ability, to each according to his wo.'.

NEW NATIONS IN
EUROPE RISE AND FALL

IN THE SAME MONTH of the same year that the Armistice was signed, General Jan Christian Smuts, a founder of the future League of Nations released a plan for peace. Since a number of peoples in the defeated empires had been living under governments they did not choose, General Smuts suggested that these peoples be allowed to form new countries of their own. He wrote this section in his proposal for peace:

That there shall be no annexation of any of those territories to any of the victorious Powers, and secondly, that in the future government of these territories and peoples the rule of self-determination or the consent of the governed to their form of government, shall be fairly and reasonably applied.

Czar Nicholas II, ruler of Russia, and his wife and children were murdered, bringing an end to the old order in that land. Millions of Russians lost their lives through disease, starvation, and massacres during the revolution that swept over that vast country. While the government was changing from a monarchy to a Communist dictatorship, peoples living on the western boundary of the old Russian empire took advantage of the confusion to gain their liberty. Finland, Estonia, Latvia, and Lithuania along the Baltic Sea became independent countries. After years of living as a conquered people under Russian domination, Poland was a free nation again and the proud Poles rejoiced. Austria and Hungary were separate countries, and their former neighbors were in a new nation, Czechoslovakia. The map of Europe had been remade by war, again, but not for long. Men promoting Lenin's kind of government were scheming for approval, necessary for gaining the power not only to remap Europe, but the entire world in time.

In 1933, President Franklin D. Roosevelt recognized the Communist dictatorship that had taken over the Russian people as the official government.

Communists of the Union of Soviet Socialist Republics were received in Washington as ambassadors and official delegates with the same rank as these representatives from all other countries. As nations recognized the U.S.S.R. officially, Communists were located in their capitals.

New nations in Europe scarcely had time to become acquainted with their freedom when another conflict was brewing in Europe and in Asia. In this one, World War II, the Union of Soviet Socialist Republics was on the side of the United States. With this nation as an ally, officials of the United States discussed both war and peace with Soviet leaders. President Franklin D. Roosevelt of the United States, Prime Minister Winston S. Churchill of the British government, and Marshal Joseph Stalin of the Soviet Union were known as "The Big Three."

In November, 1943 these three leaders met in Teheran (Tehran), Iran. Because Stalin refused to leave his country again, the "Big Three" met next in Yalta, a port on the Black Sea, in January of 1945. After Roosevelt's death in April of the same year, Harry S. Truman, the Vice President became President and joined the "Big Three" meeting in Potsdam near Berlin, Germany. Although agreements made at these meetings considered the right of peoples to a choice of their governments, Stalin ignored them. Soviet soldiers overpowered the Baltic countries that had gained their independence after World War I. Estonia, Latvia, and Lithuania were annexed to the U.S.S.R. and Communist rule was forced upon the people. Finland lost valuable territory and, at great sacrifice, had to pay costly reparations to the Moscow government although left free in name. Poland, Czechoslovakia, Romania, Yugoslavia, Hungary, Bulgaria, Albania, and Eastern Germany fell as the U.S.S.R. was able to establish Communist governments in the defenseless nations. Communism pushed into Central Europe, leaving only a fringe of free nations bordering the Atlantic Ocean and the western Mediterranean.

On March 12, 1947 President Truman outlined to a joint session of Congress the policy of giving military and economic aid to nations threatened by powerful neighbors. The President immediately recommended advancing $400,000,000 to Greece and Turkey on the border of the Soviet Union for these nations to spend in defending themselves. A few months later General George C. Marshall, Secretary of State in President Truman's Cabinet, began developing a program for Americans to spend billions of dollars in helping war-ridden nations of Europe to rebuild their bombed-out cities, restore their ruined industries, and become self-supporting again. Under the Marshall Plan, both friends and former enemies regained prosperity. The taxpayers of the United States financed their recovery.

In 1949, the United States, Canada, The United Kingdom (Great Britain), the Netherlands, France, and Belgium founded the Atlantic Pact. Later Norway, Denmark, Italy, Iceland, and Portugal joined "The North Atlantic Treaty For Defense, Peace and Security," called NATO. The countries in NATO intended to work together in their own defense. General Dwight D. Eisenhower was selected as the first commander of the armed forces of NATO. The headquarters were near Paris, France. General Eisenhower had the task of uniting nations with different languages and customs, and peoples with strong national pride. His

successors inherited that problem. In 1967 NATO headquarters were moved to a new location near Brussels, Belgium.

History records the efforts of a number of far-seeing men who advocated a united Europe to end the wars that plagued Europe for centuries. In 1683 William Penn in his famous essay, "The Peace of Europe," had suggested that the countries of Europe:

For love of peace and order, agree to meet by their stated deputies in a general diet, estates, or parliament, and there establish rules of justice for sovereign princes to observe one to another; and thus to meet yearly, or once in two or three years at farthest, or as they shall see cause, and to be styled, the Sovereign or Imperial Diet, Parliament, or State of Europe.

A step was made in this direction in 1952 when an agreement called the European Defense Community was signed in Paris by the foreign ministers of West Germany, France, Italy, Belgium, Luxembourg, and the Netherlands. The United Kingdom refused to join lest national sovereignty be endangered, but did sign a treaty to resist aggression against anyone of the seven nations in the European Defense Community. Trade agreements are gradually bringing the free nations of western Europe closer together. Nevertheless, the burden of financing armaments for a united European defense still falls heavily upon the taxpayers of the United States. Congress appropriates huge sums of money to aid foreign nations, and supports thousands of American fighting men, ready for combat, who live in these countries to resist any attack. After two world wars, the United States shares the uneasy peace of western Europe, peace by armed might.

EUROPEAN POWERS LOSE COLONIES

AFRICA HAD long been a colonial continent with only a few independent nations. Most of Africa was claimed by France, Belgium, Great Britain, and Portugal. After World War II, unrest among the natives brought strife and revolution. Many small nations were carved from the former colonies, and their independence recognized by the former mother countries. Twenty years after World War II, Africa had only one European power holding a large block of its land. Portugal had Angola, Mozambique and Portuguese Guinea. However, these areas are overseas provinces of the homeland rather than colonies. The people in Angola, Mozambique and Guinea are Portuguese citizens, the same as people living in European Portugal.

Other countries in southern Asia that had been British colonies gained recognition as separate countries, like Canada and Australia, in the British Commonwealth, and some gained total independence. Burma became an independent republic. It was a blow to Great Britain to lose its richest colony, India. French soldiers fought for years to hold Indochina. The area was lost and broken up into small nations, Cambodia, Laos, and Vietnam. Although the peoples of the East Indies had enjoyed considerable self-government under the Dutch, they also wanted independence. The Netherlands lost these rich and populous islands, held as the nation's colonies for several centuries. The name was changed to Indonesia.

Independence did not insure peace to these new nations. Peoples without experience in self-government do not always understand that freedom is tied to responsibility. Unable to provide for themselves, emerging nations sought financial help from the United States. Congress yearly voted billions of dollars for foreign aid. Meanwhile, Communists took advantage of the confusion seeking to establish communism as the form of government in the new nations without the consent of the people. This policy involved the United States in many ways, including wars overseas.

Chapter 33

Wars in Asia Involve the United States

COMMUNISTS CAPTURE CHINA

IN THE MIDDLE of the nineteenth century, Commodore Matthew C. Perry was sent by the United States Government to visit Japan and seek trade with that Oriental country. On his second trip, he was successful. A treaty was signed opening the ports of Japan to ships from the United States. After his return, Perry said in a speech on March 6, 1856:

It seems to me that the people of America will, in some form or another, extend their domination and their power, until they shall have placed the Saxon race upon the eastern shores of Asia, and I think too, that eastward and southward will her great rival in future aggrandizement (Russia) stretch forth her power to the coasts of China and Siam; and thus the Saxon and the Cossack will meet . . . . Will it be in friendship? I fear not! The antagonistic exponents of freedom and absolutism must thus meet at last, and then will be fought the mighty battle on which the world will look with breathless interest; for on its issue will depend the freedom or slavery of the world; . . . I think I see in the distance the giants that are growing up for that fierce and final encounter; in the progress of events that battle must sooner or later be fought . . . .

At the close of World War II, the Republic of China was a nation with great

manpower, but too weak to use it in defense after years of invasions and civil wars. China was easy prey for conquest. A few days before the armistice of World War II was signed, the Soviet Union joined the war against Japan and marched soldiers into Japanese territory in Asia to put these lands under Communist control. Supplied by the Soviet Union, Chinese Communists attacked the poorly-equipped armies of Chiang Kai-shek, defeated them, and seized the government of China. In December, 1949 Chiang Kai-shek established the government of Free China on Taiwan, formerly called Formosa. The fall of the huge land mass of China with millions of people, posed a threat to small neighboring countries. Korea was the next victim of Communist expansion.

KOREA BECOMES A BATTLEGROUND

THE SOVIET UNION took undue advantage of the brief part played in the war against Japan to extend government by the Communist Party into Manchuria, China, and Korea. When Japan sued for peace, it was agreed that Japanese north of the 38th parallel on the Korean peninsula would surrender to Soviet armies, and those south of that line to the United States Army. This was to be only a temporary arrangement as independence had been promised to Korea. In 1943, at a meeting in Cairo, Egypt, President Franklin D. Roosevelt of the United States, Prime Minister Winston Churchill of Great Britain, and Generalissimo Chiang Kai-shek of China agreed that "Korea shall in due course become free and independent."

Following the surrender of Japanese troops, Soviet soldiers occupied Korea north of the 38th parallel. Soviet officials set up a government under the direction of the Communist Party. In South Korea, occupied by United States troops, American officials cooperated with native leaders to organize a constitutional republic. After forty years of Japanese occupation, Koreans lacked experience in self-government. When officials of South Korea invited political parties to register for a general election, two hundred were listed.

Since the northern part of Korea was largely industrial and the southern part agricultural, the two regions were dependent upon one another. The division of the little country prevented trade and resulted in chaos. A joint commission of the United States and the Soviet Union failed to agree upon a plan to unite Korea and make the country independent. The General Assembly of the United Nations also tried and failed. The little nation remained cut in half with two capitals, Pyongyang in North Korea and Seoul in South Korea. In August, 1948 South Korea established a constitutional republic and elected Syngman Rhee the first President. Thus divided, Korea became the "powderkeg" of Asia.

Although there were frequent clashes between soldiers along the 38th parallel, no full scale invasion took place until the summer of 1950. At four o'clock on Sunday morning, June 25, North Korean armed forces, spearheaded by Soviet tanks, crossed the border and captured Seoul, the capital of South Korea. President Harry S. Truman issued orders to General Douglas MacArthur in Tokyo to dispatch troops and supplies to the South Korean army. Overpowered by greater numbers of well-equipped soldiers from North Korea, the Americans and South Korean troops were forced to retreat.

The United Nations voted to halt this invasion and asked countries in the organization to send soldiers and supplies. So few did that over ninety percent of the fighting forces were recruited in the United States, and that nation furnished practically all of the armaments and supplies. General Douglas MacArthur was selected to be Commander in Chief of this undeclared war under the banner of the United Nations.

In September, 1950 General MacArthur made a surprise amphibious landing at Inchon behind the North Korean lines, forcing a hasty retreat of the invaders. The victorious troops of South Korea marched into North Korea and captured Pyongyang, the capital, and then moved on toward the Manchurian border.

Meanwhile, thousands of Chinese Communists with weapons and war supplies were gathering in Manchuria across the Yalu River. The policy of the government in Washington was to confine the war within the borders of Korea. General MacArthur received orders not to send American planes across the Yalu to bomb supply centers; to chase planes in "hot pursuit" attacking his army; to cripple hydroelectric plants furnishing electricity to the enemy; to destroy the bridges over the river; not to attack any target within five miles of the Manchurian border in any direction. MacArthur obeyed, as was his duty, protesting that the Chinese Communists had a "privileged sanctuary" in Manchuria.

Soon an entirely new war began when hordes of Chinese soldiers poured across the Yalu bridges in November of 1950. Hopelessly outnumbered, MacArthur's troops were forced to leave the North Korean capital and retreat below the 38th parallel. Thousands of American soldiers were evacuated by sea to escape capture by the onrushing Chinese. War swept up and down the rugged hills of Korea, spreading ruin and death in its path. Government policy in Washington remained the same, keeping the conflict within the borders of the little peninsula.

On April 11, 1951 President Truman recalled General Douglas MacArthur and gave his command to General Matthew B. Ridgway. The big war in the little country had cost about a million casualties among all the troops engaged, and among the civilians who suffered hardship and disease fleeing invading armies.

The representative of the Soviet Union to the United Nations proposed a truce in Korea. In July, 1951 officers from the armies of North Korea, the Chinese Communists, and the United Nations met to arrange for a ceasefire truce to stop the fighting while their governments debated an armistice. The negotiations dragged on for over a year without reaching an agreement of any kind while the fighting continued with increasing fury as more Chinese Com-

munists were equipped with supplies from the Soviet Union to enter the war.

On October 8, 1952 the truce talks were broken off. The Communists had demanded the return of all North Korean and Chinese prisoners, by force, if necessary. When these prisoners were asked whether or not they wanted to return to their homelands, thousands said they did not want to go home to live under communism. Refusal to return these prisoners against their wishes closed the meeting.

The Korean War became a leading issue in the national election in November of 1952. The Democratic Party, in power for twenty years, was criticized for its foreign policy resulting in the loss of China to the Communists and the war in Korea. The casualties for this undeclared war amounted to about 140,000 men in fighting units of the United States.

On the twentieth of January, 1953 Dwight D. Eisenhower, General of the United States Army during World War II, was inaugurated President. Richard M. Nixon, former Senator from California was his Vice President. President Eisenhower gave immediate attention to the Korean problem. Two months after he took office, some wounded and sick prisoners on both sides were exchanged at Panmunjom in South Korea. An early date was set to resume the truce talks.

After long and tedious argument, the Communists finally signed an armistice on July 27, 1953 without gaining their demand that prisoners held by the armies in South Korea be returned by force against their wishes. Many of the Chinese prisoners had gone to Taiwan. The shooting ended on paper, but not in fact, after three years and thirty-two days of war.

The shooting continues at intervals along the 38th parallel. United States soldiers share duty with the South Korean army on guard against another invasion. North Koreans sneak through the unreal barrier to terrorize their neighbors. Raiding parties land at night on the eastern coast to rob the villagers and burn their homes. When these acts of violence are reported at Panmunjom, North Korean officials maintain a stony silence.

In the little country of South Korea, people live in hourly peril, surrounded by Communist governments. After the war, with patient hope, they faced the task of rebuilding their war-torn land and defending their constitutional republic.

WAR SPREADS IN SOUTHEAST ASIA

COMMUNISTS ANCHORED in North Korea on the northeastern coast of Asia, next established a similar bridgehead on the southeastern coast of that continent. Before World War II Japan, the Republic of China, and Thailand (Siam) were the only independent countries in Eastern Asia. Much of the area was colonial and claimed by European nations. After the war, peoples in Asia began to seek independence. From 1946 to 1954, French soldiers fought to hold Indochina for France and failed.

Before the French were driven out, Communists were planning to take over the new governments. Since most of the natives wanted independence without outside interference in three small countries — Laos, Cambodia, and Vietnam — war was brewing before the French departed.

Vietnam was the first target. With foreign assistance, Communists created civil war in the frail new nation. In an effort to bring peace, a settlement was made in Geneva, Switzerland to divide the little country at the 17th parallel. North of the line would be a Communist dictatorship. South of the line would be a government chosen by the people. Almost a million Vietnamese fled south to escape communism under Ho chi Minh and only a few moved into the northern sector from the southern part. The United States Government furnished ships to transport refugees from the North to the South, and provided food and clothing for many while they waited to find new homes. The pattern was the same as in Korea, and developed in the same way.

In 1955, South Vietnam became a constitutional republic with Ngo dinh Diem elected President. Communists stirred up strife, intending to take over the feeble nation under its first President. Under a treaty, the United States responded to Diem's call for help, and sent military men to advise and train the Vietnamese in defense. In civil war that followed, Diem was murdered. More and more troops from North Vietnam crossed into South Vietnam to aid the local Communist guerrillas, the Viet Cong, in their terrorist campaign of burning, kidnapping, and killing. More and more American fighting men — soldiers, Marines, airmen, sailors and civilians — went to defend South Vietnam, half a million by the first day of 1968, fighting on land, sea, and in the air. Lyndon B. Johnson, President of the United States, stated again and again that the big war in the little country could end any day the invaders retreated across the 17th parallel, leaving the people of South Vietnam free to choose their own form of

591

United States Marines

GUARD DUTY IN SOUTH VIETNAM

A Marine Corporal protecting a farmer helps in harvesting the crop.

MEDICAL CARE FOR REFUGEES AT DA NANG, SOUTH VIETNAM

The United States Navy sent ambulances and medical officers to treat refugees fleeing from communism. As the war progressed, the number of displaced persons helped by the Americans increased.

United States Navy

IN SOUTH VIETNAM

**UNITED STATES
GOVERNMENT SENT WEAPONS'
INSTRUCTORS TO SOUTH VIETNAM**

An officer of the South Vietnamese Air Force receives training in air defense from an officer of the United States Air Force.

HELICOPTERS — UNITED STATES ARMY

Helicopters prepare to airlift members of Twelfth Infantry Regiment to battle zone in jungles of Vietnam.

government. Thus did Vietnam become the battleground between "freedom and absolutism," on the coast of southeastern Asia as did Korea on the northeastern coast, and both bordered China.

On January 20, 1969 Richard M. Nixon was inaugurated President of the United States. He inherited the war in Vietnam. After ten months in office, President Nixon made a report on the war in a televised speech to the people.

"How and why did America get involved in Vietnam in the first place?"

Then he answered his question, stating:

"Fifteen years ago North Vietnam, with the logistical support of Communist China and the Soviet Union, launched a campaign to impose a Communist government on South Vietnam by instigating and supporting a revolution."

Among principles for future American policy in Asia, the President listed:

"The United States will keep all of its treaty commitments."

In concluding remarks, he said:

"The wheel of destiny has turned so that any hope the world has for survival of peace and freedom will be determined by whether the American people have the moral stamina and the courage to meet the challenge of free world leadership."

As Commodore Perry foretold, "the Saxon and the Cossack" met on "the coasts of China and Siam" in "that battle" that "must sooner or later be fought."

PARTNERSHIPS FOR DEFENSE — EASTERN HEMISPHERE

THE UNITED STATES plunged into world conflicts when the nation entered World War I in 1917. Coming out of that war as a great world power, the nation shouldered world responsibilities, and the burden has increased with the years. Instead of peace, "the war to end wars" spawned a breeding ground for future wars when communism, based in Russia, set out to conquer the world.

With the United States as an ally in World War II, the Soviet Union emerged from this war as a great world power. Nation after nation in eastern Europe and eastern Asia fell to communism under Soviet might. In an effort to maintain peace the United States government entered into partnerships with small Asian countries caught in the path of the Soviet drive to the Indian Ocean.

The first security agreement in the Pacific area after World War II was the Treaty of Mutual Defense between the United States and the Philippines, signed in August, 1951. In September of the same year, a treaty of defense was signed with Japan, and was replaced by another treaty in 1960. Also in 1951, a Mutual Defense Treaty was signed at the Presidio in San Francisco between the Commonwealth of Australia and the Dominion of New Zealand. This treaty is commonly called ANZUS. These nations agreed that an armed attack on one will affect all and that each will "act to meet the common danger." Japan signed a treaty of peace with the Nationalist Government of China at Taipei, Taiwan (Formosa). In 1953, treaties to defend one another were signed by the United States and the Nationalist Government of China (Free China); and between the United States and the Republic of Korea (South Korea).

In 1954, after Communists had gained power in North Korea, another collective treaty for defense was planned. Foreign ministers of Australia, France, New Zealand, Pakistan, the Philippines, Thailand, the United Kingdom (Great Britain), and the United States met in Manila and signed the South East Asia Collective Defense Treaty on September 8, 1954. The treaty is known as SEATO, and covers one-eighth of the world's surface and approximately one-seventh of its people. The signers agreed that "they are determined to prevent or counter by appropriate means any attempt . . . to subvert their freedom or to destroy their sovereignty or territorial integrity."

On March 9, 1957 the Congress of the United States passed a resolution to "promote peace and stability in the Middle East." Small nations in the Middle East discussed ways to work together to defend themselves. They finally worked out agreements and formed the Central Treaty Organization in 1959, known as CENTO, which included Iran, Turkey, Pakistan, and the United Kingdom (Great Britain). In 1961, the governments of nations in CENTO appointed a military commander to improve their defense planning.

Thus, all over the world, nations seek security by forming alliances, agreeing to fight if any one of the group is attacked. With the United States joining a number of these associations, armed forces of this nation have served in many foreign countries since 1917. From the North Sea to the China Sea after World War II, thousands of United States troops, supplied with weapons and ready for combat duty, were stationed in the Eastern Hemisphere to protect free peoples. Small nations emerging from former colonies face the problem of forming new governments. A republic or a dictatorship? Free elections or

state control? Government by laws or the whims of men? This problem is scattering American men and American money around the world in an effort to maintain peace with freedom.

NEW COUNTRIES JOIN UNITED NATIONS

IN A WORLD sick with war, nations grab at straws and dream of peace. In 1945, peoples again risked their hopes on an international organization to end war. In this assembly, each member large or small, rich or poor, strong or weak was to have one vote. However, this rule was broken at the start when the Soviet Union added two provinces as separate states and demanded three votes.

From the beginning, opposing forms of government bid for power inside the United Nations. The side winning the most of these new countries would gain the most votes in the United Nations. On the last day of 1969, the Eastern Hemisphere held 100 votes out of 126, leaving 26 votes for the Western Hemisphere.

Who pays the bill? Being the richest member, the United States was originally assessed 32% of the budget. With expenses mounting year by year, and the refusal of some nations to pay their shares of operating costs, the taxpayers of the United States have paid more than 32% for one vote. Most of the little countries, new and not developed, are required to pay only the minimum of .04% to join the organization, and sometimes this amount is taken from foreign aid furnished by the United States. Dean Rusk, Secretary of State in President Johnson's cabinet summed up the situation during his term, with this printed statement:

A two-thirds majority of the General Assembly could be formed by nations with only 10% of the world's population, or who contribute altogether 5% of the U.N.'s budget.

A brief story of one small, independent nation illustrates the problem faced by the United Nations Organization.

The Maldive Islands form a coral chain, five hundred miles long in the Indian Ocean southwest of Ceylon. All 2000 islands total 115 square miles, and only 220 are inhabited. The population is 95,000.

Since 1887 the British Government had claimed this chain of islands, but no official had been sent to state his authority. Although a native sultan lived in the capital, Male, the people governed themselves. The only privilege required by London was the right for an air base and a broadcasting station when independence was granted. The papers of independence had been deposited for some time in the nearest British office in Colombo, Ceylon, waiting to be signed by an official of the tiny island country.

The Maldivian Prime Minister got a toothache. There were no dentists in the Maldives. In July of 1965, he set out on a three-day boat trip to visit the nearest dentist, located in Colombo. While in the capital of Ceylon, he went to the office of the British High Commissioner and signed the papers of independence. Thus did the United Nations gain a new member, the smallest and least populated to date. The Maldive Islands have one vote in the General Assembly, the same as any country of any size, except the Union of Soviet Socialist Republics with three votes.

Countries of the Western Hemisphere are outnumbered almost five to one in the United Nations. Yet, with few exceptions, their governments keep the peace in that part of the world. Though languages and national backgrounds are not alike, there is a common bond. From Alaska to Patagonia, peoples of the Americas are seeking the same goal.

MAPS:

WA54r WA55r
Atlas of American History by Edgar B. Wesley

THE UNITED NATIONS — 1969 — WESTERN HEMISPHERE

NORTH AMERICA
Canada
Mexico
United States

CARIBBEAN
Barbados
Cuba
Dominican Republic
Haiti
Jamaica
Trinidad-Tobago

CENTRAL AMERICA
Costa Rica
El Salvador
Guatemala
Honduras
Nicaragua
Panama

SOUTH AMERICA
Argentina
Bolivia
Brazil
Chile
Colombia
Ecuador
Guyana
Paraguay
Peru
Uruguay
Venezuela

THE UNITED NATIONS – 1969 – EASTERN HEMISPHERE

AFRICA

Algeria
Botswana
Burundi
Cameroon
Central African Republic
Chad
Congo (Brazzaville)
Congo (Democratic Republic of)
Dahomey
Equatorial Africa
Ethiopia
Gabon
Gambia
Ghana
Guinea
Ivory Coast
Kenya
Lesotho
Liberia
Libya
Malagasy Republic (Madagascar)
Malawi
Mali
Mauritania
Morocco
Niger
Nigeria
Rwanda
Senegal
Sierra Leone
Somalia
South Africa
Sudan
Swaziland
Togo
Tunisia
Uganda
United Arab Republic
United Republic of Tanzania
Upper Volta
Zambia

ASIA

Afghanistan
Burma
Cambodia
Ceylon
China (Free)
India
Indonesia
Iran
Iraq
Israel
Japan
Jordan
Kuwait
Laos
Lebanon
Malaysia
Maldive Islands
Mauritius
Mongolia
Nepal
Pakistan
Philippines
Saudi Arabia
Singapore
Southern Yemen
Syria
Thailand
Turkey (Europe)
Union of Soviet Socialist Republics (Europe)
Yemen

AUSTRALIA
NEW ZEALAND

EUROPE

Albania
Austria
Belgium
Bulgaria
Byelorussian Soviet Socialist Republic
Cyprus
Czechoslovakia
Denmark
Finland
France
Greece
Hungary
Iceland
Ireland
Italy
Luxembourg
Malta
Netherlands
Norway
Poland
Portugal
Romania
Spain
Sweden
Ukrainian Soviet Socialist Republic
United Kingdom (Great Britain)
Yugoslavia

Chapter 34

Western Hemisphere Pursues a Vision

BOLIVAR VISIONED
A UNITED HEMISPHERE

GENERAL FRANCISCO MIRANDA who started the revolutionary movement in South America was one of the first Pan American thinkers. He spoke of "Our Americas" instead of "My Venezuela" as if he were a citizen of every country in the Western Hemisphere. Although he was born in Caracas, South America, he was educated to feel at home on both American continents. After leaving school in his native Venezuela, he studied law for over a year at a college in Mexico City. During the summer of 1784, only a year after peace was signed between the United States and Great Britain, Miranda attended lectures at Yale University in New Haven, Connecticut.

Thomas Jefferson also had felt a common bond existing between citizens of the United States and citizens of Latin American countries. In 1808, while President of the United States, he wrote to Governor Claiborne in New Orleans about Cuba and Mexico:

We consider their interests and ours at the same time, and the object of both must be to exclude all European influence from this hemisphere.

John C. Calhoun of South Carolina showed his Pan American sympathy in a practical way. When an earthquake severely damaged Venezuela in 1812, he asked Congress to raise the relief fund from $30,000 to $50,000 to load five vessels with food and clothing for the stricken people of that country. Considering that the United States was on the brink of war with Great Britain and every penny was needed for defense, the donation was a heartfelt gesture toward a neighbor in distress.

To this day the name of Henry Clay is listed among the heroes of independence throughout Latin America. As the Spanish provinces, one by one, gained their independence from Spain, their staunch friend from Kentucky argued in Congress for their recognition as free and independent states. Sometimes it took Clay several years to win enough votes for his cause, since many Congressmen were more interested in evading war with Spain than helping that nation's colonists in gaining their freedom. Senator Clay did not relax his efforts until representatives of his Government were on their way to the capitals of new-born republics in Central and South America. Henry Clay's

598

untiring devotion to the cause of independence in the Spanish colonies paved the way for the Monroe Doctrine. To him, the United States, first country to shed the yoke of colonialism, was the "natural head of the American family."

Another dreamer of Pan American unity was Simon Bolivar, whom Clay called the Washington of South America. It was in 1815 that Bolivar planned a meeting of representatives from American countries to talk over their common problems. It was hope, born of despair, perhaps. He had gone to Jamaica seeking ships and supplies from the British governor but failed to get them. The governor explained that he could not give aid to revolutionaries in Venezuela or any other Spanish province when his country was at peace with Spain.

Ten years later Bolivar was the hero, the ruler of Peru. He rode through the streets of Lima, lined with cheering crowds, to address the Peruvian Congress. As he entered the hall the delegates shouted, "Long live Bolivar! Long live the Redeemer of Peru!" He chose this time, at the height of success, to launch his dream. He suggested that a general congress meet in Panama to discuss the problems of the newly liberated states.

In June of the following year, 1826, the meeting was held. Men gathered from Mexico, Guatemala, Colombia, and Peru to do what Bolivar had dreamed in 1815:

to deliberate upon the high interests of peace and of war not only between the American nations, but between them and the rest of the world.

The difficulty of travel in those days, no doubt, kept some representatives away. Brazil, belonging to Portugal, agreed to cooperate but did not send delegates. However, the southern countries in the region of the La Plata River refused to take any part in the congress. President John Quincy Adams accepted the invitation for the United States, but the Senate did not support him, at first. After considerable argument, the Senate voted to send two delegates. President Adams appointed the United States Ambassador in Bogota, Colombia, who died enroute to Panama, and Sergeant of Pennsylvania, who did not get started until the conference had ended. The House of Representatives delayed his departure by debating too long over paying his expenses.

The small attendance at the Congress of Panama was a great disappointment to Bolivar, who did not attend. At the time he was busy quelling a revolt among Peruvians who felt that Colombian soldiers were staying too long in Peru. Although the meeting was a failure as far as results were concerned, the idea was a success. At the opening of this first American Congress the Minister of Peru had sounded the trumpet call for future cooperation:

Above all, let us form one family and forget the names of our respective countries in the more general denomination of brothers. Let us form a body of public law, which the civilized world may admire. In it, a wrong to one state shall be regarded as an injury to all.

It was a forward step toward peace for peoples differing in language and racial backgrounds to want meetings where they could discuss their common problems. In the Congress of Panama, Bolivar planted the seed of Pan Americanism. Again, "something new" had sprouted in the New World.

THE PAN AMERICAN
WAY EVOLVED
THROUGH CONFERENCES

NOT UNTIL 1889, sixty-three years after the gathering at Panama, did Bolivar's dream of American unity show signs of becoming real. In that year James G. Blaine, Secretary of State in President Harrison's Cabinet, invited the republics of the Americas to send representatives to a meeting in the United States. The conference opened in Washington. Secretary Blaine said in his official opening speech:

No conference of nations has ever assembled to consider the welfare of territorial possessions so vast. — Those now sitting within these walls are empowered to speak for nations whose borders are on both the great oceans. The territorial extent of the nations here represented falls but little short of 12,000,000 square miles, more than three times the area of all Europe, and but little less than one-fourth of the globe.

During the conference many of the South American representatives made a tour of the country as guests of our Government. They boarded a special train in Washington. The seven cars were elegant, with furnishings of mahogany and rosewood, plush upholstery, and pots of flowers in every nook and cranny. The first call was at the Military Academy, West Point. In Boston it took a half mile parade of carriages to take the visitors to see Harvard University, Longfellow's home, and the elm under which Washington took command of the Continental Army in 1775. During the visit to Boston some factories were inspected in and near the city. A delegate from Costa Rica, worn out after a day of sightseeing, complained about the haste.

"We could have spent days in the watch factory we saw," he sighed. "The United States desires to extend her trade relations with our people. I would be glad could I have had the opportunity to ask the prices of the watches we saw, and to learn if qualities and prices might be as good or better for us than what we are able to secure in Belgium."

At a mill in Lawrence, Massachusetts, however, one of the delegates did manage to talk business with the president of the company. He had seen bolts of colorful cotton prints with yellow flowers. The fustic tree from which yellow dye could be made was common in his homeland.

"You use fustic dye-wood, do you not?" the southern delegate asked the head of the mill.

"We do — much of it," the president replied.

"There is no duty in your country on fustic and we can furnish you that," the delegate remarked, his mind on future business for his own people.

The All-American guests visited the corn state of Iowa and went as far west as Omaha. In that meat-packing center each one was given a souvenir to take away, steer horns brightly polished, decorated with ribbons, and filled with little bags of Nebraska grain. In Kentucky they visited the former home of Henry Clay, loyal friend of Latin America. There they were entertained by Clay's relatives in an old southern mansion. After a tour of nearly 6000 miles, lasting forty-two days, the tourists returned to Washington where they discussed the common welfare of states in the Western Hemisphere.

Then for the first time Latin Americans and Anglo Americans sat around a table to talk over ways and means to bring a better way of life to both groups. This First

**REPRESENTATIVES OF NATIONS IN THE WESTERN
HEMISPHERE MEETING IN WASHINGTON, D.C., 1890**

International Conference of American States was really a get-acquainted meeting, which bore fruit in good will. Little business was accomplished. The most important act of this first congress set up an International Union of American Republics to promote trade. This small commercial bureau, established on April 14, 1890, grew into the Pan American Union, uniting the peoples of the Americas in peace and in war. Now, throughout the American republics the fourteenth of April is Pan American Day.

Through future conferences in the larger capitals of the Latin countries, cooperation grew slowly but surely. For a long time the small countries were fearful that the United States, large and powerful, would dominate them. Blaine had declared at the first meeting in Washington that "all shall meet together on terms of absolute equality." At the second International American Conference in Mexico City, in 1901, President Theodore Roosevelt instructed the delegates of the United States to make it clear that the chief interest of this country was to maintain "the system of self-government by the people" throughout the Americas. Elihu Root, who was Secretary of State in Roosevelt's Cabinet, made a famous speech at the Third International Conference in Rio de Janeiro in 1906, stating the aims of the United States:

We wish for no victories but those of peace; for no territory except our own; for no sovereignty except the sovereignty over ourselves. We deem the independence and equal rights of the smallest and weakest member of the family of nations entitled to as much respect as those of the greatest empire. — We wish to increase our prosperity, to expand our trade, to grow in wealth, in wisdom, and in spirit. The true way to accomplish this is not to pull down others and profit by their ruin, but to help all friends to a common prosperity and a common growth, that we may all become greater and stronger together.

At the fourth conference in Buenos Aires in 1910, a resolution was passed for the interchange of professors and students among the universities of the Americas.

601

The most popular universities with students of the United States are Mexico in Mexico City and San Marcos in Lima, Peru.

Arguments over boundaries led to small scale wars among the Latin American nations. At the fifth conference in Santiago, Chile in 1923, a treaty was made to avoid or prevent conflicts and to settle disputes without bloodshed. The American republics also pledged themselves to work together for better health of all the peoples in the Americas; for improvement of automobile roads and airlines to encourage travel among the nations and to aid the peoples to become better acquainted; for an understanding and appreciation of the Latin American contribution to science, literature, painting, music, and world culture in general.

The lack of easy transportation between the two Americas hindered friendship and understanding. The best way for Anglo Americans to learn what the Latin Americans had accomplished was to go and see for themselves. At the Santiago meeting plans were laid for building an automobile highway from Laredo, Texas, to Buenos Aires, Argentina, a distance of almost 12,000 miles. For the first time the development of aviation was discussed as a means of increasing travel among the American countries.

Five years later the sixth conference met in Havana, Cuba, where delegates were instructed to "study means for promoting friendship among the school children of the American republics." At each meeting the representatives talked more and more about the need for Latin Americans and Anglo Americans to become better acquainted. This meeting proved that a better understanding of one another's different ways was necessary if their friendship was to continue.

At Havana the policy of intervention by the United States was openly criticized by the delegates from Central and South America. Since the peoples of the Latin states had little or no opportunity to govern themselves until they gained their freedom from Spain, they had much to learn. Therefore, some of the Latin American countries have endured more than a century of revolutions.

During these upheavals, citizens of the United States lost their property and sometimes their lives. To protect them our Government frequently landed soldiers and Marines and sent warships to the ports of Latin nations during rebellions. These armed forces did police duty to maintain order and to protect the property of United States citizens. Peoples of these countries often resented this help from outside. It happened, sometimes, that the presence of Marines who kept order prevented the people from putting out of office a president whom they did not want, since their way of doing this was revolution.

Finally, it dawned upon officials in all countries, including the United States, that the Latin American way was not the Anglo American way. During Herbert Hoover's Administration, 1929 to 1933, Marines were evacuated from Nicaragua. Progress was then made toward a better understanding between the United States and Latin America. Hoover's successor, Franklin D. Roosevelt, announced the "Good Neighbor Policy" of no intervention at all. The willingness of the United States to stand by and let the Latin Americans work out their own problems in their own way, even if the way meant revolution and violence, bore fruit in the next meeting. At the seventh conference in Montevideo, Uruguay, in 1933, the following agreement was signed by the representatives of all governments, including the United States:

No state has the right to intervene in the internal or external affairs of another.

Realizing always that true cooperation is founded on understanding and that education provides the means to acquire this understanding, the delegates at the Montevideo Conference urged the American nations to found an "Institute for the Teaching of History" of the American Republics.

Although, at Havana, war was condemned and an agreement was made to settle disputes by arbitration, the delegates at Montevideo knew full well that peace rests upon sympathetic understanding. In every Pan American conference, education for peace was stressed. Soon, however, the threat of war in Europe brought the American States closer together in the common cause of survival. The peace of the world was at stake.

AMERICAN STATES UNITE IN DEFENSE

ALTHOUGH REPRESENTATIVES of the American Republics gather regularly every five years, unless circumstances prevent it, they can meet at any time if necessary. At the suggestion of Franklin D. Roosevelt, a meeting was called in Buenos Aires, Argentina, in December 1936, at a time when dictators were on the rampage in Europe. President Roosevelt addressed the congress on keeping peace in the Western Hemisphere. At this Inter-American Conference for the Maintenance of Peace, it was agreed that the twenty-one republics would stand together and consult among themselves on what action to take if war threatened any one of them. Although they did not agree to fight for one another in the event of an attack, the principle of consultation was a step forward in defense of the hemisphere.

When the eighth conference met in Lima, Peru, exactly two years later, World War II was galloping on its way. For the opening date of this important meeting, the Government of Peru chose a national holiday, the ninth of December, the anniversary of the end of Spanish rule in South America.

The hospitable Peruvians spared neither effort nor expense in providing comfort and pleasure for their All American guests. Added to the list of banquets and receptions were parties and entertainments given by clubs and private citizens. The approaching world conflict, however, cast a pall of gloom over the gaiety. Everyone seemed to realize the danger to both North and South America with war creeping at a stealthy pace over Europe and Asia. In this emergency the American Republics agreed to stand solidly together and defend themselves "against all foreign intervention or activity that may threaten them." This statement, approved on Christmas Eve, 1938, was called the Declaration of Lima. The delegates of the American States were of one mind in uniting to maintain peace, according to speeches they made at this conference:

America continues united and vigilant in the safeguarding of our common interests in the defense of peace — .

Chairman of the Brazilian Delegation

But let it be known — that we should rise en masse to defend, if some day they should be threatened, the higher principles of liberty, equity, and justice for which we have fought in the past.

Chairman of the Delegation of Haiti

Instead of a selfish, passive attitude toward evil, let us adopt a plan for effective but free, sovereign, and spontaneous cooperation, serving the good of America and of the world.

Argentine Minister of Foreign Affairs

Less than a year later, after Germany had invaded Poland and plunged Europe into World War II, foreign ministers of the American Republics held their first emergency meeting in Panama. They agreed to remain neutral, taking neither side in the conflict. To keep the war away from their doors, the Ministers established a security zone around the Western Hemisphere. This Declaration of Panama served notice upon the nations at war that no hostile act could be "attempted or carried on from land, from sea, or from the air," within the coastal limits defined in this agreement.

In July of 1940, the second meeting of consultation took place in Havana, after France fell to German might. The main topic of this gathering of ministers was the danger of victors in the European war taking over the possessions of the vanquished in the Americas, and establishing bases for aggression in the Western Hemisphere. At the meeting of Foreign Ministers, it was agreed that the American Republics would not allow any European colonies in the Western Hemisphere to be transferred to any power outside the Americas. If any such attempt was made, the foreign possessions would be administered under a trusteeship of the American Republics. This Act of Havana made it plain that aggression in the Western

Hemisphere would not be tolerated.

The Japanese attack on Pearl Harbor ushered World War II into the Americas and hurried the foreign ministers of the American Republics to another emergency meeting in Rio de Janeiro. Sumner Welles, heading the delegation from the United States, recommended that the American States sever diplomatic relations with the aggressors, Germany, Italy, and Japan. It was stated again that an act of aggression against one state would be considered as an act of aggression against all the states.

In 1945 before World War II ended, representatives of the American Republics met in Mexico City to discuss the problems of both war and peace. By the Act of Chapultepec, approved on March 6, 1945, a treaty was made whereby acts of aggression against any one of the republics would be met with the combined efforts of all the states, even to the use of armed forces.

The Treaty of Reciprocal Assistance was signed in Rio de Janeiro, Brazil on September 2, 1947, binding the American States to defend any one of their number under armed attack. This was the strongest agreement yet made to fight for the defense of the hemisphere with an all-out attack on any enemy waging war on any country. The Rio Treaty opened the way for a permanent union.

At the Ninth Conference in Bogota, Colombia in 1948, the twenty-one republics in the Western Hemisphere established the Organization of American States (OAS), confirming the agreement made at Rio de Janeiro the year before. Slowly, step by step over 122 years, these countries gained the confidence to join a federation to achieve the goals defined in the Charter of the Organization of American States:

604

Conference in national capitol, Bogota, Colombia, where the Organization of American States was formed in 1948. Flags of the 21 nations are displayed on each side of the speaker's platform.

The painting in the center shows Simon Bolivar and Francisco P. Santander, military heroes, entering Bogota to celebrate Colombia's independence from Spain.

Convinced that the historic mission of America is to offer to man a land of liberty, and a favorable environment for the development of his personality and the realization of his just aspirations;

Conscious that that mission has already inspired numerous agreements, whose essential value lies in the desire of the American peoples to live together in peace, and, through their mutual understanding and respect for the sovereignty of each one, to provide for the betterment of all, in independence, in equality and under law;

Confident that the true significance of American solidarity and good neighborliness can only mean the consolidation on this continent, within the framework of democratic institutions, of a system of individual liberty and social justice based on respect for the *essential rights of man.*

Since Communists destroy governments successfully by boring within and gaining key positions rather than by armed attack, the Rio Treaty was amended to include communism. At the Tenth Conference in 1954 at Caracas, Venezuela, the delegates approved the following statement:

That the domination or control of the political institutions of any American State by the international communist movement, extending to this hemisphere the political system of an extracontinental power, would constitute a threat to the sovereignty and political independence of the American States, endangering the peace of America, and would call for a Meeting of Consultation to consider the adoption of appropriate action in accordance with existing treaties.

This long legal sentence simply means that a communist threat to any nation would be the same as an armed attack.

In 1969, the members of the Organization of American States were: Argentina, Barbados, Bolivia, Brazil, Chile, Colombia, Costa Rica, Cuba, the Dominican Republic, Ecuador, El Salvador, Guatemala, Haiti, Honduras, Jamaica, Mexico, Nicaragua, Panama, Paraguay, Peru, Trinidad and Tobago, the United States, Uruguay, and Venezuela.

It takes time for 24 countries to gather information and to send official representatives to discuss the problems of offering troops or any other aid to a member of the OAS in trouble. It takes time to decide whether or not violence erupting in a country is a justified rebellion to improve a government, or a Communist-inspired revolution to destroy a government.

COMMUNISM THREATENS THE AMERICAS

CUBA HAS HAD a stormy history ever since the island was discovered by Columbus, and became the base of Spanish exploration in the Western Hemisphere. Over the years, Cubans have suffered from violence and discontent, and their lot is the same today. Cuba is now the base for spreading communism in the Americas.

On the first day of January, 1959 Fidel Castro and his followers toppled the government of Cuba, promising greater liberty and a better life for the people. The following month, after Castro became the Premier, he set up his own program which followed the communist pattern of confiscating private property and arresting citizens who opposed his plans. Thousands of Cubans fled to the United States. Castro's plans for a Communist Cuba were carried out with support from the Soviet Union.

For this aid, Castro allowed the Communist dictator of the Soviet Union to build missile sites in Cuba, only ninety miles from Florida. When President John F. Kennedy learned that these deadly weapons were there, ready to launch an attack on the United States or neighboring countries, he demanded their removal. At the risk of war, the Russian dictator agreed to dismantle the sites and ship the missiles back to his homeland. President Kennedy accepted his word, without inspection, that the weapons had been removed.

In January, 1961, John F. Kennedy of Massachusetts had been inaugurated President of the United States, succeeding Dwight D. Eisenhower. On November 22, 1963, the President was shot in Dallas, Texas by a young man, a citizen of the United States who had lived in the Soviet Union for several years. Upon return to his native land, he joined a group organized to support Castro, the Communist premier of Cuba. While being moved from one jail to another, the assassin was shot by a man in the crowd. Lyndon B. Johnson, Vice President, became the President of the United States, and completed President Kennedy's term. In 1964, Johnson was elected to the office of President.

Three months after his inauguration, President Johnson dispatched United States Marines to Santo Domingo, the capital of the Dominican Republic in the West Indies. On April 24, 1965, army units overthrew the government of the Dominican Republic, and started a civil war endangering the lives of people from the United States. The President acted quickly to protect these citizens and to bring them home, and sent more troops to maintain order until the Organization of American States could act. On May 6, the OAS approved setting up an Inter-American Peace Force to restore order. By that time, 25,000 United States troops were on duty there. Although some

of these units were withdrawn, countries in the OAS sent few military forces, and the burden of keeping order and preventing a Communist takeover during the confusion fell upon the United States. For this action, the United States Government was accused of breaking the non-intervention agreement signed in 1933 in Montevideo, Uruguay.

Promises of defense on paper are not easily carried out to the satisfaction of all nations in the Organization of American States. If Communists gain control of a government in the Americas by force and violence, shall other American States be powerless to help? If a nation in the Eastern Hemisphere trains, directs, and finances a Communist revolution in a country of the Americas, what is the duty of other countries in the OAS? Shall the OAS interfere if another Communist country establishes military bases in an American nation to threaten the Western Hemisphere? Shall weak nations receive aid in maintaining their independence if under attack by people within, who are directed by Communists abroad? How can speedy assistance be given to any American government in sudden danger of a Communist takeover?

In November of 1965, after eleven years, the Foreign Ministers of the Organization of American States met in Rio de Janeiro, Brazil, to discuss ways of strengthening inter-American cooperation. Brazilian Foreign Minister, Vasco Leitao da Cunha, was president of the conference with 300 delegates in attendance. From November 17 to November 30, these representatives from nations in the Western Hemisphere talked about their problems and ways to solve them. Much discussion was heard on the Alliance For Progress, a program for aid from the United States.

During the administration of President John F. Kennedy, the Alliance for Progress was signed on August 17, 1961, in Punta del Este, near Montevideo, the capital of Uruguay. The Preamble of the Charter of Punta del Este stated:

We, the American Republics, hereby proclaim our decision to unite in a common effort to bring our people accelerated economic progress and broader social justice within the framework of personal dignity and political liberty.

Although the United States had furnished large sums of money under this agreement, the Alliance For Progress was not so successful as had been expected. On November 22, 1965, President Johnson sent a message to the Rio Conference extending the period for aid beyond 1971, the date set to end this plan originally. One act of this meeting stated an idea often expressed by the delegates:

"No system can guarantee true progress unless it affirms the dignity of the individual."

Much discussion involved ways and means to increase trade among themselves, and the manufacture of products to sell overseas. Trade would increase prosperity and lift the well-being of their peoples.

On the last day of October, 1969 President Nixon spoke to a meeting of newsmen and publishers from the Latin American countries. His main topic was trade, the popular subject dating back to 1889 when representatives of these nations had gathered in Washington for the first time.

Latin Americans are proud and patriotic people, and staunchly defend the independence of their countries, large and small. Resolutions made at the Rio Conference showed an increased willingness to work together for the welfare of all. On November 30, 1965, the Act of Rio de Janeiro was signed, adding another agreement to further cooperation among the nations of the Western Hemisphere.

Slowly and cautiously, step by step, nations of the Western Hemisphere are developing an inter-American system that was the dream of Simon Bolivar, the "Liberator." In 1822, he said:

United in heart, in spirit and in aims, this continent . . . must raise its eyes . . . to peer into the centuries which lie ahead. It can then contemplate with pride those future generations of men, happy and free, enjoying to the full the blessings that heaven bestows on this earth, and recalling in their hearts the protectors and liberators of our day.

SOMETHING NEW GREW UP IN THE NEW WORLD – A DREAM!

We hold these truths to be self-evident, that all men are created equal, that they are endowed by their Creator with certain unalienable Rights, that among these are Life, Liberty and the pursuit of Happiness. That to secure these rights, Governments are instituted among Men, deriving their just powers from the consent of the governed.

Through trial and error, success and failure, hope and despair, the vision of 1776 is the quest of a hemisphere.

Index

612

Hamilton, Andrew, Zenger's lawyer, *quoted,* 84

Hammersmith, Saugus Ironworks, 434-435, (illus. 435)

Hancock, John, in Boston Tea Party, 109; escapes British, 113; Second Continental Congress, 113; presides, 115; urges bombardment of Boston, 117; signs Declaration of Independence, 122; reception for Captain Gray, 402

Harding, Warren G., President, 557

Hargreaves, James, inventor of spinning jenny, 440, 443

Hariot, Thomas, explorer for Raleigh, 50, 434

Harrison, Benjamin, President, signs Sherman Anti-Trust Act, 519; annexes Hawaii, 537; withdraws treaty, 537; Pan American Conference, Washington, 600-601

Harrison, General William Henry, replaces Hull, 221; wins Battle of Tippecanoe, 221-222

Hartford, Connecticut, named, 63

Harvard College, 522, 600

Harvey, Charles T., construction of Soo Canal, 475

H'atira Weta Ariosa, Indian prayer, 342-343

Havana, Cuba, more supplies and men join Cortes' expedition, 4; captured by British, 214, 533; traded to Spain, *quoted,* 214; *Maine,* 535, (illus. 534); yellow fever conquered, 538; independence, 538-539

Hawaii, trade treaty, 537; Pearl Harbor ceded for naval base, 536; Queen Liliuokalani, 537; President McKinley, *quoted,* 537; annexed by Congress, 537

Hawkins, British seaman, 49

Hay-Herran Treaty, 545

Hayes, Rutherford B., President, 321-322

Hayne, Robert, Senator from South Carolina, 246

Health, 527-528

Heceta, Spanish explorer of Pacific Coast, 400

Henderson, Judge, and associates, buy Kentucky from Cherokees, 97; hire Daniel Boone, 97

Henry VII, King of England, *quoted,* 48

Henry, Patrick, speech against Stamp Act, *quoted,* 107; "We-must-fight" speech, *quoted,* 112-113; First Continental Congress, 112, (illus. 112-113); governor of Virginia, 136; aids George Rogers Clark, 136

Henry E. Huntington Library and Art Gallery, 526-527, (illus. 526)

Herefords, 348-349, (illus. 349)

Herkimer, General, 133; Battle of Oriskany, 133

Hessians, arrive with Admiral Howe, 129; defeated at Trenton, 131-132

Hidalgo, Miguel y Castilla, starts revolt in Mexico, 232-233, (illus. 232); "Father of Mexican Independence," 233

Hiroshima, Japan, first atomic bomb, 576

History of the Province of Santa Cruz by de Magalhaes, 28-29, *quoted* 29

Hitler, Adolph, 558-559; dictator of Germany, 560, 566; takes Germany out of the League of Nations, 560; annexes Austria, 560; takes part of Czechoslovakia, 560; signs non-aggression pact with Union of Soviet Socialist Republics, 566; invades Poland, 566; divides country with U.S.S.R., 566; *see also* World War II

Hoe, Richard M., inventor, 501

Holland, *see* Netherlands

Homestead Act, 350, 523

Homesteaders, Oklahoma, 351-354, (illus. 351, 352, 353); Russian Germans, 354-355, (illus. 355); Scandinavians, Finns, 354-355; Central Europeans, 355-356; Overland Trail, (illus. 423)

Honolulu, supply base, Spanish American War, 537

Hood River Valley, Oregon, (illus. 416)

Hooker, General Joseph, Union, 308-309

Hooker, Thomas, founds Connecticut, 63-64

Hoover Dam, 387-391, (illus. 390)

Hoover, Herbert, directs war relief, 557; supports flood control, *quoted,* 360; President, 562-563; depression, 562; Reconstruction Finance Corporation, *quoted,* 563; evacuates U.S. Marines from Nicaragua, 602

Hopi Indians, 438

Hopkins, Commodore Esek, commands first American Navy fleet, 125-127

Houghton, Douglas, state geologist, Michigan, 473; reports copper on upper peninsula, 473-474

House of Burgesses, Virginia, formed, 56; Patrick Henry's speech, 107; journal *quoted,* 110; members in 1774, 110

Houses of Parliament, Quebec, (illus. 582)

Houston, Sam, first President of Texas, (illus. 265)

Howe, Elias, inventor, sewing machine, 491

Howe, Admiral Richard, arrives with Hessian soldiers, 129; tries reconciliation, 130, 134

Howe, William, replaces Gage in Boston, 115; leaves Boston for Halifax, 117; returns to New York, 133-134, 142

Hudson Bay, visited by Henry Hudson, 31

Hudson's Bay Company, 250-251; Fort Vancouver, 253, (illus. 254), 401, 406, 409, 413, (illus. 412)

Hudson, Henry, discovers river named for him, 30-31; trades with Indians, 31; *Half Moon's* journal *quoted,* 31; abandoned, 31

Hull, Isaac, Captain of the *Constitution,* 223-224

Hull, General William, fails to halt British, 221

Hungary, U.S.S.R. imposes Communist government, 585-586

Huron Indians, 473

Hutchinson, Anne, banished from Massachusetts, 64

Idaho, on Oregon Trail, 255-259; gains by treaty on Canadian boundary, 269; minerals, 421; forests, 424

Illinois, Joliet and Marquette, 41-42; Northwest Territory, 149; Lincoln-Douglas Debates, 292; Lincoln elected President, 292; *see also* Chicago

Illinois Indians, visited by Joliet and Marquette, 42

Illinois River, traveled by La Salle, 44

Immigrant runner, 508, (illus. 508)

Immigration, 208; newspaper *quoted*, 208; to Central Plains, 350-357; to mill towns in New England, 446; into Ohio Valley, 460; to lumber camps, 467; building Soo Canal, 475; aliens at Ellis Island, (illus. 483); to farm and factory, 502-511; *quoted*, 502, 504; (illus. 503); to South America, 504, 507-508, 510; from Germany, 504, *quoted*, 511; to United States from England, Scotland and Ireland, 505-506, *quoted*, 505, 506; from Italy, 507-508, (illus. 508); Jews from Russia and Central Europe, 508-509, *quoted*, 510; (illus. 509)

Imperial Valley, 387, (illus. 387)

Implied powers, 210, 213

Impressment of American sailors, 220

Incas, Indians in Peru, 18-19

Incentives, bonus, 518; profit-sharing, 518

Indenture, 71-73; indenture *quoted*, (illus. 72); advertisement for runaways, *quoted*, 73; advertisement selling servant's time, (illus. 73); 105; indenture of Samuel Slater, *quoted*, 441

Indentured servants, 71-73; (illus. 72); advertisement for sale of, 78; Slater, 300

Independence Hall, Philadelphia, (illus. 121)

Independence, Missouri, starting point for Oregon Trail, 258; Santa Fe Trail, 262

Indiana, Revolutionary War, 136-138; Northwest Territory, 149; land for soldiers with George Rogers Clark, 213; Battle of Tippecanoe, 221

Indian Removal Bill, 248

Indians, taken by Columbus to Spain, 1,3; Aztecs, 7-13; Cayugas, 89; Cherokees, 97, 247-250, (illus. 249); Cheyennes, 343; Chickasaws, 248, 250; Chippewas, 474, 478; Chitimacha, (illus. 574); Choctaws, (illus. 249); Creeks, 222-223, 248; Dakotas, 343; Duwamish, 410; Flatheads, 255, (illus. 364); Hopis, 438; Hurons, 473; Illinois, 42; Incas, 18-19; Iroquois, 43, 89-90, 253; Kiowas, 341; Mandans, 251; Minquas, 35; Mohawks, (illus. 32), 89; Mohicans, (illus. 32); Muscogees, 222; Narragansetts, 62; Navajos, (illus. 574); Nez Perces, 255; Ojibwas, 474; Omahas, 266; Oneidas, 89; Onondagas, 89; Osages, 253; Ottawas, 452; Pawnees, 341, (illus. 574); Pawtuckets, 442; Pequots, 63; Pimas, 386; Poncas, 341; Seminoles, 223; Senecas, 43; Shawnees, 220; Sioux, 343; Tuscaroras, 89; Wyandots, (illus. 463); Zunis, 371-372, (illus. 370, 372)

Indian society, Plains, 341-343

Indian Territory, created by Congress, 248; 341-343

Indochina, French colony, divided into Cambodia, Laos, Vietnam, 587, 591

Industrial Revolution, 439-446

Industries, *listed separately*

Industries, growth of, in colonies, beginnings, 74-80; 107, 109; war supplies, 123

Inter-American Congress for the Maintenance of Peace, Buenos Aires, 603

Inter-American Peace Force, 607

International Conference of American States, Panama, 599; Washington, 600-601, (illus. 601); Mexico City, 601; Rio de Janeiro, 601; Buenos Aires, 601; Santiago, Chile, 602; Havana, 602; Montevideo, 603; Lima, 603; Bogota, Organization of American States Charter, *quoted*, 604-606; (illus. 605)

Interstate Commerce Commission, 519

"Intolerable Acts," 110

Invasion of Canada, 116-117

Inventions, telegraph, 484-486; Atlantic cable, 486-487; telephone, 488-489; wireless, 488-490; sewing machine, 491-492; "plow that scours," 492-494, (illus. 493); reaper, 493-494; vulcanizing rubber, 494-495; automobile, 496; screw-propellers on steamboats, 496; air brake, 497-498; sleeping car, 498; Diesel engine, 499; electric light, 499-501; phonograph, 499; electric motor, 501; rotary press, 501

Iowa, migration, 465-466; Mormon encampments, 265-266; Pacific Railroad, (illus. 333), 334

Iron, in colonies, 54, 77, 434; Principio Company, 436; iron plantations, 436-437; Hopewell Iron Plantation, (illus. 436, 437); nails, (illus. 437); Valley Forge, 437, 438; iron in Ohio Valley, 460-461; Kelly Brothers Ironworks, 469-470; Jesuit missionaries *quoted*, 473; in Michigan, 473-477, (illus. 473), Mesabi Range, 477-478; shipping ore, (illus. 477); Labrador, 479; Venezuela, 480, (illus. 479); iron business declines, 480-481

Iroquois Confederacy, 89-90, 92, 96

Isabella, Queen of Spain, 2,3

Italy, emigration to United States, 507-508, *quoted*, 507, (illus. 508); to Argentina and Brazil, 507-508

Iwo Jima, Battle of, 574, 575, (illus. 575)

Ixtaccihuatl, volcano, 8, (illus. 8)

Jackson, Andrew, defeats Creek Indians, 222-223; Battle of New Orleans, 226-227, 243; early life, 242; lawyer in Nashville, 242-243; helps write State Constitution of Tennessee, 243; first representative of Tennessee in Congress, 243; elected President, 243-244; (illus. 244); 256-257, 368, 469, 562

Jackson, General Thomas J., Confederate, 297, 308-309

Jackson Mining Company, 474

"Jacksonian Era," traditions broken, 245; inaugural address, *quoted*, 245; "spoils system," 246; nullification, 246; Jackson *quoted*, 246-247; Bank of United States destroyed, 247; "pet" banks, 247, 256-257; speculation in land, 245, 247, 256-257; Indian Removal Bill signed, 248; national debt paid, 257; specie circular, 257

James I, King of England, 50, 51, 57, 58, 64

James II, King of England, *quoted*, 82

James Fort, Jamestown, (illus. 53)

James River, named for James I, 52

214; treaty by Spain to Napoleon, 215; bought by President Jefferson, 215; Acadians, 217-218; Bayou Teche, 217; Battle of New Orleans, 226-227; oil, (illus. 367); *see also* New Orleans

Louisiana Purchase, 213-218, 250-251, 285, 288, 362

L'Ouverture, Toussaint, leader of rebellion in Haiti, 209-210; governor of French Haiti, 210, 534

Lowell, Francis Cabot, starts textile mills, 443-444; "Spindle City," 444; supports tariff of 1816, 444

Lowell Institute, for education, 445-446

Lowell, Massachusetts, early factory town, 442-446; employees, 444-445; *quoted,* 445, 446; rules *quoted,* 445; (map 445); 457, 491

Lowell Offering, magazine published by girl employees in mills, 445

Loyalists, *see* Tories

Lumbering, 53, 59, 75, 77; in Northwest, 409-411, (illus. 410, 411); newspaper ad *quoted,* 410-411; near Great Lakes, 465-468; rafting, 465; (illus. 466, 467, 468)

Lumberjacks, 467-468

Lumber schooners, 465, 466, 468

Lusitania, sunk by German torpedo, 549-550

MacArthur, Major General Arthur, call for troops, 539

MacArthur, General Douglas, trains Filipino Army, 541-542; siege of Bataan, 568; headquarters in Australia, 568; appointed Supreme Commander of Allied Forces in Southwest Pacific, 568; Leyte landing, 573; with Indians, Signal Corps, (illus. 574); armistice *quoted,* 577, (illus. 576); Independence Day, Philippine Islands, *quoted,* 579; Commander-in-Chief, United Nations troops, Korean War, 589-590; recalled by President Harry Truman, 590

McClellan, General George B., Union, 297-298, 308

McCormick, Cyrus Hall, inventor of reaper, 469, 493-494; Chicago, 494

McDowell, General Irwin, Union, Battle of Bull Run, 297

McKenzie, Sir Alexander, British fur trader, traces river named for him to Arctic Ocean, *quoted,* 401, (illus. 401)

McKinley, President, 383; 520; 534; orders Army and Navy to Cuba, 534-535; annexation of Philippine Islands, *quoted,* 537, 540; annexation of Hawaii, *quoted,* 538; assassinated, 383

McLoughlin, John, manager of Fort Vancouver, 255

McNutt, Paul V., United States High Commissioner, Philippine Islands, *quoted,* 579

Machinery, Watt, 440; spinning jenny, Hargreaves, 440; water frame, Arkwright, 440

Machu Picchu, Inca ruins, Peru, (illus. 20)

Madison, James, 57; tribute to Washington, *quoted,* 146; Virginia Plan, 151-152; biog.. 152-153, (illus, 152); *quoted,* 153; "Father of the Constitution," 153;

serves in Congress, 153; legislature of Virginia, 153; President, 153, 220; Secretary of State, 212; contributor to *The Federalist Papers,* 179; War of 1812, 220-227; Letter of Marque, (illus. 225); opposes slavery, 285

Magalhaes, Pero de, author of history of Brazil, 28-29; *quoted,* 29

Magellan, 3; sails on voyage, 26; discovers strait, 27; killed in Philippines, 27; proves earth is round, 28; journal *quoted,* 28

Magellan, Strait of, discovered, 27; 536

Maine, founded by Mason and Gorges, 68; Arnold's expedition into Canada, 116; admitted as free state, 286

Maine, battleship, blown up, 534, (illus. 534)

Malinche, interpreter, 6-7, (illus. 10); 11

Manchuria, invaded by Japan, 560; by Communists, 588

Mandan Indians, 251

Manhattan Island, purchase, 34, (illus. 32); lot sale, *quoted,* 34

"Manifest Destiny," 537, 539

Mann, Horace, appointed to State Board of Education, Massachusetts, 278

Manrique, Marquis de Villa, Viceroy of Mexico, 21

Manufacturing, in the home, 74-76, 102-103, (illus. 437); first factories, 76-78, 123-124; colonial products, 101-105; northern mills, 204-208, 441-448; southern mills, 316-317

Maravedis, Spanish coins, 2

Marconi, Guglielmo, inventor of wireless telegraphy, 489-490

Marcos, Friar, sent with the Moor to locate Cibola, 15; guide with Coronado, 16

Marianas Islands, 536; Battle of Saipan, 572

Marietta, Ohio, founded by General Rufus Putnam, 452, (illus. 453)

Marion, Francis, the Swamp-Fox, 143; orderly book *quoted,* 143-144, (illus. 144)

Marne, Battle of, 549; second Battle of, 554

Marquette, French explorer, 41-43

"Marquis of the Valley," title granted to Cortes, 13

Marshall, General George C., Secretary of State, President Truman's cabinet, "Marshall Plan," 586

Marshall, John, discovers gold at Sutter's Mill, 269-270; Bigler's journal *quoted,* 269; companions, from Morman battalion, (illus. 271); 418

Marshall, John, XYZ Affair, 211-212; unexpected hero, 212; Chief Justice of United States, 212; rules Maryland cannot tax Bank of United States, 247; decision that rivers are free, 455

Marshall Plan, United States aid to war-ridden nations, 586

Martin, Luther, opposed to slavery, *quoted,* 284

Maryland, founded by Lord Baltimore, 64-66; General Assembly at St. Mary's, 65; Catholics, 65; oath of governors under Baltimores, 65; Protestants, 64-65;

Ponce de Leon, 7

Pontiac, chief of Ottawas, 452

Popocatepetl, volcano, 8-9, (illus. 9)

Popular sovereignty, 289-290; debated by Lincoln and Douglas, 292

Port St. Julian, winter stopover of Magellan, 26-27

Porter, Rear Admiral, Union, 301, 305

Porto Seguro, Brazil, Cabral lands, 25; journal *quoted,* 25

Portola, Gaspar de, military commander, California, 373-376; 398

Portugal, seeks trade, 22-26; claims Brazil by discovery, 25; in Moluccas, 27; Indian Ocean, 28; Dutch take trade, 28

Portuguese colonization, in America, 28-29; captaincies, 28; Negro slaves, 29

Portuguese Guinea, Overseas Province of Portugal, 587

Prescott, Colonel William, in command at Bunker Hill, 115

Presidio, Spanish fort on San Francisco Bay, 376, 377-379, 405

Prince Henry, school for navigators, 22

Princeton, Battle of, 132

Privateers, Dutch, 33; Washington's Army, 116; Revolutionary War, 127-128; War of 1812, 294-296; news item from Halifax paper *quoted,* 224; *Niles Weekly Register, quoted,* 224; attack in Azores, 226; War Between the States, 299-301

Proclamation of Neutrality, Washington, 210; Wilson, **549**

Profit-sharing, 518

Protestants in Maryland, 65

Providence, Rhode Island, founded by Roger Williams, 62

Pueblos, Spanish California, 380

Puerto Rico, 534; occupied, 536-537; ceded by Spain, 537; becomes a territory, 540

Pullman, George, inventor, sleeping car, 498

Puritans, 59-63; charter *quoted,* 60; buy land in Massachusetts, 59-60; laws *quoted,* 61; union of church and state, 60-61; in Maryland, 65

Putnam, Israel, at Bunker Hill, 115; in Pennsylvania, 172

Putnam, Rufus, Ohio Company, 452

Quakers, in New England, 64; in New York, 64; in Maryland, 65; in Pennsylvania, 66-68; Mary Dyer hanged, 67; 88-89, 130-131

Quebec, founded by Champlain, 41; Marquette and Joliet, school, 42; French and Indian War, 94-95; Plains of Abraham, 95; Americans defeated, 116-117

Quebec Act, 110

Queen Elizabeth I of England, encourages trade, 48; Spanish Armada, 49, 50

Quetzalcoatl, prophet, 4-7

Quivera, imaginary land, 17

Radium, discovered, 422

Rafting, 465

Railroads, Union Pacific, 332-340; Central Pacific, 336-340; Kansas Pacific, (illus. 341); Great Northern, 416; first railroad, 457-459; Baltimore and Ohio, 459, (illus. 458); first train to Denver, news item *quoted,* 498

Railroad Act of 1862, 333-334, 523; *quoted,* 333-334, (illus. 333)

Raleigh, Sir Walter, founds Roanoke Colony, 49; beheaded by James I, 50; 434, 438, 505

Ranchos, Spanish California, 379-382; trade, *quoted,* 381

Randolph, Edmund, biog., 150-151, (illus. 151); offers "Virginia Plan," 151; letter to House of Burgesses explaining refusal to sign Constitution, 177; first Attorney General, 203

Reaper, invented by McCormick, 293-294

Reclamation Act, 383

Reconstruction Act, 319; Fourteenth Amendment, *quoted,* 319

Reconstruction Finance Corporation, 563

Reed, Major Walter, army doctor, yellow fever in Cuba, 538, (illus. 538); 545

Religion, brought to America by Spain, 3, 5, 7, 13, 21, 522; missions established among Indians, 41-45; Mayflower Compact, 47; English clergy plan to convert natives in America, 51; prayer, first representative assembly, *quoted,* 56; Separatists, 57-58; Pilgrims, 57-59; Puritans, 59-62, 64; in Maryland, 65; Catholics in Maryland, 65; Anglican, 61, 64, 71; Mennonites, 67; Anabaptists, 67; state religions, 186-187; law for religious freedom in Virginia, written by Jefferson, *quoted,* 187; Christian Indians, 253; Northwest Tribes request Christian teachers, 253; Dr. Whitman, missionary, 253-255; Father De Smet, missionary, 255; Alamo, (illus. 264); Mormons, 265-267; Franciscans, 373; California missions, 377-378, (illus. 378, 379), 382

Republican Party, founded, 291; nominates John C. Fremont for President, 291; elects Abraham Lincoln, President, 292

Resettlement Administration, 564-565

Retail Clerks International Association, (illus. 517)

Revere, Paul, Boston Massacre, (illus. 108); messenger for letters by Samuel Adams, 109; arouses patriots, 113

Revolutionary War, Lexington, 114; Concord, 114; Bunker Hill, 114-115; Congress elects Washington as commander-in-chief, 115; invasion of Canada, 116-117; British evacuate Boston, 117; Declaration of Independence, 118-122; supplies for war, 122-125; American seamen, 125-128; war moves into middle colonies, 128-132; British plan to isolate New England, 132-135; war on western frontier, 135-138; foreigners aid Americans, 138-145; war ends in South, 138-145; Treaty of Paris, *1783,* 145

Revolution in France, 209

302; Fort Donelson, 302; Fort Wright, (illus. 302); Shiloh Church and Pittsburg Landing, 302; siege of Vicksburg, 305-306; Confederacy divided again, 306-307; Chattanooga, 306-307; Chickamauga, 306; Missionary Ridge, 306-307; Atlanta, 307; Sherman's march through Georgia, *quoted*, 307; fall of Savannah, 307; Virginia campaign, 307-313; Fair Oaks, 308; Seven Days' Battle, 308; Fredericksburg, 308; Chancellorsville, 308-309; Gettysburg, battle of, 309; Wilderness, Spottsylvania, Cold Harbor, 311; General Grant, (illus. 311); Generals Early and Sheridan in Shenandoah Valley, 311; surrender of Lee at Appomattox, 312, 313; General Lee, (illus. 312)

"War Hawks," 220-221

War of 1812, 220-227; Congress declares war on England, 221; invasion of Canada fails, 221; British burn Washington, 223; engagement between *Constitution* and *Guerriere*, 223-224; Battle of New Orleans, 226-227; *London Courier, quoted,* 226; Treaty of Ghent, 227; effect upon manufacturing, 443, 444, 447

War of Independence, *see* Revolutionary War

War of Independence, Second, *see* War of 1812

War with Mexico, trappers and traders invade Mexican territory, 260-262; Yankees settled in Texas, 262-263; Alamo, 264, (illus. 264); Santa Anna defeated at San Jacinto, 264; annexation of Texas, 264; Kearny's march to California, 265-266; General Scott captures Mexico City, 268; General Taylor invades from north, 268; Treaty of Guadalupe Hidalgo, 268; 305, 312

Warren, Dr. Joseph, killed at Bunker Hill, 115

Washburn, General Henry D., leads expedition into Yellowstone area, 427-428

Washington (State), territory divided with Oregon, 407; founding of Seattle, 410; lumbering, 409-411; salmon industry, 412-414, (illus. 412, 413); farming, 414-416; gold mining, (illus. 415); Interstate Compact Commission, 416; 424; Mt. Rainier, (illus. 430)

Washington, Augustine, Principio Iron works, 436

Washington, Booker T., Negro educator founds Tuskegee Institute, 324, (illus. 322, 323)

Washington, George, 57; 74; journey to Ohio country, 91-92, *quoted,* 91, (illus. 91); Braddock's Army, 94-95; with General Forbes, 94-95; House of Burgesses, 110; (illus. 110); First Continental Congress, 110; hears Patrick Henry speak, 112; Commander-in-Chief, 115, *quoted,* 115; takes command of Continental Army, 115-118; evening before Battle of Long Island, *quoted,* 128; 128-132; 134; 140; 142-143; Yorktown, 145; (illus. 145B); presides at Constitutional Convention, 150; *quoted,* 176; elected President, journey to New York, inauguration, 198-203; *quoted,* 198-199; 202; (illus. 199, 200, 201); *Gazette of the United States, quoted,* 202;

appoints cabinet, 203; journey to factories in New England, diary *quoted,* 204-205; *quoted,* 210; Henry Lee's tribute *quoted,* 210; slaves freed in will, *quoted,* 285; coal, diary *quoted,* 439; 460; 515; *quoted,* 552; 600

Washington, National Capital site, 204

Watt, James, inventor, 440, 443

Wayne, Major General Anthony, defeats Indians, 453-454

Webster-Ashburton Treaty, 472-473

Webster, Daniel, opposes nullification, 246, *quoted,* 246; "Defender of the Constitution," 246; opposes Indian Removal Bill, 248; Compromise of 1850, *quoted,* 288-289; Secretary of State Tyler's cabinet, 472-473; makes border treaty with England, 472-473; lawyer defending Goodyear's patent, 495

Webster-Hayne Debate, 246

Weiser, Conrad, interpreter, 89

West Indies, visited by Columbus, 3

Westinghouse, George, invents airbrakes, 497-498, (illus. 497, 498)

West Virginia, statehood, *1863,* 297, 303; does not secede, 297

Westward Movement, crossing Allegheny Mountains, 87-98, 135-136; Louisiana Purchase, 213; Lewis and Clark Expedition, 215-217; fur traders to Pacific Coast, 250-253; crossing plains to Oregon, 255-259; Mexican War, 260-265; Mormon migration, 265-267; California gold rush, 269-276; Compromise of 1850, 289; continental railroad, 332-340; Homestead Law, 350; homesteading, 350-354; immigration, 354-356; 460; along rivers and Great Lakes, 460-480

"What hath God wrought," first telegram, Washington to Baltimore, 485, (illus. 486)

Whigs, blame Jackson for Panic of 1837, 256; nominate Henry Clay for President, 264; oppose annexation of Texas, 264; 485

Whiskey Ring, 321

White, Josiah, manufacturer, 447; *quoted,* 448

White Plains, Battle of, 130

Whitman, Dr. Marcus, missionary to Oregon, 253

Whitman, Mrs., *quoted,* 253, 254

Whitney, Eli, invents cotton gin, 283-284; on Greene Plantation, 283-284, 285; 317

Whittier, John G., poems against slavery, *quoted,* 290; poem on first trans-Atlantic cable, 487, *quoted,* 487

Wilderness Road, gateway to west, 96; trail blazed by Boone, 97; 213, 216, 238, 258

Williams, Roger, 61-63; arrival, 61; Winthrop diary *quoted,* 61; opposes union of church and state, 62; trial, *quoted,* 62; letter *quoted,* 62; founds Rhode Island, 61-63, 67

Williamsburg, capital of Virginia, 91, 136

Wilson, James, biog., 183-184, (illus. 183); *quoted,* 182, 183, 184; studies law with John Dickinson, 184; teaches law in College of Philadelphia, 260; signs